1990

Medical and Health Annual

Encyclopædia Britannica, Inc.

CHICAGO

AUCKLAND•GENEVA•LONDON•MADRID•MANILA•PARIS•ROME•SEOUL•SYDNEY•TOKYO•TORONTO

1990 Medical and Health Annual

Editor	Ellen Bernstein
Senior Editor	Linda Tomchuck
Contributing Editors	David Calhoun, Charles Cegielski, Barbara Whitney
Editorial Adviser	Drummond Rennie, M.D. Professor of Medicine Institute for Health Policy Studies University of California, San Francisco; Deputy Editor, *The Journal of the American Medical Association* (West Coast)
Art Director	Cynthia Peterson
Planning Analyst	Marsha Check
Senior Picture Editor	Holly Harrington
Picture Editors	Cathy Melloan, April A. Oswald
Art Production Supervisor	Richard A. Roiniotis
Layout Artist	Dale Horn
Illustrator	Anne H. Becker
Art Staff	Amy I. Brown, Daniel M. Delgado, Patricia A. Henle, Kathy Kalinowski
Manager, Copy Department	Anita Wolff
Senior Copy Editor	Barbara Whitney
Copy Staff	Naomi Cohn, Ellen Finkelstein, Thomas J. Riggs, Peter Shrock
Manager, Production Control	Mary C. Srodon
Production Control Staff	Marilyn L. Barton, Vernetta McCoy, Yvonne G. Pua
Manager, Composition and Page Makeup	Melvin Stagner
Coordinator, Composition and Page Makeup	Michael Born, Jr.
Composition Staff	Duangnetra Debhavalya, Morna Freund, John Krom, Jr., Thomas Mulligan, Gwen Rosenberg, Tammy Tsou
Page Makeup Staff	Griselda Cháidez, Arnell Reed, Danette Wetterer
Director, Corporate Computer Services	Michelle J. Brandhorst
Computer Services Staff	Steven Bosco, Philip Rehmer, Vincent Star
Manager, Index Department	Carmen-Maria Hetrea
Senior Index Editor	Martin L. White
Index Staff	Sheila M. Vasich
Librarian	Terry Miller
Associate Librarian	Shantha Uddin
Curator/Geography	David W. Foster
Assistant Librarian	Robert M. Lewis
Secretarial Staff	Dorothy Hagen, Kay Johnson

Editorial Administration

Philip W. Goetz, Editor in Chief
Michael Reed, Managing Editor
Karen M. Barch, Executive Director of Editorial Production
Carl Holzman, Director of Budgets and Controller

Encyclopædia Britannica, Inc.
Robert P. Gwinn, Chairman of the Board
Peter B. Norton, President

Foreword

Ten years ago the 1980 *Medical and Health Annual* featured a symposium on Diet and Health. An article entitled "How Little We Know" examined the status of knowledge about cholesterol and its link to heart disease. It summed up the situation as follows: "Thus far our efforts to make dietary intervention a rational approach to the treatment or prevention of coronary atherosclerosis have resulted in confusion. There is no established valid basis for any theory that represents atherosclerosis as a nutritional disease." Another article in the symposium—"Should There Be a Law?"—concerned itself with the U.S. government's 1977 publication of *Dietary Goals for the United States*, a short document that made the simple recommendations that Americans reduce their consumption of calories, sugar, salt, fats, and cholesterol and increase their consumption of complex carbohydrates. The response to those recommendations was a great storm of protest; members of the scientific community and public policy officials alike questioned whether the evidence for establishing such goals was "scientifically adequate."

The opening feature article in this volume once again turns to the subject of diet and health. "Food for Thought" begins by looking at three reports issued in 1988 and 1989 (two in the U.S. and one in Europe) that also made recommendations for dietary changes. Unlike the relatively skimpy 1977 publication, these recent reports were each several hundred pages in length. One of them—"the size of the Manhattan phone book"—analyzed some 5,000 studies. Taken together, the new reports provide overwhelming evidence that changes in diet *can* reduce the risk of certain chronic diseases—in particular, atherosclerosis, the major cause of heart disease. No longer is the "adequacy" of the data supporting such changes as a means of improving the health of the general population in question, and the wrangling among scientists appears to have abated.

This very noteworthy progress in a decade's time should not suggest that *all* dietary questions have been answered. Indeed, the subject of what people should and should not eat continues to provoke many disputes, even among experts. With advances in the understanding of nutritional diseases have come new questions. In the past year the public has been conspicuously anxious about the safety of the food supply—among other things, it has been fearful of outbreaks of food-borne disease and alarmed by media reports about pesticide residues on fruits and vegetables (*e.g.,* Alar on apples). "Food for Thought" also addresses these and numerous other prominent concerns on the minds of today's consumers.

Three feature articles in this volume consider the well-being of the youngest generations. One of the world's most eminent child psychologists addresses the many ways youngsters today are being deprived of childhood. A status report on the psychological functioning of teenagers reveals that adolescents across the globe are neither "mixed-up" nor maladjusted. And noted exercise physiologists propose creative remedies for the "fitness crisis" that is presently threatening the health of American youth.

Readers who think there is nothing new to be said about smoking and health will undoubtedly be enlightened by "Till Death Do Us Part." This article chronicles the history of cigarette smoking in the U.S.—its precipitous rise and its slow-but-steady decline. It then goes on to predict smoking's future: as fewer and fewer Americans are lighting up, U.S. tobacco companies are passionately courting new "flames" in other parts of the world.

"Tomorrow's Forecast: Hot, with a Chance of Malaria," the title of another feature, is not a joke. The spread of malaria and other truly ominous infectious diseases is indeed a feared consequence if, as many experts are now predicting, the climatic changes that are associated with the so-called greenhouse effect come to pass.

"Oscar Wilde's Fatal Illness: The Mystery Unshrouded" provides irrefutable evidence that Victorian England's most notorious literary figure did *not* die of syphilis, as many who knew him and a number of biographers have espoused. The author of this feature had special access to a medical certificate signed by a Parisian neurologist and dated Nov. 27, 1900—three days before Wilde's death. For allowing him to study and reproduce that crucial document, the author is grateful to the Viscountess Eccles, proprietor of the Hyde Collection.

These are only a few of the feature articles that make up just one part of the 1990 *Medical and Health Annual*. In addition, the 170-page, alphabetically organized "World of Medicine" offers a roundup of recent developments in many of the medical specialties and allied health fields (from "Accidents and Safety" to "Veterinary Medicine"). The section includes nine timely Special Reports on topics as diverse as medical preparation for "the big quake" in California, the previously unrealized potential of children with Down syndrome, and fraud in the biomedical sciences.

The 15 articles in the "Health Information Update" provide reliable and up-to-date information meant to help people live healthy lives. Subjects include physical fitness, medical procedures, child care, drugs, nutrition, preventive medicine, and other matters of personal health.

*   *   *

Recently in Washington, D.C., participants at a symposium considered how the press and the public handle the assessment of health risks. A correspondent from the *Washington Post* perceptively pointed out that journalists frequently "do a poor job of putting health risks in perspective. Deadlines," she emphasized, "leave little time to focus on the big picture." One of the express purposes of the *Medical and Health Annual* is to "put in perspective" the host of health-related stories that make news each year. The *Annual* turns to authorities—physicians and medical scientists who are among the most knowledgeable in their fields—to assess risks as well as to evaluate "breakthroughs"—in other words, to provide "the big picture."

We hope that the efforts of our many contributors will not only bring a reasonable perspective to important matters of health but help readers keep pace with the rapidly evolving developments in the exciting field of medicine. The editors and artists who worked on this volume have attempted to prepare a yearbook of medicine that is timely, stimulating, and attractive. We hope we have succeeded.

Ellen Bernstein

—Editor

Contents

Food for Thought

by Marion Nestle, Ph.D., M.P.H.

HAZARD REPORTED IN APPLE CHEMICAL
—New York Times, Feb. 2, 1989
CHILEAN FRUIT PULLED FROM SHELVES AS U.S. WIDENS
INQUIRY ON POISON
—New York Times, March 15, 1989
SHOPPERS EXASPERATED BY NEW PERIL
—New York Times, March 15, 1989
HEALTH OFFICIAL REBUKES SCHOOLS OVER APPLE BANS
—New York Times, March 16, 1989
U.S. AGENCIES TO ALLAY FEARS, PROCLAIM APPLES SAFE TO EAT
—New York Times, March 17, 1989
COMPANIES TEST FOOD TO CALM THE PUBLIC
—New York Times, March 25, 1989
FEARS OF PESTICIDES THREATEN AMERICAN WAY OF FARMING
—New York Times, May 1, 1989

Outbreaks of food-borne disease and concern over pesticide residues on fruits and vegetables have become an increasing focus of public attention during the past two or three years. Consumers not only ask the experts which foods are "healthy" to eat but also ask which—if any—are safe. The need to improve regulatory policies and to assess the risk of food contamination is now high on the national agendas of countries in Europe and North America. Calling on the British government to allay public fears about food safety, an editorialist in the medical journal *The Lancet* declared in February 1989 that "shopping for food should not be a source of undue anxiety." This opinion is heartily endorsed by consumers and public health officials alike.

Whereas public anxiety about the food supply focuses on environmental contaminants, medical and health authorities are far more concerned about fat intake and other dietary excesses. This concern received special impetus with the recent publication of three remarkably similar reports on the subject of diet and health that, taken together, provide overwhelming evidence that dietary changes can reduce the risk of certain chronic diseases.

Marion Nestle, Ph.D., M.P.H., is Professor and Chair, Department of Home Economics and Nutrition, New York University, New York City.

(Overleaf) "Still Life with Ham" by Pieter Claesz, 1650, oil on canvas, 36³/₈ × 55 in. Collection, Sarah Campbell Blaffer Foundation, Houston, Texas

Three comprehensive reports on the subject of diet and health, published in Europe and the U.S. in 1988 and 1989, were notably consistent in their recommendations—namely, that people reduce their intake of saturated fat, cholesterol, salt, and sugar and increase consumption of fiber and complex carbohydrates. The process of educating the public about making healthy food choices is an ongoing effort, one that has already had some striking successes, as illustrated by the graph below showing increasing "cholesterol consciousness."

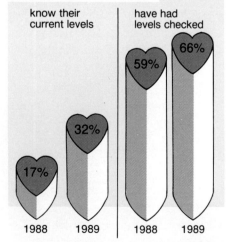

Cholesterol consciousness of U.S. adults

know their current levels

have had levels checked

17% 1988
32% 1989
59% 1988
66% 1989

Source: Gallup Organization/Voluntary Hospitals of America; © 1989 Whittle Communications

New dietary recommendations: remarkable consensus

Historically, governmental and health agencies have issued dietary recommendations for the purpose of encouraging people to consume the foods needed to prevent nutritional deficiencies. With increasing recognition that the primary causes of death in industrialized countries are coronary heart disease (CHD), certain cancers, diabetes, and stroke—all of which are related at least to some extent to what people eat—the focus of dietary recommendations in these countries began to shift toward prevention of chronic, rather than deficiency, diseases.

Since 1977 the U.S. government, for example, has advised the public to reduce overall intake of dietary fat, saturated fat, cholesterol, sugar, salt, and alcohol; to increase consumption of foods containing complex carbohydrates and fiber; and to balance caloric intake and expenditure to maintain an appropriate body weight. These recommendations have elicited considerable controversy. Because the recommendations call for changes in established family eating patterns that could have potentially significant economic consequences, the food industry generally has opposed them. Scientists have questioned the validity of the findings on which some of these recommendations are based, and some health professionals have argued that restrictive diets are unnecessary for the general public and should be recommended only for individuals who have specific risk factors for disease.

The three major reports on diet and health published in 1988 and 1989 should put an end to the scientific controversy. In July 1988 the U.S. Public Health Service issued *The Surgeon General's Report on Nutrition and Health,* a 700-page, heavily referenced review of research that links specific dietary factors to a wide range of chronic diseases. The report identifies reduction of fat intake as the primary dietary priority for the U.S. population and supports earlier dietary recommendations. It also notes the consistency of such recommendations for the prevention of several chronic diseases and draws far-reaching policy implications from these conclusions.

Later in 1988 the World Health Organization (WHO) Regional Office for Europe released *Healthy Nutrition,* a report designed to improve dietary patterns throughout the populations of WHO's 32 European member nations. This report establishes intermediate and ultimate goals for reducing the intake of fat, saturated fat, cholesterol, salt, and sugar along lines similar to the U.S. surgeon general's recommendations; it also includes goals for dietary fiber and guidelines for fluoride and, where necessary, iodine supplementation.

Finally, early in March 1989, the U.S. National Research Council (NRC) released its even more comprehensive study, entitled *Diet and Health,* a document roughly the size of the Manhattan telephone directory. The overall conclusions of *Diet and Health* are virtually identical to those of *The Surgeon General's Report on Nutrition and Health,* and its quantitative guidelines for intake of fat (that 30% or less of daily energy intake be derived from fat), saturated fat (10% of daily intake), cholesterol (limited to 300 milligrams per day), and salt (6 grams per day) support previous U.S. recommendations as well as those of the WHO report.

Health-conscious Americans continue to explore various ethnic cuisines as they search for ways to reduce the amount of fat—and calories—in their diets and eat more foods that are rich in fiber. Oriental-style dishes are popular because they tend to be low in cholesterol and saturated fats. Stir-frying has the advantage of using only a small amount of cooking oil; vegetables cook quickly, stay crisp, and retain their appealing natural color.

The overall acceptance of these recommendations by the scientific community may owe as much to their familiarity as to the impressive quantity of supporting evidence; *Diet and Health* analyzed 5,000 studies to reach its conclusions. Despite some lingering doubts about scientific inconsistencies, all the reports agree that the preponderance of evidence favors dietary changes as a means of improving the health of the general population. The next step is to identify effective strategies for putting the recommendations into practice. Toward this end, the NRC is preparing a further report on implementation of its dietary guidelines, which is scheduled for release in 1990.

Dietary fats—not all equal

Dietary recommendations to eat less fat address specifically the risks of high blood cholesterol (which contributes to CHD), high blood pressure, certain cancers, and diabetes. They are also aimed at preventing obesity, which is known to be a risk factor for other, more serious conditions. The current guidelines suggest that consumers choose lean meats and low-fat dairy products to reduce total fat in their diets and that they replace animal fats with those from vegetable sources to reduce the overall intake of saturated fat. This advice, although still appropriate, has been complicated somewhat by new research on dietary fat sources.

In attempting to categorize and classify the dietary properties of various fatty acids, researchers observed that replacing dietary palmitic acid with either stearic acid or oleic acid could reduce blood cholesterol levels by as much as 14 and 10%, respectively. Thus, they concluded, not all saturated fats are equal in terms of their ability to raise cholesterol levels.

Because stearic acid is a principal fatty acid component of meat and chocolate and oleic acid is the principal fatty acid of olive oil, these findings have been interpreted—especially by meat, candy, and olive oil producers—as evidence that these foods reduce disease risk and can be

Many people are confused about what dietary changes to implement in order to reduce blood cholesterol. The results of one poll (below) indicate that more than a third of Americans believe that decreasing dietary intake of cholesterol alone is the best method. As The Surgeon General's Report on Nutrition and Health *emphasized, however, it is the overall intake of saturated fat that contributes most to elevated cholesterol levels.*

What is the single most important dietary change a person can make to lower an elevated cholesterol level?	
dietary change	percentage who favor change
less cholesterol	36
more fiber	26
less saturated fat	18
less fat	17
do not know	3

consumed with impunity. However, the fats in any given food contain many different kinds of fatty acids. Of the fatty acids in beef, for example, 31% are known to raise blood cholesterol levels. The overall effects of olive oil remain to be determined, however. Recently replacement of other dietary fats with olive oil has been reported to promote better control of blood sugar levels in patients with diabetes mellitus. Nevertheless, an editorial in the *New England Journal of Medicine,* the source of these 1988 studies, noted that until more is known about the various subclassifications of fatty acids in foods, physicians "should not change [their] chief dietary message to the American public"—that is, to reduce *total* fat in the diet.

Fish: on today's menu

Whether the message to eat less fat applies to fish oils containing the fatty acids called omega-3 fatty acids (so named for their particular molecular structure and also found in some vegetable oils) has also been under investigation. When substituted for saturated fatty acids, omega-3 fatty acids reduce blood cholesterol levels and the corresponding risk of CHD. Reports that they prevent or reduce symptoms of a host of other problems—asthma, skin conditions, diabetes, rheumatoid arthritis, and Raynaud's disease (a vascular disorder)—and help to control blood sugar and blood pressure levels in patients with diabetes are less well established, however. *The Surgeon General's Report on Nutrition and Health* notes that the evidence is "too preliminary" for changes in average intake of these substances to be recommended; *Diet and Health* concludes that there is insufficient evidence for the beneficial effects of fish oil supplements (*not* fish itself) and that the absence of long-term adverse effects has not been demonstrated. Both reports recommend that while awaiting the results of further research, people include fish on the menu at least once a week.

Tropical oils: health versus economics

Recommendations to reduce intake of saturated fats by replacing them with fats from vegetable sources have brought the issue of "tropical" oils—coconut, palm, and palm-kernel oils—to public attention. The series of full-

"I see Dr. Koop's office is getting serious about the nutrition issue . . ."

H. Payne; © 1988 Scripps Howard. Reprinted by permission of United Feature Syndicate

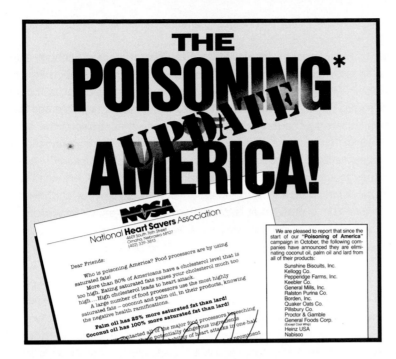

page advertisements on the subject that appeared in major U.S. newspapers indicates the level of passion aroused today by food-related subjects. The first of the ads, which ran in the *New York Times,* the *Wall Street Journal,* and several other widely circulated papers, was bought and paid for by a single person, an American named Phil Sokolof. In the ads he charged that several U.S. manufacturers of cereals, cookies, and other snack foods prepared with tropical oils were responsible for the "Poisoning of America." The reaction on the part of producers and manufacturers was swift. Pepperidge Farm, Keebler, General Mills, and Quaker Oats were among the 13 major manufacturers who eventually announced that they would reformulate products with other, less saturated oils. In retaliation, the Malaysian Oil Palm Growers' Council sponsored another full-page ad to give the American people their version of "The Facts About Palm Oil," which they characterized as "healthy and nutritious."

Unlike most other vegetable oils, tropical oils are exceptionally high in saturated fatty acids. As a result, they are solid at room temperature, melt in the mouth (as, for example, in chocolate), and impart crispness and long shelf-life to such items as cereals, crackers (biscuits), and other packaged goods—qualities favored by manufacturers. At the heart of the debate are three issues: health effects, labeling, and economic policy. Tropical oils are higher in cholesterol-raising fatty acids than butter or beef fat, and their consumption might be expected to increase the risk of CHD. In the past, however, American consumers have not found it easy to avoid them; they are commonly indicated on package labels only as one of several possible alternative ingredients ("vegetable shortening [contains one or more of the following: partially hydrogenated cottonseed oil, partially hydrogenated soybean oil, coconut oil or palm oil]"), a maneuver that allows manufacturers to select the fats to be used in any given product on the basis of seasonal availability and price.

While it is true that tropical oils are usually less expensive than soy and

As consumers become more knowledgeable about the health effects of what they eat, it is inevitable that there will be changes in family eating habits and that these will eventually have an impact on food growers and processors. The issue of tropical oils is a case in point. Although they are of vegetable origin, tropical oils—in particular palm and coconut oil—are very high in cholesterol-raising fatty acids. Until quite recently they were widely used in a variety of processed foods—especially such snack foods as cookies, crackers, and chips—because they contribute to flavor and extend shelf life. They are also low in cost. Following the publication of a series of full-page newspaper ads accusing major food companies that used tropical oils of "poisoning" the American public, many leading companies agreed in 1989 to reformulate some products using less saturated kinds of fats. For the workers on a Malaysian palm oil plantation (below), the campaign against tropical oils represents a threat to their very existence. Palm and coconut oil are major cash crops for a number of third world countries, including Malaysia, Indonesia, and the Philippines.

(Above) Reprinted with permission of Phil Sokolof, National Heart Savers Association

Carl Mydans—Black Star

Scientists are continuing to study the properties of various kinds of fats, searching, among other things, for some that may be "heart friendly." In their quest they have turned up some surprising facts. Olive oil, for example, which has a high proportion of monounsaturated fatty acids, was shown in one study to help control blood sugar levels in persons with diabetes. In another study researchers compared the various fatty acid components of different saturated fats; they found that cholesterol levels were lowered in subjects placed on a liquid diet high in stearic acid, a principal fatty acid component of beef and chocolate. (Although the stearic acid found in beef and chocolate may have beneficial effects, the foods themselves also contain large amounts of other fatty acids known to contribute to elevated cholesterol levels.) While investigations like these may someday result in the formulation of revised dietary guidelines, for the time being, consumers are advised to stick with the recommendation to reduce dietary intake of saturated fats to no more than 10% of total calories and to limit the amount of total fat in the diet to 30% or less of calories.

corn oils, other economic considerations are also germane. Although they make up less than 3% of the total oils available in the U.S. food supply, tropical oils are important sources of income for the countries that produce them, namely, Malaysia, Indonesia, and the Philippines. Thus, while one side of the controversy charges that tropical oils are virtual "poison," the other side claims that they are benign foods and vital to the economy of less developed nations. As noted above, the controversy has already induced numerous manufacturers to switch to other types of fat. More important than the controversy itself is the fact that such arguments can distract consumers from more critical issues—the needs to reduce intake of the more prevalent saturated fats obtained from meat and dairy products and to improve information about fat content on food package labels.

Food labels: room for improvement

Those consumers who would like to follow current dietary recommendations need to know how much fat is in the food they eat and how saturated it is. Both *The Surgeon General's Report* and *Diet and Health* call for the development of new food package labeling regulations; those now in force have not changed substantially since 1971. As many as 70 to 80% of U.S. consumers say that they read labels and that they use them to make food choices. Advocates of new labeling standards want mandatory disclosure of the types of fat, total fat content, and the amount of saturated fat, cholesterol, sodium, calories, and fiber contained in foods.

Until recently the U.S. Food and Drug Administration (FDA) prohibited health claims on food labels, contending that such claims constituted "misbranding" (as the FDA put it) and would make foods subject to the same regulations as drugs. In 1987, in reaction to a highly successful Kellogg

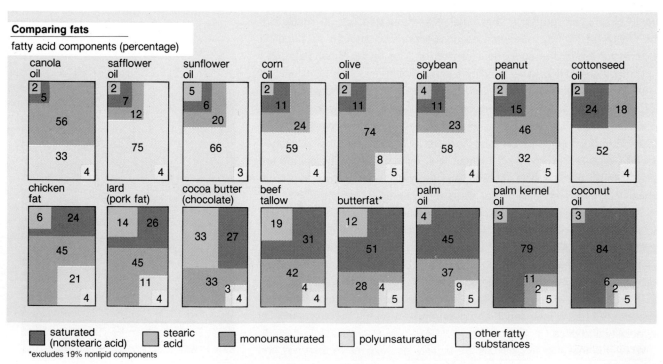

Comparing fats

fatty acid components (percentage)

Source: USDA

campaign implying that one of its high-fiber breakfast cereals might reduce cancer risk, the FDA developed a new policy that would permit food products to carry health messages on their labels. A summary of the more than 500 comments received on the proposed policy suggests that the food industry favors it, consumer advocates are opposed to it, and nutrition professionals are divided on the issue. A revised FDA proposal to restrict health messages to a limited number of topics (e.g., fiber as helping to prevent cancer of the bowel, calcium as having a role in the prevention of osteoporosis) has been awaiting approval since the fall of 1988.

In the meantime, the makers of food products have developed some new and ingenious ways of exploiting current labeling regulations. Thus, a cereal may carry a message in bold print advertising its high fiber content, but a careful reading of all the nutritional information—the small print—shows that high-fiber cereals may also be high in salt, sugar, calories, or saturated fats. The fact that a package label prominently displays the phrase "no cholesterol" does not necessarily mean that the product inside is low in fat. In another example, a major U.S. company advertised that its soups were low in fat and cholesterol and made a positive contribution to heart disease prevention. What the ad neglected to mention was that the high sodium content of the soups might increase the risk of heart disease by raising blood pressure. Such examples make it abundantly clear that new rules for food labeling are necessary if consumers are to be able to make intelligent, informed choices.

Alcohol and stroke risk

Dietary recommendations to restrict alcohol consumption are based on well-established links between drinking and the development of cirrhosis of the liver, nervous system disorders, birth defects, osteoporosis, hypertension, and cancers of the mouth, larynx, and esophagus. Associations with increased risk of stroke, CHD, and cancers of the bowel and breast, however, are less certain.

There is substantial epidemiological evidence to support a relationship between drinking—especially binge drinking—and stroke. Population studies, which look at the overall alcohol intake of large groups of people, demonstrate that the risk of stroke increases with progressively higher levels of alcohol intake. Case-control studies, in which the drinking habits of individuals who have had strokes (cases) are compared with those of people who have never had strokes (controls), show that both chronic heavy drinking and binge drinking are linked to increased overall risk of this condition, especially in younger persons. These same studies show links with increases in both hemorrhagic stroke (i.e., stroke caused by bleeding) and thrombotic stroke (caused by a blood clot). Prospective, community-based studies (which follow a group of initially healthy people over a period of time) demonstrate that the risk of hemorrhagic, but not thrombotic, stroke increases with alcohol use and that this risk rises independently of other known risk factors, such as high blood pressure or cigarette smoking. Just exactly how alcohol acts to increase the risk of stroke has not yet been determined.

Nutrition information per serving	
serving size	6 oz (170 g)
servings per container	2
calories	250
protein	xx g
carbohydrate	xx g
fat	15 g
sodium	xxx mg

Ingredients: water, beef fat, hydrogenated vegetable oil, salt, carrots, onions, food starch, tomato paste, spices, caramel color

Knowing how to evaluate the fat content of processed foods can be a challenge for even the best-informed consumer. There are four basic questions to ask: (1) Is fat a major ingredient? The label must list all ingredients by weight. In the above product, the greatest ingredient is water. Beef fat and hydrogenated vegetable oil are next; therefore, this is likely to be a high-fat product; (2) Is there more than one kind of fat in the product? If several high-fat ingredients are listed, the product probably contains an undesirable amount of fat; (3) How many calories come from fat? This product has 15 grams of fat per serving (one gram of fat equals nine calories). Out of a total of 250 calories per serving, 135—more than 50%— come from fat; (4) Is the serving size appropriate? There are two six-ounce servings in the container. Six ounces may be a smaller-than-average serving. Thus, an average serving might have more calories—and more fat—than indicated.

CONTAINS NO COCONUT OIL

Drawing by C. Barsotti; © 1988 The New Yorker Magazine, Inc.

From A. G. Shaper et al., "Alcohol and Mortality in British Men...." The Lancet, vol. II, no. 8623 (Dec. 3, 1988), pp. 1267–73

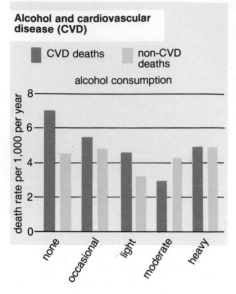

Alcohol and cardiovascular disease (CVD)

A British study supports the finding that the risk of cardiovascular disease is elevated in heavy drinkers, whereas people who drink moderately are at relatively low risk. Researchers are uncertain how to interpret the apparent increase in risk among abstainers and those who drink only occasionally. Possibly, ill health is a reason for decreased intake of alcohol. Studies that separate nondrinkers from former drinkers show that the former drinkers are at greatest risk.

In a study of stroke incidence among nearly 8,000 men who were followed over a 12-year period in the Honolulu Heart Program, researchers found that light drinkers had more than double the risk of hemorrhagic stroke than nondrinkers. Among heavy drinkers the risk was nearly triple. The relationship between excessive alcohol consumption and increased risk of stroke is less certain than the link that has been established for such chronic diseases as cirrhosis of the liver, hypertension, and nervous system disorders.

Drinking and heart disease

On the basis of evidence from many studies, the relationship between alcohol consumption and CHD risk, if plotted on a graph, describes a J-shaped curve. People who drink moderately have relatively low rates of CHD compared with people who drink less and compared with those who drink more. Risk is elevated in both lifetime abstainers and former drinkers—at least in populations with relatively high mean serum cholesterol levels (greater than 200 milligrams per deciliter). This pattern of higher risk at low intake levels has been shown to be consistent across many different population groups, true of women as well as men, and independent of many other risk factors. It is explained, at least in part, by the fact that nondrinkers and those who drink only occasionally have reduced blood levels of high-density lipoprotein (HDL), the so-called good cholesterol.

In other words, it appears that moderate alcohol consumption might actually decrease coronary risk (by raising HDL levels), a notion many health professionals find difficult to accept. The deleterious effects of alcohol on other medical conditions and the relationship of drinking to accidents, suicide, and violence argue against recommending its consumption under any circumstances. In addition, there is also some contrary evidence—for example, the risk of CHD is reduced in Seventh Day Adventists, who abstain from alcohol. The higher risk observed in other groups of abstainers may perhaps be a function of their previous drinking history; the results of studies that separate nondrinkers from former drinkers indicate that the former drinkers are at greater risk. Another possibility is that the type of HDL affected by alcohol is not the one normally associated with heart disease prevention.

Alcohol and cancer: related, but only weakly

At least 21 separate studies have examined the association between alcohol and colon cancer. Of these, 12 suggest a relationship, but 9 do not. A report in the May 1988 *American Journal of Epidemiology* suggested that alcohol may be more clearly related to rectal than to colon cancer. Studies of the relationship of alcohol to breast cancer also display inconsistencies. Most evidence comes from case-control studies in which the reported alcohol consumption of women with breast cancer is compared

Alcohol and stroke incidence

rate of stroke per 1,000 by age and drinking status

age (years)	hemorrhagic strokes		thromboembolic strokes		all strokes	
45–49	8.2	0.0	12.2	13.4	21.2	13.4
50–54	9.4	6.3	17.7	12.6	28.7	20.9
55–59	15.9	3.2	30.8	32.3	47.7	37.1
60–64	21.3	5.5	38.6	31.0	67.8	47.4
65–69	17.3	15.2	69.3	60.9	99.6	81.2

drinkers   nondrinkers

From Richard P. Donahue et al., "Alcohol and Hemorrhagic Stroke," JAMA, vol. 255, no. 17 (May 2, 1986), pp. 2311–14; © 1988 American Medical Association

"It's called a dry Martini. When Grandpa was a young man, all the young men on the move drank dry Martinis."

with the drinking histories of women who do not have breast cancer. Of 15 such studies, only 8 have found any association, and these suggest that moderate drinking doubles the risk, at most.

That the association is weak was confirmed by a meta-analysis (a quantitative review of data from various studies) published in the Aug. 5, 1988, issue of the *Journal of the American Medical Association.* The authors concluded that only 13% of all cases of breast cancer in the United States "might be attributable to alcohol consumption." Many other observations support the view that drinking and breast cancer are only weakly related: the absence of experimental data in animals; the lack of a clear increase in cancer rate with increased alcohol intake; studies of British barmaids that show a higher death rate from cirrhosis of the liver in this group but lower mortality from breast cancer; and the relatively low rates of breast cancer in France and Italy—countries with the highest per capita rates of alcohol consumption.

The new sobriety

Alcohol contributes to an estimated 100,000 deaths per year in the U.S. and more than $130 billion in economic losses. Perhaps in response to these grim statistics, Americans have been steadily reducing their consumption of beer, wine, and hard liquor in the past decade. Between 1980 and 1987, beer consumption fell by 7%, wine by 14%, and hard liquor by 23%; these trends are expected to continue. Other suggestions of a new temperance movement are the doubling of membership in Alcoholics Anonymous from 1977 to 1987 and the 17% drop in alcohol consumption in restaurants since 1987.

The "new sobriety" can be accounted for in part, at least, by increasing

15

public awareness of the hazards associated with drinking. Some hard-hitting advertising campaigns have brought home the tragedies wrought by drunk drivers, and the social acceptability of driving under the influence is waning. As further evidence that abstention is an idea whose time has come, the U.S. will in November 1989 become the first country to require a health warning on all containers of alcoholic beverages. The label is to read as follows:

GOVERNMENT WARNING: (1) According to the Surgeon General, women should not drink alcoholic beverages during pregnancy because of the risk of birth defects. (2) Consumption of alcoholic beverages impairs your ability to drive a car or operate machinery, and may cause health problems.

China: an epidemiologist's paradise

For answers to many of the pressing questions about dietary habits and the development of diverse diseases, some medical scientists have turned to China. The size, geographic diversity, and stability of its population and the availability of national data on illness and death rates make China an ideal site for epidemiological investigations of diet and disease. In 1989 scientists at Cornell University, Ithaca, New York, the University of Oxford, and two medical centers in Beijing (Peking) published the first results of their joint study of more than 300 dietary, life-style, and mortality characteristics of groups living in 65 widely disbursed rural areas throughout China. Because these local populations demonstrate far greater variation in eating habits and in disease prevalence than is found in industrialized countries, these data should permit investigators to clarify some of the more puzzling diet-disease relationships. Fat intake across the 65 areas, for example, ranged from 6 to 45% of total calories, and some regions exhibited a death rate from cancer that was 350 times that of other regions.

The study has already generated more than 100,000 correlations between specific dietary factors (*e.g.*, alcohol, vitamin A), biochemical indexes of nutritional status (blood cholesterol, iron), demographic variables (age, gender), life-style characteristics (physical activity, smoking history), and dis-

Several recent events have shaken consumer confidence both in the safety of the food supply and in the ability of the government to ensure that the food that reaches the marketplace is free of contamination. Anxiety was heightened in late February 1989 when a report by the environmentalist organization the National Resources Defense Council was made public. It predicted that several thousand U.S. schoolchildren could eventually develop cancer as a result of exposure to chemical residues, in particular a substance known as Alar, which was being widely used on red apples. Subsequently, American apple growers decided to discontinue the use of Alar, but not before some school cafeterias stopped serving apples. Then, only a few weeks later, two grapes in a shipment from Chile were found to have been injected with cyanide, evidently by a terrorist. While investigating the incident, the Food and Drug Administration impounded two million crates of grapes and other fruit from Chile, and stores all over the country removed all Chilean produce from the shelves. Fortunately, no more poisoned fruit was found.

Steve Leonard—Black Star

Compared with the risks from chemical residues or tampering, microbial contamination of food poses a considerably more urgent health hazard. In 1988 the contamination of eggs with Salmonella *organisms was a major focus of concern. In April 1988 the U.S. Centers for Disease Control reported on 65 outbreaks of* Salmonella *that had caused 2,119 cases of illness; of those that could be traced to a specific food, more than 75% had been caused by uncracked, fresh eggs. Much microbial contamination is a consequence of the close-quarter conditions in the centralized production of eggs and poultry, where infections tend to spread rapidly.*

ease (heart disease, cancer). Analysis of correlations among these factors is certain to provide otherwise unavailable information on, for example, the relationship of diet to cancer, thus permitting more definitive understanding of how fat, alcohol, pesticide residues on food, and other factors might affect the risk of this disease.

Food safety: cause for anxiety in the supermarket

Several events in 1989 revealed profound, ongoing public fears about the safety of the food supply. The U.S. Food Marketing Institute's 1989 trends survey reported, for the fifth year in a row, that at least 75% of American consumers view pesticide and herbicide residues in food as a serious health hazard. These views were reinforced by three events that happened in rapid succession: a report that Alar, a pesticide used on red apples in the U.S., might increase cancer risk in children caused school boards throughout the country to withdraw the fruit from lunch menus; the governments of the U.S., Japan, and Canada refused to permit the import of a billion dollars' worth of Chilean grapes because cyanide had been found in two of them; and the state of Arkansas ordered the destruction of 400,000 chickens contaminated by heptachlor, an insecticide banned from food crops in 1978 but still permitted for use on seeds.

These events, however, were only the latest in a series that have deeply shaken the confidence of consumers throughout the U.S., Europe, and the U.K. In December 1988 a political furor developed in the United Kingdom when Edwina Currie, a junior health minister, remarked that "most" of the country's egg production was, in her words, "sadly infected with *Salmonella.*" Shortly afterward, Currie was forced to resign. Although her comments were considered irresponsible, the public's concern was not unfounded. The number of isolations of one particular type of *Salmonella* from poultry and intact eggs in the U.K. had increased from under 400 to more than 10,000 between 1981 and 1988 and had doubled between 1987 and 1988.

A March 1989 Gallup poll shows that while most U.S. consumers believe, on the whole, that their food is safe, they are more concerned about the issue than ever before.

Consumer confidence in 1989

concerns about food supply in general

more worried than ever before about pesticides and other chemical residues	38%
less worried	6%
no change	53%
want food free of chemicals even if price is higher	73%
often or occasionally buy organic	45%
never or hardly ever buy organic	47%

concerns about specific foods

worried about or have cut purchases of

apples	44%
vegetables	41%
eggs and poultry	23%
fish	25%
milk	9%

confidence in regulatory processes

feel that government ensures safety of food produced in U.S.	52%
feel that imported food is safe	44%

From the *Newsweek* Poll, conducted by the Gallup Organization (March 16–17, 1989); © 1989 by Newsweek, Inc.

In the U.S. the authority for food inspection is fragmented among a number of disparate federal, state, and local agencies. The Department of Agriculture is charged with inspecting meat and poultry; the Food and Drug Administration is responsible for fruits, vegetables, and eggs and partly responsible for seafood and milk. Federal inspection of seafood, however, is not mandatory. Furthermore, in none of the various regulatory agencies is the staff large enough to do the job. If fish is inspected at all, it is done at the local level. Rudolph Albanese (below) is a fish inspector for New York City.

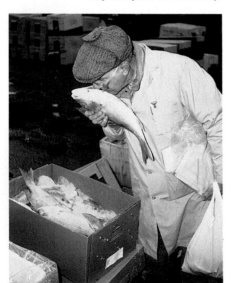

In the U.S., where numerous egg-related outbreaks of *Salmonella* have been reported in recent years, the Department of Agriculture (USDA) revealed that a third of the poultry currently being sold is contaminated by these or other bacteria, viruses, or parasites. The FDA has estimated that food-borne illness affects 33 million Americans annually, and epidemiologists from the Centers for Disease Control have reported the number and severity of food-borne illnesses to be increasing every year. Much microbial contamination is a consequence of the increasingly centralized production and processing of eggs and poultry. Infections spread rapidly under assembly-line conditions.

Current government regulations are apparently insufficient to prevent outbreaks of food-borne illness. In the U.S., authority for food inspection is fragmented among disparate federal, state, and local agencies. The USDA inspects meat and poultry; the FDA is responsible for fruits, vegetables, and eggs and partially responsible for seafood and milk. Federal inspection of seafood is not mandatory, however, a situation that was of particular concern to consumers in 1989, and the primary responsibility for milk inspection is at the local level. In none of these agencies are staffing levels adequate to the task.

Consumers *can* be educated to wash, cook, and store poultry and eggs appropriately, but economic pressures are now forcing food producers and processors to take steps to prevent the initial contamination. They are currently considering such methods as disinfection of animals, feed, and processing equipment; immunization of animals; and the addition of competitive intestinal microorganisms to animal feed.

Hormones and livestock: more "health versus economics"

In January 1989 the European Communities (EC) instituted a ban on imports of beef from the U.S. The ban was in response to complaints by groups in West Germany and Italy about the potential health hazards of hormones currently being used by U.S. cattle producers to increase the lean weight

18

of beef prior to slaughter. The ban placed the billion-dollar American beef export trade at risk and caused the U.S. to retaliate by proposing an increase in taxes on foods and beverages imported from Europe.

European health concerns about the use of hormones in livestock stem from an incident that took place in Italy in 1981 in which premature sexual maturation of infants was attributed to baby food made from veal treated with the synthetic estrogen diethylstilbestrol; the substance had been banned (both in Europe and the U.S.), and its use would have been strictly illegal. As a result of this incident, however, the EC in 1985 outlawed *all* use of hormones in livestock and gave U.S. meat exporters until 1989 to comply. Hormones continue to be used legally in the U.S. Most are synthetic derivatives of estrogen and progesterone that authorities agree pose no threat to human health when used properly (in accepted amounts and only at specific times in the animal's life cycle).

From the standpoint of the U.S. meat industry, much is at stake in the dispute with the EC. The use of hormones is said to save the $23 billion-a-year U.S. cattle industry at least $650 million annually. Americans are already concerned about the cholesterol in beef and discouraged by beef's high price; publicity about hormones will not help sales. The underlying issue in the international dispute is more one of trade policy than of health.

Pesticides keep apples away

Consumers who wish to improve their health by cutting down on meat and dairy foods and increasing complex carbohydrate and fiber intake must now confront another issue—widespread contamination of fruits and vegetables by fungicides, herbicides, insecticides, and plant-growth regulators. In February 1989 a report from a U.S. environmental group, the Natural Resources Defense Council (NRDC), declaring that American children face intolerable risks of cancer from pesticide residues was publicized on the popular television show "60 Minutes" and given front-page attention in national newspapers and magazines. According to the NRDC estimate, up to 6,200 preschool youngsters in the U.S. will develop cancer later in life from exposure to pesticides. The NRDC attributed nearly all of the risk to a substance called Alar (daminozide), a growth regulator that is used on

MY MOM WON'T LET ME EAT APPLES 'CAUSE THEY MAY CONTAIN ALAR.

MY MOM WON'T LET ME EAT ANY GRAPES 'CAUSE THEY MAY HAVE CYANIDE.

SO MY MOM'S LETTING ME EAT CANDY BARS!

Brian Basset; © 1989 The Seattle Times

Irradiated strawberries stored in the refrigerator for four weeks still look firm and edible; berries that were not irradiated have become moldy. The potatoes on the left were irradiated; those on the right, which were not treated, had begun to sprout after two months. Exposure of foods to the level of radiation needed to produce these beneficial effects does not make them radioactive; it can, however, alter flavor and slightly reduce nutrient content.

red apples to promote firmness, enhance color, and reduce spoilage. The NRDC report stated that children are at higher risk than adults because they consume more calories relative to body weight, eat six or seven times more fruit, drink 18 times more apple juice, have longer potential life-spans, and have less well-developed bodily detoxification systems.

The NRDC risk estimates are difficult to evaluate. First, Alar itself does not appear to be carcinogenic; rather, it breaks down to a carcinogenic substance when heated. Second, the widely respected National Research Council reported in 1987 that even the most carcinogenic pesticide residues would increase the lifetime risk of cancer, which is already about 25%, only by 0.1%—to 25.1%. However, this claim too is difficult to evaluate. As stated in the March 17, 1989, issue of *Science,* these kinds of numbers are "squishy"—there are no hard figures on either side on which to base enlightened public policy.

Consumer anxieties about pesticides are heightened by the lack of ability to control their use; people cannot see, smell, or taste pesticide residues on food and must rely on regulatory processes to screen them out of the food supply. In the U.S. alone, however, pesticide use has more than doubled in the last 20 years to about 372 million kilograms (820 million pounds) per year; these substances pervade the food supply. Alar, unlike some other agricultural chemicals, penetrates the skin of apples and cannot be washed off. In May 1989 *Consumer Reports* identified Alar residues in three-quarters of the apple juice samples surveyed. The U.S. Environmental Protection Agency (EPA) insists that the 320 pesticides now approved for use on food crops pose little hazard to health, but 66 of these substances have been identified as carcinogens. Knowledge about their long-term health effects is based mainly on extrapolation of data from tests using laboratory animals. No epidemiological studies have yet demonstrated correlations between pesticide consumption and cases of human cancer. Data on levels of pesticide intake also are meager. A 1988 study in the *American Journal of Public Health* found that blood levels of 11 pesticides and their metabolites (substances into which they are broken down within the body) increased with age in individuals living in rural areas. The authors were unable to evaluate the health risks of such exposures, however. The EPA's reassurances are inconsistent with its own regulatory policies; the

20

agency has attempted to prohibit the use of Alar three times since 1979.

What of the American consumer who must choose between the unknown risks of pesticide-treated produce and the benefits of increased fruit and vegetable consumption? One food columnist in the *New York Times* advised readers to wash and peel fresh fruits and vegetables, to demand organically grown produce, and, whenever possible, to grow their own food. This advice is hardly practical for most people. It is also worth noting that 60–80% of all pesticides in use today in the U.S. are used to enhance the appearance of fruits and vegetables by heightening their color and keeping them relatively free of blemishes. If consumers want produce without pesticide residues, they will have to learn to accept fruits and vegetables that look less than perfect.

Food irradiation: is it safe or necessary?

Whether food irradiation is a safe—and acceptable—alternative to pesticides is uncertain. The process kills insects, molds, and bacteria, can be effective against *Salmonella* organisms, and slows ripening. It does so by bombarding foods with gamma rays from one of two radioactive isotopes, cobalt-60, a by-product of nuclear power, or cesium-137, a waste product from nuclear weapons production. These sources induce formation of electrically charged highly reactive molecules that damage living cells. This damage either kills microbial cells outright or prevents them from reproducing. The degree of sterilization of exposed foods increases with radiation

Irradiation: what it can and cannot do

suggested dose in kilograys	benefits	limitations
0.05–0.75	sterilizes insects	reinfestation possible
0.05–0.15	inhibits sprouting of root crops and elongation of asparagus	potatoes must cure before irradiation
0.1–0.75	delays ripening of some fruits	successful for only limited number of fruits
0.3–0.5	inactivates parasites in meat	refrigeration still necessary
1–2	kills spoilage microorganisms in fish and fungi in fruits	recontamination possible for all foods; foods still need refrigeration
2–4	reduces microorganisms causing public health problems in meat and poultry	above certain doses, causes softening, pitting, and other problems in fruits; above certain doses, affects color and flavor of meat and poultry
23–57	sterilizes food for unrefrigerated storage	food must be irradiated frozen to minimize undesirable changes in quality

1 kiloray = 100 rads

From R. M. Morrison, "Irradiation Potential for Preserving Food," *National Food Review*, NFR-3, USDA, Spring 1986

At present the only foods that may legally be irradiated in the U.S. are dehydrated spices, teas, and seeds; certain fruits and vegetables; and fresh pork. Packaged foods must be clearly labeled to indicate that they have been treated by irradiation, and the label must display the flowerlike food-irradiation logo that has been adopted internationally.

"You figure it. Everything we eat is 100 percent natural yet our life expectancy is only 31 years."

dose. Since 1981 the World Health Organization has approved dose levels up to 10 kilograys as safe. One kilogray (1,000 grays) is equal to 100,000 rads (radiation absorbed dose), the form of measurement commonly used in the past. Exposure from a chest X-ray would be about 0.1 to 0.5 rads. Exposure to this level of radiation does not make food radioactive, although it does alter flavor, reduce nutrient content, and cause other, not completely understood changes in molecular structure. The loss of nutritional value is minimal, however, and the so-called induced radiolytic products, the substances formed in response to the radiation, are unlikely to be harmful.

By 1989, 33 countries had approved at least some irradiated foods for human consumption, but some of these countries permit only limited use of the process. For example, the U.K. restricts irradiated food to that used

In 1989 a food columnist for the New York Times *advised consumers to carefully wash or peel all fresh fruits and vegetables, to demand that stores stock more organically grown produce, and, wherever possible, to grow their own food. Certainly, the call for organic fruits and vegetables has been given impetus by recent events. Correspondingly, interest in pesticide-free agriculture is increasing among food producers. However, a majority of the herbicides and pesticides used in the U.S. today are employed for "cosmetic" purposes. If consumers want foods free of chemical residues, they may have to settle for fruits and vegetables that are less than perfect in appearance. This is a compromise many consumers are apparently ready to make.*

Herman Kokojan—Black Star

in hospital diets, The Netherlands to chicken, and the U.S. to dehydrated herbs and spices, seeds, teas, vegetable seasonings, certain fruits and vegetables, and fresh pork.

The debate over food irradiation centers on issues of human safety. The major proponents include food producers, who seek an efficient means of preventing microbial contamination, and nuclear power producers, who seek a market for nuclear waste products. These groups contend that irradiation extends the storage life of foods without microbiological, toxicological, or nutritional risk. Opposed are consumer groups who question the effects of ionizing radiation on food quality and cite the disasters at Three Mile Island and Chernobyl as examples of the inability of the nuclear power industry to maintain adequate safety standards.

Consumers' fears that irradiated foods are radioactive or toxic are not justified by current data. More realistic are concerns that unsanitary food handling subsequent to irradiation might lead to recontamination or that transportation, storage, use, and disposal of radioactive source materials will pose a public risk. Whether mandatory labeling of irradiated foods might resolve public anxiety is uncertain. Consumer resistance to food irradiation is strong. Perhaps for this reason, the international symbol chosen to represent the process resembles a flower, with all of its connotations of peace and safety. To increase consumer acceptance, proponents have suggested that food irradiation be referred to by some other term, such as "cosmic processing," "picowave processing," or the designation "processed with ionizing energy."

A reasonable perspective

Experts agree that the health risks of pesticide residues in foods are real but finite and that they are small in comparison with the risks posed by cigarettes, alcohol, saturated fats, or cholesterol. Population studies convincingly demonstrate an association between diets high in fruits and vegetables and protection against certain cancers and other chronic diseases. Public alarm about pesticides and irradiation emphasizes the need for better regulatory policies and safer food-production methods, and public pressure may be the most effective way to achieve these ends. A case in point: the proportion of apples treated with Alar in the U.S. reportedly decreased from 40 to 5% between 1985 and 1989. After the public outcry in the spring of 1989, U.S. apple growers announced that they would voluntarily stop using the chemical; subsequently, the manufacturer of Alar discontinued its sale in the U.S. With more consumers asking for organically grown produce, interest in pesticide-free agriculture is increasing among policymakers and food producers.

Placing these issues in reasonable perspective is a challenge to all concerned—government officials, scientists, and consumer advocates. All of the experts agree that microbial contamination poses the most urgent health hazard. Consumers can prevent food-borne infection by storing, washing, and cooking foods properly, but in the long term, the problems of microbial contamination demand political solutions based on improved inspection and regulation of food production and processing methods.

HORN OF MODERATION

Drawing by Stevenson; © 1989 The New Yorker Magazine, Inc.

23

Johns Hopkins: Celebrating a Century of Medicine

by A. McGehee Harvey, M.D., and Susan L. Abrams

By the late 19th century, American medicine was ripe for an explosion of progress. According to one theory, medical science advances in cycles: relatively quiet periods are characterized by growing dissatisfaction with the status quo; new approaches are tried and modified during the ensuing period of experimentation. When a satisfactory compromise is reached, the ferment ceases, things settle down, and the process begins again.

The state of medical education and practice in the United States before the turn of the century was, in a word, deplorable. Entrance requirements for medical schools were shockingly low; most medical students had completed only elementary school. Medical schools generally offered an eight-month program, and students were awarded the medical degree if they could answer a few questions at the end of the course. Students received little or no practical experience in clinical subjects, and effective licensing of physicians did not exist.

At the same time, however, interest in bacteriology had reached a critical level, and in the 1880s the bacterial causes of many diseases would be discovered. Technological innovation was also leading Americans to appreciate the place of science in an industrial society, while improvements in public education were preparing more and more students for advanced work. Moreover, a growing amount of private wealth was available to support new philanthropic enterprises. It was at that time, in Baltimore, Maryland, that plans for the Johns Hopkins University, the Johns Hopkins Hospital, and a school of medicine had come to fruition—against many odds. The hospital opened in 1889 and the medical school in 1893. The first president of the university, Daniel C. Gilman, advanced a vision of medicine at Johns Hopkins vastly different from the prevailing views of medical education and patient care. Today, at the centennial of medicine at Johns Hopkins, Gilman's then advanced notions are taken for granted as integral parts of American medicine.

Baltimore's greatest philanthropist

The man who endowed the university, medical school, and hospital that bear his name was neither a scholar nor a physician. Johns Hopkins was a

A. McGehee Harvey, M.D., is Distinguished Service Professor of Medicine at the Johns Hopkins School of Medicine.
Susan L. Abrams is an editor at the Johns Hopkins School of Medicine.

(Opposite page) In a photograph taken in 1962, a pediatric nurse and a young patient hospitalized for cardiac surgery watch the construction of the new Children's Medical and Surgical Center. Photograph, Robert Phillips, the Alan M. Chesney Medical Archives, the Johns Hopkins Medical Institutions

25

The Johns Hopkins
Medical Institutions; photograph, Bert Glinn

Johns Hopkins, a Quaker who rose from a grocer's helper to the most powerful financier in Victorian Baltimore, chose to leave his $7 million fortune for the creation of two closely linked institutions—a university that would be distinguished for excellence and a hospital that would be staffed by doctors "of the highest character and greatest skills."

Quaker from a Maryland plantation family that fell on hard times when, in accordance with Quaker beliefs, it freed its slaves. The plantation could no longer support the family, and young Johns was sent to Baltimore to live with his uncle, a wholesale grocer. "Thee has business ability and thee must go where the money is," his mother urged him. However, when this uncle refused him permission to marry his daughter (the Society of Friends did not permit marriages between first cousins), Johns moved out of the house and set up his own business. He prospered, eventually becoming a banker, but he never married. With no direct heirs, he intended to dispose of his entire fortune in accordance with the principles of the Society of Friends, and he believed that he would be "given to see" the best use of his money. He talked with other philanthropists and with friends and acquaintances, and he read extensively—about medicine and many other subjects. Then, in 1867, Hopkins decided to donate $7 million in two equal portions—one part for the founding of a hospital and the other for a university. It was the largest endowment ever made for medical purposes up to that time. Hopkins next selected 12 trustees and placed them on interlocking boards to govern the two institutions, which was concrete evidence that he wanted the hospital and the university to be closely linked.

Hopkins gave careful consideration to ideas that he intended to incorporate into this new endeavor. He instructed the trustees to obtain the advice and help of experts from around the world in planning the hospital so that it would "compare favorably with any institution of like character in this country or in Europe." The trustees were told to staff the hospital with physicians and surgeons "of the highest character and greatest skills."

University, hospital, medical school: realizing Hopkins's dream

When the Johns Hopkins University opened in 1876 under Gilman's direction, it was the first modern university in the United States—the first to adopt the European idea of university education, which insisted on the importance of research and required all its faculty members to be investigators. Gilman emphasized not simply the transmittal of what was known but the discovery of new information.

The multitalented architect who was selected to design the hospital that Johns Hopkins endowed was John Shaw Billings. Billings had been a battlefield surgeon during the Civil War and was a pioneer in public health and a medical bibliographer and bibliophile who later became the first director of the New York (City) Public Library. In the fall of 1876 he visited hospitals and medical schools in London, Leipzig, Berlin, Vienna, and Paris; he returned to the United States having absorbed the best of European approaches, which he then applied to his plans for the Johns Hopkins Hospital.

National Library of Medicine, Bethesda, Maryland

Students came to Hopkins to "learn by doing," a process that required them to acquire knowledge rather than receive it passively. Through small classes and individual laboratory work, they learned how to learn and how to continue the process of self-education once their formal schooling was over.

This spirit of unity was fostered by fortunate circumstances. The university's substantial financial resources were accompanied by a freedom from religious and governmental control. There was also freedom from the hindrance of tradition—freedom from the handicap of antiquated ideas.

The same emphasis upon research and advanced instruction that marked the Johns Hopkins University was also to become the center of the program of medical education and medical research at the Johns Hopkins Hospital. In accordance with Hopkins's wishes, the trustees set out to find the best person available to design the hospital. Five men were invited to submit plans; four were experts in hospital design, but the fifth—John Shaw Billings—was one of the outstanding men of his generation. An army surgeon during the Civil War, Billings became an authority in public health, medical education, and medical bibliography; his later career included his pioneering work as the organizer and first director of the New York (City) Public Library.

It was obvious to the trustees that Billings would be more than merely an architect, and in 1876 he began to supervise the hospital's construction. The facilities that Billings designed were the most advanced for the time. An elaborate ventilating system would prevent the spread of disease, and rounded corners where walls and floors met would keep dirt from accumulating and be easy to clean. More important, however, Billings's plans made the hospital a place for teaching and research as well as for patient care.

Construction of the hospital began under John Shaw Billings's supervision in 1876; the new medical facility formally opened on May 7, 1889. The leading article in the next day's Baltimore American *began, "Magnificent in her beauty and her glory stood The Johns Hopkins Hospital yesterday." In 1976, at the time of the university's centennial, the original Queen Anne-style domed administration building was officially named the John Shaw Billings Building and was added to the National Register of Historic Buildings.*

27

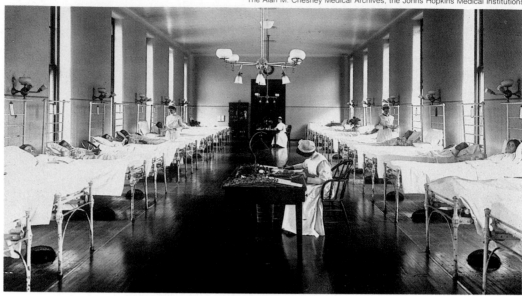

While the hospital was under construction, plans for the medical school were also under way. The founding faculty—consisting of Billings, Ira Remsen, and Henry Newell Martin—was appointed by Gilman in 1883, but ten years elapsed before the school opened, and by then none of the founders was available to serve on the faculty.

The first member of the faculty actually to serve in the medical school was William H. Welch. Appointed professor of pathology in 1884, he was to be Johns Hopkins's guiding spirit until his death in 1934 at age 84. Other faculty members were appointed during the next few years: William Osler as professor of medicine, William S. Halsted as professor of surgery, and Howard A. Kelly as professor of gynecology. With Welch, they were the "Four Doctors," the subject of a famous painting by John Singer Sargent,

(Above) Common wards in the original hospital were designed to avoid the buildup of dust and dirt and thus were kept scrupulously clean. Many large windows allowed abundant natural lighting, and individually regulated ventilators under the beds provided fresh air for each patient.

Plans for the medical school were in progress a full decade before it actually was able to open in 1893. Pictured are members of the founding medical faculty—Basil Gildersleeve (seated left), Ira Remsen (seated right), Henry A. Rowland (standing left), and William H. Welch (standing right)—all of whom were appointed by Daniel C. Gilman (seated center), the first president of the Johns Hopkins University.

which now hangs in the medical school's library—the Welch Medical Library. Not only were Osler, Halsted, and Kelly professors in the medical school, they were also chiefs of their respective departments in the hospital.

A women's committee to the rescue

Financial disaster struck the Johns Hopkins University in the late 1880s when the Baltimore and Ohio Railroad, whose stock represented all of the university's endowment, stopped paying dividends. As part of the university, the medical school could not open without the railroad's funds. Into the picture stepped a group of trustees' daughters. Led by Martha Carey Thomas, who later became president of Bryn Mawr (Pennsylvania) College, the women formed a committee to raise the rest of the money needed to open the medical school. Women nationwide rallied to the cause; among the subscribers was First Lady Caroline Harrison. One of the trustees' daughters, Mary Garrett, herself contributed $50,000, and in the fall of 1890, the Women's Fund Committee was able to offer the trustees $100,-000. This donation came with one stipulation: women had to be admitted to the medical school on equal terms with men.

The trustees accepted the contribution, but the school could not open until a total of $500,000 had been raised. By December 1892 less than half the necessary amount was in hand. Garrett then offered to contribute the remaining money—but her offer came with additional stipulations. Garrett insisted that entering medical students have a bachelor's degree from a first-rate college and a reading knowledge of French and German. The trustees and faculty were aghast. Although the founding faculty had advocated these entrance requirements in 1884, they now feared that in practice, few students would be qualified for or interested in attending Johns Hopkins under these conditions. The unprecedented character of these conditions led Osler to remark to Welch that they had been lucky to get in as professors because neither of them could have got in as students!

The Johns Hopkins
Medical Institutions; photograph, Guy Pease

The "Four Doctors" immortalized in the famous portrait by John Singer Sargent (1906) were (left to right): William Welch, William Halsted, William Osler, and Howard Kelly. The painting now hangs in the library of the School of Medicine, named the Welch Medical Library.

Had it not been for the money provided by the Women's Fund Committee, the medical school could not have opened when it did. Mary E. Garrett (seated center) herself contributed a major portion of the $500,000 that was needed. Others on the committee were (clockwise from lower left) Elizabeth King, Julia Rogers, Mary Gwinn, and Martha Carey Thomas. One of the stipulations that went with the money was that women were to be admitted to the medical school on an equal footing with men.

The Alan M. Chesney Medical Archives,
the Johns Hopkins Medical Institutions

Photograph, Frederick Gutekunst, from *Description of the Johns Hopkins Hospital* by John Shaw Billings; Baltimore: the Johns Hopkins Hospital, 1890

Hospitals in the late 19th century commonly were breeding grounds for pestilence. John Shaw Billings, in designing the Johns Hopkins Hospital, zealously guarded against contagion. The "isolating ward" at right consisted of 20 private patient rooms, each with its own ventilation and chimney, and, as Billings described it, all the rooms opened onto a corridor "through which the wind is always blowing."

In 1890, when William S. Halsted was surgeon in chief, he commissioned the Goodyear Rubber Co. to produce two pairs of rubber gloves. These were to be worn by the head operating room nurse, who had developed a serious rash from vigorous presurgical scrubbing with a mercuric chloride solution. Some seven years later it became routine for all members of the surgical team to wear gloves (below). Today the Johns Hopkins staff uses well over seven million rubber gloves in a single year.

The Alan M. Chesney Medical Archives, the Johns Hopkins Medical Institutions

First medical school class: 18 students

Mary Garrett's contribution allowed the trustees to recruit the rest of the medical school's first faculty. Welch was already in place as the school's first dean. Franklin P. Mall was appointed professor of anatomy; William H. Howell became professor of physiology; and John J. Abel went to Baltimore as professor of pharmacology.

But would they have any students? The opening of the medical school was announced in February 1893. On October 2 of that year, the official opening day, 16 applicants took their credentials to Welch's office, all of whom were admitted (some provisionally); 2 more were admitted a few days later. The first class of the Johns Hopkins University School of Medicine therefore comprised 18 students, including 3 women.

These students were plunged into rigorous, exciting, informal courses that took them out of the classroom and into the laboratory. There was no formal meeting of Mall's anatomy class, for example. Each student was given a part of a cadaver and told to get to work. In the third and fourth years—the so-called clinical years—students turned from the laboratories to the hospital wards. In most other medical schools, attending physicians only rarely allowed the students to come in contact with patients on the wards. Consequently, students generally graduated from medical school lacking any experience with living patients. At Johns Hopkins, in contrast, the students became part of the machinery of the hospital. Osler's fourth-year students examined patients and performed laboratory tests, and the histories they took and the reports they made became part of the patients' records.

Halsted's world-renowned school of surgery

Perhaps the most dramatic of all the stories related to the advance of medical knowledge in the early days of the Hopkins hospital and medical school is that of Halsted, its first surgeon in chief. Halsted struggled throughout most of his career to overcome his accidental addiction to cocaine, acquired

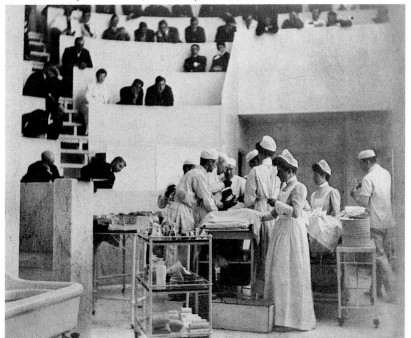

The operating theater was often filled to capacity when William S. Halsted performed a surgical procedure (left). Halsted's knowledge of surgical anatomy and dissection, which he passed on to his students by operating before them, was unparalleled. He revolutionized surgery—emphasizing skill and technique—and was the innovator of many operations. William Osler (below) became physician in chief at Johns Hopkins in 1888. World renowned as a superb clinical teacher, Osler largely dispensed with didactic lecturing and took his students to the patients' bedsides. An Osler maxim was: "He who studies medicine without books sails an uncharted sea, but he who studies medicine without patients does not go to sea at all."

when he was experimenting with the drug as a local anesthetic before its addictive properties were known.

In the process of controlling this problem, Halsted underwent a total change in personality. Before his addiction he was described by a friend as "a bold, daring and original surgeon; a prodigious worker; a gay, cheerful soul, intimate with his students, holding open house for his friends, giving concerts at his home, enjoying people, and apparently one of them in their sports and pleasures." His career was so full of activity that had he continued on this path, he would probably have contributed little in the way of profound creative work.

After his addiction was under control, Halsted became "a thoughtful, cautious, meticulous and pre-eminently safe surgeon; . . . a worker, indeed, but one who avoided hospital appointments; who limited his operative work, who sought leisure for study and reflection and became a profound thinker and surgical philosopher; and a man in relations with others, shy, retiring, and remote, avoiding the crowd and its plaudits and preferring a seclusion which only a few choice friends were able to invade."

When Halsted began his work at Hopkins, surgeons were just beginning to understand the basic principles of successful and safe surgery. Halsted extended these basic principles, teaching an entire generation of surgeons his approaches and techniques.

One important principle was the prevention of infection. Even with the best precautions, it was impossible to make the skin of the patient and the hands of the surgeon germfree. Halsted therefore turned to a study of the tissue itself and discovered that the best approach was to disturb the tissues as little as possible during operation. He devised a clamp—known as the Halsted artery forceps—that would hold tissues gently; he also used

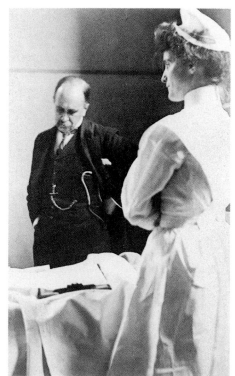

Howard A. Kelly was brought to Johns Hopkins by William Osler in 1889. Kelly is credited with the establishment of gynecology as a true specialty. He concentrated on gaining an understanding of the underlying pathology of women's diseases and on new surgical approaches. Here he is shown (center, facing forward) performing a laparotomy—in the days before surgeons and their assistants wore masks or gloves. A fundamentalist Christian, Kelly is said to have called a prayer meeting before every operation.

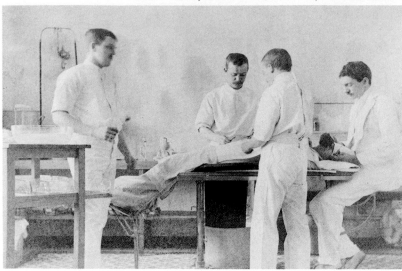

the finest silk for sutures, having found that silk causes less reaction in the tissue than catgut.

Halsted's innovations spanned many areas of surgical practice. He devised a suture that could be used to reconnect parts of the intestine; his operation for breast cancer—the Halsted radical mastectomy—revolutionized the surgical treatment of that disease; his experimental works on the thyroid gland were classics.

Under Halsted's direction, the large field of surgery developed into smaller specialties, and part of Halsted's genius was his ability to identify outstanding young surgeons to develop these new areas. One such area was neurosurgery. Harvey Cushing was placed in charge of this specialty. Cushing's experiments on the pituitary gland were landmarks in the history of endocrinology.

The nature of discovery

It was the emphasis on the discovery of new information that set the fledgling Johns Hopkins University School of Medicine apart from other medical schools of the day. The grandfather of medical research at Hopkins was Welch, whose Pathological Laboratory was the training ground for many Hopkins investigators in the early years of the hospital. Investigations that were carried out in the Pathological Laboratory over many years illuminate the nature of discovery at Hopkins.

A pioneering scientific achievement was the development of tissue culture—the growing of tissue outside the body. Attempts had been made as early as 1885 to grow tissue *in vitro,* but without success. In 1907 Ross G. Harrison, a student of Mall, became the first scientist to devise a simple, practical method for propagating living tissue in the laboratory. His particular interest was the development of the nervous system in the embryo. Harrison had been struggling with two conflicting theories of how nerve fibers grow and connect. Some scientists believed that each fiber grew from its own cell and thus extended for great lengths until it reached

(Opposite page, bottom) The first graduating class of the School of Medicine—the class of 1897—was a notably brilliant group, comprising many who made lasting contributions to the medical knowledge. Pictured are faculty member William Welch (second row, center) along with the male members of the class and an unidentified dog. The only graduate not in the picture is Mary S. Packard.

32

its destination. Others were sure that nerve fibers were built in segments, which formed short lengths of tissue that somehow joined end to end. Neither idea had been subjected to scientific experiment.

Harrison found the answer by actually observing nerve fibers grow. He removed a tiny portion of spinal cord from a frog embryo and placed it in a drop of nourishing lymph (the pale coagulable fluid that bathes the tissues) on a hollowed-out slide. Day after day he watched the living fibers as they spread across the slide. His experiment proved that these fibers develop by outward growth from one particular nerve cell, and his discovery revolutionized neurology.

Harrison's work was extended by the husband-and-wife team of Warren and Margaret Lewis, who also used the tissue culture technique to investigate the nature of cells. The Lewises modified Harrison's method by using blood plasma instead of lymph and concocted a nourishing artificial medium in which the cells could grow. They were able to accumulate full descriptions of different types of living cells, with all their parts, and went on to discover how these cells perform their different functions in the body. The technique of tissue culture thus became the basis for pioneering studies in the new science of cell biology.

George O. Gey, a student of the Lewises, worked with tissue culture at Hopkins for more than 40 years. Gey's best known contribution was the establishment of the so-called HeLa cell culture line, the first established human cell line. Gey was trying to grow cells from women with carcinoma-in-situ of the cervix (i.e., a cancer in a stage of development where it was still contained within the uterine cervix) but was unsuccessful until he obtained tissue from a 31-year-old woman with intermenstrual spotting, who turned out to have cancer. Gey named the cell culture after the patient, Henrietta Lacks. HeLa cell cultures have been used for studies of the nutritional requirements of cells in culture, of viral growth, of drug

William H. Welch was appointed professor of pathology in 1884 and was the guiding spirit of the medical school for half a century. Welch's Pathological Laboratory was the training ground for dozens of investigators who made pioneering scientific discoveries. Welch is caricatured by Max Broedel, the lively artist who established the country's first department of medical illustration at Johns Hopkins in 1911.

effects, and of genetic control mechanisms and mutations at the cellular level. At Harvard University John Enders, in his Nobel Prize-winning work, used Gey's technique to show that the poliomyelitis virus would grow in cells that came from outside the nervous system, thus opening the way for the development of the polio vaccine. The usefulness of the cell line to molecular and cell biology can hardly be overestimated.

The first graduating class: leaders in discovery

It was not surprising that the first class of medical students at Johns Hopkins comprised an unusually talented group. They had braved the university's daunting entrance requirements, and they had been admitted for their sound background in science as well as their intelligence. Three members of this first class made scientific discoveries whose importance endures to this day.

Thomas R. Brown was a fourth-year student taking Osler's clinical clerkship when he encountered a patient with an unusual group of signs and symptoms. The patient, a Baltimore hobo, complained of generalized muscle pains; his white blood cell count was higher than normal and contained a large number of eosinophils, a particular kind of white blood cell; and he had a fever. Brown questioned the patient closely and learned that he had eaten incompletely cooked pork a few weeks earlier. Examining the patient's muscle cells under the microscope, Brown found what he had suspected: the encysted larval worms that signal the diagnosis of trichinosis. Although this disease was well known, it was Brown who related its diagnosis to an elevated level of eosinophils. Brown later made the important observation that eosinophilia can also be found in patients with adrenal insufficiency.

At the same time that Brown was investigating eosinophilia, Bailey Ashford, a colonel in the United States Army, was baffled by a devastating epidemic of anemia sweeping through Puerto Rico. Reading about the eosinophilia produced by one parasitic infestation stimulated Ashford to search the stools of his own patients, and he discovered that another parasite—hookworm—was responsible for their anemia. Ashford proceeded to treat and eventually prevent hookworm infestations in Puerto Rico.

Another Hopkins medical student, William G. MacCallum, developed an interest in parasitic infections during his third year of medical school. Malaria was endemic in Baltimore in those days, and several physicians at Hopkins, including Osler, were studying the disease. It was known that birds carried a parasite similar to the malarial parasite in humans, and MacCallum's fellow student Eugene L. Opie had already identified two forms of the parasite in crows. MacCallum found that development of these parasites in both birds and humans was a sexual process—a discovery with enormous implications for treatment of the disease.

Opie described two forms of the parasite: one hyaline, the other granulated. MacCallum observed that only the hyaline forms developed tails (flagellae); the granular forms were extruded and came to rest as spheres beside the free nuclei of the red corpuscles, which had recently contained them. MacCallum's key observation was that one flagellum proceeded to each granular sphere and plunged itself into the sphere. He recognized that

In the early part of this century, the Johns Hopkins nursing service regularly made house calls; they were often called upon to help deliver babies at home.

this was a sexual process and later demonstrated its occurrence in a case of human malaria.

MacCallum later concentrated on the parathyroid glands, studying the influence of various factors, including diet, on tetany, a disease characterized by painful muscle spasms. He corroborated the findings of others that the injection of an extract of the parathyroid gland would cause symptoms of tetany to disappear. When a patient who developed tetany after subtotal thyroidectomy (nearly total excision of the thyroid gland) was given an injection of a preparation made from four or five bovine parathyroid glands, symptoms disappeared within several hours.

In collaboration with Carl Voegtlin, head of the Chemical Laboratory, MacCallum demonstrated that tetany was due to dysfunction of the nervous system, not the muscles themselves. They showed that transfusion of a sufficiently large amount of blood from a normal dog would suppress symptoms in a dog with tetany. Their later experiments conclusively demonstrated the immediate and specific curative effect of a soluble calcium salt upon the tetany that followed removal of the parathyroid glands. These studies clarified the role of the parathyroid glands at a time when there was great confusion about their function in the human body.

By studying microscopic sections from the pancreases of patients with diabetes, MacCallum's classmate Opie demonstrated for the first time that obliteration of the islet cells of Langerhans is followed by the onset of diabetes. Reasoning from Opie's discovery, MacCallum decided that to prove the relation between these islets and diabetes, he would need to isolate them so that they could be studied independently of all other body tissues. To do this, he took advantage of the recent demonstration by Joseph von Mering and Oscar Minkowski at the University of Strasbourg, France, that removal of the whole pancreas led to severe diabetes.

First, MacCallum separated a portion of the pancreas and tied off (ligated) its duct. As a result, the secreting (acinar) cells atrophied, leaving only islet tissue. When he then removed the rest of the pancreas, no diabetes developed. Next, he took the mass of pure islet tissue away—and diabetes ensued. Thus, MacCallum proved the specific control of the islet cells over carbohydrate metabolism. This technique of duct ligation leading to atrophy of acinar tissue while leaving the islet intact was used by Frederick Banting and Charles Best at the University of Toronto in their successful attempt to isolate insulin.

Later students were also pathbreaking investigators. In 1915 heparin, a natural substance in the blood that prevents it from clotting, was discovered by a second-year medical student, Jay McLean. A medical student at Hopkins helped discover the first molecular disease; in the mid-1930s Irving J. Sherman, an undergraduate at the Johns Hopkins University, became interested in sickle-cell anemia and in the sickle-cell trait. In an advanced genetics course, he began to study their pattern of transmission. When Sherman entered the Hopkins medical school the following year, he continued his investigations in the laboratory of hematologist Maxwell Wintrobe. Using polarized light, Sherman saw that the hemoglobin molecule seen only in sickle cells split the ray of light in two, a finding that indicated an

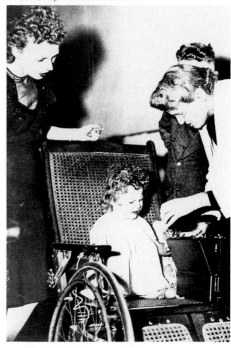

Pediatric cardiologist Helen B. Taussig is pictured with one of her "blue baby" patients. Taussig had many young patients with a congenital malformation of the ductus arteriosus and with narrowing of the aorta, a condition that resulted in an inadequate blood flow to the lungs. These babies developed cyanosis—a lack of oxygen causing a bluish cast to the fingernails and lips. In conjunction with surgeon Alfred Blalock and his technician, Vivien Thomas, Taussig helped devise an operation that would join the subclavian artery to the pulmonary artery to correct the cyanotic disorder. On Nov. 29, 1944, they performed their first—and completely successful—operation on a very ill child. They were immediately gratified when their patient's lips turned pink. Since then, thousands of babies the world over have been saved by the procedure, which paved the way for the era of modern heart surgery. (The black box Taussig is carrying is a hearing aid; she was partially deaf at the time.)

An open chest defibrillator (below left) was developed by William B. Kouwenhoven and his colleagues in the 1950s. By applying an AC current to the chest wall of electric shock victims, they were able to restore cardiac contractions and thus dramatically revive these patients. Other cardiac advances that were made by Johns Hopkins investigators include development of the closed-chest heart massage technique (cardiopulmonary resuscitation) in the mid-1950s, development of the first rechargeable pacemaker in the late '60s, and the implantation of an automatic defibrillator to correct irregular heartbeats in 1980. The contemporary photograph (below right) shows a patient in the Heart Center at Johns Hopkins undergoing echocardiography, which uses sound waves to provide a two-dimensional picture that shows precise details of the heart muscle. The noninvasive and completely painless procedure allows frequent monitoring of a patient's heart in order to evaluate the effectiveness of cardiac therapy.

abnormality in the physical state of sickle hemoglobin. His observations on this unique finding were incomplete at the time he finished medical school, but he published them anyway, hoping that someone would continue to pursue the problem.

The scientist who extended this finding was Linus Pauling. He learned about Sherman's results from William B. Castle, a renowned Harvard hematologist, when the two were traveling together to a committee meeting. Basing their work on Sherman's findings, Pauling and his colleagues at the California Institute of Technology demonstrated the presence of an electrophoretically abnormal hemoglobin in sickle-cell disease, and in 1949 they published their epoch-making article on sickle-cell anemia—the first molecular disease. This event demonstrated unequivocally that on occasion, even if rarely and inadvertently, committee meetings may lead to valuable contributions.

The pioneering and vital contributions made in a century of medicine at Johns Hopkins include dozens of firsts—many of which have already been noted. Numerous lifesaving treatments for previously untreatable diseases have been developed by Hopkins faculty and practitioners.

The "blue baby" operation

Before 1944 operations on the heart were highly risky, largely unsuccessful, and rarely performed. In that year, however, two Hopkins doctors—Helen B. Taussig and Alfred Blalock—with the help of Blalock's talented technician, Vivien Thomas, devised an operation on the heart that allowed many formerly doomed infants to live.

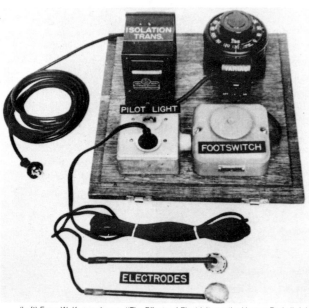

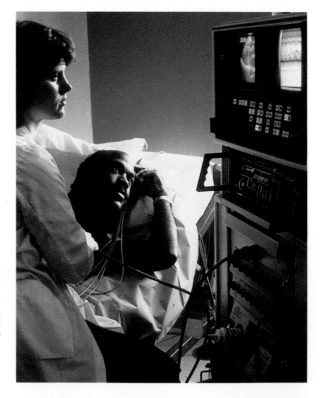

(Left) From W. Kouwenhoven, "The Effects of Electricity on the Human Body," *Johns Hopkins Medical Journal*, 115 (1964). Reprinted by permission of the Johns Hopkins Press; (right) the Johns Hopkins Medical Institutions; photograph, Bert Glinn

Blalock was the chief of surgery, and Taussig was head of the Pediatric Cardiac Clinic. In the clinic, Taussig examined many young patients with malformations of the ductus arteriosus and with narrowing of the aorta. As long as the ductus was open, she observed, children did not become cyanotic. Cyanosis—a bluish look particularly to the lips and fingernails—was the result of a lack of oxygen due to inadequate blood flow to the lungs. A surgeon in Boston was then performing an operation in which he would tie off the ductus in patients in whom too much blood was going to the lungs; Taussig wondered whether it would be possible to *build* a ductus for patients with the opposite problem.

Blalock, meanwhile, had been trying to use another artery to bypass constricted aortas; his work was still in the experimental stage, as his animal subjects were developing problems after operation. When Taussig asked whether a similar operation could be devised to improve the circulation to the lungs in children with pulmonary stenosis, Blalock invited her to join him in working on the problem in his laboratory. After many difficult months, they felt that they had found a procedure that would work.

On Nov. 29, 1944, Blalock and Taussig decided to go ahead with an operation that would join the subclavian artery to the pulmonary artery in a cyanotic child. Despite the technical problems of operating on a very small and very ill child, Blalock was able to carry out the procedure successfully. "Oh, his lips are pink!" Taussig remembered the anesthetist saying as the immediate success of the operation became apparent. The "blue baby" operation, which brought deserved fame to Taussig and Blalock, inaugurated the modern era of cardiac surgery, which later included coronary artery bypasses and heart transplants.

Reviving victims by cardiopulmonary resuscitation

There is no more dramatic contribution to the technology of medicine than that which restores a failure of the pumping action of the heart by the simple application of physical pressure to the victim's chest wall. In the 1920s the electric utility companies were concerned about the rising number of linemen killed by electric shock. It had been demonstrated that ventricular fibrillation (a condition in which the heartbeats are random and fluttery and there is no effective circulation of the blood) that was induced by electric shock could be reversed by an electric countershock. William B. Kouwenhoven began work to devise a practical method of applying this knowledge. In collaboration with William Milnor, also of Johns Hopkins, they discovered that an AC current applied to the chest wall would restore effective cardiac contractions. The Hopkins AC defibrillator was tested hundreds of times in the laboratory before it was successfully used on a patient on March 28, 1957.

In tests with the defibrillator, G. Guy Knickerbocker, another Hopkins faculty member, noted that there was a significant rise in blood pressure when the electrodes of the defibrillator were pressed against a test animal's chest even before the countershock was applied. Pursuing this observation, he showed that external manual chest massage could raise blood pressure to 40% of normal. On Feb. 15, 1958, Henry T. Bahnson, a surgeon at

The diagnostic use of X-rays was perfected at Johns Hopkins by Russell H. Morgan, who in 1946 became the first director of the department of radiology. He utilized his knowledge of mathematics, physics, and engineering to create a timer that automatically regulated a patient's exposure to radiation and increased the accuracy of X-ray images, thus reducing the need for retakes.

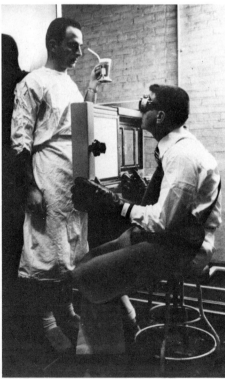

Bill Denison

Hopkins, successfully used this technique of external cardiac massage to resuscitate a two-year-old child whose heart was in ventricular fibrillation.

External chest massage could be used immediately, until an external defibrillator was brought in; a third method of restoring heart and lung function was mouth-to-mouth resuscitation, developed earlier by two Baltimore anesthetists (not at Hopkins), James Elam and Peter Safer. Thanks to these three procedures, thousands of lives have been saved.

Presidents' sons and a crucial drug

The striking difference in the course of disease in two U.S. presidents' sons, incidents occurring 12 years apart, illustrates the signal advance in the treatment of infection with one type of drug—the sulfonamides. Calvin Coolidge, Jr., died of blood poisoning in 1924; Franklin D. Roosevelt, Jr., was cured of the same condition by a drug supplied by Perrin H. Long and Eleanor A. Bliss of Johns Hopkins.

Early work on the parent compounds, the sulfonamides, had been done in Germany in the mid-1930s. In the United States, Long and Bliss had been investigating the treatment of streptococcal infections when they learned about the German drug Prontosil. They obtained some, and in studying its structure they confirmed that sulfanilamide is the effective portion of the Prontosil molecule and proposed that it acts by preventing the growth of bacteria rather than by killing bacteria already present.

Their immediate results in treating laboratory animals with the drug seemed miraculous, and they soon decided to try the drug on patients. Again, the results were spectacular as patients near death from previously untreatable illnesses—streptococcal tonsillitis, erysipelas, acute otitis media, blood poisoning—were cured. Long and Bliss's report of their studies

Victor A. McKusick and his students take in the Baltimore panorama from atop the dome of the historic hospital administration building. McKusick, who holds the position of University Professor of Medical Genetics, is renowned for his work in clinical genetics. His catalog of genetic disorders and genetic factors in disease is an essential tool used by geneticists worldwide. In 1988 McKusick became president of the Human Genome Organization, an international group of scientists that has undertaken the major project of mapping and sequencing the human genome.

38

began the era of the sulfonamide derivatives, a long series of effective drugs in the sulfonamide family.

The benefits of sulfonamide in the prevention of chronic rheumatic heart disease was also discovered by a Hopkins faculty member, Caroline B. Thomas. When Long mentioned at lunch in the doctor's dining room at the hospital that he had successfully used the drug to prevent fatal streptococcal infections in mice, Thomas thought of her many young patients with recurrent rheumatic fever. She decided to try to prevent these infections by giving patients a small amount of sulfanilamide every day. The regimen indeed prevented acute infections; not a single recurrence of rheumatic fever occurred in patients who took the drug.

Serendipitous insights

Not all medical advances occur because scientists set out to attack a specific problem. Serendipity has played an important part in a number of the discoveries made by medical scientists at Johns Hopkins.

Chance played an important part in William S. Tillett's discovery of streptokinase and its use in patients. While working with hemolytic streptococci in the 1930s, Tillett noticed that normal human plasma could make these organisms clump together, while human serum could not. He therefore expected that adding streptococci to plasma would make the plasma clot. To his disappointment he found that clotting occurred just as rapidly in the control preparation. Later he was surprised to find that the formerly clotted plasma had turned liquid again. Through further experiments Tillett isolated the agent that caused the plasma to liquefy, a substance that became known as streptokinase.

The discovery of a remedy for motion sickness also came about through a fortunate accident. Leslie N. Gay, head of the Allergy Clinic at Hopkins, was trying a new antihistamine drug on a patient with hives. The patient was very enthusiastic about this new treatment, telling Gay that she had always been incapacitated by motion sickness whenever she rode a trolley car. All that had changed, however, since she started taking the drug. Gay tested her reaction experimentally—he gave her sugar pills (placebos) for a while, and she returned after two or three days, very disappointed that her motion sickness had returned.

From chemical scissors to mapping the human genome

The Nobel Prize for Physiology or Medicine was awarded in 1978 to two Hopkins scientists, Daniel Nathans and Hamilton O. Smith, who along with Werner Arber of Switzerland discovered so-called restriction enzymes and applied them to the study of the gene. These enzymes—chemical scissors—can cut the gene into pieces of manageable size, allowing scientists to analyze the chemical structure of the gene and of other DNA regions that help regulate gene expression. Building on Arber's work, Smith discovered the first site-specific restriction enzyme in the late 1960s, demonstrating that it cut DNA in the middle of a specific, symmetrical sequence. Smith later found this type of enzyme useful for studying the ways in which proteins interact with specific sequences of DNA.

The Johns Hopkins
Medical Institutions; photograph, Bert Glinn

The Maumenee Building, with its dramatic two-story lobby, opened in 1982. It houses the Wilmer Eye Institute as well as the genetic eye division and the new center for retinal degeneration. Wilmer ophthalmologists have pioneered and perfected treatments for a wide range of eye diseases and visual disorders, and every year patients travel from many parts of the world to be treated by specialists at the institute.

The Harriet Lane Home for Invalid Children served as a "family doctor" for children from east Baltimore from the time it opened in 1912. The crowded waiting room scene below was typical in the 1930s and '40s. This role of serving the community was strictly in accordance with the instructions that Johns Hopkins left to the hospital's original trustees in 1873: "The indigent sick of this city and its environs, without regard to sex, age, or color, who may require surgical or medical treatment . . . shall be received into the Hospital without charge." Today needy children from the community are cared for in the Children's Medical and Surgical Center, which opened in 1964.

Nathans's pathbreaking work on the mapping of DNA was based on Smith's findings. Nathans used these enzymes to isolate specific pieces of chromosome from a tumor virus and then mapped the virus's genes. With this information, he could identify the genes that direct the manufacture of the tumor-producing protein.

These discoveries marked the beginning of a new era in medicine, the era of recombinant DNA. Restriction enzymes are at the center of most research in molecular genetics. Huntington's disease, thalassemia, and colon cancer are only three of the disorders whose secrets are yielding to the use of DNA technology.

Since the early 1960s another Hopkins scientist, Victor A. McKusick, professor of medical genetics, has been a world leader in mapping the gene locations of inherited diseases on chromosomes and cataloging genetic traits and defects. In 1988 he was elected president of the Human Genome Organization (HUGO), a group of scientists from around the world who have joined to promote international collaboration on mapping and sequencing the human genome. The project represents an effort to assign all of the 50,000 to 100,000 human genes to their proper chromosomal location. Mapping the human genome is one of the major scientific undertakings of the remainder of the 20th century.

Johns Hopkins today

In the century since its founding, the Hopkins model of medical education and research has spread throughout the United States. As Hopkins graduates helped to create other strong medical schools, the uniqueness of the Johns Hopkins Medical Institutions diminished. Now one of many excellent institutions in the United States, Johns Hopkins has entered its second century by adapting the principles of its founder to the requirements of a changing society.

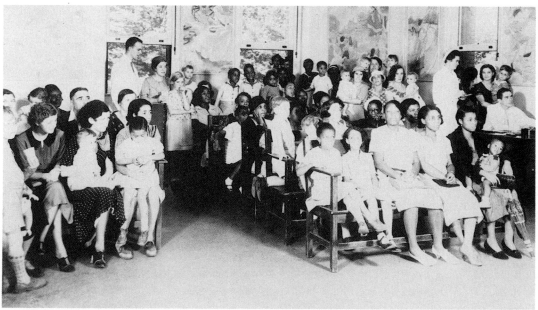

The Alan M. Chesney Medical Archives, the Johns Hopkins Medical Institutions

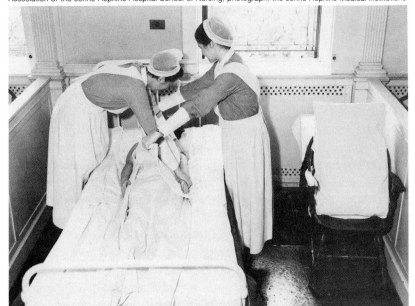

This undated photograph shows nurses applying a sedative pack to a patient in the Henry Phipps Psychiatric Clinic, which opened in 1913. The Phipps clinic was notable in its day because it sought to remove the stigma of asylums and to provide proper care for any type of mental disorder—from the slightest to the most grave—in a modern hospital setting. In 1982 the clinic was replaced by the Adolf Meyer Center for Psychiatry and the Neurosciences, named for the Swiss psychiatrist who was the first chairman of psychiatry at Johns Hopkins.

Numbers tell a large part of the story. When the Johns Hopkins Hospital opened, it had 220 hospital beds; now it has over 1,000. In its first year of operation, the hospital provided 43,000 days of inpatient care; in 1988 it provided almost half a million days of inpatient care and received an equal number of outpatient visits. It was 1890 when Halsted commissioned the Goodyear Rubber Co. to produce two pairs of rubber gloves for an operating room nurse; now 7,219,200 rubber gloves are used at Hopkins in a single year.

The medical school faculty has grown from 18 members in 1893 to 2,440 full- and part-time members today. There were 18 medical students in the first entering class; in 1989 the total number of medical students at Hopkins was 459.

Today the hospital and medical school comprise more than 340 separate divisions, spread over 21 hospital buildings that encompass 232,250 square meters (2.5 million square feet) of space. With all of its affiliated hospitals, the Johns Hopkins Medical Institutions occupies 17.8 hectares (44 acres).

Yet the story of the past century is one of development as well as growth. Although the trend toward specialization in medicine has produced many new departments and centers at Johns Hopkins, some of its most outstanding components are extensions of ones created early in its history.

The Children's Medical and Surgical Center, which opened in 1964, is an outgrowth of the Harriet Lane Home for Invalid Children, founded in 1912. The Adolf Meyer Center for Psychiatry and the Neurosciences, founded in 1982, was an outgrowth of the Phipps Psychiatric Clinic, established in 1913. The Brady Urological Institute was dedicated in 1915 in honor of the famous philanthropist James Buchanan ("Diamond Jim") Brady. Brady was a grateful patient of Hugh H. Young, a member of the department of surgery at Hopkins who became the institute's first director. The director today, Patrick Walsh, is known for his pioneering work in prostate surgery. The

41

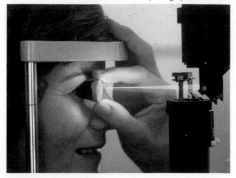

Argon laser treatment to seal off bleeding vessels in the eye was developed by Arnall Patz, director of the Wilmer Eye Institute. Wilmer ophthalmologists continue to pioneer new uses for lasers in the treatment of eye diseases.

At the Adolf Meyer Center for Psychiatry and the Neurosciences, physicians are investigating the neurological causes of Alzheimer's disease. Meanwhile, social workers at the center help Alzheimer's patients cope with their physical and mental impairment.

Wilmer Eye Institute, opened in 1925 and named for William H. Wilmer, the first director, is in the forefront of ophthalmologic treatment and research. Wilmer specialists were among the first to use laser surgery to treat leading causes of blindness, including glaucoma.

Two parts of the Johns Hopkins Medical Institutions that have also grown to meet changing times are the School of Nursing and the School of Hygiene and Public Health. Like the hospital, the School of Nursing was founded in 1889 in accordance with the wishes of Johns Hopkins. Its early leaders—Isabel Hampton, M. Adelaide Nutting, and Lavinia Dock—put in place an unusual program for the time, one that combined classroom education of nurses with the conventional bedside training. Today the school carries on its academic tradition by offering baccalaureate, master's, and postdoctoral programs.

The School of Hygiene and Public Health was founded in 1916 with a grant from the Rockefeller Foundation. Under the leadership of William H. Welch, it was the first institution of its kind in the world. The school's "mission," said Welch, was to recognize that "there are no social, no industrial, no economic problems which are not related to problems of health." In 1989 the school awarded 20% of all doctoral degrees given by schools of public health worldwide, and its 7,000 living graduates represent every state in the U.S. and a great many foreign countries.

Building for the future: reaching into the community

The hospital's most recent program is the Johns Hopkins Health System, which has extended Hopkins's reach into the community in order to offer a broader range of services for the care of the sick, as well as extended facilities for teaching and research. Through this organization Hopkins has acquired three other Baltimore hospitals—Francis Scott Key Medical Center, Wyman Park Medical Center (the old U.S. Public Health Service Hospital), and North Charles Hospital. The last two were consolidated in 1988 into the Homewood Hospital Center. Hopkins also formed its own health maintenance organization (HMO), with more than 20 outlets around the region. In addition, Hopkins has begun construction of one of the largest medical research parks in the country. Under the aegis of the Hopkins Health System, the 52.6-hectare (130-acre) Bayview Research Campus will take ten years and $500 million to complete. Its planned tenants include a national center for asthma research, private biomedical firms, a hotel, and a conference center. They will join the Francis Scott Key Medical Center, clinical research centers for the National Institute on Aging and the National Institute on Drug Abuse, and facilities of the Nova Pharmaceutical Corp., all of which are already on site.

Major investment in AIDS

The Johns Hopkins Medical Institutions has developed new patterns of organization to meet important current problems. One example is the response to the epidemic of AIDS (acquired immune deficiency syndrome), which coordinates programs in the hospital, the School of Medicine, and the School of Hygiene and Public Health.

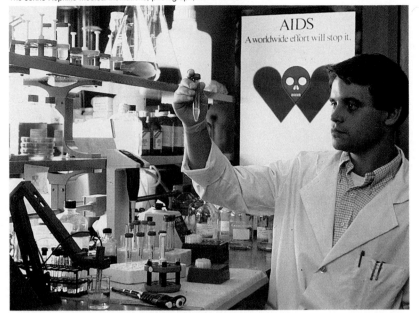

Responding to important new health problems has always been a top priority of the Johns Hopkins Medical Institutions. Investigations into AIDS began early—in 1983. In the ensuing years programs have expanded in research, education, and patient care. AIDS research, which is coordinated in the hospital, the School of Medicine, and the School of Hygiene and Public Health, is now funded by more than $11 million annually.

AIDS programs at Hopkins began in 1983, even before there were a sizable number of AIDS patients in the Baltimore area. A longitudinal study initiated in that year, organized and directed by the late B. Frank Polk, recruited 1,200 homosexual men as participants. Early research in the School of Hygiene and Public Health concentrated not only on the natural history of the disease but on drug-using populations, prisoners, and educational programs. In the ensuing six years, programs at Hopkins have expanded to meet the burgeoning need for investigation, education, and care. In 1984 only 250 patients with HIV (human immunodeficiency virus) infection were seen in the hospital's outpatient service, but by 1988 this number had climbed to almost 7,000. AIDS research is now funded by more than $11 million a year in grants and contracts, distributed in the departments of medicine, pediatrics, ophthalmology, neurology, comparative medicine, psychiatry, oncology, and emergency medicine.

Enduring vitality

Over the past century the form of Johns Hopkins's service to the community has changed to meet changing times, populations, and needs. Hopkins himself stated that "the primary mission of the Johns Hopkins Hospital is patient care." The intellectual architect of the Hopkins Hospital, Billings, expressed the hope of many when he wrote that the new institution in Baltimore should "produce investigators as well as practitioners, to give to the world men who can not only sail by the old charts, but who can make new and better ones for the use of others." It is the triad of medical research, patient care, and teaching that has become the hallmark of the Johns Hopkins Medical Institutions. To coordinate these three facets of medicine, as its founder and early leaders specified, is the goal of the present and the future.

Johns Hopkins stipulated that teaching and learning should be closely allied with patient care. Today this link continues and was distinctly realized in the opening of the combined Russell A. Nelson Patient Tower and A. McGehee Harvey Teaching Tower.

43

Turning Kids On to Fitness

by Patty S. Freedson, Ph.D.,
James M. Rippe, M.D., and
Ann Ward, Ph.D.

In the 1970s and 1980s many adults in Western countries started exercising on a regular basis, participating in a widespread "fitness boom." People had become conscious that life-style has much to do with their health; they stopped smoking, changed their diets, and began exercising. By the mid-1980s, however, some experts began to sound the alarm that the so-called fitness boom appeared to be largely confined to economically advantaged, highly educated individuals.

Even more alarming was the fact that by the end of the decade of the 1980s, a number of reports had emerged suggesting that the fitness boom had not touched children at all. In fact, the *fitness* levels of U.S. children had severely declined while their *fatness* had increased. The United States Department of Health and Human Services reported that children in the 1980s were less fit than the children of the 1960s.

The decline in fitness could be seen in a variety of areas. Measures of cardiorespiratory fitness and strength both declined. The President's Council on Physical Fitness and Sports reported that half of the girls in the United States between the ages of 6 and 17 and 30% of boys between 6 and 12 could not run a mile in less than ten minutes; 55% of girls and 25% of boys were not strong enough to do a single pull-up. Perhaps most alarming was that by the time they reach the age of 12, over 40% of U.S. children have at least one major risk factor for coronary heart disease (CHD).

Youngest generation: fat and unfit

Why are these statistics cause for such concern? There are two reasons. First, the Western world is in the midst of a major epidemic of CHD. It is the number one killer of adults in developed countries. Moreover, it is now understood that CHD has its origins in childhood rather than in middle age or the older years. Thus, the high percentage of children with major risk factors for CHD places a whole generation at increased risk for perpetuating this epidemic.

Patty S. Freedson, Ph.D., is Associate Professor in the Department of Exercise Science at the University of Massachusetts at Amherst.
James M. Rippe, M.D., is Associate Professor of Medicine (Cardiology) and Director of the Exercise Physiology Laboratory at the University of Massachusetts Medical School, Worcester.
Ann Ward, Ph.D., is Assistant Professor of Medicine and Director of Research in Exercise Physiology at the University of Massachusetts Medical School, Worcester.

(Overleaf) Photograph, Mike Habermann

Second, many habits, practices, and characteristics carried into adulthood are firmly established during the childhood years. Inactive, overweight children are likely to become inactive, overweight adults with all the attendant health risks of obesity and a sedentary life-style. Many experts fear that children who do not get a taste for activity in childhood will never acquire it as adults.

Despite being faced with this dilemma, many schools have turned their backs on fitness. Only 5 of the 50 U.S. states require physical education for all 12 grades, and only one (Illinois) requires it on a daily basis. Faced with budget constraints, many schools have chosen to eliminate or curtail physical education. This point of view was articulated by New Jersey Gov. Thomas Kean, who in 1989 led the drive to make physical education optional in his state. Governor Kean declared: "We require as much phys ed as English. . . . Let parents and children choose between dodgeball and Dickens, relay races and relativity."

Unfortunately, this type of sentiment appears to be growing at the very time when epidemiological studies in adults have clearly begun to show the important links between activity, fitness, and health and, conversely, between inactivity, lack of fitness, and the development of serious chronic diseases. Similar intuitive associations about fitness and health of children appear obvious, and scientific proof is slowly beginning to emerge.

One of the proudest achievements of Western civilization has been the improved health of children. It is a sad irony that at a time when many of the problems of childhood infectious disease have been largely eradicated in developed countries, a whole other set of potentially equally serious health risks to children has emerged. Paradoxically, these risks seem intertwined with many of the advances in Western civilization: too many calories, too much leisure, and not enough activity.

When the President's Council on Physical Fitness and Sports measured the fitness levels of U.S. children in the late 1980s, it found that among other things, significant numbers did not have the stamina to pass a running test or the strength to do even a single pull-up. Clearly the fitness boom that in the past decade has motivated Americans to take up exercise on a regular basis has not included the youngest generation.

Robert E. Daemmrich—TSW/Click-Chicago Ltd.

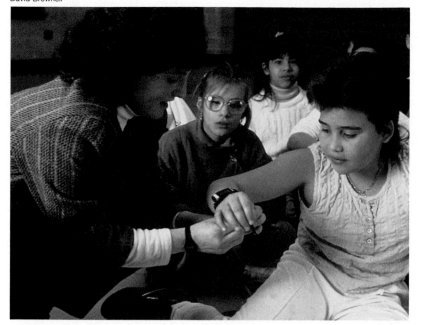

The President's Council's most alarming finding about the fitness of today's children was that by age 12 over 40% already have at least one major risk factor for coronary heart disease (CHD)—the number one killer of American adults. Early intervention with a program of exercise that promotes cardiorespiratory fitness will minimize children's risk of becoming adult CHD victims. Youngsters participating in a fitness program at the University of Massachusetts at Amherst have their initial heart rates measured before they begin a regimen of progressive aerobic exercise. Regular monitoring of heart rate during the course of an exercise program is the best way to determine if a child is placing enough—but not too much—demand on the heart.

The current trends are unlikely to change unless society begins to understand the important ties between childhood habits and health. The alarm has been sounded and the timing is urgent. The health of a whole generation may rest in the balance.

Fitness goals established

The topic of health, fitness, and exercise for youth is particularly timely and important in the year 1990. In 1980 the United States Department of Health and Human Services designated the so-called Health Objectives for the Nation—specific public health goals for the nation to achieve by 1990. Goals were established for 15 target areas—one of the 15 being physical fitness and exercise. Eleven objectives were listed, three of which dealt specifically with exercise-related objectives for 10–17-year-old children. These objectives, set forth in the publication *Promoting Health/ Preventing Disease 1990: Objectives for the Nation,* were: (1) by 1990 a methodology for systematically assessing the physical fitness of children should be developed; at least 70% of children and adolescents aged 10 to 17 should participate in such an assessment; (2) by 1990 the proportion of children and adolescents aged 10 to 17 participating regularly in appropriate physical activities, particularly cardiorespiratory fitness programs that can be carried into adulthood, should be greater than 90%; and (3) by 1990 the proportion of children and adolescents aged 10 to 17 participating in daily physical education programs should be greater than 60%.

Other goals that were established for youth fitness included the acquisition of information regarding participation rates in regular physical activity and the evaluation of the short-term and long-term health benefits of exercise. A decade has passed, and it must now be asked: Will these goals be met? The answer is a resounding no!

Body fatness of children: skin fold scores* 1960s versus 1980s

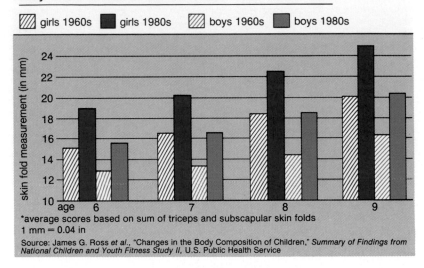

*average scores based on sum of triceps and subscapular skin folds
1 mm = 0.04 in

Source: James G. Ross *et al.*, "Changes in the Body Composition of Children," *Summary of Findings from National Children and Youth Fitness Study II*, U.S. Public Health Service

Not only are American children today resoundingly unfit, they are also fatter than ever before. In two separate surveys—in 1984 and in 1987—the National Children and Youth Fitness Study assessed the body fatness of children, measured by the sum of skin-fold thicknesses of the triceps and the subscapula (below the shoulder blade). Skin folds are a practical index of body composition that provide a more accurate estimate of body fatness than simple weight–height ratios. Marked increases in fatness were evident when these measures were compared with skin-fold thicknesses of similarly aged girls and boys in the 1960s.

Because there is a clear trend toward obesity in U.S. children, and because atherosclerosis (plaque buildup in arteries) has its origins in childhood, it is of concern that many of the most widely consumed foods in the American child's diet not only contain too many calories but are especially high in saturated fat, which raises blood cholesterol. It is generally recommended that children aged 6–11 consume no more than 22 grams of saturated fat daily. The maximum for boys 12–17 is 30 grams and for girls 24 grams.

Favorite foods of kids

food	calories	saturated fat (grams)
cheeseburger, ¼ lb	629	17.2
chocolate chip cookies, 4 small	200	2.8
cola drink, 12 oz	145	0
cupcake with icing	130	2.0
French fries, 10 strips	135	1.7
hotdog, 2 oz, with bun	290	6.1
ice cream, 1 cup	270	8.9
macaroni & cheese, 1 cup	230	4.2
milkshake (thick), 11 oz	350	5.9
peanut butter, 2 tbs	190	3.0
pizza (cheese), 1 slice	145	1.7
potato chips, 10	115	2.1
tomato soup (with milk)	175	3.4

Source: USDA *Nutritive Value of Foods*

Assessment of progress: not encouraging

In the 1980s the U.S. Public Health Service's Office of Disease Prevention and Health Promotion, which has the responsibility of monitoring the nation's progress toward the established objectives, conducted two studies to assess the status of exercise-related objectives for youth. The National Children and Youth Fitness Study (NCYFS I) began formulating the testing protocol in 1982 and over a four-month period in 1984 collected data on a national random sample of 5th- through 12th-grade students from 140 public and private schools in 19 states. Of the 10,275 students selected for evaluation, 8,800 agreed to participate in the investigation. The results that specifically address the youth, exercise, and fitness objectives were:

● Only about 60% of youth participate in activity that promotes cardio-respiratory fitness.

● Fewer than 40% of 5th through 12th graders have daily physical exercise.

● There is a steep decline in physical education after grade school, where 98% of 5th graders are enrolled in physical education; the participation rate drops to 50% by 12th grade.

● Current physical education activities emphasize games, relays, and competitive sports that are unlikely to be carried on in adult life.

● Physical education relates directly to physical fitness. Youth that scored in the top 25% on the fitness tests have more days of physical education classes per week and are involved in a greater variety of activities, including lifetime fitness activities.

● Body fatness, as measured by the sum of the triceps and subscapular skin folds, was higher than in similarly aged youth measured in the 1960s.

The National Children and Youth Fitness Study II (NCYFS II) followed; 4,678 six–nine-year-old boys and girls from 19 states were tested in 1985 and 1986. The study was extended to younger children to obtain data on a segment of the population that had never been evaluated for fitness. It was felt that extending the knowledge about fitness and exercise as related to this youngest group would help in the development of optimal health and exercise attitudes and practices in youth.

In addition to the information that was collected in NCYFS I, data were obtained from the parents and teachers about the children's free play and organized sport activity levels, factors that affect fitness, television watching habits, and parents' activity patterns. The major findings were:

- Body fat was higher than that measured on a sample of six–nine-year-old children over 20 years ago, suggesting a higher level of body fatness for this age group today in comparison with 20 years ago.
- Ninety-seven percent of the children were enrolled in physical education classes, which met an average of 3.1 times per week.
- Fewer than 50% had regular fitness testing, and a large majority of the testing evaluated motor skills rather than health-related items.
- At grade three there was a shift toward competitive team sports in the physical education curriculum, and there was no focus on lifetime fitness activities.
- Almost 85% of the children participated in competitive sports through community- or agency-sponsored activities.
- Fewer than 30% of the parents engaged in regular moderate-to-vigorous exercise.
- Parents exercised with their children less than one day per week.
- Kids who performed better in a cardiovascular fitness test (a one-mile walk/run [one mile equals about 1.6 kilometers]) were more physically active.
- Kids who were more active spent less time watching television.

Historical perspective

In the early 1950s the results of a fitness test administered to U.S. and European youth revealed that nearly 60% of U.S. children failed the test. In sharp contrast, only 9% of European children failed. One can speculate that this difference reflected different physical activity patterns and less focus on fitness development in the U.S. In 1956 Pres. Dwight D. Eisenhower, alarmed by the poor performance of the U.S. youth in contrast to their European counterparts, formed what was then called the President's Council on Youth Fitness (presently the President's Council on Physical Fitness and Sports).

In 1960 a standardized battery of fitness tests was developed by the American Association for Health, Physical Education, and Recreation (AAHPER) and adopted by the President's Council on Youth Fitness. The purposes of those tests were to identify areas of poor performance and to recognize with an award those individuals who had high performances. The original test battery was very skill-oriented, including such tests as pull-ups for boys and flexed arm hang for girls, standing long jump, sit-ups, 30-yard (one yard equals about 0.9 meter) agility shuttle run, 50-yard dash, softball throw, and the 600-yard run. Because of the strong skill component, performance on the individual test items was related to a child's level of skill. The test was modified in 1964, then again in the years 1974 and 1980, and became known as either the AAHPER Skill Related Fitness Test or the President's Council Youth Fitness Test.

In recent years greater emphasis has been placed on health-related fitness tests. Instead of agility, speed, power, and balance, attention has

In the early 1950s only 40% of U.S. children were able to pass a physical fitness test, while by notable contrast, 91% of European youth passed the same test. Although programs were established to improve American youth fitness, the goals of these programs have not been met, and despite students' poor physical performance levels, many school physical education programs are currently being curtailed. European schools, on the other hand, have traditionally emphasized physical education in grammar school curricula. Soccer (football), which originated as a team sport in English schools, is the most widely played game in Europe. French schoolboys (below) exhibit the fast footwork and control that are the foundation of the game. Children who grow up playing soccer not only develop skills and coordination at an early age, which are manifested in overall physical fitness, but most important, they acquire the habit of exercise, which they are likely to carry into adulthood.

Patrick Vielcanet—Allsport

been redirected toward cardiorespiratory endurance, body fatness, muscular strength, and flexibility. Experts believe that good scores on these tests may reduce the future risk of a variety of problems and diseases that emerge later in life.

The four most popular health-related fitness test components are cardiorespiratory endurance, a measurement of physical work capacity; body composition, a measure of body fatness; muscular strength, a measure of ability to exert a force against a resistance; and flexibility, a measure of range of motion. The reasons these items are being measured today can be summarized as follows: High cardiorespiratory endurance is associated with reduced fatigue and a lower risk for coronary heart disease. Low body fat is associated with reduced risks for CHD, hypertension (high blood pressure), and diabetes. A high level of strength is associated with enhanced ability to lift and carry as well as a reduced incidence of musculoskeletal pain. High flexibility is associated with reduced risk of low back pain and other musculoskeletal problems.

The specific tests used to measure the four components vary slightly among different youth fitness testing programs; six of these are listed in the table below. The so-called Physical Best test is the most recent version of the American Alliance for Health, Physical Education, Recreation and Dance health-related fitness test. The Fitnessgram is also a health-related fitness

Standardized fitness tests developed in the 1960s were largely skill oriented—testing agility, speed, power, and balance. Today the most widely used fitness tests for children are health oriented. As shown in the table below, they measure cardiorespiratory endurance, muscular strength of the upper body and abdomen, body composition, flexibility, and agility.

Fitness test components and measures

test component	Physical Best	Fitnessgram	Fit Youth Today	President's Challenge	NCYFS I	NCYFS II
cardio-respiratory endurance	1-mile walk/ run for time	1-mile walk/ run for time	20-minute constant-pace jog	1-mile walk/ run for time	1-mile walk/run for time	0.5-mile walk/run (6–7 years)
flexibility	sit and reach	sit and reach	sit and reach	v-sit and reach	sit and reach	sit and reach
muscular strength/ endurance						
upper body	pull-ups	pull-ups or flexed arm hang	not tested	pull-ups or flexed arm hang	chin-ups	modified pull-ups
abdomen	sit-ups (number in 1 minute)	sit-ups (number in 1 minute)	sit-ups (number in 2 minutes)	sit-ups (number in 1 minute)	sit-ups (number in 1 minute)	sit-ups (number in 1 minute)
body composition	sum of triceps and calf or triceps and subscapula skin folds or body mass index (height and weight)	sum of triceps and calf skin folds or body mass index	sum of triceps and calf skin folds	not measured	sum of triceps and sub-scapula skin folds	sum of triceps and sub-scapula skin folds
agility	not tested	shuttle run (optional)	not tested	shuttle run	not tested	not tested

Adapted from R. Pate and R. J. Shephard, "Characteristics of Physical Fitness in Youth" in *Perspectives in Exercise Science and Sports Medicine: Youth, Exercise and Sport* (Indianapolis: Benchmark Press, Inc., 1989), pp. 1–45

The University of Massachusetts tested over 380 6–13-year-olds to develop norms for a youth walking-fitness program. Skin-fold thicknesses assessed body composition; sit-ups tested for abdominal strength; and heart rate taken during vigorous pedaling on a stationary cycle measured cardiorespiratory fitness.

test and was developed by the Institute for Aerobics Research through support from the Campbell Soup Co. The Fit Youth Today test is the health-related fitness test being used in the state of Texas. The most recent version of the president's council fitness test presented in 1985 (President's Challenge) has begun to focus on more health-related items. The biggest differences between the President's Challenge and other testing programs is that it omits a measure of body fatness and continues to test agility. The NCYFS I and II tests were those used to assess the previously described goals established in 1980 for youth fitness by 1990.

Childhood: the start of heart disease

Atherosclerosis (plaque buildup in arteries) has its origins very early in childhood. Although the clinical signs and symptoms of atherosclerosis do not appear until adulthood, the fatty streaks that signify the first stages of the atherosclerotic process have been seen as early as 10 to 20 years of age. In fact, significant atherosclerosis was observed in approximately one-third of the young U.S. soldiers killed in Korea and Vietnam. It is important to identify risk factors for cardiovascular disease early in life and to offer preventive options. It makes sense to encourage *children* to establish healthy habits so as to minimize the likelihood of their becoming victims of cardiovascular disease as *adults*.

How prevalent are the risk factors for heart disease in children? Two studies in the mid-1970s reported that over 46% of 7–12-year-old children had at least one CHD risk factor (*i.e.,* high blood pressure, elevated cholesterol and triglyceride levels, family history of heart disease, or obesity). In another study of over 4,800 schoolchildren in Muscatine, Iowa, nearly 25% had elevated cholesterol. Thus, the incidence and prevalence of CHD risk factors is alarmingly high; efforts therefore must be directed toward modifying risk factors that can be controlled by the individual. That rule applies to every risk factor listed except, of course, family history. The

51

earlier the intervention begins, the more effective it is likely to be, since atherosclerosis progresses relentlessly yet remains silent until the middle or later years of life.

Fat children: already at risk?

While overfatness in and of itself is generally not considered a disease, its relationship to CHD, to high blood pressure, and to diabetes has been well documented. In developed countries the levels of body fatness among youth have increased dramatically over the last 20 years. The long-term health implication of this obesity epidemic will remain unknown until these children reach the age where the health risks associated with CHD, high blood pressure, and diabetes emerge. There are good reasons for advocating exercise intervention in the current generation rather than waiting to see the *likely* adverse effects and then acting to reduce body fat levels in the next generation of youth. A strategy should be undertaken to reduce body fat levels to at least the levels of the 1960s.

It has been established that the number of fat cells an individual carries is determined during early childhood. Therefore, the youth of today probably have larger numbers of fat cells than their 1960s counterparts. Will that make them more susceptible to higher body fat levels as adults—putting them at higher risk for diseases such as CHD, high blood pressure, and diabetes? It seems reasonable to expect that such unfortunate consequences *will* follow. Body fatness has a tendency to "track" from childhood to adulthood. Simply put, this means that overweight children are likely to become overweight adults. If exercise intervention programs to control body fat levels are used for youth today, the apparently greater risk for them in later life may be substantially reduced. Increasing daily energy expenditure through regular moderate to vigorous physical activity may not modify fat-cell number, but it can probably aid in reducing fat-cell size.

Exercise intervention

Numerous studies on adults have established a strong relationship between physical activity, fitness, and health (particularly reduced risk of CHD). However, uncertainty persists concerning the most appropriate type of activity. This results partially from confusion between short-term training and lifelong activity for cardiovascular health. Short-term training emphasizes exercise designed to improve cardiovascular fitness. This involves exercising at least three times a week for 20 minutes at 70 to 85% of maximum heart rate. Only 20% of the U.S. adult population has adopted this regimen. Furthermore, of the people who begin an exercise program of this type, 50% drop out within six months.

On the other hand, physical activity that involves sustained exercise may not be of sufficient intensity to improve cardiovascular fitness, but most population studies have linked health to consistent lifelong physical activity rather than the shorter-term achievement of cardiovascular fitness. The Harvard Alumni Study examined the relationship between physical activity and incidence of heart attacks among more than 16,000 men who entered college between 1916 and 1950. These men were followed for more than

25 years, and it was found that compared with individuals who expended less than 500 kilocalories per week, those who regularly expended 2,000 kilocalories or more in physical activity each week showed significant reductions in heart attacks. While a number of important questions remain (such as the level and intensity of activity that are optimal for health), there is a broad consensus that activity in and of itself *is* linked to health.

What can be done to get kids active? Children acquire habits and practices from their parents. Therefore, encouraging parents to be physically active and to involve their kids represents an attractive and simple way to get kids moving—enhancing their fitness and promoting lifelong health.

It may be incorrectly assumed that children's level of activity is more than adequate to provide protection against the progression of CHD. A common perception is that they are always moving around and thus are very active. However, a study investigating the quality of young children's

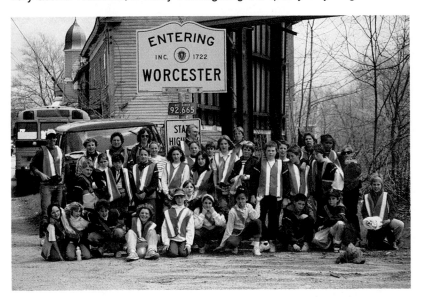

activity revealed that during normal free play, they rarely have heart rates in excess of 160 beats per minute. In other words, their exercise is not vigorous, nor is it prolonged (20 to 30 minutes); thus, they are not reaping the benefits of their activity.

The walking rage: not for adults only

A recent study conducted in the exercise science department at the University of Massachusetts at Amherst affirmed that children who come from families where parents are physically active are indeed much more likely to be active than children who come from families where parents are inactive. One obvious means of getting kids to be more active and concerned about their own level of physical fitness is through family fitness programs. One type of family exercise that can be classified as an appropriate lifetime fitness activity is a walking program. One might predict that kids would consider walking dull and would not be motivated to participate. Wrong! Walking can be made both challenging and fun for children.

In the mid-1980s a craze for walking as a major fitness and health-promoting activity swept America. In one survey in 1983, an estimated 55 million adults reported that they participated in walking as exercise—more than twice the number of joggers. The sudden surge of interest in walking coincided with mounting scientific evidence that an active life-style improves mental well-being, promotes weight loss, helps prevent bone thinning (osteoporosis), increases strength, decreases the likelihood of developing coronary heart disease, and may be associated with increased longevity. Walking is an ideal way to achieve these major health benefits. But how do children take to walking as a health-promoting activity? At the Fort River Elementary School in Amherst, Massachusetts, the fifth-grade class accepted the challenge proposed by their physical education teacher, Joanne Witek, to discover just how rewarding walking can be. Twenty-eight students signed contracts to walk for their health. Over a 16-week period, they trained every day after school in preparation for a 48-mile, four-day walk across the state to Worcester. (Opposite page and left) On April 26, 1988, the 28 students and five adults, wearing shining orange vests and Gore-Tex jackets, began their "Big Walk," heading eastward along the historic Old Boston Post Road (Highway 9). On day three it poured the entire day, but continue they did. For some of the walkers, the day they were drenched was—if not the best day—the most memorable. On day four, however, the sun shone; excitement mounted as the fifth graders and their adult companions covered their last 11 miles. The Amherst-to-Worcester walk was a definite success; all 28 students emerged wholeheartedly enthusiastic about their accomplishment.

Terry Angelides

53

The experiences of a group of fifth-grade students clearly verify this fact. In 1988, 28 10- and 11-year-old students and their physical education teacher from the Fort River Elementary School in Amherst, Massachusetts, walked 48 miles in four days from Amherst to Worcester, Massachusetts. The students maintained a high level of motivation and enthusiasm throughout the program, in which they trained for 16 weeks in preparation for the walk—averaging 10–36 miles per week. None of the children dropped out of the program. Each training day presented a new challenge—with the big challenge at the end of the program—the four-day trip—the most effective motivator of all. All children received a tremendous amount of support and encouragement from family and friends. Their experience is best told by the students themselves.

One year after their trek, students recalled their walk with fond memories. These were some of their comments:

I really enjoyed the walk to Worcester. I think the walk really helped me physically because it put my muscles back in work and got me in shape and I would do it right away if there was another walk.

The training was hard but it kept me fit during the winter. The walk was hard too but it was definitely fun. I would do the walk again, but a different one and longer. The rainy day was the funnest! I had a fun time with everybody and got a lot closer to them.

I'm glad I did the walk to Worcester because it's a once in a lifetime experience. It also is great for your health and walking is enjoyable too. You get to meet people you didn't really know before.

Starting a children's fitness walking program

Prior to starting a walking program, it is a good idea to measure the child's initial level of cardiovascular fitness. The field test used most often to measure cardiovascular fitness is the one-mile walk/run test referred to previously. The object of this test is to complete the one-mile distance in as fast a time as possible; most commonly this involves running. A running test may not be appropriate for all children, however—especially if they have not been involved in a regular exercise program. In fact, the running test may be demotivating since it involves all-out exertion that may be uncomfortable for some children, thus starting them off with the wrong ideas about fitness.

The University of Massachusetts recently completed a study that was funded by the Ronald McDonald Children's Charities to develop a walking test for 6–13-year-old children. At the present time, this program has established walk-time categories that are age and gender specific so that parents and teachers can administer the test to children and determine an appropriate walking program. More than 380 6–13-year-old children were tested to develop the norms for the program. Any parents can adapt such a walking program for their own children by simply following the steps outlined. There is nothing more gratifying to a parent than helping a child achieve a measure of self-confidence and mastery over his or her world. This simple, easy-to-follow fitness walking exercise program can set youngsters on a road that will carry them for life; it is a program that is likely to have lifelong beneficial consequences for their health and well being.

Everyone is a winner: a walking program for children

Step one: administering the test. The walking test covers a half mile for 6–9-year-olds and one mile for 10–13-year-olds. Kids between the ages of 9 and 10 should be classified with the younger age group.

1. Initially a measured track should be located (quarter-mile tracks can usually be found at high schools and recreation facilities), or a familiar flat surface can be measured out to determine a half-mile or mile distance.

2. Children should stretch for five to ten minutes to warm up their muscles before doing the test, concentrating in particular on stretching their legs and lower back. Once in a stretch position, the child should hold the position for five seconds, then release. (No bouncing!) This should be repeated ten times on each leg. The lower back stretch should also be repeated ten times, holding the stretch for five seconds at a time.

3. As they walk, kids should be instructed to maintain the fastest pace possible throughout the prescribed distance, but they should not run! (A consistent walking pace is very important for accurate test results, so it is a good idea for children to practice their walking pace before they actually take the test.)

4. The child's time should be recorded at the end of the walk in minutes and seconds. As a general rule, the half mile should take between 5 and 10 minutes, the mile between 10 and 20 minutes.

5. After completing the test, youngsters should cool down by walking for two to three minutes at a slower pace and then should stretch again for five minutes.

Step two: interpreting the test results. 1. The walk test tables (Tables 1 and 2) should be used to find the appropriate age and gender category for each child. The performance table for six–nine-year-olds is not broken down by gender because when the test was developed, there were no differences in walk times between the boys and girls in this age group. (Note: Youngsters who are between age groups should be classified with the younger age group; for example, a child who is 6 years and 11 months old will fall into the 6-year-old category.)

2. The youngster's walk time should be matched with the appropriate symbol and color category (red hearts, green diamonds, purple squares, blue circles, orange stars, and yellow triangles). Here it is important to stress that a child cannot do poorly on the test! The times listed are standards only; they are to be used to identify the appropriate walking program and to measure improvement in walk test time after regular participation in the fitness walking program.

3. The appropriate symbol and color code in the walk test table should be matched to the same code in the walking prescriptions. The child is now ready to begin his or her program.

Step three: progressing through the walking program. 1. Not all children will engage in fitness walking the same number of times per week. These guidelines should be followed for progressing through the different phases presented in the fitness walking prescriptions. A child who walks one day per week should complete each phase three times, then progress to the next phase. A child who walks two days per week should complete each

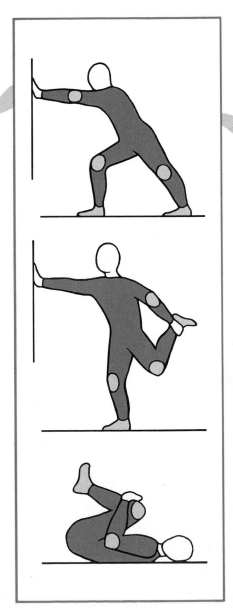

Stretching to warm up muscles is important before any exercise. Before taking the walking test, children should concentrate on stretching their legs and lower back. The stretching maneuvers below are (top to bottom) the Achilles tendon and calf stretch, the quadriceps stretch, and the lower back stretch.

phase twice, then progress to the next phase. A child who walks three or more days per week can progress to a new phase every week.

2. The walking test should be readministered after 18 sessions of fitness walking (or after 28 sessions of another high-activity exercise program) and improvement in walk time measured.

3. After a child completes all six phases of the program, his or her walking time or distance or both should be increased. The fitness walking prescriptions—by color/symbol program (Tables 3–5 for 6–9-year-olds and Tables 6–8 for 10–13-year-olds)—will serve as guides.

Establishing target heart rate. While time and distance are important indicators of overall fitness, no factor gives better information on intensity

Table 1: Half-mile walk time categories

age	red	green	purple
6–7 years	less than 7:15	7:15–8:40	greater than 8:40
8–9 years	less than 6:40	6:40–8:00	greater than 8:00

Table 2: One-mile walk time categories

age	blue	orange	yellow
10–11 years			
boys	less than 12:45	12:45–16:00	greater than 16:00
girls	less than 13:20	13:20–16:10	greater than 16:10
12–13 years			
boys	less than 12:20	12:20–15:05	greater than 15:05
girls	less than 12:55	12:55–15:10	greater than 15:10

Fitness walking prescriptions
6–9-year-old children

♥ Table 3: Red program ♥

phase	1	2	3	4	5	6
time	9 min	12 min	15 min	18 min	21 min	24 min
distance	0.5 mi	0.7 mi	0.9 mi	1.1 mi	1.3 mi	1.5 mi

◆ Table 4: Green program ◆

phase	1	2	3	4	5	6
time	9 min	12 min	15 min	18 min	21 min	24 min
distance	0.4 mi	0.6 mi	0.8 mi	1 mi	1.2 mi	1.4 mi

■ Table 5: Purple program ■

phase	1	2	3	4	5	6
time	9 min	12 min	15 min	18 min	21 min	24 min
distance	0.3 mi	0.5 mi	0.7 mi	0.9 mi	1.1 mi	1.3 mi

of effort than heart rate (or pulse) measured during exercise. Although the youngest children (those aged 6 to 9) may not be able to determine their own heart rates accurately, it is a good idea for 10–13-year-olds to learn how to do this as part of the walking and fitness program. Initially many children (and adults!) may find it difficult to locate their pulse, but with practice they will soon master it. The best way is to place two fingers lightly on the inside of the wrist (below the thumb) and count "pulses."

As a rule, during the fitness walking program a child's heart rate should fall into a "target heart rate" range of between 31 and 42 beats per 15 seconds (or 124 and 168 beats per minute). These figures represent approximately 60–80% of the maximum heart rate range. The target heart rate chart (Table 9) should be used for determining the appropriate range.

After walking at the prescribed pace for five minutes, the child should then stop and take his or her pulse for 15 seconds (or be assisted by someone else in doing this). If the heart rate is lower than indicated above, the pace should be picked up and the pulse checked again after five minutes. If the heart rate exceeds the prescribed guidelines, the heart rate should be retaken after a slowed-down five-minute walk. This monitoring of the heart rate ensures that a child is placing enough demand on the heart.

Photographs, David Brownell

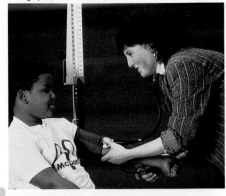

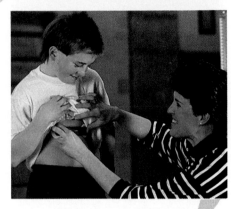

Walking is a great activity for youngsters, particularly those who do not participate in organized athletics. Walking is easy; there are no complex rules to learn or complicated movements to master. It can be done indoors or outdoors, alone or with others. When youngsters are active, they feel good about themselves, and it has been well established that walking is great for health both in the short term and in the long term. The children above participated in studies that were carried out in the exercise science department at the University of Massachusetts with a grant from the Ronald McDonald Children's Charities. A series of walking tests and a six-phase walking program that promote fitness and are suitable for boys and girls aged 6 to 13 were developed, in the process of which extensive monitoring was done of the children's vital signs before, during, and after various levels of exercise. For any parents or teachers who want to start a fitness walking program for children, the tests on the preceding pages are easily administered and do not require any special equipment.

10–13-year-old children

Table 6: **Blue program**

phase	1	2	3	4	5	6
time	9 min	12 min	15 min	18 min	21 min	24 min
distance	0.6 mi	0.8 mi	1 mi	1.2 mi	1.4 mi	1.6 mi

★ Table 7: **Orange program** ★

phase	1	2	3	4	5	6
time	9 min	12 min	15 min	18 min	21 min	24 min
distance	0.5 mi	0.7 mi	0.9 mi	1.1 mi	1.3 mi	1.5 mi

Table 8: **Yellow program**

phase	1	2	3	4	5	6
time	9 min	12 min	15 min	18 min	21 min	24 min
distance	0.4 mi	0.6 mi	0.8 mi	1 mi	1.2 mi	1.4 mi

Table 9: **Target heart rate***
beats per 15 seconds
(beats per minute in parentheses)

	phases 1 & 2	phases 3 & 4	phases 5 & 6
△ yellow program	31–34 (124–136)	31–37 (124–148)	35–40 (140–160)
★ orange program	31–37 (124–148)	35–37 (140–148)	35–42 (140–168)
● blue program	35–37 (140–148)	35–40 (140–160)	38–42 (152–168)

*children aged 6–9 too young to monitor own heart rate accurately

Upper-body strength is necessary for many activities of daily living—lifting, carrying, reaching, and so forth—and a youngster who has developed strong arms and shoulders is unlikely to suffer musculoskeletal injuries. Doing chin-ups or even playing on a jungle gym will help children to attain this important aspect of fitness.
Exercise need not be boring, painful, or competitive. Aerobic dancers get the most out of their workout as they kick, flex, swivel, jump, lift their knees, and wave their arms—all in step to upbeat music.

Muscular strength: not to be neglected

Children who take up walking as a way to fitness will most likely derive many benefits in terms of lifelong health. Walking, however, involves primarily the legs and does not affect upper-body strength, but this aspect of fitness is important, too. Results from the research literature clearly show that upper-body strength for children is very low. In fact, 30% of 10–11-year-old boys and 60% of 10–18-year-old girls were not able to do even one chin-up! Upper-body strength is essential both for the activities of daily living and for injury prevention. In the quest for increased levels of physical activity and improved fitness among youth, it is important not to neglect the upper body.

Examples of activities that can be used to develop muscular strength and endurance are playing on a monkey bar, where a child uses his or her arms and upper body to move across a horizontal ladder that is suspended above the ground, and playing on a jungle gym. Exercises that can be done to promote development of upper-body strength and endurance include push-ups, pull-ups, and sit-ups (bent knees, of course), as well as resistance-training exercises using light weights—*e.g.,* bench press exercises that use a resistance, where the child can comfortably complete 10–15 repetitions. If resistance training is used, the child should be trained to use the equipment and should have proper supervision to ensure safety and minimize the risk of injury.

Education + activity = health

Besides encouraging children to exercise and exercising with them, what other strategies can adults use to promote physical activity among school-age youth? Youngsters not only should be encouraged to become active and fit but should learn why exercise is important.

Certainly the school offers the ideal environment for imparting knowledge about exercise. Both physical education programs and the classroom can be effective settings for instruction. In science classes, for example,

Thumbs up to the active life. The childhood fitness crisis can be averted. Children who give up their sedentary life-styles discover just how horizon-expanding exercising can be; not only are the immediate pleasures and benefits innumerable but youngsters who become active are taking a major step toward ensuring that they will enjoy good health in the future.

children can study anatomy and physiology—*e.g.,* they can learn how the heart works and, in the process, how exercise affects the heart and skeletal muscles. The physical education teacher can then provide information about what constitutes proper exercise training specifically to promote cardiovascular fitness. Students can use their own bodies as experimental laboratories—progressing through structured exercise programs and discovering the physical effects on the body of various activity regimens. Such an approach will do much more toward getting children to truly appreciate that exercise is indeed worthwhile for them than will merely preaching the benefits of activity.

In many schools specific health education classes are included in the curriculum. The goal of such health education programs is to reach children before they pick up bad habits and to find creative ways to instill lifelong habits that are healthy. Such programs *are* effective. This was shown in a recent survey conducted by Metropolitan Life Foundation and Louis Harris & Associates that assessed the extent and effectiveness of health education for nearly 5,000 pupils in 199 U.S. public schools. It was found that youngsters in the 3rd through the 12th grades who had at least three years of health education in their school curricula were, among other things, less likely to drink alcohol, smoke, or take drugs. And, notably, they were more likely to exercise regularly.

Reversing the trend

The goals for youth fitness established in 1980 for the year 1990 were not met. It seems ironic that Western civilization, which is said to place great value on young people, has not done more to promote their fitness. If adults truly want to leave the world a better place for the youngest generation—if they want their children to be able to enjoy their health as they experience their future—the time to act is now. Only creative and concerted efforts will enable the as-yet-unachieved goals for the fitness of all children to be met before the turn of the century.

Till Death Do Us Part:
America's Turbulent Love Affair with the Cigarette

by Kenneth E. Warner, Ph.D.

Kenneth E. Warner, Ph.D., is Professor, Department of Public Health Policy and Administration, School of Public Health, University of Michigan, Ann Arbor. He served as Senior Scientific Editor of the 25th-anniversary Surgeon General's Report on Smoking and Health.

(Opposite page) The tobacco industry must go to great lengths to perpetuate its products; some 3,000–5,000 young people must be persuaded to start smoking each day in order to replenish the market depleted through death and quitting by adults. Illustration, "Replacement Smoker" by Vern Herschberger; Stop Teenage Addiction to Smoking (STAT), P.O. Box 60658, Longmeadow, Massachusetts

A hundred years from now, when historians look back upon America in the 20th century, they will surely rank the rise and fall of the cigarette as one of the most intriguing social phenomena of the period. Medical historians will rank the growth of smoking in the United States as among the most tragic developments. In a century plagued by warfare, it is sobering to reflect, as Sen. Robert F. Kennedy did in 1967, that "every year cigarettes kill more Americans than were killed in World War I, the Korean War, and Vietnam combined; nearly as many as died in battle in World War II."

Today cigarette smoking annually claims 390,000 U.S. lives, accounting for more than one-sixth of all deaths. Smoking is responsible for fully 30% of all cancer deaths, including almost 90% of lung cancer mortality, the leading cause of cancer death in both men and women; a fifth of deaths from coronary heart disease, the nation's leading disease cause of death; almost a fifth of stroke deaths; and over four-fifths of deaths from chronic obstructive pulmonary disease—primarily emphysema and chronic bronchitis. Smoking is also the leading cause of nonfatal illness.

The hazards of tobacco use have been suspected for almost four centuries. In 1604 Britain's King James I described smoking in his *Counterblaste to Tobacco* as "a custome Lothsome to the eye, hatefull to the Nose, harmfull to the braine, [and] dangerous to the Lungs." A contemporary, the Ottoman Empire's Sultan Murad IV, believed that tobacco caused infertility and reduced the fighting capabilities of his soldiers. In 1633, when he decreed its use punishable by death from hanging, beheading, or starvation, he in fact "proved" tobacco was hazardous to health.

True scientific appreciation of the health effects of smoking, however, is a product only of the present century, dating primarily from the middle of the century, when a series of well-designed epidemiological studies demonstrated the strong association between smoking and lung cancer. Until the mid-1950s the public remained blissfully ignorant of the dangers of smoking. Widespread public concern about those dangers dates only from the mid-1960s. So does the turnaround in America's love affair with tobacco.

60

The cigarette's rise . . .

While tobacco smoking and chewing were popular among adult males in the 1800s, *cigarette* smoking—the most dangerous form of tobacco use—is a phenomenon of the present century. The popularity of cigarette smoking was made possible by two technological developments: invention of the Bonsack cigarette-rolling machine in 1880, a device that automated cigarette manufacture (and thus permitted a quantum leap in the production of cigarettes), and development of American blended cigarette tobacco, a blend mild enough to permit deep inhalation, the most efficient means of delivering nicotine into the bloodstream.

In 1913 the R. J. Reynolds Tobacco Co. introduced Camel cigarettes, the first major cigarette brand successfully employing the American blend of tobacco. Camel is universally regarded as the product and marketing innovation that ushered in the modern era of the cigarette. (Ironically, 1913 also witnessed the birth of the American Cancer Society.) When American men marched off to war soon thereafter, the highly convenient manufactured cigarette went with them. The rest, as they say, is history.

From 1900 through 1963 annual adult per capita consumption of manufactured cigarettes in the U.S. (defined as total cigarette consumption divided by the population 18 years of age and older) climbed steadily from 54 cigarettes to 4,345 cigarettes. By the early 1920s over half of all American men were smokers. (Including pipe and cigar smoking and tobacco chewing, 87% of adult males consumed tobacco products.) By the mid-1930s, 70% of men were smokers at the age of peak smoking rates—in their twenties and early thirties.

While a sizable majority of men smoked in 1935, they were joined by fewer than a fifth of the adult female population. At that time smoking by women was generally regarded as socially unacceptable. Beginning around

Tobacco was popular among adult males in the 1800s (it was smoked in pipes or chewed). Well before clear scientific evidence linked its use to various forms of cancer and other disease, it was known that tobacco was habit-forming and that nicotine was the addictive component. Although this 19th-century advertisement claimed that No-To-Bac was "guaranteed" to "kill the tobacco habit," this was at a time before medicines were regulated, and nostrums that purported to cure every imaginable ill flooded the market. Such patent medicines ranged from the useless to the deadly, but few were legitimate remedies and actually did what they claimed. Today drug innovators are still searching for a product that will be a truly effective treatment for nicotine dependence.

Philadelphia Museum of Art; given by William H. Helfand

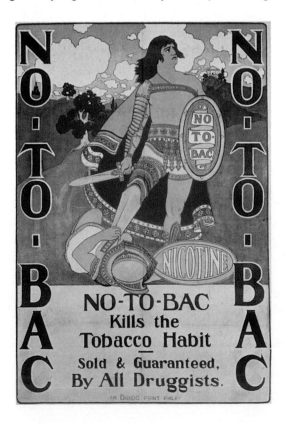

The roles that American heroes and heroines played in promoting cigarette smoking should not be underestimated. Smoking could hardly have been seen as anything but utterly romantic—not to mention sexy and sophisticated—when Humphrey Bogart lighted Lauren Bacall's cigarette in the 1944 motion picture To Have and Have Not. *In the 1940s and '50s, Edward R. Morrow was undoubtedly the best known and most influential American commentator—first on CBS radio and then on CBS-TV. In the minds of his viewers, Morrow's chain-smoking most certainly became associated with his reputation for intellectual integrity, taste, and restraint.*

World War II, however, the norm began to change; smoking diffused among women as it had several decades earlier among men, to the point that a third of all women were smokers by the mid-1960s.

America's romance with the cigarette touched virtually every sphere of modern life, and seemingly every celebrity. The idols of the silver screen conveyed the message that smoking was macho (John Wayne, Gary Cooper) and sexy and sophisticated (Humphrey Bogart and Lauren Bacall). Sports stars associated the product with athletic prowess (Joe DiMaggio, Ted Williams, Stan Musial, and Mickey Mantle). Newscaster Edward R. Murrow's on-the-air chain-smoking lent cigarettes an intellectual quality. Pres. Franklin D. Roosevelt's cigarette-holder smokes exuded confidence, leadership, and even a certain elegance. Eleanor Roosevelt's smoking helped to "liberate" women from the shackles of the nonsmoking norm. Smoking was ordinary, expected, and respectable; simply put, it was all-American. In magazine ads, the "Gipper," Ronald Reagan, told the U.S. that he was "sending Chesterfields to all my friends" for Christmas.

America's increasingly amorous affair with the cigarette was jolted by the scientific revelations in the early 1950s of the relationship between smoking and lung cancer. The cigarette industry's response was swift and effective. While denying the link and mounting a campaign to cloud the evidence, the industry also produced cigarettes with "miracle" filter tips and marketed them, either implicitly or explicitly, as reducing or removing exposure to the hazardous products of combustion. (Ironically, asbestos comprised a third of the original Kent Micronite Filter.) With the smoking population (and the population of potential smokers) reassured, cigarette consumption resumed its seemingly inexorable climb to ever higher levels.

The industry persists in denying that smoking has ever been proved to cause any disease. Presumably, this official denial is intended to perpetuate the industry's myth that there is a scientific "controversy" concerning the health issue, long a strategic element in the effort to keep the U.S. smoking.

63

In addition, it is a necessary position for guarding against judgments of liability in the scores of product-liability lawsuits now filed against the cigarette companies and the thousands more that would surely follow the industry's admission of long-standing knowledge of the dangers of smoking.

. . . and its fall

If the scientific findings of the 1950s unsettled America's romance with the cigarette, an event in early 1964 put the relationship permanently on the skids. On January 11 of that year, U.S. Surgeon General Luther Terry released *Smoking and Health,* the report of the Advisory Committee to the Surgeon General of the Public Health Service. Destined to become a landmark public health document, the first "Surgeon General's Report," as it became known, enunciated the then-known dangers of smoking in unequivocal terms. Press coverage of the long-anticipated report was extensive; release of the report would later be ranked as one of the leading news stories of 1964. Illustrative of the importance attached to the surgeon general's press conference announcing publication of the report was the fact that it was scheduled on a Saturday, to guard against a precipitous reaction on Wall Street.

Release of the first "Surgeon General's Report" inaugurated the national "antismoking campaign," a period of sustained, if often uncoordinated, effort on the part of numerous government agencies and private-sector health organizations to educate the public about the hazards of smoking. The result has been striking ever since. Per capita cigarette consumption fell by 3.5% in 1964, one of only a handful of annual decreases throughout the first two-thirds of the century. (The decrease that year was driven by consumption's plummeting 15% in the first three months following issuance of the report.) While consumption recovered slightly during the next two years,

What could be more all-American than smoking Chesterfields—especially when endorsed by the dashing actor Ronald Reagan in this Christmastime magazine advertisement, c. 1950?

Photograph, DOC Archive

it fell annually from 1967 through 1970, a period of government-mandated antismoking messages on television and radio, rose briefly during 1971 through 1973, and then began an annual downward spiral that has never stopped. The rate of per capita consumption realized in 1963, the year prior to the first "Surgeon General's Report," turned out to be the peak.

By the end of the 1980s, per capita consumption had fallen fully 30%, to a level last experienced in 1944. The percentage of adults smoking had dropped from 40% in 1965 to 29% in 1987, the lowest figure recorded since surveys of smoking began. The decrease was especially dramatic among men, from over 50% in 1965 to close to 30% in 1987. While the decline was much more modest among women, the antismoking campaign had clearly stalled and reversed the escalation in women's smoking rates observed in the postwar era. In its own right, the precipitous decline in smoking is as fascinating a phenomenon as its surge in the first part of the century.

Call for a smoke-free society

In 1984 Surgeon General C. Everett Koop issued a call for a smoke-free society by the year 2000. He has since defined a "smoke-free society" as one in which smoking is restricted to consenting adults in the privacy of their own homes. By this definition, consumption trends suggest that a smoke-free society is a goal that can be closely approximated within the next two decades, if not necessarily by the year 2000. Certainly the rapid growth of "clean indoor air" laws and private-sector smoking-restriction policies reflects, and contributes to, changing social norms consistent with the vision of a "smoke-free society." However, the steady reversal of the popularity of smoking in the aggregate masks specific trends that augur less progress against smoking, or at least more difficult progress, in the coming decades. In addition, the long lag between quitting smoking and the elimination of its deleterious effects on health assures that the burden of smoking will remain a fundamental ingredient in the vital statistics of the U.S. until well into the next century.

Tobacco's toll: public perception versus reality

Smoking has long held the dubious distinction of being society's leading cause of preventable death, a fact established by the most substantial body of scientific knowledge ever amassed linking a product to disease. The enormity of the toll of smoking is obscured for the average American, however, by (1) the imponderable nature of the large number that summarizes the mortality burden—390,000 deaths per year, (2) the familiarity and ubiquity of smoking, and (3) the glamorization of smoking by an industry that spends $2.6 billion annually to recruit and retain consumers. The imagery of cigarette advertising and the implicit message of its legality foster the impression that "smoking can't be really all that dangerous" (as 44% of smokers responded to a poll conducted in the U.K.). The tobacco industry attempts to reinforce this perception through its persistent denial that the dangers of smoking have been proved. The perception may be reinforced further by self-imposed restrictions on coverage of the hazards of smoking by publications dependent on tobacco advertising revenues.

Until the early 1960s most Americans remained blissfully unaware of the explicit dangers of smoking. Yet even when there were only preliminary reports that linked smoking with various health problems, the tobacco industry seemed to feel a need to stress that its products were not *unhealthy. Throughout the 1940s and '50s, cigarette manufacturers used doctors in advertisements to convey the message that smoking was safe; doctors not only recommended it, they did it themselves.*

Photograph, DOC Archive

65

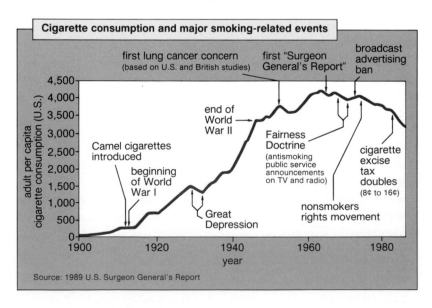

On Jan. 11, 1964, U.S. Surgeon General Luther Terry issued the long-awaited 150,000-word report Smoking and Health, *which had been prepared by a special committee of scientists and physicians at the request of Pres. John F. Kennedy. Terry announced that smoking was "a health hazard of sufficient importance in the United States to warrant appropriate remedial action"; at the time, 70 million Americans were believed to be habitual smokers.* Smoking and Health *was the landmark public health document that indicted smoking as the chief cause of lung cancer in men, as the most important cause of chronic bronchitis in men and women, and as a cause of cancer of the larynx. The experts also found an association between smoking and emphysema, peptic ulcers, delivery of premature infants, and cancer of the esophagus and bladder. Cigarette consumption in the U.S. plummeted 15% in the first three months following the surgeon general's announcement, and the country would never again see per capita cigarette consumption rates higher than those in 1963—the year before the report.*

Combined, these factors contribute to Americans' substantial underestimation of the relative importance of smoking in the hierarchy of disease-causing behaviors and substances. This is illustrated by a 1983 poll in which health experts ranked "not smoking" as the most important of 24 health and safety factors while lay public respondents ranked it tenth, behind such factors as "having smoke detectors in the home." While home fires are a serious risk, cigarettes annually claim 65 times more lives. Also, ironically, the leading cause of home-fire deaths is the cigarette.

Analogies help to convey the significance of a number like 390,000 deaths. Senator Kennedy's aforementioned war dead comparison is one example. Another is the observation that cigarettes cause as many deaths as three jumbo jet crashes a day would. A particularly striking comparison is that cigarettes kill more Americans than all of the following combined: AIDS, cocaine, heroin, alcohol, automobiles, homicide, suicide, and (of course) fire. As surgeon general, Koop, who had identified AIDS as the nation's most pressing emergent public health crisis, was quick to point out in 1988 that cigarettes killed more Americans every month than AIDS had killed since it was first reported in 1981.

Changing demographics

Ignorance of the full extent of smoking's hazards is found in all socio-economic and demographic groupings, but depth of knowledge varies significantly with level of education. The smoking-and-health message has been conveyed most successfully to college graduates, whose smoking prevalence (*i.e.,* the percentage of the group smoking at a given point in time) has declined by more than half since the mid-1960s, falling from 34% in 1965 to 16% in 1987. In sharp contrast, the prevalence of smoking among Americans lacking a high school diploma has remained virtually unchanged over the same period, falling only from 37 to 36%.

Similarly, rates of smoking are higher among blue-collar workers than among white-collar workers. (Physicians have exhibited the greatest propensity of any profession or occupation to "kick the habit." While their smoking prevalence exceeded 50% in the early 1950s, today it appears to be in the vicinity of 10%, with younger generations of physicians and medical

Cigarette consumption and major smoking-related events

first lung cancer concern
(based on U.S. and British studies)

first "Surgeon General's Report"

broadcast advertising ban

end of World War II

Fairness Doctrine
(antismoking public service announcements on TV and radio)

Camel cigarettes introduced

beginning of World War I

cigarette excise tax doubles
(8¢ to 16¢)

Great Depression

nonsmokers rights movement

adult per capita cigarette consumption (U.S.)

4,500 · 4,000 · 3,500 · 3,000 · 2,500 · 2,000 · 1,500 · 1,000 · 500 · 0

1900   1920   1940   1960   1980
year

Source: 1989 U.S. Surgeon General's Report

students having smoking rates closer to 5% or less.) Among ethnic groups, proportionately more blacks than whites smoke, a reversal of the pattern existing before mid-century. Hispanic men appear to fall in between white and black men in terms of smoking prevalence, while Hispanic women smoke at lower rates than do either white or black women.

The most striking shift in the demographic patterns of smoking is found in the gender mix of the smoking population. In the mid-1930s the proportion of the male population smoking was three times that of the female population. Two decades later it was still twice as large. Currently, the two prevalence rates are approaching parity. And since the percentage of high school girls who smoke is now larger than that of boys who do so (a phenomenon dating from the late 1970s), the rate of smoking among women is projected to exceed that of men sometime in the 1990s.

Drastic consequences for women and blacks

The importance of the changing demographics of smoking resides in the illness and death trends now evident or predictable. Two trends in particular have captured attention—and created alarm—within the public health community. One is the role of smoking in the growing "health gap" between society's haves and have-nots. Perhaps most disturbing is the fact that blacks experience higher death rates than whites for most of the major smoking-related causes of death. While other factors contribute to this gap, there is little doubt that blacks' higher smoking rates exacerbate their mortality and morbidity outcomes in such smoking-related diseases as lung cancer and heart disease. In the mid-1980s the incidence of lung cancer among white males began declining, reflecting the substantial cessation of smoking that began among white males in the mid-1960s. Among black males, however, lung cancer incidence continued to rise.

The second trend causing consternation among health professionals is the rapidly escalating rate of smoking-produced disease among women. Combined with indications of decreases in smoking-related disease in men, this escalation has led to the projection that in the coming decades women will lose half of their seven-year life-expectancy lead over men.

The rising toll of smoking by women is most noticeable in the most obvious disease marker of smoking: lung cancer. In the middle of the 1980s, lung cancer surpassed breast cancer as the leading cause of cancer death in women. While age-adjusted death rates for all other major cancers have been steady or falling over the past several decades, the lung cancer death rate among smoking women has escalated rapidly, from 24 deaths per 100,000 women in 1960–64 to 130 in 1982–86. That the lung cancer epidemic is attributable almost exclusively to smoking is demonstrated by the fact that during that same period, the lung cancer death rate among nonsmoking women remained unchanged at 12 per 100,000 population—one-eleventh of the rate among smokers in 1982–86.

Just as the prevalence of smoking by women lagged behind that of men by about three decades, women's lung cancer death pattern is paralleling that of men three decades earlier. The implication for women is frightening since lung cancer today accounts for 35% of all cancer deaths among

Public education has been the consistent and unifying theme in the war against smoking throughout the quarter of a century since the first "Surgeon General's Report." In reviewing the changes in smoking and health during that time, U.S. Surgeon General C. Everett Koop noted the major successes of the antismoking campaign. For example, decisions that Americans made between 1964 and 1985 to quit or not to start smoking will have led to the avoidance or postponement of almost three million smoking-related deaths by the year 2000. In appraising the contemporary situation, however, Koop added a sobering note: "Smoking will continue as the leading cause of preventable, premature death for many years to come." During the Great American Smokeout of 1987, Koop confronted a life-sized Mr. Potato Head and challenged the popular toy to surrender his pipe. The gesture was meant to set an example for the nation's children. The document that Koop is holding says: "The Surgeon General of the United States in conjunction with the American Cancer Society proudly bestow the title of Official Spokespud of the 1987 Great American Smokeout upon Mr. Potato Head."

In 1984 Surgeon General C. Everett Koop called for a smoke-free society by the year 2000. The clean indoor air laws that have been enacted throughout the country and the smoking restrictions that have been imposed in public places are in keeping with such a vision. These patrons of a club in Atlanta, Georgia, must do their smoking outside the establishment.

men, a figure so dominant among cancer causes of death that each of the next closest "contenders"—colorectal and prostate cancer—accounts for only 11% of male cancer deaths. Lung cancer was first listed as an official cause of death in the International Classification of Diseases in 1930. The disease was virtually unknown at the turn of the century.

Ironic cancer phobia

Exposed to a daily barrage of media stories on environmental toxins and chemical carcinogens, the American public believes it is in the midst of a man-made cancer epidemic. The belief is technically correct—the cancer death rate has been rising since mid-century, and the increase is indeed man-made—but the perceived source and the extent of the "cancer epidemic" are quite wrong. Since 1950 the age-adjusted cancer death rate has risen by 9%. However, excluding lung cancer—the source of 25% of all cancer deaths and a disease that is caused almost exclusively by smoking—the age-adjusted cancer death rate has actually fallen by 13%. There is no cancer epidemic; rather, there is an epidemic of smoking-produced cancer death, man-made by the manufacturers of cigarettes. Increasingly, the burden of this epidemic is being placed on women, minorities, and Americans in blue-collar occupations.

To bring the U.S.'s chemical phobia full circle, it is interesting to note that the everyday cigarette, a product once characterized as a "prolific chemical factory," itself emits over 4,000 chemicals, 43 of which have been identified as carcinogens. There is ten times more cyanide in *every puff* on a standard filtered cigarette than was found in each of the two Chilean grapes that provoked the "fruit poisoning scare" in March 1989.

Youthful initiation, insidious addiction

The persistence of widespread smoking in the U.S. in the face of over-whelming evidence of its dangers reflects a complex web of sociological and

Youngsters in a first-grade class at a public school in Boston had a "graduation" ceremony in May 1989; they are among 800,000 pupils from 28,000 U.S. schools who make up the "Smoke-Free Class of 2000." The students are participating in a nationwide program sponsored by the American Cancer Society, the American Heart Association, and the American Lung Association.
Its aim is to convey to children in their first school year the message that they should not start smoking—before cigarette advertising persuades them to do otherwise—and to keep them from smoking throughout their years in school.

psychological factors, the biochemistry of the lit cigarette, and the marketing efforts of the tobacco industry. The initiation of smoking begins almost invariably in the teenage years or even earlier, when the behavior is viewed as a symbol of rebellion and independence and a step toward adulthood.

While children acknowledge the hazards of smoking, they see them as applying only to "old people." Imbued with a sense of immortality and convinced that they will be able to quit smoking "at will," children begin smoking with no perception of the personal relevance of its hazards; most believe that they will quit smoking a few years later. The facts belie that expectation. While many will eventually quit, large numbers will find themselves chained to an addiction the surgeon general has characterized as comparable to addiction to cocaine and heroin. The behavior that begins innocently, if mischievously, enough ends as what the National Institute on Drug Abuse has characterized as the most widespread form of drug dependence in the U.S.—and the most fatal.

Youthful initiation and nicotine addiction are the primary ingredients perpetuating smoking. While the former is influenced by a myriad of role models, including peers, parents, and selected celebrities, the social environment in which smoking begins is also defined by the marketing activities of the tobacco industry. Those activities include conventional print advertising of cigarettes and, increasingly, a variety of other promotional techniques. They also include the introduction of a diverse set of new nicotine-delivering products designed to respond to nicotine dependence in the U.S. in a social environment increasingly hostile toward smoking in public places.

Selling death: the marketing of cigarettes in the U.S.

The $2.6 billion in advertising and promotion expenditures by the cigarette manufacturers—more than $10 for every man, woman, and child, or $50 for every smoker—constitutes one of the largest marketing efforts ever devoted to a consumer product. The effort takes many shapes, ranging from conventional advertising in the print media to distribution of free product samples, sponsorship of sports events (*e.g.,* Virginia Slims tennis, Marlboro Cup racing, and Winston soccer) and cultural activities (major art exhibits, tours of ballet companies and modern dance troupes, and jazz

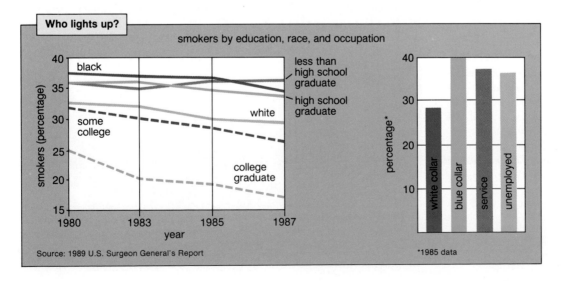

Who lights up?

smokers by education, race, and occupation

Source: 1989 U.S. Surgeon General's Report

*1985 data

April A. Oswald

and symphony orchestra concerts), and support of educational and health care institutions. (Virginia Slims held a benefit for Children's Hospital in Oakland, California, which introduces a certain irony, in that smoking is a leading cause of pregnancy outcomes leading to hospitalization of infants.) In addition, tobacco companies and their public relations arm, the Tobacco Institute, invariably rank near the top of special interest group contributions to members of Congress in the form of honoraria and lecture fees.

Although aided by nicotine's addictiveness, the tobacco industry confronts a unique problem in the attempt to perpetuate use of its products— it loses more of its customers every year than any other major industry. The industry's product kills many more of its consumers than does any other product, and an average of 1.5 million Americans have quit smoking each year since 1964. Because "replacement smokers" are drawn primarily from the ranks of children, 3,000 to 5,000 children have to start smoking each and every day, year in and year out, for the aggregate number of smokers not to plummet. Survey data indicate that this number of children *does* replenish the market depleted through death and quitting by adults.

The need for "replacement smokers" does not in and of itself prove that the tobacco industry targets children or, necessarily, that targeting would work. It does demonstrate, however, that the industry has a powerful incentive—its very survival—to ensure the continuation of the flow of new child entrants into the tobacco marketplace.

In recent years the cigarette companies have shifted from concentrating on conventional print advertising to emphasizing other promotional techniques. The reasons for the shift appear to be numerous and varied. Promotional techniques permit more specific targeting of consumers and potential consumers. Some experts see the distribution of free product samples (directly or through coupons) as a more efficient means of encouraging initiation of product use by adolescents than is the conventional print ad. Sports sponsorship has provided a vehicle for tobacco companies to exhibit product names and logos on television, despite the ban on broadcast advertising of cigarettes. In addition, it has been suggested that sponsorship of social and cultural activities is an efficient, even inexpensive means for

The smoking patterns of blacks—in particular, black men—and women are alarming. Smoking prevalence has been consistently higher among black men, who also suffer from a disproportionate share of risk factors and illness, than among white men—41% compared with 31% in 1987. In women lung cancer—almost exclusively attributable to smoking— has now surpassed breast cancer as the leading cause of cancer deaths; it has been predicted that in the coming decades women will lose half of their seven-year life-expectancy edge over men.

Brad Bower—Picture Group

the industry to buy the loyalty of diverse organizations and interest groups. More generally, sponsorship of socially meaningful endeavors may lend the cigarette manufacturers an aura of legitimacy.

In recent years the tobacco industry in various fashions has supported black, Hispanic, and women's organizations. It is notable that these groups have failed to address the issue of the marketing of cigarettes to their members. As lung cancer has surpassed breast cancer as the leading cause of cancer death among women, major national women's organizations and publications with wide audiences, such as *Ms.* magazine, *Cosmopolitan,* and *Redbook,* have not voiced concern about the increasing targeting of women by the cigarette companies. Similarly, with tobacco supporting such institutions as the NAACP, the United Negro College Fund, the National Urban League, and such prominent black-oriented magazines as *Jet* and *Ebony,* the nation's leading black organizations have remained silent about the excessive death rates experienced by cigarette-smoking blacks.

The demographics and economics of smoking go hand in hand. As smoking has become increasingly rare in the higher socioeconomic strata, marketing increasingly has targeted minority and blue-collar populations. The industry claims it is simply competing for a market where it already exists. Critics argue that the industry is attempting to maintain and expand markets among the more vulnerable members of society.

New generations of "smokes": responding to health concerns

In contemplating issues of smoking and health, one is tempted to think of the cigarette as a single, unchanging entity. Even acknowledging that American smokers now have a choice of well over 200 brands, all appear to be variations on the same theme.

In fact, however, historically "the cigarette" has undergone four changes of such qualitative importance as to constitute new generations of the product category. The original product—the roll-your-own cigarette, accompanied by handmade manufactured cigarettes—yielded to the first generation of machine-made cigarettes in the early years of the 20th century. The two most recent generational changes—filter-tipped cigarettes, introduced in the 1950s, and low-tar-and-nicotine cigarettes, dating from the late 1960s—represented industry (and consumer) response to health concerns. Each of

Cancer-causing factors: relative importance		
	percentage of all cancer deaths (U.S.)	
factor	best estimate	range
tobacco	30	25–40
alcohol	3	2–4
diet	35	10–70
food additives	<1	−5–2
reproductive history and sexual behavior	7	1–13
occupation	4	2–8
pollution	2	<1–5
industrial products	<1	<1–2
drugs and medical procedures	1	0.5–3
geophysical factors (*e.g.,* ionizing radiation)	3	2–4
infection	10?	1–?

Adapted from R. Doll and R. Peto, *Journal of the U.S. National Cancer Institute,* June 1981

While the American public tends to perceive that a wide array of chemicals and environmental pollutants are the cause of a man-made cancer epidemic, the fact remains that none of the many known cancer-causing factors is as substantial as tobacco. A single cigarette is a veritable chemical factory—emitting more than 4,000 chemicals, 43 of which are known carcinogens.

(Left) Pascal Rondeau—Allsport; (right)
photograph, DOC Archive

In the 1930s and '40s, sports heroes appeared in ads for virtually every brand of cigarette; they attributed their very success—if not explicitly, then by implication—to the particular brand they smoked. In recent years cigarette marketing has largely shifted away from print advertising to the sponsorship of a wide range of sports and cultural events.

In sponsoring events that involve risk taking (such as automobile racing), the cigarette companies appeal in particular to a large and seducible adolescent market. Despite the 1971 federal law banning cigarette advertising on television, sports sponsorship enables cigarette companies to emblazon their names and their logos across the bodies of race cars, on drivers' helmets, and on banners, signs, and scoreboards—all of which are viewed by vast TV audiences.

these new cigarette types became the dominant product on the market within approximately a decade of its introduction.

As part of its current strategy for dealing with the hostile environment toward smoking, the tobacco industry is working feverishly on the next generation of "the cigarette," as well as on nicotine-delivering alternatives to the cigarette and other conventional tobacco products. Still in the research-and-development stage, the next generation, like its two predecessors, may well be designed with the health-conscious smoker in mind. Unlike the previous two generational innovations, however, the next generation seems destined to address a social issue as well as, or instead of, a health concern; it will attempt to reduce concerns about passive smoking, the involuntary exposure of nonsmokers to the smoke from lit cigarettes.

Two prototypes were introduced by the R. J. Reynolds Tobacco Co. for test marketing in 1988 and 1989. The first was by far the more radical and ambitious innovation. Dubbed the "cleaner smoke" by its manufacturer and the "smokeless cigarette" by the media, Premier was a "high-tech" device apparently intended to address both smokers' health fears and nonsmokers' objections to tobacco smoke pollution. The device was designed to heat, rather than burn, its ingredients. Tipped with a carbon heat source, the device volatilized nicotine and "flavoring agents" contained on small alumina beads in an aluminum capsule. The effluent was passed through a tobacco paper cooling chamber, then a polypropylene mouthpiece, and the resultant aerosol was inhaled by the smoker.

While the device produced nicotine and carbon monoxide—the former being the addicting agent in tobacco and each being a contributor to heart disease—the absence of actual burning of the tobacco greatly reduced the products of combustion most directly associated with lung cancer.

72

R. J. Reynolds referred to these as the "controversial compounds" found in cigarette smoke. While the company refused to acknowledge that these "controversial compounds" were in fact dangerous, the product's promotion was widely interpreted as attempting to convey to smokers that Premiers were "safer" to smoke than conventional cigarettes. The fact that Premier produced little visible sidestream smoke was interpreted as a concession to nonsmokers. (Sidestream smoke is emitted directly into the air from a lit cigarette, while mainstream smoke is inhaled by a smoker, filtered in the lungs, and then exhaled.)

Premier failed its test marketing and was withdrawn by the company, a product failure costing R. J. Reynolds an estimated $300 million. At about the same time, the company introduced Vantage Excel, a low-tar cigarette advertised as producing less visible smoke from the lit end of the cigarette. No apparent health theme—for the smoker—has accompanied the early promotion of this product. Rather, it appears to be intended to diminish the sidestream smoke issue. Thus, this more modest innovation is apparently designed to appeal to smokers concerned about offending their nonsmoking family, friends, and co-workers.

While Premier has been the most radical and publicized departure from the fourth-generation cigarette, it was not the first "smokeless cigarette." That distinction belongs to Favor, a hollow cylindrical tube approximating a cigarette in external appearance that contained nothing but a plug of plastic foam impregnated with nicotine. The idea was that the "smoker" would suck on the mouthpiece end and inhale nicotine vapors. Produced by a small start-up company in the mid-1980s, Favor was declared a drug-delivery system by the Food and Drug Administration (FDA) and was withdrawn from the market. The FDA is responsible for regulating drugs and drug-delivery devices for safety and efficacy. The FDA has refused, however, to regulate conventional cigarettes, claiming that they are neither a food nor drug nor drug-delivery device.

Alternative nicotine products

The desire to cater to a market of 50 million Americans addicted to nicotine, in a social environment increasingly hostile to smoking, has led numerous entrepreneurs to develop an intriguing array of alternative nicotine-delivery systems (ANDS). In addition to Premier and Favor, two that have received some public attention are Masterpiece Tobacs and Ipco Creamy Snuff.

April A. Oswald

It might seem ironic that the Feb. 8, 1988, cover of Newsweek, *with the headline "What You Should Know About Heart Attacks," carried on its back cover an ad for Malibu cigarettes. Actually, the placement of cigarette ads side by side with stories about smoking-related disease creates complacency about smoking— making it appear that cigarettes, by their very ubiquity, cannot really be all that dangerous. It is notable that such a smoking-relevant story (which on the cover cited cholesterol, diet, and exercise as risk factors for heart disease) ignored smoking—probably the most important avoidable risk factor. The fact that magazines often downplay smoking in their coverage of health matters is probably not coincidental; rather, it is done so as not to offend a major source of advertising revenues.*

(Below) Mike Keefe; © 1987 The Denver Post

Late in 1988 the R. J. Reynolds Tobacco Co. test marketed Premier, a new genre of cigarette designed with the health-conscious smoker in mind and meant to be a more socially acceptable tobacco product. While, according to its maker, the cigarette eliminated many deadly compounds found in regular cigarette smoke, it still provided smokers with high levels of nicotine and carbon monoxide. The smoker lighted the end of the "smokeless cigarette," which ignited the carbon heat source just inside the lighted end (see diagram). The warmed air was sucked through the cigarette, passing through tobacco and tobacco extract in order to pick up nicotine and flavoring. Air was then cooled in two filters—first a tobacco-paper filter and then a polypropylene filter. What was unique about this product—variously called a "nicotine stick," the "high-tech cigarette," and the "cleaner smoke"— was that the only part that burned was the carbon heating element. There was no ash. The cigarette did not shrink; it just ran out of fuel. The $300 million experiment, however, failed its test marketing; smokers who tried Premier evidently were not satisfied, and sales were poor. The product was subsequently withdrawn by the manufacturer.

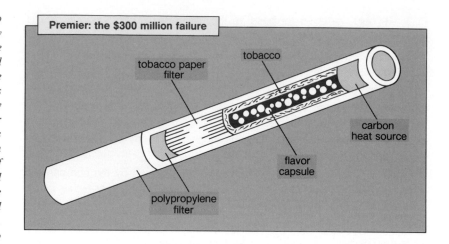

Premier: the $300 million failure

tobacco paper filter

tobacco

carbon heat source

flavor capsule

polypropylene filter

A chewing gum containing a small amount of tobacco, Masterpiece Tobacs was produced by the Pinkerton Tobacco Co. with the apparent intent of appealing to smokers who wanted to get nicotine into their systems without smoking. A major feature of the product was that the consumer could use the product without the unseemly spitting that accompanies use of conventional smokeless tobacco products. Masterpiece Tobacs was withdrawn from the market after the FDA declared it a food product adulterated with tobacco. (The FDA regulates gum as a food product.)

Ipco Creamy Snuff is produced in India by Asha Industries and is exported to the United States. Ipco, which as of the summer of 1989 had not been banned by the FDA, is a dark tobacco product in toothpaste form. It promises that "daily regular use of the paste will have many beneficial effects in cases of extreme dental pain, toothaches, swollen, bleeding, and spongy gums, and pyorrhea." The same themes were employed in selling dental snuff in the 19th and early 20th centuries. The product permits absorption of nicotine through the mucous membranes of the inside of the cheek and gums.

Tobacco toothpaste is not the only tobacco toiletry available in the U.S. A Greek company, P. D. Papoutsanis, sells Tabac soap—a product that one health professional has characterized as being "for the person who wants to smell like the Marlboro Man but not die like him."

Nicotine for those trying to quit

Expected in the near future are nicotine aerosols and dermal patches. Unlike the previous ANDS, however, these are intended to be used as adjuncts in the medical management of nicotine dependence. Interest in such drugs has heightened considerably recently, given the successful marketing of Nicorette, a nicotine-bearing gum. Since the product's introduction in the U.S. in 1984, it has been estimated that approximately 10% of all smokers have used it. Controlled trials have suggested that combined with proper behavioral counseling, use of the gum can increase smoking cessation success rates.

Given the number of nicotine-dependent consumers and the general distaste for smoking among smokers and nonsmokers alike, the market for the dollars of the nicotine-dependent population in the U.S. will not be the exclusive province of those who wish to perpetuate the addiction. There can be little doubt that future competition will intensify among innovators looking to capitalize on the cessation market.

David versus Goliath: the battle against smoking in the U.S.

The persistence of 50 million Americans remaining addicted to nicotine and the fact that tobacco continues to account for more than one-sixth of all American deaths provide stark evidence that in the U.S. the battle against tobacco-produced death and disease is far from over. Nevertheless, continuing annual declines in smoking prevalence and the emergence of a social environment increasingly antagonistic toward smoking indicate that the tide has turned. The first half of this century witnessed the relentless growth of what would prove to be history's most deadly man-made epidemic; the second half is presiding over the gradual demise of the epidemic in the U.S.

Reinforced by the addictiveness of nicotine, the seductive appeal of tobacco to each new generation of children retards progress toward achieving the surgeon general's goal of a smoke-free society. The health community faces its most formidable barrier, however, in the wealth and power of the tobacco industry. The industry's efforts to sell its products are as dominant in the marketing field as cigarettes are dominant among the causes of death.

Compared with this economic behemoth, the forces pitted against tobacco seem paltry. Collectively, the financial resources available to antismoking

Despite the fact that for over two decades cigarette consumption in the U.S. has been steadily declining, the tobacco industry has remained stunningly resilient. In fact, the antismoking movement faces its most formidable hurdle in the industry's wealth and its power. Hefty price increases on its products have more than compensated for the declining volume of smokers. Just over a decade ago a pack of cigarettes cost about 55 cents; now it may cost as much as $2. In 1988 the volume of cigarette sales of American tobacco companies was 558 billion (down from 619 billion in 1980); nonetheless, industrywide profits tripled to $11.55 per 1,000 cigarettes— up from $3.80 in 1980. A further reason for the industry's ability to withstand the declining volume of smokers is that foreign sales now constitute an increasingly important market—one that the industry is depending upon to be a major source of profits well into the 21st century.

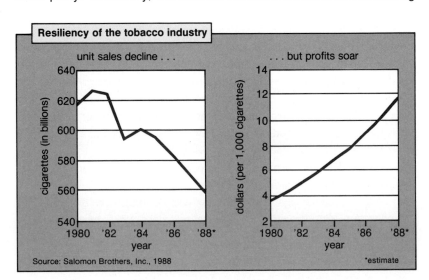

Resiliency of the tobacco industry

unit sales decline . . .

. . . but profits soar

Source: Salomon Brothers, Inc., 1988

*estimate

The smoking-and-health message has been conveyed most successfully to college graduates. Among young women with some college education, initiation of smoking decreased between 1974 and 1985, but among non-college-educated women, it increased to an all-time high. The most striking shift in overall demographic patterns is in the gender mix of smokers, which clearly indicates that the antismoking message is not being heeded by a substantial proportion of the female population. Currently the prevalence of female smokers is about equal to that of males. Since the 1970s more high-school-age females have begun smoking than young males; consequently, it has been predicted that before the end of the century, the rate of smoking among women will exceed that of men.

U.S. Department of Health and Human Services

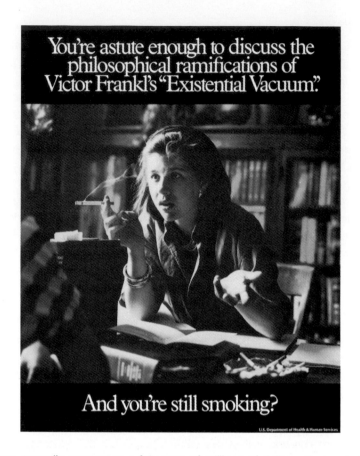

groups annually amount to a few tens of millions of dollars, the equivalent of a few days' worth of tobacco industry advertising and promotion. Yet as indicated by the data on cigarette smoking trends presented earlier, the battle for the hearts and minds of smokers is being won, gradually, by the health community. The antismoking David is slaying the tobacco Goliath, although the confrontation is decidedly a protracted one.

Scholars who have studied the antismoking "campaign" have concluded that the increasing social unacceptability of smoking and the associated decreases in smoking prevalence have derived from the persistence of the educational campaign against smoking. Changes in smoking behavior reflect the cumulative impact of development of public knowledge of the dangers of smoking, followed by changes in attitudes toward smoking, and eventually converted into reductions in smoking.

While public education has been the persistent theme, over time the battlefield has shifted to the public policy arena. For example, in the decade of the 1980s, the cigarette excise tax has been identified not simply as a revenue-raising device but also as a powerful tool for decreasing cigarette consumption, and particularly for dissuading children from starting to smoke. By one prominent estimate, every 10% increase in the price of a pack of cigarettes will decrease cigarette consumption by 4% among adults and by 14% among children and teenagers.

In 1983 the federal cigarette excise tax was doubled, from 8 to 16 cents per pack, the first increase in the federal tax since 1951. In a few states

CITIZENS' ARREST

DANZIGER
The Christian Science Monitor

The financial resources available to antismoking groups annually are paltry compared with the expenditures of the tobacco companies on advertising and promotion. The industry spends more than $10 for every American man, woman, and child in what constitutes one of the largest marketing efforts ever devoted to a consumer product. Nevertheless, slowly but surely the battle for the hearts and minds of smokers is being won by the health community. Changes in smoking behavior reflect the cumulative impact of public knowledge of the dangers, followed by changes in attitudes toward smoking and ultimately by reductions in the numbers of those who smoke. As restrictions on public smoking have become more and more widespread, they have had a decidedly negative effect on how society views not only smoking in public but smoking in general. It seems inevitable that in the coming years cigarette smoking will be regarded as unacceptable social behavior.

(Above) Jeff Danziger; © 1988 The Christian Science Monitor; (below) U.S. Department of Health and Human Services

portions of the proceeds from increases in excise taxes have been earmarked to health research and antismoking education. In November 1988, for example, Californians passed a ballot initiative raising their state tax from 10 cents per pack to 35 cents per pack, with new revenues estimated at $650 million annually, including the largest pool of funds ever earmarked for public health. The tax increase of 25 cents per pack—the largest single increase in U.S. history—was passed despite a tobacco-industry-funded lobbying and advertising campaign against the initiative, estimated at up to $20 million.

Other public policy efforts have concentrated on restricting smoking in public places, regulating the advertising and promotion of tobacco products, restricting children's access to tobacco, and improving and adding warning labels to tobacco-product packages and ads. At the federal level, Congress passed two major pieces of tobacco-and-health legislation in 1984 and 1986 pertaining to the labeling of cigarettes and smokeless tobacco products. Bills currently in both the Senate and the House of Representatives propose a variety of restrictions on tobacco advertising and promotion, including a complete ban. Recently legislation prohibited smoking on domestic airline flights of two hours or less, effective in 1988 for a two-year trial period. Congress is reviewing the issue of airline smoking, since the temporary measure is scheduled to expire.

Throughout the 1980s some states and localities banned the distribution of free samples of tobacco products, while other jurisdictions banned advertising in particular locales (e.g., public transit systems). Selected jurisdictions have placed restrictions on sales of cigarettes through vending machines, and several states have debated raising the minimum age of legal purchase or developing means of putting teeth into the enforcement of existing laws.

The hallmark of the antismoking campaign in the 1980s has been the "nonsmokers' rights movement," the effort to provide nonsmokers with a smoke-free environment through the adoption of clean indoor air laws and private business policies. Having proliferated throughout the country, such laws and policies both contribute to and reflect a social environment in which smoking is becoming increasingly unacceptable. Indeed, smoking is

Smoking used to be in step, too.

The Marlboro Man looms large over a street in Shen-chen (Shenzen), China— an unmistakable sign that "Marlboro Country" is without borders. Indeed, Marlboro, long the leading cigarette in the United States, is now the best-selling cigarette worldwide. In 1980 Philip Morris became one of the first U.S. cigarette companies to open shop in China—a country in which an estimated 70% of men are currently smokers and the female and youth populations are increasingly taking up the habit.

fading into the sunset of American social history, but it leaves a legacy of death and despair that will be revisited for decades to come.

Selling death abroad

Sunset in the U.S., it must be remembered, is dawn in Asia. The "brown plague" of tobacco-produced death is spreading transcontinentally, from the developed societies of the Western world to the less developed countries of Asia and the third world. Several years ago the emerging pattern of rapid growth in smoking abroad led William Foege, then the director of the U.S. Centers for Disease Control, to conclude that smoking will be the leading cause of premature, preventable death in the third world by the turn of the century. The potential toll of tobacco in less developed countries is illustrated by the estimate that 70% of Chinese men currently smoke cigarettes, a figure that translates into at least a quarter of a billion smokers among adults of one sex in a single country.

The international cigarette market is dominated by a handful of major multinational companies based in the U.S. and the U.K. Increasingly, stagnation of the market in countries like the U.S. has led these companies to seek to develop and expand overseas markets.

Overseas expansion has not always come easily. In countries in Asia, through the mid-1980s, hefty tariffs and restrictions on advertising impeded the free flow of U.S. cigarettes across the border. Congressmen from tobacco-growing states worked aggressively to apply political pressure to open up these markets. In 1986, for example, Sen. Jesse Helms (Rep., N.C.) wrote a letter to Japan's then prime minister, Yasuhiro Nakasone, threatening trade sanctions if the Japanese did not open their cigarette market to U.S. brands. He wrote a similar letter to South Korea's president in 1987. The office of the U.S. trade representative in the White House has been enlisted by Senator Helms and his colleagues—and has worked diligently—to eliminate barriers to the marketing of U.S. cigarettes in Japan, Taiwan, South Korea, and, most recently, Thailand.

The pressure has worked. Japan, for example, imported 6.5 billion U.S. cigarettes in 1985 and 32 billion in 1987. South Korea's importation of U.S. cigarettes rose from 312 million in 1987 to 2.4 billion a year later. Among its other successes, U.S. pressure opened up print advertising to U.S. cigarettes in South Korea, a country in which cigarette advertising previously had been virtually banned. In Taiwan imports leaped from 209 million cigarettes in 1986 to 5.1 billion in 1987. The value of exports of U.S. cigarettes worldwide doubled between 1986 and 1988, from $1.3 billion to $2.6 billion. The quantity of cigarettes nearly doubled, rising from 64.3 billion to 118.5 billion. As a consequence, while cigarette consumption continues to decline in the U.S., production of U.S.-brand cigarettes is actually rising.

Critics of overseas marketing of U.S.-brand cigarettes observe that the U.S. is exporting its epidemic of lung cancer to Asia and Africa. Noting the government's "pushing" of U.S. cigarettes abroad, and the fact that U.S. law does not require exported cigarettes to bear health warnings, Rep. Chester Atkins (Dem., Mass.) has said that the message of U.S. policy is that "Asian lungs are somehow more expendable than American lungs."

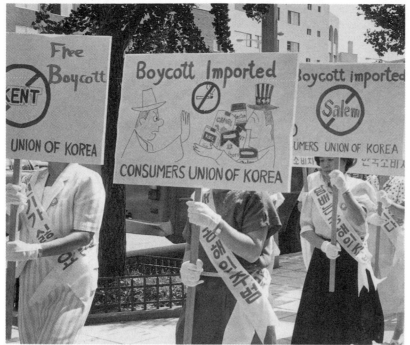

In 1986 members of a consumers union of South Korea demonstrated against the action that approved the importation of U.S. cigarettes into that country. Through the mid-1980s high tariffs and restrictions on advertising impeded the marketing of U.S. cigarettes in most Asian countries. However, congressmen from Southern tobacco-growing states led an aggressive effort, which included threats of trade sanctions, to force Asian governments to lift trade barriers. The political pressure worked; once the market opened in South Korea, U.S. cigarette imports rose from 312 million in 1987 to 2.4 billion in 1988. The fact that U.S. cigarettes sold abroad are not required to carry health warnings prompted Chester Atkins, a Democratic representative from Massachusetts, to comment that the message of U.S. policy is that "Asian lungs are somehow more expendable than American lungs."

In particular, critics note that contemporaneous with the aggressive marketing of U.S. cigarettes in Asian countries has come the spread of smoking among adolescents and adult women; until recently, very few children and adult females smoked in most Asian countries. Television advertising of U.S. cigarettes on Japanese TV has become a leading source of TV ad revenue; much of that revenue comes from ads for U.S. cigarettes targeted at Japanese adolescents and women.

The tobacco industry denies that its marketing efforts affect the amount and age-sex distribution of cigarette smoking abroad. As in the U.S., they claim that U.S. cigarettes are merely competing with indigenous brands for shares of a market whose size is not influenced by the industry's marketing efforts. Industry representatives also emphasize the economic benefits of tobacco's contribution to reducing the United States' international trade deficit. Philip Morris proudly boasts that Marlboro, the leading cigarette at home, is also the number-one-selling cigarette throughout the world. Indeed, Marlboro's international significance extends beyond its dominance of the cigarette market; Marlboro is the world's largest selling packaged good of any kind.

Critics have also noted that there is great hypocrisy in the fact that the U.S. government threatens countries that export cocaine to U.S. shores while simultaneously threatening countries that attempt to maintain barriers to "our own deadly drug pushing."

In the concluding decade of the 20th century, as the developed nations are witnessing the gradual fall of tobacco, the rest of the world reenacts its tragic rise. American visionaries can dream of a smoke-free society in the foreseeable future. To their counterparts in much of the rest of the world, however, the vision of tobacco's future is an emerging nightmare.

79

Health for All:
Illusory Goal in a
World at War

by Alex Poteliakhoff, M.D.

Scientific progress in the past several decades has engendered a vision of the future that is confident of improvement in human well-being. Such hopes have been embodied in the resolve of nations to achieve "Health for All by the Year 2000." This goal was declared in 1978 at a conference sponsored by the World Health Organization (WHO) and the United Nations Children's Fund (UNICEF), held at Alma-Ata, Kazakh S.S.R.; 134 nations agreed to promote and protect the health of all people of the world. In the declaration, the countries affirmed that primary health care (PHC) is the key to attaining the goal. PHC may be defined as essential health care, scientifically sound and socially acceptable, delivered at a cost that the community and country can afford. It comprises adequate nutrition, safe water and basic sanitation, maternal and child care including family planning and immunization, education in prevalent health problems, treatment of common diseases and injuries, and, finally, control of locally endemic diseases, including the provision of essential drugs.

In reality, however, instability and turbulence in so many regions of the world make hopes recede and progress almost a delusion. Natural disasters and mismanagement of the ecology have acted as brakes to development and, as if these destructive forces were not enough, armed conflicts on a vast scale have added to the global chaos. Perhaps the historic moment has come when humanity should pause to look at all the factors that hold progress back and begin to tackle those ingrained patterns of human behavior that can no longer be afforded.

After World War I—described as the war to end all wars—and then the immense destruction of World War II, it should seem shocking that some 150 wars, with a loss of life of at least 20 million people, have been fought since 1945. However, loss of life is only one indicator of damage and destruction. In all regions where wars have raged, carefully elaborated health care structures have crumbled, infant and maternal mortality rates have soared, and physical and mental trauma on a vast scale have resulted in invalidism and gross deterioration of health standards.

Alex Poteliakhoff, M.D., is Vice Chairman of the London-based Medical Association for Prevention of War. The association was founded in 1951; among its aims are to formulate the ethical responsibilities of doctors in relation to war, to oppose the use of medical science for any purpose other than the prevention and relief of human suffering, and to urge that all nations divert energies and money from the preparation for war toward the fight against disease and malnutrition.

(Overleaf) Echo of a Scream *by David Alfaro Siqueiros, 1937, duco on wood, 48 × 36 in. Collection, Museum of Modern Art, New York; gift of M. M. Warburg*

In the aftermath of a truck bombing in Kabul, Afghanistan, an injured civilian is carried from the rubble. During the nine-year-long seige of this nation by Soviet forces, more than one million civilians lost their lives and countless others were maimed and injured. Even after the Soviet withdrawal in February 1989, guerrilla fighting continued to rage. The International Committee of the Red Cross estimated that tens of thousands of Afghans would need corrective surgery or other treatment for injuries when the war finally ended.

The statistics on the effects of war are not easy to come by, as it is often not in the national interest to divulge figures of military and civilian casualties during the course of a war, and this makes it difficult to report on some conflicts. Because it is impossible in this relatively short article to even begin to cover all the wars ongoing in the world today, it is hoped that the limited selection here will give a representative picture of the cruelty of war and its calamitous effects on health care.

Afghanistan: foreign aid to a shattered nation

Since the Soviet invasion of 1979, the mountains of Afghanistan have echoed to the sound of guns and bombs. Out of a total population of some 18 million, one million have lost their lives in the war and at least 5 million have been forced to take refuge in other lands—3 million in Pakistan and 2 million in Iran. From 1978 to 1984 military expenditure rose from $70 million to $340 million and the armed forces swelled from 46,000 to 110,000 troops. Meanwhile, expenditure on health care remained almost static, hovering between $1 and $2 a year per person. Infant mortality rates improved only slightly from the abysmal figure of 226 per 1,000 live births to 182 per 1,000, while life expectancy dropped from 42 to 37 years, presumably because of war deaths of people in the prime of life.

An evaluation of the progress in primary health care in Afghanistan, made for WHO's recently released *Seventh Report on the World Health Situation,* covering the years 1978 to 1984, points to a lack of managerial skills, of resources, and of community involvement. Owing to the demands of the military sector, expenditure on public health was low—indeed, less than 1% of the gross national product (GNP). Although there had been some aid

Andy Hernandez—Picture Group

from WHO, UNICEF, and various foreign voluntary aid agencies, this had raised annual public health expenditure only from $1 to $1.30 per person. Moreover, the report conceded that health care coverage exists in only 65% of urban areas and in 45% of rural areas and that safe water is available to an even smaller proportion of the population. In Kabul, the capital, 45% of children are immunized, while in the provinces this falls to 10%. Yet in that section of the *Seventh Report* relating to Afghanistan, there is, curiously, not a single mention of the effects of war on health care. Only the statistics give mute evidence of this.

The British writer Doris Lessing visited Afghan relief camps in Pakistan in 1986 on behalf of the organization Afghan Relief, a London-based charity. Following her experience she wrote the book *The Wind Blows Away Our Words,* in which she reported how "Beautiful parts of Afghanistan have been reduced to desert; ancient towns, full of art treasures bombed flat. One out of three Afghans is now dead or in exile or living in a refugee camp. And the world remains largely indifferent."

In Afghanistan agricultural production depends on good irrigation of the land with water that comes from the snow-covered mountains through a system of irrigation channels. The war has caused destruction of these channels—the result being near famine in three of the country's eight regions. According to UNICEF statistics, 39% of Afghan children under age five weigh less than they should for their height. An important contributing factor is the deficiency of their diets. For all too many children, the daily diet consists of nothing more than a kind of flat bread (*nan*), a few vegetables, and tea.

UNICEF has provided $2 million in aid to Afghanistan, but without foreign medical help the people in the zones held by the resistance—and this accounts for 85% of the country—would have had little in the way of effective health care. Foreign assistance to Afghanistan has come from several quarters of the world, but principally from French and American voluntary groups. What is the motivation for this arduous and hazardous work? Probably the doctors and medical assistants who have risked their lives to treat both soldiers and civilians amid unremittent killing and destruction are driven by various combinations of compassion, justice, adventure, and the wish to see and live among different cultures.

From France three groups have given aid to Afghanistan. One of these is Médecins sans Frontières, formed in 1971, now with 3,500 volunteers and a budget of $25 million. Two others—Médecins du Monde and Aide Médicale Internationale, which were established later and are somewhat smaller—have also been major sources of aid. In the past decade these three French organizations have sent doctors and nurses abroad not only to such wartorn countries as Afghanistan but also to refugee camps in Thailand and to drought areas in Africa. They give help without regard to race, religion, or politics. Sometimes they supplement the work of the Red Cross; at other times they fill the void left when political or legal constraints have impinged on the work of the Red Cross—requiring it to limit or withdraw aid. Unlike the Red Cross, which relies on the backing of the governments in the places it serves, groups such as these from France place medicine *above*

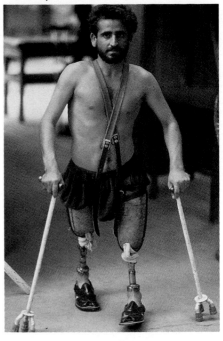

An Afghan refugee learns to walk again as a double-amputee at an orthopedic clinic run by the Red Cross in Peshawar, Pakistan. Because millions of undetectable antipersonnel mines have been laid throughout Afghanistan—both by the government and by guerrilla forces—civilians suffering traumatic injuries will not be uncommon in years to come; the Red Cross predicts that the need for trauma surgery and artificial limbs will extend well into the next century.

Jana Schneider—SIPA

Afghan mothers and children gather to receive nan, *a type of bread, at a food-distribution outpost in Kabul. For years the capital has been hard hit by food shortages—in part due to the collapse of agriculture and in part due to the frequency of roads being closed off by guerrilla attacks. Malnutrition is exceptionally common among Afghanistan's 6.8 million children under age 16—children who, according to the latest UNICEF statistics, rank among the world's least privileged.*

During the initial years of the war in Afghanistan, many doctors were executed, imprisoned, or driven into exile, and numerous hospitals and clinics were demolished. Without foreign medical aid, the country would have had virtually no effective health care. The International Medical Corps, a group of American volunteer doctors and nurses, has responded by providing medical assistance inside the country's most devastated regions. (Right) A major IMC project has been the immunization of 10,000 Afghan children against measles, tetanus, and tuberculosis, for which it trained Afghan medics to help administer the shots.

state affairs; they do not wait for a government's invitation to treat the suffering in the world's trouble spots.

One team sent to Afghanistan by Médecins sans Frontières was headed by physician Paul Ickx, who along with three nurses took 46 days to reach the hospital at Zari in rebel territory from a base in Pakistan. For 11 days they struggled through snow-covered mountain passes. When they eventually reached their destination, they gave invaluable medical and surgical help for the eight months of their stint, seeing up to 200 patients a day.

The group Médecins du Monde established a one-story mud-thatch clinic 129 kilometers (80 miles) southwest of Kabul in an area of intense fighting; for nearly a decade it has provided free treatment, food, and transportation to hospitals in Peshawar, Pakistan, for thousands of patients—wounded guerrillas (Afghan freedom fighters, known as mujahideen) as well as civilian women and children.

The British medical journal *The Lancet* in 1988 described the work done by one U.S. international relief agency, International Medical Corps. Realizing that the most effective health care system would be one run by the indigenous people, the agency sent a group of committed doctors, nurses, and teachers who worked with the mujahideen and trained nearly a hundred Afghan volunteers, some already medically qualified, in the basic elements of public health, medicine, and surgery over a period of eight months. Around 30 medical-surgical units are now operating within Afghanistan at various levels of expertise ranging from administering first aid and treating common complaints to performing major surgery. Because the units operate without electricity, sterilization of surgical instruments has to be carried out by primitive methods. The units were established in "safe" locations—*i.e.,* settings well camouflaged, known as "cave clinics." The hope is that once hostilities cease, these facilities will be able to come out into the open and function as centrally located vital health care centers for the Afghan people.

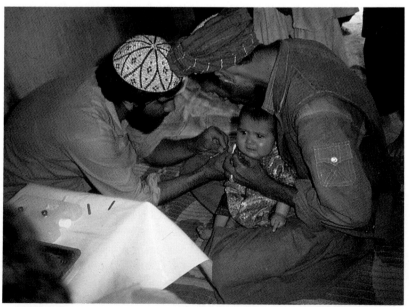

International Medical Corps

It is not yet known if the final withdrawal of Soviet forces in February 1989—after nine years of battle, frustration, and defeat—will lead to a more stable situation. An initial lull in fighting followed the pullout of the last 50,000 Soviet troops from a shattered Afghanistan, but soon the guerrilla attacks resumed and the war loomed ever larger; there was every indication that the internal conflict would continue raging for untold months to come. If stability finally *does* ensue, there is likely to be ample goodwill on the part of many foreign medical aid groups to help the Afghans reconstruct their ailing health services.

Eritrea: a country waiting to exist

Eritrean nationalist groups have been struggling for independence from the Ethiopian Empire since 1961. The Eritrean People's Liberation Front (EPLF) has become the leading political group. In spite of great poverty and a high illiteracy rate, the Eritrean people have succeeded in building an impressive health care structure. At the first International Conference on Health in Eritrea, held in Milan, Italy, in 1986, Asefaw Tekeste, president of the Eritrean Medical Association, said that several factors had been helpful in the implementation of a PHC program: the democratic nature of the village health councils, the fact that the program is regarded as being an essential part of the political strategy of the EPLF, the abolition of bureaucracy and corruption, and the absence of private medical practice. On the other hand, there are factors that inhibit its implementation—*e.g.,* the continuing state of war, the destruction of the infrastructure by Ethiopian forces, the lack of adequate resources, and the occupation of some 15% of Eritrea by the enemy. The nomadic life of many of the farmers adds to the difficulty of providing health care, but that problem has been partly solved by the organization of mobile medical teams based at health centers.

In 1985 alone more than 1,000 civilians were wounded and more than 200 were killed. Casualties arose from various kinds of bombs, machine gun bullets, antipersonnel mines, and—most horrible of all—napalm, which caused 82 cases of severe burns in that year alone.

The simplest level of care was at village health clinics, which were each staffed by two primary health workers. Next came health stations serving some 10,000 people. Of 42 such stations that had been established, 30 were in operation and 5 of these possessed simple laboratory equipment. At an even higher level, there were 22 functioning health centers caring for around 700,000 people, but only 14 of these were fully equipped and staffed. Each health center had a maternal and child unit, mobile teams, and a polyclinic. Finally there were six regional hospitals.

The central hospital at Orotta has been graphically described by orthopedic surgeon H. D. W. Powell in the *British Medical Journal* in an article entitled "The Forgotten War in the Hidden Valley." Powell was part of a British medical team funded by International Medical Relief and sent to Eritrea in 1987. This base hospital had been set up in 1981, and its 1,200 beds were distributed among numerous small buildings dug out of rock and hidden by thorn trees. In this unlikely setting—"a barren rocky valley in the far north west of what had been Eritrea, uninhabited except by nomads

During their ongoing struggle for independence from Ethiopia, the people of the province of Eritrea have succeeded in building an impressive health care structure. (Below) A wounded patient is cared for in a narrow passageway in one of the buildings that make up the fully functioning base hospital, established by the Eritrean People's Liberation Front at Orotta, near the Sudan border.

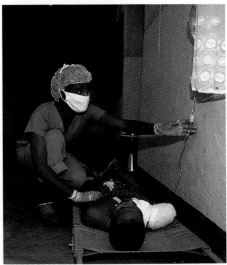

Anthony Suau—Black Star

85

The orthopedic ward at the hospital at Orotta is filled to capacity. The ward itself is housed in a building that has been dug into the side of a riverbank and is completely camouflaged by dense thorn trees. This remarkable hospital has 1,200 beds and full medical and surgical capabilities, including a maternity ward where 500 babies are delivered each year, three operating theaters that are kept busy day and night, a modern prosthetics workshop, and a pharmacy that uses sophisticated Italian equipment to manufacture its own antibiotics.

with herds of goats and cows"—is a functioning hospital with neurosurgical, cardiovascular, maxillofacial and dental, ophthalmologic, orthopedic, pediatric, obstetric-gynecologic, and general medical departments, as well as a central pharmacy that uses Italian equipment to manufacture essential drugs, including antibiotics. Three major operating theaters are kept busy. Extra power is derived from several solar panels and windmills. The team noted that there was no shortage of food in "Hospital Valley," as sufficient sorghum was grown locally.

Because of the disruption caused by the ongoing war, medical attention is directed mainly at the treatment of sickness rather than on the prevention of disease and the maintenance of health. Immunization has been possible only in the base area around the central hospital, and no national evaluation of the progress of the PHC program has been practical. There is also a tacit admission that more hospital beds are needed; it is hoped that six further regional hospitals can be established.

In spite of the obvious efforts, commitment, and achievements of the Eritrean people and health planners, no one can be satisfied with the present situation. There is a shortage of equipment and staffing at all levels. As the area has not yet achieved international recognition, statistics on health care are not to be found in WHO or UNICEF reports. Health planners in Eritrea give the infant mortality rate as around 200 per 1,000 and the mortality of children under age five as about 420 per 1,000. These figures are far too high and would not be tolerated in peacetime.

While a peace proposal was put forward by the EPLF in 1980, there was no response from Ethiopia. The sad fact remains that without peace, real progress in health care *cannot* be achieved.

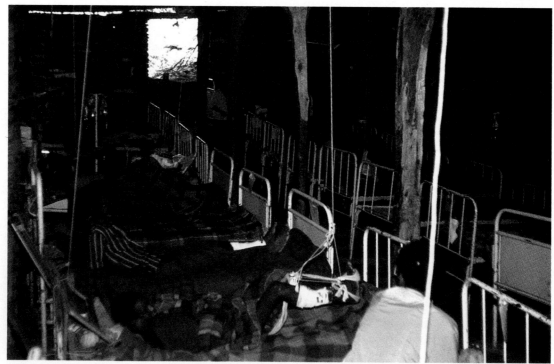

Médicins sans Frontières

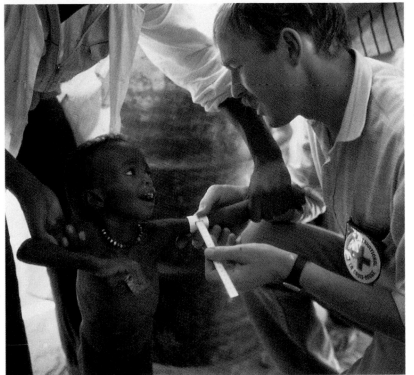

(Left) A Red Cross worker monitors an Eritrean child's growth. As in all war-torn areas, the health status of children has suffered greatly in this Ethiopian province. With most medical service going to the care of the sick and injured, very little progress has been made in primary health care. Because Eritrea has not achieved international recognition, statistics on child health are not available from either UNICEF or the World Health Organization. Nonetheless, infant and child mortality rates are assumed to be unacceptably high.

Lebanon: prosperity laid waste by war

In the early 1970s Lebanon had a progressive and effective health care system. The general picture of health care until 1984 in Lebanon, a country of some three million people, was depicted in WHO's *Seventh Report on the World Health Situation.* Resources devoted to health care were, in general, reasonable. More than 10% of the nation's GNP (if private spending is added to public spending) went to health care. Vital statistics could be termed acceptable, with an infant mortality rate of 48 per 1,000 and life expectancy of 66 years. According to the WHO report, however, internal strife has resulted in the disintegration of the Ministry of Health, in an inability to plan for medium- and long-term programs, and in the interruption of ongoing health programs due to loss of personnel, equipment, and property. All sectors of health care delivery were preoccupied with the immediate problems of war and safety.

The suffering of innocent victims of war and the courage and dedication of doctors and nurses in the battle areas cannot be conveyed by statistics. If one looks to a single small plot of land engulfed in the war, however—a plot measuring only 0.08 square mile (0.2 square kilometer) that is temporary "home" to some 9,000 refugees—one can begin to appreciate the tragedy, the pain, and the heroism. Such a drama was recounted by Pauline Cutting in her book *Children of the Siege,* which describes the plight of Palestinians in the Bourj al-Barajneh area of Beirut under siege by Amal militiamen during a period of 18 months in 1985–87. Cutting is a British doctor who offered her expertise in trauma surgery at a hospital established by the Palestine Red Crescent Society at the camp.

In 1988 close to three million people were at risk of dying from starvation in drought-stricken northern Ethiopia. Because the area was in the control of insurgents and vital roads were under seige, much of the food provided by international relief agencies remained stockpiled at Asmera, the capital of Eritrea, and could not be transported to the remote villages where it was needed.

87

Heavy artillery battles in the mountains surrounding Beirut, Lebanon, are a familiar sight. In the residential areas of the city itself, 14 long years of civil strife have made shellings that leave streets littered with debris, buildings shattered, and the air thick with gunpowder, dust, and smoke the norm. In a passionate appeal for a cease-fire in April 1989, Christian members of Lebanon's National Assembly called for an end to "the barbaric bombardment of innocent people."

Aubert/Keystone-Paris—Picture Group

There were two periods of actual war during those 18 months, and in that time 181 people died and 1,200 were wounded. Cutting and her assistants performed 300 operations under general anesthesia. Often there was a shortage of fuel for the electric generator, resulting in darkness and water shortage. At the height of the siege, food supplies ran out, and starvation delayed healing and recovery in wounded patients. Cutting herself lost 10% of her own body weight. At that point she decided to let the outside world know of the plight of the camp population. The spotlight of the world press concentrated on Bourj al-Barajneh, and the interest and compassion thus generated brought relief at last to the hospital and its gallant and exhausted staff. A truce was arranged between the combatants, and aid agencies were allowed to bring in food and medical supplies; typically this did not last and hostilities flared, engulfing the camp once more in war and suffering.

Mention must be made of the valuable and brave work of the International Committee of the Red Cross in the unhappy country of Lebanon. Under the provisions of the 1949 Geneva Conventions and additional Protocols of 1977, the Red Cross can give relief to members of the armed forces and to civilians—in the case of both international and civil wars—and its work has been welcomed and encouraged for decades in all parts of the world. The International Red Cross began its relief work in Lebanon in 1967, and its efforts had increased with the outbreak of civil war in 1975.

In the latter part of 1988, it had some 30 Swiss nationals in the field and was employing about 100 Lebanese workers to distribute food and much-needed medicines to war victims and to provide logistic support to the Lebanese Red Cross. Then in November 1988, seemingly out of the

88

blue, a Red Cross representative in southern Lebanon, Peter Winkler, was kidnapped by the Organization of Socialist Revolutionaries. The Red Cross responded by withdrawing some of its staff and suspending its operations. Although Winkler was released a month later, threats continued to be made against the lives of Red Cross staff, and so, for the first time in its 125 years of respected service, the International Committee was obliged to withdraw its remaining workers. In later negotiations the Red Cross expressed its willingness to resume its work in Lebanon.

Mozambique: unmatched toll of human suffering

In London in 1988 at a conference of the Medical Association for Prevention of War, Derek Summerfield, a British physician who has practiced medicine in southern Africa, reported on the grim situation in Mozambique. After a ten-year war of liberation, the people of Mozambique had gained their hard-won independence from colonial rule. The new government inherited an inadequate, poorly distributed health service that was concentrated mainly in the urban centers, leaving the country as a whole relatively bare; some 70% of the population was not cared for, while sophisticated hospitals in the towns provided a curative type of medicine and preventive medicine was neglected. Moreover, 25% of children died before their fifth birthday. Then, from 1975 onward, health services were reorganized. A shift took place toward primary health care with emphasis on rural needs rather than urban and preventive services rather than curative. Hundreds of midwives, primary health care workers, and students in maternal and child welfare were trained. The improvement gained could not be consolidated, however. Civil war has raged since the early 1980s between the rebel Mozambique National Resistance (MNR, known as Renamo) and Frelimo, the Mozam-bique Liberation Front, and the horrors and suffering of war have fallen *not* to any significant extent on the contending soldiers but largely on the civilian population.

AFP Photo

Red Cross ambulances evacuated the wounded from Shatila, a Palestinian refugee camp, in April 1987 after Syrian troops broke a five-month-long seige of the camp by Amal militia. The International Committee of the Red Cross had been providing relief and logistic support to the Lebanese Red Cross since the outbreak of civil war in 1975. In the latter part of 1988, continued threats against the lives of Red Cross staff serving in Lebanon caused the organization to withdraw its workers. This was the first time in its 125-year history that the Swiss-based humanitarian organization had been forced out of a war-torn country where it was providing aid.

In Mozambique even the children have been dragged into the fighting that has raged since the early 1980s. They have been taught to kill, burn, and commit untold acts of brutality. At the Lhanguene orphanage in Maputo, Neil Boothby, an American child psychologist, has established a unique program for treating children who have been mentally scarred by the war—children who were victims of brutality and those who were victimizers. (Below left) Boothby (center) and Abubakar Sultan, national director of the Lhanguene rehabilitation program, talk with two former child soldiers, Fernando (left) and Firinice (right). Fernando, at age 14, was leader of a group of Renamo soldiers—all younger than himself. By age 13 he had committed six murders. At age six, Firinice was kidnapped by Renamo bandits, forced to set his own house on fire, then made to witness the killing and dismemberment of his parents and five brothers and sisters. Then he too became a soldier. Boothby encourages the children not only to talk about what they have suffered but to act out or to draw the horrors they have endured (below right).

It appears that MNR's aim is the disruption and paralysis of the economy and destabilization of political organization. There has been wholesale terrorization of the civilian population with torture and mutilations, often of individuals in the presence of their families. The Geneva Conventions, which should protect the civilian population, have been ignored or swept aside, assuming that the Renamo rebels were even aware of their existence. Communications with health posts and hospitals have been interrupted by mines; Red Cross planes have been attacked; and health workers have been abducted or killed.

Indeed, the brutality, depravity, and perversity of war are well illustrated by this particular conflict, where even young children have been dragged into the war. They have been taught to fight, to kill, and to burn. By threats, by punishment, by the offer of food and drugs, and by other forms of coercion, they have been enticed into the commission of brutal acts. Writing in the *New Internationalist,* the Mozambican journalist Orlanda Mendes tells how Fernando, a boy aged 14, was forced to join the "bandits" under threat of death. He became chief of a group of boy soldiers fighting government troops. Sickened by the bloodshed, he finally escaped—after killing two bandits—and gave himself up to Frelimo soldiers. He and other children traumatized by brutal killings, rape, and the disintegration of their communities were being cared for in a special rehabilitation center in Maputo, run by Mozambican teachers with the help of psychiatric advisers from the United States and England. The return of these youngsters—victims and victimizers—to some semblance of mental health will be a slow process.

Between 1982 and 1987, 595 Mozambican primary health care units were destroyed or closed. Hospitals suffered as well, by both direct attack and the mining of their approaches, so that by 1986 some two million people had lost access to health care. The number of doctors working in the rural areas dropped sharply. In some areas mothers have been too frightened to attend maternity units, and on one terrible occasion when a massacre took place in the town of Homoine, even pregnant women were murdered.

Photographs, Bill Pierce—Sygma

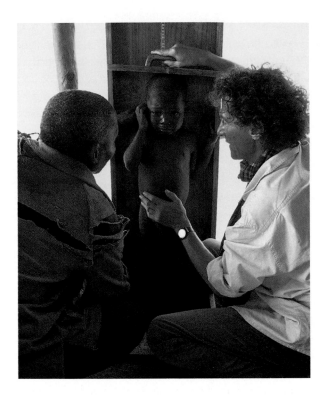

Médecins sans Frontières (Doctors Without Borders) has been treating, healing, and feeding the victims of war, natural disasters, epidemics, dictatorships, and hunger since 1971. In the southeastern African country of Malawi, this French volunteer medical aid organization provides comprehensive health care for Mozambican refugees. (Left) A youngster has his height and weight measured. MSF volunteer medical workers also provide immmunizations against childhood diseases and treat refugee children suffering from malnutrition.

Photograph, Peter Turnley—Black Star

In the countryside, immunization programs have been disrupted, although this has been counterbalanced to some extent by their acceleration in the towns. A UNICEF report, "Children on the Front Line," attributes 320,000 child deaths between 1981 and 1986 to the war. The infant mortality rate in 1985 was as high as 200 per 1,000, while the mortality of children under age five was 325–375 per 1,000; 8.4% of children in the war-affected areas were acutely malnourished.

Before the war the health service had established sound vaccination programs and a satisfactory distribution of drugs and had brought tuberculosis and leprosy under reasonable control. Now, owing to terrorist attacks, scarcity of foreign currency and fuel, and disruption of communications, these programs have largely lapsed. Epidemics of communicable diseases, such as measles and diphtheria, are commonplace, and the incidence of tuberculosis and leprosy is rising again. In financial terms the cost of damage to health buildings was estimated at $21.5 million through 1986, while damage to the contents cost an additional $3.8 million. The economic crisis and shortage of foreign currency preclude replacement of the lost equipment.

The 1988 UNICEF report on "The State of the World's Children" has this to say about Mozambique and the other states that border South Africa: "Peace and an end to apartheid are the prerequisites for both health and development in southern Africa. In the meantime, millions of children could be saved from the worst consequences of the conflict if the international community were to provide urgently needed finance, food, drugs, vaccines, transport, water supplies and help for improving food production." The International Committee on Crisis Control has ranked Mozambique, of all countries in the world, as the one with the greatest toll of human suffering.

At a clinic for refugees run by Médecins sans Frontières, a Mozambican woman receives treatment for a leg wound.

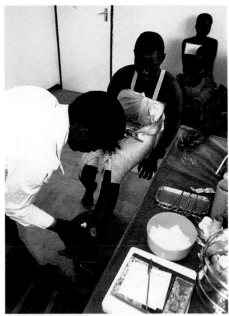

Photograph, Peter Turnley—Black Star

Nicaragua: creative solutions dashed

Nicaragua wasted no time after the fall of the hated Anastasio Somoza regime in 1979 to organize a nationwide public health program. In spite of the depletion of the country's resources and the exodus of doctors in the course of the civil war, a national health system was inaugurated and the private sector was allowed to supplement the public system. Primary health care services were quickly created by the training of so-called multipliers; *i.e.,* rapidly taught volunteers who passed on their new knowledge and eventually created a force of 100,000 health workers known as *brigadistas*. So effective were these measures that WHO gave special recognition to Nicaragua in 1982 as a model country for its progress in primary health care. Improvement in hygiene, simple treatment regimes of common diseases, and mass immunization campaigns led quickly to a fall in infant mortality rates from 120 per 1,000 live births in the three years preceding the revolution to 75 per 1,000 in 1983.

The Nicaraguans skillfully used a literacy campaign to augment the health program by employing health material as basic reading material. Health and hygiene consciousness became the bonus of literacy.

These gains in living and health standards were not to last, however. *Contra* incursions have taken a grave toll. In disregard of the Geneva Conventions, health posts and hospitals have been attacked and destroyed. According to Paula Braveman and David Siegel, two U.S. doctors reporting in the *International Journal of Health Services,* by 1985 the *contras* had killed 38 civilian health workers, wounded 11, and kidnapped 28, while 61 health institutions had been completely or partially destroyed and 37 others intermittently or totally closed. Moreover, because of the need for health workers at the front, over 5,000 had left their civilian jobs for service in combat zones. Health promotion in the civilian population thus has suffered as *brigadistas* have had to shift their efforts to the treatment of war casualties.

Some 35,000 people lost their lives in the revolution to oust Somoza. More than 30,000 have been killed since then, half of them civilians. Out of a total population of 3.5 million, over 6,000 soldiers and 5,000 civilians have been disabled; legs blown off by land mines are the most common injuries. Mental scarring goes hand in hand with physical scarring, and the survivors of such brutal events as rape and the punitive amputation of limbs relive and retell their horrible experiences.

Nicaraguan children have by no means been spared. Long-term "hysterical mutism and blindness" have been reported in children forced by guerrillas to witness or perform murders of family. Some 7,580 children have been orphaned and are considered psychologically at risk.

Diseases that had previously been under control have once more asserted themselves. The incidence of childhood diseases and of malaria is rising. The lack of insecticides in addition to war conditions has hampered vector control, and dengue fever (a viral infection spread by mosquitoes) attacked 600,000 people in 1985.

Stewart Britten, a British psychiatrist, visited Nicaragua in 1988 and saw many disabled patients. He was impressed by the psychiatric attention the mentally disabled were receiving. He noted that Nicaraguan medical

Since the fall of the Anastasio Somoza regime in 1979, a decade of contra *incursions has taken a huge toll on the civilian population of Nicaragua. More than 15,000 civilians have lost their lives; over 5,000 civilians have been disabled; and an estimated 8,000 children have been orphaned. Many of these orphans are now suffering mental scars that are the result of having been forced to witness rapes and murders of their own family members. The armed woman below protects her children and guards her home, which bears the Sandinista National Liberation Front flag.*

Gerald Williams—SIPA

92

services had become largely self-sufficient in terms of doctors, nurses, and physiotherapists, but help was still needed from abroad in specialty services such as orthopedic surgery, neurosurgery, and speech therapy.

To sum up, the health services of Nicaragua have responded to the challenge of civil war in what must be seen as an imaginative and intelligent way, but hopes for a brighter future and for the attainment of higher standards of health care have been dashed by the continuing conflict. As it was so succinctly put in *The Lancet* by three U.S. physicians in 1985: "We feel it is safe to conclude that Nicaragua's major health concern is war and that war involves not only the direct effects of bombs and bullets but also the indirect effects of aggression on the nation's economy and corresponding physical and psychological health."

(Above) Nicaraguan schoolchildren run for their lives, fleeing from a barrage of contra *bullets. The hospitalized child below was not lucky enough to have escaped injury; all too frequently it is the children who are caught—the innocent victims in brutal guerrilla attacks.*

Hellish poisons: the martyrdom of Halabjah

Probably the greatest fear of humankind since the dropping of a nuclear bomb on Hiroshima on Aug. 6, 1945, has been that of a nuclear holocaust. That Sword of Damocles, fortunately, has not fallen; instead the world is witnessing a new face of war, what Winston Churchill called "that hellish poison"—*i.e.,* the scourge of chemical weapons. With one or two exceptions, less developed countries do not have the scientific or economic resources to make nuclear weapons, but many of them can manufacture chemical weapons—called "the poor man's atomic bomb." Any country that has a pesticide-manufacturing factory is capable of making the deadly gases, which are both simple and cheap to produce.

The Geneva Conventions outlaw all weapons of mass destruction; therefore, neither nuclear nor chemical weapons can be morally or legally justified. Nevertheless, nations threatened with defeat will use any means

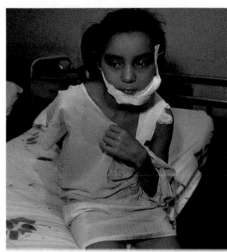

93

Dead, bloated bodies lay strewn on the ground of the small town of Halabjah in northern Iraq. In March 1988 this Iranian-held village was bombed with a sinister combination of cyanide poison and mustard and nerve gases, leaving 5,000 civilians dead.

to ensure survival. Increasingly over the past half decade, this is what Iraq has done. Faced with a numerically superior enemy (Iran), Iraq began using chemical weapons against Iran in 1983, at first defensively as an act of desperation against waves of Iran's Revolutionary Guards, then later in a planned manner to help its own offensive. For the former purpose, so-called persistent chemicals were used, such as mustard gas, which would contaminate an area for long periods. When on the offensive, the Iraqis employed more insidious means—*i.e.,* systematically targeting the enemy's command posts and artillery and supply points with dissipating chemicals, which kill and disable but vanish by the time the attacking troops themselves arrive on the scene. There are no reliable estimates of Iranian casualties that can be attributed to chemical weapons—poison gas effects

Shown at right are American victims of mustard gas, which was first used as a weapon by the Germans in World War I. The poison penetrates uniforms, blisters skin, and burns lungs.

Photograph, The Bettmann Archive

are exceedingly difficult to diagnose, especially after victims have left the site of the attack—but it is likely that they are in the tens of thousands.

Halabjah has now joined the list of towns, such as Hiroshima and Dresden, that are notorious for suffering inflicted upon their inhabitants. In March 1988 this town in northern Iraq, which had been in Iranian hands, was bombed by Iraqi warplanes in its most brutal assault. First, conventional bombs were used; then, when its people had sought shelter in cellars, a sinister combination of chemical weapons, including mustard gas, nerve gas, and hydrogen cyanide, was dropped. The heavier poison gas seeped into the cellars, resulting in the deaths of some 5,000 civilians— men, women, and children—with many more injured. The bloated bodies of Kurdish victims were left literally littering the streets.

The agonies of those affected by mustard gas are terrible. Exposed skin is blistered and burned, leaving ulcers; eyelids swell and vision can be temporarily or permanently lost; and the lungs are congested and airways obstructed. If the poison is swallowed, nausea, vomiting, and diarrhea add to the distress. The bone marrow may be damaged, lowering resistance to infection. The effects of nerve gases are even more horrible. They induce asphyxiation and wheezing. Muscle cramps are followed by paralysis, and many victims die after a period of restlessness, confusion, and coma. Cyanides, which block the uptake of oxygen into the tissues, can kill in five minutes, with the victim's symptoms progressing from headache to violent convulsions and coma.

The people of Halabjah were taken by surprise. They had no protective clothing, no gas masks, no antidote—in fact, no defense whatsoever. Iran has protested to the international community on many occasions, and its accusations have been upheld by United Nations investigators. At the same time, Iran cannot be regarded as totally innocent; it too has probably used

Two Kurdish survivors from Halabjah bear the physical and mental scars of that harrowing spring day when the people of their small village were taken utterly by surprise in the most brutal attack in the eight years of fighting between Iran and Iraq.

Photographs, (below left) Moradabadi—Reflex/Picture Group; (below right) Susan May Tell—Picture Group

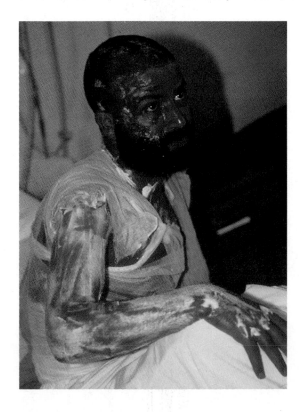

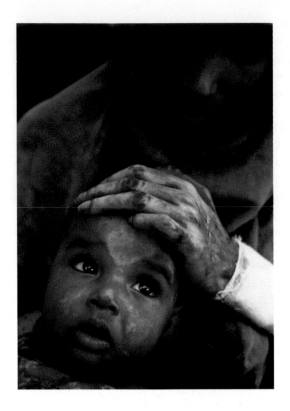

chemical weapons in retaliation. It is to be hoped that Iraq and Iran—and indeed all nations—have now been shamed into ceasing to use these hellish weapons against defenseless people—that the carnage of Halabjah will not soon be forgotten by the international community.

War and the innocents

Children are never the initiators or instigators of war; they are its innocent victims. Their right to protection in times of war is recognized in many of the Geneva Conventions and Protocols. Nonetheless, millions suffer through war and in the preparation for war.

Amal Shamma', head of the department of pediatrics at Berbir Medical Centre, Beirut, described the impact of war on children in *World Health* magazine, pointing out how one of the problems in estimating the extent of child suffering in war is the absence of exact data. In the international classification of diseases, war is not even listed as an official cause of death. Shamma' has rightly demanded that war injuries to children be officially listed as such.

Of the estimated 120,000 people who died in Lebanon between 1975 and 1986, from 18,000 to 40,000 were children under 15 years of age. The social and economic effects of war on children were even more difficult to measure than the physical. Children suffer from economic deprivation, the deaths of their parents and providers, malnutrition, homelessness, lack of medical care, interrupted formal education, and stunted growth.

Shamma' cited several studies that have been carried out on the psychological effects of war on Lebanese children. G. Yacoub examined a group of 30 children living in war zones and found that fearfulness, insecurity, regression in behavior, sleep disturbances, and nightmares occurred frequently. He also observed in some children a perversion of moral attitudes. "Some of the children had shown fascination with, and a desire for, participation in acts of killing." In another study, J. Abu Nasr and colleagues concentrated on the effects of war on moral judgment in 548 children between the ages of 11 and 14. They found that 26% of the children had changed their judgment from a moral to an immoral one in regard to the acceptability of killing.

In 1983 in Finland at a symposium on Children and War, Raija-Leena Punamaki, a psychologist, described the psychological reactions of Palestinian and Israeli children to war and violence. The hard realities of the conflict situation—the sense of patriotism and cohesion that had developed in children of both nationalities—had brought about an acceptance of war, but this acceptance of violence and aggression did not eliminate fear. In many of the Palestinian children, aggression and anger alternated with crying spells and restlessness. Some were almost paralyzed by fear, while others found it difficult to concentrate. There were symptoms of mental illness. Some 17% were significantly depressed, and one in five suffered from extreme fatigue and lack of initiative. By day many of the children displayed outwardly courageous behavior, confronting Israeli soldiers, but at night they lay restless and sleepless or tortured by nightmares. A mother described her daughter's pathological fears: "If it happens that she sees soldiers or even their jeep on the way to school, she runs home with a white face and refuses to go to school for weeks."

Another particularly distressing occurrence, which has already been illustrated in the case of Mozambique, is that children are being dragged into the actual fighting and killing and are dying by the thousands, sometimes

Studies of children who must face war as an everyday reality have shown that there is often an acceptance of violence and aggression and in some cases even a fascination with brutality and a desire to participate in it. On a deeper level, however, many of these children are tormented by fear, which may express itself in sleeplessness, nightmares, and regressive behavior.

The 1977 Protocols to the Geneva Conventions specifically state that children under age 15 should not be recruited into a country's armed forces. In Iran children aged 13 and younger are indoctrinated with concepts of martyrdom and are prepared mentally, physically, and spiritually to be soldiers. Because enrollment in the Army does not require the consent of parents, many children volunteer to be sent to the front. During the Iran–Iraq war, Iran suffered huge losses; not surprisingly, the death toll was highest among the youngest fighters. Pictured at left are a group of Iranian prisoners of war—some as young as nine or ten.

Honorable Mention:
Proper Names in the Medical Lexicon

by John H. Dirckx, M.D.

"I've got Bright's disease," lamented a 19th-century wit, "and he's got mine!" Appellations like Bell's palsy, Clutton's joints, and Hutchinson's teeth seem to provide an unfailing source of amusement, at least for those who do not happen to have the designated conditions. Modern medical dictionaries and textbooks teem with such terms—names for anatomic structures, diagnostic tests, diseases, drugs, organisms, and surgical procedures and instruments—incorporating and forever commemorating the names of their discoverers or inventors. Technically they are known as eponyms.

Behind each name a story

Behind every eponym lies a story—sometimes quite a different story from what one might suppose. Scientific investigators, bitter rivals throughout their professional careers, may ultimately find themselves linked in eternal partnership by a hyphen because no one knew for certain which of them was the first to make a crucial discovery. Some familiar eponyms honor people who merely rediscovered things that were well known to the ancients, and some memorialize individuals who actually pilfered discoveries or inventions from less ambitious colleagues. A few medical eponyms owe their origin to the vanity or commercial enterprise of physicians who put their own names on products or methods in an attempt to secure, if not everlasting glory, at least exclusive profits. Nonetheless, most medical eponyms have been created by common consent of the medical profession or the public at large to honor the innovative, ingenious, painstaking, or perhaps simply lucky person who first observed the body part, physiological function, or disease process or who devised the test, instrument, or treatment that now bears his or her name.

Welcome relief from lexical jawbreakers

The wish to recognize the achievements and perpetuate the names of venerated anatomists, physicians, and surgeons is not the sole motivation behind

John H. Dirckx, M.D., is Medical Director, C. H. Gosiger Memorial Health Center, University of Dayton, Ohio, and author of The Language of Modern Medicine: Its Evolution, Structure, and Dynamics.

(Opposite page, clockwise from upper left), Photograph, National Library of Medicine; photograph, World Health Organization; William H. Helfand Collection

Richard Bright
(1789–1858)

cinchona plant
(*Cinchona ledgeriana*)

patent medicine trade card
(late 19th century)

Dr. Hand's Remedies for Children
Pleasant Physic,   Colic Cure,
Teething Lotion,   Worm Elixir,
Diarrhœa Mixture,   General Tonic,
Cough and Croup Medicine, Chafing Powder

the continued use of proper names in medical terminology, nor is it even the most cogent one. Every physician knows something about Addison's and Hodgkin's diseases, but probably not one in a thousand knows anything about Addison and Hodgkin themselves. If eponyms have been kept in regular use by the medical profession long after their historical associations have been lost to all but the historian, it is chiefly because they inject a little warmth, color, and variety into medical terminology, affording a welcome change from the frigid pomposity of jawbreaker words—for example, agammaglobulinemia, choledocholithiasis, pseudo-pseudohypoparathyroidism—derived from Greek and Latin.

For the same reason, physicians and lay people have also fashioned terms from the names of biblical figures (Adam's apple, onanism) and characters from classical mythology (Achilles tendon, morphine) and even modern literature. Munchausen's syndrome, for example, is the name given to a mental disorder whose victims typically go from hospital to hospital convincingly retailing fabricated medical histories and often undergoing the most radical and invasive treatments. The syndrome is named after a literary character, Baron Munchausen (loosely modeled after a real-life German baron), whose outrageous fictional exploits were recounted by Rudolf Erich Raspe, an 18th-century storyteller. Corpulent persons who experience drowsiness and lethargy because of inadequate lung expansion are said to suffer from Pickwickian syndrome. The term refers not to Mr. Pickwick, the title character of Charles Dickens's *Pickwick Papers,* but to a minor character in the chronicle, Joe, the fat boy, who was always falling asleep. Sadism and masochism are named after European novelists—the French Count (usually called Marquis) de Sade and the Austrian writer Leopold von Sacher-Masoch—whose characters displayed these psychological aberrations.

Modern medical dictionaries teem with names derived from a variety of sources, medical and nonmedical. Among the most memorable are those with origins in classical mythology. A case in point is the structure known as the Achilles tendon, the powerful tendon that connects the calf muscles to the bone of the heel (shown below in an illustration from a 19th-century anatomy text). Myth holds that Achilles was the offspring of a mortal, King Peleus, and the sea nymph Thetis. Thetis, in seeking immortality for her infant son, dipped him into the River Styx while holding him by the heel—the only part of his body that was untouched by the waters and thus unprotected. As a celebrated warrrior in the army of Agamemnon, Achilles was fatally wounded when Paris—his arrow guided by the god Apollo—shot him in the very spot where he was vulnerable.

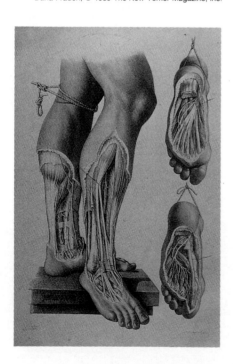

"Achilles! How's the wife? The kids? The heel?"

Modern literature has inspired many colorful medical eponyms. Munchausen's syndrome, for example, a mental disorder whose victims convincingly fabricate all sorts of illnesses, is named for a memorable literary character called Baron Munchausen. In the stories, written by Rudolph Erich Raspe, Munchausen regaled his friends with outrageously improbable tales of his life as a soldier and sportsman. (Left) Raspe's gallant fictional baron made a dashing reappearance in the 1989 film The Adventures of Baron Munchausen.

Esteem for the ancients

The earliest medical authority who is honored eponymically is the father of medicine himself, the Greek physician Hippocrates, who lived and practiced in the 5th century BC. The pinched and drawn facial expression of the dying patient, vividly described by Hippocrates in his *Prognostics,* is to this day called the hippocratic facies. A distinctive enlargement, or clubbing, of the fingertips that Hippocrates observed in patients with empyema (a respiratory condition) is still known as hippocratic clubbing; the phenomenon has since been found to occur in other chronic ailments affecting the heart or lungs.

Galen, who lived in the 2nd century AD, was unquestionably the most influential medical writer of all time. He was born in Asia Minor but practiced in Rome, becoming court physician to the emperor Marcus Aurelius. The leaders of Roman society attended his lectures on anatomy and physiology.

In Pickwick Papers, *Charles Dickens described the character Joe, a "fat and red-faced boy in a state of somnolence." This was the first literary depiction of the malady today known as Pickwickian syndrome, a condition of drowsiness and lethargy experienced by corpulent persons whose lungs cannot expand sufficiently to allow proper respiration.*

Although he dissected goats, pigs, and Barbary apes rather than human cadavers, the dissection of the human body being strictly forbidden by the Roman religion, Galen carried the science of anatomy further than any previous investigator. He did pioneering work on the bones, muscles, and nerves, and his demonstration that the arteries carry blood and not air, as had been believed for centuries, paved the way for the discovery of the circulation of the blood. In his honor a major vessel draining the blood from the brain is called the great cerebral vein of Galen, or Galen's vein. Galen also advocated the use of medicines of vegetable origin; formulas containing such ingredients are known even today as galenicals.

For many centuries after Galen, European civilization practically stood still. The works of the old authorities were translated and annotated, analyzed and memorized, but very little original investigation was carried out in medicine or in any of the other sciences. As a consequence, virtually no eponyms in current use honor physicians of that era.

The Renaissance: eponyms by the dozens

The resurgence of learning and the reawakening of scientific curiosity in the Renaissance led to an explosion of new medical information. With the approval of civil and religious authorities, anatomists began to dissect human bodies. The 16th-century physician Andreas Vesalius, a native of Belgium, taught for many years at the University of Padua, Italy, and published the first authoritative illustrated textbook of anatomy ever to issue from a printing press. Vesalius and his students and successors corrected many of the anatomic errors made by Galen and his school. Every year brought

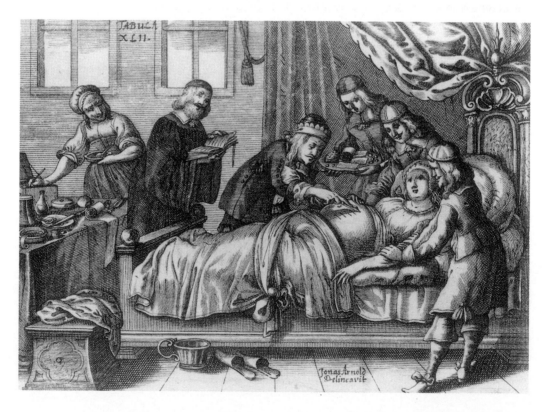

forth new discoveries in anatomy and physiology, and medical eponyms were created by the dozens.

Vesalius's pupil Gabriel Fallopius made important discoveries about the anatomic structures of the nervous system and the female reproductive system, including the uterine tubes, still usually called the fallopian tubes. Bartolomeo Eustachio, a rival of Vesalius who taught in Rome, is credited with the discovery of the auditory tube that bears his name (eustachian tube), even though the structure was known to Aristotle almost 2,000 years earlier. Nicolaus Steno, or Stensen, a native of Denmark, made vital contributions to geology, crystallography, and the study of fossils as well as to anatomy. Steno was the first to publish the concept that the heart is a muscle, another critical step toward the understanding of the circulation. However, his discovery of the duct carrying saliva from the parotid gland to the mouth (made during his dissection of a sheep) embroiled him in acrimonious conflict with his teacher, Blasius of Amsterdam, who claimed to have made the discovery first. To this day, however, the structure is universally known as Stensen's duct.

Nomenclature in modern times

The invention of the microscope unlocked a whole new realm of anatomic information and gave rise to histology, the study of the fine structure of tissues. Many terms still in daily use bear witness to the pertinacity and acumen of early histologists: the graafian follicles of the ovary, discovered by Dutch anatomist Reinier de Graaf, author of a celebrated treatise on the female reproductive organs; the haversian canals of bone, named for British osteologist Clopton Havers; the Malpighian corpuscles of the spleen and the kidney, honoring Italian anatomist Marcello Malpighi, regarded as the founder of histology.

In the early 19th century the science of pathology began to flourish as signs and symptoms of disease in living patients were carefully observed and correlated with microscopic examination of autopsy specimens. René-Théophile-Hyacinthe Laënnec, the Breton clinician best remembered for having invented the stethoscope, was also one of the founders of modern pathology. He was the first to recognize and clarify the common features of the various forms of tuberculosis and the first to describe the liver disorder still known as Laënnec's cirrhosis. Rudolf Virchow, the 19th-century German physician who introduced the concept of cellular pathology, was an indefatigable researcher and prolific writer. Virchow dabbled in many fields besides medicine, including art, history, anthropology, and archaeology. In response to his outspoken opposition to the administration of Prussian Chancellor Otto von Bismarck, the chancellor challenged him to a duel, an invitation Virchow politely declined. He elucidated several important pathological processes and coined the terms embolism, granuloma, and leukemia, among others. He recognized that the enlargement of a particular lymph node, thenceforth known as Virchow's node, might indicate a malignancy in an internal organ.

Numerous personal names have found their way into Linnean taxonomy, the elaborate system for classifying and naming living things devised by

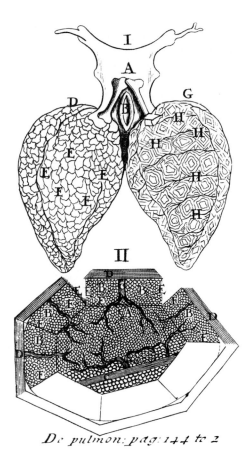

De pulmon: pag: 144 tc 2

Histology, the study of the fine structure of tissues, was made possible by the invention of the microscope. Many medical and anatomic terms still in use today bear witness to the acumen of the early histologists. The Italian physician Marcello Malpighi is widely regarded as the founder of the science. Malpighi studied the microscopic anatomy of human systems and organs, including the brain, spinal cord, and secretory glands, and produced a classic treatise on the the structure of the liver, cerebral cortex, kidney, and spleen. Several structural units of these organs bear his name, among them the Malpighian pyramid, or renal pyramid, and the Malpighian corpuscles of the spleen and kidney. Pictured above is Malpighi's study, c. 1687, of the cardiovascular system of a frog, which includes a microscopic view of the lung tissue showing the capillaries.

Photograph, National Library of Medicine

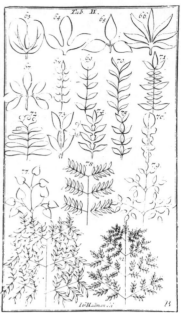

The taxonomic names of plants, animals, bacteria, fungi, and parasites often include the names of those who first recognized or described them. Organisms of the genus Escherichia, *which includes the common intestinal bacillus* E. coli *(below), are named for the German pediatrician Theodor Escherich, who first described these bacteria in 1886.*

Howard Sochurek—Medichrome

the 18th-century Swedish naturalist Linnaeus (Carl von Linné). Taxonomic terms for many disease-causing bacteria, fungi, and parasites include the names of the early microbiologists who first identified these organisms. In fact, a majority of the eponymic bacterial genus names in current use commemorate members of a single generation of scientists, all born in the mid- to late 19th century: *Brucella* for British surgeon Sir David Bruce; *Escherichia* for Theodor Escherich and *Klebsiella* for Edwin Klebs, both German physicians; *Neisseria* for Albert Neisser, German bacteriologist; *Salmonella* for U.S. pathologist Daniel E. Salmon; and *Shigella* for Japanese bacteriologist Kiyoshi Shiga.

Enduring ointments

Although nowadays medicinal preparations are usually named according to their chemical composition, it was customary at one time for inventors of new medicines to market them under their own names, often keeping the formulas secret for business reasons. In the early part of the 20th century, textbooks of therapeutics contained many eponymic drug names, such as Brandreth's pills, Dover's powder, Glauber's salt, and Hoffman's anodyne. Most of these have now gone the way of Lydia Pinkham's Vegetable Compound and Dr. Williams' Pink Pills for Pale People, but dermatologists still employ a number of eponymic terms for skin preparations, such as Burow's solution, Castellani's paint, and Whitfield's ointment.

Indexer's headache and related disorders

The enduring popularity and steady proliferation of eponyms have created some formidable problems for students of medicine. Technical terms derived from classical languages display a certain regularity of spelling and pronunciation; no such regularity can be expected among personal names culled from dozens of the world's languages. The medical student is expected

106

to learn to spell correctly names from Czech, French, German, Japanese, Spanish, Swedish, and Turkish, with all their accents, umlauts, diaereses, tildes, and cedillas appropriately placed. Moreover, the medical student must learn to pronounce these names, if not as they are pronounced in their countries of origin, at least as they are pronounced by physicians in the country where he or she intends to practice.

Eponyms create a different set of headaches for medical editors, bibliographers, catalogers, indexers, and librarians. There is, for example, the seemingly simple question of alphabetization. A Hispanic surname typically includes the surnames of both the mother's and the father's family. Should the method of staining nerve cells devised by the Spanish histologist Santiago Ramón y Cajal be indexed with the *R*'s or with the *C*'s? Or with the *Y*'s? Names from many languages include particles like "von" and "de," which may or may not deserve capitalization and may or may not be separable for purposes of alphabetization. The neurological disease first described by the 19th-century French physician Georges Gilles de la Tourette has at various times and places been called Gilles de la Tourette's syndrome, de la Tourette's syndrome, la Tourette's syndrome, and Tourette's syndrome— and indexed accordingly. Similar problems are presented by von Recklinghausen's disease, von Graefe's sign, and van den Bergh's test.

107

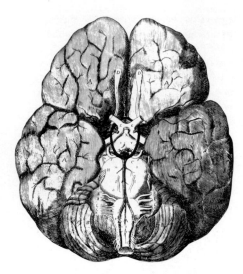

Blood is supplied to the brain by two paired arteries that communicate with each other at the base of the brain to form the so-called circle of Willis. This structure was described by British physician Thomas Willis in 1664 in his Cerebri Anatome *("Anatomy of the Brain"). In the drawing of the brain (above), the circle of Willis is highlighted in red.*

Drawing by Sir Christopher Wren; photograph, the Bodleian Library, Oxford

Among the most enduring medical eponyms are those for instruments so simple they cannot be improved upon; e.g., the Kelly clamp, Penrose drain, and Foley catheter, to mention but a few. The Ayers examining table, c. 1858 (opposite page, bottom), is one piece of equipment that has not withstood the test of time.

A hyphenated eponym referring to more than one person, such as Hand-Schüller-Christian disease, is alphabetized according to the first name in the series. A hyphenated eponym referring to a single person, such as Albers-Schönberg disease (a condition described by Heinrich Albers-Schönberg and also known as osteopetrosis) is indexed by the former element of the compound name. However, the British custom of calling a man by his middle and last names when the middle name is a family name (Conan Doyle for Arthur Conan Doyle, Bernard Shaw for George Bernard Shaw) has carried over into medical cataloging practice, adding a further element of confusion. For example, the characteristic skin discoloration first reported by George Grey Turner is often called Grey Turner's sign and alphabetized with the G's; likewise, the vascular disease described by Frederick Parkes Weber often figures in published literature as Parkes Weber's disease and is so indexed. An even more peculiar custom is that of treating first names as integral parts of some eponymic terms even for purposes of alphabetization. The Austin Flint cardiac murmur, Cornelia de Lange's syndrome, Dorothy Reed cells, Gordon Holmes's sign, and Graham Steell's murmur are cases in point.

Irksome inconsistencies

The traditional use of the possessive case, formed with 's, to create eponyms has been a frequent source of annoyance and contention among medical writers, editors, and lexicographers. For one thing, the practice frequently leads to spelling errors; for example, the apostrophe is often wrongly inserted before a final s that is part of a surname, as in Coomb's test for Coombs test and as in Wilm's tumor instead of Wilms' tumor. And on the other hand, the apostrophe before the s may be left out when the s is thought to belong to the name, as in the incorrect Downs syndrome rather than Down's syndrome (or, as it is now often alternatively called, Down syndrome) or Potts instead of Pott's fracture.

There has never been much consistency in the use of the possessive form. The 's is seldom used with hyphenated eponyms, as in Letterer-Siwe disease and Laurence-Moon-Biedl syndrome. It appears in Paget's cells and Jendrassik's maneuver but not in Hürthle cells or Kocher maneuver. A few eponymic terms are almost invariably formed by the addition of the preposition of: the circle of Willis, the crypts of Lieberkühn, the foramen of Magendie, the island of Reil, the islets of Langerhans, the organs of Zuckerkandl, the tetralogy of Fallot. In the names pons varolii (the bridge of Varolio) and corpora arantii (the bodies of Aranzi), the Latin possessive (genitive) case is used.

These inconsistencies have irked some editors, who have argued, moreover, that a phrase like Cushing's disease is illogical because it is not Cushing who has the disease. A few have made the experiment of decreeing possessive eponyms out of existence. However, this arbitrary legislation not only does violence to established customs and traditions but also forces writers and readers to endure such absurdities as Courvoisier law, devil grip, and housemaid knee. Small wonder if these editorial decrees seldom remain in force for long.

Variations sometimes whimsical

On being turned into eponyms, proper names often undergo modification or distortion. Adjectives and derivative nouns based on proper names usually start with lowercase letters: hippocratic, mendelian, parkinsonism, roentgenogram. In addition, units of measure based on proper names are not capitalized and may be truncated as well, as in torr (a unit of pressure equal to one millimeter of mercury), named for the 17th-century Italian physicist Evangelista Torricelli. The name of George Papanicolaou, a pioneer in the study of cancer at the cellular level, is usually cut down to its first syllable, as in Pap test. An abnormal bulging of Descemet's membrane in the eye is called a descemetocele, and a nodule forming at the site of infection in Chagas' disease is known as a chagoma. A patient whose middle ear has been insufflated with air by means of a Politzer bag is said to have been politzerized. Inflammation of Skene's glands is skenitis, and surgical removal of Bartholin's gland is a bartholinectomy.

Because a method of gel electrophoresis for studying chromosomes is called Southern blot after its originator, Edward Southern of Edinburgh, Scotland, variations on this method have acquired the whimsical names northern, western, and even southwestern blot. A test for elevated prostatic acid phosphatase in the serum, an indication of prostatic cancer, has been dubbed the male PAP test.

Medical instruments are commonly named for those who invented them. On being turned into eponyms, however, proper names often undergo modification—e.g., changing the first letter from capital to lowercase. The roentgenogram (the original name for the photographic image produced by X-rays) was named for the German physicist Wilhelm Conrad Roentgen, who won the Nobel Prize for Physics in 1901 for his discovery of the X-ray.

Semantic drift

Whether an eponym survives the centuries or falls into lexical obscurity is largely dependent on circumstance. The English physician Richard Bright first reported the frequent association of dropsy, or edema (swelling due to fluid retention), with kidney disease, as manifested by protein in the urine, in 1827. For many decades thereafter this condition was called Bright's disease. Today, however, a variety of disorders are known to induce pro-

While attending the wounded at Corunna and Waterloo, Charles Bell, Scottish physician and an accomplished artist, made a number of oil sketches of injured British soldiers. The above sketch shows a man who has suffered a head wound caused by the penetration into his skull of a musket ball. Although he was an able surgeon, Bell became best known as an anatomist, principally of the nervous system. His Nervous System of the Human Body *(1830) contained the first detailed description of the facial nerve and of the facial distortion and paralysis—now known as Bell's palsy—that results when this nerve is damaged.*

tein loss by the kidney accompanied by generalized edema; thus, the term Bright's disease has gone out of fashion.

Other eponyms, however, remain in use even when their purport or bearing has radically changed. In 1704 the Italian anatomist Antonio Maria Valsalva published an important treatise on the human ear, in which he described a simple means of clearing a blocked eustachian tube: exhale forcefully while keeping the lips and nostrils compressed. In his honor this procedure (which was probably first practiced by Adam and Eve) is known as the Valsalva maneuver. A later generation of medical specialists became interested in the effects of the Valsalva maneuver on the circulation, particularly its usefulness in distinguishing various kinds of heart murmur. Thus, during the course of the physical examination, modern cardiologists sometimes instruct their patients to exhale against closed vocal cords, a procedure that avoids the unpleasant popping sensation caused by the sudden inflation of the middle ears. Although this alternative procedure is expressly designed to leave the ears unaffected, it is still called the Valsalva maneuver.

Another example of the staying power of some eponyms is that of Hodgkin's disease, named for the English physician Thomas Hodgkin, who in 1829 described the malignancy of the spleen and lymph nodes that bears his name. Some 97 years later Herbert Fox, a pathologist in Philadelphia, obtained access to tissue specimens (which had been kept in preservative in the intervening years) from Hodgkin's original seven patients and published a paper showing that only four of them had Hodgkin's disease!

An eponym applied to a surgical operation usually remains in use only until someone develops a better operation, but names for surgical instruments, particularly those that are so simple they cannot be improved upon, enjoy greater longevity. Nearly all surgical instruments in modern use have eponymic names. To the surgeon and his assistants, an Adson tissue forceps is just an Adson, a Foley catheter just a Foley, a Kelly clamp a Kelly, and a Penrose drain a Penrose.

Nouns, common and uncommon

An eponym is not expected to have any inherent semantic content, but it may seem to do so if it contains a proper name that can easily be mistaken for a common noun. For many years the Sippy diet was a staple in the hospital treatment of peptic ulcer. Granted that it consisted largely of liquids that could be sipped, the diet in fact was named for the U.S. physician who developed it, Bertram W. Sippy. The Quick test, a blood test that measures prothrombin, is indeed expeditious, taking just 12 seconds when the prothrombin level is normal, but it gets its name from its originator, the U.S. biochemist Armand J. Quick. Similarly, Cork leg, Heads zones, Milkman's syndrome, Minor tremors, Ribbing syndrome, Rotors syndrome, Shaver's disease, and Stills murmur, all named for individual practitioners, can easily be misinterpreted by being taken too literally.

The occurrence of terms such as these, together with the huge number of eponyms in modern use, sometimes seduces the unwary reader (or hearer) into taking a term for an eponym when it is not one. Thus, caisson

110

disease (decompression sickness) occasionally turns up in print as Caisson's disease, though the term refers to the caisson, or air-filled chamber, in which workers can carry on excavation under water. A special type of urethral catheter with a curved tip, called a coudé catheter from the French for "bent," is now and then fathered on a nonexistent Dr. Coudé. Brown cough mixture and brown tumors of bone are so called simply because they are brown. The gurney, the wheeled cot of the type used in hospitals to transport patients, is officially spelled with a small g, pending any evidence that it commemorates some doctor, nurse, orderly, or hospital handyman named Gurney.

The German practice of beginning common as well as proper nouns with capital letters has led many to mistake purely descriptive terms for eponyms. Grenz rays have a wavelength on the *borderline* (German *Grenze*) between X-rays and ultraviolet rays. No one named Grenz had anything to do with their application to medicine. Misinterpretation of the phrase Jod-Basedow's disease—hyperthyroidism induced by *iodine* (German *Jod*)—often compels the 19th-century German physician Karl von Basedow to share the honors for identifying this condition with an imaginary doctor by the name of Jod. The 19th-century parasitologist Jaroslav Hlava of Prague, Bohemia (now Czechoslovakia), suffered an even harsher fate when all credit for his work on amebic dysentery was transferred to a chimerical physician, O. Uplavici. Actually, "O Uplavici" was the title of Hlava's published paper. It means "On Dysentery" in Czech but became the author's name through a printer's

The 19th-century French physician Jean-Martin Charcot was one of the founders of modern neurology. In his clinic at the Salpêtrière Hospital in Paris, Charcot identified a number of neurological, neuromuscular, and psychiatric conditions. One of his major contributions was his vivid description of hysterical disorders—psychoneurotic conditions whose symptoms typically mimicked those of organic disorders. In the painting below, by Pierre-André Brouillet (c. 1887), Charcot lectures to a group of physicians on the manifestations of hysteria. Of the many medical eponyms that bear witness to his eminence are Charcot's triad (three diagnostic signs seen in multiple sclerosis), Charcot's joint (a destructive joint condition occurring in association with diseases of the spinal cord), and Charcot-Marie-Tooth disease, a form of muscular atrophy that was described in 1866 by Charcot and Pierre Marie and, independently, by the British physician Howard Henry Tooth.

Ordinarily a medical scientist stakes a claim to eponymous fame by being the first to publish a report of a given disease or phenomenon. This is not always the case, however. Sister Joseph (above), the nursing superintendent at St. Mary's Hospital in Rochester, Minnesota, was also principal assistant to surgeon William J. Mayo. She noticed that some patients with abdominal cancer had growths near the navel that indicated the spread of the malignancy, and she shared this observation with Mayo. When Mayo published a report of the phenomenon in 1928, he gave her credit for the discovery, thus establishing in the medical lexicon the term Sister Joseph's sign.

error when an abstract of the report was published in the more widely spoken German language.

If eponymic terms often perplex or mislead students and practitioners of medicine, what pitfalls do they create for members of the laity? The conversion of Alzheimer's disease into "old-timer's disease" was perhaps inevitable, and "change strokes" (for Cheyne-Stokes) breathing seems almost too apt a translation to be true. Since Legg-Calvé-Perthes disease affects the femur (thigh bone), the lay alternative "leg of Perthes" possesses a certain logical appeal, but surely fancy has triumphed over sober reflection when Charcot's joint is recast as "charcoal joint," Rorschach test as "roaring shock test," and Sengstaken tube as "silk stocking tube."

Who saw it first?

The existence of several eponyms referring to the same thing usually means a dispute over priority. Sometimes the availability of equivalent or "synonymous" eponyms has amusing consequences. In the English-speaking world, hyperthyroidism accompanied by the ocular condition exophthalmos is called Graves' disease, after the 19th-century Irish physician Robert Graves, who published one of several early descriptions of this disorder. Speakers of German, however, refer to the same disorder as Basedow's disease, in honor of Karl von Basedow, mentioned above, while to speakers of Italian it is Flajani's disease (for the Italian surgeon Giuseppe Flajani).

Ordinarily one stakes one's claim to a disease or observation by being the first to publish a report of it, but this is not always so. Sister Joseph (born Mary Dempsey in 1856), who was nursing superintendent at St. Mary's Hospital in Rochester, Minnesota, for several decades, served during much of that time as surgeon William J. Mayo's principal assistant. Having noticed that some patients with abdominal cancer had growths near the navel representing spread of malignancy to the body wall, she mentioned this observation to Mayo. He published a report of it in 1928, giving credit where it was due, and since then the phenomenon has been called Sister Joseph's sign.

The South African surgeon C. F. M. Saint was a keen observer and a gifted teacher who often drew the attention of his students to unusual or significant combinations of physical findings or abnormal conditions. After he had remarked several times on the frequency with which three conditions—hiatus hernia, gallbladder disease, and colonic diverticulosis—occur together, one of his students published a paper on the subject, calling it Saint's triad. Saint himself, either careless of fame or doubtful that the combination meant anything (doctors still are), seems not to have taken the paper very seriously. On one occasion he reportedly asked another of his students, "What the hell *is* Saint's triad?"

Taxonomic terms for disease-causing germs have sometimes been named for celebrated figures in medical history who played no role in their discovery. Such is the case with *Listeria* and *Pasteurella*. Bacteria of the genus *Serratia,* which cause blotchy red discoloration of bread and pasta, were first isolated by an Italian pharmacist, Bartolomeo Bizio, in 1819. Bizio named the organisms after his compatriot Serafino Serrati, a physicist

112

who Bizio believed should have been honored as the principal developer of the steamship!

Celebrated patients

Occasionally the medical profession or the general public has seen fit to name a disease after one or more persons who have been afflicted by it. This is particularly likely to happen when the patient is a prominent public figure. The French poet Alfred de Musset suffered from incompetence of the aortic valve. As a result, his head constantly nodded in time with his heartbeat. This indication of cardiac disease now bears the name Musset's sign, among others.

The most common form of color blindness is sometimes called daltonism after the English scientist John Dalton, whose inadvertent mixing and matching of gaudy hues in his wardrobe sometimes shocked his fellow Quakers. He published a report of his vision problem in 1794, noting that his brother also had the condition.

Lou Gehrig, the "Iron Horse" of the New York Yankees, hit 493 home runs during his illustrious baseball career. In 1941 at age 38, he died of amyotrophic lateral sclerosis, a progressive neurological disorder of unknown cause that has since become known as Lou Gehrig's disease.

Some familial diseases are known by the names of the families in which they were first noted or investigated. Examples are Hartnup disease, a metabolic disorder, and Christmas disease, a form of hemophilia. The Duffy, Kell, Kidd, Lewis, and Lutheran blood groups bear the surnames of the persons in whom they were first found. Legionnaires' disease and the germ that causes it, *Legionella pneumophilia,* are named after the American

Occasionally the medical profession or the general public has seen fit to name a disease after an individual afflicted by it. This is particularly likely to happen when the patient is a prominent public figure. Baseball hero Lou Gehrig, the "Iron Horse" of the New York Yankees, hit 493 home runs and played in 2,130 consecutive games before his death in 1941, at age 38, from the progressive neurological disorder called amyotrophic lateral sclerosis. Today the disorder is probably more widely known as Lou Gehrig's disease. A postage stamp honoring the late champion was issued in 1989 in celebration of the 50th anniversary of the Baseball Hall of Fame in Cooperstown, New York.

U.S. Postal Service

Photograph, courtesy of
The Star, Hansen's Disease Center

When the name of a disease is inextricably associated with long-standing misconceptions about it, the name itself can become stigmatizing and an alternative name may be sought. Such has been the case with leprosy, since biblical times widely but mistakenly regarded as a highly contagious affliction of mysterious origin. Although the causative organism, a bacillus, was discovered in 1873 by a Norwegian physician, Armauer Hansen, and successful antibiotic treatment was developed, an irrational fear of the disease—and those afflicted—persisted. In the 1940s Stanley Stein, a patient at the Carville, Louisiana, leprosarium, led a successful campaign to have leprosy officially renamed Hansen's disease. Stein is shown above in a photo taken in the 1950s with actress Tallulah Bankhead, who championed the effort to remove the age-old stigma from the disease by renaming it.

Legion, at whose Pennsylvania state convention in Philadelphia in 1976 the first recognized outbreak of the disease occurred, killing 29 persons.

According to a venerable but almost certainly spurious legend, the countess of Chinchón, wife of a 17th-century Spanish viceroy in Peru, contracted malaria and was cured with doses of Peruvian bark (Jesuits' bark), now known to be a source of quinine. Whether this tale is true or not, Linnaeus apparently believed it, for he named the genus of the plant *Cinchona* in honor of the countess.

A few people have achieved a unique kind of immortality by serving as sources of cells or infective organisms that continue to reproduce or replicate indefinitely, even long after the death of the individual. In 1951 an American woman named Henrietta Lacks died in Baltimore of cancer of the uterine cervix. Living cells taken from her tumor gave rise to the first continuously cultured strain of cancerous cells—a strain that is still going strong in hundreds of laboratories throughout the world under the name of HeLa cells. Most of the mumps vaccine used in the U.S. consists of attenuated live virus from the Jeryl Lyn strain, named after the child from whom the original infectious material was cultured. The name of the antibiotic bacitracin commemorates a patient, Margaret Tracy, from whose tissues the parent strain of *Bacillus subtilis* was isolated in 1945.

Physician-patients commemorated

In some notable instances of medical eponymy, doctor and patient were one and the same. The term Pott's fracture of the ankle commemorates the 18th-century English surgeon Percivall Pott, who sustained such an injury when thrown by a horse and devised a successful means of treating it. Pott's student John Hunter, one of the greatest anatomists in history, performed a remarkable experiment on himself, inoculating his genitals with infectious material taken from a prostitute. As a consequence of this rash deed, he contracted both gonorrhea and syphilis, a fact that lent weight at the time to the erroneous belief that these were two different manifestations of the same disease. Now that they have been distinguished, the primary lesion of syphilis is known as a hunterian chancre.

Other researchers have paid even more dearly for their boldness in quest of medical knowledge. Daniel Carrión, a Peruvian medical student in the 19th century, inoculated himself with blood from a patient with verruga peruana, a seemingly benign skin infection. His subsequent development of Oroya fever, which helped to prove that this disease is caused by the same parasitic organism as verruga, led to his death at the age of 26 from what is now called Carrión's disease. In 1910 the U.S. pathologist Howard T. Ricketts, who had demonstrated the transmission of Rocky Mountain spotted fever by ticks, was in Mexico studying a similar disease (tabardillo) when he contracted it himself and died of it. In his memory the genus embracing the microorganisms that cause these diseases is known as *Rickettsia*. Five years after the death of Ricketts, one of these organisms, the cause of epidemic typhus now known as *Rickettsia prowazekii*, claimed the life of Stanislas von Prowazek, a German zoologist who had been engaged in the laboratory study of the disease.

114

Pride of place

Although the great majority of proper nouns that have found their way into the medical lexicon are the names of persons, a few are geographic terms. In recent years it has become customary in the U.S. to name new infectious diseases or their causative agents after the cities or locales in which outbreaks were first recognized or cases first diagnosed. Coxsackie viruses, a group of related viruses that cause several acute communicable diseases, are named for a town in New York where the first of the group was isolated; Norwalk agent, a frequent cause of outbreaks of acute diarrheal disease in children, gets its name from a city in Ohio; and Lyme disease, a recently recognized syndrome of fever, rash, and arthritis caused by a tick-borne bacterium, is named for Old Lyme, Connecticut, the town where many of the first cases occurred. Similarly, San Joaquin fever bears the name of the California river valley where it is endemic. The names of the infectious disease tularemia and the bacterium that causes it, *Francisella tularensis,* commemorate Tulare County, California, where the disease was first studied. Medicines and other forms of treatment may also bear eponymic place names, as in the cases of Epsom salts (magnesium sulfate, named after the English town once famous for its mineral springs) and the Milwaukee brace for correcting scoliosis.

Sometimes regional eponyms in medicine turn out to be misleading. The identification of a disease with a specific locale may even interfere with its diagnosis in cases that occur far from the recognized epicenter. Rocky Mountain spotted fever is currently more prevalent in the Appalachians than in the Rockies, and Lyme disease has now been identified in at least 43 U.S. states and in Europe and Australia. Most of the balsam of Peru in use today comes from El Salvador. And whatever the source of any given batch of plaster of paris, it is almost certainly not from Paris.

The names of hospitals, medical centers, and other institutions also have occasionally been taken into medical parlance. The name of the Hospital of

Photograph, World Health Organization

This engraving shows a soldier being "treated" for syphilis; the sign identifies him as "a Spaniard afflicted with Naples disease." Probably no other disease has borne such a variety of national appellations or thereby engendered such intense animosity. Most modern authorities agree that syphilis was introduced into Europe by Spanish sailors following their return from the New World in 1493. Spanish soldiers who were dispatched to Naples to repel a French invasion carried the infection into Italy. Subsequently, defeated French forces took it home with them. Each country named the new plague after one of its less-esteemed neighbors.

St. Mary of Bethlehem in London, founded in the 13th century and early devoted to the care of the mentally ill, was, by the 18th century, corrupted into Bedlam and became a generic term for any lunatic asylum. Today the word bedlam still implies a scene of general uproar and confusion, such as was common in early asylums. A pain-relieving mixture containing narcotics and cocaine, first used at London's Brompton Hospital in 1896, is called Brompton cocktail and is widely employed today in the treatment of patients with terminal cancer. Eusol, the name of an antiseptic fluid for wound irrigation, is an acronym for Edinburgh University solution of lime. A liniment composed of linseed oil and lime water, once enormously popular, was called carron oil after the Carron Iron Works in Scotland, where it was a standard treatment for burns.

Dubious distinctions

Medical terms connecting diseases with particular races or countries have often been perceived as ethnic or national slurs, not without some justification. After all, calling pellagra "Italian leprosy" and typhus "Hungarian disease" hardly confers on these countries the kind of recognition they would be expected to appreciate. In Germany, The Netherlands, and Scandinavia, rickets has been styled the English disease, an expression that never appears in the English medical literature or English translations of foreign medical works. Mongolism was an unfortunate choice of term for the genetic aberration now known as Down's syndrome, but it reflected an ignorance of racial differences that was typical in the English-speaking world at the time the term was coined. Somewhat less opprobrious is the expression Siamese twins for conjoined twins. This phrase harks back to Chang and Eng, twins joined by a ligament from the breastbone to the navel, who were born in 1811 in Siam (now Thailand) and were for many years a major attraction in P. T. Barnum's sideshows. It is not known just why rubella ever came to be designated German measles, but during World

The tick-borne infection called Lyme disease is named for Old Lyme, Connecticut, the town where many of the first cases were seen in the mid-1970s. Sometimes such regional eponyms can be misleading, occasionally even interfering with the diagnosis of cases that occur far from the recognized epicenter. Lyme disease has now been identified in at least 43 states, but many people still think of it as a disease confined primarily to the Northeast. These unsuspecting hikers in a national park in California receive instructions on how to prevent tick bites; in recent years significant outbreaks of Lyme disease have occurred on the West Coast in both California and Oregon.

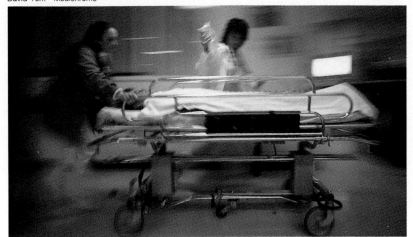

The gurney, the wheeled cot used in hospitals to transport patients, is officially spelled with a lowercase g, pending evidence that it commemorates some doctor, nurse, orderly, or hospital handyman named Gurney.

War I the latter term aroused such consternation and indignation in the U.S. that it was changed temporarily to "liberty measles."

No disease has borne such a variety of national appellations, or engendered such intense animosity thereby, as syphilis. Most modern authorities agree that syphilis was introduced into Europe by Spanish sailors returning from Hispaniola with Christopher Columbus in 1493. A body of Spanish soldiers dispatched to Naples to repel a French invasion carried the infection into Italy. The defeated French army took it back home with them, and from there it quickly spread to the rest of Europe, including England. Each country named the new plague after one of its less-esteemed neighbors (among the Turkish Muslims, it was the Christian disease), but the term French disease—or morbus gallicus—achieved the widest currency and was for centuries a source of embarrassment and annoyance to the French.

The game of the name

The International Anatomical Nomenclature Committee, which has convened every five to ten years since 1950 to standardize and revise anatomic nomenclature, has dealt a severe blow to the practice of eponymy by rigorously excluding personal names from the quasi-official word list of human anatomy. Not that there will ever be a shortage of eponyms in the day-to-day spoken and written language of medicine. Physicians and medical writers will continue to use terms like eustachian tube, malpighian corpuscles, foramen of Monro, islets of Langerhans, and organ of Corti, even though these and all other eponyms have been purged from the *Nomina Anatomica,* the international "bible" of anatomists.

Thousands of medical researchers publish millions of words each year, reporting the discovery or rediscovery of anatomic structures and "new" diseases, instruments, procedures, and treatments. There can be little doubt that the hope of achieving lasting fame eponymically acts as a powerful spur to many of these investigators. Though some modest souls might prefer oblivion, many more would gladly purchase immortality by being the first to describe some unique variety of wart, boil, or malignant growth—perhaps even by being the first to die of it.

117

TOMORROW'S FORECAST:

Hot, with a Chance of Malaria

by Laurence S. Kalkstein, Ph.D.

Laurence S. Kalkstein, Ph.D., *is Professor at the Center for Climatic Research, Department of Geography, University of Delaware, and an Adviser to the U.S. Environmental Protection Agency's Office of Policy Analysis.*

(Opposite page) Carbon dioxide and pollutants spew into the air from an industrial plant in Baltimore, Maryland. Experts fear that changes in the composition of the atmosphere due to human activity may soon lead to an Earth that is both hotter and less protected from the damaging effects of solar radiation. Photograph, Paul Souders—Picture Group

In December 1988 throngs of participants and observers attended an international conference held in Washington, D.C., on the topic of preparing for a change in the Earth's climate. The meeting drew 750 leading scientists involved in research on the effects of a possible global warming and a depletion of stratospheric ozone. About 125 reporters also attended, clearly indicating that the prospect of a major climate change had captured the attention of a concerned public. The reporters did not go home empty-handed. A headline in the *Washington Post* proclaimed, "Disease, Disruption Tied to Global Warming"; the *New York Times* warned, "Ferocious Storms and Droughts Seen"; and the *Philadelphia Inquirer* cautioned, "Ozone-Layer Damage May Be Understated, Experts Warn."

The reason for pessimism was probably well founded. During the three-day conference, experts predicted significant rises in sea level, which would inundate coastal cities; reduced agricultural yields, which would particularly affect North America; the spread of infectious diseases that are now limited to tropical regions; dramatic decreases in water and air quality; and increases in skin cancer and other diseases related to exposure to sunlight. Especially troubling is the time scale of the predictions—within the next 80–100 years—indicating that a global policy to mitigate the effects will have to be in place almost immediately if the potential for catastrophe is to be avoided. Such a task presently appears almost insurmountable, considering that many scientists are in disagreement over the magnitude, or even the existence, of a global climate threat. In addition, international cooperation involving virtually any environmental problem historically has been almost impossible to achieve.

What is causing the celebrated greenhouse effect and the depletion of ozone in the stratosphere? What would be the impact of these perceived atmospheric changes on human health? How many people would die as a result of large-scale climatic change? What policies should be instituted to counter the potential problem? These are the questions vexing medical experts, climatologists, policymakers, and, possibly most important, the general public, who are bombarded with catastrophic and conflicting viewpoints from the media.

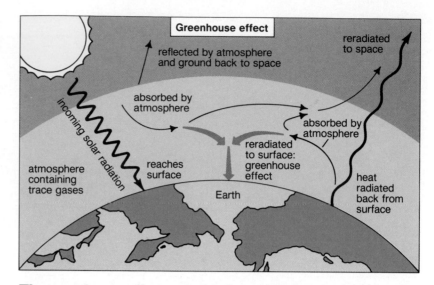

(Above) Adapted from an illustration by Peter Gardiner, *Inside Science*, no. 13, Oct. 22, 1988; © New Scientist, London. (Below) Graph sources: Charles D. Keeling, Scripps Institution of Oceanography and National Oceanic and Atmospheric Administration

The fate of the energy that reaches the Earth from the Sun is traced in the diagram at right. Incoming solar radiation is rich in short-wavelength energy, chiefly visible light and near-infrared radiation. On the way to the surface, it passes through the atmosphere, which contains carbon dioxide (CO_2), water vapor, and other trace gases nearly transparent to the shorter wavelengths; roughly half of the incoming radiation penetrates to the surface, while the rest is reflected back to space or absorbed by the atmosphere. Most of that which reaches the surface is absorbed and then radiated as long-wavelength infrared, or heat, energy. It is this form of energy that the atmospheric trace gases readily absorb and return to the surface (more than 80%), keeping the surface warmer on average than it would be otherwise— the greenhouse effect. The more trace gases there are in the atmosphere, the greater the warming is. (Below) A plot of continuous measurements of atmospheric CO_2 made at a mountaintop observatory in Hawaii shows a rise of nearly 10% between 1960 and 1988. Measurements of atmospheric methane, nitrous oxides, and chlorofluorocarbons around the world likewise reveal recent increases.

The greenhouse effect and global warming

There is little doubt that the greenhouse effect exists and that all life on Earth depends on it. Scientists estimate that in its absence the Earth would be approximately 58° C (104° F) colder than it is. Its name derives from the observation that the Earth's surface and atmosphere, considered as a single system, indeed acts like an enormous greenhouse. Solar radiation, which is rich in short-wavelength energy emitted by a very hot Sun, enters the system through an atmosphere (analogous to the glass of a greenhouse) that is transparent to much of that energy. The same atmosphere is much less transparent to heat energy, which is long-wavelength radiation emitted by a comparatively much cooler Earth, and consequently a significant portion of the heat is trapped within the Earth-atmosphere system. So-called trace gases in the atmosphere, mainly carbon dioxide (CO_2) and water vapor, are responsible for the atmosphere's ability to permit the differential movement of short- and long-wavelength radiation. Thus, temperatures at the Earth's surface average about 16° C (61° F), while stratospheric temperatures (about 32 kilometers [20 miles] above the surface) are an inhospitable −40° C (−40° F), as trace gases are much less prevalent there.

The greatest question surrounding the greenhouse effect involves whether a human-induced change in trace-gas concentration in the atmosphere is sufficient to raise average temperatures and cause large-scale changes in global climate. Measurements indicate that the amount of CO_2 in the atmosphere has increased from about 315 parts per million in the late 1950s to about 350 parts per million in the late 1980s, a rise of more than 10%. Most scientists believe that the rise is due to the burning of fossil fuels (a by-product of burning is CO_2) and deforestation (the burning of trees adds CO_2 to the atmosphere; in addition, fewer trees mean less photosynthesis, which absorbs CO_2 and releases oxygen). It is estimated that if this increase continues, the atmospheric CO_2 concentration will double by the middle of the 21st century, exceeding any values of CO_2 concentrations in at least the last 200,000 years as determined by analyses of air trapped in ice layers cored from the polar caps.

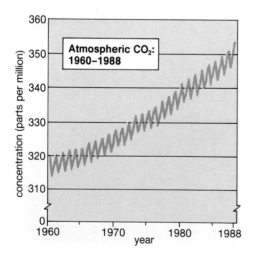

In addition, other trace gases that might influence the greenhouse effect are increasing because of human activities. Chlorofluorocarbons (CFCs), used as refrigerants and in insulating material, aerosols, and sprays, are increasing in the atmosphere at a rate of 5–7% per year. Methane, a gas produced by natural microbiological processes and by such human activities as coal mining, oil production, and cattle raising, has risen about 1.1% per year since 1976. Nitrous oxides, whose sources include biological matter in the oceans, fossil-fuel and forest burning, and agricultural fertilizers, recently have been rising by about 0.3% per year. Taken together, these three gases add about as much to potential global warming as CO_2.

Scientists have been attempting to assess the possible effects of trace-gas increases on climate by developing models of the Earth-atmosphere system that account for changes in atmospheric gas concentrations. These general circulation models (GCMs), however, are only approximations of reality because of scientists' less-than-exact knowledge of the processes involved. Most of the developed GCMs predict that a doubled atmospheric CO_2 concentration will cause mean global temperatures to rise 2° to 4° C (3.6° to 7.2° F). Additionally, the increase will be most pronounced over polar regions, with the most ambitious GCMs estimating a mean temperature rise of as much as 14° C (25.2° F) in some polar regions.

In addition, certain feedback mechanisms that are not well expressed in the GCMs may lead to more rapid warming. For example, as oceans warm, their capacity to hold dissolved CO_2 diminishes, potentially resulting in more atmospheric CO_2. The melting of ice caps and glaciers, which strongly reflect solar radiation, might permit more absorption of radiation at the surface and thus hasten warming. Moreover, polar thawing might speed the decay and release of carbon now held in permafrost.

The endangered ozone layer

Projected depletion of stratospheric ozone poses a second threat to the stability of the Earth's environment. Ozone, a molecule comprising three

A human activity thought to be raising the concentration of atmospheric CO_2 and thereby influencing the greenhouse effect is large-scale deforestation (left), particularly in the tropical countries. Burning of trees adds CO_2 directly to the atmosphere and removes large tracts of plant life, which normally consumes CO_2 in carrying out photosynthesis. Furthermore, deforestation is often a prelude to cattle ranching, a significant source of another atmospheric trace gas—methane—since cattle generate and release hundreds of liters of the gas per day per animal as part of their normal digestive process. Rice paddies (below) are an additional source of methane, which is produced by microorganisms growing in the oxygen-poor mud below the water's surface.

Photographs, (left) Loren McIntyre—Woodfin Camp & Associates; (right) Chuck O'Rear—West Light

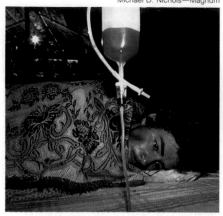

Michael D. Nichols—Magnum

Victims of malaria may become a more common sight in lower-latitude temperate regions like the southern U.S. if global warming occurs. Higher temperature and humidity favor the malarial parasite and its mosquito vector and thus may allow their proliferation in regions whose milder climate now helps suppress the disease.

Researchers have used information on climatic sensitivity of the tsetse fly, the carrier of trypanosomiasis (sleeping sickness), to predict changes in its distribution in sub-Saharan Africa, given the 2° C (3.6° F) temperature increase for the region that is expected from global warming. According to the analysis, tsetse flies may become less common in western Africa and in portions of central Africa, but they may multiply in eastern regions where population densities of humans and domestic animals are high.

ozone-hole skeptics note that during 1988 ozone concentration actually increased over the Antarctic. Whether this single-year increase is an aberration or the sign of a new trend is impossible to determine at present.

In spite of scientists' disagreements, the U.S. Environmental Protection Agency (EPA) is officially proceeding as if global warming and continued ozone depletion do lie ahead. Policies are presently under development to help society adjust to these potential detrimental changes in climate. Determination of the health effects of a possible climate change is but one of the priorities being addressed by the EPA and other national and international agencies.

Present research is concentrating on three anticipated effects of a significantly warmer Earth on human health. First, infectious diseases affecting humans and their livestock should increase in geographic range and intensity. Second, human mortality (number of deaths) should rise substantially, as present-day weather seems to have major effects on day-to-day variations in mortality. Third, the concomitant increase in air pollution on a warmer Earth should increase the frequency of illnesses associated with such pollution.

Spread of infectious diseases

Since the introduction of vaccines and improved nutrition and sanitation, such once-devastating infectious diseases as influenza and tuberculosis are no longer among the leading causes of death in the developed nations. Given the current standard of living, it is unlikely that a climate change will significantly affect this situation. Although these diseases are much more common in the third world, there is little evidence that a warmer Earth will increase their impact in disadvantaged areas.

More threatening are the infectious diseases that are strongly related to variations in temperature and moisture conditions; these diseases are often not affected by immunization or improvements in living conditions. A large majority are vector-borne, in which an infectious agent (typically a bacterium, virus, or parasite) is transmitted to a human or animal host by means of a carrying vector. Typical vectors include such arthropods as

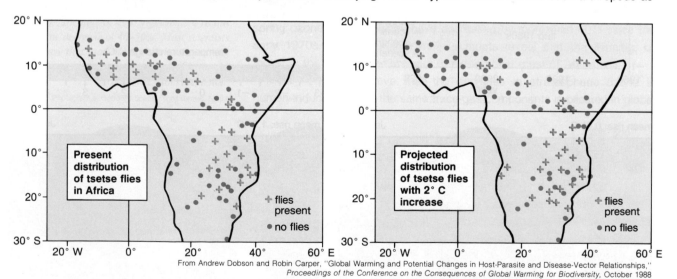

From Andrew Dobson and Robin Carper, "Global Warming and Potential Changes in Host-Parasite and Disease-Vector Relationships," *Proceedings of the Conference on the Consequences of Global Warming for Biodiversity*, October 1988

mosquitoes, ticks, and fleas, which transmit diseases like malaria, dengue fever, trypanosomiasis, and Chagas' disease. Global changes in temperature and moisture may alter the geographic regions in which the vectors and agents of these diseases are able to survive. In the U.S., for example, a warmer climate is likely to allow the northward spread of such afflictions as yellow fever, dengue fever, and Chagas' disease from Central and South America. In many Latin-American countries, the proportion of people afflicted by these diseases approaches 50%, which contrasts sharply with the present 1–3% incidence in the U.S.

It is feared that at least three vector-borne diseases will become particularly troublesome if global warming occurs. One of them, malaria, will likely menace the southern U.S., especially if resistance of mosquitoes to pesticides continues to increase. The infectious agent of malaria is any of four species of parasitic microorganisms of the genus *Plasmodium*. The primary vectors are species of *Anopheles* mosquitoes, some of which are present in the U.S. The malarial parasite requires a temperature of at least 15° C (59° F) to complete its development within the mosquito, while the mosquito vector requires a temperature of at least 16° C (61° F) and prefers a relative humidity above 60%. The parasitic agent develops more quickly with elevated temperatures; at 30° C (86° F) its reproduction rate is more than twice that at 20° C (68° F). Thus, abundance of both the agent and the vector could increase considerably under warmer conditions. Moreover, increased use of irrigation, a prediction of some future climate scenarios for the U.S., has the potential for creating numerous new breeding grounds for mosquitoes. Thus, under certain scenarios much of the southeastern U.S. from Richmond, Virginia, to Nashville, Tennessee, and southward could expect moderate to large increases in cases of malaria.

Trypanosomiasis (sleeping sickness) is a major disease of humans and their domestic animals in Africa. It is of particular importance since its presence may preclude human habitation from areas where wild animals act as a reservoir of the disease. Its agents are various species of parasitic microorganisms of the genus *Trypanosoma*. *Trypanosoma* is transmitted by an insect vector, the tsetse fly, and its spread depends on the fly's range. Research has indicated that mortality rates of the tsetse fly are closely related to humidity and, to a lesser extent, temperature. Information on the climatic sensitivities of the insect has been used to construct a possible distribution, given the mean 2° C (3.6° F) increase in temperature expected for sub-Saharan Africa if global warming occurs. The analysis suggests that tsetse flies may become less common in western Africa and across portions of sub-Saharan central Africa. This decrease, however, may be offset by a spread farther south in portions of eastern Africa having high densities of human and domestic animal populations.

Given a warmer climate, another *Trypanosoma* species may present similar problems in North America. Chagas' disease, caused by the blood-borne protozoan *Trypanosoma cruzi,* exists throughout much of Central and South America, where it exacts a high toll in sickness and death. The range of the agent is constrained by the distribution of the vector, the assassin bug, which cannot tolerate cold temperatures. The disease is transmitted to

Swollen joints caused by Lyme disease afflict the dairy cow above, one of a Wisconsin herd struck hard by the bacterial infection. A serious problem for livestock and domestic pets as well as humans, Lyme disease is transmitted by a tick, and fears have been voiced that climatic warming may encourage the spread of the vector in the populated mid-latitudes.

125

Still barren debris deposited at the foot of an Alaskan glacier offers evidence of recent glacial retreat caused by global warming. Should the trend continue, melting glaciers and polar ice caps coupled with thermal expansion of the ocean could raise sea levels high enough to flood large areas of coastal land now heavily populated or devoted to farming. On a worldwide scale such changes would strongly influence the numbers of deaths and illnesses related to malnutrition and poor sanitation.

less dramatic but still rather pessimistic—an average of 345 weather-induced deaths per season in New York City and nearly 5,000 deaths for the 15-city total.

Higher levels of air pollution

Current research suggests that global warming may increase the atmospheric concentrations of certain pollutants. Smog chamber studies have shown that oxidants in the lower atmosphere tend to rise with temperature. These oxidants generate ozone, which at ground level is considered a pollutant because it can irritate the eyes and worsen respiratory problems. In addition, warmer temperatures can speed the formation of sulfur dioxide (SO_2) and acidic materials, particularly sulfurous and sulfuric acid. Stagnating atmospheric conditions are yet another cause for concern. Some GCMs employed for future climate predictions indicate that stationary cells of high pressure, which contribute to warm, humid conditions and poor atmospheric ventilation, will be more frequent and remain intact longer. The inefficient dispersal of smoke particles and noxious gases that would result could significantly lower atmospheric quality, especially in the summer. It seems likely that global warming will create a more polluted environment, which in turn will increase the incidence of respiratory and other illnesses.

An EPA draft report to the U.S. Congress on global warming, issued in March 1989, suggested that deaths from lung cancer, emphysema, chronic bronchitis, and asthma will rise significantly within 100 years if air pollution

128

concentrations increase as predicted. In addition, evidence exists that increased air pollution affects much more than respiratory illnesses. Recent studies on mortality in London suggest that deaths from all nontraumatic causes increase as suspended-particle and SO_2 concentrations rise.

Further health effects of global warming

Other environmental changes expected from global warming may have significant effects on human health and thus complicate the already difficult task of making realistic predictions. For example, thermal expansion of the ocean and melting polar ice caps and glaciers may raise the level of the world's oceans by 0.5–1.5 meters (one meter is approximately 3.3 feet), inundating large areas of low-lying land that is now densely populated or devoted to agriculture. Certain third world nations such as Bangladesh would be particularly hard hit by as little as a half-meter rise in sea level. Millions of Bangladeshi live near the mouth of the Ganges River at elevations of just a few meters; slight sea-level alterations could flood nearly a fifth of the country's habitable land with salt water, displacing a large proportion of the population inland and wiping out huge tracts of farmland. Such changes, particularly if considered on a worldwide scale, would have a powerful influence on the number of deaths and illnesses related to malnutrition and lack of sanitation.

The effect of climate change on agricultural productivity is yet another potentially serious and complicating factor. Predicted temperature increases are not necessarily associated with concomitant increases in precipitation, raising the possibility of more frequent, and more severe, droughts for some farmlands. The corn belt of the midwestern U.S. appears particularly vulnerable, and a change in summer temperatures of only a few degrees might shift it into the Prairie Provinces of Canada. Some scientists predict that surplus grain supplies in North America (and thus exports to third world and Communist bloc nations) would vanish, adding nutritional stresses to areas that do not possess an agricultural base to support the population.

The vulnerability of human health and livelihood to potential climate change was demonstrated by extreme weather conditions in 1988, which brought intense drought to many U.S. farmlands (left) and triggered extensive flooding in low-lying areas of Bangladesh (below). Whether these disasters were related to a greenhouse-induced warming was unclear, but they served to focus international attention on the implications of a hotter Earth.

Photographs, (left) Jim Richardson—West Light; (right) Chip Hires—Gamma/Liaison

in rabbits by exposure to ultraviolet radiation. The retina is particularly sensitive to damage from UVB. Two recent studies have raised the possibility that ocular melanoma, a relatively rare but serious cancer, is related to sunlight exposure.

As with global warming, assessing the health effects of ozone depletion and a consequent increase in UV exposure is a risky business fraught with uncertainty. The Environmental Defense Fund, nevertheless, has ventured some dire predictions about increases in skin cancer in the U.S. if ozone depletion continues. Even if global CFC emissions are constrained to 1980 levels, the erosion of stratospheric ozone could result in 141,900 new cases of skin cancer annually by the year 2025. Alternately, if CFC emissions continue to increase at their present rate, then by 2075 the annual number of new cases of UV-induced skin cancer could reach 256,400. Put another way, a total of 1,660,000 skin-cancer cases could be prevented in the next 35 years if CFC emissions were stabilized at 1980 levels.

Although it is difficult to quantify increases in eye damage and in infectious diseases attributed to a breakdown in the immune functions of the skin, the outlook does not seem good. That some groups of people appear very vulnerable to even slight increases in exposure to UVB and that protective clothing seems impractical in many of the hot, tropical, infectious-disease-prone agricultural regions of the world underscores the need for immediate action to limit ozone loss.

Need for a global awakening

An enormous amount of research to anticipate and reverse the possible effects of global warming and ozone depletion has been initiated. Also under way are attempts to develop national and international consensuses on how best to attack the problems. The recent Montreal Protocol, signed by a number of nations and in effect as of Jan. 1, 1989, set quotas for the signatories on the manufacture and consumption of CFCs to 1986 levels. Further reductions are required under the protocol for 1993 and 1998. A recent action by the Du Pont Co. to remove CFCs from all of its products

may set the stage for other major industries to do the same. In March 1989, at a conference on the ozone layer, the European Communities proposed a total ban on CFCs by the end of the century. Four months later in Paris, the seven participants of an economic summit—the U.S., Japan, West Germany, France, the U.K., Italy, and Canada—devoted a third of their final communiqué to the environment, calling for "decisive action" to protect the global ecological balance. Among the specific topics addressed were climate change, limiting of trace-gas emissions, reversing of deforestation, and development of substitutes for CFCs and other ozone-destroying gases.

The March 1989 draft report by the EPA on global warming resulted from a congressional request in 1986 for the agency to present policy choices designed to stabilize critical trace-gas concentrations in the atmosphere. The EPA's plan for reduction calls for radical steps by the year 2000, including highly fuel-efficient cars and homes that cut present energy consumption by 90%. It also urges governments to raise fossil-fuel prices, limit CFC production, halt deforestation, and replant trees on a large scale.

Implementation, however, is usually a much more difficult matter. Past history has shown that the public will not reduce consumption unless there are severe shortages in energy or raw materials. This is clearly illustrated in the readoption of energy-wasting practices by Western society since the "oil crunch" of the 1970s ended. Today, with people once again allowed to make wider decisions about life-style, they are driving bigger automobiles, raising speed limits, and burning more fuel with disregard to conservation issues or environmental degradation.

The chances for further international cooperation on these issues also seem bleak at present. International agreements involving conservation and energy topics have been few and far between, and implementation of the agreements is even less common. Yet, as the EPA report stresses, all nations must become involved if climate change is to be effectively limited. The necessity for an integrated approach to solving the world's environmental problems has never seemed clearer.

Richard M. Glass, M.D., is Associate Professor of Psychiatry at the University of Chicago.

(Overleaf) Photograph, "Guaranteed Winner," Las Vegas © 1987 Jay Wolke

Three meanings of "compulsive"

One source of confusion about the term compulsive is that it is used to describe three kinds of behaviors that are only partially overlapping. Adding to the confusion is the fact that each of these phenomena can occur in a range of severity stretching from normal to clearly abnormal.

True compulsions, one of the hallmarks of obsessive compulsive disorder, are defined as follows in the most recent edition (1987) of the American Psychiatric Association's *Diagnostic and Statistical Manual of Mental Disorders,* known as *DSM-III-R:*

Compulsions are repetitive, purposeful, and intentional behaviors that are performed in response to an obsession, according to certain rules, or in a stereotyped fashion. The behavior is designed to neutralize or to prevent discomfort or some dreaded event or situation. However, either the activity is not connected in a realistic way with what it is designed to neutralize or prevent, or it is clearly excessive. The act is performed with a sense of subjective compulsion that is coupled with a desire to resist the compulsion (at least initially). The person recognizes that his or her behavior is excessive or unreasonable (this may not be true for young children and may no longer be true for people whose obsessions have evolved into overvalued ideas) and does not derive pleasure from carrying out the activity, although it provides a release of tension. The most common compulsions involve hand-washing, counting, checking, and touching.

In the 1st century AD, the Apostle Paul delineated a universal human experience when he described his own self-defeating impulse—a compulsion to do things he knew quite well were not really in his best interest (Romans 7:15–17).

Alinari/Art Resource

Defined in this way, true compulsions are to be distinguished from normal, often rational and adaptive rituals, such as routinely checking to make sure the car doors are locked.

A second use of "compulsive" is to describe certain behaviors that, like true compulsions, are excessive and maladaptive but, unlike true compulsions, are engaged in for pleasure, excitement, or escape. Examples are compulsive gambling, compulsive drug use, and compulsive sexual behavior. Rather than being incorporated into the activity itself, the struggle against such behaviors is usually due to their adverse consequences.

Finally, "compulsive" is used to describe a cluster of personality traits including perfectionism, orderliness, preoccupation with details, and conscientiousness. Adding to the terminological confusion is the fact that pervasive and extreme degrees of these traits constitute obsessive compulsive *personality* disorder, which must be distinguished from obsessive compulsive disorder.

The *DSM-III-R* defines obsessive compulsive personality disorder as "a pervasive pattern of perfectionism and inflexibility" that begins by early adulthood. Further, at least five of the following nine criteria must be present: (1) perfectionism that interferes with task completion; (2) preoccupation with details, rules, lists, order, organization, or schedules to the extent that the major point of the activity is lost; (3) unreasonable insistence that others submit to exactly one's way of doing things or unreasonable reluctance to allow others to do things; (4) excessive devotion to work and productivity to the exclusion of leisure activities and friendships (not accounted for by obvious economic necessity); (5) indecisiveness—decision making is avoided, postponed, or protracted, owing to excessive ruminating about priorities; (6) overconscientiousness, scrupulousness, and inflexibility about matters of morality, ethics, or values that are not accounted for by cultural or religious identification; (7) restricted expression of affection; (8) lack of generosity in giving time, money, or gifts when no personal gain is likely to result; and (9) inability to discard worn-out or worthless objects even when they have no sentimental value.

With compulsive personality traits, the range from normal to abnormal is particularly important to emphasize since having compulsive traits is, to a certain extent, not only normal but highly adaptive. The degree of compulsiveness, then, is the key. The relationship between the degree of compulsive personality traits and the effectiveness of an individual's performance appears to have the following pattern: at very low levels, carelessness and low standards usually lead to poor outcomes; with increasing degrees of compulsiveness, an optimal level is reached where effort, conscientiousness, and high standards tend to lead to good results. As compulsive traits become more extreme, however, performance tends to deteriorate as perfectionism, indecision, and preoccupation with details begin to interfere with getting a job done. As far as the personality trait of compulsiveness goes, some activities and even professions *require* a moderate degree of such perfectionist behavior for successful accomplishment. Most people, for example, would want their doctor to have some compulsive traits in order to properly and thoroughly evaluate abnormalities in a physical examination. Certainly one would want one's accountant to exhibit compulsiveness in identifying unbalanced financial statements; one would not want an accountant who did *not* worry about misplacing a few numbers.

If, however, the compulsive personality traits are too extreme and inflexible, an obsessive compulsive personality disorder may be present, and that usually has adverse effects on both occupational functioning and personal relationships. In addition to the diagnostic personality traits cited above, persons with obsessive compulsive personality disorder typically have great difficulty expressing emotions—especially tender feelings. They also have a strong need to be in control of situations, so even simple conversations with them begin to feel like struggles.

It must be emphasized that as a personality trait, compulsiveness is pervasive, affecting almost all of the individual's functioning. Furthermore, personality traits endure throughout the person's life history, usually becoming apparent in childhood, certainly by adolescence, and persisting throughout adulthood. Changes in personality traits, whether from treatment or from life experiences, are usually gradual and modest. This contrasts sharply with the true compulsions of persons with OCD. Although their severity may devastate the individual's life, true compulsions are limited to a specific activity (usually washing, counting, or checking), may not start until adulthood, and sometimes completely cease, either through treatment or spontaneously. Thus, the time course and pervasiveness of true compulsions are also quite different from compulsive personality traits. In fact, the majority of persons with OCD are not particularly compulsive in areas of their lives outside their specific obsessive or compulsive activities.

In summary, one must be careful to distinguish the three different meanings of the term compulsive: the true compulsions of OCD, the obsessive

Keeping track of one's money may be a reasonable and purposeful pursuit, but it crosses the bounds of normality if counting it and recounting it become a full-time occupation.

While it is quite normal to check that doors are locked, one can also carry concern about personal security to a pathological extreme.

137

Table 1: **Features of obsessive compulsive disorder**

Obsessions: repetitive, persistent, distressing thoughts, images, or impulses that are recognized as senseless and are resisted yet continue to recur

typical obsessions
- thoughts of violence (*e.g.,* killing one's child)
- contamination (*e.g.,* becoming infected from doorknobs)
- doubts (*e.g.,* persistent concerns about having hit someone while driving although no apparent accident occurred)

Compulsions: repetitive, purposeful, intentional behaviors that are recognized as unreasonable and resisted (at least initially) and yet are performed with a subjective sense of necessity

typical compulsions
- touching
- excessive washing
- counting
- hoarding
- checking

Recurrent obsessions or compulsions that are extreme enough to cause marked distress, that consume a great amount of time, or that interfere with normal routines, occupational functioning, or personal relationships are the hallmark of obsessive compulsive disorder. (Below) Fear of contamination—e.g., exposure to germs on doorknobs—is a typical obsession, *and incessant checking to see that the gas is off—never being able to trust one's own senses or sureness— is a common* compulsion. *The need for fastidious order is another compulsion that a person may manifest by constantly aligning objects, seeking perfect symmetry.*

The most famous hand-washing case in literature, that of Shakespeare's Lady Macbeth, illustrates the point that other possible causes of obsessive thoughts and ritualistic behaviors must be ruled out before a diagnosis of OCD can be made. At least while sleepwalking, Lady Macbeth had a delusional belief that her hands were bloody, which then led to her hand-washing motions. Although complete diagnostic information is lacking, from the context of *Macbeth,* the hand-washing could be taken as a manifestation of a major depression with psychotic features, triggered by her increasing guilt about persuading Macbeth to murder the king of Scotland. Her subsequent apparent suicide would also fit with the diagnosis of a psychotic depression, as suicide in such cases is not uncommon.

Common and treatable. As previously noted, two recent developments have increased interest in OCD. First, the disorder had been thought of as uncommon, but a recently reported large-scale survey conducted in the United States of the prevalence of psychiatric disorders in the general population found that the lifetime prevalence of OCD, excluding the presence of other disorders that might account for similar symptoms, was 1.7%. In other words, about 3 out of every 200 people in the U.S. may have OCD in their lifetime. Although the methods of sampling and diagnosis in this survey were very careful, some questions have been raised about whether

  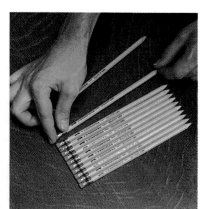

Photographs, (left) Barbara Whitney; (center and right) Cathy Melloan

this high rate of obsessive compulsive symptoms could really reflect the severe, sometimes incapacitating disorder seen much less frequently by clinicians. Nevertheless, it seems clear that OCD, at least in milder forms that are often kept secret from even family and friends, is much more common than had been previously assumed.

Second, two very different forms of treatment have been demonstrated to be effective for many patients with OCD. One of these, behavior therapy, based on a careful analysis of the behaviors themselves and also the antecedents and consequences of the behaviors, includes a variety of methods designed to modify maladaptive behavior patterns. It is usually much more difficult to modify thoughts than overt actions by means of such techniques, so behavior therapy is generally more appropriate for compulsions than for obsessions. However, a technique known as aversive conditioning—for example, having the patient snap a rubber band on his or her wrist after every obsessive thought—is sometimes helpful for obsessions.

For compulsions a process called "exposure with response prevention" is usually employed. This involves having a patient exposed to graduated doses of whatever cues typically lead to the compulsion while preventing the compulsive action from being carried out; e.g., a patient with a washing compulsion might agree to have his hands repeatedly exposed to dirt without washing them for progressively longer periods of time. While such techniques sound simple, they require careful individual assessment before being applied and depend on a great deal of cooperation from the patient.

The second new therapy is drug treatment with clomipramine (Anafranil). This is a drug that has been available as an antidepressant in many countries outside the United States for a number of years. Although its chemical structure and its effects as an antidepressant are quite similar to those of other antidepressants available in the U.S., e.g., desipramine (Norpramin, Pertofrane) and imipramine (Tofranil), several controlled research trials have shown that clomipramine is unique in its effectiveness for OCD. This may be because it has predominant effects on the neurotransmitter

One of the treatments that now appear to be helpful for many patients with OCD is with clomipramine, a drug that has been available as an antidepressant in Europe and currently has "treatment investigational new drug" status in the U.S. Although its chemical structure is similar to that of other antidepressants of the tricyclic family (see below), clomipramine appears to be unique in its ability to relieve obsessive and compulsive symptoms. Clomipramine and the tricyclic desipramine were given to two groups of OCD patients in a study at the National Institute of Mental Health. For one week patients took no drugs. Then, after two weeks in which both groups received a placebo (an inert substance), one group took clomipramine for five weeks and the other group took desipramine. The groups then "crossed over"—the members of each group taking the drug the other group had taken for another five-week period. The results, shown in the graph below, were dramatic: patients who took clomipramine first improved but then relapsed; those who took desipramine first began to improve only after receiving the second drug. (The global OCD score is a general rating of the severity of an individual patient's disorder—at 10 a symptom, such as hand-washing, is at its most severe; at 0 the symptom is virtually absent.)

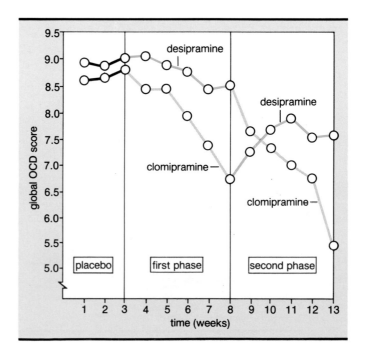

The three-dimensional view of a human brain below shows the neuroanatomy of basal ganglia. The basal ganglia, which are connected to the frontal lobe by a number of pathways, consist of several structures that lie under the cerebral cortex. The aberrations that can occur in this brain circuitry may underlie the symptoms of OCD.

serotonin, which has been implicated in the biology of OCD. Clomipramine was recently made available in the U.S. as a "treatment investigational new drug" for use by physicians who meet requirements established by the Food and Drug Administration; it may be more widely available in a few years.

Research trials indicate that about 70% of OCD patients receive at least some benefit from the drug—usually a gradual reduction of the intensity of obsessions and compulsions, with some fortunate patients becoming almost free of symptoms. The side effects of clomipramine are typical of all the tricyclic antidepressants: dry mouth, drowsiness, dizziness, excessive sweating, and tremor. Impotence and delayed ejaculation can sometimes occur in men; in fact, clomipramine has been tested as a treatment for premature ejaculation. The severity of side effects varies considerably among different individuals. As is true of most drug treatments, weighing the balance between benefits and unwanted side effects is often an important issue for a doctor and patient to consider carefully. Another drug, fluoxetine (Prozac), is a recently marketed antidepressant that is now being tested for OCD, as it also has prominent serotonin effects.

A biology of compulsions. Until recently psychological theories about OCD were dominant. Although Sigmund Freud considered the possibility of biological causes, subsequent psychoanalysts stressed psychodynamic theories. Compulsions about dirt, cleanliness, and order were seen as reflecting developmental problems during the "anal" phase of childhood psychosexual development. Furthermore, obsessions and compulsions, like other "neurotic" symptoms, were viewed as symbolic expressions of unconscious forbidden wishes. Despite the intuitive appeal of such theories, systematic studies did not find a history of unusual problems in toilet training among OCD patients, and psychotherapy designed to unravel the unconscious conflicts, although helpful for other psychological problems, usually did not prove beneficial for obsessions and compulsions.

Now a growing body of evidence is suggesting a biological basis for OCD. One important observation has been that obsessions and compul-

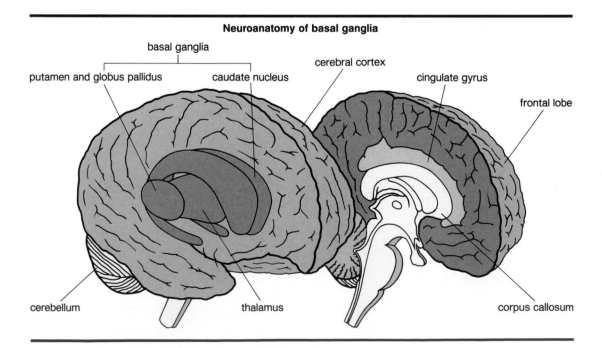

Neuroanatomy of basal ganglia

basal ganglia

putamen and globus pallidus   caudate nucleus   cerebral cortex   cingulate gyrus   frontal lobe

cerebellum   thalamus   corpus callosum

sions share many features of tics, which are clearly neurological symptoms consisting of recurrent, nonrhythmic, stereotyped motor movements or vocalizations. Like tics, obsessions and compulsions are involuntary and experienced as irresistible but can be suppressed for varying lengths of time. (The subjective experience of a tic is similar to that associated with a sneeze or cough.) The connection of obsessions and compulsions with tics is supported by the observations that many OCD patients have mild motor tics and that about one-third of patients with Tourette's syndrome, which is characterized by the childhood onset of multiple motor and vocal tics, have obsessions and compulsions. Furthermore, OCD and Tourette's syndrome tend to occur in the same families.

Second, some specific lesions of the brain, such as those that occur in certain forms of encephalitis, can cause typical OCD. Other specific brain lesions, such as surgical prefrontal lobotomy, can relieve obsessions and compulsions. (Lobotomy, however, can also lead to severe personality changes and therefore has largely been abandoned as a treatment for OCD.)

Third, there is indirect evidence that aberrations of the brain neurotransmitter serotonin are involved in OCD. As previously noted, drugs that affect serotonin neurons seem to be uniquely effective with OCD. Furthermore, investigators at the National Institute of Mental Health have recently found that a synthetic drug that mimics the effects of serotonin produces a marked worsening of OCD symptoms, suggesting that OCD patients may be "supersensitive" to serotonin effects.

Finally, new brain-imaging techniques, including positron emission tomography (PET) scans, have shown abnormalities of parts of the frontal lobes and a brain area called the basal ganglia in patients with OCD. Significantly, serotonin neurons are present in the basal ganglia. Rapoport has noted the similarity of compulsions to such instinctual animal behaviors as grooming, licking, and hoarding and has suggested that the basal ganglia may be the site of a "biology of knowing," which, when deranged in OCD, releases primitive behavior patterns and obsessions that higher centers of the hu-

Because obsessions and compulsions appear to have many features in common with tics, which are recurrent nonrhythmic motor movements of neurological origin, many psychiatrists now see OCD as having a biological basis. This has been supported by the fact that approximately one-third of patients with the rare neurological disorder Tourette's syndrome have obsessions and compulsions, and OCD and Tourette's syndrome often occur in the same families. (Above) People with Tourette's syndrome are subject to sudden, involuntary motions and utterances—e.g., jerks, grimaces, twitches, and curses.

Positron emission tomography (PET) scans have shown abnormalities in an area of the frontal lobe and in the pathway connecting the frontal lobe and the basal ganglia in the brains of patients with OCD. The PET scans at left reveal metabolic differences in the brains of a control subject (top) and in a patient with OCD (bottom). Red indicates the highest level of metabolic activity and blue the lowest.

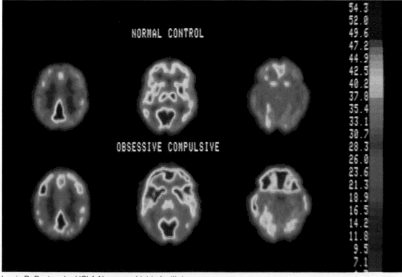

OCD is classified as an anxiety disorder that is "ego-dystonic"—it is experienced as something unpleasant and to be resisted. Pathological gambling, however, is classified as an impulse control disorder that is "ego-syntonic"—the activity is consonant with the gambler's conscious wishes, and at the time it is carried out, it is experienced as both pleasurable and gratifying.

man brain recognize as senseless yet cannot control. Presumably, effective drug treatment corrects those abnormal biological functions, while behavior therapy provides a gradual "deconditioning" of the biologically based behavior patterns.

Against the odds: the realities of pathological gambling

Because of the high levels of anxiety associated with true obsessions and compulsions, OCD is classified as an "anxiety disorder" in *DSM-III-R*. As specified previously, obsessive compulsive personality disorder is a "personality disorder." The next example that will be considered is the ultimately self-destructive "compulsive" behavior that occurs in pathological gambling (PG), which is classified as an "impulse control disorder." A key distinction from OCD is that while true obsessions and true compulsions

Kleptomania, the recurrent impulse to steal items that one does not need, is another impulse control disorder. The kleptomaniac derives a sense of pleasure or relief at the time of the theft.

Photograph, Jean-Loup Charmet, Paris

are "ego-dystonic," *i.e.,* experienced as an unpleasant "foreign body" to be resisted, the activities of the impulse control disorders are "ego-syntonic." This means they are consonant with the individual's conscious wishes and are experienced as pleasurable and gratifying at the time of the activity, even though their negative consequences may subsequently produce regret and guilt. Two of the other disorders that *DSM-III-R* classifies with pathological gambling as impulse control disorders "not elsewhere classified"—kleptomania and pyromania—clearly fit this characteristic. In kleptomania there are recurrent impulses to steal objects not needed for personal use or monetary gain, with a sense of pleasure or relief at the time of the theft. In pyromania there is pleasure in recurrent fire setting, which is not done for monetary gain, revenge, or in response to a delusion or hallucination. The appropriateness of including two other conditions classified in *DSM-III-R* as impulse control disorders is less certain. Trichotillomania involves what appears to be a true compulsion to pull out one's own hair and thus may be a particular form of OCD. Intermittent explosive disorder is a controversial diagnostic category described as involving discrete episodes of loss of control of aggressive impulses resulting in serious assaultive acts or destruction of property. Some psychiatrists question the validity of this diagnosis as a separate category, and it is also not clear that sudden violent outbursts are gratifying or pleasurable in the same sense as the actions of the other impulse control disorders.

The diagnosis of PG. The *DSM-III-R* criteria for PG require at least four of the following: (1) frequent preoccupation with gambling or with obtaining money to gamble; (2) frequent gambling of larger amounts of money or over a longer period of time than intended; (3) a need to increase the size or frequency of bets to achieve the desired excitement; (4) restlessness or irritability if unable to gamble; (5) repeated loss of money by gambling and returning another day to win back losses ("chasing"); (6) repeated efforts to reduce or stop gambling; (7) frequent gambling when expected to meet social or occupational obligations; (8) sacrifice of some important social, occupational, or recreational activity in order to gamble; and (9) continuation of gambling despite inability to pay mounting debts or despite other significant social, occupational, or legal problems that the person knows to be exacerbated by gambling.

Pathological gambling's distinctions from obsessive compulsive disorder are clear and important, but there are also some interesting parallels. Both have normal counterparts—the ordinary rituals of everyday life for OCD and controllable social gambling for PG. Both have recently been found to be considerably more common than previously suspected—recent estimates place the prevalence of PG at a rather astounding 2 to 3% of the adult population of the U.S. As mentioned above, OCD has affected famous persons; so, too, has PG—*e.g.,* Russian writer Fyodor Dostoyevsky wrote a short novel called *The Gambler* that was based on his own personal pursuit of gambling.

PG-alcoholism parallels. Parallels between PG and what *DSM-III-R* classifies as "substance abuse disorders" are even more striking. The addictive quality of PG is quite clear. There is tolerance (the need for increasingly

Trichotillomania, an irresistible urge to pull out one's own hair (eyebrows and eyelashes as well as head hair), is classified in the American Psychiatric Association's Diagnostic and Statistical Manual of Mental Disorders (DSM-III-R) *as an impulse control disorder, but evidence now suggests that it may have more in common with obsessive compulsive disorder (an anxiety disorder). Results of recent drug trials have shown that clomipramine, the same drug that has been so effective in treatment trials for OCD, appears to be similarly effective in the management of trichotillomania. (Again, another antidepressant—the drug desipramine—was not effective.) With clomipramine, patients reported that they were better able to resist the urge to tear out their hair and also that the urge itself decreased in intensity. Trichotillomania is surprisingly common. It has been estimated that two million to eight million Americans—virtually all of them women—may be afflicted. While in some patients the problem is relatively mild, others are tormented by the disorder, which may start just after puberty and last throughout their lives; they must incessantly struggle against the compulsion to do something that is both painful and mutilating.*

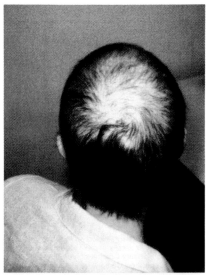

Judith L. Rapoport, National Institute of Mental Health

145

The natural history of pathological gambling is remarkably similar to that of alcoholism. Both disorders involve progressive loss of control and increasingly adverse consequences from activities that do not have notably deleterious effects if engaged in in moderation. Psychiatrist Robert L. Custer has described a progression of pathological gambling with three descending phases—from winning to losing to desperation. Once the gambler "hits bottom," there is a way out; recovery has also been delineated by Custer in three progressive phases. The most successful treatment programs for gamblers have been modeled on alcoholism treatment. A 12-step, self-help Gamblers Anonymous program, based on the well-established Alcoholics Anonymous approach, was begun in 1957. There are now some 600 GA groups in the U.S., and there are also two related organizations with many groups—GamAnon for family members and GamAteen for children and teenagers of pathological gamblers. A crucial step to recovery in both alcoholism and pathological gambling is the acceptance that abstinence is essential.

Illustration source: Robert L. Custer

genetically determined biological vulnerability that presumably interacts with psychosocial factors to lead to the disorder. There is also some evidence that PG tends to run in families (which is often true with alcoholism), suggesting at least the possibility of a genetic component.

Investigators at the National Institute on Alcohol Abuse and Alcoholism have recently reported on an extensive biological study of a group of 24 carefully diagnosed patients with PG. They found that the pathological gamblers had significantly higher urinary output of the neurotransmitter norepinephrine than normal control subjects, as well as higher levels of MHPG, a norepinephrine metabolite, in their cerebrospinal fluid. One impetus for this study was that several previous studies had found low levels of cerebrospinal fluid 5-HIAA, a serotonin metabolite, in persons who had engaged in impulsive violent acts. The investigators hypothesized that PG, as a different type of impulse control disorder, might also be associated with this abnormality in serotonin metabolism. Instead, they found evidence of possible malfunction of the norepinephrine system, which has previously been suggested as the biological substrate of sensation-seeking and risk-taking behavior—important components of PG. This finding must be interpreted cautiously; it has yet to be replicated or shown to be specific to PG. Furthermore, an abnormality in norepinephrine functioning could be a *consequence* of PG rather than a cause of it.

It is also notable that the search for possible biological bases for compulsive drug abuse has not led to definitive results. Although it is possible that a specific biological vulnerability will eventually be established for PG and compulsive drug use, it is likely that important roles for psychological, behavioral, and social factors in the development of those disorders will also be confirmed.

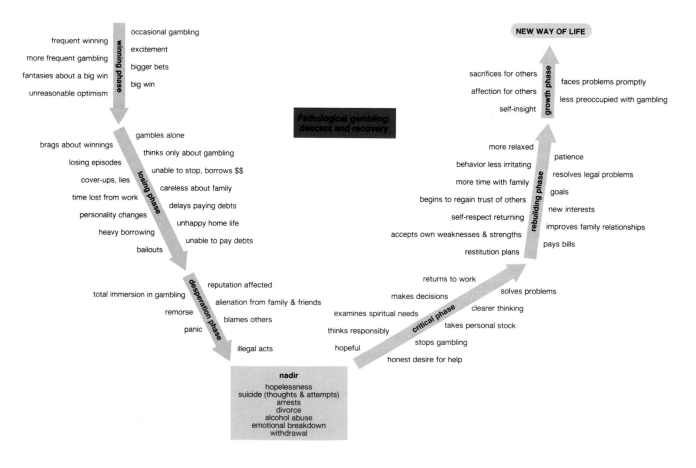

The causes of pathological gambling are unknown. Some interesting investigations currently under way are looking into the possibility that it has biological origins. Whether or not such a basis is established, it is likely that important roles for specific psychological, behavioral, and social factors will be further delineated and that ultimately there will be not only better understanding of the disorder but better means of preventing and treating it.

FOR FURTHER INFORMATION:
Diagnostic and Statistical Manual of Mental Disorders, 3rd Edition, Revised. American Psychiatric Association, Washington, D.C., 1987.

Obsessive compulsive disorder:

Karno, M., *et al.* "The Epidemiology of Obsessive-Compulsive Disorder in Five U.S. Communities," *Archives of General Psychiatry,* vol. 45 (December 1988, pp. 1094–99).
Rapoport, Judith L. *The Boy Who Couldn't Stop Washing.* New York: E. P. Dutton, 1989.

Obsessive Compulsive Foundation, Inc.
P.O. Box 9573
New Haven, CT 06535
1-203-772-0565

Anafranil (clomipramine) Treatment Program
c/o CIBA-GEIGY Pharmaceutical Co.
556 Morris Avenue
Summit, NJ 07901
1–800–842–2422

Pathological gambling:

Custer, Robert L., and Milt, Harry. *When Luck Runs Out: Help for Compulsive Gamblers and Their Families.* New York: Facts on File Publications, 1985.
Lesieur, Henry R. *Understanding Compulsive Gambling.* Center City, Minnesota: Hazeldon Educational Materials, 1986.
Roy, A., *et al.* "Pathological Gambling: A Psychobiological Study," *Archives of General Psychiatry*, vol. 45 (April 1988, pp. 369–373).

Gamblers Anonymous International Service Office
P.O. Box 17173
Los Angeles, CA 90017
1–213–386–8789

On the Job in JAPAN

by Howard Frumkin, M.D., M.P.H.

Over the past century, and especially since the end of World War II, the rapid development of Japanese industry has stunned the rest of the world. Many nations, East and West, now look to Japan as a model for economic growth and management techniques. The "typical" Japanese worker, at least as pictured in Western minds, has a kind of job security undreamed of in Europe and the United States, and the worker, in return, rewards the company with a fierce loyalty beyond the imagination of most Western observers. Problems regarding working conditions are generally solved peacefully, through consensus, and the relationship of labor and management is amicable.

This view of life and work in Japan is more a stereotype than a reality; it is a rule to which there are many exceptions. To get a more accurate picture, it is necessary to examine some specific aspects of Japanese social and economic history. While the safeguarding of worker safety and health has been and continues to be a high priority, industrialization has not been achieved without some cost to Japanese workers in terms of illness and injury.

In the late 19th century, progressive-minded Japanese coined an expression for their approach to modernization: *wakon yosai,* which means "Japanese spirit, Western techniques." Thus, while learning and borrowing prodigiously from the West, Japan retained its unique cultural values. These values have shaped the Japanese way of viewing and responding to issues of occupational health and safety. In some ways the Japanese approach has been quite effective in addressing these issues. In other respects certain ingrained traditions are responsible for the failure to remedy problems faced by some segments of the Japanese work force.

From isolation to modernization

The history of modern Japan began officially with the coronation of the emperor Meiji in 1868, an event known as the Meiji Restoration. The feudal regime of the Tokugawa shogunate was dismantled, thus ending a period of more than two centuries of isolation from the rest of the world. Japan

Howard Frumkin, M.D., M.P.H., *is Assistant Professor of Medicine at the University of Pennsylvania School of Medicine, Philadelphia.*

(Opposite page) Assembly line, Mazda Motor Corp.; photograph, Nik Wheeler— Black Star

150

In 1853 Commodore Matthew C. Perry arrived in Japan as an official emissary of U.S. Pres. Millard Filmore. Perry's mission was to establish diplomatic and trade relations with the reluctant officials of the Tokugawa shogunate, a feudal regime that had ruled Japan in splendid isolation for more than two centuries. The Japan that Perry landed in had not even begun to enter the modern era; the economy was almost entirely agrarian, and the countryside was dominated by local war lords, each supported by his own army of samurai. The lithograph above, first published in 1856 in Perry's official report to the U.S. Congress, shows his meeting with the Japanese imperial commissioners at Yokohama.

at this time was much like medieval Europe. It was an agrarian society ruled by feudal lords (daimyo), whose domains were protected by their own armies of samurai; more than 80% of the Japanese people were rural peasants. In 1853 Commodore Matthew Perry had arrived, demanding that Japan establish relations with the United States. Five years later Tokugawa officials concluded a commercial treaty with the United States; ten years later still, a group of Western-minded reformers gained control of the government, ushering in the Meiji era.

Modernization was a top priority of the Meiji government. An economic superstructure was rapidly developed; before long, railroads, ports, roadways, shipyards, telegraph lines, mines, and a banking system were in place. The existing silk industry was greatly expanded, and a cotton textile industry was quickly established. By 1913 Japan was producing a third of the world's raw silk and exporting a quarter of its cotton yarn.

Most of the workers in these early industries were poorly paid peasants who migrated from rural areas to the growing factory districts of such cities as Tokyo, Osaka, and Nagoya. Many of the problems of rural life—including malnutrition, poor hygiene, and rampant tuberculosis—were compounded in the city by crowding, lack of sanitation, industrial accidents, and occupational exposures to such toxic materials as cotton dust. Women were employed in vast numbers, and child labor was common; workdays were typically 12 to 14 hours long, and health and safety standards were nonexistent. In 1897 when the metalworkers' union, one of the earliest labor unions in Japan, established a fund to help its members, the fund was financially decimated by the high incidence of beriberi, a vitamin-deficiency disease. Tuberculosis grew to epidemic proportions among factory workers.

Hard life of the "factory girls"

Evidence of the wretched conditions of early factory workers exists in the form of government reports from the time and accounts left by the workers themselves. In his book *Peasants, Rebels, and Outcastes* (1982), Japanese writer Mikiso Hane recounts some of the grim details of life in the dormitories where female factory workers were housed. Strict curfews were imposed in these prisonlike residences, and in many, except for going to work, "factory girls" were allowed to leave the premises only a few times each month. Visitors were limited, and mail was censored. Workers were punished with verbal abuse, withholding of food, and beatings.

A government report dated 1901 describes the disciplinary measures enforced in a small textile plant in a village in Saitama prefecture. The plant's 24 female employees, aged 14 to 25, were locked inside and forced to labor—often from 5 AM until late at night—until they had completed a prescribed amount of work. Those who did not meet their individual quotas were not fed. The report tells how one worker, who had run away twice and been brought back each time, was beaten with an iron rod. When she failed to meet her work quotas, the punishment was repeated, and she was burned with moksa weed. The woman tried to hide from her employer but was found and dragged through the snow by her hair and then made to stand outside in the cold for an hour. As a result of her severe treatment, she was blinded.

Recognition of the social problems of the new laboring class came slowly. A series of sensational newspaper articles about conditions in the Takashima mines prompted the government to enact mining laws in 1890 and 1905. Exposés about the appalling conditions in factories and industrial slums continued to appear over the next few years, and the government continued to carry out official investigations. Still, labor unrest increased in the early years of the 20th century. Not until 1911 was an act finally passed that had some weak provisions to limit working hours, curtail child

Only a little more than a decade after Matthew Perry's arrival, a new government—the progressive-minded Meiji regime—was to propel Japan out of the Middle Ages and into the modern world. Industrialization was a major priority of the Meiji government. It quickly developed railroads, ports, telegraph lines, and a banking system. The silk industry, already established in Japan, was expanded and modernized. (Below) A Japanese woodblock print, c. 1875, depicts, in a somewhat idealized version, an early silk-reeling factory. The design of the building clearly shows the influence of Western factory architecture. A 1919 photograph, also showing silk production, better conveys the working conditions in Japanese factories of the early 20th century—crowded, fast-paced, and leaving no time for idle conversation. The hours of work were long, and some factories had production quotas that kept workers laboring well into the night. Women workers like those pictured in the photo—"factory girls," as they were called—were often housed in cheerless dormitories, where mail was censored and visitors forbidden.

Photographs, (left) UPI/Bettmann Newsphotos; (right) Laurie Platt Winfrey, Inc.

Most of the laborers in early Japanese industries were poorly paid peasants who had left the land in search of a better life. In the burgeoning factory districts of Tokyo and other major cities, however, the problems of rural life—malnutrition, poor hygiene, rampant tuberculosis—were compounded by crowding, inadequate sanitation, and exhausting 14-hour workdays. In the photo above, which was taken earlier in this century, a peasant woman and her children, possibly recent arrivals from the country, crowd close to the stove in their squalid apartment in a tenement in Osaka.

labor, and regulate working conditions. A factory inspection system had been established by 1915.

New industries, new hazards

From the 1920s through the beginning of World War II, Japanese industry continued to grow, and the social and economic status of workers improved. With new industries, however, came new health and safety hazards—for example, carbon disulfide poisoning among workers in rayon and fertilizer manufacturing, lead poisoning in printing plants, and arc flash (a form of conjunctivitis) among welders. As Japan's military effort intensified, the regulation and control of workplace hazards became lower priorities, sacrificed to the goal of maximum wartime productivity.

The next major advances in occupational health came about at the end of World War II with the implementation of a new constitution and a raft of new legislation. The Trade Union Law of 1945 guaranteed workers the right to organize, bargain collectively, and strike; the Labor Standards Law of 1947 elaborated basic principles of worker protection. These statutes established a framework of worker rights that was to facilitate specific safety and health measures in the years to come.

A period of explosive economic growth began in the 1950s. Steel, coal, electric power, fertilizer, cement, and shipbuilding production developed rapidly at first, followed by the chemical, automobile, machinery, plastics, synthetic rubber, and electronics industries. Once again, new industries brought with them a variety of new occupational hazards. In the 1950s and '60s, a combination of forces—the growing electronic communications media, some highly publicized environmental disasters, a newly vocal labor movement, and growing national prosperity—brought about quicker recognition and acknowledgement of these hazards than in earlier times. Thus were enacted the Pneumoconiosis Law of 1960, which recognized such dust diseases of the lungs as silicosis and provided for their surveillance; the Industrial Injury Prevention Organization Law of 1964, which promoted voluntary safety and health activities by employers; the Industrial Homework Law of 1970, which set labor standards for cottage industries, particularly in the areas of electronics and textile manufacturing; and the major piece of Japanese occupational health legislation, the Industrial Safety and Health Law of 1972.

"Wholesome and cultural living" for all

The Japanese today enjoy a very high standard of health. Life expectancy at birth is 75.2 years for men and 80.9 years for women, among the world's highest (the corresponding figures for the United States are 71 and 78.1, respectively). The infant mortality rate, a key indicator of public health, is among the world's lowest; according to the latest statistics available, it was 5.8 deaths per 1,000 live births, compared with 10.2 in the United States. As in other industrialized nations, the major causes of death in Japan today are heart disease, cancer, and stroke. Mortality from cancer and heart disease has risen steadily over the past few decades. On the other hand, the death rates from pneumonia, gastroenteritis, and tuberculosis have

154

declined sharply since World War II, reflecting the conquest of infectious disease that typically accompanies increasing national prosperity.

The national government plays a major role in health care. According to the constitution, all Japanese citizens are entitled to "minimum standards of wholesome and cultured living," and the government is responsible for "the promotion and extension . . . of public health." Most health services are delivered privately, through individual medical practitioners, clinics, and hospitals, but they are funded by comprehensive, universal, compulsory health insurance, administered by the Ministry of Health and Welfare. This health insurance originated as an employment-based system with the Employees' Health Insurance Law of 1922, which guaranteed medical insurance to most employed persons and their dependents. Certain excluded groups of workers, such as day laborers and seamen, were later covered by special categorical insurance bills. Unemployed persons, agricultural workers, and others without health insurance were finally enfranchised under the National Health Insurance Law in 1958 and the Inhabitants' Health Insurance Law of 1961.

Workers' compensation: virtually universal

Limited workers' compensation, covering the costs of medical care associated with work-related injuries and illnesses, was a part of the Mines Act of 1905 and the Factories Act of 1911. The Health Insurance Law enacted in 1922 covered the costs of both occupational and nonoccupational ailments, so it served a workers' compensation function for those who were covered. Several additional social insurance schemes were adopted during the 1930s and '40s, providing pension support to disabled workers and their survivors. Under these programs the government gradually assumed more of the responsibilities previously assigned to employers.

All of the various workers' compensation and pension schemes were superseded by postwar legislation, however. In 1947 a labor standards law established a legal framework for workers' compensation and acknowledged the "compensation" rather than the "assistance" aspects of the

Distribution of workers in Japan and the U.S.		
industry	percentage of work force	
	Japan	U.S.
agriculture, forestry, fishing	8.4	3.1
mining	0.1	0.8
manufacturing	24.7	19.1
electricity, gas, water	0.5	1.3
construction	9.1	6.6
trade, restaurants, hotels	22.9	20.8
transport, communication	6.0	5.7
finance, insurance, real estate, business services	7.1	10.7
community, social, and personal services	20.7	31.9

Source: International Labour Office, *Year Book of Labour Statistics*, 1987, pp. 364, 373

Recognition of the social problems of the new laboring class was slow to develop. As in the United States, journalists played an important part in exposing abusive practices in specific industries. In Japan at the turn of the century, a series of newspaper articles on the shocking conditions in the Takashima mines prompted the government to enact laws protecting mine workers. Nevertheless, despite the passage of legislation to improve working conditions, labor unrest grew in the early years of the 20th century. (Left) Women workers at a labor rally, c. 1930, were striking for higher wages.

The Mansell Collection

Mitsuhiro Wada

For the most part, Japanese university graduates do not go looking for jobs; instead, the jobs come looking for them, in the form of company recruiters who tour campuses throughout the country and speak before assemblies of new graduates like this class at Tokyo's Meiji University. In recent years there have been many more job openings than entry-level personnel to fill them. As a result, the recruitment of new employees can be a highly competitive business, involving parties, gifts, and other enticements.

A hokan, or professional jester, entertains business executives at an exclusive banquet. Not only do Japanese workers typically put in much longer hours than their Western counterparts but they may also be required to attend a variety of after-hours social events, which, regardless of the time, are viewed as being all in a day's work.

Photograph, *Train Vert*

program. An accident compensation law, also passed in 1947, established a fund supported by compulsory employer contributions but administered by the government. Over the next few decades, the present system gradually took shape. It now covers almost all Japanese workers and provides medical care, partial wage replacement, and pensions to those injured or made ill on the job. Treatment is generally provided at one of 36 hospitals nationwide that specialize in occupational injuries and rehabilitative care.

Unique patterns of employment

The distribution of employment by industry in Japan is roughly comparable to that of the United States. In both countries close to one-quarter of all those employed work in manufacturing. The most significant difference is in the percentage of the work force involved in agriculture and related activities: more than 8% (4,950,000 workers) in Japan, compared with only 3.1% (3,350,000) in the U.S.

If the basic distribution of workers in Japan is similar to that of the U.S. and other developed countries, however, the patterns of employment in Japan are, in contrast, unique. The prototype pattern for the Japanese worker is a lifetime of work with a single employer, job security and adequate retirement benefits being virtually guaranteed. (As will be made clear below, this image, this ideal, is a popular conception that is not necessarily borne out in reality.) Under this system a typical Japanese student would enter the job market upon graduation, whether from high school or university. Big companies hire large numbers of new graduates every year; the number is determined not by how many specific job openings are to be filled but by overall personnel needs. Thus, the "typical" worker would probably be trained to fill several posts, giving the company the advantage of a certain amount of flexibility in employee assignments. Continuing the prototypical pattern, the worker would advance through the company ranks, and to comparably higher wage levels, in a more or less predictable sequence, based on seniority. He would remain with the company until retirement, some time between the ages of 55 and 60.

The prototypical company in Japan, at least as it is viewed in this idealized scenario, is also quite different from its U.S. counterpart. It would be rare for such a company to lay off or fire a worker, except in cases of gross misbehavior or in time of severe economic hardship. The Japanese company plays a paternalistic role in the life of its employees. A manager might, for example, participate in his workers' weddings, family funerals, and other ceremonial events; the company might offer the worker continuing education opportunities; benefits might include housing allowances and access to sports facilities; and after retirement, if the worker needed some extra income, the company might even offer part-time employment.

Longer days, longer weeks

Another important difference is that the hours of work in Japan are considerably longer than in other industrialized nations. On average, Japanese workers spend 200 more hours on the job each year than their counterparts in the U.S. and Great Britain. The "weekend" is not universally observed; only one Japanese worker in three works a five-day week. And for those in sales and various other white-collar jobs, the workday often extends into after-hours meetings and social events.

Corresponding to these differences, labor unions have played a different role in Japan than in other developed nations. Of the 28% of Japanese workers who are now unionized, 90% belong to so-called enterprise unions. These are unions that represent the employees of a single company, bargaining with considerable autonomy from national federations. Perhaps because Japanese employment has entailed greater job security than is the rule in other nations, perhaps because of the company-based nature of the unions, and perhaps for other, more obscure reasons, there has been less of a tradition of an open labor-management struggle in Japan than elsewhere. According to International Labor Office statistics for 1986, approximately 4 workdays were lost to strikes for every 1,000 Japanese workers; in the United States the comparable figure was 99 workdays. In the typically more contentious manufacturing sector, the difference was even more striking: for every 1,000 Japanese workers, only 7 workdays were lost to strikes in 1986; their U.S. counterparts lost 277.

Popular misconceptions: the prototype debunked

In recent years it has become clear that some of these accepted generalizations about Japanese employment are only partially accurate. Four phenomena are especially pertinent examples of exceptions to the general rule: (1) the existence of the so-called dual economy, consisting of very large companies and much smaller ones; (2) the presence of a sizable number of temporary workers; (3) the emergence of the mobile worker who changes jobs to get ahead; and (4) the campaign to encourage leisure-time activities. Each of these has its effect on worker safety and well-being.

First, within the "dual economy" of Japan, the patterns of lifetime employment and paternalistic benefits are much more typical of large companies than of small ones. Early in Japan's modernization, huge conglomerates of manufacturing, trading, and financial companies, called *zaibatsu*, developed.

Tetsuya Yamada/*Trendy* Magazine, March 1989; © Nikkei Home Publishing Co., Ltd.

The majority of unionized workers in Japan belong to so-called enterprise unions, which represent all of the employees of a single company rather than individuals who perform similar types of jobs. Union membership can bring with it considerable benefits. (Above) A benefit that members of the Matsushita Co.'s labor union and their families enjoy is a holiday at the "Carnival Show Case," a vacation village that offers among its many attractions a heated swimming pool, a botanical garden, and a French restaurant.

157

Injuries on the job: downward trend		
	injury rate (number of injuries per million hours worked)	
industry	1973	1983
all industries	6.67	3.03
underground coal mining	92.75	19.42
forestry	19.86	18.06
wood products	13.98	6.07
transit	19.06	5.21
fabricated metal products	8.21	4.09
foundry	22.00	4.09
construction	14.22	2.12

Source: Labor Ministry of Japan and Japan International Cooperation Agency, *Industrial Safety and Health*, 1985

Despite an encouraging downward trend in the total number of occupational injuries in Japan, the forestry industry remains one of the most hazardous, second only to underground coal mining. So-called vibration disease, a combined disorder of the circulatory and nervous systems, is one of the major occupational hazards of forestry workers and others who use vibrating tools. In order to reduce the trauma to chainsaw operators, the tool has been redesigned so that it is smaller than previous models, and the amount of time the worker is required to operate it has been reduced.

Forestry Agency of Japan

Although the *zaibatsu* were formally disbanded after World War II, corporate giants such as Mitsubishi, Kawasaki, and Sumitomo continue to dominate the Japanese economy. This pattern is repeated in many sectors of industry; the automobile industry comprises several large manufacturers—including Toyota, Nissan, Honda, and Mazda—while the electric machinery and appliance industry is led by Toshiba, Hitachi, Sony, Sanyo, Matsushita, and Mitsubishi. These large firms do indeed provide stable employment and extensive benefits to their workers.

However, a key feature of the Japanese economy is the parallel existence of small companies that are subsidiary to large manufacturers in fact if not in name. Each automobile manufacturer, for example, depends upon scores of small companies to supply parts. The same is true in the construction, shipbuilding, iron and steel, chemical, and electrical industries. The small companies are economically more marginal than the larger ones. Accordingly, they provide fewer employment benefits, less-stable terms of employment, and, as will be discussed later, working conditions in these companies are more hazardous.

"Invisible" workers

A second exception to common views of Japanese employment is the existence of a fairly large population of temporary employees, who function as a "shock absorber" for economic changes. Although the majority of Japanese workers hold secure, long-term positions, as many as 20% work in temporary jobs. They are hired for limited periods, from a few weeks to a few months, and when economic conditions demand, they are simply discharged. Like the employees of small companies, the temporary workers do not enjoy the many benefits commonly associated with work in the prosperous Japanese economy. In fact, they are partly invisible; the Japanese method of tabulating unemployment does not count anyone who has worked at all, even for a few hours, during the survey week. Nor does it count persons who were laid off, unpaid family workers working fewer than 15 hours per week, or those who may be seeking work through family contacts or friends rather than through official channels. As a result, there is probably considerably more unemployment in Japan than official statistics reveal, but little is known about this segment of the population.

Changing jobs, taking holidays

A third departure from the commonly held ideas about Japanese employment is a trend toward growing job mobility in the work force. As a labor surplus turned to a labor shortage in about 1960, some workers began to break with tradition by changing companies in search of better opportunities. Today this trend is especially prominent among younger workers, who increasingly place personal advancement and job satisfaction ahead of security and stability. A young Japanese worker may now expect to change jobs every few years, including switching from one company to its competitors, a not uncommon practice in other industrial nations.

Finally, and most recently, an increase in disposable income among Japanese workers and the need to develop domestic markets for Japanese

158

consumer goods have led to a drive toward limiting work hours and increasing leisure time. In 1988 the Ministry of Labor launched a campaign to persuade companies to schedule more holiday time and to persuade workers to use this time, which some are loathe to do. At the time, only 6% of Japanese companies considered Saturday to be a day off. The move to increase holiday time—and the remarkable resistance of many workers to do so—resonates with a popular perception that stress is a major occupational health hazard in contemporary Japan. There is even a new Japanese word for death from overwork: *karoshi*. It can be anticipated that in the coming years there will be both a greater recognition of the health consequences of stress and a growing tendency to limit work hours.

Hazards of the Japanese workplace

About one million Japanese workers are injured on the job each year—about 3,000 of them fatally—in accidents ranging from falling from heights, being struck by flying objects, and being caught in machinery to slipping and falling, receiving acid or thermal burns, or being involved in work-related motor vehicle accidents. The highest rates of injury occur in mining and forestry. Almost all Japanese industries have reported a significant decrease in accident rates over the past decade. Rates are highest in very small companies, becoming progressively lower with increasing company size. Similarly, the accident rate is several times higher in the smaller sub-contractor firms than in the large companies that they supply. Both of these observations testify to the adverse impact of the "dual economy" on the safety of Japanese workers; the smaller companies tend to perform more dangerous operations, provide fewer safeguards, and have fewer resources for assisting workers injured on the job. Japanese labor statistics show that accidents are more common among the youngest and oldest groups of workers, while middle-aged workers have lower risk. This situation may reflect lack of experience or more reckless behavior among the young and a slowing of response time with age. In general, however, the rate and type of accidents are comparable to those seen in other industrialized countries,

Tsukasa Matsumoto,
Department of Orthopedics, Tokyo Rosai Hospital

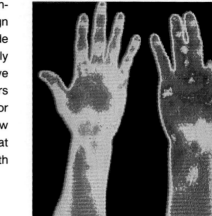

Compensation and rehabilitative care for injured workers are virtually guaranteed by the Japanese system of universal medical insurance. Thermography, a diagnostic technique that measures the heat of the tissues—and, hence, the amount of blood circulation through them—is used to assess the extent of vibration disease in one worker's hands (above). The blue areas indicate poor circulation. Circulation to the index finger of the right hand is so impaired that it does not even appear in the image. (Below) A doctor examines the hands of a worker claiming compensation for a job-related injury. (Below left) A patient at a Tokyo hospital works to improve the range of motion of his injured shoulder.

Photographs, Mitsuhiro Wada

The Labor Standards Bureau, operating within the Japanese Ministry of Labor, is responsible for enforcing health and safety standards in the country's six million workplaces. Its inspectors conduct about 200,000 inspections a year, usually targeting industries known to be hazardous. The two inspectors with the camera and clipboard (above left) are investigating an accident in which a construction worker fell from a scaffold. Another inspector (above right) checks a safety mechanism on a punch press; the machine stops automatically when the worker's hands come within a certain proximity, a safeguard that has been successful in decreasing traumatic loss of fingers, arms, and hands.

Photographs, Jijigaho-sha/Yoshiharu Ishii

except the disparity between large and small companies may be more striking in Japan than elsewhere.

The pneumoconioses, or dust diseases of the lungs, are a major category of occupational disease recognized in Japan. In these disorders inhaled dusts lead to scarring and stiffening of the lung tissue, which impairs oxygen exchange and causes shortness of breath and reduced capacity for physical exercise. Inhaled asbestos causes the chronic scarring disease called asbestosis; silica causes silicosis; beryllium causes berylliosis; coal dust causes coal worker's pneumoconiosis, otherwise known as black lung disease. All of these maladies occur among Japanese workers: shipbuilding entails asbestos exposure; construction workers engaged in tunnel building are exposed to silica; coal mining is still an active industry; and beryllium, used in the manufacture of various alloys, is prominent in electronics. In 1983 about 260,000 Japanese workers at risk of pneumoconioses underwent routine surveillance examinations; of these, 44,440 (or 17%) were found to have one of the diseases.

When a carcinogen encountered in the workplace causes an increase in the rate of occurrence of an otherwise common type of cancer, such as lung cancer, it is difficult to attribute specific cases to the workplace or to count the number of cases due to occupational exposure. On the other hand, rare tumors caused by occupational exposures can more easily be

160

tracked and the magnitude of the problem estimated. The number of cases of mesothelioma diagnosed in Japan has increased each year since the early 1970s and had reached more than 50 cases annually by 1980. As this tumor almost always occurs as a result of asbestos exposure, the increase may be interpreted as evidence that at least one significant occupational cancer problem exists in Japan.

Dermatitis (any inflammatory skin reaction), the most common occupational disease in a number of countries, is also common in Japan, as are toxic reactions to organic solvents, causing such symptoms as difficulty in concentrating, dizziness, blurred vision, and other neurological problems. "Vibration disease," a combined disorder of the circulatory and nervous systems, occurs among chainsaw and pneumatic drill operators, postal employees who ride about on motorcycles all day, and other workers subjected to constant vibration; the Japanese have been pioneers in recognizing this syndrome. So-called ergonomic disorders—basically, musculoskeletal problems such as cumulative trauma disorders and repetitive motion injuries— are also well established in the lexicon of Japanese occupational diseases; these conditions occur in a variety of occupations, ranging from assembly-line work to data and word processing.

As mentioned earlier, stress has only recently been recognized as a major occupational health problem in Japan. Medical scientists everywhere are finding growing evidence that stress and fatigue can contribute to a variety of health problems, including gastritis and ulcers, sleep difficulties, high blood pressure, heart attacks, stroke, and drug and alcohol abuse. Studies of job-related stress have identified several contributing factors, among them the irregular schedule associated with shiftwork, uncertainty

A poster issued by the Ministry of Labor shows two safari-suited Japanese tourists, accompanied by a leopard, taking their ease as antelope roam in the distance and Mt. Fuji looms benevolently. The poster says, "We order you to take one week of vacation." Japanese workers on average take only about half of the 15 paid holidays most companies offer each year. Diligence is one important reason cited to explain the reluctance to use vacation time, but holiday crowds, traffic jams, and the high cost of traveling within the country also play a part in discouraging people from taking advantage of time off. A growing appreciation of the health effects of work-related stress is undoubtedly a factor in the government's campaign to popularize vacations.

Poster, Labor Ministry of Japan

about the future, lack of control, lack of interpersonal interaction, boredom or monotony, excessive job demands, and ambiguous or conflicting role definitions. Although larger Japanese companies offer the advantages of clear role definitions, ample opportunity to learn new skills, and a high degree of job security, the problems of excessive demands and lack of control may be severe in a big corporation. Currently, about 250 workers' compensation claims are filed in Japan each year for deaths related to workplace stress; about 10% are ruled valid and awarded judgment.

Setting workplace standards

The legal framework for the government's role in occupational safety and health is the Industrial Safety and Health Law (ISHL) of 1972. This law is analogous to the U.S. Occupational Safety and Health Act of 1970, on which it was partly based. The ISHL functions in several ways. It enables the Ministry of Labor to set standards and to inspect workplaces. It requires employers to maintain safe workplaces, comply with national standards, perform medical and environmental surveillance, keep records of employee injuries, and organize health and safety committees and educational programs. The law also requires employees to cooperate in these efforts and to comply with workplace rules.

The Ministry of Labor sometimes issues mandatory workplace standards. More often, however, standards are based on so-called technical recommendations. These are developed by expert panels, which include representatives of labor and management and scientist-consultants, and operate through consensus. The standards may be challenged in court, but in sharp contrast to the U.S. experience, this rarely occurs in Japan.

The Labor Standards Bureau, within the Ministry of Labor, is responsible for enforcing the standards. Several thousand inspectors conduct about 200,000 inspections each year in Japan's six million workplaces. These inspections are targeted at the most hazardous industries in each locality, although worker complaints may trigger an inspection at any workplace. Inspections are announced beforehand, and the inspectors often limit their

Life in Japan is typically seen as much less stressful than life in the Western world. Economic miracles have their price, however, and one of them is an increased pace of life. These Tokyo commuters at the evening rush hour look every bit as harried and exhausted as homeward-bound city dwellers anywhere else in the world.

visits to reviewing records rather than actually touring the plants. For these reasons, some health hazards do go unnoticed. If a violation is found during an inspection, the company is requested to correct it and to notify the Labor Standards Inspection Office when this has been done. Reinspections are conducted in the case of serious violations. This system does not always result in strict enforcement of standards, however.

Campaign against "white finger disease"

Union activism in Japan is limited by the enterprise union system, by the low proportion of workers who are unionized, and by a relatively weak sense of workers' rights on matters concerning working conditions. However, unions have contributed to important advances in safety and health. Two specialized laws, the Silicosis Law of 1955 and the Pneumoconiosis Law of 1960, owe their passage to vigorous union support, especially from several mine workers' unions. Regulations to prevent solvent poisoning were adopted in 1960, also as the result of union support. In the mid-1960s the All Forestry Workers' Union successfully campaigned to have "white finger disease," a vibration-related condition, recognized as a compensable occupational disorder.

Many Japanese companies, especially the larger ones, have health and safety staffs that include company physicians. These staffs are responsible for developing educational programs and conducting medical surveillance and environmental monitoring within the plant or office. In addition, trade associations in such major industries as steel and automobile manufacture are active in promoting safety and health.

Job-related stress has only recently been recognized as an important health problem in Japan. Although the larger corporations do offer stable employment, clear role definitions, and a high degree of job security, the problems of excessive demands on individual workers and their lack of control over their own situations can be severe. Currently about 250 workers' compensation claims are filed each year for deaths related to workplace stress. A new word has even been coined for death from overwork: karoshi. *A poster showing a frenzied-looking white-collar worker emphasizes the importance of order. "Looking for something again?" it asks. "Always keep your workplace neatly arranged."*

Poster, Japan Industrial Safety and Health Association

Women workers: still in second place

Women have traditionally been relegated to secondary positions in Japanese society; a Confucian adage holds that a woman should in youth obey her father, in maturity her husband, and in old age her son. Although the constitution guarantees equality of the sexes, social inequities survive. Many more men than women complete university educations, are hired into "career-track" jobs, and advance up the corporate ladder. Until recently, a woman would typically work at a menial job after finishing school, marry, and leave the work force to raise a family.

The pattern of women's participation in the Japanese economy has changed dramatically with modernization. When Japan was largely an agricultural society, most women worked at home and in the fields and rice paddies; during the early phases of industrialization, women went to work in textile factories or replaced their husbands at agricultural work while the men took factory jobs. Today almost half of all adult women work, and they constitute 40% of the nation's labor force.

Women are concentrated in a small number of job categories, primarily clerical, sales, and service work. In textile production and other light industries, they represent an important part of the work force. In other industries and in the professions, however, women are sharply underrepresented, although this situation is slowly changing. Moreover, women are more likely than men to be hired on a temporary or part-time basis and to have limited opportunities for advancement. And women, on average, earn significantly less than men. Thus, in many ways employment patterns continue to reflect the long-standing cultural tradition of male dominance.

Labor laws officially ban wage discrimination against women and restrict overtime and some nighttime and hazardous work. The law also guarantees six weeks of prenatal and eight weeks of postnatal leave, nursing time off for women who are breast-feeding, and time off for menstruation-related problems. An equal employment opportunity law, adopted in 1985, rein-

At an early-morning meeting in Tokyo's Mitsukoshi department store, "elevator girls"—young women who greet the store's customers, operate elevators, and staff information booths—receive their daily briefing. Just as women have traditionally been relegated to subordinate positions in Japanese society, so too have they been restricted to a secondary place in the economy. While women continue to be concentrated in a small number of job categories—primarily in clerical, sales, and service jobs—there are beginning to be signs of change as growing numbers of women enter the professions.

164

forced already existing antidiscrimination provisions but did not establish any significant new rights for women.

Several special occupational health problems of women may be noted. The first is "homework." As noted earlier, Japan has sizable cottage industries in textiles, electronics, toys, and electrical equipment. In sandal manufacturing, for example, a huge load of sandals might move from one residence to another, each family performing one specific task—stamping out foot pieces, punching holes for straps, riveting, and so on. The workplace is typically crowded and hot, and the machines used in homework can be dangerous. Further, no health or safety regulations apply in the home workshop. Well over one million women work under these circumstances, being exposed to high risks of accident and ergonomic injury.

Unequal opportunity: Japan's minorities

Minority workers have received less attention in Japan than in other nations because of Japan's relative racial homogeneity, but they do, nonetheless, exist. One important minority group is the Korean community, which numbers over 700,000. Japan annexed Korea in 1910 and began confiscating land; many Koreans then migrated to Japan in search of work. Later, during World War II, large numbers of Koreans were imported to replace Japanese workers serving in the armed forces. Koreans worked primarily on road gangs, in mines, and at other hard labor during the early decades of the 20th century and took over industrial jobs during World War II. Currently Koreans remain the victims of employment discrimination, but since most lack Japanese citizenship, even if born in Japan, they have little legal recourse. Sweatshop districts can be seen in the Korean sections of big cities, such as Osaka, where residents work under primitive, dangerous conditions at such jobs as sandal and garment manufacturing.

A second minority of note is the *burakumin,* Japan's traditional untouchable caste. Comprising about 2% of the population (three million people), these people are descendants of those who traditionally performed such loathsome jobs as butchering and leather work (occupations tabooed by orthodox Shinto and Buddhism), street cleaning, and handling of the dead. Discrimination against *burakumin* is now illegal, but it continues to exist. In particular, *burakumin* have difficulty finding jobs in the larger, more prestigious corporations and thus tend to be concentrated in smaller, more marginal companies, where the risks of accident and disease are greater.

The price of prosperity

Almost all productive human activities, from agriculture to transportation, mining to manufacturing, pose hazards for the people who work at them. Even in a thriving economy like that of Japan, prosperity has its price, including the health costs borne by working people. In general, the health risks to workers in Japan closely parallel those faced by their counterparts in Western industrial nations. How the Japanese have coped with this consequence of prosperity has been, to a great extent, shaped by their unique social and cultural traditions.

Poster, Japan Industrial Safety and Health Association

"Safety comes from following the proper procedure," says the characteristically Japanese motto on the poster. For a country that has enjoyed unprecedented economic growth, Japan does not seem to have paid disproportionately in terms of worker health and safety.

Letting Children Be Children . . .
While They Can

by Bruno Bettelheim, Ph.D.

We could never have loved the earth so well if we had had no childhood in it.
—George Eliot

At the very beginning of this century, the Swedish reformer and author Ellen Key published *Barnets århundrade* (*The Century of the Child*), a book that was to gain her world fame and that would be translated into many languages. In it she stated her hope that the 20th century would bring about the liberation of children and would make their lot much better than it had been in past times. And it is true, in much of the world: universal education has replaced child labor; psychologists specializing in child development have taken the place of the rod or the ruler; and routine immunizations have virtually eliminated the infectious diseases that were major cripplers and killers of children 100 years ago. But now, approaching the end of the century, scholars and investigators of the problems of childhood are coming to the conclusion that far from being the century of the child, this century is raising *Children Without Childhood* (which is the title of a recent book by Marie Winn, who spent ten years collecting evidence about how children's lives and adults' attitudes toward child rearing have changed). Indeed, it is this century that has seen *The Disappearance of Childhood,* as the title of Neil M. Postman's recent book asserts.

What accounts for vanished childhood?

These two authors—and others—have given a variety of reasons for childhood's disappearance. One factor, which most child development specialists agree has much to do with this undesirable phenomenon, is television. This, in fact, was the central thesis of Postman's book. According to Postman, who is professor of media ecology and communications at New York University, television has opened to children knowledge of matters that, before the age of mass media, were carefully hidden from them. It was this difference between what was known by children and what was known only by adults that to an important extent created the very phenomenon of childhood, and this distinction accounted for much of the respect that children had for adults. By contrast, Postman found that there is very little that youngsters today are not exposed to at a very early age. He points

Bruno Bettelheim, Ph.D., is Distinguished Service Professor of Education Emeritus and Professor Emeritus of Psychology and Psychiatry at the University of Chicago, a member of the National Academy of Education, and the author of many books on child psychology. He is perhaps best known for his pioneering work with treating and educating emotionally disturbed children, but his studies of how disturbed children react to shortcomings in their upbringing have thrown light on the raising of normal children. Successful parenting is the subject of his most recent book, A Good Enough Parent, published in 1987.

(Opposite page) "Freedom from Fear" by Norman Rockwell; printed by permission of the Estate of Norman Rockwell; copyright © 1943 Estate of Norman Rockwell

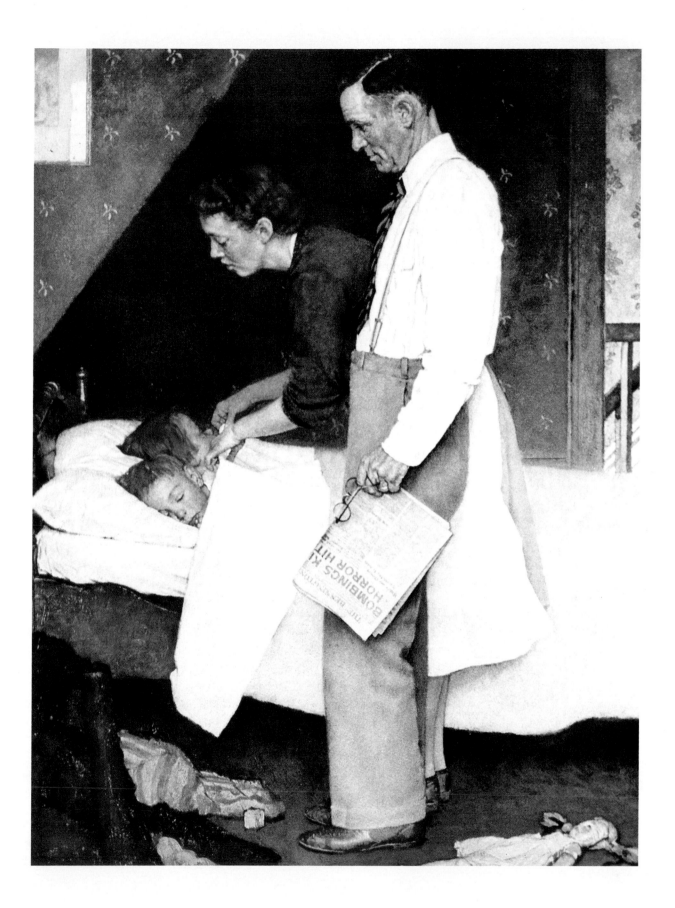

April A. Oswald

in particular to what they learn about sex on TV; there are now "very few expressions of human sexuality that television regards as serious enough to keep private, that is to say as inappropriate for use as a theme for a program or as the focal point of a commercial. From vaginal spray commercials to discussion of male strippers, from programs preoccupied with the display of buttocks and breasts to documentaries on spouse swapping, the secrets unfold one by one. In some cases, to be sure, a subject such as incest, lesbianism or infidelity is treated with seriousness and even dignity, but this is quite beside the point."

Indeed, the ubiquitous influences affecting the sanctity of childhood today are all too familiar. Today children are encouraged by parents and teachers to engage in dating at an age where a few decades ago dating was out of the question. Drugs, which in earlier decades of this century were unknown to children, now play an important and destructive role in their lives. The frequency of unstable marriages and divorce means that children are being drawn into their parents' conflicts, and in many cases children have to split their lives into the time spent with one parent and that spent with the other. Consequently, children are growing up emotionally neglected and without the sense that is so vital to a young person's identity—that of belonging.

While in the past, great efforts were made to shield children from worrying about life's inherent dangers, now they are deliberately made aware of them. The threat of nuclear war and the risk and dangers of AIDS are especially timely examples. The *New York Times* recently reported how in Palo Alto, California, the Board of Education wanted to introduce instruction about the dangers of AIDS into kindergarten classes in the district's 14 elementary schools. Outraged teachers protested the proposed step, declaring: "Our society has gradually chipped away at the very essence of childhood. Children are no longer free to walk down the street unaccompanied, to talk to strangers, or even to enjoy their Halloween candy. We must now teach children to prepare for disasters, to be suspicious of others, to be concerned about the changing environment. Introducing one more issue over which children have no control can only diminish their sense of self."

What makes a child a child?

A few years ago *Time* magazine ran a cover story with the headline "Children Having Children." Numerous other publications have told similar stories. There is no denying that pregnancies in young adolescents have become a very serious problem; in New York City, for example, they account for as many as 15% of all pregnancies. Moreover, inadequate prenatal care and poor nutrition among very young mothers contribute to high rates of babies born prematurely, who start life at a disadvantage. Offspring of these youngest mothers have high rates of illness and mortality, and in later life they have serious emotional and educational problems. Keeping these youngest mothers in school to complete their education is yet another serious part of the problem.

But is it really true that *children* are having children? The answer to this question depends on how one defines childhood and adulthood. The problem of defining these two periods of life is not new; even the ancients

Many specialists in child development have recently addressed the problem of children being deprived of their childhood. One important contributing factor, many agree, is television, with the fare it offers. The average child spends 25 hours a week in front of the television set, and because parents often use TV as a surrogate baby-sitter, youngsters today are exposed to "adult" subjects that in previous eras they would not have known about until they were older and more mature. From sexuality and immorality to blood, violence, and death—they witness it all.

168

Dressed for success? One has to wonder. In his book The Disappearance of Childhood, *author Neil M. Postman decries the fact that children are encouraged to mimic adult behaviors and likewise that adult sensibilities are becoming more and more childish. He enumerates ways in which the differences between children and adults have been eradicated—citing the TV programs they watch, their manners, the food they eat, and the clothes they wear as examples. "The children's clothing industry," writes Postman, "has undergone vast changes. . . . What was once unambiguously recognized as 'children's' clothing has virtually disappeared. Twelve-year-old boys now wear three-piece suits to birthday parties, and sixty-year-old men wear blue jeans to birthday parties."*

Nancy Brown

recognized it. The great Byzantine emperor Justinian asserted in his collection of laws that sexual maturity was what separated children from adults. This question was also discussed at the Council of Trent (1545–63), and there the Roman Catholic Church arrived at the same conclusion, namely, that sexual maturity indicates adulthood. By notable contrast, *Time* and the other popular media of today, in decrying the fact that children are having children, are—since it is obvious that only sexually mature females can conceive and bear children—pointing to the young ages of those having babies. Such a chronological basis for deciding who is and who is not a child, however, is largely an illusion—and one that creates difficult problems for children and adults alike.

It is important to emphasize that in past times "children having children" was hardly a problem. For example, in Norway in the mid-1840s, girls reached menarche (the onset of the menstrual cycle) on the average at about 17 years of age; now Norwegian girls do so four years earlier. The great grandmothers of today's American teenagers, who reached puberty around the turn of the century, did so at about age 14½; their great granddaughters now do so at least one or two years earlier.

In the early 1970s James M. Tanner, working at the Institute of Child Health at the University of London, compared statistics from the U.K., the U.S., and several European countries (Denmark, West Germany, Sweden, Finland, Norway, and The Netherlands). In some countries statistics were available from 1840 to the mid-1960s, in others only from the 1940s to the mid-'60s; however, Tanner found marked similarities among the various nations, with comparable reductions (of three to four months for each decade) in the age of the first menstruation.

The age at which boys reach maturity is not as easy to be certain about as the beginning of menstruation permits in girls, but all studies of growth and development have shown that a parallel process of reduction in the age at which boys reach sexual maturity has taken place. Over the

169

Illicit drugs, which in earlier decades of this century were virtually unknown to children, now play an important and destructive role in their lives. After crack dealers in Washington, D.C., approached 12-year-old Atiba Miller (right), he was forbidden by his father to go outside alone.

In many cases youngsters who become drug addicts during their pubertal years were as children given drugs by their parents—most often to make the *parents'* lives easier. Very young children, for example, are often given sedatives to help them sleep. When they have nightmares, parents give them drugs to help them get back to sleep rather than spending the necessary time with them during the night to ease their terrors and reassure them that "it was only a dream." They give drugs to provide the feeling of security; before such drug use was widespread, children could gain that comfort only from loving closeness to their parents.

Other drugs are widely used to manipulate children's behavior in school. Methylphenidate (Ritalin) is prescribed by pediatricians to settle down so-called hyperactive children; unruly youngsters are thus "disciplined" with a potent drug. This practice has been used as a "quick fix," though, thereby setting yet another example for children that behavior change is most readily and easily achieved through the use of drugs.

It is not that youngsters do not know that taking drugs is injurious to their health. In this author's work with juvenile drug addicts at the Sonia Shankman Orthogenic School at the University of Chicago, not a single young addict was encountered who did not know the detriment to his or her health that using drugs entailed. The reason that these children took drugs despite this knowledge was, as they explained, that they could not manage life without them; life was just "too difficult." It was not an easy task to get them to give up using drugs. For them to reach the point where they could cope without drugs, it was necessary to simplify their lives so that they could handle their problems with help; sadly, this meant removing them from their homes, where they were exposed to pressures and negative messages from their parents, which only contributed to the desire to "escape" by using drugs.

In one case an adolescent girl addicted to heroin fought treatment fiercely, even physically attacking the Orthogenic School's staff members who were striving to help her. In her first several days at the school, she

The epidemic of substance abuse among young people can in part be attributed to the "drug culture" in which they are growing up. Too often parents themselves are drug abusers; their use of alcohol, cigarettes, and pills for every ill conveys the message to children that drugs are the answer to every problem.

Michael Weisbrot—Stock, Boston

172

suffered terribly from withdrawal, but eventually she accepted help and overcame her addiction. The key to the change in this young girl was that she learned to believe that she was a lovable child and a worthwhile human being who could gain life's rewards without the "escape" that large doses of heroin had previously provided.

Procreation: a solution to alienation?

As has been explained, children are reaching puberty at younger and younger ages. It is not just that youngsters today mature so much earlier, however; the provocative images they see on the television screen and that they are bombarded with in magazines and at movies make sexual behavior attractive to them. (One survey found that in a year's time the average young viewer sees more than 9,000 scenes of suggested sexual intercourse on prime-time TV.) Certainly, these two forces together help explain why girls and boys are engaging in sex—and consequently many are also having children.

Like drug use, teen pregnancy is a growing concern in the United States. Half a million babies are born to teenagers a year. Despite the availability of birth control, the rate of pregnancy in unmarried teens is much higher than in most other developed countries. Parents, who should be a reliable source

About half of young sexually active girls do not use any form of birth control. When they become pregnant, many hope having a baby will fill a void in their lives. Instead, they find that their lives are terribly confined. They are both overwhelmed by and ill-equipped to handle the responsibility of caring for an infant.

Having a baby when you're a teenager can do more than just take away your freedom, it can take away your dreams.

THE CHILDREN'S DEFENSE FUND

Several generations ago life itself was not as complex or precarious as it is today, and most parents' efforts were concentrated on giving their children the feeling that life was safe and good. In the 1950s "Father Knows Best" presented the quintessential wholesome family, the Andersons. The popular situation comedy saw the children—Betty, Kathy, and James, Jr. (not pictured)—through the normal trials and tribulations of growing up. When difficulties arose at school, with friends, or with members of the opposite sex, the Anderson children knew that they could always turn to their parents for the best advice. Jim and Margaret Anderson encouraged them to face their problems honestly and not to take the easy way out, and in the end the younger generation always gained by the experience.

Photograph, Photofest

While it is virtually impossible for parents today to shield their children from the increasingly menacing influences in the world, they can still provide a stable family life that enables children to feel rooted and secure. In order for parents to gain the trust and respect of their children, it is important that they spend meaningful time together.

Billy E. Barnes—TSW/Click—Chicago Ltd.

174

of sexual information, too often are squeamish or judgmental in talking with their children about the subject. Therefore, they are not providing the necessary balance to the media's barrage of sexual messages and innuendos or to what children learn from peers. Professionals who work with "troubled" young people agree that adults often maintain a double standard about sex. They convey the message that if a teenage girl protects herself by using birth control, then she is looking for sex. Parents reinforce the message that contraception is bad by failing to discuss it, by being loath to admit that their children may be sexually active.

Studies of young teenagers who became pregnant and wanted to keep their babies have shown that they felt terribly lonely and subconsciously hoped that a baby would love them and give them the companionship they needed. It was a rude awakening for them when the baby was born and, instead of comforting them as they had hoped, the infant required a great deal of care, which they were unable or unwilling to provide. Some then gave the infant up for adoption or, more frequently, turned it over to their own mothers.

That pregnancy becomes an accessible means of fulfillment was illustrated by comments of young mothers in the *Time* article mentioned earlier: "My life was getting boring. I wanted a baby." "Before I was pregnant, I was nothing. Now I am somebody. I'm a mother." These were typical expressions of girls who felt that there was an absence of interesting alternatives to childbearing for them and who imagined a baby would fill the void in their lives.

Frequently youngsters who get pregnant have been neglected children. Many have been abused. They look to having their own baby as a way to get the attention they feel they deserve, to meet their own nurturing needs. Nevertheless, one of the serious problems is that these alienated young parents often express their frustrations by abusing their children. Child abuse is usually a two- or three-generation problem; those parents who tend to abuse their children often have been abused themselves. Thus, the best way to prevent perpetuation of child abuse is to treat abused children *before* they have babies—to help victims overcome the hurt that the abuse has wrought, to attempt to alleviate the damage it did to them.

A sad state of family life

There is no doubt that life has become more complicated and precarious than it was in past times. Parents themselves are living more isolated lives. Because so few of them reside close to their own parents, they lack an important support system that in previous eras afforded a sense of root-edness. Not surprisingly, parents are finding it more difficult to give *their* children security. Such an atmosphere is essential, though, for endowing young people with the self-assuredness that makes it possible for them to meet life's challenges and master their problems.

The deeper parents are committed to each other, the more ready and able they are to commit themselves to their children. It is nearly impossible in this day and age to shield one's child against the pernicious impact of the media. Still, the child who feels rooted and self-confident because of the security he or she experienced while growing up is better able to do well in life, despite the anxieties the mass media create. In short, only a stable family will create stable children.

The trouble is that so many families are lacking stability. One need only witness the number of marriages that end in divorce—in any given year, for every two marriages that occur, there is one divorce. Even in families that stay together, more and more women are now working outside the home. Mothers as well as fathers now spend less time with their children. In many families parents share with their children only in leisure-time activities, on weekends, or during vacations. While it is important, of course, that parents spend at least their leisure time with their children, these activities generally are not treated by parents or perceived by children as "really serious"; the "serious" work of their parents remains a closed book to children.

One of the most troubling phenomena affecting children today is the lack of family stability. Recent studies have found that children whose parents divorce suffer lasting wounds in the form of anger, depression, anxiety, feelings of betrayal and rejection, self-deprecation, and underachievement.

Illustration by Eugene Mihaesco

With children today maturing so much earlier than in previous generations and being exposed to worldly anxieties at such young ages, they are cheated out of much of what childhood truly should be. Even their play is adultlike. The most popular dolls are no longer simple Raggedy Anns or baby dolls but Barbies, with their well-developed bodies and high-fashion adult wardrobes. Little League baseball, too, is a game that stresses adult values— competition and winning—and in many cases it seems to be played more for the fulfillment of parents than for the sheer fun of children.

By contrast, in times past, when children could observe the working lives of both their parents, respect was the result. For example, when the boy growing up on a farm observed his father hitching a team of oxen to the plow and plowing a straight furrow, he could not help admiring his parent for his prowess. The same was true for children observing their mothers taking care of the home, sewing clothes for the family, or preparing their meals—meals that were *not* bought at the store and cooked in a microwave oven. Rather, meals were prepared from scratch, and often many of the ingredients were home grown. When mothers chiefly stayed at home, their children could observe them in their work—could even participate in it— and this then became a bond between them.

When parents and children spent more time together, the parents were the main instructors of their children; the child learned from observation and instruction how to do things. Moreover, previously parents raised children as they had been raised; they had tradition and the example of the extended family to guide them. Now those supports are gone. It is difficult to replace the ties that previously served to bind children and their parents— particularly now that food, clothing, shelter, and even health care for the children are more or less taken as their inalienable rights. Not too long ago these were viewed by children as special gifts from their parents, for which they were grateful.

With so much gone from family life, with its weakened support systems, parents are finding it difficult to guide their children; yet children need to be understood. When parents fail to provide a stable family environment, children are alienated and seek other outlets, which too often are self-destructive.

Lost innocence: can it be restored?

A hundred years ago the span of childhood was more than 10 or 11 years; now the years from about age 5 or 6 to 13 years constitute childhood— at best some 8 years. So while childhood has not disappeared, it has been nearly cut in half and, what is worse, even those few years are encumbered by adult concerns. Today's children are all too often cheated out of their childhood because too many parents (and the media) worry them with adult problems, such as threats to the environment and anxieties about the future, not to mention parental separation and divorce.

What can be done about these changes, which, so it seems, have deprived children of their childhood? It is doubtful that the hands of the biological time clock will be turned back; on the contrary, all indications are that in the next decades youngsters may mature sexually even earlier than they do at present. Thus, society will have to accept and live with the fact that 13-year-old youngsters will be sexually mature. Parents, society, and most of all the educational system will have to change their attitudes and procedures accordingly. Nonetheless, this author firmly believes there is good reason to protect in every way possible whatever short-lived "innocence" parents and society are able to bestow upon children.

Childhood is a time of dependency, a time when children need to be enveloped by loving, tender care and made to feel secure in their world.

If the family provides this crucial base of security, children will not feel a need to have babies of their own in the false hope that a baby will provide it for them. The more they can enjoy the now-so-much-shorter period of childhood, the less they will feel an urgency to make use of their physiological potentialities.

Because the period of childhood has been so much shortened, all efforts should be made to make it a successful childhood. Children should not be pressured to achieve and to mature before they are ready. For one thing, they should be allowed to play as children naturally play. Freud in "The Poet and Fantasy" wrote: "Should we not seek the first traces of poetic activities already in the child? Perhaps we may say: Every child in his play behaves like a poet, as he creates his own world, or to put it more correctly, as he transposes the elements forming his world into a new order, more pleasing and suitable to him." It is regrettable, however, that many popular games and toys today mimic adult ways of life or emphasize competition over enjoyment. As long as they are children, why not encourage them to play with childlike toys? Barbie dolls, with their well-developed chests, ample hips, and slim waistlines, garbed in highest-fashion wardrobes, made their debut in 1959 and have endured as "best-sellers" in the toy world. Barbie and her beau, Ken, however, are certainly a world apart from Raggedy Ann and baby dolls of yesteryear.

Little League baseball provides an especially good example of a highly competitive game that was created by parents and seems to be more for the enjoyment and fulfillment of parents than of the children who play it. How some children really feel about such competition was brought home to one mother when she reminded her nine-year-old son that he had a Little League game that afternoon. His response was, "Damn! Again no time for play!"—and this despite the fact that he was the star of his team and received much praise for his skill in playing the game.

The challenge of being a good parent

Finally, it is worth reminding all parents that it *is* within their power to arrange the lives of their children in such a way that they can enjoy them to the fullest despite the sway of the mass media. Even in this era of AIDS, rampant drug abuse, a depleting ozone layer, fruit maliciously contaminated by cyanide, and the threat of nuclear war, parents still have the means to predominate over contemporary evils—weighty as those evils may be.

The best preparation for parenthood is realizing there will be problems. A Chinese proverb stated that "Nobody's family can hang out the sign 'Nothing the matter here.'" There are no shortcuts—no easy solutions—and immediate satisfactions are not always attainable. This author's lifelong effort to discover and test what is involved and required for successful child-rearing—from over half a century of dealing with children professionally, and from experience with my own children and grandchildren—has convinced me that living means struggling, and that parents who are willing to accept the challenge and guide their youngsters through the normal struggles of childhood, and attempt to spare them at least a few years of worldly anxieties, *will* be "good enough" parents.

Improving the lives of children has been the focus of Bruno Bettelheim's life and work for well over half a century. He firmly believes that despite all the changes that have affected the world in which today's youngest generation is growing up, parents can still provide the crucial base of security that enables children to experience innocence and goodness. Bettelheim, at age 85, is as devoted as ever to the well-being of children. Here he gets a hug from a particular favorite child, his granddaughter Aurelia Flaming.

Lester Sloan—Woodfin Camp & Associates

The year 1985 was designated International Youth Year by the United Nations. The year's aims included further integrating young people into society and increasing worldwide awareness of their enormous potential. On April 7, 1985, the World Health Organization held festivities to celebrate the joyous and explosive energy of the international youth population, described by Halfdan Mahler, WHO's director-general, as the "best crop of young people in history . . . with better access to the world's store of knowledge." Said Mahler, "Every community should take stock of its youthful resource and nurture it for all its promise." The animated teens above are from the Canary Islands.

future to prepare for by acknowledging their special responsibility to help the human race avoid war and any use of nuclear weapons. The bottom line today for both public education and institutions of higher learning is that they must commit themselves to the principle "that young people, in particular, should be educated to live in peace," which was an objective stated at the time the UN inaugurated the International Youth Year.

Challenging the popular image: survey of teens in ten countries

How do today's teenagers around the world really feel about their lives and about their challenges for the future? Until recently, societies had little way of knowing for sure.

The 1988 publication of an extensive international study was the first large cross-cultural sampling of teenagers, in which they had the chance to participate in taking a carefully translated, standardized self-image questionnaire. In the study, directed by Daniel Offer of the Center for the Study of Adolescence at Michael Reese Hospital and Medical Center in Chicago, some 6,000 teenagers residing in urban centers with lower- to upper-middle-class backgrounds from ten countries described themselves in relation to their families and peers. Their attitudes, values, and coping styles were also explored. Countries participating in the study were determined by the cooperation of local investigators who had previously shown an interest in the Offer Self-Image Questionnaire. The questionnaire, which has been administered to over 400 samples of adolescents worldwide since 1962 and translated into 22 languages, comprises 130 items concerning teens' feelings about their psychological world. The strength of such self-report questionnaires is that each teenager responds anonymously to the same items, all of which are designed to cover important areas of adolescent functioning. Five "selves" are probed: the psychological self, the social self, the sexual self, the familial self, and the coping self.

The results of this study, together with other surveys of over 20,000 normal adolescent students using the same instrument, are significant in that they are remarkably consistent in showing that 20% of the adolescents—a clear minority—report disturbing feelings of loneliness, emptiness, confusion, or depression. This group, however, is far outnumbered by the

	Population characteristics and number of participants				
country	population (in millions, 1984)	per capita income (in U.S. dollars)	quality-of-life index	female participants	male participants
Australia	16	9,820	96	285	194
Bangladesh	100	120	36	202	190
Hungary	10	4,180	91	592	565
Israel	4	4,500	92	307	273
Italy	57	6,480	95	616	634
Japan	120	9,890	98	209	202
Taiwan	19	2,579	88	180	183
Turkey	50	1,460	62	218	232
United States	237	11,360	96	245	246
West Germany	61	13,590	94	199	166

Source: Daniel Offer, Eric Ostrov, Kenneth Howard, and Robert Atkinson, *The Teenage World: Adolescents' Self-Image in Ten Countries* (New York and London: Plenum Medical Book Co., 1988).

80% who do cope well with the teenage years and who make a relatively smooth transition to adulthood. This 80% who adjust well to the adolescent experience represent the norm. They are generally relaxed under everyday circumstances, can control their day-to-day trials, and have confidence in their ability to deal with stress. The vast majority of teenagers do successfully achieve the developmental tasks facing them, while only a subgroup experience serious turmoil or disturbance.

Subjects in all the countries attended high school at the time they responded to the questionnaire. While the test-taking experience was more novel to the teenagers in Bangladesh, all participants in the survey were eager and cooperative. The questionnaire itself not only functioned as an instrument that tapped areas of universal concern to adolescents but also invited them to express in a nonthreatening way what they really feel about their lives.

Noting a few distinguishing factors of each country and how teenagers reacted to specific statements makes universal aspects of the teen experience apparent. The table provides a selection of items from the survey, encompassing all five areas of psychological functioning and showing how international participants compared in their responses.

Australia. With a per capita income that is among the highest in the world, Australia enjoys a quality-of-life index of 96 (based on 100, using a measurement developed by the UN—a composite index calculated by averaging three indexes: life expectancy, infant mortality, and literacy). About nine out of ten Australians live in the urban centers along the coasts; the teenagers who were part of this study were from a suburb of Melbourne. Of this group, 83% reported they enjoy life. Australian teens appear to be well-adjusted; for example, the vast majority report that a job well done gives them pleasure (95%), that they like to help a friend whenever they can (94%), that being together with other people gives them a good feeling (93%), and that at times they think about what kind of work they will do in the future (91%). When a tragedy occurs to one of their friends, 88% reported also feeling sad; 87% feel there is plenty they can learn from others; and 63% would not like to be associated with those kids who "hit below the belt."

Before the mid-1980s, international studies assessing the attitudes and values of adolescents had not been undertaken. In 1988 the results of the first such study were published. A cross-cultural sample of 6,000 teenagers from urban centers in ten countries (table, opposite page) responded to a standardized self-image questionnaire that had been carefully translated into the languages of all the participating nations. The profile that emerged is quite different from the image of adolescent turmoil that is widely held.

One of the countries that participated in the international study was Australia. It was found that Australian teens on the whole are conscientious and hard working; 95% reported that a job well done gives them pleasure, and 91% reported that they think about what kind of work they will do in the future. Like those who participated in the survey, the Australian high school students pictured here, who have part-time jobs as newspaper sellers, are enthusiastic, industrious, and attuned to what is happening in the world at large.

James Pozarik—Gamma/Liaison

The adolescent self-image study that sought to characterize the "core" adolescent found today's teenagers to be compassionate and oriented toward others. This was evident on May 25, 1986, when teenagers throughout the U.S. joined hands with literally millions of like-minded Americans—young and old—who believed that no one should go hungry or be without shelter. The transcontinental Hands Across America drive raised an estimated $32 million.

Youth represents a tremendous potential for society, and teenagers around the world are participating in community activities aimed at helping others. In many less developed countries, young people are taking an active role in primary health care and health education.

Taiwan. This small island country with a high population density has overtaken China in many areas of manufacturing and is well on its way to becoming a fully developed country, with a quality-of-life index of 88. Coming from the modern city of T'ai-chung, 71% of the teens in this study said they enjoy life. Their social adjustment and empathic inclinations are very close to those of Japanese youth. A higher proportion (33%), however, feel way behind sexually. Emotional emptiness was reported by 47% (the highest in the study), but a below-average 25% report frequently feeling sad.

Turkey. Still considered to be a less developed country, Turkey has a relatively low per capita income ($1,460 in 1980) and a quality-of-life index of only 62. Coming from the city of Adana, 86% of the teens in the study reported enjoying life. Turkish youth can be considered above average in their social and sexual adjustments. They are the most empathic (94%) and quite eager to learn. Their tendency toward depression, however, is high: 42% feel emotionally empty and 33% frequently sad. Turkish youth also were higher than average in feeling life is beset with unsolvable problems.

United States. The U.S. has a per capita income of $11,360 and a quality-of-life index of 96. In a sample of 491 teens primarily from the Chicago, New York, and Baltimore, Maryland, areas, 92% reported that they enjoy life. Contrary to the common perception, these American adolescents are also very well-adjusted socially. Comparatively, teenagers in the U.S. have higher than average negative feelings toward their mothers (13%) and toward their fathers (15%). Sexually 24% feel that they lag behind. However, below-average numbers report feeling emotionally empty most of the time (19%) and frequently sad (23%).

West Germany. Among the ten countries, West Germany has the highest per capita income ($13,590); its quality-of-life index is 94. The teens in the sample come from schools in West Berlin, and 85% report enjoying life. And again these youths were found to be quite well-adjusted socially, sexually, and academically. Finally, West Germany teens come out the least depressed, with 8% feeling emotionally empty and 17% frequently sad.

Universal aspects of the adolescent experience

Attempts to understand adolescents through the use of standard psychological measurements reveal many common developmental patterns as well as feelings, concerns, and interests.

The actual span of years of adolescent development varies in different cultures and with different definitions. In this study 13- to 19-year-olds were included, and "adolescence" was viewed as a psycho-social-biological stage of development corresponding to changes in many areas that accompany the transition from childhood to adulthood. Once in high school, the majority of teenagers have already undergone the biological changes of puberty. At the end of high school, the process of separation from the family, which has already begun, continues—obviously not in identical ways in all countries.

It is quite evident that today's teens are more alike than they are different. Even with varying cultural norms and expectations, they show broad agreement when it comes to family and social relationships, vocational and educational goals, and even individual values.

The vast majority of teenagers feel there is plenty they can learn from others. They value work and school. They enjoy doing a job well, think about the kind of work that they will do in the future, and would rather work than be supported.

In fact, adolescents seem to have little difficulty understanding each other. Teenagers today have a body of knowledge that is shared across many cultures, owing largely to the emergence of what may be seen as a world culture. With television and other media often having global audiences, one event or idea can influence an entire global cohort of adolescents in the same way at the same time. An excellent example of this phenomenon was the Live Aid Concert in the summer of 1985. This was probably the biggest and the most spectacular event in the entire history of pop music, as well as a triumph of a kind of new idealism among the world's youth population. On July 13, 72,000 people packed Wembley Stadium in London, and a further 90,000 packed the John F. Kennedy Stadium in Philadelphia, for a 16-hour concert that took place on both sides of the Atlantic and was televised live around the world. In all, it was watched by over 1.5 billion people. More remarkable still was the fact that this was a charity concert, at which all performers and technicians gave their services free, to raise money for the Band Aid fund to combat starvation in Africa. The two Live Aid shows raised over $71.5 million from viewers around the world.

Empirical studies verify that worldwide today's teenagers do share a collective personality as well as a collective consciousness. They have assimilated common elements of human nature, culture, and civilization, as well as a common pattern of meanings that have been dispersed and spread throughout the world. The media transmit ideas and events to all corners of the globe, defining what is new or desirable, and these aspects of life are adopted by young developing minds.

A self-portrait of the core adolescent has emerged in which important psychosocial factors are widely shared. Today's teens who have the most in common with their peers describe themselves as being happy most of the time. They enjoy life, perceive themselves as able to exercise self-control, and are caring and oriented toward others. They care about how others might be affected by their actions, prefer not to be alone, derive a good feeling from being with others, and like to help a friend whenever they can. They feel there is plenty they can learn from others. They value work and school. They enjoy doing a job well, think about the kind of work that they will do in the future, and would rather work than be supported.

The international sampling of teens in the ten countries revealed that they feel confident about their body image and hold age-appropriate sexual attitudes. Overall, they do not feel far behind sexually, are not afraid to think or talk about sex, and do not feel they are boring to the opposite sex.

In the family, again, the large majority have positive feelings toward their parents. Both parents are viewed by teens as basically good, and the majority feel their parents will not be disappointed or ashamed of them in the future. For the most part they do not carry a grudge against their parents; rather, they feel that their parents are usually patient and satisfied with them most of the time.

The world's teenagers cope well with life's vicissitudes, are able to make decisions, feel talented, like to put things in order and make sense of them, do not give up after their first failure, try to prepare in advance for new situations, and feel that they will be able to assume responsibilities for themselves in the future.

While teenagers in Bangladesh, Japan, Taiwan, and Turkey tend to be more prone to loneliness and depression than the subjects in other countries, those who would be considered "troubled" are still a clear minority. This profile of the universal adolescent contrasts sharply with popular conceptions of adolescence as a time of alienation from parents and as a time of self-centeredness and directionlessness. Instead, adolescents do generally accept their parents' attitudes and values, respecting them as well as their own responsibilities. Importantly, the aspects of their experience they agree most upon are relationships, goals, and values.

It should be emphasized that the methodology of the ten-country study did not ensure universal agreement; the questionnaire allowed for as much agreement about negative feelings and poor adjustment as about positive feelings and good adjustment. Furthermore, the conclusions regarding universals were checked in multiple ways across all ten countries. Hypoth-

Teenagers today, as Marshall McLuhan predicted, are influenced more and more by global events and issues, and they are growing up with a sense of camaraderie with other teens around the world. Such fellowship was in force on Dec. 1, 1988, when an international group of young people gathered at the World Health Organization's headquarters in Geneva for a World AIDS Day youth forum. Speakers included Jonathan Mann, director of WHO's Global Program on AIDS and a health educator from West Berlin who himself has AIDS. The young people had come together to discover what roles they could play in helping stem the AIDS epidemic.

World Health Organization; photograph, T. Farkas

esizing a "universal" bright outlook for the world's teenagers, therefore, appears justified.

Prospects for the future

The basic family-and-other orientation of this generation of teenagers is reason for optimism. Teenagers express love and respect for their parents and affirm good feelings toward their peers. They appear well on their way to mastering the universal tasks of adolescent development—forming a clear, coherent view of self, separating from their family of origin, relating well to others, preparing to form a conjugal family of their own, and developing a viable psychosocial identity that will synthesize personal characteristics with an acceptable social role. The well-adjusted adolescent will be the one who accepts developmental changes and also has the help of parents who offer support when it is needed but allow the teenager enough independence to be challenged by these tasks.

Another reason for optimism is that today's teens do appear to be much more influenced by global events and issues than just by their local cohorts. In fact, as researchers notice fewer differences across cultures, it is becoming more evident that people today are living in a global village, as McLuhan predicted. As the final decade of the 20th century begins, this process is one that will in all likelihood have an even greater impact on the generation of teenagers to follow the present one; it is a phenomenon that will only grow in impact. The global village now being glimpsed will become even smaller in the decades to come.

It may be that the teenagers of the 1980s, especially those in the less developed, non-Western countries, are among the first who really have grown up with a sense of camaraderie with teenagers from others parts of the world. They are probably more aware that some of what they are experiencing has also been experienced by other teenagers around the world. The idea of a global cohort would not have been possible to consider a decade or two ago. In fact, this global interaction could serve to at least maintain the current gap between the 80% who are healthy and well-adjusted and the 20% who experience serious difficulties during the crucial adolescent years, if not make it even greater.

In his speech on World Health Day in 1985, WHO Director-General Mahler stressed that "the potential of youth, if it is to be properly tapped, requires understanding and support. Youth is a very special time with special challenges. . . . Studies have shown that a majority of youngsters want to help others and want to assume responsibility. . . . The joyous and explosive energy of youth and its natural curiosity are there to be exploited to build a better world."

Indeed, it would appear that the experiences of the world's teenagers make them capable of the kind of commitment hoped for when the UN declared its International Youth Year—a commitment to a world community. Signs of this are evident in the significant number of common values they share. As an awareness of the world as one intercommunicating global village continues to grow, these universal attitudes may no longer seem unusual. They may rather become commonplace.

A young couple traveling in Spain take a break from a crowded agenda of sight-seeing in Madrid's Retiro Park. Today's teenagers are more influenced by events around the world than any previous generation has been; not surprisingly, they share many common attitudes, values, and goals. A decade or so earlier, this realization of a "global village" would not have been possible. What teenagers learn about their counterparts in other nations stimulates their curiosity to know more— to expand their horizons further. Those who are fortunate enough to travel gain a fuller appreciation of other cultures but are also likely to discover that other people in other places are not so very different from themselves.

189

Oscar Wilde's Fatal Illness:
The Mystery Unshrouded

by Macdonald Critchley, M.D.

I was a problem for which there was no solution.

—Oscar Wilde

That's the way of the world: we work, we scheme, we plan one way. Fate finishes it all off in another.

—Pierre-Augustin Caron de Beaumarchais in *The Marriage of Figaro,* 1784

Among the abundance of literary figures who flourished in England in the Victorian era, few have attracted more attention than Oscar Fingal O'Flahertie Wills Wilde. Biographies and critical studies have accrued—some adulatory, some hostile, only a few being wholly detached. The reasons for such interest lie not so much in the merits of his writings as in his notoriety as a bold and brilliant conversationalist whose imperious and sometimes effeminate manner, and whose scandalous sexual proclivities, led to his eventual disgrace and imprisonment. To many, Oscar Wilde represents the quintessence of the decadent fin de siècle, the world-weary artist martyred by an establishment of hypocrisy. An even more potent cause for the diversity of acclaim is the unsatisfactory nature of the material available for the biographer.

Historical and literary research is at all times bedeviled by the fallibility of human memories. It is a psychological truism that any individual's recall of past events is scarcely, if ever, wholly accurate. As the eminent English psychologist Hans Eysenck once remarked: "Memory is an active process, not a passive one; it changes, distorts, and adapts the remembered materials so that they will fit better into preconceived schemata."

Abundance of accounts, paucity of facts

What is actually known about Oscar Wilde is, in essence, little more than a myth, created upon "evidence" that is indirect, unreliable, uncorroborated, and often blindly accepted and transmitted. Wilde himself was no stickler for the truth, as he admitted. In a letter to the novelist Arthur Conan Doyle, Wilde wrote, "Between me and life there is a mist of words always. I throw probability out of the window for the sake of a phrase, and the chance of an

Macdonald Critchley, M.D., is Consultant Neurologist at the National Hospital, London, President Emeritus of the World Federation of Neurology, and a Commander of the Order of the British Empire.

(Opposite) The tomb of Oscar Wilde in the Père Lachaise cemetery in Paris was created by the sculptor Jacob Epstein. The figure carved on the monument is a debauched-looking angel with bags under the eyes and personifications of the Seven Deadly Sins in a crown upon the head. On the back side of the tomb is an inscription from Wilde's last work, The Ballad of Reading Gaol, *published in 1898:*

> *"And alien tears shall fill for him*
> *Pity's long-broken urn*
> *For his mourners will be outcast men,*
> *And outcasts always mourn."*

Photograph, Jean-Loup Charmet, Paris

191

epigram makes me desert truth." Wilde is also reputed to have confessed: "I do not remember anything. The artist must destroy memory. The truth about the life of a man is not what he does, but the legend which he creates around himself. Legends should never be destroyed."

George Bernard Shaw was shrewd when he wrote in a letter dated April 16, 1933, to Wilde's young protégé Lord Alfred Douglas ("Bosie"): "It is a pity that Wilde still tempts men to write lives of him. If ever there was a writer whose prayer to posterity might well have been 'Read my works; and let my life alone,' it was Oscar."

Not only has there been seemingly endless speculation about the events in Wilde's notorious life but there has also been wide conjecture as to the circumstances that brought about his demise at the early age of 46. It is Wilde's last illness and death that are dealt with here.

One of the more colorful commentators, St. John Ervine, wrote of the dying Oscar Wilde:

His debt to Death was due and must soon be paid. It was not a peaceful death but one of dreadful pain. . . . Wilde died dreadfully. All the splendour and applause in great mansions and famous theatres where people talk long and well, had fallen down to this shabby room in a poor apartment-hotel . . . where a stricken man in exile held his tormented head in his hands and blasphemed against himself and God.

These words, however, were written half a century after the demise of their subject, and their author had not been present at the scene. What, in fact, were the circumstances surrounding Wilde's death—the actual clinical data?

Wilde's physical health

From a purely physical standpoint, Wilde was constitutionally fit, even robust. He was tall and heavily built, and from what is known of his under-graduate days at the University of Oxford, he was well able to take care of himself. Despite his apparent physical well-being, his life-style and habits (by today's standards at least) would not be looked upon as "healthy." For one

thing, he was a great trencherman. For another, he was a chain smoker. Although he had a powerful build, he took no pleasure in sport, saying that his favorite outdoor pursuit was dominoes. Not only did he relish and partake of hearty meals, he also had a strong head for liquor. This was evidenced many times in his life. On one occasion, during his lecture tour to the U.S. in 1882, in the company of a tough gang of miners in Colorado, he was plied with whiskey, but despite his heavy consumption, he was unaffected. On the same trip, at the Bohemian Club in San Francisco (founded in 1872 and comprising writers, artists, and musicians), some of the younger members set out to make their guest drunk. Although each of the hosts succumbed to the many rounds of drinks, Wilde alone was unaffected and later walked back to his hotel from his evening's entertainment by himself. With one possible exception, discussed later, Wilde escaped serious illness and bodily injury.

A complex and stormy emotional makeup

Although endowed with more than average physical strength, Wilde was emotionally and psychologically vulnerable. Beneath his obvious charismatic qualities lay many problems; these were concealed only in part.

Wilde was gifted with a very high intelligence. His well-known talents were reflected in the quality of his prose and in his scintillating wit, which secured for him a very special place in society. Around him gathered a coterie of writers and artists who became intimates—among them the aforementioned Bosie, Robert Ross, Robert Sherard, Reginald Turner, More Adey, Frank Harris, Pierre Louÿs, and André Gide.

At Trinity College, Dublin, where he was a Queen's scholar (1871–74), he was awarded the prestigious Berkeley Gold Medal for Greek. A demy-ship (scholarship) took him to Magdalen College, Oxford (1874–78), where he obtained a double first-class degree in classical moderations and in Litterae Humaniores (liberal arts) and won the coveted Newdigate Prize for poetry. Wilde used to pretend that he attained these awards without resort to study. However, according to David Hunter Blair, a fellow student at Oxford, Wilde actually devoted hours to assiduous and laborious reading, usually well into the early morning.

Although intellectually gifted, Wilde often behaved foolishly. He was a practicing homosexual who made little if any attempt to conceal his activities at a time when such propensities were both unacceptable and unlawful. Gradually his fastidiousness declined, and he began to cause scandal by openly consorting with youngsters who were inferior to him intellectually and socially—"stable-boys and painted pimps," as St. John Ervine put it. "Feasting with panthers," Wilde himself wrote when he was in prison. He had also commented that "I have never learned anything except from people younger than myself" and that an "inordinate passion for pleasure" was "the secret of remaining young."

Wilde was fundamentally a kind man and, apart from his sexual pro-clivities, one who scrupulously avoided vulgarity in speech and detested it in others. Perhaps he was best known for his style; foppish in dress and comportment, he was one of the most extravagant exponents of *art*

(Opposite page, top) Oscar Wilde poses in 1882, at age 28, looking in fine fettle. Yet in spite of his apparent physical well-being, his life-style was far from healthy. Although he had a powerful build, he took no pleasure whatsoever in sport. The cartoon (opposite page, bottom) is titled "Aesthetics v. Athletics" and shows Wilde—the aesthete—complaining: "This is indeed a form of death, and entirely incompatible with any belief in the immortality of the soul." Furthermore, he was a chain smoker. Rarely was he seen without a cigarette in hand or mouth. In the March 5, 1892, issue of Punch, *Wilde was caricatured (above) addressing a group of ladies and puffing upon a cigarette. "Quite too-too puffickly precious!!" ran the caption.*

Wilde was well known for his flamboyant wit; he was clever and charismatic and was always surrounded by a great number of friends. He often acted foolishly, however. He was cavalier about his homosexuality at a time when it was both unacceptable and unlawful. His long-time infatuation with young Lord Alfred Douglas ("Bosie") began in 1891. As a lover, however, Douglas proved to be vain, spoiled, devious, and ultimately vengeful. It was Douglas's father, the marquess of Queensberry, who in 1895 brought Wilde to trial for sexual indecency. The photograph above is of Wilde and Bosie early in their relationship at a farmhouse in Norfolk, England, which Wilde had rented following the orders of his doctor to take a rest cure. Wilde had been ill after his play Salome *was censored in England.*

nouveau. His biographer Frank Brennand epitomized him in the following terms: "Oscar was many persons in one: poseur, liar, moral coward, conceited, vain, arrogant, intolerant, insincere, faithless. Brave, gentle, lovable, forgiving, generous, gay, irresistible, genius, bringer of laughter and giver of grief. This was Oscar Wilde."

In assessing Wilde's character, psychologists would find it important to recall details of his parentage. His father, Sir William Wilde, was a gifted oddity—by profession a leading Dublin eye specialist and laryngologist, he also published books on archaeology, folklore, and the satirist Jonathan Swift. At the same time, though, he was also grubby and sexually promiscuous. Before marrying Oscar's mother, he fathered three illegitimate children.

Oscar's mother, Lady Wilde, was at least as eccentric. In her adolescence she attained notoriety as a bluestocking and a revolutionary poet, naming herself Speranza (claiming descendancy from Dante). After her marriage her political fervor abated, but she became more and more unbalanced. As a widow residing in Chelsea, the section of London that had long been the home of numerous artists and that was famous for its bohemian atmosphere, Lady Wilde attained quite a reputation for her unconventional dress and manners.

The parents had two other children. Oscar had an older brother, William—widely known as "Wuffalo Will"—who grew up a genial, able, but intemperate ne'er-do-well. His younger sister, Isola, died at age nine; Oscar was deeply affected by her death.

The key, however, to the psychological makeup of Wilde is to be found in his hysterical personality. According to the textbooks, this is a condition (now termed histrionic personality disorder in the American Psychiatric Association's *Diagnostic and Statistical Manual of Mental Disorders,* 1987) that is characterized by dramatic, reactive, and intensely expressed emotional behavior as well as by immaturity and emotional instability. The quick responses of individuals with hysterical, or histrionic, personality disorder are shown in eager but evanescent enthusiasms, infatuations, and easy laughter and tears. Typically, hysterical individuals are egocentric: the whole world is seen only in the light of how much they personally are involved. In personal relationships they are possessive and demanding. Everything is valued in superlatives. They feel quite at home in the stormiest situations, which they endow with a stagey, dramatic quality. Readily deceived by others, they also have an abundant capacity for deceiving themselves. Those with a hysterical personality must always be playing a part, making themselves interesting—even at the cost of honor and good name.

Wilde speaks best for himself, however. Typical of the hysterical personality, he was both actor and audience:

The gods had given me almost everything. I had genius, a distinguished name, high social position, brilliancy, intellectual daring: I made art a philosophy, and philosophy an art: I altered the minds of men and the colours of things; there was nothing I said or did that did not make people wonder: I took the drama, the most objective form known to art, and made it as personal a mode of expression as the lyric or the sonnet, at the same time that I widened its range and enriched its characterisation: Drama, novel, poem in rhyme, poem in prose, subtle or fantastic dialogue, whatever

194

I touched, I made beautiful in a new mode of beauty. . . . I awoke the imagination of my century so that it created myth and legend around me. I summed up all systems in a phrase and all existence in an epigram. . . . But I let myself be lured into long spells of senseless and sensual ease. I amused myself by being a *flâneur*, a dandy, a man of fashion. I surrounded myself with the smaller natures and the meaner minds. I became the spendthrift of my own genius, and to waste an eternal youth gave me a curious joy. Tired of being on the heights, I deliberately went to the depths in the search for new sensation. What the paradox was to me in the sphere of thought, perversity became to me in the sphere of passion. Desire, at the end, was a malady, or a madness, or both. I grew careless of the lives of others. I took pleasure where it pleased me, and passed on. . . . I ceased to be lord over myself. I was no longer the captain of my soul, and did not know it. I allowed pleasure to dominate me. I ended in horrible disgrace. There is only one thing for me now, absolute humility.

These words, from the first complete version of *De Profundis,* published in London in 1949, are poignant and revealing for they demonstrate Wilde's introspection, his dubious sincerity, and his self-tormenting egocentricity. They also betray his inordinate vanity. He boasted, for example, that he had written comedies that outdid William Congreve for brilliancy, Alexandre Dumas *fils* for philosophy, and everybody else for every other quality.

Disgrace and doom

On May 25, 1895, when he was 40 years of age, Wilde was sentenced at the Central Criminal Court, London, to two years' imprisonment with hard labor, on charges of having committed acts of gross indecency. The circumstances of his imprisonment constituted a brutal psychic trauma. Allegedly, six months later when he was transferred from Wandsworth Prison to Reading prison, Wilde was forced to stand shivering on the Clapham Junction train platform in London, handcuffed to an authority or chained with other convicts or manacled between two warders (the accounts differ). He was said to be the focus of gaping travelers who tittered and made

Wilde's wit and high intelligence secured him a very special place in society. His circle of intimates comprised many writers and artists, including the journalist Frank Harris (below left) and French novelist André Gide (right).

Oscar's father, Sir William Wilde (1815–76), was an esteemed Irish physician and the author of numerous medical and nonmedical books. However, he led a dissipated life, and before marrying Oscar's mother, he was father to three illegitimate children. Oscar's mother (1826–96) was a poet, known for her eccentricity and her unconventional dress and manners. Lady Wilde remained supportive of Oscar throughout the ordeal caused by his scandalous sexual activities. "Even if you go to prison, you will always be my son. It will make no difference to my affection," she told him.

crass comments. One allegation is that someone spat in his face. It is not known whether these charges are accurate. It is known, however, that the abrupt translation of a pampered aesthete from his life of self-indulgence to a harsh regimen of compulsory labor was inordinately distressing for Wilde. The coarse clothing of a convict and meager and distasteful food caused him enormous suffering; conversation, reading, and writing were forbidden; and for months visitors were not allowed.

Only toward the end of his incarceration did matters become somewhat better. When he could not overindulge himself—being deprived of tobacco and alcohol as well as rich food—he lost his surplus fat and was physically better for it. On the advice of a visiting alienist (psychiatrist), he was finally allowed to have books; the principal factor in his betterment, however, was the privilege of being able to write again. Each day he was issued with pen and ink and one or two sheets of paper. These were collected in the evening and retained by the prison governor; they were returned to him when he left jail. What he had written in those months was a bitter denunciation of Bosie—his vain, spoiled, rich, and ultimately vicious friend—a diatribe that became known and was later published as *De Profundis* but that Wilde had entitled *Epistola: In Carcere et Vinculis* ("Letter: In Prison and in Chains").

He left prison on May 19, 1897; he had been granted no shortening of his sentence for good conduct. Immediately he left England, never to return. Crossing to France, he stayed first at Berneval, near Dieppe, but he soon moved on, meandering through Provence to Italy, Capri, and Switzerland, finally settling in Paris, staying at the Hôtel d'Alsace—a modest establishment—under the pseudonym Melmoth.

Last years: "a kind of suicide"

He was to survive for another three and a half years. During this time a physical and moral disintegration became evident. In the words of his French biographer Philippe Jullian, Wilde's last years were *"une manière de suicide"* ("a kind of suicide"). On his release he resumed his worst habits and overindulgences to an even greater extent than before incarceration. He was dogged by financial difficulties, and he was obliged to cadge

196

money from loyal friends and acquaintances. According to Evelyn Waugh, he became a professional sponge. His letters reveal that he had by no means lost his wit, and they betray no hint of intellectual decline. The lamp of his creative genius, however, was almost extinguished. The only serious product of his final years was *The Ballad of Reading Gaol.* At Reading, Wilde was profoundly moved when another prisoner was executed for the murder of his young sweetheart. This was the subject of the *Ballad.* This was essentially a sentimental work of questionable merit. "A vivacious poem of the third class" was the assessment of Harold Nicolson, who reviewed the *Ballad of Reading Gaol* for the London newspaper *The Observer.*

Wilde also reverted to his homosexual practices, with total lack of discrimination as to his choice of partners. He was now drinking hard liquor in great quantities—at least four liters of Courvoisier cognac a week. At a Paris café he found a rare old cognac and indulged himself in drinking it greedily when he was in funds. At the same time, he took to drinking absinthe, a particularly toxic libation; in addition to having a high alcohol content, it is rich in wormwood, which contains a toxic agent. When it is taken in quantity, this poison can cause diarrhea and vomiting, kidney damage, personality changes, convulsions, and permanent damage to the nervous system.

Once again Wilde put on weight—but now to considerable excess. His features had become high-colored and bloated: "the sort of face one expects to find on a coin," according to Henri de Régnier in his *Figures et caractères,* or, as Frank Harris described him, "like a Roman Emperor of the decadence."

Fatal progression of symptoms

It is not easy to detect the precise point when vague ill health signified the beginning of Wilde's fatal malady. A possible early intimation of malaise

Max Beerbohm, the English caricaturist, writer, and dandy, was best known for his drawings that parodied the pretentious, affected, and absurd qualities of his famous and fashionable contemporaries, and Wilde was certainly among the most famous and fashionable men of the day. Beerbohm had great admiration for Wilde's brilliance and his art but at the same time was disgusted by his sordid sexual escapades. "Aspects of Wilde" (left) is one of many caricatures Beerbohm rendered of Oscar.

Aspects of Wilde by Max Beerbohm; collection, the Ashmolean Museum, University of Oxford

OSCAR WILDE'S CRIME

The Diletante of Two Hemispheres Landed Neck and Crop in Jail.

Branded As a Self-Confessed Apostle of the "Third Sex," He Languishes in Prison, While the Marquis of Queensberry, Who Pluckily Stood By His Accusations, Is Hailed as a Public Benefactor in Exposing the Vile and Unnatural Practices of Wilde.

is to be found on a postcard that Wilde sent from Berneval to the art critic and journalist Robert Ross on May 23, 1897: "I observe a slight tendency to Mrs. Daubeny's ailments." Mrs. Daubeny was a character in Wilde's play *A Woman of No Importance.* Wife of an archdeacon, she never appears onstage, but references to her are made several times in the play as a chronic but self-satisfied invalid who is a martyr to headaches, dizziness, poor hearing, dim vision, sleeplessness, gout, and memory loss (except for childhood events) and is unable to eat anything more solid than jelly. A physician reading this postcard would most likely have seen this reference to Mrs. Daubeny as a light-hearted commentary not to be taken seriously and thus not subject to interpretation as a harbinger of Wilde's terminal illness.

Wilde was now hard of hearing in one ear, a symptom that was first noted by Douglas in April 1895, just before Wilde went to jail. According to Harris, some months later Wilde developed earache, sickness, and giddiness one morning. The visiting prison doctor thought he was shamming and made him get up and go to the service in the jail's chapel. In chapel Wilde felt dizzy and fainted, striking the side of his head. For some time afterward he had a bloodstained discharge from the ear on that side. These symptoms suggest there was a flare-up of his chronic otitis media—an inflammation of the middle ear marked by pain, fever, dizziness, and abnormalities of hearing—which Wilde had had for some time.

The next clinical event in Wilde's medical history was a skin rash he developed after release from prison. Details are lacking as to its precise appearance. Presumably it was widespread and involved unexposed areas of the body; Wilde wrote in a letter to Ross from the Hôtel d'Alsace that in the bath he looked like a leopard. (This letter was undated but probably was written on Feb. 28, 1900.) In this same correspondence Wilde men-

tioned various other symptoms, which were distressing but unspecific. "My throat is a lime kiln, my brain is a furnace and my nerves a coil of angry adders." He also stated that his doctor was visiting him and had prescribed arsenic and strychnine, but without much success. Whether itching was a symptom is not known. Wilde described the rash as being "painful" and spoke only once of its being irritating. The explanation remains a matter of conjecture. Wilde himself ascribed the rash to poisoning from eating mussels, but perhaps he was being facetious. Certainly it was long-lasting, but it vanished shortly after a visit to the Vatican. In a letter to Ross dated April 21, 1900, he wrote: "By the way, did I tell you that on Easter Sunday I was completely cured of my mussel poisoning? It is true, and I always knew I would be: five months under a Jewish physician not merely did not heal me, but made me worse: the blessing of the Vicar of Christ made me whole." (The Jewish doctor who had been unsuccessful was no doubt the Paris practitioner Maurice a'Court Tucker, whose patients were largely among the English colony in Paris, including diplomatic staff and tourists.)

The rash, however, reappeared in August 1900, three months before his death; moreover, by then it apparently caused itching. The dermatologic diagnosis is not obvious. Indeed, Wilde might well have been correct, for the rash could have been an allergic response to shellfish, but such reactions do not usually last many weeks. Some medical writers have suggested that the rash was due to a vitamin deficiency following alcohol abuse. If such a rash were seen in a patient today, it would be common to suspect a drug sensitivity. The drugs that might cause such a reaction, however, were not in use a century ago; very few of the medicaments that were popular in 1900 produced skin reactions. The bromides were an exception, but a bromide eruption is commonly facial in site and pustular in character, which was not true of Wilde's rash.

Wilde himself came round to the opinion that he had neurasthenia, thus raising the possibility of a dermatologic neurosis. "Neurasthenia" was a term much in use by both laity and doctors a hundred years ago. It never

Disgrace and doom were Oscar Wilde's fate for the last five years of his life. Just when he was at the pinnacle of his worldwide fame as a poet, author, and dramatist, he plummeted to the quintessence of depravity. The headline and illustration (opposite page) from the New York Illustrated News, *April 18, 1895, typified the popular revulsion to Wilde's "crimes" at the time of his conviction. The* News, *in a lengthy account of Wilde's trial, described the convicted criminal as "the most shunned man in all the world—an unclean thing— set apart as the personification of a phase of immorality too disgustingly filthy and nauseating to be more than alluded to in print."*

(Opposite page) Photographs, Culver Pictures

The Illustrated Police News—Law Courts and Weekly Record, *in its May 4, 1895, issue in the U.K., depicted the demise of Wilde from his arrest and trial to his wretched time in prison (when signs of what would be his fatal illness began to be evident). In jail he experienced earaches, nausea, and giddiness—symptoms of chronic otitis media—but the visiting prison doctor (left) was convinced that Wilde was shamming.*

Photograph, reproduced by permission of the British Library

The Absinthe Drinker by Édouard Manet, 1859.
Collection, The Ny Carlsberg Glyptotek, Copenhagen

obtained the approval of psychiatric purists. A century ago the British neurologist Sir William Gowers wrote:

The history of the word "neurasthenia" is noteworthy. It is a contribution to medical nomenclature which we owe to our transatlantic brethren, and it attained universal use with the utmost celerity. The concise and concrete character of the word gives it a satisfying definiteness. This depends to a large extent on its classical and somewhat graceful sound. Not only is it graceful to the ear, but it is graceful to the mind of the patient who suffers and longs to know from what, who longs to have a name for that which he, or more often she, feels must be a more definite malady than is suggested by the commonplace designation of "nervous weakness." It has firmly established itself in current clinical terminology. But it often tends to be too satisfying. Men are apt to rest on it as they would not on its English equivalent. . . . Words are our servants, but they often exert a very masterly influence upon us, none the less effective because we are not conscious of it. . . . The general use of the word "neurasthenia" was in spite of a strong objection to it which was felt by many. The Royal College of Physicians of London could not include it in their "Nomenclature of Disease," and yet it is one of the most common of medical words in every language. . . . Remember that the word is a name which should have little meaning even to those who used it. You may employ it to collect the symptoms of the case under a general designation, but do not let it cover them as a cloak.

Wilde was also developing other vague symptoms that were not necessarily organic in character. He was becoming increasingly reluctant to write letters, especially long letters, a disinclination that he described as a *cacoethes tacendi* ("an itch to be silent"). Toward the end of 1897, he complained to his publisher Leonard Smithers that his handwriting "once Greek and gracious," as he described it, was becoming illegible.

To an experienced diagnostician, the most meaningful symptom of Wilde's fatal illness was an excruciating and persistent pain in the head. True, he had mentioned headache as far back as 1897, but in such flippant terms as to suggest that this symptom was then neither intense nor incapacitating. Headache is a commonplace complaint, often quite benign in nature. However, when the pain becomes intense, overpowering, and resistant to all attempts at relief, it may augur impending doom. This is especially so when it is associated with drowsiness and a high temperature. Such was the case with Wilde.

He was now spending much of the day in bed, taking large quantities of opium by mouth for the relief of pain. Chloral, which was taken in liquid form, was given to help him sleep. He was also injected with morphine for his pain, but without benefit. The doctor applied mustard plasters to the limbs—the idea behind this treatment being that of a counterirritant. (Hippocrates taught that a person does not have an equal amount of pain simultaneously in two places.) Ice packs were placed on his head, in the belief that congestion was thereby relieved. The doctor also used leeches (*Hirudo medicinalis,* an aquatic bloodsucking worm)—a common practice then. The leeches were attached to the patient's skin in order that they should withdraw blood from the inflamed tissues; it was believed that this relieved local congestion. Apart from the use of morphine, these treatments are now out of fashion.

Wilde's right ear was continuing to give him trouble, and on Oct. 10, 1900, some form of surgical intervention was carried out. It is not clear just

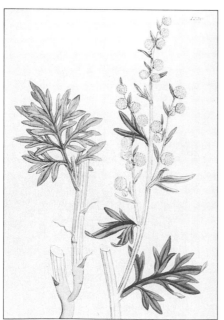

Linda Hall Library, Kansas City, Missouri

what operation was performed or by whom, but from a letter to Harris it is known that the fee was 1,500 francs, later reduced to 750 francs. It seems probable that a paracentesis tympani had taken place and that it was carried out under general anesthesia. This procedure involves a surgical incision into the eardrum in order to release underlying pus.

Because the ear suppurated—*i.e.*, discharged pus—daily dressings were required. Wilde's general condition rapidly deteriorated, and he was now bedfast and, at times, not fully conscious. Even in his semicoma, as Reginald Turner, visiting Wilde at the Hôtel d'Alsace, noted in a letter to Ross, he would move his hand feebly toward his head. Wilde was then also running a high fever. Off and on he was delirious, and his speech became faint and rambling; moreover, incoherent phrases in both Latin and Greek would be detected, while the words uttered in English were marked by an Irish brogue, which was not his usual way of speaking. Reversion to more common forms of speech (demotic speech) during an illness is a phenomenon well known to neurologists.

On November 27 a consulting physician was called in. After the consultation the attending physician, Tucker, and the consultant drew up and signed a brief report in which they wrote that their patient had "a suppurative meningoencephalitis consequent upon aural disease." This means that the ear infection had spread to the brain and had involved the meninges— the covering of the brain—and the brain itself. Often this produces a brain abscess. Such a diagnosis is a fairly straightforward one for the doctor because of the characteristic symptoms and signs. (Since the 1930s and the introduction of the sulphonamide drugs, meningitis secondary to aural disease has become treatable.)

At 2 PM on Nov. 30, 1900, Wilde died in the presence of his friends Turner and Ross and the proprietor of the Hôtel d'Alsace, Jean Dupoirier. No autopsy was performed.

The Granger Collection

When Wilde was released from prison on May 19, 1897, he left England, never to return. He spent time in Switzerland and Italy before settling in Paris. For his last three and a half years of life, he resumed his very worst habits, overindulging in food, drink, and promiscuous sex. He is pictured in Rome late in 1897 with his former lover Bosie. Like many artists of his day, Wilde took to drinking absinthe. "A glass of absinthe is as poetical as anything in the world. What difference is there between a glass of absinthe and a sunset?" was how Wilde spoke of this cloudy green aperitif. (Opposite page) In the late 19th century in France, absinthe was the subject of many well-known paintings, including Édouard Manet's "The Absinthe Drinker." The highly intoxicating libation is made from the herb Artemisia absinthium *(wormwood), the toxic component of which is thujone, and it can cause gastrointestinal symptoms, hallucinations, convulsions, and permanent damage to the kidneys and the nervous system.*

In prison, where the food was meager and distasteful, Wilde lost weight. Upon his release, however, he once again became the great trencherman, consuming great quantities of liquor and partaking of rich and hearty meals. He soon put on substantial excess weight. Frank Harris described Wilde's bloated and high-colored appearance as "like a Roman Emperor of the decadence." The photograph above was taken in 1897 when the portly Wilde was visiting the Vatican.

Did syphilis kill Oscar Wilde?

The distinguished London otologist Sir Terence Cawthorne (who died in 1970) published some careful studies of Wilde's fatal illness in the *Proceedings of the Royal Society of Medicine* (1959) and in the *Annals of Otology, Rhinology, and Laryngology* (1966). He had no doubt that death was caused by the cerebral complications of a septic infection of the ear. In Cawthorne's opinion there might have been an actual abscess in the left temporal lobe of the brain.

Harris referred darkly to a dreadful disease that weakened all the tissues of Wilde's body—a disease, however, that he did not name. Douglas believed that Wilde was a victim of demoniac possession. A similar idea was advanced by the British writer Coulson Kernahan, who wrote that Wilde was being subjugated by forces of darkness.

A number of biographers have ventilated quite another idea: that Wilde died from tertiary syphilis. Even the diagnosis of general paralysis of the insane (dementia paralytica), a form of tertiary syphilis, has been invoked. Of all the speculations about what caused Wilde's death, the most widely mentioned hypothesis, namely syphilis, raises several points for discussion. Three important questions must be asked. First, did Wilde die directly of tertiary syphilis? Second, was syphilis an indirect cause of death? Third, did Wilde ever actually contract syphilis or any other venereal disease?

It is important to understand that syphilis is a complicated disease—one that comprises three stages. First comes the primary lesion, usually due to sexual contact with an infected partner. It takes the form of a penile or vaginal sore (chancre), which may be quite mild; it heals spontaneously, sometimes leaving a tiny scar. Weeks or months later comes the secondary stage, consisting of a mild fever, lasting for a few weeks, and skin rashes. The patient is contagious during both the primary and the secondary stages. There is then a latent period, which may last for many years, and finally the tertiary stage, which can be fatal, develops.

The tertiary stage may take several forms, and any organ of the body may be affected. The principal manifestation is the development of lumps of connective tissue, which are called gummas. They occur principally in the lower leg. The spinal cord may undergo degeneration, causing tabes dorsalis (locomotor ataxia), which is marked by wasting, pain, and lack of coordination of voluntary movements and reflexes, as well as disorders of sensation and sometimes vision. Tertiary syphilis may affect the brain, causing a progressive dementia known as general paralysis of the insane. A common site of tertiary syphilis is in the heart, especially the aorta (the great vessel leading out of the heart). An aortic aneurysm, which can lead to rupture, is a common late manifestation. Now syphilis responds well to penicillin, but antibiotics were not available until the 1940s.

In the latest and most voluminous Wilde biography (1987), *Oscar Wilde* by Richard Ellmann, widely regarded as the definitive work, the author wrote: "Opinion on the subject [of whether Wilde contracted syphilis] is divided, and *some authorities do not share my view of Wilde's medical history.* Admittedly the evidence is not decisive—it could scarcely be so, given the aura of disgrace, shame, and secrecy surrounding the disease in Wilde's time and after—*and might not stand up in a court of law. Nevertheless I am convinced that Wilde had syphilis, and that conviction is central to my conception of Wilde's character* and my interpretation of many things in his later life" [this author's italics].

Various statements have been made—but none by any physician—that Wilde contracted a luetic (syphilitic) infection when he was an undergraduate at Oxford. Some, like the journalist Robert Sherard, have gone so far as to identify the local prostitute who, he said, was probably responsible.

Dental arguments have been adduced as corroboration of an indirect kind. Wilde's teeth were often described as irregular and discolored. This appearance has been attributed by some to a gingivostomatitis, a common side effect of excessive treatment then in vogue for syphilis, namely, inunctions of mercury. However, this is no more than a specious assumption. Whether Wilde's teeth were obviously unsightly before he went to Oxford is not known. (Photographs do not reveal any evident discoloration or irregularity.) The earliest record is the observation by the actress Lily Langtry that his teeth were greenish in hue. This was in 1876, two years before he left the university.

It is known, too, that for some reason or other in his last years in Paris, Wilde underwent prolonged treatment at the hands of M. Du Bouche, a dental surgeon. The fee, which amounted to 600 francs, was eventually paid after Wilde's death. Dental care must not, however, be regarded as supporting the idea of a previous mercurial overdosage.

It has furthermore been alleged that before Wilde's marriage to Constance Lloyd in 1884, he consulted a doctor and was given a medical clearance. No clinical confirmation of this assertion has emerged. The London practitioner Charles de Lacy Lacy, who was the Wildes' family doctor, apparently left no written case records. However, something of his sexual health is known; his two healthy sons, Cyril and Vyvyan, were born in 1885 and 1886.

In the late summer of 1900, Wilde had a recurrence of a skin rash, accompanied by a host of other symptoms, including a persistent pain in the head, drowsiness, a high temperature, dizziness, and discharge from his ear. He was generally bedridden and received an array of "treatments" that were in fashion at the time but are no longer used today. One of these was mustard plaster applied to his limbs—presumably to reduce pain in his head by providing a counterirritant. The drawing (below left), from 1889, is a spoof on mustard plaster therapy. It was titled "Letting Bad Enough Alone." The "exceedingly long patient" says to the doctor, "I say, doctor, are you going to put that mustard plaster on my feet to draw the pain from my head?" "Yes. Why?" replies the doctor, to which the patient responds, "Well, I object. I'd rather have it where it is than drawn down through six feet and five inches of new territory." Wilde's doctor also applied leeches (Hirudo medicinalis) to the skin to suck blood from inflamed tissues and thereby relieve local congestion. Bloodletting with leeches is illustrated in the 17th-century woodcut below. The technique was so favored in Europe in the 19th century that France imported 40 million leeches in a single year.

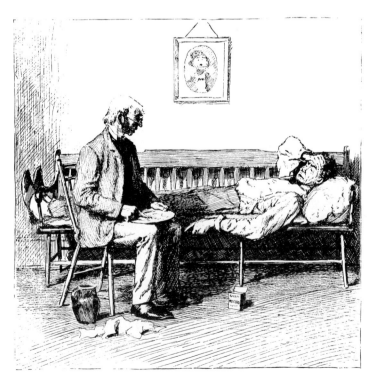

Yet another syphilis-related allegation came about and found a place in many biographies. This was that Wilde's syphilis, presumed to have been cured, relapsed. Again, no medical confirmation of such a recrudescence has materialized, yet the condition has been blamed for the breakup of Wilde's marriage and for an intensification of his deviant sexual behavior.

As already noted, at the bedside of the dying Wilde were his friends Turner and Ross. They observed the clinical charade silently performed by the two doctors, and Ross recorded that the pupils of the patient's eyes did not contract to a beam of light. Inactive pupils are typical in neurosyphilis, but such an explanation is ruled out by the fact that Wilde's pupils "no longer responded." In other words, there had been a change in their functional activity. Terminal coma adequately explains this phenomenon.

Is it possible to trace the origins of the idea that Wilde became syphilitic? Arthur Ransome, one of the first to undertake a critical evaluation of Wilde's work, stated dogmatically in *Oscar Wilde: A Critical Study* (1912) that Wilde died from tertiary syphilis. In a second edition of his book issued in 1913, however, Ransome omitted all references to syphilis. Ransome did not know Wilde personally. The request for him to write his book came directly from Martin Secker, the publisher. In order to gather material, Ransome got in touch with Ross, Wilde's intimate friend and confidant. In a preliminary note to his biography, Ransome wrote, "I wish to thank Mr. Robert Ross, Wilde's literary executor, who has helped me in every possible way, allowed me to read many of the letters that Wilde addressed to him, and gave me much time out of a very busy life to the verification, from documents in his possession, of the biographical facts included in my book."

It is difficult to escape the conclusion that it was Ross who was responsible for the supposition that Wilde had contracted syphilis, that he had

died from this disease, and that the original infection had occurred while he was a student at Oxford. But was Ross a credible witness? Ten days after Ross and Turner witnessed Wilde's death, Ross wrote at length to More Adey, describing in dramatic terms what had transpired. When Turner read this letter, however, he proclaimed that much of it was inaccurate and grossly exaggerated.

Reference has earlier been made to Wilde's circle of artistic friends. Many of them gave him financial as well as moral support during his last years. Wilde's biographers have compiled their material largely from the writings and correspondence of these friends, which were based upon little more than vague reminiscence and anecdotal chitchat. Unfortunately, as witnesses these friends are unreliable and often inconsistent. United in their affection for Wilde, they were also inflamed with jealousy and in many instances were at serious odds with one another. Indeed, their quarrels occasionally spilled over into the courts of law. The writer Lewis Broad, in *The Friendships and Follies of Oscar Wilde* (1954; later [1957] published as *The Truth About Oscar Wilde*), has ably discussed what he called "the battles of the friends."

A terminal ear infection: the wisdom of Wilde's doctors

On the basis of the available evidence, most astute medical men today would have to concur with the diagnosis arrived at by the doctors in attendance at Wilde's deathbed. Their report read:

The undersigned doctors, having examined M. Oscar Wilde (called Melmott) on Sunday 25th November, have recognized serious cerebral disorders resulting from a long-standing infection of the right ear despite treatment for several years. On the 27th the symptoms became much worse. The diagnosis of meningoencephalitis must undoubtedly be made. In the absence of any signs of localized disorder one cannot contemplate trephination. The treatment advised is purely medical. Surgical intervention seems not to be possible.

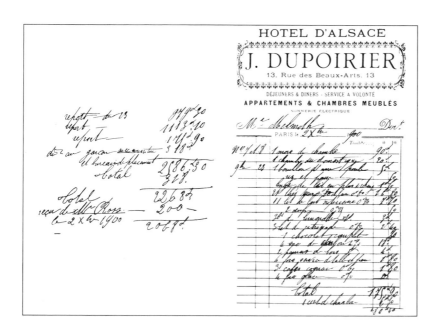

Wilde's death was the result of a long-standing infection of the right ear, despite treatment over several years. The ear infection led to an inflammation of the meninges, the membranes that envelop the brain. In 1900, before antibiotics were available, middle ear infections could be very serious, leading to fatal meningitis and encephalitis, as Wilde's did. Microorganisms from a suppurating middle ear infection (one that discharges pus) may gain access to the inner ear through the oval and round windows at the broad end of the cochlea. The infection can spread to the brain because the inner ear is separated from the brain cavity by only a thin layer of bone.

For many years the identity of the final consultant on Wilde's case, who was called in by Tucker and was cosigner of the death certificate, had been a matter of conjecture. The mystery was solved in 1983 after Mary Hyde, proprietor of the Hyde Collection of historical materials in New Jersey, showed this author the actual certificate signed by the two doctors and generously provided him with a photocopy of it. Because the first signature on the certificate was not clear, it was enlarged and then sent to an eminent French neurologist, François Lhermitte at the Hopîtal Salpêtrière in Paris. Lhermitte verified at the Académie Nationale de Médecine that the name of Tucker's cosigner was Paul Claisse.

Claisse was clearly an appropriate consultant to be called upon to diagnose Wilde's last illness. He had gained the coveted Gold Medal for interns in the Paris faculty and had published widely in the medical literature. Among his papers were, significantly, one that concerned meningitis, another that dealt with skin disorders, and yet another about tertiary syphilis—all conditions that were alleged to have played a part in the fatal malady of Wilde. This author feels certain that a man of Claisse's experience and distinction, given the special areas of medicine to which he gave attention during his career, would not have lightly cast aside the other possible—or at least, widely alleged—causes of Wilde's symptoms, especially tertiary syphilis. One can quite confidently assume that Claisse would not have made a mistaken diagnosis. The suggestion that Wilde had contracted syphilis at some time in his life still rests on hearsay, but the statement that tertiary syphilis was the cause of his death was clearly and convincingly refuted by his highly competent doctors.

Today it might surprise people that someone could die of an ear infection. Before antibiotics, however, infections of the middle ear were very serious; they could lead to fatal meningitis or encephalitis.

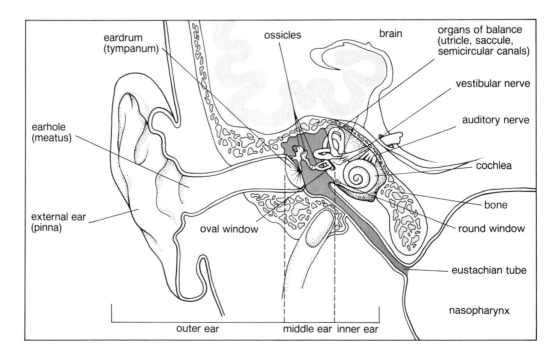

Speculation about the cause of Oscar Wilde's death has ranged from demoniac possession to the most widely espoused theory, tertiary syphilis. However, recent assessment by qualified physicians of the progression of symptoms and of the events in Wilde's life surrounding his final fatal illness has effectively ruled out the possibility that he suffered from any of the forms that tertiary syphilis can take. The now accepted diagnosis is the one reached by Wilde's long-time physician and by the eminent Parisian neurologist who was called in as a consultant. That diagnosis holds that Wilde died as the direct result of his chronic middle ear infection that ultimately spread to his brain. The photograph of Wilde on his deathbed was taken on Nov. 30, 1900.

To appreciate that one could die of an untreated middle ear infection, one should have an understanding of the basic structure of the ear and its location near the brain. The ear comprises a pinna (external ear), which funnels sound waves into the meatus (earhole). The waves impinge upon a taut membrane of tissue, which is the tympanum (eardrum). Beyond the eardrum is the middle ear, which connects with the nasopharynx through a narrow tube, the eustachian tube. (This is why upper respiratory infections so often spread to the ear.) Then comes the cochlea (inner ear), which is a complicated shell-like structure in which lie the tiny endings of the auditory nerves. These nerve endings pick up and convey sound messages to the brain. Adjacent to the cochlea are the minute ossicles, or bony structures, that play an important part in registering sound waves. Another adjacent structure comprises the organs of balance (utricle, saccule, and semicircular canals). It is especially important to appreciate that the inner ear is separated from the intracranial cavity only by a thin and fragile layer of bone.

There may never be conclusive medical evidence, but the common forms of cerebral syphilis—general paralysis of the insane and meningovascular syphilis—can be eliminated. There was no falling off of Wilde's intellectual capacity to support a diagnosis of general paralysis of the insane. No stroke occurred to suggest meningovascular syphilis, nor did the clinical evidence favor a diagnosis of gumma in the brain (a rare form of cerebral syphilis). The balance of probabilities is strongly in favor of a terminal meningoencephalitis, the direct result of his chronic suppurative otitis.

Because of the discovery of the sulphonamide drugs and penicillin, Wilde's terminal illness would not be likely to cause death nowadays. Moreover, had Wilde been born a century later, he probably would not have been imprisoned. Readers then might be the richer by reason of further lasting literary works but, by the same token, two of his most powerful books—*The Ballad of Reading Gaol* and *De Profundis*—would never have been written. Whatever future biographers may have to say about Oscar Wilde and his works, there is unlikely to be further speculation about his death.

Legal
Remedies

by George J. Annas, J.D., M.P.H.

Since judges do not possess any special expertise for evaluating new medical technologies, why, one might ask, do so many controversial medical developments ultimately end up in the courts? In the U.S. the judiciary is the branch of government designated to articulate and protect the rights of the individual. And in the U.S. both individual liberty and economic opportunity are highly prized. It becomes logical therefore for medical disputes that impinge upon individual rights and involve potentially large sums of money to result in confrontation in the courts. Contrary to what one might expect, it is not only the failures of medical science that come to court; success also breeds contention.

Two endeavors in recent medical research illustrate the role of law in modern medicine: the production of commercially valuable cell lines and the search for drugs to treat the deadly disease AIDS (acquired immune deficiency syndrome). The following discussion will examine each of these developments as a source of legal debate that is likely to have enduring consequences for both medicine and law.

The case of the patented cells

An "immortal" human cell line is a laboratory-grown population of cells, derived from one individual's tissues, that can reproduce continuously and indefinitely in culture. One such cell line now in existence has been continuously cultured since 1951. Most of these cell lines are cultured from tumors. Cell lines have many uses in research, perhaps the most valuable of which is to serve as "biological factories" to produce various products such as human proteins or genetic material. In 1980 the U.S. Supreme Court ruled that microorganisms produced by man-made processes could be patented under the Patent Act. As a result, cell lines that produce valuable substances are themselves very valuable commercially.

A natural question arises: If a physician or research scientist succeeds in producing a valuable immortal cell line from a patient's tumor, is the patient

George J. Annas, J.D., M.P.H., is Utley Professor of Health Law, Boston University Schools of Medicine and Public Health. He is the author of Judging Medicine *(1988) and* The Rights of Patients *(1989).*

(Opposite page) Illustration by Dale Horn

208

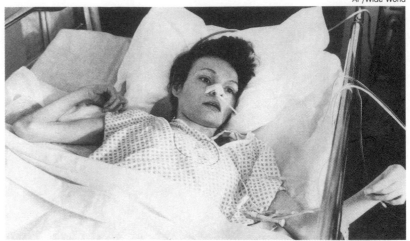

In 1986 a California appeals court ruled that Elizabeth Bouvia, a patient in a Lancaster, California, hospital, had the right to refuse to be force-fed. Bouvia, a quadriplegic cerebral palsy victim who was in constant pain, had first sought— but was denied—court permission to starve to death in 1983. The 1986 decision represented the culmination of a court battle during which she became a symbol of the right-to-die movement. The questions raised by her case go to the heart of some of the most challenging issues that physicians, judges, and ethicists must face.

(Opposite page, top) The first human cell line was established in 1951 by George Gey, a cancer researcher at the Johns Hopkins University School of Medicine, Baltimore, Maryland. Gey named the cell line HeLa after the patient, Henrietta Lacks, from whose tumorous tissue the first cells were taken. Immortal cell lines, populations of laboratory-grown cells capable of reproducing indefinitely in culture, can be extremely useful in research. They may also be commercially valuable. (Opposite page, bottom) In 1980 the U.S. Supreme Court ruled that the General Electric Co. could patent a genetically engineered bacterium—a form of the common Pseudomonas genus— with a potential for cleaning up oil spills. In ruling that new life forms created in the laboratory could be patented, the court opened an entirely new area of legal dispute: Who has the right to own the biological products of these cell lines, and who should be allowed to profit from them?

entitled to receive a share of the profits? This perplexing question was presented to the courts for the first time in 1984 in the case of John Moore.

In 1976 John Moore, then a surveyor on the Alaskan pipeline, sought medical treatment at the University of California at Los Angeles (UCLA) for a form of leukemia. He was treated by hematologist-oncologist David W. Golde. As is an accepted procedure in the disease, Golde removed Moore's spleen, which had enlarged from the normal size of about 0.2 kilogram (0.5 pound) to about 6.35 kilograms (14 pounds). Moore quickly improved. Golde took a tissue sample from the spleen and from it isolated and cultured an immortal cell line that was capable, through genetic engineering techniques, of producing a variety of valuable products. On Golde's suggestion, UCLA applied for a patent on the cell line, which was granted in 1984. The value of this cell line is today put at many millions of dollars.

In September 1983 Moore learned, rather by chance, of the existence of the cell line (the Mo cell line, named after him) and filed suit against Golde and the university. A trial court threw the suit out, but in July 1988 a three-member panel of the California.Court of Appeals, in a 2–1 decision, reversed that ruling and determined that Moore should be able to present his case to a jury. To reach this conclusion the appeals court had had to answer three key questions: Were the spleen cells used to produce the cell line Moore's property? Did Golde wrongfully take them? And did Moore suffer financial harm as a result of a wrongful taking?

The body: whose property?

The property issue is a difficult question, as the human body is not usually legally considered as property. Nonetheless, the appeals court had no sympathy whatsoever with the position that researchers, doctors, universities, and companies can own human cells but individuals cannot. Similarly, the contention that a diseased spleen is a thing of no value was negated by the fact that cells from the spleen had been the foundation of a multimillion-dollar industry. The court was equally unimpressed with the argument by the UCLA researchers that permitting Moore to participate in economic gain from his cells would inhibit scientific progress. It stated:

210

... biotechnology is no longer a purely research oriented field in which the primary incentives are academic or for the betterment of humanity. Biological materials no longer pass freely to all scientists. As here, the rush to patent for exclusive use is rampant. The links being established between academics and industry to profitize biological specimens are a subject of great concern. If this science has become science for profit, then we fail to see any justification for excluding the patient from participation in the profits.

Was not Moore's spleen simply "medical waste," which he had abandoned for the surgeons to dispose of as they saw fit—not unlike hair that has been cut in a barber shop? This has certainly been the traditional legal view. For example, in 1974 when another patient sued a surgeon and hospital for cremating his amputated leg, the knowledge of which action he said caused him to have hellish nightmares, the Kentucky Supreme Court was unsympathetic. It ruled that, in the absence of "any specific reservation, demand, or objection to some normal procedure," the patient accepts the "standard method" the hospital uses to dispose of amputated body parts when he or she consents to surgery. (Moore had, in fact, at the time of the original surgery, signed a form authorizing the hospital to dispose of severed tissue from his body by cremation.)

The California court reached a similar conclusion in the Moore case, but it decided that this case was different from that of the amputee in Kentucky. The court concluded that "interment or incineration" would have been proper disposal methods for Moore's spleen. But, the court said, "It cannot be seriously asserted that a patient abandons a severed organ to the first person who takes it, nor can it be presumed that the patient is indifferent to whatever use might be made of it." The conclusion follows naturally: "commercial exploitation" of human tissue is improper "without the consent of the living patient." The court ruled that the matter of exactly how much Moore should be paid was an issue for a jury to decide. The one judge who dissented would have thrown the case out because, in his opinion, Moore's claim was trivial. He thought Moore's contribution to the value of the cell line was minimal, and he likened Moore's spleen tissue to "unformed clay or stone transformed by the hands of a master sculptor into a valuable work of art."

Physician as gardener

No matter how the Moore case is ultimately decided—and it may be some time before all legal avenues have been pursued—the California legislature can, by statute, determine the rights and responsibilities of all parties in such disputes. Physicians and hospitals can also adopt research policies spelling out the ground rules in advance, and biotechnology companies can develop (as some already have) explicit guidelines for their own conduct. But what should the statute, policy, or guideline be? Is there a fair and reasonable solution?

The law often develops by using analogies. The California court suggested the following analogy to help clarify the legal thinking about the issues in the Moore case: Suppose that crude oil in the ground is ruining a farmer's corn crop and that the farmer may even be willing to pay a refinery

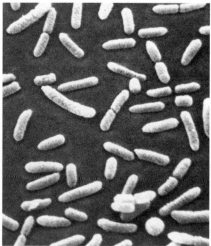

General Electric Research and Development Center

211

to take the oil off his land. Even though the farmer cannot make any use of the oil without the aid of the refinery, the farmer is, nonetheless, entitled to a share in the refinery's profits from the product of his land.

Several other agricultural analogies have been suggested in connection with the Moore case. For example, under Roman law, as long as crops remain in the ground, they are generally owned by the person who owns the land. If they are removed, ownership depends upon whether they are *fructus naturales* (a category that would include perennials such as trees and grasses) or *fructus industriales* (annuals such as corn). The distinction is based on the amount of human input: the more labor is expended, the more likely ownership is to reside with the gardener. Severed fruits thus belong to the gardener, whereas severed trees belong to the landowner. When applied to Moore, this analogy favors the physician as the party who has contributed the most effort in the "harvesting" of the tissues. So does a similar Roman doctrine, specification, which holds that when an entirely new product—for example, a statue—is fashioned by one person out of products—such as a stone—belonging to another, the person who performs the transformation owns the final product.

Of progeny and profit

Neither of the above doctrines settles the question of profit sharing. Even if the physician-researcher now owns the cell line, he or she may still owe the patient something. The dissenting judge in the Moore case thought that "something" would be the value of the portion of the spleen at the time it was taken; *i.e.,* nothing or virtually nothing. This is not clear, however. Since the cells are living, and they reproduce, a more apt agricultural analogy may be one applying to livestock. In this context the progeny of the mating of domestic animals are the property of the female animal's owner, under the maxim *partus sequitur ventrem* ("the birth comes from the womb"). In addition, an owner who is wrongfully deprived of livestock can get recompense for the value of, say, the eggs from stolen chickens or milk from stolen cows. These animal progeny cases support a claim by

In the late 1970s John Moore (below) underwent treatment for leukemia, including the removal of his spleen, at the University of California at Los Angeles (UCLA). Several years later Moore discovered that cells from his spleen had been used by David Golde (below, right), the hematologist-oncologist who had treated him, to produce a substance that boosts the immune system and might be useful in fighting AIDS and other diseases. UCLA, seeing it as potentially worth millions of dollars, patented the cell line that Golde developed from Moore's spleen cells, and a biotechnology firm and a major pharmaceutical company invested hundreds of thousands of dollars for exclusive access to the so-called Mo cell line. A suit filed by Moore in 1983 that claimed he had been exploited by Golde and the university was unsuccessful; however, in July 1988 a California appeals court ruled that Moore should have a chance to present his case before a jury. His day in court is yet to come.

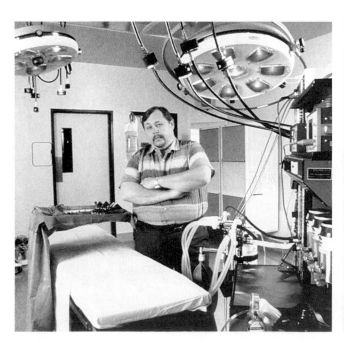

the patient on the value of the substances produced by the cell line grown from wrongly taken tissues or cells.

This line of thinking suggests yet another analogy. Suppose a farmer's cow is dying of a contagious disease that threatens to infect the rest of the herd. A neighbor agrees to care for the cow on his (the neighbor's) farm, both of them believing the animal's illness to be fatal. Under the neighbor's care, however, the cow unexpectedly recovers. Instead of informing the farmer and returning the cow, the neighbor keeps the animal and breeds it. Over the years it has a dozen calves before the farmer discovers what the neighbor has done. Under animal progeny precedents the farmer should be able to get the cow back, along with the value of the calves.

Discarded organs: garbage or gold?

But what about the question of body parts removed during surgery being regarded as medical waste? The problem with treating Moore's spleen like garbage is that Moore did not abandon his spleen—he assumed the surgeon would do what would customarily have been done to it—and had he known the organ was valuable, he would not have voluntarily let his doctors use it. This is a critical point in the case made by the UCLA researchers. It is precisely because medical scientists fear that patients will not voluntarily relinquish their rights to commercial products resulting from manipulation of their cells that researchers oppose even discussing the potential value of such cells with patients.

Perhaps the following analogy would be more appropriate to the case: A person is usually happy to have someone dispose of his garbage; but if there are two competing garbage companies, and one of them will pay to take the garbage away (or will do it less expensively than the other), people will certainly choose to do business with the company that will pay. If yet a third company discovers a way to turn garbage into gold, most people would want that company to pay them even more. And if someone's garbage were unique, he or she might well hold out for a share of the garbage company's profits.

Whereas medicine has yet to develop a cure for AIDS or a vaccine to prevent people from becoming infected, the law has at least been able to provide legal remedies for some persons with the disease. Betty Dale (above) is one of hundreds of people who have contracted AIDS from a blood transfusion received prior to 1985, the time when U.S. blood banks began to routinely screen donated blood for the AIDS virus. Some blood banks have settled out of court in cases like Dale's, and in many instances juries have granted sizable awards to people who became infected via transfusion.

Three brothers—all hemophiliacs—apparently became infected with the AIDS virus through a blood product. Randy (left) and Robert Ray are shown with their sister Candy at a congressional hearing in 1987. (Brother Ricky is not pictured.) After the boys were barred from school in their home town of Arcadia, Florida, the family obtained a court order enabling them to return to classes. Then someone set fire to their house. The family finally moved. In September 1988 the Rays, who charged that their civil rights had been violated, reached a $1.1 million settlement with the school district for Arcadia. It was the first major monetary award in an AIDS discrimination case.

Garbage collection companies have no obligation to tell their clients what is being done with their waste—but physicians do. The doctor-patient relationship is often described as a "fiduciary," or trust, relationship. Part of that trust rests on the assumption that anything the physician does not disclose to the patient is withheld on the understanding that the information would not affect the patient's decision about his or her own care. Further, it is assumed that the undisclosed information is, in any event, about something done for the patient's benefit. This is hardly the case when a patient's organ is "mined" for biological gold.

A potential solution

The California court seems correct in its decision in the Moore case. If human cells are to be profited from, patented, or both, the person from whom these cells are derived should have at least as much legal right to own and profit from their commercial exploitation as the physician-researcher and the biotechnology company. Thus, there are two possible ways to resolve the situation: all those involved—patient, physician, researchers, drug manufacturer—profit, or none profit. The preference of this author, as one who is concerned with the ethical issues raised by the burgeoning of biotechnology, is to discourage the increasing commercialization of the body and its tissues by amending the Patent Act to explicitly prohibit the patenting of human cells and the Organ Transplant Act to include a prohibition on the sale of human tissue and cells for any purpose (not just, as the law now stands, when they are intended for transplantation).

In the absence of such statutory controls, however, some guidelines need to be developed. Fairness and respect for persons require that pa-

In October 1988 AIDS activists demonstrated at the headquarters of the U.S. Food and Drug Administration (FDA) in Rockville, Maryland, to show their anger at the FDA's insistence that drugs going through the approval process be tried in humans before they become legally available to AIDS patients. Ironically, it was the advent of the AIDS epidemic itself—and protests of AIDS activists—that had earlier prompted the first major change in the FDA's rigorous drug-approval process; under a new rule announced in May 1987, promising but still experimental drugs were to be made available to persons with life-threatening diseases. The rule applies only to drugs that are currently under investigation in controlled clinical trials on human subjects, thus excluding substances being tested in countries other than the U.S., as well as substances deemed to be potentially harmful or of doubtful value.
AP/Wide World

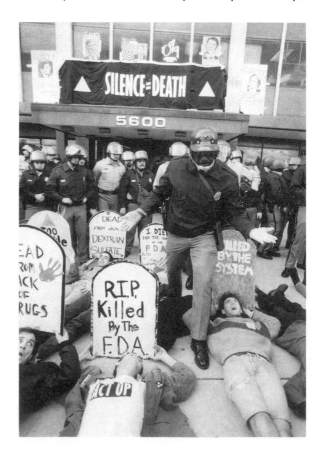

tients be explicitly informed that their organs, tissues, and cells may be used for commercial purposes when such use is intended. Patients should have a right to accept or reject this use and should be offered reasonable compensation if they agree to it. This compensation could be in the form of a small percentage of profits (or gross sales) and would accrue to the patient in the highly unlikely event that a commercially successful product were to be developed.

AIDS—when medicine fails

One of the products that the Mo cell line produces is a lymphokine (a type of blood protein) known as GM-CSF (granulocyte-macrophage colony-stimulating factor), which is currently being tested as a possible treatment for AIDS. As a universally fatal and frightening disease, AIDS has forced society into a confrontation with the mortality of the individual, the limits of modern medicine, and the frontiers of human compassion. In contrast to the success of science in producing products such as cell lines that function as biological factories, medical research has yet to discover a cure for AIDS (although the drug known as zidovudine, or AZT, can prolong the lives of some patients). Scientific and medical strategies for dealing with the AIDS epidemic must thus far be considered unsuccessful. In the light of medicine's apparent failure in the conquest of AIDS, what role has the law assumed for the ever increasing number of AIDS patients?

The primary role of the law in the AIDS epidemic is to protect the public's health and the civil rights of those suffering from the disease. Since AIDS can be acquired only by sexual or blood-to-blood contact, such traditional public health measures as mandatory screening and quarantine have been deemed neither necessary nor helpful. Instead, the public health community has adopted a strategy focusing on education about how the virus is transmitted and methods (such as condom use and screening of the blood supply) of preventing transmission. Despite the campaign to educate the public at large, however, there remains a deep-seated fear on the part of

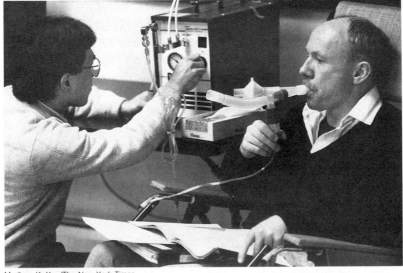

Marilynn K. Yee/The New York Times

In 1988, in a case brought by the Dallas (Texas) Gay Alliance, a judge ruled that AIDS patients in that city should have access to the then-experimental drug aerosol pentamidine, which was believed to be effective in preventing a deadly type of pneumonia to which persons with AIDS are particularly vulnerable. Subsequently, in February 1989, the FDA broadened its research protocol governing aerosol pentamidine, making the as-yet-unproven drug more widely available. The drug received formal approval the following June.

In the 1970s cancer patients from the U.S. were flocking to a clinic in Tijuana, Mexico (above), to receive laetrile (amygdalin), a controversial drug made from apricot pits (above right). In 1979 a group of patients sued to prevent the Food and Drug Administration from interfering with the importation of the drug. The FDA vigorously defended its position, emphasizing that there had been no clinical trials to establish the safety or effectiveness of laetrile. Further, it was felt that making this unproven treatment available might divert patients from seeking other, established therapies.

The Supreme Court upheld the FDA's stand, pointing out that because of their desperation, patients with incurable diseases—perhaps more than others— need the protection of the law to keep them from falling prey to false claims and quack cures. Even today, however, in a much more relaxed regulatory climate, the FDA continues to protect AIDS patients and others from expensive, unproven, and, in some cases, dangerous therapies, such as the "ozone machine" pictured at right, being touted for treatment of AIDS because of its reputed antiviral properties.

many individuals that they might contract this deadly illness through various kinds of casual contact. As a result, persons with AIDS have been the subject of discrimination in such areas as housing, education, employment, medical care, and insurance.

This discrimination can be personally devastating, and it often deprives infected individuals of basic civil and human rights. For the time being, at least, medicine can provide no cure for their illness. Nor can the law cure AIDS. It can, however, discourage discrimination and provide redress where discrimination exists. Successful lawsuits have been brought to require public schools to admit children with AIDS to their classrooms, to prevent employers from arbitrarily firing AIDS patients, and to prevent discrimination in housing and insurance. AIDS is one illness for which lawyers have so far been able to provide more help to patients than physicians have.

Examples abound. In one case a U.S. Circuit Court of Appeals concluded that a teacher who had tested positive for the AIDS virus was a handicapped person under federal law and that the teacher's job was therefore protected (since the teacher did not present a significant risk of harm to students). In another case a federal court concluded that a child with AIDS had a right to continue to be a student in a kindergarten classroom, even though the child had previously bitten a classmate. In arriving at this

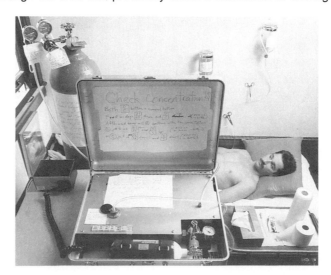

conclusion, the court put the burden of proving danger of transmitting AIDS on those who sought to exclude the child from the classroom.

Responding to hope—or hype?

Because of its universally fatal prognosis, AIDS has also caused a reconsideration, in the United States at least, of the basic laws on drug safety and efficacy—in a way that no other disease, no matter how negative the outlook, has been able to do. The general rule in the U.S. has been that, except in carefully controlled and approved research programs, experimental drugs are not to be made available to patients until such drugs have been proved both safe and effective to the satisfaction of the U.S. Food and Drug Administration (FDA). AIDS, however, because of its epidemic spread, rapid course, and universal fatality, has prompted many to ask if this policy makes sense. Would it not perhaps be kinder and more compassionate, they ask, to permit those suffering from AIDS to have access to various unapproved drugs? In July 1985 the late film star Rock Hudson made headlines when he went to Paris to obtain HPA-23, a drug he was convinced could save his life. Should he have been able to obtain this medication at home in the U.S.?

In 1988, in a lawsuit brought by the Dallas (Texas) Gay Alliance, a judge decided that AIDS patients in Dallas should have access to one experimental and, at that time, unapproved drug (aerosol pentamidine); the decision was based on compassionate reasons. "This Court is not a physician," the judge declared, "nor is it a hospital administrator, but it must be to some extent a voice of the conscience of the community. That voice . . . must be raised in favor of life." (The drug in question received FDA approval in June 1989.) Using a similar rationale, FDA Commissioner Frank Young announced in July 1988 that U.S. citizens would thenceforth be permitted to import unapproved drugs from abroad, in small quantities for their personal use, because, in Young's words, "There is such a degree of desperation, and people are going to die, and I'm not going to be the commissioner that robs them of hope." Are these legal actions a response to hope or hype, to real science or quackery? The question is not a new one.

In the 1970s thousands of U.S. cancer patients traveled to Mexico and Canada to obtain laetrile, touted by some as a useful anticancer drug. Laetrile was not available in the U.S., and in 1979 a group of terminally ill cancer patients sued to prevent the FDA from interfering with their importing it. The FDA defended its ban on the basis that there had been no adequate, well-controlled studies of laetrile's safety or effectiveness. Another important issue was that it diverted patients from other, established (if not necessarily curative) therapies then available in the U.S. Thus, many physicians saw it as at best an unproven treatment (or at worst a hoax) that seduced desperate people hoping for a miracle cure.

The U.S. Supreme Court upheld the FDA's position. It noted that safety and effectiveness have meaning for the terminally ill as well as for those with curable diseases, pointing out that the terminally ill are especially vulnerable to exploitation by all manner of false claims and promises. In the court's words:

The complex legal issues surrounding death may soon seem simple in comparison with the questions that— as a result of the techniques of in vitro fertilization (IVF)—are being raised about the beginning of life. In 1986 Risa and Steven York (above) entered an IVF program in Norfolk, Virginia. Several attempts at embryo implantation failed. In 1988, having moved to California, they requested that the clinic in Norfolk ship their one remaining frozen embryo to a Los Angeles IVF center. The Norfolk facility refused, claiming the Yorks had no rights to the embryo outside that institution's jurisdiction. It is not yet clear what part the law will play in disputes raised by the technology of IVF. That the law will have a part, no one doubts.

Since the turn of the century, resourceful entrepreneurs have advertised a wide variety of purportedly simple and painless cures for cancer, including . . . peat moss; . . . colored floodlamps; pastes made from . . . Limburger cheese; mineral tablets. . . . Congress could reasonably have determined to protect the terminally ill, no less than other patients, from the vast range of self-styled panaceas that inventive minds can devise.

Was the FDA right on cancer and wrong on AIDS, or is there a fundamental difference between the two diseases that accounts for the different positions? One possible explanation is that society now places a higher value on individual autonomy than it did a decade ago and that trust in the government's protective role has diminished. A more likely reason is that, unlike cancer, AIDS has been totally resistant to attempts to cure it, and those suffering from AIDS have been much more effective than cancer patients in mobilizing public support for their plight. Political demonstrations by gay activist groups, for example, have influenced FDA policy in a way that the advocates of laetrile never could.

The AIDS activists have succeeded in forcing a change in the policies of the FDA, but whether this is a victory only history will be able to determine. With underground and unapproved drugs becoming so freely available that few persons with AIDS do not take some kind of medication, it may be impossible to conduct valid clinical trials of experimental treatment drugs. That is, it might become completely impossible for researchers to establish a control group—patients receiving placebo therapy under strict supervision—to compare with a group of patients taking an experimental drug. And without a control group for comparison, it will be much more difficult to demonstrate that any given drug is actually effective in fighting AIDS. In short, what appears compassionate in the short run may turn out to be devastatingly destructive in the long run.

Judging medicine: crucial decisions ahead

The law cannot create new "wonder" products, such as immortal cell lines, nor can it cure deadly diseases such as AIDS. The law can, however, help to ensure that the profits from scientific products are fairly distributed and that those suffering from feared diseases are not subjected to unfair discrimination. The law must be responsive to new scientific developments. Nonetheless, in protecting human rights strongly and consistently, its rightful goal is to establish a permanent climate in which, no matter what the successes or failures of modern medicine may be, basic human rights will continue to be highly valued and protected.

One way to test the views on the two seemingly unrelated topics of cell lines and AIDS sufferers is to think about the fate of a person who might be discovered to have a natural immunity to the AIDS virus. Would society imprison this person and force him or her to participate in research? Would the person be permitted to sell his or her priceless cells to the highest bidder? How such an individual would be treated in any given society is a measure of both its humanity and its common sense. Because society is often ruled by neither, judges will undoubtedly be called upon again and again to help make crucial decisions about medical issues involving human rights.

218

ENCYCLOPÆDIA
BRITANNICA

MEDICAL
UPDATE

From the 1989 Printing of *Encyclopædia Britannica*

The purpose of this section is to introduce to continuing *Medical and Health Annual* subscribers selected *Macropædia* articles or portions of articles that have been completely revised or rewritten in the most recent edition of the *Encyclopædia Britannica*. It is intended to update the *Macropædia* coverage of medical and health-related topics, and it offers a longer and more comprehensive treatment than can be accomplished fully by the yearly review of significant developments in the *Annual*.

The article chosen from the 1989 printing is RESPIRATION AND RESPIRATORY SYSTEMS. This selection includes the parts of the *Britannica* article that concern human respiration. It is the work of distinguished scholars and represents the continuing dedication of the *Encyclopædia Britannica* to bringing texts that provide authoritative interpretation as well as pertinent data and examination of timely issues to the general reader.

Respiration and Respiratory Systems

Respiration is the process by which animal organisms take up oxygen and discharge carbon dioxide in order to satisfy their energy requirements. In the living organism, energy is liberated, along with carbon dioxide, through the oxidation of molecules containing carbon. The term respiration also denotes the exchange of the respiratory gases (oxygen and carbon dioxide) between the organism and the medium in which it lives and between the cells of the body and the tissue fluid that bathes them.

With the exception of energy used by animal life in the deep ocean, all energy used by animals is ultimately derived from the energy of sunlight. The carbon dioxide in the atmosphere in conjunction with the energy of sunlight is used by plants to synthesize sugars and other components. Animals consume plants or other organic material to obtain chemical compounds, which are then oxidized to sustain vital processes.

The article is divided into the following sections:

General features of the respiratory process

Although the acquisition of oxygen and the elimination of carbon dioxide are essential requirements for all animals, the rate and amount of gaseous exchange vary according to the kind of animal and its state of activity. In the Table the oxygen consumption of various animals is expressed in terms of millilitres of oxygen per kilogram of body fluid, reflecting the gas demands of different species at rest and in motion. A change in the chemical composition of the body fluids elicits a response from the central nervous system, which then excites or depresses the machinery of external respiration.

Oxygen Consumption of Various Animals and Its Variation with Rest and Activity		
	weight (grams)	oxygen consumption (millilitres per kilogram of weight per hour)
Paramecium	0.000001	500
Mussel (*Mytilus*)	25	22
Crayfish (*Astacus*)	32	47
Butterfly (*Vanessa*)	0.3	
resting		600
flying		100,000
Carp (*Cyprinus*)	200	100
Pike (*Esox*)	200	350
Mouse	20	
resting		2,500
running		20,000
Human	70,000	
resting		200
maximal work		4,000

Source: A. Krogh, *The Comparative Physiology of Respiratory Mechanisms* (1959).

THE GASES IN THE ENVIRONMENT

The range of respiratory problems faced by aquatic and terrestrial animals can be seen from the varying composition and physical characteristics of water and air. Air contains about 20 times the amount of oxygen found in air-saturated water. In order to extract an equivalent amount of oxygen as an air breather, an aquatic animal may find it necessary to pass across the respiratory surfaces a relatively larger volume of the external medium. Moreover, the diffusion rate of oxygen is much lower in water than in air. The problem is further compounded by the higher density (1,000 times air) and viscosity (100 times air) of water, which impose on the machinery of aquatic respiration a much greater work load. Thus, fish may expend about 20 percent of their total oxygen consumption in running the respiratory pump, as compared with about 1 to 2 percent in mammals, including humans.

The carbon dioxide content of most natural waters is low compared with air, often almost nil. In contrast to oxygen, carbon dioxide is extremely soluble in water and diffuses rapidly. Most of the carbon dioxide entering water combines either with the water (to form carbonic acid) or with other substances (to form carbonates or bicarbonates). This buffering capacity maintains a low level of free carbon dioxide and facilitates the maintenance of a favourable diffusion gradient for carbon dioxide exchange by water breathers. In general, oxygen exchange, which is strongly dependent on the oxygen content of the water, is more critically limiting for aquatic forms than is the exchange of carbon dioxide.

Temperature exerts a profound effect on the solubility of gases in water. A change from 5° to 35° C (41° to 95° F) reduces the oxygen content of fresh water by nearly half. At the same time, a rise in body temperature produces an increase in oxygen consumption among animals that do not closely regulate their body temperatures (so-called cold-blooded animals). A fish experiencing both rising water and body temperatures is under a double handicap: more water must be pumped across its gill surfaces to extract the same amount of oxygen as was needed at the lower temperature; and the increased metabolism requires greater quantities of oxygen.

The amount of oxygen available in natural waters is also limited by the amount of dissolved salts. This factor is a determinant of oxygen availability in transitional zones between sea and fresh water. Pure water, when equilibrated with oxygen at 0° C, for example, contains about 50 millilitres of oxygen per litre; under the same conditions, a solution containing 2.9 percent of sodium chloride contains only 40 millilitres of oxygen per litre. Bodies of water may have oxygen-poor zones. Such zones are especially evident in swamps and at the lower levels of deep lakes. Many animals are excluded from such zones; others have become remarkably adapted to living in them.

The Earth's atmosphere extends to a height of many miles. It is composed of a mixture of gases held in an envelope around the globe by gravitational attraction. The atmosphere exerts a pressure proportional to the weight of a column of air above the surface of the Earth extending to the limit of the atmosphere: atmospheric pressure at sea level is on average sufficient to support a column of mercury 760 millimetres in height (abbreviated as 760 mm Hg—the latter being the chemical symbol for mercury). Dry air is composed chiefly of nitrogen and inert gases (79.02 percent), oxygen (20.94 percent), and carbon dioxide (0.03 percent), each contributing proportionately to the total pressure. These percentages are relatively constant to about 80.5 kilometres in altitude. At sea level and a barometric pressure of 760 millimetres of mercury, the partial pressure of nitrogen is 79.02 percent of 760 millimetres of mercury, or 600.55 millimetres of mercury; that of oxygen is 159.16 millimetres of mercury; and that of carbon dioxide is 0.20 millimetres of mercury. *Composition of air*

The existence of water vapour in a gas mixture reduces the partial pressures of the other component gases but does not alter the total pressure of the mixture. The importance of water-vapour pressure to gas composition can be appreciated from the fact that at the body temperature of humans (37° C, or 98.6° F) the atmospheric air drawn into the lungs becomes saturated with water vapour. The water-vapour pressure at 37° C is 47 millimetres of mercury. To calculate the partial pressures of the respiratory gases, this value must be subtracted from the atmospheric pressure. For oxygen, 760 (the atmospheric pressure) − 47 = 713 millimetres of mercury, and 713 × 0.209 (the percentage of oxygen in the atmosphere) = 149 millimetres of mercury; this amounts to some 10 millimetres of mercury lower than the partial pressure of oxygen in dry air at 760 millimetres of mercury total pressure.

Atmospheric pressures fall at higher altitudes, but the composition of the atmosphere remains unchanged. At 7,600 metres (25,000 feet) the atmospheric pressure is 282 millimetres of mercury and the partial pressure of oxygen is about 59 millimetres of mercury. Oxygen continues to constitute only 20.94 percent of the total gas present. The rarefaction of the air at high altitudes not only limits the availability of oxygen for the air breather, it also limits its availability for aquatic forms, since the amount of dissolved gas in water decreases in parallel with the decline in atmospheric pressure. Lake Titicaca in Peru is at an altitude of about 3,810 metres; one litre of lake water at this altitude (and at 20° C, or 68° F) holds four millilitres of oxygen in solution; at sea level, it would hold 6.4.

The variations in the characteristics of air and water suggest the many problems with which the respiratory systems of animals must cope in procuring enough oxygen to sustain life.

Human respiration

THE DESIGN OF THE RESPIRATORY SYSTEM

The human gas-exchanging organ, the lung, is located in the thorax, where its delicate tissues are protected by the bony and muscular thoracic cage. The lung provides the organism with a continuous flow of oxygen and clears the blood of the gaseous waste product, carbon dioxide. Atmospheric air is pumped in and out regularly through a system of pipes, called conducting airways, which join the gas exchange region with the outside of the body (Figure 8). The airways can be divided into upper and lower airway systems. The transition between the two systems is located where the pathways of the respiratory and digestive systems cross, just at the top of the larynx.

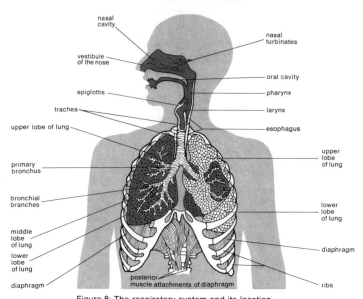

Figure 8: The respiratory system and its location.

From (head and throat areas only) J. Sobotta and H. Becher in H. Ferner and J. Staubesand (eds.), *Atlas der Anatomie des Menschen*, vol. 2 (1972), © Urban & Schwarzenberg, Munich

Upper and lower airways

The upper airway system comprises the nose and the paranasal cavities, called sinuses, the pharynx, or throat, and partly also the oral cavity, since it may be used for breathing. The lower airway system consists of the larynx, the trachea, the stem bronchi, and all the airways ramifying intensively within the lungs, such as the intrapulmonary bronchi, the bronchioles, and the alveolar ducts. For respiration, the collaboration of other organ systems is clearly essential. The diaphragm, as the main respiratory muscle, and the intercostal muscles of the chest wall play an essential role by generating, under the control of the central nervous system, the pumping action on the lung. The muscles expand and contract the internal space of the thorax, whose bony framework is formed by the ribs and the thoracic vertebrae. . . .

Morphology of the upper airways. *The nose.* The nose is the external protuberance of an internal space, the nasal cavity (Figure 9). It is subdivided into a left and right canal by a thin medial cartilaginous and bony wall, the nasal septum. Each canal opens to the face by a nostril and into the pharynx by the choana. The floor of the nasal cavity is formed by the palate, which also forms the roof of the oral cavity. The complex shape of the nasal cavity is due to projections of bony ridges, the superior, middle, and inferior turbinate bones (or conchae), from the lateral wall. The passageways thus formed below each ridge are called the superior, middle, and inferior nasal meatuses.

On each side, the intranasal space communicates with a series of neighbouring air-filled cavities within the skull (the paranasal sinuses) and also, via the nasolacrimal duct, with the lacrimal apparatus in the corner of the eye. The duct drains the lacrimal fluid into the nasal cavity. This fact explains why nasal respiration can be rapidly impaired or even impeded during weeping: the lacrimal fluid is not only overflowing into tears, it is also flooding the nasal cavity.

Paranasal sinuses

The paranasal sinuses are sets of paired single or multiple cavities of variable size. Most of their development takes place after birth, and they reach their final size toward the age of 20 years. The sinuses are located in four different skull bones—the maxilla, the frontal, the ethmoid, and the sphenoid bones. Correspondingly, they are called the maxillary sinus, which is the largest cavity; the frontal sinus; the ethmoid sinuses; and the sphenoid sinus, which is located in the upper posterior wall of the nasal cavity. The sinuses have two principal functions: because they are filled with air, they help keep the weight of the skull within reasonable limits, and they serve as resonance chambers for the human voice.

The nasal cavity with its adjacent spaces is lined by a respiratory mucosa. Typically, the mucosa of the nose contains mucus-secreting glands and venous plexuses; its top

cell layer, the epithelium, consists principally of two cell types, ciliated and secreting cells. This structural design reflects the particular ancillary functions of the nose and of the upper airways in general with respect to respiration. They clean, moisten, and warm the inspired air, preparing it for intimate contact with the delicate tissues of the gas-exchange area. During expiration through the nose, the air is dried and cooled, a process that saves water and energy.

Two regions of the nasal cavity have a different lining. The vestibule, at the entrance of the nose, is lined by skin that bears short thick hairs called vibrissae. In the roof of the nose, the olfactory organ with its sensory epithelium checks the quality of the inspired air. About two dozen olfactory nerves convey the sensation of smell from the olfactory cells through the bony roof of the nasal cavity to the central nervous system.

The pharynx. For the anatomical description, the pharynx can be divided into three floors (see Figure 9). The upper floor, the nasopharynx, is primarily a passageway for air and secretions from the nose to the oral pharynx. It is also connected to the tympanic cavity of the middle ear through the auditory tubes that open on both lateral walls. The act of swallowing opens briefly the normally collapsed auditory tubes and allows the middle ears to be aerated and pressure differences to be equalized. In the posterior wall of the nasopharynx is located a lymphatic organ, the pharyngeal tonsil. When it is enlarged (as in tonsil hypertrophy or adenoid vegetation), it may interfere with nasal respiration and alter the resonance pattern of the voice.

The middle floor of the pharynx connects anteriorly to the mouth and is therefore called the oral pharynx or oropharynx. It is delimited from the nasopharynx by the soft palate, which roofs the posterior part of the oral cavity.

Middle and lower floors

The lower floor of the pharynx is called the hypopharynx. Its anterior wall is formed by the posterior part of the tongue. Lying directly above the larynx, it represents the site where the pathways of air and food cross each other: Air from the nasal cavity flows into the larynx, and food from the oral cavity is routed to the esophagus directly behind the larynx. The epiglottis, a cartilaginous, leaf-

From E. Pernkopf in H. Ferner (ed.), *Atlas der Topographischen und angewandten Anatomie des Menschen*, vol. 1 (1980), © Urban & Schwarzenberg, Munich

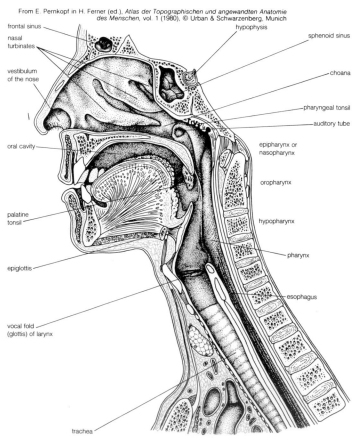

Figure 9: Upper airways with nasal and oral cavities, pharynx, and larynx.

shaped flap, functions as a lid to the larynx and, during the act of swallowing, controls the traffic of air and food.

Morphology of the lower airways. *The larynx.* The larynx is an organ of complex structure that serves a dual function: as an air canal to the lungs and a controller of its access, and as the organ of phonation (see Figure 10). Sound is produced by forcing air through a sagittal slit formed by the vocal cords, the glottis. This causes not only the vocal cords but also the column of air above them to vibrate. As evidenced by trained singers, this function can be closely controlled and finely tuned. Control is achieved by a number of muscles innervated by the laryngeal nerves. For the precise function of the muscular apparatus, the muscles must be anchored to a stabilizing framework (Figure 10). The laryngeal skeleton

From J.W. Rohen and C. Yokochi, *Anatomie des Menschen*, vol. 1 (1982); © F.K. Schattauer Verlag, Stuttgart

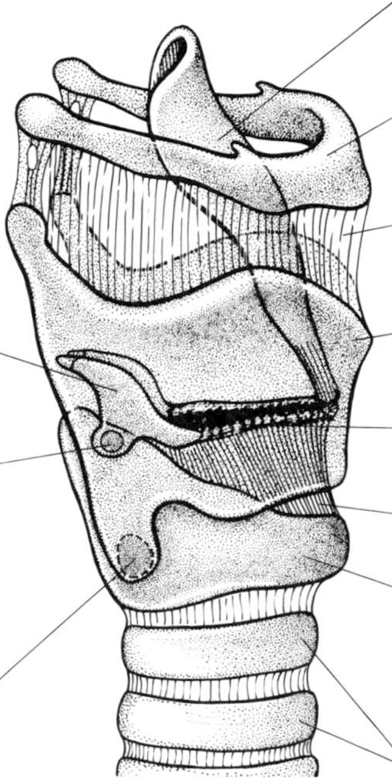

Figure 10: Larynx with major cartilages, hyoid bone, and vocal cords.

consists of almost a dozen pieces of cartilage, most of them very small, interconnected by ligaments and membranes. The largest cartilage of the larynx, the thyroid cartilage, is made of two plates fused anteriorly in the midline. At the upper end of the fusion line is an incision, the thyroid notch; below it is a forward projection, the laryngeal prominence. Both of these structures are easily felt through the skin. The angle between the two cartilage plates is sharper and the prominence more marked in men than in women, which has given this structure the common name of Adam's apple. Behind the shieldlike thyroid cartilage, the vocal cords span the laryngeal lumen. They correspond to elastic ligaments attached anteriorly in the angle of the thyroid shield and posteriorly to a pair of small pyramidal pieces of cartilage, the arytenoid cartilages. The vocal ligaments are part of a tube, resembling an organ pipe, made of elastic tissue. Just above the vocal cords, the epiglottis is also attached to the back of the thyroid plate by its stalk. The cricoid, another large cartilaginous piece of the laryngeal skeleton, has a signet-ring shape. The broad plate of the ring lies in the posterior wall of the larynx and the narrow arch in the anterior wall. The cricoid is located below the thyroid cartilage, to which it is joined in an articulation reinforced by ligaments. The transverse axis of the joint allows a hingelike rotation between the two cartilages. This movement tilts the cricoid plate with respect to the shield of the thyroid cartilage and hence alters the distance between them. Because the arytenoid cartilages rest upright on the cricoid plate, they follow its tilting movement. This mechanism plays an important role in altering length and tension of the vocal cords. The arytenoid cartilages articulate with the cricoid

Adam's apple

plate and hence are able to rotate and slide to close and open the glottis.

Viewed frontally, the lumen of the laryngeal tube has an hourglass shape, with its narrowest width at the glottis. Just above the vocal cords there is an additional pair of mucosal folds called the false vocal cords or the vestibular folds. Like the true vocal cords, they are also formed by the free end of a fibroelastic membrane. Between the vestibular folds and the vocal cords, the laryngeal space enlarges and forms lateral pockets extending upward. This space is called the ventricle of the larynx. Because the gap between the vestibular folds is always larger than the gap between the vocal cords, the latter can easily be seen from above with the laryngoscope, an instrument designed for visual inspection of the interior of the larynx.

The muscular apparatus of the larynx comprises two functionally distinct groups. The intrinsic muscles act directly or indirectly on the shape, length, and tension of the vocal cords. The extrinsic muscles act on the larynx as a whole, moving it upward (*e.g.,* during high-pitched phonation or swallowing) or downward. The intrinsic muscles attach to the skeletal components of the larynx itself; the extrinsic muscles join the laryngeal skeleton cranially to the hyoid bone or to the pharynx and caudally to the sternum (breastbone).

Muscular apparatus

The trachea and the stem bronchi. Below the larynx lies the trachea, a tube about 10 to 12 centimetres long and two centimetres wide. Its wall is stiffened by 16 to 20 characteristic horseshoe-shaped, incomplete cartilage rings that open toward the back and are embedded in a dense connective tissue. The dorsal wall contains a strong layer of transverse smooth muscle fibres that spans the gap of the cartilage. The interior of the trachea is lined by the typical respiratory epithelium. The mucosal layer contains mucous glands.

Size and shape

At its lower end, the trachea divides in an inverted Y into the two stem (or main) bronchi, one each for the left and right lung. The right main bronchus has a larger diameter, is oriented more vertically, and is shorter than the left main bronchus. The practical consequence of this arrangement is that foreign bodies passing beyond the larynx will usually slip into the right lung. The structure of the stem bronchi closely matches that of the trachea.

Structural design of the airway tree. The hierarchy of the dividing airways, and partly also of the blood vessels penetrating the lung, largely determines the internal lung structure. Functionally the intrapulmonary airway system can be subdivided into three zones, a proximal, purely conducting zone, a peripheral, purely gas-exchanging zone, and a transitional zone in between, where both functions grade into one another (Figure 11). From a morphological point of view, however, it makes sense to distinguish the relatively thick-walled, purely air-conducting tubes from those branches of the airway tree structurally designed to permit gas exchange.

The structural design of the airway tree is functionally important because the branching pattern plays a role in determining air flow and particle deposition. In modeling the human airway tree, it is generally agreed that the airways branch according to the rules of irregular dichotomy. Regular dichotomy means that each branch of a treelike structure gives rise to two daughter branches of identical dimensions. In irregular dichotomy, however, the daughter branches may differ greatly in length and diameter. The models calculate the average path from the trachea to the lung periphery as consisting of about 24–25 generations of branches. Individual paths, however, may range from 11 to 30 generations. The transition between the conductive and the respiratory portions of an airway lies on average at the end of the 16th generation, if the trachea is counted as generation 0. The conducting airways comprise the trachea, the two stem bronchi, the bronchi, and the bronchioles. Their function is to further warm, moisten, and clean the inspired air and distribute it to the gas-exchanging zone of the lung. They are lined by the typical respiratory epithelium with ciliated cells and numerous interspersed mucus-secreting goblet cells. Ciliated cells are present far down in the airway tree, their height decreasing with the narrowing of the tubes, as does

Irregular dichotomy of airway tree

Conducting airways

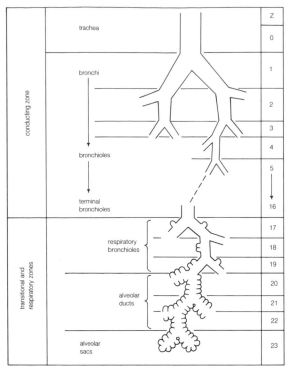

Figure 11: Model of airway branching in the human lung, assuming regular dichotomy (see text).

the frequency of goblet cells. In bronchioles the goblet cells are completely replaced by another type of secretory cells named Clara cells. The epithelium is covered by a layer of low-viscosity fluid, within which the cilia exert a synchronized, rhythmic beat directed outward. In larger airways, this fluid layer is topped by a blanket of mucus of high viscosity. The mucus layer is dragged along by the ciliary action and carries the intercepted particles toward the pharynx, where they are swallowed. This design can be compared to a conveyor belt for particles, and indeed the mechanism is referred to as the mucociliary escalator.

Whereas cartilage rings or plates provide support for the walls of the trachea and bronchi, the walls of the bronchioles, devoid of cartilage, gain their stability from their structural integration into the gas-exchanging tissues. The last purely conductive airway generations in the lung are the terminal bronchioles. Distally, the airway structure is greatly altered by the appearance of cuplike outpouchings from the walls (see Figure 11). These form minute air chambers and represent the first gas-exchanging alveoli on the airway path. In the alveoli, the respiratory epithelium gives way to a very flat lining layer that permits the formation of a thin air–blood barrier. After several generations (Z) of such respiratory bronchioles, the alveoli are so densely packed along the airway that an airway wall proper is missing; the airway consists of alveolar ducts. The final generations of the airway tree end blindly in the alveolar sacs.

The lungs. *Gross anatomy.* The organ lung is parted into two slightly unequal portions, a left lung and a right lung, which occupy most of the intrathoracic space (see Figure 8). The space between them is filled by the mediastinum, which corresponds to a connective tissue space containing the heart, major blood vessels, the trachea with the stem bronchi, the esophagus, and the thymus gland. The right lung represents 56 percent of the total lung volume and is composed of three lobes, a superior, middle, and inferior lobe, separated from each other by a deep horizontal and an oblique fissure. The left lung, smaller in volume because of the asymmetrical position of the heart, has only two lobes separated by an oblique fissure. In the thorax, the two lungs rest with their bases on the diaphragm, while their apexes extend above the first rib. Medially, they are connected with the mediastinum at the

Right and left lung volumes

hilum, a circumscribed area where airways, blood and lymphatic vessels, and nerves enter or leave the lungs. The inside of the thoracic cavities and the lung surface are covered with serous membranes, respectively the parietal pleura and the visceral pleura, which are in direct continuity at the hilum. Depending on the subjacent structures, the parietal pleura can be subdivided into three portions: the mediastinal, costal, and diaphragmatic pleurae. The lung surfaces facing these pleural areas are named accordingly, since the shape of the lungs is determined by the shape of the pleural cavities. Because of the presence of pleural recesses, which form a kind of reserve space, the pleural cavity is larger than the lung volume (Figure 12).

During inspiration, the recesses are partly opened by the expanding lung, thus allowing the lung to increase in volume. Although the hilum is the only place where the lungs are secured to surrounding structures, the lungs are maintained in close apposition to the thoracic wall by a negative pressure between visceral and parietal pleurae. A thin film of extracellular fluid between the pleurae enables the lungs to move smoothly along the walls of the cavity during breathing. If the serous membranes become inflamed (pleurisy), respiratory movements can be painful. If air enters a pleural cavity (pneumothorax), the lung immediately collapses owing to its inherent elastic properties, and breathing is abolished on this side.

Pulmonary segments. The lung lobes are subdivided into smaller units, the pulmonary segments. There are 10 segments in the right lung and, depending on the classification, eight to 10 segments in the left lung. Unlike the lobes, the pulmonary segments are not delimited from each other by fissures but by thin membranes of connective tissue containing veins and lymphatics; the arterial supply follows the segmental bronchi. These anatomical features are important because pathological processes may be limited to discrete units, and the surgeon can remove single diseased segments instead of whole lobes.

The intrapulmonary conducting airways: bronchi and bronchioles. In the intrapulmonary bronchi, the cartilage rings of the stem bronchi are replaced by irregular cartilage plates; furthermore, a layer of smooth muscle is added between the mucosa and the fibrocartilaginous tunic. The bronchi are ensheathed by a layer of loose connective tissue that is continuous with the other connective tissue elements of the lung and hence is part of the fibrous skeleton spanning the lung from the hilum to the pleural sac. This outer fibrous layer contains, besides lymphatics and nerves, small bronchial vessels to supply

Structure

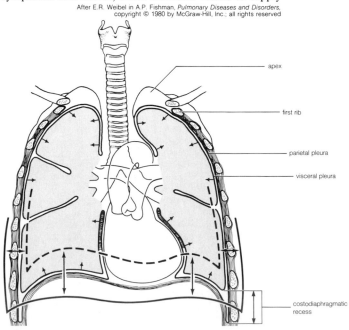

Figure 12: *Frontal section of chest.*
Pleural space and lobar fissures are shown. Single arrows represent retractive forces. Double arrows indicate the expansion of the lung into recesses during deep inspiration.

the bronchial wall with blood from the systemic circulation. Bronchioles are small conducting airways ranging in diameter from three to less than one millimetre. The walls of the bronchioles lack cartilage and seromucous glands. Their lumen is lined by a simple cuboidal epithelium with ciliated cells and Clara cells, which produce a chemically ill-defined secretion. The bronchiolar wall also contains a well-developed layer of smooth muscle cells, capable of narrowing the airway. Abnormal spasms of this musculature cause the clinical symptoms of bronchial asthma.

The gas-exchange region.   The gas-exchange region comprises three compartments: air, blood, and tissue. Whereas air and blood are continuously replenished, the function of the tissue compartment is twofold: it provides the stable supporting framework for the air and blood compartments, and it allows them to come into close contact with each other (thereby facilitating gas exchange) while keeping them strictly confined. The respiratory gases diffuse from air to blood, and vice versa, through the 140 square metres of internal surface area of the tissue compartment. The gas-exchange tissue proper is called the pulmonary parenchyma, while the supplying structures, conductive airways, lymphatics, and non-capillary blood vessels belong to the non-parenchyma.

Paren-
chyma

The gas-exchange region begins with the alveoli of the first generation of respiratory bronchioles. Distally, the frequency of alveolar outpocketings increases rapidly, until after two to four generations of respiratory bronchioles, the whole wall is formed by alveoli. The airways are then called alveolar ducts (Figure 13) and, in the last generation, alveolar sacs. On average, an adult human lung has about 300,000,000 alveoli. They are polyhedral structures, with a diameter of about 250 to 300 micrometres, and open on one side, where they connect to the airway. The alveolar wall, called the interalveolar septum, is common to two adjacent alveoli. It contains a dense network of capillaries, the smallest of the blood vessels, and a skeleton of connective tissue fibres (Figure 14). The fibre system is interwoven with the capillaries and particularly reinforced at the alveolar entrance rings. The capillaries are lined by flat endothelial cells with thin cytoplasmic extensions. The interalveolar septum is covered on both sides by the alveolar epithelial cells. A thin, squamous cell type, the type I pneumocyte, covers between 92 and 95 percent of the gas-exchange surface; a second, more cuboidal cell type, the type II pneumocyte, covers the remaining surface. The type I cells form, together with the endothelial cells, the thin air–blood barrier for gas exchange; the type II cells

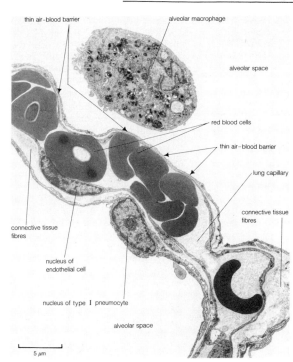

Figure 14: Electron micrograph of part of the interalveolar septum of the adult human lung. The lung capillary contains red blood cells interlaced with connective tissue fibres. The alveolar macrophage normally lies within the surfactant layer, which is not preserved here.

From P.H. Burri, "Lung Development and Growth," in A.P. Fishman and A.B. Fisher (eds.), *The Respiratory System*, vol. 1; © copyright 1985, American Physiological Society

are secretory cells. Type II pneumocytes produce a surface-tension-reducing material, the pulmonary surfactant, which spreads on the alveolar surface and prevents the tiny alveolar spaces from collapsing. Before it is released into the airspaces, pulmonary surfactant is stored in the type II cells in the form of lamellar bodies. These granules are the conspicuous ultrastructural features of this cell type. On top of the epithelium, alveolar macrophages creep around within the surfactant fluid. They are large cells, and their cell bodies abound in granules of various content, partly foreign material that may have reached the alveoli, or cell debris originating from cell damage or normal cell death. Ultimately, the alveolar macrophages are derived from the bone marrow, and their task is to keep the air–blood barrier clean and unobstructed. The tissue space between the endothelium of the capillaries and the epithelial lining is occupied by the interstitium. It contains connective tissue and interstitial fluid. The connective tissue comprises a system of fibres, amorphous ground substance, and cells (mainly fibroblasts), which seem to be endowed with contractile properties. The fibroblasts are thought to control capillary blood flow or, alternatively, to prevent the accumulation of extracellular fluid in the interalveolar septa. If for some reason the delicate fluid balance of the pulmonary tissues is impaired, an excess of fluid accumulates in the lung tissue and within the airspaces. This condition is called pulmonary edema. As a consequence, the respiratory gases must diffuse across longer distances, and proper functioning of the lung is severely jeopardized.

Pulmonary
surfactant

Blood vessels, lymphatic vessels, and nerves.   With respect to blood circulation, the lung is a complex organ. It has two distinct though not completely separate vascular systems: a low-pressure pulmonary system and a high-pressure bronchial system. The pulmonary (or lesser) circulation is responsible for the oxygen supply of the organism. Blood, low in oxygen content but laden with carbon dioxide, is carried from the right heart through the pulmonary arteries to the lungs. On each side, the pulmonary artery enters the lung in the company of the stem bronchus and then divides rapidly, following relatively closely the course of the dividing airway tree. After numerous divisions, small arteries accompany the alveolar ducts and split up into the alveolar capillary networks.

Lung
vascular
systems

From P.H. Burri, "Morphology and Respiratory Function of the Alveolar Unit," *International Archives of Allergy and Applied Immunology*, no. 76, suppl. 1, March 1985; © 1985, S. Karger AG, Basel

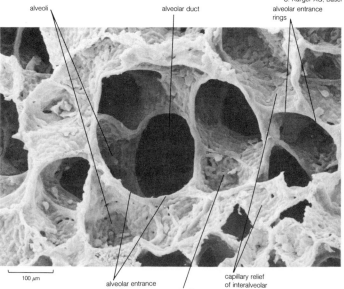

Figure 13: Scanning electron micrograph of the adult human lung showing alveolar duct with alveoli. Capillary relief of interalveolar septa is clearly visible because alveolar surfactant has not been preserved by fixation procedures.

Because intravascular pressure determines the arterial wall structure, the pulmonary arteries, which have on average a pressure five times lower than systemic arteries, are much flimsier than systemic arteries of corresponding size. The oxygenated blood from the capillaries is collected by venules and drained into small veins. These do not accompany the airways and arteries but run separately in narrow strips of connective tissue delimiting small lobules. The interlobular veins then converge on the intersegmental septa. Finally, near the hilum the veins merge into large venous vessels that follow the course of the bronchi. Generally, four pulmonary veins drain blood from the lung and deliver it to the left atrium of the heart.

The bronchial circulation has a nutritional function for the walls of the larger airways and pulmonary vessels. The bronchial arteries originate from the aorta or from an intercostal artery. They are small vessels and generally do not reach as far into the periphery as the conducting airways. With a few exceptions, they end several generations short of the terminal bronchioles. They split up into capillaries surrounding the walls of bronchi and vessels and also supply adjacent airspaces. Most of their blood is naturally collected by pulmonary veins. Small bronchial veins exist, however; they originate from the peribronchial venous plexuses and drain the blood through the hilum into the azygos and hemiazygos veins of the posterior thoracic wall.

The lymph is drained from the lung through two distinct but interconnected sets of lymphatic vessels. The superficial, subpleural lymphatic network collects the lymph from the peripheral mantle of lung tissue and drains it partly along the veins toward the hilum. The deep lymphatic system originates around the conductive airways and arteries and converges into vessels that mostly follow the bronchi and arterial vessels into the mediastinum.

Filtering action of lymph nodes

Within the lung and the mediastinum, lymph nodes exert their filtering action on the lymph before it is returned into the blood through the major lymphatic vessels, called bronchomediastinal trunks. Lymph drainage paths from the lung are complex. The precise knowledge of their course is clinically relevant, because malignant tumours of the lung spread via the lymphatics.

The pleurae, the airways, and the vessels are innervated by afferent and efferent fibres of the autonomic nervous system. Parasympathetic nerve fibres from the vagus nerve (10th cranial nerve) and sympathetic branches of the sympathetic nerve trunk meet around the stem bronchi to form the pulmonary autonomic nerve plexus, which penetrates into the lung along the bronchial and vascular walls. The sympathetic fibres mediate a vasoconstrictive action in the pulmonary vascular bed and a secretomotor activity in the bronchial glands. The parasympathetic fibres stimulate bronchial constriction. Afferent fibres to the vagus nerve transmit information from stretch receptors, and those to the sympathetic centres carry sensory information (e.g., pain) from the bronchial mucosa.

Lung development. After early embryogenesis, during which the lung primordium is laid down, the developing human lung undergoes four consecutive stages of development, ending after birth. The names of the stages describe the actual morphology of the prospective airways. The pseudoglandular stage exists from five to 17 weeks; the canalicular stage, from 16 to 26 weeks; the saccular stage, from 24 to 38 weeks; and finally the alveolar stage, from 36 weeks of fetal age to about 1 1/2 to two years after birth.

First development

The lung appears around the 26th day of intrauterine life as a ventral bud of the prospective esophagus. The bud separates distally from the gut, divides, and starts to grow into the surrounding mesenchyme. The epithelial components of the lung are thus derived from the gut (*i.e.,* they are of endodermal origin), and the surrounding tissues and the blood vessels are derivatives of the mesoderm.

Following rapid successive dichotomous divisions, the lung begins to look like a gland, giving the first stage of development (pseudoglandular) its name. At the same time, the vascular connections also develop and form a capillary plexus around the lung tubules. Toward week 17, all the conducting airways of the lung are preformed, and it is assumed that, at the outermost periphery, the tips of the tubules represent the first structures of the prospective gas-exchange region.

During the canalicular stage, the future lung periphery develops further. The prospective airspaces enlarge at the expense of the intervening mesenchyme, and their cuboidal epithelium differentiates into type I and type II epithelial cells or pneumocytes. Toward the end of this stage, areas with a thin prospective air–blood barrier have developed, and surfactant production has started. These structural and functional developments give a prematurely born fetus a small chance to survive at this stage.

During the saccular stage, further generations of airways are formed. The tremendous expansion of the prospective respiratory airspaces causes the formation of saccules and a marked decrease in the interstitial tissue mass. The lung looks more and more "aerated," although it is filled with fluid originating from the lungs and from the amniotic fluid surrounding the fetus. Some weeks before birth, alveolar formation begins by a septation process that subdivides the saccules into alveoli. At this stage of lung development, the infant is born.

Changes at birth

At birth the intrapulmonary fluid is rapidly evacuated and the lung fills with air with the first breaths. Simultaneously, the pulmonary circulation, which before was practically bypassed and very little perfused, opens up to accept the full cardiac output.

The newborn lung is far from being a miniaturized version of the adult lung. It has only about 20,000,000 to 50,000,000 alveoli, or 6 to 15 percent of the full adult complement. Therefore, alveolar formation is completed in the early postnatal period. Although it was previously thought that alveolar formation could continue to the age of eight years and beyond, it is now accepted that the bulk of alveolar formation is concluded much earlier, probably before the age of two years. Even with complete alveolar formation, the lung is not yet mature. The newly formed interalveolar septa still contain a double capillary network instead of the single one of the adult lungs. This means that the pulmonary capillary bed must be completely reorganized during and after alveolar formation; it has to mature. Only after full microvascular maturation, which is terminated sometime between the ages of two and five years, is the lung development completed, and the lung can enter a phase of normal growth.

CONTROL OF BREATHING

Breathing is an automatic and rhythmic act produced by networks of neurons in the hindbrain (the pons and medulla). The neural networks direct muscles that form the walls of the thorax and abdomen and produce pressure gradients that move air into and out of the lungs. The respiratory rhythm and the length of each phase of respiration are set by reciprocal stimulatory and inhibitory interconnection of these brain-stem neurons.

An important characteristic of the human respiratory system is its ability to adjust breathing patterns to changes in both the internal milieu and the external environment. Ventilation increases and decreases in proportion to swings in carbon dioxide production and oxygen consumption caused by changes in metabolic rate. The respiratory system is also able to compensate for disturbances that affect the mechanics of breathing, such as the airway narrowing that occurs in an asthmatic attack. Breathing also undergoes appropriate adjustments when the mechanical advantage of the respiratory muscles is altered by postural changes or by movement.

This flexibility in breathing patterns in large part arises from sensors distributed throughout the body that send signals to the respiratory neuronal networks in the brain. Chemoreceptors detect changes in blood oxygen levels and change the acidity of the blood and brain. Mechanoreceptors monitor the expansion of the lung, the size of the airway, the force of respiratory muscle contraction, and the extent of muscle shortening.

Although the diaphragm is the major muscle of breathing, its respiratory action is assisted and augmented by a complex assembly of other muscle groups. Intercostal muscles inserting on the ribs, the abdominal muscles, and muscles such as the scalene and sternocleidomastoid that

Non-respiratory functions of respiratory muscles

attach both to the ribs and to the cervical spine at the base of the skull also play an important role in the exchange of air between the atmosphere and the lungs. In addition, laryngeal muscles and muscles in the oral and nasal pharynx adjust the resistance of movement of gases through the upper airways during both inspiration and expiration. Although the use of these different muscle groups adds considerably to the flexibility of the breathing act, they also complicate the regulation of breathing. These same muscles are used to perform a number of other functions, such as speaking, chewing and swallowing, and maintaining posture. Perhaps because the "respiratory" muscles are employed in performing nonrespiratory functions, breathing can be influenced by higher brain centres and even controlled voluntarily to a substantial degree. An outstanding example of voluntary control is the ability to suspend breathing by holding one's breath. Input into the respiratory control system from higher brain centres may help optimize breathing so that not only are metabolic demands satisfied by breathing, but ventilation is accomplished with minimal use of energy.

Central organization of respiratory neurons. The respiratory rhythm is generated within the pons and medulla. Three main aggregations of neurons are involved: a group consisting mainly of inspiratory neurons in the dorsomedial medulla, a group made up of inspiratory and expiratory neurons in the ventrolateral medulla, and a group in the rostral pons consisting mostly of neurons that discharge both in inspiration and in expiration. It is currently thought that the respiratory cycle of inspiration and expiration is generated by synaptic interactions within these groups of neurons.

The inspiratory and expiratory medullary neurons are connected to projections from higher brain centres and from chemoreceptors and mechanoreceptors; in turn they drive cranial motor neurons, which govern the activity of muscles in the upper airways and the activity of spinal motor neurons, which supply the diaphragm and other thoracic and abdominal muscles. The inspiratory and expiratory medullary neurons also receive input from nerve cells responsible for cardiovascular and temperature regulation, allowing the activity of these physiological systems to be coordinated with respiration.

Neurally, inspiration is characterized by an augmenting discharge of medullary neurons that terminates abruptly. After a gap of a few milliseconds, inspiratory activity is restarted, but at a much lower level, and gradually declines until the onset of expiratory neuron activity. Then the cycle begins again. The full development of this pattern depends on the interaction of several types of respiratory neurons: inspiratory, early inspiratory, off-switch, post-inspiratory, and expiratory.

Early inspiratory neurons trigger the augmenting discharge of inspiratory neurons. This increase in activity, which produces lung expansion, is caused by self-excitation of the inspiratory neurons and perhaps by the activity of an as yet undiscovered upstream pattern generator. Off-switch neurons in the medulla terminate inspiration, but pontine neurons and input from stretch receptors in the lung help control the length of inspiration. When the vagus nerves are sectioned or pontine centres are destroyed, breathing is characterized by prolonged inspiratory activity that may last for several minutes. This type of breathing, which occasionally occurs in persons with diseases of the brain stem, is called "apneustic" breathing.

Post-inspiratory neurons

Post-inspiratory neurons are responsible for the declining discharge of the inspiratory muscles that occurs at the beginning of expiration. Mechanically, this discharge aids in slowing expiratory flow rates and probably assists the efficiency of gas exchange. It is believed by some that these post-inspiratory neurons have inhibitory effects on both inspiratory and expiratory neurons and therefore play a significant role in determining the length of the respiratory cycle and the different phases of respiration.

As the activity of the post-inspiratory neurons subsides, expiratory neurons discharge and inspiratory neurons are strongly inhibited. There may be no peripheral manifestation of expiratory neuron discharge except for the absence of inspiratory muscle activity, although in upright humans the lower expiratory intercostal muscles and the abdominal muscles may be active even during quiet breathing. Moreover, as the demand to breathe increases (for example, with exercise), more expiratory intercostal and abdominal muscles contract. As expiration proceeds, the inhibition of the inspiratory muscles gradually diminishes and inspiratory neurons resume their activity.

Chemoreceptors. One way breathing is controlled is through feedback by chemoreceptors. There are two kinds of respiratory chemoreceptors; arterial chemoreceptors monitor and respond to changes in the partial pressure of oxygen and carbon dioxide in the arterial blood, and central chemoreceptors in the brain respond to changes in the partial pressure of carbon dioxide in their immediate environment. Ventilation levels behave as if they were regulated to maintain a constant level of carbon dioxide partial pressure and to ensure adequate oxygen levels in the arterial blood. Increased activity of chemoreceptors caused by hypoxia or an increase in the partial pressure of carbon dioxide augments both the rate and depth of breathing, which restores partial pressures of oxygen and carbon dioxide to their usual levels. Too much ventilation, though, depresses the partial pressure of carbon dioxide, which leads to a reduction in chemoreceptor activity and a diminution of ventilation. During sleep and anesthesia, lowering carbon dioxide levels three to four millimetres of mercury below values occurring during wakefulness can cause a total cessation of breathing (apnea).

Peripheral chemoreceptors. Hypoxia, or the reduction of oxygen supply to tissues to below physiological levels (produced, for example, by a trip to high altitudes), stimulates the carotid and aortic bodies, the principal arterial chemoreceptors. The two carotid bodies are small organs located in the neck at the bifurcation of each of the two common carotid arteries into the internal and external carotid arteries. This organ is extraordinarily well perfused and responds to changes in the partial pressure of oxygen in the arterial blood flowing through it rather than to the oxygen content of that blood (the amount of oxygen chemically combined with hemoglobin). The sensory nerve from the carotid body increases its firing rate hyperbolically as the partial pressure of oxygen falls. In addition to responding to hypoxia, the carotid body increases its activity linearly as the partial pressure of carbon dioxide in arterial blood is raised. This arterial blood parameter rises and falls as air enters and leaves the lungs, and the carotid body senses these fluctuations, responding more to rapid than to slow changes in the partial pressure of carbon dioxide. Larger oscillations in the partial pressure of carbon dioxide occur with breathing as metabolic rate is increased. The amplitude of these fluctuations, as reflected in the size of carotid body signals, may be used by the brain to detect changes in the metabolic rate and to produce appropriate adjustment in ventilation.

The carotid bodies

The carotid body communicates with medullary respiratory neurons through sensory fibres that travel with the carotid sinus nerve, a branch of the glossopharyngeal nerve. Microscopically, the carotid body consists of two different types of cells. The type I cells are arranged in groups and are surrounded by type II cells. The type II cells are generally not believed to have a direct role in chemoreception. Fine sensory nerve fibres are found in juxtaposition to type I cells, which, unlike type II cells, contain electron-dense vesicles. Acetylcholine, catecholamines, and neuropeptides such as enkephalins, vasoactive intestinal peptide, and substance P, are located within the vesicles. It is believed that hypoxia and hypercapnia (excessive carbon dioxide in the blood) cause the release of one or more of these neuroactive substances from the type I cells, which then act on the sensory nerve. It is possible to interfere independently with the responses of the carotid body to carbon dioxide and oxygen, which suggests that the same mechanisms are not used to sense or transmit changes in oxygen or carbon dioxide. The aortic bodies located near the arch of the aorta also respond to acute changes in the partial pressure of oxygen, but less well than the carotid body responds to changes in the partial pressure of carbon dioxide. The aortic bodies are responsible for many of the cardiovascular effects of hypoxia.

The aortic bodies

Central chemoreceptors. Carbon dioxide is one of the most powerful stimulants of breathing. As the partial pressure of carbon dioxide in arterial blood rises, ventilation increases nearly linearly. Ventilation normally increases by two to four litres per minute with each one millimetre of mercury increase in the partial pressure of carbon dioxide. Carbon dioxide increases the acidity of the fluid surrounding the cells but also easily passes into cells and thus can make the interior of cells more acid. It is not clear whether the receptors respond to the intracellular or extracellular effects of carbon dioxide or acidity.

Even if both the carotid and aortic bodies are removed, inhaling gases that contain carbon dioxide stimulates breathing. This observation shows that there must be additional receptors that respond to changes in the partial pressure of carbon dioxide. Current thinking places these receptors near the undersurface (ventral part) of the medulla. However, microscopic examination has not conclusively identified specific chemoreceptor cells in this region. The same areas of the ventral medulla also contain vasomotor neurons that are concerned with the regulation of blood pressure. Some investigators argue that respiratory responses produced at the ventral medullary surface are direct and are caused by interference with excitatory and inhibitory inputs to respiration from these vasomotor neurons. They believe that respiratory chemoreceptors that respond to carbon dioxide are more diffusely distributed in the brain.

Muscle and lung receptors. Receptors in the respiratory muscles and in the lung can also affect breathing patterns. These receptors are particularly important when lung function is impaired, since they can help maintain tidal volume and ventilation at normal levels.

Changes in the length of a muscle affect the force it can produce when stimulated. Generally there is a length at which the force generated is maximal. Receptors, called spindles, in the respiratory muscles measure muscle length and increase motor discharge to the diaphragm and intercostal muscles when increased stiffness of the lung or resistance to the movement of air caused by disease impedes muscle shortening. Tendon organs, another receptor in muscles, monitor changes in the force produced by muscle contraction. Too much force stimulates tendon organs and causes decreasing motor discharge to the respiratory muscles and may prevent the muscles from damaging themselves.

Inflation of the lungs in animals stops breathing by a reflex described by the German physiologist Ewald Hering and the Austrian physiologist Josef Breuer. The Hering-Breuer reflex is initiated by lung expansion, which excites stretch receptors in the airways. Stimulation of these receptors, which send signals to the medulla by the vagus nerve, shortens inspiratory times as tidal volume (the volume of air inspired) increases, accelerating the frequency of breathing. When lung inflation is prevented, the reflex allows inspiratory time to be lengthened, helping to preserve tidal volume.

There are also receptors in the airways and in the alveoli that are excited by rapid lung inflations and by chemicals such as histamine, bradykinin, and prostaglandins. The most important function of these receptors, however, may be to defend the lung against noxious material in the atmosphere. When stimulated, these receptors constrict the airways and cause rapid shallow breathing, which inhibits the penetration of injurious agents into the bronchial tree. These receptors are supplied, like the stretch receptors, by the vagus nerve. Some of these receptors (called irritant receptors) are innervated by myelinated nerve fibres, others (the J receptors) by unmyelinated fibres. Stimulation of irritant receptors also causes coughing.

Variations in breathing. *Exercise.* One of the remarkable features of the respiratory control system is that ventilation increases sufficiently to keep the partial pressure of carbon dioxide in arterial blood nearly unchanged despite the large increases in metabolic rate that can occur with exercise, thus preserving acid–base homeostasis. A number of signals arise during exercise that can augment ventilation. Sources of these signals include mechanoreceptors in the exercising limbs; the arterial chemoreceptors, which

The Hering-Breuer reflex

can sense breath-by-breath oscillations in the partial pressure of carbon dioxide; and thermal receptors, because body temperature rises as metabolism increases. The brain also seems to anticipate changes in the metabolic rate caused by exercise, because parallel increases occur in the output from the motor cortex to the exercising limbs and to respiratory neurons. Changes in the concentration of potassium and lactic acid in the exercising muscles acting on unmyelinated nerve fibres may be another mechanism for stimulation of breathing during exercise. It remains unclear, however, how these various mechanisms are adjusted to maintain acid–base balance.

Sleep. During sleep, body metabolism is reduced, but there is an even greater decline in ventilation so that the partial pressure of carbon dioxide in arterial blood rises slightly and arterial partial pressure of oxygen falls. The effects on ventilatory pattern vary with sleep stage. In slow-wave sleep, breathing is diminished but remains regular, while in rapid eye movement sleep, breathing can become quite erratic. Ventilatory responses to inhaled carbon dioxide and to hypoxia are less in all sleep stages than during wakefulness. Sufficiently large decreases in the partial pressure of oxygen or increases in the partial pressure of carbon dioxide will cause arousal and terminate sleep.

During sleep, ventilation may swing between periods when the amplitude and frequency of breathing are high and periods in which there is little attempt to breathe, or even apnea (cessation of breathing). This rhythmic waxing and waning of breathing, with intermittent periods of apnea, is called Cheyne-Stokes breathing, after the physicians who first described it. The mechanism that produces the Cheyne-Stokes ventilation pattern is still argued, but it may entail unstable feedback regulation of breathing. Similar swings in ventilation sometimes occur in persons with heart failure or with central nervous system disease.

In addition, ventilation during sleep may intermittently fall to low levels or cease entirely because of partial or complete blockage of the upper airways. In some individuals, this intermittent obstruction occurs repeatedly during the night, leading to severe drops in the levels of blood oxygenation. The condition, termed sleep apnea syndrome, occurs most commonly in the elderly, in the newborn, in males, and in the obese. Because arousal is often associated with the termination of episodes of obstruction, sleep is of poor quality, and complaints of excessive daytime drowsiness are common. Snoring and disturbed behaviour during sleep may also occur.

Sleep apnea syndrome

In some persons with sleep apnea syndrome, portions of the larynx and pharynx may be narrowed by fat deposits or by enlarged tonsils and adenoids, which increase the likelihood of obstruction. Others, however, have normal upper airway anatomy, and obstruction may occur because of discoordinated activity of upper airway and chest wall muscles. Many of the upper airway muscles, like the tongue and laryngeal adductors, undergo phasic changes in their electrical activity synchronous with respiration, and the reduced activity of these muscles during sleep may lead to upper airway closure.

THE MECHANICS OF BREATHING

Air moves in and out of the lungs in response to differences in pressure. When the air pressure within the alveolar spaces falls below atmospheric pressure, air enters the lungs (inspiration), provided the larynx is open; when the air pressure within the alveoli exceeds atmospheric pressure, air is blown from the lungs (expiration). The flow of air is rapid or slow in proportion to the magnitude of the pressure difference. Because atmospheric pressure remains relatively constant, flow is determined by how much above or below atmospheric pressure the pressure within the lungs rises or falls.

Alveolar pressure fluctuations are caused by expansion and contraction of the lungs resulting from tensing and relaxing of the muscles of the chest and abdomen. Each small increment of expansion transiently increases the space enclosing lung air. There is, therefore, less air per unit of volume in the lungs and pressure falls. A difference in air pressure between atmosphere and lungs is created, and air flows in until equilibrium with atmospheric pressure is restored at a higher lung volume. When the muscles of inspiration relax, the volume of chest and lungs decreases, lung air becomes transiently compressed, its pressure rises above atmospheric pressure, and flow into the atmosphere results until pressure equilibrium is reached at the original lung volume. This, then, is the sequence of events during each normal respiratory cycle: lung volume change leading to pressure difference, resulting in flow of air into or out of the lung and establishment of a new lung volume.

The lung–chest system. The forces that normally cause changes in volume of the chest and lungs stem not only from muscle contraction but from the elastic properties of both the lung and the chest. A lung is similar to a balloon in that it resists stretch, tending to collapse almost totally unless held inflated by a pressure difference between its inside and outside. This tendency of the lung to collapse or pull away from the chest is measurable by carefully placing a blunt needle between the outside of the lung and the inside of the chest wall, thereby allowing the lung to separate from the chest at this particular spot. The pressure measured in the small pleural space so created is substantially below atmospheric pressure at a time when the pressure within the lung itself equals atmospheric pressure. This negative (below-atmospheric) pressure is a measure, therefore, of the force required to keep the lung distended. The force increases (pleural pressure becomes more negative) as the lung is stretched and its volume increases during inspiration. The force also increases in proportion to the rapidity with which air is drawn into the lung and decreases in proportion to the force with which air is expelled from the lungs. In summary, the pleural pressure reflects primarily two forces: (1) the force required to keep the lung inflated against its elastic recoil and (2) the force required to cause airflow in and out of the lung. Because the pleural pressure is below atmospheric pressure, air is sucked into the chest and the lung collapses (pneumothorax) when the chest wall is perforated, as by a wound or by a surgical incision.

The force required to maintain inflation of the lung and to cause airflow is provided by the chest and diaphragm (the muscular partition between chest and abdomen), which are in turn stretched inward by the pull of the lungs. The lung–chest system thus acts as two opposed coiled springs, the length of each of which is affected by the other. Were it not for the outward traction of the chest on the lungs, these would collapse; and were it not for the inward traction of the lungs on the chest and diaphragm, the chest would expand to a larger size and the diaphragm would fall from its dome-shaped position within the chest.

The role of muscles. The respiratory muscles displace the equilibrium of elastic forces in the lung and chest in one direction or the other by adding muscular contraction. During inspiration, muscle contraction is added to the outward elastic force of the chest to increase the traction on the lung required for its additional stretch. When these muscles relax, the additional retraction of lung returns the system to its equilibrium position.

Contraction of the abdominal muscles displaces the equilibrium in the opposite direction by adding increased abdominal pressure to the retraction of lungs, thereby further raising the diaphragm and causing forceful expiration. This additional muscular force is removed on relaxation and the original lung volume is restored. During ordinary breathing, muscular contraction occurs only on inspiration, expiration being accomplished "passively" by elastic recoil of the lung.

At total relaxation of the muscles of inspiration and expiration, the lung is distended to a volume—called the functional residual capacity—of about 40 percent of its maximum volume at the end of full inspiration. Further reduction of the lung volume results from maximal contraction of the expiratory muscles of chest and abdomen. The volume in these circumstances is known as the residual volume; it is about 20 percent of the volume at the end of full inspiration (known as the total lung capacity). Additional collapse of the lung to its "minimal air" can be accomplished only by opening the chest wall and creating a pneumothorax.

The membranes of the surface of the lung (visceral pleura) and on the inside of the chest (parietal pleura) are normally kept in close proximity (despite the pull of lung and chest in opposite directions) by surface tension of the thin layer of fluid covering these surfaces. The strength of this bond can be appreciated by the attempt to pull apart two smooth surfaces, such as pieces of glass, separated by a film of water.

The respiratory pump and its performance. The energy expended on breathing is used primarily in stretching the lung–chest system and thus causing airflow. It normally amounts to 1 percent of the basal energy requirements of the body but rises substantially during exercise or illness. The respiratory pump is versatile, capable of increasing its output 25 times, from a normal resting level of about six litres (366 cubic inches) per minute to 150 litres per minute in adults. Pressures within the lungs can be raised to 130 centimetres of water (about 1.8 pounds per square inch) by the so-called Valsalva maneuver—*i.e.,* a forceful contraction of the chest and abdominal muscles against a closed glottis (*i.e.,* with no space between the vocal cords). Airflow velocity, normally reaching 30 litres per minute in quiet breathing, can be raised voluntarily to 400 litres per minute. Cough is accomplished by suddenly opening the larynx during a brief Valsalva maneuver. The resultant high-speed jet of air is an effective means of clearing the airways of excessive secretions or foreign particles. The beating of cilia (hairline projections) from cells lining the airways normally maintains a steady flow of secretions toward the nose, cough resulting only when this action cannot keep pace with the rate at which secretions are produced.

An infant takes 33 breaths per minute with a tidal volume (the amount of air breathed in and out in one cycle) of 15 millilitres, totaling about 0.5 litre—approximately one pint—per minute as compared to adult values of 14 breaths, 500 millilitres, and seven litres, respectively.

If the force of surface tension is responsible for the adherence of parietal and visceral pleurae, it is reasonable to question what keeps the lungs' alveolar walls (also fluid-covered) from sticking together and thus eliminating alveolar airspaces. In fact, such adherence occasionally does occur and is one of the dreaded complications of premature births. Normal lungs, however, contain a substance—a phospholipid surfactant—that reduces surface tension and keeps alveolar walls separated.

GAS EXCHANGE

Respiratory gases—oxygen and carbon dioxide—move between the air and the blood across the respiratory exchange surfaces in the lungs. The structure of the human lung provides an immense internal surface that facilitates gas exchange between the alveoli and the blood in the pulmonary capillaries. The area of the alveolar surface in the adult human is about 100 square metres. Gas exchange across the membranous barrier between the alveoli and capillaries is enhanced by the thin nature of the membrane, about 0.5 micrometre, or $\frac{1}{100}$ of the diameter of a human hair.

Respiratory gases move between the environment and the respiring tissues by two principal mechanisms, convection and diffusion. Convection, or mass flow, is responsible for movement of air from the environment into the lungs and for movement of blood between the lungs and the tissues. Respiratory gases also move by diffusion across tissue barriers such as membranes. Diffusion is the primary mode of transport of gases between air and blood in the lungs and between blood and respiring tissues in the body. The process of diffusion is driven by the difference in partial pressures of a gas between two locales. In a mixture of gases, the partial pressure of each gas is directly proportional to its concentration. The partial pressure of a gas in fluid is a measure of its tendency to leave the fluid when exposed to a gas or fluid that does not contain that gas. A gas will diffuse from an area of greater partial pressure to an area of lower partial pressure regardless of the distribution of the partial pressures of other gases. There are large changes in the partial pressures of oxygen and carbon dioxide as these gases move between air and the respiring tissues. The partial pressure of carbon diox-

Elastic properties of lung

Functional residual capacity

Airflow velocity

Convection and diffusion

ide in this pathway is lower than the partial pressure of oxygen, due to differing modes of transport in the blood, but almost equal quantities of the two gases are involved in metabolism and gas exchange.

Oxygen and carbon dioxide are transported between tissue cells and the lungs by the blood. The quantity transported is determined both by the rapidity with which the blood circulates and the concentrations of gases in blood. The rapidity of circulation is determined by the output of the heart, which in turn is responsive to overall body requirements. Local flows can be increased selectively, as occurs, for example, in the flow through skeletal muscles during exercise. The performance of the heart and circulatory regulation are, therefore, important determinants of gas transport.

Oxygen and carbon dioxide are too poorly soluble in blood to be adequately transported in solution. Specialized systems for each gas have evolved to increase the quantities of those gases that can be transported in blood. These systems are present mainly in the red cells, which make up 40 to 50 percent of the blood volume in most mammals. Plasma, the cell-free, liquid portion of blood, plays little role in oxygen exchange but is essential to carbon dioxide exchange.

Transport of oxygen. Oxygen is poorly soluble in plasma, so that less than 2 percent of oxygen is transported dissolved in plasma. The vast majority of oxygen is bound to hemoglobin, a protein contained within red *Hemo-* cells. Hemoglobin is composed of four iron-containing *globin* ring structures (hemes) chemically bonded to a large pro- *and oxygen* tein (globin). Each iron atom can bind and then release an oxygen molecule. Enough hemoglobin is present in normal human blood to permit transport of about 0.2 millilitre of oxygen per millilitre of blood. The quantity of oxygen bound to hemoglobin is dependent on the partial pressure of oxygen in the lung to which blood is exposed. The curve representing the content of oxygen in blood at various partial pressures of oxygen, called the oxygen-dissociation curve (Figure 15), is a characteristic S-shape because binding of oxygen to one iron atom influences the ability of oxygen to bind to other iron sites. In alveoli at sea level, the partial pressure of oxygen is sufficient to bind oxygen to essentially all available iron sites on the hemoglobin molecule.

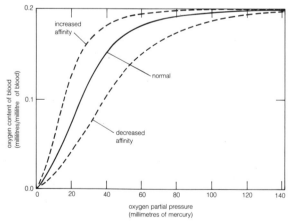

Figure 15: The oxygen-dissociation curve, which shows the relationship between the oxygen content of blood (ml O_2/ml blood) and the partial pressure of oxygen. An increase in the temperature or in the concentrations of 2,3-diphosphoglycerate (2,3-DPG), carbon dioxide (CO_2), or hydrogen ions will decrease the affinity of hemoglobin for oxygen and shift the curve to the right. Conversely, a decrease in the above variables will result in increased affinity and therefore shift the curve to the left.

Not all of the oxygen transported in the blood is transferred to the tissue cells. The amount of oxygen extracted by the cells depends on their rate of energy expenditure. At rest, venous blood returning to the lungs still contains 70 to 75 percent of the oxygen that was present in arterial blood; this reserve is available to meet increased oxygen demands. During extreme exercise the quantity of oxygen

remaining in venous blood decreases to 10 to 25 percent. At the steepest part of the oxygen-dissociation curve (the portion between 10 and 40 millimetres of mercury partial pressure), a relatively small decline in the partial pressure of oxygen in the blood is associated with a relatively large release of bound oxygen.

Hemoglobin binds not only to oxygen but to other *Hemo-* substances such as hydrogen ions (which determine the *globin* acidity, or pH, of the blood), carbon dioxide, and 2,3- *and other* diphosphoglycerate (2,3-DPG; a salt in the red blood cells *substances* that plays a role in liberating oxygen from hemoglobin in the peripheral circulation). These substances do not bind to hemoglobin at the oxygen-binding sites; however, with the binding of oxygen, changes in the structure of the hemoglobin molecule occur that affect its ability to bind other gases or substances. Conversely, binding of these substances to hemoglobin affects the affinity of hemoglobin for oxygen. (Affinity denotes the tendency of molecules of different species to bind to one another.) Increases in hydrogen ions, carbon dioxide, or 2,3-DPG decrease the affinity of hemoglobin for oxygen, and the oxygen-dissociation curve shifts to the right. Because of this decreased affinity, an increased partial pressure of oxygen is required to bind a given amount of oxygen to hemoglobin. A rightward shift of the curve is thought to be of benefit in releasing oxygen to the tissues when needs are great in relation to oxygen delivery, as occurs with anemia or extreme exercise. Reductions in normal concentrations of hydrogen ions, carbon dioxide, and 2,3-DPG result in an increased affinity of hemoglobin for oxygen, and the curve is shifted to the left. This displacement increases oxygen binding to hemoglobin at any given partial pressure of oxygen and is thought to be beneficial if the availability of oxygen is reduced, as occurs at extreme altitude.

Temperature changes affect the oxygen-dissociation curve similarly. An increase in temperature shifts the curve to *Effect of* the right (decreased affinity; enhanced release of oxygen); *tempera-* a decrease in temperature shifts the curve to the left (in- *ture* creased affinity). The range of body temperature usually encountered in humans is relatively narrow, so that temperature-associated changes in oxygen affinity have little physiological importance.

Transport of carbon dioxide. Transport of carbon dioxide in the blood is considerably more complex. A small portion of carbon dioxide, about 5 percent, remains unchanged and is transported dissolved in blood. The remainder is found in reversible chemical combinations in red blood cells or plasma. Some carbon dioxide binds to blood proteins, principally hemoglobin, to form a compound known as carbamate. About 88 percent of carbon dioxide in the blood is in the form of bicarbonate ion. The distribution of these chemical species between the interior of the red blood cell and the surrounding plasma varies greatly, with the red blood cells containing considerably less bicarbonate and more carbamate than the plasma.

Less than 10 percent of the total quantity of carbon dioxide carried in the blood is eliminated during passage through the lungs. Complete elimination would lead to large changes in acidity between arterial and venous blood. Furthermore, blood normally remains in the pulmonary capillaries less than a second, an insufficient time to eliminate all carbon dioxide.

Carbon dioxide enters blood in the tissues because its local partial pressure is greater than its partial pressure in blood flowing through the tissues. As carbon dioxide enters the blood, it combines with water to form carbonic acid (H_2CO_3), a relatively weak acid, which dissociates into hydrogen ions (H^+) and bicarbonate ions (HCO_3^-). Blood acidity is minimally affected by the released hydrogen ions because blood proteins, especially hemoglobin, *Buffering* are effective buffering agents. (A buffer solution resists *effect of* change in acidity by combining with added hydrogen ions *hemo-* and, essentially, inactivating them.) The natural conver- *globin* sion of carbon dioxide to carbonic acid is a relatively slow process; however, carbonic anhydrase, a protein enzyme present inside the red blood cell, catalyzes this reaction with sufficient rapidity that it is accomplished in only a fraction of a second. Because the enzyme is present only inside the red blood cell, bicarbonate accumulates

Chloride shift

to a much greater extent within the red cell than in the plasma. The capacity of blood to carry carbon dioxide as bicarbonate is enhanced by an ion transport system inside the red blood cell membrane that simultaneously moves a bicarbonate ion out of the cell and into the plasma in exchange for a chloride ion. The simultaneous exchange of these two ions, known as the chloride shift, permits the plasma to be used as a storage site for bicarbonate without changing the electrical charge of either the plasma or the red blood cell. Only 26 percent of the total carbon dioxide content of blood exists as bicarbonate inside the red blood cell, while 62 percent exists as bicarbonate in plasma; however, the bulk of bicarbonate ions is first produced inside the cell, then transported to the plasma. A reverse sequence of reactions occurs when blood reaches the lung, where the partial pressure of carbon dioxide is lower than in the blood.

Hemoglobin acts in another way to facilitate the transport of carbon dioxide. Amino groups of the hemoglobin molecule react reversibly with carbon dioxide in solution to yield carbamates. A few amino sites on hemoglobin are oxylabile, that is, their ability to bind carbon dioxide depends on the state of oxygenation of the hemoglobin molecule. The change in molecular configuration of hemoglobin that accompanies the release of oxygen leads to increased binding of carbon dioxide to oxylabile amino groups. Thus, release of oxygen in body tissues enhances binding of carbon dioxide as carbamate. Oxygenation of hemoglobin in the lungs has the reverse effect and leads to carbon dioxide elimination.

Only 5 percent of carbon dioxide in the blood is transported free in physical solution without chemical change or binding, yet this pool is important, because only free carbon dioxide easily crosses biologic membranes. Virtually every molecule of carbon dioxide produced by metabolism must exist in the free form as it enters blood in the tissues and leaves capillaries in the lung. Between these two events, most carbon dioxide is transported as bicarbonate or carbamate.

Gas exchange in the lung. The introduction of air into the alveoli allows the removal of carbon dioxide and the addition of oxygen to venous blood. Because ventilation is a cyclic phenomenon that occurs through a system of conducting airways, not all inspired air participates in gas exchange. A portion of the inspired breath remains in the conducting airways and does not reach the alveoli where gas exchange occurs. This portion is approximately one-third of each breath at rest but decreases to as little as 10 percent during exercise, due to the increased size of inspired breaths.

Cyclic nature of ventilation

In contrast to the cyclic nature of ventilation, blood flow through the lung is continuous, and almost all blood entering the lungs participates in gas exchange. The efficiency of gas exchange is critically dependent on the uniform distribution of blood flow and inspired air throughout the lungs. In health, ventilation and blood flow are extremely well matched in each exchange unit throughout the lungs. The lower parts of the lung receive slightly more blood flow than ventilation because gravity has a greater effect on the distribution of blood than on the distribution of inspired air. Under ideal circumstances, partial pressures of oxygen and carbon dioxide in alveolar gas and arterial blood are identical. Normally there is a small difference between oxygen tensions in alveolar gas and arterial blood because of the effect of gravity on matching and the addition of a small amount of venous drainage to the bloodstream after it has left the lungs. These events have no measurable effect on carbon dioxide partial pressures because the difference between arterial and venous blood is so small.

Abnormal gas exchange. Lung disease can lead to severe abnormalities in blood gas composition. Because of the differences in oxygen and carbon dioxide transport, impaired oxygen exchange is far more common than impaired carbon dioxide exchange. Mechanisms of abnormal gas exchange are grouped into four categories—hypoventilation, shunting, ventilation–blood flow imbalance, and limitations of diffusion.

If the quantity of inspired air entering the lungs is less than is needed to maintain normal exchange—a condition known as hypoventilation—the alveolar partial pressure of carbon dioxide rises and the partial pressure of oxygen falls almost reciprocally. Similar changes occur in arterial blood partial pressures because the composition of alveolar gas determines gas partial pressures in blood perfusing the lungs. This abnormality leads to parallel changes in both gas and blood and is the only abnormality in gas exchange that does not cause an increase in the normally small difference between arterial and alveolar partial pressures of oxygen.

In shunting, venous blood enters the bloodstream without passing through functioning lung tissue. Shunting of blood may result from abnormal vascular (blood vessel) communications or from blood flowing through unventilated portions of the lung (e.g., alveoli filled with fluid or inflammatory material). A reduction in arterial blood oxygenation is seen with shunting, but the level of carbon dioxide in arterial blood is not elevated even though the shunted blood contains more carbon dioxide than arterial blood.

Shunting

The differing effects of shunting on oxygen and carbon dioxide partial pressures are the result of the different configurations of the blood-dissociation curves of the two gases. As noted above, the oxygen-dissociation curve is S-shaped and plateaus near the normal alveolar oxygen partial pressure, but the carbon dioxide-dissociation curve is steeper and does not plateau as the partial pressure of carbon dioxide increases. In the example in Figure 16, blood perfusing the collapsed, unventilated area of the lung, labeled A, leaves the lung without exchanging oxygen or carbon dioxide. The content of carbon dioxide, indicated by the letter A next to the carbon dioxide-dissociation curve, is greater than the normal carbon dioxide content, indicated by the square. The remaining healthy portion of the lung, labeled B in the figure, receives both its usual ventilation and the ventilation that normally would be directed to the abnormal lung. This lowers the partial pressure of carbon dioxide in the alveoli of the normal area of the lung. As a result, blood leaving the healthy portion of the lung, indicated by the letter B next to the carbon dioxide-dissociation curve, has a lower carbon dioxide content than normal. The lower carbon dioxide content in this blood counteracts the addition of blood with a higher carbon dioxide content from the abnormal area, and the composite arterial blood carbon dioxide content remains normal, as indicated by the arrow next to the carbon dioxide-dissociation curve. This compensatory mechanism is less efficient than normal carbon dioxide exchange and requires a modest increase in overall ventilation, which is usually achieved without

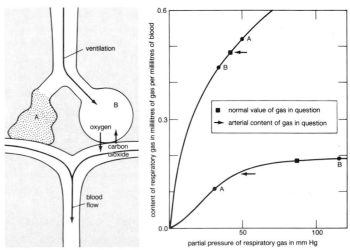

Figure 16: *The effect of shunting of blood through nonfunctioning lung tissue on oxygen and carbon dioxide exchange.*
(Left) Distribution of ventilation and blood flow. (Right) The oxygen- (lower curve) and carbon dioxide- (upper curve) dissociation curves of blood showing the relationships between blood contents and partial pressures of the respiratory gases (see text).

difficulty. Because the carbon dioxide-dissociation curve is steep and relatively linear, compensation for decreased carbon dioxide exchange in one portion of the lung can be counterbalanced by increased excretion of carbon dioxide in another area of the lung.

In contrast, shunting of venous blood has a substantial effect on arterial blood oxygen content and partial pressure. Blood leaving an unventilated area of the lung has an oxygen content (indicated by the letter A next to the oxygen-dissociation curve) that is less than the normal content (indicated by the square). In the healthy area of the lung, labeled B in the figure, the increase in ventilation above normal raises the partial pressure of oxygen in the alveolar gas and, therefore, in the arterial blood. The oxygen-dissociation curve, however, reaches a plateau at the normal alveolar partial pressure, and an increase in blood partial pressure results in a negligible increase in oxygen content. Mixture of blood from this healthy portion of the lung (with normal oxygen content) and blood from the abnormal area of the lung (with decreased oxygen content) produces a composite arterial oxygen content that is less than the normal level, indicated by the arrow next to the oxygen-dissociation curve. Thus, an area of healthy lung cannot counterbalance the effect of an abnormal portion of the lung on blood oxygenation because the oxygen-dissociation curve reaches a plateau at a normal alveolar partial pressure of oxygen. This effect on blood oxygenation is seen not only in shunting but in any abnormality that results in a localized reduction in blood oxygen content.

Venti-lation-blood flow imbalance

Mismatching of ventilation and blood flow is by far the most common cause of a decrease in partial pressure of oxygen in blood. There are minimal changes in blood carbon dioxide content unless the degree of mismatch is extremely severe. Inspired air and blood flow normally are distributed uniformly, and each alveolus receives approximately equal quantities of both. As matching of inspired air and blood flow deviates from the normal ratio of 1 to 1, alveoli become either overventilated or underventilated in relation to their blood flow. In alveoli that are overventilated, the amount of carbon dioxide eliminated is increased, which counteracts the fact that there is less carbon dioxide eliminated in the alveoli that are relatively underventilated. Overventilated alveoli, however, cannot compensate in terms of greater oxygenation for underventilated alveoli because, as is shown in the oxygen-dissociation curve, a plateau is reached at the alveolar partial pressure of oxygen, and increased ventilation will not increase blood oxygen content. In healthy lungs there is a narrow distribution of the ratio of ventilation to blood flow throughout the lung that is centred around a ratio of 1 to 1. In disease, this distribution can broaden substantially so that individual alveoli can have ratios that markedly deviate from the ratio of 1 to 1. Any deviation from the usual clustering around the ratio of 1 to 1 leads to decreased blood oxygenation—the more disparate the deviation, the greater the reduction in blood oxygenation. Carbon dioxide exchange, on the other hand, is not affected by an abnormal ratio of ventilation and blood flow as long as the increase in ventilation that is required to maintain carbon dioxide excretion in overventilated alveoli can be achieved.

A fourth category of abnormal gas exchange involves limitation of diffusion of gases across the thin membrane separating the alveoli from the pulmonary capillaries. A variety of processes can interfere with this orderly exchange; for oxygen, these include increased thickness of the alveolar–capillary membrane, loss of surface area available for diffusion of oxygen, a reduction in the alveolar partial pressure of oxygen required for diffusion, and decreased time available for exchange due to increased velocity of flow. These factors are usually grouped under the broad description of "diffusion limitation," and any can cause incomplete transfer of oxygen with a resultant reduction in blood oxygen content. There is no diffusion limitation of the exchange of carbon dioxide because this gas is more soluble than oxygen in the alveolar–capillary membrane, which facilitates carbon dioxide exchange. The complex reactions involved in carbon dioxide transport proceed with sufficient rapidity to avoid being a significant limiting factor in exchange.

INTERPLAY OF RESPIRATION, CIRCULATION, AND METABOLISM

The interplay of respiration, circulation, and metabolism is the key to the functioning of the respiratory system as a whole. Cells set the demand for oxygen uptake and carbon dioxide discharge, that is, for gas exchange in the lungs. The circulation of the blood links the sites of oxygen utilization and uptake. The proper functioning of the respiratory system depends on both the ability of the system to make functional adjustments to varying needs and the design features of the sequence of structures involved, which set the limit for respiration.

Role of respiration

The main purpose of respiration is to provide oxygen to the cells at a rate adequate to satisfy their metabolic needs. This involves transport of oxygen from the lung to the tissues by means of the circulation of blood. In antiquity and the medieval period, the heart was regarded as a furnace where the "fire of life" kept the blood boiling. Modern cell biology has unveiled the truth behind the metaphor. Each cell maintains a set of furnaces, the mitochondria, where, through the oxidation of foodstuffs such as glucose, the energetic needs of the cells are supplied. The precise object of respiration therefore is the supply of oxygen to the mitochondria.

Cell metabolism depends on energy derived from high-energy phosphates such as adenosine triphosphate (ATP), whose third phosphate bond can release a quantum of energy to fuel many cell processes, such as the contraction of muscle fibre proteins or the synthesis of protein molecules. In the process, ATP is degraded to adenosine diphosphate (ADP), a molecule with only two phosphate bonds. To recharge the molecule by adding the third phosphate group requires energy derived from the breakdown of foodstuffs, or substrates. Two pathways are available: (1) anaerobic glycolysis, or fermentation, which operates in the absence of oxygen; and (2) aerobic metabolism, which requires oxygen and involves the mitochondria. The anaerobic pathway leads to acid waste products and is wasteful of resources: The breakdown of one molecule of glucose generates only two molecules of ATP. In contrast, aerobic metabolism has a higher yield (36 molecules of ATP per molecule of glucose) and results in "clean wastes"—water and carbon dioxide, which are easily eliminated from the body and are recycled by plants in the process of photosynthesis. For any sustained high-level cell activity, the aerobic metabolic pathway is therefore preferable. Since oxidative phosphorylation occurs only in mitochondria, and since each cell must produce its own ATP (it cannot be imported), the number of mitochondria in a cell reflects its capacity for aerobic metabolism, or its need for oxygen.

The supply of oxygen to the mitochondria at an adequate rate is a critical function of the respiratory system, because the cells maintain only a limited store of high-energy phosphates and of oxygen, whereas they usually have a reasonable supply of substrates in stock. If oxygen supply is interrupted for a few minutes, many cells, or even the organism, will die.

Route of oxygen

Oxygen is collected from environmental air, transferred to blood in the lungs, and transported by blood flow to the periphery of the cells where it is discharged to reach the mitochondria by diffusion. The transfer of oxygen to the mitochondria involves several structures and different modes of transports. It begins with ventilation of the lung, which is achieved by convection or mass flow of air through an ingeniously branched system of airways; in the most peripheral airways ventilation of alveoli is completed by diffusion of oxygen through the air to the alveolar surface. The transfer of oxygen from alveolar air into the capillary blood occurs by diffusion across the tissue barrier; it is driven by the oxygen partial pressure difference between alveolar air and capillary blood and depends on the thickness (about 0.5 micrometre) and the surface area (about 130 square metres in humans). Convective transport by the blood depends on the blood flow rate (cardiac output) and on the oxygen capacity of the blood, which is determined by its content of hemoglobin in the red blood cells. The last step is the diffusive discharge of oxygen from the capillaries into the tissue and cells, which is driven by the oxygen partial pressure difference and depends on the quantity of capillary blood in the tissue. In this process the blood plays a central role and affects all transport steps: oxygen uptake in the lung, transport by blood flow, and discharge to the cells. Blood also serves as carrier for both respiratory gases: oxygen, which is bound to hemoglobin in the red blood cells, and carbon dioxide, which is carried by both plasma and red blood cells and which also serves as a buffer for acid-base balance in blood and tissues.

Metabolism, or, more accurately, the metabolic rate of the cells, sets the demand for oxygen. At rest, a human consumes about 250 millilitres of oxygen each minute. With exercise this rate can be increased more than 10-fold in a normal healthy individual, but a highly trained athlete may achieve a more than 20-fold increase. As more and more muscle cells become engaged in doing work, the demand for ATP and oxygen increases linearly with work rate. This is accompanied by an increased cardiac output, essentially due to a higher heart rate, and by increased ventilation of the lungs; as a consequence, the oxygen partial pressure difference across the air–blood barrier increases and oxygen transfer by diffusion is augmented. These dynamic adjustments to the muscles' needs occur up to a limit that is twice as high in the athlete as in the untrained individual. This range of possible oxidative metabolism from rest to maximal exercise is called the aerobic scope. The upper limit to oxygen consumption is conferred not by the ability of muscles to do work but rather by the limited ability of the respiratory system to provide or utilize oxygen at a higher rate. Muscle can do more work, but beyond the aerobic scope they must revert to anaerobic metabolism, with the result that waste products, mainly lactic acid, accumulate and limit the duration of work.

Aerobic scope

The limit to oxidative metabolism is therefore set by some features of the respiratory system, from the lung to the mitochondria. Knowing precisely what sets the limit is important for understanding respiration as a key vital process, but it is not straightforward, because of the complexity of the system. Much has been learned from comparative physiology and morphology, based on observations that oxygen consumption rates differ significantly among species. For example, the athletic species in nature, such as dogs or horses, have an aerobic scope more than twofold greater than that of other animals of the same size; this is called adaptive variation. Then, oxygen consumption per unit body mass increases as animals become smaller, so that a mouse consumes six times as much oxygen per gram of body mass as a cow, a feature called allometric variation. Furthermore, the aerobic scope can be increased by training in an individual, but this induced variation achieves at best a 50 percent difference between the untrained and the trained state, well below interspecies differences.

Within the aerobic scope the adjustments are due to functional variation. For example, cardiac output is augmented by increasing heart rate. Mounting evidence indicates that the limit to oxidative metabolism is related to structural design features of the system. The total amount of mitochondria in skeletal muscle is strictly proportional to maximal oxygen consumption, in all types of variation. In training, the mitochondria increase in proportion to the augmented aerobic scope. Mitochondria set the demand for oxygen, and they seem able to consume up to five millilitres of oxygen per minute and gram of mitochondria. If energy (ATP) needs to be produced at a higher rate, the muscle cells make more mitochondria. It is thus possible that oxygen consumption is limited at the periphery, at the last step of aerobic metabolism. But it is also possible that more central parts of the respiratory system may set the limit to oxygen transport, mainly the heart, whose capacity to pump blood reaches a limit, both in terms of rate and of the size of the ventricles, which determines the volume of blood that can be pumped with each stroke. The issue of peripheral versus central limitation is

Limits to oxidative metabolism

still under debate. It appears, however, that the lung as a gas-exchanging organ has sufficient redundancy that it does not limit aerobic metabolism at the site of oxygen uptake. But, whereas the mitochondria, the blood, the blood vessels, and the heart can increase in number, rate, or volume to augment their capacity when energy needs increase, such as in training, the lung lacks this capacity to adapt. If this proves true, the lung may well constitute the ultimate limit for the respiratory system, beyond which oxidative metabolism cannot be increased by training.

ADAPTATIONS

High altitudes. Ascent from sea level to high altitude has well-known effects upon respiration. The progressive fall in barometric pressure is accompanied by a fall in the partial pressure of oxygen, both in the ambient air and in the alveolar spaces of the lung; and it is this fall that poses the major respiratory challenge to humans at high altitude. Humans and some mammalian species like cattle adjust to the fall in oxygen pressure through the reversible and non-inheritable process of acclimatization, which, whether undertaken deliberately or not, commences from the time of exposure to high altitudes. Indigenous mountain species like the llama, on the other hand, exhibit an adaptation that is heritable and has a genetic basis.

Respiratory acclimatization in humans is achieved through mechanisms that heighten the partial pressure of oxygen at all stages, from the alveolar spaces in the lung to the mitochondria in the cells, where oxygen is needed for the ultimate biochemical expression of respiration. The decline in the ambient partial pressure of oxygen is offset to some extent by greater ventilation, which takes the form of deeper breathing rather than a faster rate at rest. Diffusion of oxygen across the alveolar walls into the blood is facilitated, and in some experimental animal studies the alveolar walls are thinner at altitude than at sea level. The scarcity of oxygen at high altitudes stimulates increased production of hemoglobin and red blood cells, which increases the amount of oxygen transported to the tissues. The extra oxygen is released by increased levels of inorganic phosphates in the red blood cells, such as 2,3-diphosphoglycerate. With a prolonged stay at altitude, the tissues develop more blood vessels, and, as capillary density is increased, the length of the diffusion path along which gases must pass is decreased—a factor augmenting gas exchange. In addition, the size of muscle fibres decreases, which also shortens the diffusion path of oxygen.

Respiratory acclimatization

The initial response of respiration to the fall of oxygen partial pressure in the blood on ascent to high altitude occurs in two small nodules, the carotid bodies, attached to the division of the carotid arteries on either side of the neck. As the oxygen deprivation persists, the carotid bodies enlarge but become less sensitive to the lack of oxygen. The low oxygen partial pressure in the lung is associated with thickening of the small blood vessels in pulmonary alveolar walls and a slight increase in pulmonary blood pressure, thought to enhance oxygen perfusion of the lung apices.

Indigenous mountain animals like the llama, alpaca, and vicuña in the Andes or the yak in the Himalayas are adapted rather than acclimatized to the low oxygen partial pressures of high altitude. Their hemoglobin has a high oxygen affinity, so that full saturation of the blood with oxygen occurs at a lower partial pressure of oxygen. In contrast to acclimatized humans, these indigenous, adapted mountain species do not have increased levels of hemoglobin or of organic phosphates in the red cells; they do not develop small muscular blood vessels or an increased blood pressure in the lung; and their carotid bodies remain small.

Native human highlanders are acclimatized rather than genetically adapted to the reduced oxygen pressure. After living many years at high altitude, some highlanders lose this acclimatization and develop chronic mountain sickness, sometimes called Monge's disease, after the Peruvian physician who first described it. This disease is characterized by greater levels of hemoglobin. In Tibet some infants of Han origin never achieve satisfactory acclimatization on ascent to high altitude. A chemodectoma, or benign tumour, of the carotid bodies may develop in native highlanders in response to chronic exposure to low levels of oxygen.

Swimming and diving. Fluid is not a natural medium for sustaining human life after the fetal stage; human respiration requires ventilation with air. Nevertheless, all vertebrates, including humans, exhibit a set of responses that may be called a "diving reflex," which involves cardiovascular and metabolic adaptations to conserve oxygen during diving into water. Other physiological changes are also observed, either artificially induced (as by hyperventilation) or resulting from pressure changes in the environment at the same time that a diver is breathing from an independent gas supply.

Hyperventilation, a form of overbreathing that increases the amount of air entering the pulmonary alveoli, may be used intentionally by swimmers to prolong the time they are able to hold their breath under water. Hyperventilation can be dangerous, and this danger is greatly increased if the swimmer descends to depth, as sometimes happens in snorkeling. The increased ventilation prolongs the duration of the breath-hold by reducing the carbon dioxide pressure in the blood, but it cannot provide an equivalent increase in oxygen. Thus the carbon dioxide

Hazards of breath holding

that accumulates with exercise takes longer to reach the threshold at which the swimmer is forced to take another breath, but concurrently the oxygen content of the blood falls to unusually low levels. The increased environmental pressure of the water around the breath-holding diver increases the partial pressures of the pulmonary gases. This allows an adequate oxygen partial pressure to be maintained in the setting of reduced oxygen content, and consciousness remains unimpaired. When the accumulated carbon dioxide at last forces the swimmer to return to the surface, however, the progressively diminishing pressure of the water on his ascent reduces the partial pressure of the remaining oxygen. Unconsciousness may then occur in or under the water.

Hazards due to pressure

Divers who breathe from an apparatus that delivers gas at the same pressure as that of the surrounding water need not return to the surface to breathe and can remain at depth for prolonged periods. But this apparent advantage introduces additional hazards, many of them unique in human physiology. Most of the hazards result from the environmental pressure of water. Two factors are involved. At the depth of a diver, the absolute pressure, which is approximately one additional atmosphere for each 10-metre increment of depth, is one factor. The other factor, acting at any depth, is the vertical hydrostatic pressure gradient across the body. The effects of pressure are seen in many processes at the molecular and cellular level and include the physiological effects of the increased partial pressures of the respiratory gases, the increased density of the respiratory gases, the effect of changes of pressure upon the volumes of the gas-containing spaces in the body, and the consequences of the uptake of respiratory gases into, and their subsequent elimination from, the blood and tissues of the diver, often with the formation of bubbles. The multiple effects of submersion upon respiration are not easily separated from one another or clearly distinguishable from related effects of pressure upon other bodily systems.

The increased work of breathing, rather than cardiac or muscular performance, is the limiting factor for hard physical work underwater. Although the increased work of breathing may be largely due to the effects of increased respiratory gas density upon pulmonary function, the use of underwater breathing apparatus adds significant external breathing resistance to the diver's respiratory burden.

Arterial carbon dioxide pressure should remain unchanged during changes of ambient pressure, but the impaired alveolar ventilation at depth leads to some carbon dioxide retention (hypercapnia). This may be compounded by an increased inspiratory content of carbon dioxide, especially if the diver uses closed-circuit and semiclosed-circuit rebreathing equipment or wears an inadequately ventilated helmet. Alveolar oxygen levels can also be disturbed in diving. Hypoxia may result from failure of the gas supply and may occur without warning. More commonly, the levels of inspired oxygen are increased. Oxygen

in excess can be a poison; at a partial pressure greater than 1.5 bar ("surface equivalent value" = 150 percent), it may cause the rapid onset of convulsions, and after prolonged exposures at somewhat lower partial pressures it may cause pulmonary oxygen toxicity with reduced vital capacity and later pulmonary edema. In mixed-gas diving, inspired oxygen is therefore maintained at a partial pressure somewhere between 0.2 and 0.5 bar, but at great depths the inhomogeneity of alveolar ventilation and the limitations of gas diffusion appear to require oxygen provision at greater than normal levels.

The maximum breathing capacity and the maximum voluntary ventilation of a diver breathing compressed air diminish rapidly with depth, approximately in proportion to the reciprocal of the square root of the increasing gas density. Thus the practice of using an inert gas such as helium as the oxygen diluent at depths where nitrogen becomes narcotic, like an anesthetic, has the additional advantage of providing a breathing gas of lesser density. The use of hydrogen, which in a mixture with less than 4 percent oxygen is noncombustible, provides a greater respiratory advantage for deep diving.

Effects on pulmonary function

At the extreme depths now attainable by humans—some 500 metres in the sea and more than 680 metres in the laboratory—direct effects of pressure upon the respiratory centre may be part of the "high-pressure neurological syndrome" and may account for some of the anomalies of breathlessness (dyspnea) and respiratory control that occur with exercise at depth.

The term carbon dioxide retainer is commonly applied to a diver who fails to eliminate carbon dioxide in the normal manner. An ability to tolerate carbon dioxide may increase the work capacity of a diver at depth but also may predispose him to other consequences that are less desirable. High values of end-tidal carbon dioxide with only moderate exertion may be associated with a diminished tolerance to oxygen neurotoxicity, a condition that, if it occurs underwater, places the diver at great risk. Nitrogen narcosis is enhanced by the presence of excess carbon dioxide, and the physical properties of carbon dioxide facilitate the nucleation and growth of bubbles on decompression.

Independent of the depth of the dive are the effects of the local hydrostatic pressure gradient upon respiration. The supporting effect of the surrounding water pressure upon the soft tissues promotes venous return from vessels no longer solely influenced by gravity; and, whatever the orientation of the diver in the water, this approximates the effects of recumbency upon the cardiovascular and respiratory systems. Also, the uniform distribution of gas pressure within the thorax contrasts with the hydrostatic pressure gradient that exists outside the chest. Intrathoracic pressure may be effectively lower than the pressure of the surrounding water, in which case more blood will be shifted into the thorax, or it may be effectively greater, resulting in less intrathoracic blood volume. The concept of a hydrostatic balance point within the chest, which represents the net effect of the external pressures and the effects of chest buoyancy, has proved useful in designing underwater breathing apparatuses.

Intrapulmonary gas expands exponentially during the steady return of a diver toward the surface. Unless vented, the expanding gas may rupture alveolar septa and escape into interstitial spaces. The extra-alveolar gas may cause a "burst lung" (pneumothorax) or the tracking of gas into the tissues of the chest (mediastinal emphysema), possibly extending into the pericardium or into the neck. More seriously, the escaped alveolar gas may be carried by the blood circulation to the brain (arterial gas embolism). This is a major cause of death among divers. Failure to exhale during ascent causes such accidents and is likely to occur if the diver makes a rapid emergency ascent, even from depths as shallow as two metres. Other possible causes of pulmonary barotrauma include retention of gas by a diseased portion of lung and gas trapping due to dynamic airway collapse during forced expiration at low lung volumes.

Decompression illness

Decompression sickness may be defined as the illness, following a reduction of pressure, that is caused by the formation of bubbles from gases that were dissolved in the tissues while the diver was at an increased environmental pressure. The causes are related to the inadequacy of the diver's decompression, perhaps failure to follow a correct decompression protocol, or occasionally a diver's idiosyncratic response to an apparently safe decompression procedure. The pathogenesis begins both with the mechanical effects of bubbles and their expansion in the tissues and blood vessels and with the surface effects of the bubbles upon the various components of the blood at the blood–gas interface. The lung plays a significant role in the pathogenesis and natural history of this illness and may contribute to the clinical picture. Shallow, rapid respiration, often associated with a sharp retrosternal pain on deep inspiration, signals the onset of pulmonary decompression sickness, the "chokes." Whether occurring alone or as part of a more complex case of decompression sickness, this respiratory pattern constitutes an acute emergency. It usually responds rapidly to treatment by recompression in a compression chamber.

Diseases and disorders of respiration

Diseases of the respiratory system may affect any of the structures and organs that have to do with breathing—the nasal cavities, the throat (pharynx), the larynx, the windpipe (trachea), the airways (bronchi), and the lung tissue. In addition, respiration is dependent on normal functioning of the muscles in the chest wall and the diaphragm, which may also be affected by disease. The respiratory tract is the site of an exceptionally large range of disorders for three main reasons: first, it is exposed to the environment and therefore may be affected by dust or gases in the air; second, it possesses a large network of capillaries through which the entire output of the heart has to pass, which means that diseases that affect the small blood vessels are likely to affect the lung; and third, it may be the site of "sensitivity" or allergic phenomena that may profoundly affect function.

SIGNS AND SYMPTOMS

By contrast, the symptoms of lung disease are relatively few. Cough is a particularly important sign of all diseases that affect any part of the bronchial tree. A cough productive of sputum is the most important manifestation of disease of the major airways, of which bronchitis is a common example. In severe bronchitis the mucous glands lining the bronchi enlarge greatly, and up to a cupful of sputum may be produced in a few hours; more commonly, 30 to 60 millilitres of sputum are produced in a 24-hour period, particularly in the first two hours after awakening in the morning. An irritative cough without sputum may be caused by extension of malignant disease to the bronchial tree from nearby organs. The presence of blood in the sputum (hemoptysis) is an important sign that should never be disregarded. Although it may result simply from an exacerbation of an existing infection, it may also indicate the presence of inflammation, capillary damage, or tumour. It is also a classic sign of tuberculosis of the lungs.

Blood-stained sputum

The second most important symptom of lung disease is dyspnea, or shortness of breath. This sensation, of complex origin, may arise acutely, as when a foreign body is inhaled into the trachea, or with the onset of a severe attack of asthma. More usually, it is insidious in onset and slowly progressive. What is noted is a slowly progressive difficulty in completing some task, such as walking up a flight of stairs, playing golf, or walking uphill. The shortness of breath may vary in severity, but in diseases such as emphysema (described below), in which there is irreversible lung damage, it is constantly present. It may become so severe as to immobilize the victim, and tasks such as dressing cannot be performed without difficulty. Severe fibrosis of the lung, resulting from occupational lung disease or arising from no identifiable antecedent condition, may also cause severe and unremitting dyspnea. Dyspnea is also an early symptom of congestion of the lung as a result of impaired function of the left ventricle of the heart. When this occurs, if the right ventricle that

Dyspnea

pumps blood through the lungs is functioning normally, the lung capillaries become engorged, and fluid may accumulate in small airways. It is commonly dyspnea that first causes a patient to seek medical advice, but absence of the symptom does not mean that serious lung disease is not present, since, for example, a small lung cancer that is not obstructing an airway will not produce shortness of breath.

Chest pain may be an early symptom of lung disease, but it is most often associated with an attack of pneumonia, in which case it is due to an inflammation of the pleura that follows the onset of the pneumonic process. This pain is characteristically felt when a deep breath is taken, and it disappears when fluid accumulates in the pleural space, a condition known as a pleural effusion. Acute pleurisy with pain may signal a blockage in a pulmonary vessel, which leads to acute congestion of the affected part, sometimes with a pleurisy over it. Severe chest pain may by occasioned by the spread of malignant disease to involve the pleura, or by a tumour, such as a mesothelioma, arising from the pleura itself. Severe, intractable pain caused by such conditions may require surgery to cut the nerves supplying the affected segment to give relief. Fortunately, pain of this severity is rare.

Chest pain

To these major symptoms of lung disease—coughing, dyspnea, and chest pain—may be added several of less importance. A wheeziness in the chest may be heard. This is caused by airway obstruction, such as occurs in asthma. Some diseases of the lung are associated with the swelling of the fingertips (and, rarely, of the toes) called "clubbing." Clubbing may be a feature of bronchiectasis (chronic inflammation and dilation of the major airways), diffuse fibrosis of the lung from any cause, and lung cancer. In the case of lung cancer, this unusual sign may disappear after surgical removal of the tumour. In some lung diseases, the first symptom may be a swelling of the lymph nodes that drain the affected area, particularly the small nodes above the collarbone in the neck; enlargement of the lymph nodes in these regions should always lead to a suspicion of intrathoracic disease. Not infrequently, the presenting symptom of a lung cancer is caused by spread of the tumour to other organs. Thus, a hip fracture from bone metastases, cerebral signs from intracranial metastases, or jaundice from liver involvement may all be the first evidence of a primary lung cancer, as may sensory changes in the legs, since a peripheral neuropathy may also be the presenting evidence of these tumours.

The generally debilitating effect of many lung diseases is well recognized. A person with primary lung tuberculosis or with lung cancer, for example, may be conscious only of a general feeling of malaise, unusual fatigue, or seemingly minor symptoms as the first indication of disease. Loss of appetite and loss of weight, a disinclination for physical activity, general psychological depression, and some symptoms apparently unrelated to the lung such as mild indigestion or headaches, may be diverse indicators of lung disease. Not infrequently, the patient may feel as one does when convalescent after an attack of influenza. Because the symptoms of lung disease, especially in the early stage, are variable and nonspecific, physical and radiographic examination of the chest are an essential part of the evaluation of persons with these complaints.

General effects of lung disease

THE DEFENSES OF THE LUNG

Exposed as it is to the outside environment, the respiratory tract possesses a complicated but comprehensive series of defenses against inhaled material. The cells that form the first line of defense in the smaller radicles of the airway and in the alveoli of the lung are the alveolar macrophage cells. These cells can ingest and destroy bacteria and viruses and can remove small particles. They also secrete chemicals that attract white blood cells to the site, and hence they can initiate an inflammatory response in the lung. Particles picked up by macrophages are removed by them into the lymphatic system of the lung and stored in adjacent lymph glands. Soluble particles are removed into the bloodstream, to be finally excreted by the kidney. This is the route followed by the small lead particles emitted in automobile exhaust, which are inhaled, ingested by macrophages, cleared into the bloodstream, and finally

The macrophages

excreted. The half-life of these particles in the lung is about 12 hours.

METHODS OF INVESTIGATION

Physical examination of the chest remains important, as it may reveal the presence of an area of inflammation, a pleural effusion, or an airway obstruction; the first two of these conditions will be visible on chest radiographs, but the third is usually audible only. Examination of the sputum for bacteria allows the identification of many infectious organisms and the institution of specific treatment; sputum examination for malignant cells is occasionally helpful. The conventional radiological examination of the chest has been greatly enhanced by the technique of computerized tomography, which shows small lesions and permits their precise location to be defined. The introduction of the flexible bronchoscope (in place of a rigid instrument) has greatly lessened the discomfort and danger associated with visual inspection of the bronchi and allows small tissue samples to be taken for histological study at the same time.

Tests of lung function

A number of tests are available to determine the functional status of the lung and the effects of disease on pulmonary function. A simple ventilatory test, the measurement of the velocity of a forced maximal expiration after a full inspiration, allows the degree of airway obstruction to be quantified. Airflow obstruction occurs in asthma and emphysema. A related test, of ventilatory capability, measures the volume that can be forcibly expired in one second after a full inspiration. Ventilatory capability can be simply measured with a spirometer or flow meter, and these devices are widely used in field studies. More complex laboratory equipment is necessary to measure the volumes of gas in the lung; the distribution of ventilation within the lung; airflow resistance; the stiffness of the lung, or the pressure required to inflate it; and the rate of gas transfer across the lung, which is commonly measured by recording the rate of absorption of carbon monoxide—used for this purpose because of the high affinity of hemoglobin for it. Gas transfer is impaired in diseases that destroy the lung or cause severe generalized thickening. Arterial blood gases and pH values indicate the adequacy of oxygenation and ventilation and are routinely measured in intensive care unit patients. Tests of exercise capability, in which work load, total ventilation, and gas exchange are compared before and in response to exercise, are useful in assessing disability.

MORPHOLOGICAL CLASSIFICATION OF RESPIRATORY DISEASE

Overview of the respiratory system

It is helpful to recall the main divisions of the respiratory system as a basis for the morphological description of respiratory system diseases. The upper airway consists of the nose, nasopharynx, and larynx. Below these structures lies the trachea, or windpipe. Thereafter the airway divides into two major airways, right and left, then into progressively smaller tubes, until finally the terminal bronchioles, which are about one millimetre in diameter, are reached. On average, 16 generations of division occur between the trachea and the terminal bronchioles. Although there is only one airway at the beginning—the trachea—there are about 650,000 terminal bronchioles. The cross-sectional area of the bronchial tree increases with increasing subdivision. The end of each terminal bronchiole opens into an acinus, so called because the structure resembles a cluster of grapes, and from this point onward the gas-exchanging portion of the lung is reached. The alveoli or air sacs, which are divided into groups or lobules by fibrous partitions, or septa, are small hexagonal structures forming a blind end to the acinus. The wall of the acinus consists of blood capillaries, and the remaining structures are extremely thin, only providing supporting tissue for the rich capillary bed that constitutes the parenchyma, or the essential tissue of the lung itself. The parenchyma is the gas-exchanging tissue of the lung and has a surface area roughly comparable to that of a tennis court. Blood is distributed to the lung through the branching pulmonary artery, which subdivides with the bronchial tree and accompanies the smaller bronchioles into the region of the acinus to supply the capillaries of the alveolar wall. Oxygenated blood from the acini is collected into pulmonary veins, which run at some little distance from the bronchioles. An interstitial space exists around the alveoli and around the bronchioles and blood vessels, and this connects the lymph nodes (the small masses of lymphatic tissue that occur along the course of the lymph vessels) situated in the midline of the thoracic cavity and extending in a chain up into the neck and down into the abdomen.

The lung is covered by a protective membrane, the pleura, and the inner lining of the chest wall consists of a similar membrane. The space between these two fibrous coverings, called the intrapleural space, normally contains no air, and only a few millilitres of fluid for lubrication purposes, as during breathing one layer must slide on another. The pleurae may become involved by inflammation or neoplastic disease, in which case an effusion of fluid may occur between the two layers.

From this general description, diseases of the respiratory system may be grouped into the following categories.

Upper airway disease. The nasal sinuses are frequently the site of both acute and chronic infections. In common with the palate and the nasopharynx, they are also the site of malignant neoplastic changes. Cancer of the larynx is much more common in smokers than in nonsmokers; and cancers of other parts of the upper respiratory tract, some of which may be caused by exposure to dusts and metals, are also more likely to develop in smokers.

Sleep apnea syndrome

The occurrence of upper airway obstruction (particularly common in people who snore) has been documented in sleep laboratory studies. In the sleep apnea syndrome, episodes of obstruction are accompanied by cessation of breathing for up to half a minute and a marked fall in blood oxygen levels, terminating in arousal from sleep. The sleep apnea syndrome is not uncommon. It is not confined to the very obese, although it forms part of the syndrome of severe obesity in which sleep disturbance is common; and it is associated with the daytime somnolence known as the pickwickian syndrome, after Charles Dickens' description of the fat boy in *The Pickwick Papers.* Sleep apnea is caused by relaxation of muscles around the pharynx and obstruction of the airway by the palate. It is related to narrow anatomical dimensions in this area but is also more likely to occur if alcohol is ingested shortly before sleep. Sleep apnea is more than a medical curiosity: it may cause a rise in systemic blood pressure, and the daytime somnolence may occur while the affected person is at work.

Diseases of major bronchi. The major bronchi can become the seat of chronic inflammation, as in chronic bronchitis or bronchiectasis. The latter disease is not uncommonly caused by the familial disease of cystic fibrosis. The major bronchi may also be the site of development of malignant disease.

Asthma

Diseases of smaller bronchi and bronchioles. It is in the smaller bronchi that major obstruction commonly occurs in asthma, since these bronchioles contain smooth muscle in their walls and the muscle may contract, causing airway obstruction. The small radicles of the bronchial tree, the bronchioles, are commonly involved in infective processes such as viral infections; they are also the primary site of deposition of inhaled dust and particles. Because of the large cross-sectional area of this part of the airway, considerable disease may be present in the bronchioles without affecting the expiratory flow rate. The bronchioles are occasionally the site of a primary noninfective bronchiolitis in persons with rheumatoid arthritis.

The alveolar ducts and alveoli. These structures are the site of primary involvement in many infections, including pneumonia, and it is on the parenchyma of the lung that the main effects of blockage of a pulmonary artery (pulmonary embolus) occur. The capillary bed surrounding the alveoli is subject to damage, and fluid may leak through the alveolar capillaries to accumulate in the lungs (pulmonary edema). The capillary bed is also extensively damaged in the condition known generally as acute respiratory distress syndrome; the exact mechanism of the damage is not yet fully understood. The alveolar walls themselves may undergo diffuse interstitial thickening, a characteristic of diseases grouped under the heading of "diffuse interstitial fibrosis"; interstitial thickening may also occur as a manifestation of collagen diseases such as scleroderma. One of the common forms of emphysema, in which alveolar destruction occurs, entails early loss of tissue at the point where the bronchiole ends in the acinus, resulting in a punched-out lesion in the centriacinar region. It is believed that this form is the one that most commonly develops after years of cigarette smoking.

The lung parenchyma is the site of the discrete aggregations of cells, usually giant cells, that form the granulomas characteristic of the generalized disease known as sarcoidosis, and it is in the lung parenchyma that nodules caused by the inhalation of silica particles are found.

The lymphatic system. The system of channels draining the lung may be involved in primary disease of the lungs, but more commonly it is involved in metastatic invasion by distant tumours arising in the breast, stomach, or pancreas.

The pleura. The pleura may be involved in inflammatory or neoplastic processes, either of which may lead to fluid accumulation (pleural effusion) between the two layers.

Although these divisions provide a general outline of the ways in which diseases may affect the lung, they are by no means rigid. It is common for more than one part of the system to be involved in any particular disease process, and disease in one region not infrequently leads to involvement of other parts.

Interdependence of respiratory sites

VIRAL INFECTIONS

A wide variety of viruses are responsible for acute respiratory disease. The common cold—frequently of viral origin—can cause inflammation of the trachea and laryngitis, and these processes may extend to involve the lower bronchial tree. After such episodes the ciliary lining of the bronchial tree may be damaged, but the repair process is usually rapid.

Infections with rhinoviruses and adenoviruses are especially important in children, in whom they cause a febrile illness, occasionally with severe bronchiolar involvement. Although recovery is usually rapid, in some infections with respiratory syncytial virus an extensive bronchiolitis develops that may be severe enough to threaten life. In epidemics of these diseases, occasional cases occur in which the course is complicated by inflammation of the pericardium—the membrane enclosing the heart—or by a pleural effusion.

Influenza and parainfluenza viruses are capable of causing severe illness. The influenza virus attacks many systems of the body simultaneously, but the primary site of viral replication appears to be the alveolar cells of the lung. There the virus multiplies many times over within a 24-hour period, and the pulmonary involvement may begin in the parenchyma and cause considerable consolidation and inflammation of lung tissue. It is common for there to be severe tracheitis, bronchitis, and bronchiolitis at the same time. Another form of the disorder is that described as viral pneumonia, in which a distinguishing feature is the presence of patchy areas of atelectasis or partial collapse of lung tissue, without extensive involvement of the bronchial tree. All of these conditions are more dangerous in small children and in the elderly, and the lung that is the seat of a severe attack of influenza may quickly become secondarily infected.

It was secondary bacterial infection that accounted for the high mortality in the influenza epidemic of 1918 and 1919, one of the worst human catastrophes on record. It has been estimated that more than 20,000,000 people around the world died during the epidemic, and of the 20,000,000 people who suffered from the illness in the United States, approximately 850,000 died. It was a characteristic of this epidemic that young people were commonly severely affected. The high mortality resulted from the lack of antibiotics for treating the secondary bacterial infection; widespread malnutrition probably also contributed to the death rate.

There are three immunologically distinct types of influenza virus, designated A, B, and C; parainfluenza viruses

Influenza viruses

Three types of influenza virus

are designated by the letter D. Types A, B, and D cause epidemic disease. Within type A there are now known to be at least four distinct strains. The "Asian" strain of type A was responsible for the 1957 influenza epidemic. Epidemic influenza tends to occur in two- or three-year cycles; careful study has allowed predictions to be made of their future occurrence. Although infected individuals develop lasting immunity to a particular strain following an attack of influenza, the immunity is highly specific as to type, and no protection is afforded against even closely related strains. Artificial immunization with high potency vaccines is of value in protecting against previous strains, and the vaccines have been shown to ameliorate the infection in the general population. Their use is particularly indicated in elderly people whose cardiac or lung function is already compromised.

Mycoplasma, identified in 1944 as responsible for a group of pneumonias previously thought to be of viral origin, is a member of a group of organisms known as the pleuropneumonia-like organisms and has also been termed the "Eaton agent" after the scientist who first described it. *Mycoplasma pneumoniae* is the single most common cause of pneumonia in school-age children and young adults. The infection produces soft patchy shadows on the chest radiograph and relatively few signs on physical examination. A nonproductive cough and fever occur for a few days. Familial spread is common, and disease occurs in epidemic form in young healthy people brought together in clusters, as in military recruit camps and colleges, where a number of outbreaks have been documented. It is not usually a life-threatening disease, but in rare cases it may progress to cause acute respiratory distress syndrome.

Psittacosis and ornithosis, primarily infections of birds, and particularly common among parakeets and parrots, are transmitted to human beings by inhalation of dust particles from the droppings of infected birds. The onset of psittacosis may be quite severe, with headache, insomnia, and even delirium. Gastrointestinal symptoms such as vomiting and pain are frequent, and a cough productive of clear sputum usually develops after a few days. Mild attacks are often unrecognized and dismissed as due to influenza. Recovery is usually complete, but convalescence may be slow. A pandemic of this disease in 1929 was caused by the shipment of 5,000 parrots into Argentina from Brazil for auction. Many of the birds died, and there was considerable human mortality.

Q fever is an infection with *Coxiella burnetii.* The disease was first described in Queensland, Australia; areas in which Q fever is now known to be endemic include Australia, the western United States, Africa, England, and the Mediterranean countries. Animal infection is widespread and involves a large variety of domestic farm animals, particularly cattle and sheep, and some wild animals. Transmission is believed to occur between mammals through ticks and mice. Human disease, which is uncommon, is probably acquired through inhalation of infected material. Laboratory workers and employees in slaughterhouses are particularly at risk. Q fever is usually a mild and self-limited disease, requiring only symptomatic treatment.

The disease chickenpox (varicella), particularly when it occurs in adults, may affect the lung. Acute lesions may occur in the lung parenchyma, leading to a transient but significant fall in arterial oxygen tension (hypoxemia), occasionally necessitating oxygen therapy. Recovery may be slow but is usually complete, although shadows may remain on the radiograph as a result of it.

Whooping cough occurs in epidemic form among children and appears to be linked to the later development of the chronic infective process known as bronchiectasis, which occurs as a result of bronchial damage. In western countries, both whooping cough and measles (which causes an acute bronchiolitis) have been controlled by effective vaccines. In developing countries, where these vaccines are not administered, these diseases are still a major cause of mortality in children. Resistance to acute respiratory diseases is reduced when there is malnutrition.

Lung repair after viral infection. The reparative processes in the lung after any viral attack may be quite slow. Apparent clinical recovery may occur relatively quickly

Whooping cough

Slow
process of
repair

and the radiograph may show no remaining shadows, yet repair and restitution of the alveolar wall may take several additional weeks. There is speculation that the occurrence of a severe viral infection in childhood may impair subsequent development of the lung or even set the stage for chronic respiratory disease in later life, but this has not been proved.

BACTERIAL PNEUMONIA

Before effective antibiotics became available, pneumonia was the respiratory disease responsible for the greatest mortality and consequently was one of the most feared diseases. Because it frequently led to the death of severely disabled, elderly people, it was also known as the "old man's friend." The most common form of the disease is caused by a streptococcus, *Diplococcus pneumoniae.* Infection is followed by an acute illness of sudden onset with high fever, involvement of one or more lobes of the lung with resultant consolidation of the lung tissue, followed by complications such as a lung abscess, pleurisy, or heart failure; but terminating naturally after about seven days with a high peak of fever and a sudden crisis, followed by a sharp fall in temperature and slow resolution. The classic form of the disease is now rarely seen, since prompt antibiotic therapy controls the acute process within 24 hours. Streptococci cause a diffuse type of bronchopneumonia, and it is this condition that is most likely to occur as a consequence of forced recumbency in elderly people. The infection probably develops in those parts of the lung where airway closure has occurred and where some extravasation of fluid is present. Streptococcal pneumonia may also occur as a complication of an acute attack of influenza, and the much lowered mortality of influenza is to be explained by effective antibiotics against streptococci. Staphylococcal pneumonia occurs as an acute illness in small children and may lead to rapid destruction of lung tissue with abscess formation; however, if the acute state is survived, as it usually is with chemotherapy, the lung recovers fully. This type of pneumonia may also occur as a complication of preexisting lung disease of any kind and may follow aspiration of stomach contents into the lung. The development of antibiotic-resistant staphylococci has meant that this form of pneumonia may be a problem in the hospital environment, complicating other lung disease or occurring postoperatively. Pneumonia due to infection with *Klebsiella pneumoniae* may be difficult to treat and characteristically may occur as a repetitive series of episodes of pneumonia, each running a rather long course with slow resolution. The organism *Hemophilus influenzae* is commonly isolated from the sputum of patients with chronic bronchitis during acute exacerbations of infection, but its exact role as a cause of disease is not well understood.

In all these bacterial pneumonias, the diagnosis may be made from the characteristic radiographic pattern, together with isolation from the sputum of the bacterium primarily responsible.

Legion-
naires'
disease of
1976

Legionnaires' disease. In July 1976, an outbreak of severe pneumonia occurred among U.S. veterans attending a convention of the American Legion in Philadelphia. Of the 147 persons admitted to hospitals, 29 died. Identification of the organism responsible (subsequently named *Legionella pneumophila*) constituted a classic medical detective story. The bacterium had evaded detection before because it does not stain with the usual stains used in sputum examination. It is now known that this bacterium may grow in air-conditioning systems or on shower heads, and it has been shown to be responsible for sporadic but severe outbreaks of pneumonia, particularly but not exclusively in older people. Fortunately, the bacterium is sensitive to erythromycin.

Pneumonia of any cause can lead to the development of the serious state known as adult respiratory distress syndrome, which is discussed in detail in a later section.

Pneumonia in immunocompromised persons. For some years prior to 1980, it had been known that if the immune system was compromised by immunosuppressive drugs (given, for example, before organ transplantation to reduce the rate of rejection), the patient was at risk for developing pneumonia from organisms or viruses not normally pathogenic. Patients with AIDS may develop pneumonia from cytomegalovirus or *Pneumocystis* infections, capable of causing invasive pneumonic lesions in the setting of reduced immunity. Such infections are a major cause of illness in these patients, are difficult to treat, and may prove fatal. Infections with fungi such as *Candida* also occur. The diagnosis and management of these cases has become a challenging and time-consuming responsibility for respiratory specialists in cities with large numbers of AIDS cases.

Pulmonary
tubercu-
losis

Of all the lung diseases caused by bacteria, pulmonary tuberculosis is historically by far the most important. Particular features of this dreaded condition, to which many writers of the last hundred years have turned for dramatic material, include the severe general debilitation and weakness that it may cause; the insidious nature of the onset of its initial symptoms, which may not be pulmonary in nature; the familial tendency; the long-drawn-out course of the disease and the distressing nature of many of its manifestations, particularly severe hemorrhage from the lung and from tuberculous involvement of the brain (meningitis), or involvement of the adrenal gland leading to adrenal insufficiency (Addison's disease); and, above all, the general inefficacy of medical treatment before effective antibiotic therapy became available. Antibiotics have greatly reduced the mortality from pulmonary tuberculosis in all developed countries, but the decline in mortality began well before their introduction, and it is clear that improved diet and housing were responsible for this. With antibiotic therapy, however, the bacilli quickly disappear from the sputum and the spread of infection is quickly controlled.

In its classic form, tuberculosis first causes pulmonary inflammation at the apices (upper portions) of the lungs, and it may progress slowly to form a chronic cavity in this region. Secondary infection of the cavity may occur and may be difficult to eradicate. When still active, pulmonary tuberculosis is a constant threat to the patient, because blood-borne spread may occur at any time. Diffuse spread of tuberculosis in the lung (known as miliary tuberculosis) may occur at the onset of the disease. The chest radiograph reveals many small and diffuse shadows. The exact sequence of events that leads to this disseminated form of disease is not understood, but prompt treatment is required to prevent spread to the brain and other organs. Pulmonary tuberculosis remains an important disease.

Treatment
of tubercu-
losis

Streptomycin was the first clinically successful antituberculous drug, and it is still occasionally used. More commonly, rifampin together with isonicotinic hydrazide (isoniazid, or INH) is used first, and ethambutol may be used in addition. INH is never given alone as the tubercle bacilli acquire resistance to it; hence it is often combined with another drug, para-aminosalicylic acid (PAS). It is important to stress that there is no one "best" regimen preferable to all others in every case. Tubercle bacilli can acquire resistance to most of the antituberculous drugs, and skillful treatment consists in combining antibiotics so that resistant bacilli are less likely to be produced. The development of resistance to antibiotics can be delayed by the concomitant use of two or more drugs, by continuous treatment without significant interruption until all bacterial growth has ceased, and by the use of bed rest and resectional surgery in a few selected cases. Surgery may be indicated when a chronic cavity has developed. In most newly diagnosed cases, a year of antibiotic therapy is recommended, although recent observations have suggested that with modern treatment regimens, effective control may be achieved in a shorter period.

The major problem in treating pulmonary tuberculosis is ensuring continued medication and supervision. This may be very difficult in developing countries and in indigent and alcoholic populations of large cities in developed countries. Detection and treatment also pose problems in native communities living in isolated regions, such as the Canadian Eskimos. Although the death rate from respiratory tuberculosis in the Western world has fallen greatly since 1900, it remains a serious and difficult problem in some underprivileged communities, in many tropical countries, and in any population with inadequate medical care and poor diet and hygiene. In addition, pulmonary tuberculosis has reappeared in the West in persons with AIDS, in whom treatment is complicated by diminished immunity.

ALLERGIC LUNG DISEASES

There are at least three reasons why the lungs are particularly liable to be involved in allergic reponses to proteins. First, the lungs are exposed to the outside environment, and hence particles of foreign protein—e.g., in pollen—may be deposited directly in the lung; second, the walls of the bronchial tree contain smooth muscle that is very likely to be stimulated to contract if histamine is released by cells affected by the allergic reaction; and third, the lung contains a very large vascular bed, which may be involved in any general inflammatory response. It is therefore not surprising to find that sensitivity phenomena are common and represent an important aspect of pulmonary disease as a whole. The most common and most important of these is asthma. This word is loosely applied to all kinds of conditions in which there is airflow obstruction, but it is better reserved for those conditions in which an allergic component of the bronchial obstruction is likely to be present.

Asthma. Spasmodic asthma is characterized by contraction of the smooth muscle of the airways and, in severe attacks, by airway obstruction from mucus that has accumulated in the bronchial tree. This results in a greater or lesser degree of difficulty in breathing. One approach to classifying asthma differentiates cases that occur with an identifiable antigen, in which antigens affect tissue cells sensitized by a specific antibody, and cases that occur without an identifiable antigen or specific antibody. The former condition is known as "extrinsic" asthma and the latter as "intrinsic" asthma. Extrinsic asthma commonly manifests in childhood because the subject inherits an "atopic" characteristic: the serum contains specific antigens to pollens, mold spores, animal proteins of different kinds, and proteins from a variety of insects, particularly cockroaches and mites that occur in house dust. Exacerbation of extrinsic asthma is precipitated by contact with any of the proteins to which sensitization has occurred; airway obstruction is often worse in the early hours of the morning, for reasons not yet entirely elucidated. The other form of asthma, intrinsic, may develop at any age, and there may be no evidence of specific antigens. Persons with intrinsic asthma experience attacks of airway obstruction unrelated to seasonal changes, although it seems likely that the airway obstruction may be triggered by infections, which are assumed to be viral in many cases.

Asthma acquired as the result of occupational exposure (a special form of intrinsic asthma) is now recognized to be more common than previously suspected. Exposure to solder resin used in the electronics industry, to toluene diisocyanate (used in many processes as a solvent), to the dust of the western red cedar (in which plicatic acid is the responsible agent), and to many other substances can initiate an asthmatic state, with profound airflow obstruction developing when the subject is challenged by the agent.

It is a characteristic of all types of asthma that those with the condition may exhibit airflow obstruction when given aerosols of histamine or acetylcholine (both normally occurring smooth muscle constrictors) at much lower concentrations than provoke airflow obstruction in normal people; affected individuals may also develop airflow obstruction while breathing cold air or during exercise. These characteristics are used in the laboratory setting to study the airway status of patients. As a result of much recent work, it is thought that the diagnosis of asthma of any kind is difficult to sustain in the absence of a general increase in airway reactivity.

The acute asthmatic attack is alarming both for the sufferer and for the onlooker. There is acute difficulty in breathing, and the chest assumes a more and more inspiratory position. Despite the severe respiratory difficulty, the patient remains fully conscious. The most dangerous form of the condition is known as status asthmaticus. The bronchial spasm worsens over several hours or a day or so, the bronchi become plugged with thick mucus, and airflow is progressively more obstructed. The affected person becomes fatigued; the arterial oxygen tension falls still further, carbon dioxide accumulates in the blood (leading to drowsiness), and the acidity of the arterial blood increases to dangerous levels and may lead to cardiac arrest. Prompt treatment with intravenous corticosteroids and bronchodilators is usually sufficient to relieve the attack, but in occasional cases ventilatory assistance is required. In a few cases, death from asthma is remarkably rapid—too rapid for this complete sequence of events to have occurred, although at autopsy the lungs are overinflated. The exact mechanism of death in these cases is not completely understood.

Although the state of the airway is influenced by psychogenic factors, asthma is not correctly regarded as a disease commonly caused by psychological factors. It may interrupt normal activities and schooling to such an extent that it casts a shadow over the development of the personality. More commonly, it tends to diminish in severity with age, and people who had quite severe asthma in childhood may lead normal lives after the age of 20. It is now known that asthma attacks may be precipitated by food—in small children, possibly by milk; and some adults are extremely sensitive to sulfite compounds in food or wine. A subgroup of asthmatics are so sensitive to aspirin (acetylsalicylic acid) that ingestion of this chemical may lead to a life-threatening attack.

Changes in mortality from asthma in different countries have been closely studied, but the causes are obscure. It is clear, however, that there has been a considerable increase in the rate of hospital admissions for asthma in children and in adults up to the age of 60. Because there is now more effective treatment for asthma than was available previously, it is not clear why this should be occurring. Unless the asthma is complicated by infection (of which that by the fungus *Aspergillus* is common in damp climates), the chest radiograph remains normal. Asthma does not lead to the destructive lesions of emphysema (described below), although the physical appearance of the patient and the sounds of airflow obstruction in the lung may be similar in the two conditions.

Hay fever. Hay fever is a common seasonal condition caused by allergy to grasses and pollens. It is frequently familial, and the sensitivity is often to ragweed pollen. Conjunctival infection and edema of the nasal mucosa lead to attacks of sneezing. Allergic inflammation and the development of polyps in the nasal passages represent a severer form of hay fever that is often associated with asthma.

Hypersensitivity pneumonitis. This is an important group of conditions in which the lung is sensitized by contact with a variety of agents and in which the response consists of an acute pneumonitis, with inflammation of the smaller bronchioles, alveolar wall edema, and a greater or lesser degree of airflow obstruction due to smooth muscle contraction. In more chronic forms of the condition, granulomas, or aggregations of giant cells, may be found in the lung. One of these illnesses is the so-called farmer's lung, caused by the inhalation of spores from moldy hay (thermophilic *Actinomyces*). This causes an acute febrile illness with a characteristically fine opacification in the basal regions of the lung on the chest radiograph. Airflow obstruction in small airways is present, and there may be measurable interference with diffusion of gases across the alveolar wall. If untreated, the condition may become chronic, with shortness of breath persisting after the radiographic changes have disappeared. Farmer's lung is common in Wisconsin, on the eastern seaboard of Canada, in the west of England, and in France. Education of farmers and their families and the wearing of a simple mask can completely prevent the condition.

A similar group of diseases occurs in those with close contact with birds. Variously known as pigeon breeder's lung or bird fancier's lung, these represent different kinds of allergic responses to proteins from birds, particularly proteins contained in the excreta of pigeons, budgerigars (parakeets), and canaries. An acute hypersensitivity pneumonitis may also occur in those cultivating mushrooms

Extrinsic and intrinsic forms of asthma

Status asthmaticus

Farmer's lung

Bird fancier's lung

(particularly where this is done below ground), after exposure to redwood sawdust, or in response to a variety of other agents. An influenza-like illness resulting from exposure to molds growing in humidifier systems in office buildings ("humidifier fever") has been well-documented. It is occasionally attributable to *Aspergillus*, but sometimes the precise agent cannot be identified. The disease may present as an atypical nonbacterial pneumonia and may be labeled a viral pneumonia if careful inquiry about possible contacts with known agents is not made.

BRONCHITIS AND BRONCHIOLITIS

Acute bronchitis. Acute bronchitis most commonly occurs as a consequence of viral infection. It may also be precipitated by acute exposure to irritant gases, such as ammonia, chlorine, or sulfur dioxide. In people with chronic bronchitis—a common condition in cigarette smokers—exacerbations of infection are common. The bronchial tree in acute bronchitis is reddened and congested, and minor blood streaking of the sputum may occur. Most cases of acute bronchitis resolve over a few days, and the mucosa repairs itself.

Bronchiolitis refers to inflammation of the small airways. Bronchiolitis probably occurs to some extent in acute viral disorders, particularly in children between the ages of one and two years, and particularly in infections with respiratory syncytial virus. In severe cases the inflammation may be severe enough to threaten life, but it normally clears spontaneously, with complete healing in all but a very small percentage of cases. In adults, acute bronchiolitis of this kind is not a well-recognized clinical syndrome, though there is little doubt that in most patients with chronic bronchitis, acute exacerbations of infection are associated with further damage to small airways. In isolated cases, an acute bronchiolitis is followed by a chronic obliterative condition, or this may develop slowly over time. This pattern of occurrence has only recently been recognized. In addition to patients acutely exposed to gases, in whom such a syndrome may follow the acute exposure, patients with rheumatoid arthritis may develop a slowly progressive obliterative bronchiolitis that may prove fatal. An obliterative bronchiolitis may appear after bone marrow replacement for leukemia and may cause shortness of breath and disability.

Exposure to oxides of nitrogen, which may occur from inhaling gas in silos, when welding in enclosed spaces such as boilers, after blasting underground, or in fires involving plastic materials, is characteristically not followed by acute symptoms. These develop some hours later, when the victim develops a short cough and progressive shortness of breath. A chest radiograph shows patchy inflammatory change, and the lesion is an acute bronchiolitis. Symptomatic recovery may mask incomplete resolution of the inflammation.

Early changes due to smoking

An inflammation around the small airways, known as a respiratory bronchiolitis, is believed to be the earliest change that occurs in the lung in cigarette smokers, although it does not lead to symptoms of disease at that stage. The inflammation is probably reversible if smoking is discontinued. It is not known whether those who develop this change (after possibly only a few years of smoking) are or are not at special risk of developing the long-term changes of chronic bronchitis and emphysema.

Chronic bronchitis. The chronic cough and sputum production of chronic bronchitis were once dismissed as nothing more than "smoker's cough," without serious implications. But the striking increase in mortality from chronic bronchitis and emphysema that occurred after World War II in all Western countries indicated that the long-term consequences of chronic bronchitis could be serious. This common condition is characteristically produced by cigarette smoking. After about 15 years of smoking, a blob of mucus is coughed up in the morning, owing to an increase in size and number of mucous glands lining the large airways. The increase in mucous cells and the development of chronic bronchitis may be enhanced by breathing polluted air (particularly in areas of uncontrolled coal burning) and by a damp climate. The changes are not confined to large airways, though these produce the dom-

inant symptom of chronic sputum production. Changes in smaller bronchioles lead to obliteration and inflammation around their walls. All of these changes together, if severe enough, can lead to disturbances in the distribution of ventilation and perfusion in the lung, causing a fall in arterial oxygen tension and a rise in carbon dioxide tension. By the time this occurs, the ventilatory ability of the patient, as measured by the velocity of a single forced expiration, is severely compromised; in a cigarette smoker, ventilatory ability has usually been declining rapidly for some years. It is not clear what determines the severity of these changes, since many people can smoke for decades without evidence of significant airway changes, while others may experience severe respiratory compromise after 15 years or less of exposure.

Pulmonary emphysema. This irreversible disease consists of destruction of alveolar walls. It occurs in two forms, centrilobular emphysema, in which the destruction begins at the centre of the lobule, and panlobular (or panacinar) emphysema, in which alveolar destruction occurs in all alveoli within the lobule simultaneously. In advanced cases of either type, this distinction can be difficult to make. Centrilobular emphysema is the form most commonly seen in cigarette smokers, and some observers believe it is confined to smokers. It is more common in the upper lobes of the lung (for unknown reasons) and probably causes abnormalities in blood gases out of proportion to the area of the lung involved by it. By the time the disease has developed, some impairment of ventilatory ability has probably occurred. Panacinar emphysema may also occur in smokers, but it is the type of emphysema characteristically found in the lower lobes of patients with a deficiency in the antiproteolytic enzyme known as alpha$_1$-antitrypsin. Like centrilobular emphysema, panacinar emphysema causes ventilatory limitation and eventually blood gas changes. Other types of emphysema, of less importance than the two major varieties, may develop along the dividing walls of the lung (septal emphysema) or in association with scars from other lesions.

Types of emphysema

A major step forward in understanding the development of emphysema followed the identification, in Sweden, of families with an inherited deficiency of alpha$_1$-antitrypsin, an enzyme essential for lung integrity. Members of affected families commonly developed panacinar emphysema in the lower lobes, unassociated with chronic bronchitis but leading to ventilatory impairment and disability. Intense investigation of this major clue led to the "protease-antiprotease" theory of emphysema. It is postulated that cigarette smoking either increases the concentration of protease enzymes released in the lung (probably from white blood cells), or impairs the lung's defenses against these enzymes, or both. Although many details of the essential biochemical steps at the cellular level remain to be clarified, this represents a major step forward in understanding a disease whose genesis was once ascribed to overinflation of the lung (like overdistending a bicycle tire).

Theories concerning smoking and emphysema

Chronic bronchitis and emphysema are distinct processes. Both may follow cigarette smoking, however, and they commonly occur together, so determination of the extent of each during life is not easy. In general, significant emphysema is more likely if ventilatory impairment is constant, gas transfer in the lung (usually measured with carbon monoxide) is reduced, and the lung volumes are abnormal. The radiological technique of computerized tomography may improve the accuracy of detection of emphysema. Many people with emphysema suffer severe incapacity before the age of 60; thus, emphysema is not a disease of the elderly only. A reasonably accurate diagnosis can be made from pulmonary function tests, careful radiological examination, and a detailed history. The physical examination of the chest reveals evidence of airflow obstruction and overinflation of the lung, but the extent of lung destruction cannot be reliably gauged from these signs, and therefore laboratory tests are required.

The prime symptom of emphysema, which is always accompanied by a loss of elasticity of the lung, is shortness of breath, initially on exercise only, and associated with loss of normal ventilatory ability. The severity of this loss is a predictor of survival in this condition. But once venti-

Signs and symptoms

latory ability is reduced to less than half the normal value, what determines outcome is the severity of the changes in blood gases, chiefly the lowering of arterial blood oxygen tension. The chronic hypoxemia (lowered oxygen tension) is believed to lead to the development of increased blood pressure in the pulmonary circulation, which in turn leads to failure of the right ventricle of the heart. The symptom (subjective evidence perceived by the patient) of right ventricular failure is swelling of the ankles; the signs (objective evidence discovered by the examining physician) are engorgement of the neck veins and enlargement of the liver. These are portents of advanced lung disease in this condition. The hypoxemia may also lead to an increase in total hemoglobin content and in the number of circulating red blood cells, as well as to psychological depression, irritability, loss of appetite, and loss of weight. Thus the advanced syndrome of chronic obstructive lung disease may cause not only such shortness of breath that the afflicted person is unable to dress without assistance, but also numerous other symptoms.

The slight fall in ventilation that normally accompanies sleep may exacerbate the failure of lung function in chronic obstructive lung disease, leading to a further fall in arterial oxygen tension and an increase in pulmonary arterial pressure.

Unusual forms of emphysema also occur. In one form the disease appears to be unilateral, involving one lung only and causing few symptoms. Unilateral emphysema is believed to result from a severe bronchiolitis in childhood that prevented normal maturation of the lung on that side. "Congenital lobar emphysema" of infants is usually a misnomer, since there is no alveolar destruction. It is most commonly caused by overinflation of a lung lobe due to developmental malformation of cartilage in the wall of the major bronchus. Such lobes may have to be surgically removed to relieve the condition.

Bronchiectasis. Bronchiectasis is believed usually to begin in childhood, possibly after a severe attack of whooping cough or pneumonia. It consists of a dilatation of major bronchi. The bronchi become chronically infected, and excess sputum production and episodes of chest infection are common. The disease may develop as a consequence of airway obstruction or of undetected (and therefore untreated) aspiration into the airway of small foreign bodies such as plastic toys.

Bronchiectasis may also develop as a consequence of inherited conditions, of which the most important is the familial disease of cystic fibrosis. The essential defect in this condition probably has to do with the transport of sodium and other ions across the wall of membranes, but it is not yet completely understood. The most important consequence of cystic fibrosis, apart from the malnutrition it causes, is the development of chronic pulmonary changes, with repetitive infections and bronchiectasis as characteristic features. This condition does not progress to pulmonary emphysema but rather causes obliteration and fibrosis of small airways and dilation and infection of the larger bronchi. Thick, viscid secretions in the bronchial tree are difficult to expectorate. However, the modern management of the condition, with the control of pulmonary infections, has markedly improved survival in affected persons, many of whom, who would formerly have died in childhood, now reach adult life.

Cystic fibrosis

OCCUPATIONAL LUNG DISEASE

Silica dust produces a distinctive reaction in the lung that eventually leads to the development of masses of fibrous tissue and distinctive nodules of dense fibrosis, which, by contracting, distort and damage the lung. Silicosis is a hazard in any occupation in which workers are exposed to silica dust, particularly rock drilling above or below ground, quarrying, or grinding with a wheel containing silica. Cases have also been reported in dental technicians, who use the material ground into a fine powder. Silicosis is usually fairly easy to detect on radiographs, and in its later stages it causes considerable shortness of breath and reduction of the vital capacity (a maximal breath). Sandblasting without respiratory protection is exceedingly dangerous, and fatal cases of acute silicosis caused by un-

Silicosis

protected sandblasting have been reported. The dangers of silica are generally well recognized, and better protection has reduced the incidence of this condition. The disease may advance, with increasing disability, for years after the person has stopped inhaling the dust.

Coal dust alone, even if its silica content is very low, causes a distinctive pattern of change in the lung known as coalworker's pneumoconiosis (also called black lung). Initially the dust is deposited in the terminal bronchioles, where it causes a fibrotic reaction. At this stage there is little disability, but later the disease may progress to a more generalized form, and in some instances large masses of fibrotic tissue form in the lung. This condition, known as progressive massive fibrosis, is usually associated with severe disability and the risk of a secondary heart failure. It is not clear whether this stage is more likely to develop if pulmonary tuberculosis is superimposed on the respiratory damage caused by coal dust inhalation.

The widespread use of asbestos as an insulating material during World War II, and later in flooring, ceiling tiles, brake linings, and as a fire protectant sprayed inside buildings, led to a virtual epidemic of asbestos-related disease 20 years later. At first only the form of disease known as asbestosis, with radiographic changes and impaired function at an early stage, was recognized. Then it became apparent that exposure to much less asbestos than was needed to cause asbestosis led to thickening of the pleura, and, when both cigarette smoking and asbestos exposure occurred, there was a major increase in the risk for lung cancer. It is currently believed that the risks from smoking and from significant asbestos exposure are multiplicative in the case of lung cancer. Finally, a malignant tumour of the pleura known as mesothelioma was found to be caused almost exclusively by inhaled asbestos. Often a period of 20 years or more elapsed between exposure to asbestos and the development of the tumour.

Asbestosis

As far as is known, all the respiratory changes associated with asbestos exposure are irreversible. Malignant mesothelioma is rare and unrelated to cigarette smoking, but survival after diagnosis is less than two years. Usually the pleural thickenings are not associated with disturbance of function or symptoms, although in occasional cases the pleuritis is more aggressive, in which case both may occur. It is not yet understood why asbestos causes such devastating changes. Furthermore, not all types of asbestos are equally dangerous; the risk of mesothelioma in particular appears to be much higher if crocidolite, a blue asbestos that comes from South Africa, is inhaled than if chrysotile is inhaled. But exposure to any type of asbestos is believed to increase the risk of lung cancer when associated with cigarette smoking. There has been much discussion of the advisability of removing asbestos from all buildings. It has been argued on the one hand that this is the only responsible policy, and on the other that more exposure might follow the careless removal of the material than would occur if it were left in place. All industrialized countries have imposed strict regulations for handling asbestos, and the work force is generally aware of the material's dangers.

The increasing use of man-made mineral fibres (as in fibreglass and rock wool) has led to concern that these may also be dangerous when inhaled; present evidence suggests that they do increase the risk of lung cancer in persons occupationally exposed to them. Standards for maximal exposure have been proposed.

The toxicity of beryllium was first discovered when it was widely used in the manufacture of fluorescent light tubes shortly after World War II. Beryllium causes the formation of granulomas in the lung and alveolar wall thickening, often with considerable disability as a result. Although beryllium is no longer used in the fluorescent light industry, it is still important in the manufacture of special steels and ceramics, and new cases of beryllium poisoning are occasionally reported.

It is not only inorganic minerals and dusts that may affect the lung. The dust produced in the processing of raw cotton may cause chronic obstructive lung disease. This does not have a characteristic pathology, however, and it does not give rise to emphysema. It is unclear whether cotton dust alone or the combination of cigarette smoke

Byssinosis

and cotton dust is particularly dangerous. The disease that results is known as byssinosis, or "brown lung." Workers in cotton plants in England used to complain of "Monday morning fever" and were found to suffer an easily measurable decrement in ventilatory function when they returned to work after spending a weekend away from the plant. The active particle or contaminant in the cotton dust that is responsible for the syndrome has not yet been identified.

The dust from western red cedar may cause occupational asthma, and dust from the redwood and other trees may cause an acute hypersensitivity pneumonitis. Workers in the sugarcane industry may be affected by a similar syndrome, known as bagassosis; sisal workers also develop airflow obstruction.

Toluene diisocyanate, used in the manufacture of polyurethane foam, may cause occupational asthma at very low concentrations; in higher concentrations, such as may occur with accidental spillage, it causes a transient flulike illness associated with airflow obstruction. Prompt recognition of this syndrome has led to modifications in the industrial process involved.

Although the acute effects of exposure to many of these gases and vapours are well-documented, there is less certainty about the long-term effects of repeated low-level exposures over a long period of time. This is particularly the case when the question of whether work in a generally dusty environment has contributed to the development of chronic bronchitis or later emphysema—in other words, whether such nonspecific exposures increase the risk of these diseases in cigarette smokers. There is little unanimity on this question, but it is generally recognized that the differentiation is difficult.

Many chemicals can damage the lung in high concentration: these include oxides of nitrogen, ammonia, chlorine, oxides of sulfur, ozone, gasoline vapour, and benzene. In industrial accidents, such as occurred in 1985 in Bhopāl, India, and in 1976 in Seveso, near Milan, people in the neighbourhood of chemical plants were acutely exposed to lethal concentrations of these or other chemicals. The custom of transporting dangerous chemicals by rail or road has led to the occasional exposure of bystanders to toxic concentrations of gases and fumes. Although in many cases recovery may be complete, it seems clear that long-term damage may occur.

Assessment of disability

The assessment of disability and the writing of opinions on attributability have become important tasks for many respiratory specialists. Disability consequent upon a specific lung disease can be assessed by pulmonary function testing and in some cases by tests of exercise capability; these measures provide a good indication of the impact of the disease on the physical ability of the patient. It is much more difficult to decide how much of the disability is attributable to occupational exposure. If the exposure is historically known to cause a specific lesion in a significant percentage of exposed persons, such as mesothelioma in workers exposed to asbestos, attribution may be fairly straightforward. In many cases, however, the exposure may cause only generalized pulmonary changes leading to airflow obstruction or may cause lung lesions of multifactorial etiology, the precise cause of which cannot be determined by histological examination of the tissue. The question of attributability in these instances, already diffuse, may be complicated by a history of cigarette smoking, which may be mild or moderate, or of short or long duration. Physicians asked to give opinions on attributability in multifactorial disease processes before a legal body frequently must rely on the application of probability statistics to the individual case, a not wholly satisfactory procedure to those who must assign compensation and disability benefits.

LUNG CANCER

Cigarette smoking and lung cancer

Up to the time of World War II, cancer of the lung was a relatively rare condition. The increase in its incidence in Europe after World War II was at first ascribed to better diagnostic methods, but by 1956 it had become clear that the rate of increase was too great to be accounted for in this way. At that time the first epidemiological studies began to indicate that a long history of cigarette smoking was associated with a great increase in risk of death from lung cancer. By 1965 cancer of the lung and bronchus accounted for 43 percent of all cancers in the United States in men, an incidence nearly three times greater than that of the second most common cancer (of the prostate gland) in men, which accounted for 16.7 percent of cancers. The 1964 *Report of the Advisory Committee to the Surgeon General of the Public Health Service* (United States) concluded categorically that cigarette smoking was causally related to lung cancer in men. Since then, many further studies in diverse countries have confirmed this conclusion.

The incidence of lung cancer in women began to rise in 1960 and continued rising through the mid-1980s. This is believed to be explained by the later development of heavy cigarette smoking in women compared with men, who greatly increased their cigarette consumption during World War II. By 1988 there was evidence suggesting that the peak incidence of lung cancer due to cigarette smoking in men may have been passed. The incidence of lung cancer mortality in women, however, is increasing.

The reason for the carcinogenicity of tobacco smoke is not known. Tobacco smoke contains many carcinogenic materials, and although it is assumed that the "tars" in tobacco smoke probably contain a substantial fraction of the cancer-causing condensate, it is not yet established which of these is responsible. In addition to its single-agent effects, cigarette smoking greatly potentiates the cancer-causing proclivity of asbestos fibres, increases the risk of lung cancer due to inhalation of radon daughters (products of the radioactive decay of radon gas), and possibly also increases the risk of lung cancer due to arsenic exposure. Cigarette smoke may be a promoter rather than an initiator of lung cancer, but this question cannot be resolved until the process of cancer formation is better understood. Recent data suggest that those who do not smoke but who live or work with smokers and who therefore are exposed to environmental tobacco smoke may be at increased risk for lung cancer, eloquent testimony to the power of cigarettes to induce or promote the disease.

Varied symptoms of lung cancer

Because lung cancer is caused by different types of tumour, because it may be located in different parts of the lung, and because it may spread beyond the lungs at an early stage, the first symptoms noted by the patient vary from blood staining of the sputum, to a pneumonia that does not resolve fully with antibiotics, to shortness of breath due to a pleural effusion; the physician may discover distant metastases to the skeleton, or in the brain that cause symptoms unrelated to the lung. Lymph nodes may be involved early, and enlargement of the lymph nodes in the neck may lead to a chest examination and the discovery of a tumour. In some cases a small tumour metastasis in the skin may be the first sign of the disease. Lung cancer may develop in an individual who already has chronic bronchitis and who therefore has had a cough for many years. The diagnosis depends on securing tissue for histological examination, although in some cases this entails removal of the entire neoplasm before a definitive diagnosis can be made.

Survival from lung cancer has improved very little in the past 40 years. Early detection with routine chest radiographs has been attempted, and large-scale trials of routine sputum examination for the detection of malignant cells have been conducted, but neither screening method appears to have a major impact on mortality. Therefore, attention has been turned to prevention by every means possible. Foremost among them are efforts to inform the public of the risk and to limit the advertising of cigarettes. Steps have been taken to reduce asbestos exposure, both in the workplace and in public and private buildings, and to control air pollution. The contribution of air pollution to the incidence of lung cancer is not known with certainty, though there is clearly an "urban" factor involved.

Exposure to radon

Persons exposed to radon daughters are at risk for lung cancer. The hazard from exposure was formerly thought to be confined to uranium miners, who, by virtue of their work underground, encounter high levels of these radioactive materials. However, significant levels of radon daughters have been detected in houses built over natural sources, and with increasingly efficient insulation of houses, radon daughters may reach concentrations high enough to place the occupants at risk for lung cancer. A recent survey of houses in the United States indicated that about 2 percent of all houses had a level of radon daughters that posed some risk to the occupants. Major regional variations in the natural distribution of radon occur, and it is not yet possible to quantify precisely the actual magnitude of the risk. In some regions of the world (such as the Salzburg region of Austria) levels are high enough that radon daughters are believed to account for the majority of cases of lung cancer in nonsmokers.

Workers exposed to arsenic in metal smelting operations, and the community around the factories from which arsenic is emitted, have an increased risk for lung cancer. Arsenic is widely used in the electronics industry in the manufacture of microchips, and careful surveillance of this industry may be needed to prevent future disease.

Some types of lung cancer are unrelated to cigarette smoking. Alveolar cell cancer is a slowly spreading condition that affects men and women in equal proportion and is not related to cigarette smoking. Pulmonary adenocarcinoma of the lung also has a more equal sex incidence than other types, and although its incidence is increased in smokers, it may also be caused by other factors.

It is common to feel intuitively that one should be able to apportion cases of lung cancer among discrete causes, on a percentage basis. But in multifactorial disease, this is not possible. Although the incidence of lung cancer would probably be far lower without cigarette smoking, the contribution of neither this factor nor any of the other factors mentioned can be precisely quantified.

MISCELLANEOUS PULMONARY CONDITIONS

Nonoccupational diffuse interstitial fibrosis. This condition has many names, including cryptogenic fibrosing alveolitis. It is a diffuse disease characterized by thickening of the alveolar walls, which may become so severe as to interfere with gas transport, and hypoxemia (reduced oxygen supply to tissues) results. Hypoxemia particularly occurs with exercise, since exercise reduces the time the blood spends in the alveolar capillary; and when the wall is thickened, there is insufficient time for oxygen to pass into the blood and achieve full saturation. Thus an early indication of abnormality in this condition is a significant fall in the pressure of oxygen in the arterial blood during exercise. The pulmonary diffusing capacity is usually reduced when this occurs.

Early indications

The cause of diffuse interstitial fibrosis is not known, although it sometimes appears after a viral infection; it also occurs in some diseases of the collagen system. It may run a relatively short course, but often it is slowly progressive over several years and leads eventually to secondary heart failure. The radiographic appearances are characteristic, although in some instances a lung biopsy may be necessary to establish the diagnosis. In a few patients the course of the disease seems to be improved by steroid treatment, but in many cases the downhill course of the disease is uninfluenced by it.

Sarcoidosis. Sarcoidosis is a disease characterized by the development of small aggregations of cells, or granulomas, in different organs; the lung is commonly involved. Other common changes are enlargement of the lymph glands at the root of the lung, skin changes, inflammation in the eye, and liver dysfunction; occasionally there is inflammation of nerve sheaths, leading to signs of involvement in the affected area. The kidney is not commonly involved, but some changes in blood calcium levels occur in a small percentage of cases. The disease seems to affect the Scandinavian population more often than other Caucasians; and in the North American population it is more severe in blacks than in whites. In most cases the disease is first detected on chest radiographs. Evidence of granulomas in the lung may be visible, but often there is little interference with lung function. The disease usually remits without treatment within the next year or so, but in a small proportion of cases it progresses, leading finally to lung fibrosis and retraction.

Eosinophilic granuloma. This disease causes granulomas associated with masses of eosinophil cells, a subgroup of the white blood cells. It also causes lesions in bone. Eosinophilic granuloma is a lung condition that may spontaneously "burn out," leaving the lung with some permanent cystic changes. Its cause is not known.

Alveolar proteinosis. Alveolar proteinosis is characterized by accumulation of protein-rich material in the alveolar spaces of the lung. It is not usually associated with irreversible changes in the lung but runs a remittent course and finally may resolve completely. Its cause is unknown. It is often treated by lavage (washing out) of the lung with saline during bronchoscopy. The disease produces a characteristic radiographic picture and is not associated with changes in any other organ.

Immunologic conditions. The lung is often affected by generalized diseases of the blood vessels. Periarteritis nodosa, an acute inflammatory disease of the blood vessels believed to be of immunologic origin, is an important cause of pulmonary blood vessel inflammation. Acute hemorrhagic pneumonitis occurring in the lung in association with changes in the kidney is known as Goodpasture's syndrome. The condition has been successfully treated by exchange blood transfusion, but its cause is not fully understood. Pulmonary hemorrhage also occurs as part of a condition known as pulmonary hemosiderosis, which results in the accumulation of the iron-containing substance hemosiderin in the lung tissues.

The lung may also be involved in a variety of ways by the disease known as systemic lupus erythematosus, which is also believed to have an immunologic basis. Pleural effusions may occur, and the lung parenchyma may be involved. These conditions have only recently been recognized and differentiated; accurate diagnosis has been much improved by refinements in radiological methods, by the use of pulmonary function tests, and especially by improvement in thoracic surgical techniques and anesthesia that have made lung biopsy much less dangerous than it formerly was.

The common condition of rheumatoid arthritis may be associated with scattered zones of interstitial fibrosis in the lung or with solitary isolated fibrotic lesions. More rarely, a slowly obliterative disease of small airways (bronchiolitis) occurs, leading finally to respiratory failure.

Radiation damage. The lung may be damaged by irradiation of the chest wall in the treatment of cancer of the breast and other conditions. About three weeks or so after the end of the treatment, a pneumonitis may develop in the underlying lung, signaled by an irritant and unproductive cough. The condition may resolve, although in a few cases the lung becomes fibrotic and contracts to a small fraction of its normal volume. There is considerable individual variation in the response to the same dose of radiation.

Circulatory disorders. The lung is commonly involved in disorders of the circulation. The most important and common of these is blockage of a branch of the pulmonary artery by blood clot, which has usually formed in the veins of the legs or the pelvis. The resulting pulmonary embolus leads to changes in the lung supplied by the affected artery. These changes are known as a pulmonary infarction. The consequences of embolism range from sudden death, when the infarction is massive, to an increased respiratory rate, slight fever, and occasionally some pleuritic pain over the site of the infarction. People are at increased risk for pulmonary embolism whenever they are immobilized in bed and the circulation is sluggish, and particularly during the postoperative period. Early mobilization after surgery or childbirth is considered an important preventive measure. Repetitive small emboli may lead to pulmonary thromboembolic disease, in which the pressure in the main pulmonary artery is permanently increased. This disease is believed to be more common in women who have regularly used birth-control pills, but it is not confined to them.

Pulmonary embolism

In primary pulmonary hypertension, a condition of unknown origin, a marked increase in pulmonary arterial pressure occurs, with changes in the small radicles of the pulmonary artery that may not be clearly embolic in nature. Both repetitive thromboembolic disease and primary pulmonary hypertension eventually lead to failure of the right ventricle of the heart, usually after increasing disability with severe shortness of breath.

Congestion of the lungs and the development of fluid in the pleural cavity, with consequent shortness of breath, follows left ventricular failure, usually as a consequence of coronary arterial disease. When the valve between the left atrium of the heart and the left ventricle is thickened and deformed by rheumatic fever (mitral stenosis), chronic changes develop in the lung as a result of the increased pressure in the pulmonary circulation. These changes contribute to the shortness of breath in that condition and account for the not-infrequent blood staining of the sputum.

Diseases of the pleura. The pleura lining the lung may become perforated and spontaneously rupture, usually over a small collection of congenital blebs or cysts at the apex of the lung. This causes spontaneous pneumothorax, a partial or occasionally complete collapse of the lung. In the majority of cases a pneumothorax resolves slowly of its own accord, although pleural suction may be needed to expedite recovery. If repetitive attacks occur, the blebs may be removed surgically, and the pleura lining the lung may be sealed to the pleura lining the inner wall of the thorax to prevent a recurrence.

Spontaneous pneumothorax

The most common disease of the pleura is inflammatory. A pleurisy with an effusion may be the presenting symptom of pulmonary tuberculosis, and pleurisy may accompany any kind of pneumonia, though it is rare in viral infections. When a pleural effusion in a person with bacterial pneumonia becomes infected, pus accumulates in the pleural cavity (empyema). This complication, dreaded before the antibiotic era, required drainage of the pleural space. Such episodes are now rarely seen as a result of acute infections, but draining sinuses may still occur in pulmonary tuberculosis or fungal infections. Infection of the lung and later the pleural cavity by the moldlike bacteria *Actinomyces* and *Nocardia* is particularly likely to lead to this complication.

Diseases of the mediastinum and diaphragm. The mediastinum comprises the fibrous membrane in the centre of the thoracic cavity, together with the many important structures situated within it. Enlargement of lymph glands in this region is common, particularly in the presence of lung tumours or as part of a generalized enlargement of lymphatic tissue in disease. Primary tumours of mediastinal structures may arise from the thymus gland or the lower part of the thyroid gland; noninvasive cysts of different kinds are also found in the mediastinum.

The diaphragm may be incompletely formed, leading to herniation of abdominal viscera through it. In adult life the important disease involving the diaphragm is bilateral diaphragmatic paralysis. This leads to a severe reduction in the vital capacity when the subject is recumbent, although exercise capability may be relatively well preserved. In many cases the cause of the paralysis cannot be determined. The function of the diaphragm may be compromised when the lung is highly overinflated, as occurs in emphysema; diaphragmatic fatigue may limit the exercise capability of affected persons.

Acute respiratory distress syndrome of adults. Bacterial or viral pneumonia, exposure of the lung to gases, aspiration of material into the lung (including water in near-drowning episodes), or any generalized septicemia (blood poisoning) or severe lung injury may lead to capillary leakage throughout the lung, a syndrome that is known as the acute respiratory distress syndrome of adults. It was first recognized when cases occurred following septicemia induced by intrauterine birth control devices; however, this is only one of the pathways to a generalized lung injury that has many causes. Acute respiratory distress syndrome carries about a 50 percent mortality, later infection by certain types of bacteria being particularly serious. Life-support treatment with assisted ventilation rescues some patients, but there has been little improvement in survival during the 1970s and 1980s. Recovery and repair of the lung may take months after clinical recovery from the acute event.

Effects of air pollution on health. The disastrous fog and attendant high levels of sulfur dioxide and particulate pollution (and probably also sulfuric acid) that occurred in London in the second week of December 1952 led to the deaths of more than 4,000 people during that week and the subsequent three weeks. Many, but not all, of the victims already had chronic heart or lung disease. Prize cattle at an agricultural show also died in the same period as a result of the air pollution. This episode spurred renewed attention to this problem, which had been intermittently considered since the 14th century in England, and finally the passage of legislation banning open coal burning, the factor most responsible for the pollution. This form of pollution, common in many cities using coal as heating fuel, was associated with excess mortality and increased prevalences of chronic bronchitis, respiratory tract infections in the young and old, and possibly lung cancer. Many industrial cities in Western countries now have legislation restricting the use of specific fuels and mandating emission-control systems in factories.

The 1952 London epidemic

In 1952 a different kind of air pollution was characterized for the first time in Los Angeles. The large number of automobiles in that city, together with the bright sunlight and frequently stagnant air, leads to the formation of photochemical smog. This begins with the emission of nitrogen oxide during the morning commuting hour, followed by the formation of nitrogen dioxide by oxygenation, and finally, through a complex series of reactions in the presence of hydrocarbons and sunlight, to the formation of ozone and peroxyacetyl nitrite and other irritant compounds. Eye irritation, chest irritation with cough, and possibly the exacerbation of asthma occur as a result. It is now recognized that ozone is formed in many large cities of the world. Modern air pollution consists of some combination of the reducing form consequent upon sulfur dioxide emissions, and the oxidant form, which begins as emissions of nitrogen oxides. Ozone is the most irritant gas known. In controlled exposure studies it reduces the ventilatory capability of healthy people in concentrations as low as 0.12 parts per million. These levels are commonly exceeded in many places, including Mexico City, Bangkok, and São Paulo, where there is a high automobile density and the meteorologic conditions favour the formation of photochemical oxidants. Although acute episodes of communal air exposure leading to demonstrable mortality are unlikely, there is much concern over the possible long-term consequences of brief but repetitive exposures to oxidants and acidic aerosols; such exposures are now common in the lives of millions of people. Their impact has not yet been precisely defined.

Smog

The indoor environment can be important in the genesis of respiratory disease. In developing countries, disease may be caused by inhalation of fungi from roof thatch materials or by the inhalation of smoke when the home contains no chimney. In developed countries, exposure to oxides of nitrogen from space heaters or gas ovens may promote respiratory tract infections in children. Inhalation of tobacco smoke in the indoor environment by nonsmokers impairs respiration and may cause lung cancer. A tightly sealed house may act as a reservoir for radon seeping in from natural sources.

Acute carbon monoxide poisoning. Acute carbon monoxide poisoning is a common and dangerous hazard. The British physiologist J.S. Haldane pioneered the study of the effects of carbon monoxide at the end of the 19th century, as part of his detailed analysis of atmospheres in underground mines. Carbon monoxide is produced by incomplete combustion, including combustion of gas in automobile engines, and for a long period it was a major constituent of domestic gas made from coal (its concentration in natural gas is much lower). When the carbon monoxide concentration in the blood reaches 40 percent (that is, when the hemoglobin is 40 percent saturated with carbon monoxide, leaving only 60 percent available to bind to oxygen), the subject feels dizzy and is unable to perform simple tasks; judgment is also impaired. Hemoglobin's affinity for carbon monoxide is 200 times greater than for oxygen, and in a mixture of these gases hemoglobin will preferentially bind to carbon monoxide;

Mechanism of action

for this reason, carbon monoxide concentrations of less than 1 percent in inspired air seriously impair oxygen–hemoglobin binding capacity. The partial pressure of oxygen in the tissues in carbon monoxide poisoning is much lower than when the oxygen-carrying capacity of the blood has been reduced an equivalent amount by anemia, a condition in which hemoglobin is deficient. The immediate treatment for acute carbon monoxide poisoning is assisted ventilation with 100 percent oxygen.

The carbon monoxide inhaled by smokers who smoke more than two packs of cigarettes a day may cause up to 10 percent hemoglobin saturation with carbon monoxide. A 4 percent increase in the blood carbon monoxide level in patients with coronary artery disease is believed to shorten the exercise that may be taken before chest pain is felt, in those who have that symptom on exercise.

LUNG TRANSPLANTATION

Early attempts at transplanting a single lung in patients with severe bilateral lung disease were not successful, but from the late 1970s bilateral lung transplantation had some striking results. Persons severely disabled by cystic fibrosis, emphysema, sarcoidosis, pulmonary fibrosis, or severe primary pulmonary hypertension reportedly achieved nearly normal lung function several months after the procedure. Combined heart–lung transplantation has been attempted, with some good long-term results. One study of seven cases showed that ventilatory capacity after bilateral lung transplantation was about 75 percent of the normal value for that individual. Because transplantation offers the only hope for persons with severe lung disease, who may be relatively young, the techniques are being pursued aggressively in specialized centres.

WORLD
OF
MEDICINE

A review of
recent developments
in health and medicine

Accidents and Safety

Just as doctors and scientists are working to reduce deaths caused by disease, safety experts are working to reduce deaths caused by accidents, the leading cause of death in the U.S. among those 36 years old and younger. Automobile accidents, which kill around 50,000 people each year, continue to be a primary target of legislated safety efforts. It has been estimated that alcohol is a factor in 80–90% of these deaths; at some time in their lives, about 40% of Americans will be involved in an accident in which alcohol is related. In an effort to decrease these numbers, all U.S. states now have set the legal drinking age at 21; early research indicates that a drop in drunk-driving accidents has resulted. Laws requiring safety-belt use among drivers and front-seat passengers also seem to produce a drop in automobile-related deaths if the laws are strictly enforced to encourage a high rate of compliance. Safety experts are focusing their efforts on reducing other types of accidents as well—those involving older drivers, bicyclists, and young children.

Older drivers

By the year 2000 an estimated one out of every three U.S. drivers will be 55 or older. Older people want and need the freedom and mobility of driving. A study by the American Automobile Association's Foundation for Traffic Safety suggests that being able to use a car is important for the mental health of older people because of the mobility and independence it affords them. Unfortunately, older drivers tend to be involved in more accidents than their middle-aged counterparts. A 1988 federal study, conducted by the National Research Council (NRC), reported that on the basis of distance driven, drivers aged 75 and older are twice as likely to be involved in a traffic accident as middle-aged drivers. Older drivers also tend to be involved in more multiple-vehicle crashes and more low-speed crashes.

According to the National Institute on Aging, the most common cause of accidental death among persons in the 65–74 age group is motor vehicle accidents.

The reason accidents increase with age is clear—the abilities required for safe driving tend to diminish with age. Drivers must constantly respond to a large number of stimuli, about 90% of which are visual. Eyesight often deteriorates as a person ages. An older person is more likely to have developed nearsightedness or farsightedness; peripheral vision is likely to be fading; and cataracts may have led to cloudy vision. Older drivers' eyes also tend to adapt more slowly to changes in light. As a person ages, the size of the pupil may shrink from about six millimeters to about two millimeters; the effect on one's vision is akin to that of wearing dark sunglasses. Therefore, the ability to see at night is reduced.

The perceptions that do not involve seeing usually involve hearing, which also tends to become less acute with age. Thus, older people find it more difficult to recognize the warning sounds of horns, sirens, train whistles, and squealing tires. Even when older drivers do see or hear well enough to recognize an emergency situation, their reflexes tend to be slower. As a result, they may simply be unable to brake or steer quickly enough to avoid an accident.

It is not suggested, however, that driving privileges be arbitrarily curtailed or restricted by age. Age alone does not accurately predict how well a person drives; some people have noticeably poorer eyesight and reflexes by age 70, while others are as alert at 85 as they were at 55. As senior citizen groups are quick to point out, the most dangerous group of drivers continues to be teenagers.

One key to making the roads safer lies in identifying those older drivers whose abilities are deteriorating. The 1988 NRC study urged state licensing agencies to tighten their driver screening programs. In some states drivers can renew their licenses through the

In Tuscola, Illinois, a 77-year-old woman taking her road test drove through a plate-glass window of the driver-testing center, killing a woman and injuring three bystanders. Drivers aged 75 and over rank second only to 16–24-year-olds in number of accidents per mile driven. Because many of the abilities that are vital to safe driving diminish with age, some state licensing agencies are now requiring older drivers to pass both vision and road tests at more frequent intervals—for their own safety and for that of others on the roads.

mail. Others require only a vision test every four years; in that time the eyesight and reflexes of some older people can worsen considerably, perhaps without their awareness. In response to the study, some states are considering laws that would require more frequent testing of older drivers. Illinois, for example, has proposed that drivers aged 81 to 86 be required to take both a vision and on-the-road driving test every two years. The tests would be required every year beginning at age 87; drivers 87 and older are more than five times as likely to be involved in an accident as middle-aged drivers. Some older drivers would prove unable to drive safely. For others, however, the law would require only that certain restrictions be put on their licenses. An otherwise capable driver who suffered from poor night vision, for example, would most likely be issued a daylight-only license.

The NRC study also noted that states need to take older drivers' diminished abilities into account when designing road signs. The signs currently in use—most of which feature 46-cm (18-in) letters—were designed to be readable at a distance of 275 m (900 ft), but that assumes the average driver has vision correctable to 20/25. About 40% of all drivers aged 65 to 74 have vision worse than that.

Meanwhile, traffic experts suggest that those older persons who continue to drive change their driving habits; instead of the normal suggested following time of two seconds, older drivers should increase following time to three seconds during the day and four at night. (To calculate following time, a driver begins counting seconds with the "one thousand one, one thousand two" method when the car in front passes a stationary object and then stops counting when he or she passes the same object.) In practice, many older drivers already compensate for their reduced abilities. Most who give up driving currently do so voluntarily as they lose confidence in their abilities. Studies show that older drivers take fewer risks, drive less often, and obey traffic rules more consistently than younger drivers.

Bicycling boom: important safety issues

Bicycles have become enormously popular in the U.S. as an alternative to automobiles. Estimated annual sales of bicycles have topped 13 million in recent years. There are a number of reasons for their popularity. In the early 1970s, as the environment became a more prominent issue, many people took to bicycling as a pollution-free alternative to driving for short trips. The Bicycle Federation of America estimates that two million Americans commute to work on bikes.

The health concerns of Americans in the 1980s have also been a boon to bicycle sales. Fitness experts say that bicycling is an excellent exercise for developing cardiovascular fitness, toning muscles, and controlling weight. Sports physicians, in fact, report

that competitive cyclists have some of the strongest hearts they see. Many former joggers have traded in their running shoes for bicycles, and with good reason; cycling is much less likely to lead to injuries of the ankle or knee. The pounding that the feet and legs receive during jogging can lead to Achilles tendinitis, knee sprains, shin splits, and other problems. Cycling, while exercising the legs very strongly, relieves much of the pressure on the ligaments and tendons.

Bikes have been making inroads on the back roads as well—in the form of all-terrain bikes, or ATBs. These vehicles, which started out as homemade models put together by trail-riding enthusiasts, feature thick, knobby tires for better stability and traction, upright handlebars for better control, and up to 18 gears for different inclines. Although they are relative newcomers, ATBs already account for about 1.2 million sales per year.

Only about 20% of all ATBs sold end up on back roads and trails, however. City bikers have found that the same features that make ATBs stable on trails also make them comfortable and easy to ride on streets. Some manufacturers now offer "city bikes," which are basically ATBs without some of the features that trail riders desire—e.g., ultralow gears and quick-release seats.

With millions of bicycles now in use, it is not surprising that bicycles are associated with a large number of injuries. The Consumer Product Safety Commission estimates that about a million bicycle-related injuries each year require medical attention. Children and adolescents alone require about 300,000 emergency room visits per year for treatment of bicycle injuries.

The avoidance of bicycle injuries begins with the choice of the right bike. A bicycle should fit a cyclist's height, weight, and ability. Parents sometimes make the mistake of buying a bike that is too big so a youngster can "grow into it." As a result, the child tries to handle a bike that is too cumbersome and heavy; adequate control may thus be sacrificed, and falls and collisions may occur more frequently.

Perhaps nothing is as important to a cyclist's safety as wearing a helmet. A simple fall from a bike, even when it is not moving, can produce a devastating brain injury. In a 1.8-m (6-ft) fall, the average adult head slams to the ground with a force of about 4,500 kg (10,000 lb) at the point of impact; the brain then slams against the inside of the skull with a force of about 900 kg (2,000 lb). An approved helmet cuts the force at impact by 90%. A study directed by Robert S. Thompson of the Group Health Cooperative in Seattle, Wash., found that cyclists who wear helmets reduce their risk of head injury 85% and their risk of brain injury 88%. Fully 75% of all cyclist deaths—about 1,300 cyclists die in accidents in the U.S. every year—and disabling injuries are directly caused by brain injuries. In the study in Seattle, of 235 cyclists who had head

Palo Alto, California, has been described as the "most bicycle-friendly town in the U.S." A 3.2-kilometer (2-mile) stretch of Bryant Street, a main thoroughfare, is designated a "bicycle boulevard," where cars have limited access.

injuries, 99 had serious brain injury; only 4 of those 99 wore helmets.

Safety advocates say there is little reason not to wear a helmet these days. While older models produced complaints that they were too hot and bulky, current versions are much lighter but provide just as much protection. Newer models have large ventilation holes, which contribute to their comfort. Safety experts are especially targeting children for helmet-education efforts. Studies show that only about 2% of children and adolescents wear helmets when riding bicycles. Children in bicycle-mounted child seats should also wear helmets. Injuries to children riding in these seats have been increasing; in California from 1977 to 1986, for example, the rate rose from 17 to 28% of all reported bicycle-related injuries to children aged five and younger.

Cycling experts also encourage cyclists to use common sense when riding—to ride slowly and carefully on rough and uneven surfaces, such as gravel, and not to ride in wet or slippery weather. Many safety rules for cyclists are not merely common sense, however; they are the law. Cyclists are subject to the same traffic rules as car drivers. About half of all cycling injuries resulting from accidents involving bicycles and cars occur at intersections, and in over half of these accidents, the cyclist—not the motorist—violated a traffic rule. The most common violations are

failing to yield the right-of-way, driving in the middle of the street, driving too fast for conditions, disregarding traffic signs, driving against the flow of traffic, and making an improper turn.

A campaign for kids' safety

When asked what threats to their children's safety they worry most about, parents usually name drugs, kidnappers, and disease. The leading killer of children, though, is accidental injury. Accidents kill more children every year than do all childhood diseases combined. According to a study conducted by Johns Hopkins University, Baltimore, Md., each year about 10,000 children under the age of 14 die of accidental injuries. Another 50,000 are permanently disabled. The most common causes of death and injury to children are automobile accidents, falls, choking, burns and scalds, and drowning. All of these injuries are largely preventable.

In response to these alarming figures, a number of safety organizations in 1987 launched the National Safe Kids Campaign, funded largely by Johnson & Johnson and the National Safety Council. C. Everett Koop, then the U.S. surgeon general, served as honorary chairman and was a principal spokesman for the campaign. Leaders of Safe Kids announced that they intended to galvanize research efforts, identify the most common causes of childhood injuries, and distribute literature to educate parents about the dangers that surround their children.

All 50 U.S. states have now passed legislation requiring that children in cars ride in child restraints. Too often adults let children ride without restraints for short trips, buckling them up only for trips on the highway. Accident statistics suggest that this practice is misguided; most accidents occur at intersections and close to home. Thus, children should be restrained for every ride in the car. It is especially important that infants be placed in safety seats. Infants held in a passenger's lap face the greatest risk of serious injury.

More than a third of children injured or killed in traffic accidents are pedestrians. Leaders of Safe Kids urge parents to provide children with a place to play away from streets and traffic. Children also need to be properly taught how to cross the street safely. Studies have shown that children, especially those aged five and younger, have a difficult time understanding verbal-only directions. Children should be shown how to stop and look left, then right, then left again before crossing. Every year many children are killed by the family vehicle in their own driveway. Drivers should always check first to make sure children are not nearby. Drivers of trucks and vans, which offer less rear visibility, need to be especially cautious.

To prevent falls among toddlers and infants, parents are advised to take special precautions. Youngsters using walkers present a special problem; parents

Leaders of the National Safe Kids Campaign urge parents to provide children with a place to play that is away from streets and traffic. In driveways, motorists should always check to make sure youngsters are not nearby.

should use gates to keep toddlers and their walkers away from stairs. Children using walkers are actually more mobile than their natural abilities would allow, so they need to be watched carefully.

A common cause of choking among children is a piece of a toy small enough to fit in the mouth and throat. Although the U.S. Congress in 1984 passed a Toy Safety Act that is supposed to keep unsafe toys off the shelves, in practice the Consumer Product Safety Commission does not have enough staff to keep track of the 150,000 toys introduced each year. Parents, therefore, must make the choice of safe toys their responsibility. The Toy Manufacturers of America (TMA) publishes extensive safety standards for member companies. Companies that belong to TMA have a good record in following that trade group's recommendations. Manufacturers who intend to meet both TMA and federal standards subject their toys to tests designed to ensure that small parts cannot be pulled off even in rough play.

Safety experts say that the age labeling on a toy should never be ignored. What is safe for a seven-year-old may not be safe for a toddler. Parents also need to inspect toys themselves and look for small parts that could pop off.

Safe Kids recommends that for the prevention of burns, matches and lighters should be stored out of reach, children should be prevented from playing in the kitchen or near stoves and heaters, and the home should be equipped with smoke alarms and fire extinguishers. For prevention of scalds, bathwater should be tested before a child is allowed to get in

the tub, and young children who are bathing should be supervised so they do not accidentally turn on the hot water. Many safety experts also recommend setting the home water heater at no higher than about 50° C (120° F).

Children should never be alone near water. Even a few centimeters (one centimeter is about 0.39 in) of bathwater is enough to drown a small child. Swimming pools should be securely fenced so that small children cannot unlatch the gate and let themselves in; when the pool is unattended, a tamper-proof cover should be placed on it.

Air mattresses should not be relied on to keep children safe in swimming pools; children can easily slide off of them. In fact, safety experts recommend that all children who are allowed in a pool take swimming lessons as soon as possible after age three. A child who can hold his or her breath on command is considered to be ready for swimming instruction. Children should never be allowed to dive into water unless an adult is supervising, and then only if an adult has first made sure the water is deep enough.

When boating, both children and adults should avoid standing, which can tip the boat, and they should wear personal flotation devices. The devices that children wear should be specially designed for someone their size and weight.

In launching the National Safe Kids Campaign, Koop noted that if a disease killed 10,000 children each year, outraged parents would demand that the medical community take action. In the case of preventing accidents, parents must take action themselves.

—*Tom D. Naughton*

Aging

Rapid growth of the older population has increased the need for improved geriatric care and prevention of disability. The specialty of geriatric medicine focuses on the prevention, diagnosis, care, and treatment of illnesses and disabilities in older persons. This approach to promoting the health of older patients takes into account the interaction of diseases, medications, the environment, personal and social factors, and age. While geriatrics acknowledges unfavorable aspects of the aging process, it stresses that physical and mental deterioration are not inevitable.

Comprehensive Geriatric Assessment

In October 1987 the National Institute on Aging (NIA) in the United States sponsored the Consensus Development Conference on Comprehensive Geriatric Assessment. After hearing expert testimony, the consensus panel attempted to answer a series of questions that defined geriatric assessment, reviewed assessment methods, evaluated their effectiveness, and identified priorities for future research in the field. In addition, the American College of Physicians and the American Geriatrics Society have recently issued position papers regarding geriatric assessment.

The NIA defines comprehensive geriatric assessment (CGA) as "a multidisciplinary evaluation in which the multiple problems of older persons are uncovered, described, and explained, if possible, and in which the resources and strengths of the person are catalogued, need for services assessed, and a coordinated care plan developed to focus interventions on the person's problems." CGA incorporates many domains, including physical (medical problems), mental (intellectual), emotional, functional, social, economic, environmental, and quality of life (well-being). Some of these areas, especially the physical, are best assessed by physicians; others, by such professionals as social workers and nurses. The domains of CGA are assessed by specific questionnaires, interviewers, or direct observation. For example, a home visit by a visiting nurse may be the most effective means of checking for safety hazards that might increase the chance of falling in the home.

CGA begins with a complete medical evaluation to identify illnesses and medication effects that may be contributing to impairment. Mental and emotional status is evaluated to exclude the possibility of a dementing illness (such as Alzheimer's disease) or an emotional problem (such as depression).

Functional ability and social assessment. Functional assessment is the measurement of a person's ability to complete functional tasks and fulfill social roles. Functional tasks can range from the simplest self-care to executive-level occupational responsibilities and can be classified into three levels—basic, intermediate, and advanced activities.

Basic activities include self-care functions such as feeding, dressing, getting to the toilet, and bathing. Intermediate activities include shopping, taking medications, cooking, doing laundry, and getting to places that are beyond walking distance. Independence or dependence in these intermediate activities often determines whether an elderly person can continue to live alone. Advanced activities may be thought of as "luxury" items of function, those well beyond what is needed to maintain independent living. They usually relate to recreational, occupational, altruistic, or community service functions.

Social function includes social activities, relationships, community and religious involvement, and employment. At the highest levels of social and physical function, the distinction between these two spheres often disappears; *e.g.,* a tennis match represents both an advanced physical task and a social activity.

Assessment of the social domain frequently looks at the person's social support network, including current and potential care givers. Economic assessment is usually conducted by a social worker, who examines resources and care needs. Environmental assessment looks at the living environment from a safety viewpoint but also evaluates the architectural design and proximity of necessary services, such as grocery stores and pharmacies. Recently geriatricians have begun to examine the domain of "quality of life" or well-being, which is in keeping with the World Health Organization's definition of health extending beyond the absence of disease.

Limitations of assessment. The NIA consensus statement was careful to note the potential limitations of CGA. First, the process must be targeted toward older persons who are most likely to benefit from the intervention. Thus, persons who are very healthy and those who are irreversibly impaired, such as persons with severe Alzheimer's disease, are not suitable candidates. Elderly persons, particularly those over 75 years of age, with potentially reversible disorders such as acute confusion, pressure sores, or medical conditions that have resulted in prolonged bed rest are perhaps

John Sotomayor/The New York Times

Comprehensive Geriatric Assessment evaluates the problems, resources, strengths, and needs of the elderly population; this kind of broad assessment enables specialists in aging to provide interventions that will help maximize the older person's quality of life. In Manhattan men play shuffleboard at a recreation center for seniors, part of a new project that provides a safe gathering place for the elderly residents of a West Side neighborhood.

the best candidates. Approximately 5–10% of hospitalized patients and probably 2–5% of the nonhospitalized population of elderly persons appear to meet these criteria. A second caveat affecting the success of CGA programs is the linkage between assessment and follow-up services. The assessment is primarily a diagnostic rather than a therapeutic process; steps must be taken to assure that recommendations are implemented by the physicians who provide primary care to the person. Periodic reassessment may also be valuable in redirecting the treatment plan.

Several studies of CGA at the best geriatric centers using selected patients have demonstrated improvement in diagnostic accuracy, prolongation of survival, and reductions in medical care costs and acute care hospital and nursing home use.

Depression in the elderly

The term depression has been used to describe various moods and feelings ranging from transient negative feelings—the so-called blues—to a full-fledged, life-threatening psychiatric illness. Symptoms of depression such as loss of pleasure, sleep or appetite disturbances, and feeling sad may affect as many as 10% of older persons living in the community. In contrast, only 1–2% of older persons living in the community have a medical diagnosis of major depression. This figure rises to 10–20% in older persons who are hospitalized or institutionalized (usually in a nursing home).

The diagnosis of major depression is made on clinical grounds; *i.e.,* patients have a cluster of symptoms (at least five) that cannot be attributable to other causes such as medications (*e.g.,* some drugs that are used to treat high blood pressure) or other diseases (*e.g.,* hormonal imbalances caused by thyroid disorders). These symptoms are depressed mood, loss of interest or pleasure in activities, appetite disturbance, decreased energy or easy fatigability, agitation or slowing of movements or indecisiveness, insomnia or sleeping too much, decreased self-esteem, poor concentration, and recurrent thoughts of death or suicide. Most laboratory tests in patients with suspected depression are used to exclude other possible causes of the symptoms; at present there is no laboratory test that can establish the diagnosis of major depression.

Underdiagnosis. Depression in the elderly population is probably underdiagnosed because physicians and patients may incorrectly believe that symptoms of depression may be attributable to other diseases or, perhaps more commonly, to the aging process itself. In addition, depression may manifest itself with different symptoms in elderly persons. Compared with younger persons with depression, they are more likely to complain of weight loss and are less likely to report feelings of worthlessness and guilt. They may also have more problems with cognition, such as memory and higher intellectual function, than younger persons.

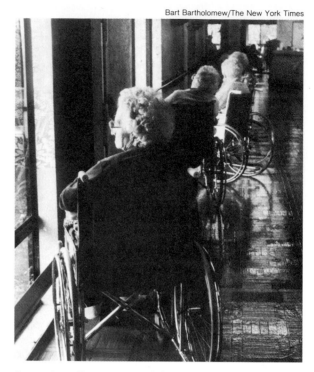

Depression affects 10–20% of elderly patients in nursing homes—compared with 1–2% of older persons living in the community. Because the problem is underdiagnosed, many residents are not getting appropriate treatment.

Other reported atypical symptoms of depression in older persons include pain syndromes, hypochondriasis, malnutrition, and alcoholism. A syndrome called pseudodementia has been described in which cognitive problems are the result of depression rather than dementia. More often, however, persons with severe memory impairment and depressive symptoms have both dementia and depression.

Appropriate treatment. The management of depression in older persons is multidimensional. Traditional insight-oriented psychotherapy does not appear to be of much benefit, but a more directive, educationally oriented, cognitive-behavioral therapy has been valuable. In this therapy, negative thoughts are challenged by the therapist, and patients are encouraged to develop new ways of adapting to situations.

Medications have been effective in treating depression in later life. These medications must be administered with caution because of potential side effects that may be more common and more severe in the elderly because of changes in the body's processing of drugs and alterations in the body's responses to drugs that accompany aging. In addition, diseases that are common in older persons, such as prostate disease, may be adversely affected by the medications. As a result, the antidepressant drugs with the fewest side effects are selected, and lower doses are usually employed. Although tricyclic antidepressants are most commonly used in treating older persons with depression, other classes of drugs including monoamine-oxidase inhibitors and psychomotor stimulants (e.g., Ritalin [methylphenidate hydrochloride], a drug commonly used for attention deficit disorders in children and for treating individuals with the neurological disorder narcolepsy) have been used effectively in some patients.

Older persons with severe depression and those who have been resistant to medication therapy have been successfully treated with electroconvulsive therapy. This procedure is safe but has side effects of transient confusion and memory loss, especially in persons with preexisting dementia. These problems have been reduced but not eliminated with newer methods of administration.

Treatment of the older person with depression must also consider the family of the patient, including family counseling and support services. Depression may be associated with loss of function and independence, which are likely to increase stress on the family and the care givers. These repercussions must be discussed openly to optimize family participation in the recovery process. Families must also be alert to the risk of suicide, which appears to increase with age, especially among white males. Generally, suicidal persons give clues to this possibility, but these clues are often unrecognized. Fortunately, this outcome is uncommon, and most older persons with depression are managed successfully with a combination of therapeutic modalities.

—David B. Reuben, M.D.

AIDS

"There simply has never been anything quite like this before," Jonathan Mann, director of the World Health Organization's (WHO's) Global Program on AIDS, has said. No other disease in history has descended upon the world so suddenly and spread so silently, striking people down in their most productive years. Even if transmission of the human immunodeficiency virus (HIV), which causes AIDS, were to stop tomorrow, there would probably be at least one million new cases of AIDS over the next five years. WHO estimates that between five million and ten million people throughout the world are already infected and that by the year 2000 the cumulative total of people infected with HIV may increase by a factor of three to four.

AIDS is here to stay. In contrast to the optimistic outlook that prevailed during the successful international campaign to eradicate smallpox, no one at WHO can envisage an end to the battle against AIDS. Despite the impending toll of disease, however, the Fifth International Conference on AIDS, which met in Montreal in June 1989, was marked by a mood of greater optimism than in many previous years. Researchers

seemed quietly confident that before long they would be able to develop a range of drugs that would treat AIDS and prevent people infected with HIV from developing immunodeficiency. Some of the earlier pessimism about the prospects of developing a vaccine had also melted away.

Progression of the disease

The virus now known as HIV was first isolated in 1983, two years after what later became known as acquired immune deficiency syndrome, or AIDS, was first described in the U.S. The disease is so new that no one knows what proportion of people infected with HIV will go on to develop AIDS. Some estimates suggest that about 50% of HIV-infected people will develop AIDS within ten years of becoming infected, although many doctors believe that most people infected with the virus will eventually develop AIDS. A recent study from San Francisco put the average incubation period, from the time of the development of antibodies to HIV to the diagnosis of AIDS, at 9.8 years.

At the moment, the strategies for controlling AIDS depend mainly on education and information. But the task of trying to change human behavior, particularly sexual behavior, is a monumental one. That is why scientists are racing to develop a vaccine to protect uninfected people from the virus. Researchers are also trying to design drugs that, even if they do not cure AIDS, could at least keep the virus in abeyance in the body, preventing or delaying the onset of severe immunodeficiency. Progress in both of these avenues of scientific research has been hampered by lack of knowledge about the virus itself and how it attacks the immune system.

New technique for detecting infection

Recent investigations have succeeded in unveiling many of the secret strategies of HIV. One key discovery has resulted from the application of a new diagnostic technique to the detection of the virus. The technique, called the polymerase chain reaction, or PCR, makes it possible to amplify minute quantities of the genetic material DNA (deoxyribonucleic acid). Using PCR, researchers have been able to seek out the tiny amounts of viral DNA derived from HIV that become incorporated into the cells of people infected by the virus.

This new test has provided some startling insights into the workings of HIV. One is the discovery that the antibodies produced in response to HIV can take months—or even years—to develop. In 1988 researchers at the Northwestern University School of Medicine, Chicago, were able, using PCR, to find viral DNA in a proportion of apparently healthy homosexual men long before their blood tested positive for antibodies to HIV. The interval between infection and appearance of antibodies ranged from 7 to 42 months.

Scientists gathering in Montreal in June 1989 for the Fifth International Conference on AIDS were greeted by the sight of a huge condom-shaped balloon bearing the motto "I save lives." The theme of prevention—including a report on the prophylactic use of drugs for some people in the early stages of the disease—was emphasized throughout the conference. The mood at Montreal was notably more optimistic than at previous international AIDS conferences.

In view of these findings, Anthony Fauci, director of the U.S. National Institute of Allergy and Infectious Diseases, Bethesda, Md., has suggested that people who have been exposed to the virus, such as the regular sexual partners of infected persons, yet have had negative tests for antibodies should be aware there is a risk that they could nevertheless be infected. When PCR becomes more widely available, these people may want to be retested, he said.

A subsequent study, reported in the *New England Journal of Medicine* in June 1989, found some men who had failed to produce antibodies for as long as three years following infection. Two similar studies, reported at Montreal, did not confirm these results, however. Leading researchers at the conference said that although they were convinced that the phenomenon of latent infection exists, they thought it was very rare. They wanted more evidence before they could draw any firm conclusions about the wider implications of the findings for the epidemic as a whole.

Effect on the immune system

What happens during the latent phase of infection? The life cycle of the virus begins when it enters certain cells of the body, mainly those bearing on their surfaces a protein called CD4, which acts as a receptor for the virus. In a process known as integration, a viral enzyme, called reverse transcriptase, makes a copy of the virus's genetic material, which the virus inserts into the DNA of the host cell. Research suggests that once incorporated into the macrophages (cells of the immune system that help to eliminate invading microorganisms), the viral DNA may remain quiescent until some trigger—perhaps another infection—sets off replication, with the result that more virus is produced.

Macrophages are not the only cells to become in-

fected with HIV. The virus also attacks the T-helper cells, which play a vital role in orchestrating the immune response. In the presence of infection, some T-helper cells become activated, producing chemicals that influence other components of the immune system. In this way T-helper cells coordinate the activities of the B cells (which produce antibodies), as well as those of another type of T cell (some of which attack infected cells) and those of the macrophages.

One of the first observations that doctors made about the earliest patients diagnosed with AIDS was that the number of T-helper cells circulating in their blood had plummeted. Surprisingly, however, only about one in 10,000 to one in 100,000 T cells in the blood of infected people seemed to be actively infected with HIV. The body could easily replace these infected T cells if they died. Thus, it was a mystery why people with AIDS lost great numbers of their T-helper cells.

One theory is that some effect on *uninfected* cells is to blame. Infected people in whom the virus is actively replicating are likely to have plenty of virus in their bloodstream, from which viral protein can easily become detached. This free-floating viral protein will bind to any cell bearing the receptor protein CD4, such as T-helper cells. This may act as an invitation to other cells of the immune system to kill them, even though they are not truly infected.

Fighting opportunistic infections

A person without the normal numbers of T-helper cells is unable to ward off certain "opportunistic" infections, so called because they take advantage of the infected person's immunocompromised status. One strategy for helping prolong the lives of people with AIDS is to prevent, diagnose, and aggressively treat those infections. In 1989 aerosol pentamidine, a drug used in the treatment of the pneumonia caused by *Pneumocystis carinii* (a respiratory infection that some people with AIDS suffer repeatedly), was approved for use by the U.S. Food and Drug Administration (FDA). Because the aerosol form of the drug is inhaled directly into the lungs, where it is needed, lower doses can be used and side effects are fewer than with oral administration. Regular use of the spray can also prevent recurrences.

Several other drugs have recently been approved or become available experimentally for the treatment of conditions associated with AIDS. In the United States doctors can now prescribe the antiviral drug ganciclovir (Cytovene) for cytomegalovirus infections of the eye, which can cause blindness; alpha interferon for Kaposi's sarcoma, the malignant skin condition that sometimes develops in persons with AIDS; and r-erythropoietin, a genetically engineered blood factor, for the anemia that persons with AIDS sometimes suffer.

Containing the virus

Another approach to the treatment of AIDS is to limit the damage that the virus does to the body. The fact that the virus integrates its own DNA into the genetic

In Tacoma, Washington, David Purchase hands out clean syringes to drug addicts. Although this practice could help check the spread of AIDS among drug abusers, such programs have been mired in controversy in most U.S. cities.

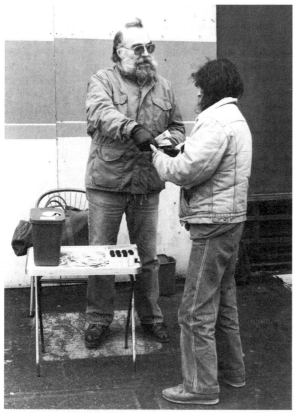

Doug Wilson/The New York Times

material of the host cell presents special difficulties for the development of drugs to treat AIDS, however. It is unlikely that it will ever be possible to use drugs to rid an infected person of the virus, although there have been intriguing reports of a few people who have naturally lost antibodies to the virus. In one U.S. study four homosexual men who had tested positive for antibodies to HIV were subsequently found to test negative; researchers found, however, that they were still positive for the virus itself when tested with PCR. Oddly, two of the men later became negative by PCR as well—that is, no traces of viral DNA could be found in their blood. The researchers had little confidence, however, that these men were cured. They suggested that the virus may have been sequestered somewhere in the body, perhaps in brain tissue, which a PCR test on the blood could not detect.

If the virus remains in the body for life, then any drug to treat it would have to be taken for life, too. Such a drug would need to be inexpensive, able to be taken by mouth, and without toxic side effects. It would also need to be able to pass from the blood circulation into the brain (not all drugs can) in order to treat the neurological effects of HIV infection. Finally, the drug would be useless if the virus could mutate to avoid its action. To develop an agent with all of these characteristics is indeed a tall order. Still, some researchers are fairly confident that they may, before long, discover substances that can block the virus and prevent it from replicating. And the fact that HIV has quite a complicated life cycle provides scientists with many more points at which to attack it.

CD4—new weapon against HIV?

Perhaps the most obvious strategy is to prevent the virus from binding to its host cell in the first place. As noted above, the surface protein of the virus binds specifically to the receptor protein CD4, which is found on T-helper cells, macrophages, and a variety of other cells. Several biotechnology companies have now produced recombinant CD4, which, when injected into the bloodstream of infected people, should act as a decoy for the virus, attracting viral particles and preventing them from infecting other cells. Human trials of recombinant CD4 began in 1988, and early results suggest that the treatment has few adverse side effects.

In 1989 researchers at the California biotechnology company Genentech announced that they had created a hybrid antibody bearing CD4 on its surface. All antibodies carry a variable region that binds to antigens. (An antigen is any substance capable of triggering an immune response.) The variety of antibodies is infinite. There is one to bind to every conceivable antigen. In the hybrid antibody made at Genentech, the variable regions have been replaced with molecules of CD4. This change confers several advantages. Antibodies are long-lived, so the body should not eliminate the

Although it accounts for only a small proportion of cases of AIDS in the U.S. and other developed countries, heterosexual transmission is increasingly a matter of concern, as evidenced by this poster in a New York City subway.

hybrids as quickly as it does molecules of CD4 alone. About two injections a week should be enough to sustain suitable levels of the hybrid antibody in the blood of a person infected with HIV. In addition, because the type of antibody used crosses the placenta, this therapy has the potential to prevent an infected woman from passing the virus on to her unborn child. It remains to be seen how the hybrid antibody will fare in human trials.

Other anti-HIV strategies

There are several proteins and enzymes vital to the survival of HIV. Without the protein encoded by the gene called *tat,* for example, it is virtually impossible for the virus to make any of its other proteins. Several groups of researchers are therefore working on ways of blocking the production of this protein. Other suitable targets for anti-HIV drug therapy are the viral enzymes. One of these enzymes, a protease, has the function of splitting the long strings of proteins that HIV initially makes. These "polyproteins" become functional only when split into their component parts. To find out how important the role of the protease is, researchers at the U.S. pharmaceutical company Merck Sharp & Dohme genetically modified the active

site of the enzyme. They found that the "offspring" of the modified virus, viral particles containing only polyproteins, could no longer infect cells that are normally susceptible to HIV. The Merck scientists are now working on identifying a substance that can inhibit the synthesis of the protease. As a first step in this task, they have already crystallized the enzyme and determined its three-dimensional structure.

The other viral enzyme that has become a target of drug researchers is reverse transcriptase, which is necessary for HIV—and, indeed, all retroviruses— to insinuate themselves into the genetic material of the host cell. The drug zidovudine (formerly known as azidothymidine, or AZT; Retrovir) acts by inhibiting this enzyme. Trials in the U.S., France, and Britain are currently under way to determine whether zidovudine can delay the onset of AIDS in people infected with HIV. Unfortunately, zidovudine is very expensive, and some people taking it suffer unacceptable side effects, primarily anemia, which necessitates periodic interruption of treatment. In addition, resistant strains of HIV can develop in people taking the drug for prolonged periods of time. This latter observation may explain why some doctors have noticed that AIDS patients receiving zidovudine sometimes relapse after a period of relatively improved health.

Vaccines—problems and prospects

Researchers are much more optimistic about the chances of soon developing a drug that infected people could take to stave off the onset of AIDS than they are about the prospects of producing a vaccine to protect against infection with HIV. Vaccines usually work by limiting infection. They prime the immune system so that when the infectious agent invades, the immune response is rapid and effective. In the case of HIV, however, a vaccine would need to prevent the initial infection completely rather than simply limiting it. If even one cell became infected as a result of exposure to the virus, the vaccine would have failed, because the virus would be permanently established in the body.

Another problem is that no one knows what kind of immune response needs to be produced in order to fight off the virus successfully. The bodies of people infected with HIV seem to respond in all the ways (producing antibodies, for example) that would normally put an end to an invading microorganism, but this virus is different. There is no record of any human patient who has recovered from infection with HIV and has developed immunity to further attacks, as is common in so many other infectious diseases.

There are several theories to explain why the immune system seems to be incapable of eliminating this particular virus. One is that the genes coding for the surface proteins of the virus mutate very quickly, several times faster, for example, than those of the influenza virus. Second, HIV can spread from cell to cell, completely avoiding the immune system, even at the initial stage of the infection. Third, it is the task of macrophages to engulf and destroy invading micro-organisms that have become coated with antibodies; in the case of HIV, however, the virus may set up a silent infection within the macrophages themselves, where, again, it is safe from destruction by the immune system. The final theory is that infected cells may find a sanctuary somewhere in the body where the cells of the immune system cannot seek them out. If infected cells migrate to the brain or the bone marrow, for example, the immune system may be powerless to act against them.

Most researchers are now agreed that to be effective against HIV, a vaccine would need to stimulate both arms of the immune system—both cells and antibodies. Several groups of investigators have already tried injecting volunteers with candidate vaccines despite the lack of evidence to suggest that the preparations will have any effect. In some cases the volunteers have been people already infected with HIV but with no symptoms of disease; the point of this experiment is to find out whether the trial vaccines can boost the subjects' immune systems and so delay the onset of AIDS. At the very least, such tests will provide researchers with valuable information on the response of the human immune system to different components of the virus.

At Montreal several teams of scientists reported advances in their work toward a vaccine. For example, Jonas Salk, inventor of the polio vaccine, said that he and his colleagues had injected two chimpanzees (both infected with HIV) with a preparation of whole inactivated HIV that had been stripped of its protein coat. Afterward the researchers were no longer able to isolate the virus from the two chimps. Salk is also testing this preparation on human volunteers infected with HIV, but it is still too early to tell if the "vaccine" will have the desired effect of boosting the immune system.

Other groups of researchers at the Montreal meeting told of their success in identifying a region of HIV's outer protein that may prove to be an important component of a vaccine. Tests on animals have shown that antibodies directed against this segment, a peptide, can neutralize the virus. Scott Putney of Repligen Corp., a biotechnology company in Cambridge, Mass., reported that he and his colleagues had analyzed the sequence of amino acids contributing to the peptide in around 100 viruses isolated from people all over the U.S. The sequence was very similar in about 40% of the viruses. Putney believes that a vaccine based on this segment of protein might protect against 40% of HIV strains found in infected people. Emilio Emini and colleagues at Merck Sharp & Dohme Laboratories in West Point, Pa., found that neutralizing antibodies directed against the peptide identified by Putney's team were effective in protecting chimpanzees against infection with HIV. Their study provides one of the first pieces of evidence that an immune response may be able to protect against HIV infection. Putney hopes that further research may identify other peptides common to a significant proportion of HIVs. The ultimate aim would be to develop a vaccine made up of a "cocktail" of peptides, which would protect against many different strains of the virus. However, even if researchers can identify the appropriate peptides, they will still face the problem of how to present them to the immune system. One way is to "display" the proteins on the surface of a particle, much as they would appear on the actual virus. As with all novel approaches, how-

Sara Krulwich/The New York Times

Alison Gertz, a 23-year-old woman from an affluent New York City family, was understandably shocked when she was diagnosed with AIDS in 1988. She had never had a blood transfusion or taken intravenous drugs and did not consider herself sexually promiscuous. Since learning that she has AIDS, Gertz has been actively working to spread the message that heterosexuals must not dismiss the threat of the disease.

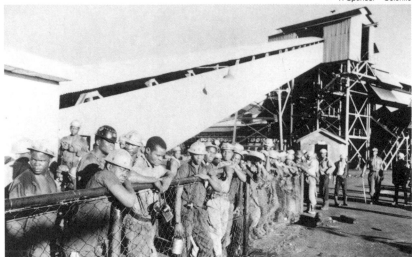

The social and financial impact of AIDS in Africa is difficult to quantify. The monetary cost of caring for individuals with AIDS does not take into account the cost to society of large numbers of people— teachers, farmers, soldiers, miners— being struck down in their most productive years.

ever, health authorities will require stringent checks on the safety of any such agents before giving approval for tests on people not infected with HIV.

Ethical dilemmas in vaccine tests

Even when scientists believe that they have a candidate vaccine worth testing for its efficacy in preventing infection with HIV, their problems will be far from over. A crucial question is who will take part in the test? One problem is that the risk of an adult's becoming infected with HIV depends largely on that person's behavior. (High-risk activities include unprotected sex with an infected person and the sharing of needles when injecting drugs.) Thus, anyone running a trial to see if a candidate vaccine may protect against infection with HIV would have to educate the participants on how to avoid becoming infected. This requirement would immediately make the trial a less powerful means of determining the effectiveness of the vaccine. The trial would have to prove that the vaccine was more effective than education alone.

The ethical issues associated with a trial of this kind are gargantuan, particularly if it were to be conducted in a less developed country—an African country, say. It would be wrong, for example, if a country that put its citizens at some risk in testing a vaccine did not benefit fully from the results of that research. Some researchers believe that there is no option but to conduct trials of candidate vaccines in Africa. Daniel Zagury, the French scientist who tested an experimental vaccine on himself, has suggested that young men coming from the countryside to live in Kinshasa, the capital of Zaire, might prove a suitable population on which to carry out tests. Zagury and his colleagues believe that people arriving in Kinshasa from rural areas are much less likely to be infected with the virus than people who have been living in Kinshasa for five years or more, of whom more than 15% are infected.

If a candidate vaccine could prevent this figure from increasing, this would provide some evidence of the vaccine's effectiveness.

The epidemiological pattern

The pattern of AIDS in Africa continues to be very different from that in the U.S. and Europe. In Africa the virus has been spread mainly by heterosexual intercourse, whereas in the U.S. and many European countries, the major high-risk activities are homosexual contact and intravenous drug use. In 1988 and 1989 public health officials in the Americas expressed alarm at the disproportionate number of AIDS cases in the Caribbean countries and the potential for an epidemic in the Americas that could parallel that in Africa. Still, few researchers were willing to commit themselves to predicting whether there would be an epidemic among heterosexuals in the developed countries.

Although heterosexual intercourse does not inevitably transmit the virus, there is no doubt that heterosexual transmission occurs. Throughout the world as a whole, transmission via heterosexual contact is probably the most common path of spread of the virus. In Africa some researchers have linked the wide spread of the virus to the prevalence of genital ulcer disease, which may facilitate transmission. According to one study, there may also be a link with the lack of circumcision—uncircumcised men being more likely to become infected.

The extent to which African countries are reporting cases of AIDS to WHO does not, in some cases, accurately reflect the true numbers. By April 1989 few African countries had reported more than 6,000 cases of AIDS to the international agency. Calculations carried out by WHO's staff, however, suggest that a hypothetical East African country with a population of 16.1 million would have had more than 24,000 cases of AIDS between the notional start of the epidemic, in

1980, and the end of 1987. This hypothetical country probably would have had about 416,000 infected people in 1986, or 2.6% of the population. About a dozen countries in Central and East Africa could be expected to have a similar pattern of infection.

The impact of AIDS in Africa is difficult to measure. The calculated monetary cost of caring for someone with AIDS does not take into account the effects on societies of people dying in their most productive years. Many babies will be born with AIDS; many children will be orphaned; many older people will lose their sons and daughters, their only social security. In countries where numerous administrators, technicians, doctors, nurses, teachers, farmers, miners, or soldiers may die young, what will happen?

It is impossible to predict the future. One encouraging aspect of AIDS in Africa is that children under the age of 15, who are largely uninfected, make up about 50% of the population of many African countries. According to some predictions, AIDS may not cause populations to dwindle; if rates of population growth do begin to decline, this trend may not occur for several decades.

The drive to educate everyone about AIDS and how to avoid becoming infected is well under way in Africa under the guidance of WHO's Global Program on AIDS. The problems of trying to spread the word in countries where the roads are bad, where not everyone has a radio, or where there are many different languages and dialects are enormous. The logistics of delivering a therapy, should the day come when one is available, will present even greater difficulties.

—*Sharon Kingman*

Allergies and Asthma

The most common chronic diseases experienced by humans are allergic in nature. About 20% of the population of the Western world suffer from allergic afflictions, including allergic rhinitis (hay fever), asthma, urticaria (hives), food allergies, reactions to insect venom, and anaphylaxis (severe, systemic allergic shock). Medical scientists believe that allergic diseases are misguided responses of an immune process that evolved to defend against parasitic organisms.

Three major elements participate in allergic reactions—allergens, immunoglobulin E (IgE) antibodies, and mast cells. Allergens are water-soluble proteins that are derived largely from airborne particles—commonly pollen, which is experienced seasonally, or perennial sources like dander, dust, and mold. In such instances it is a protein on the surface of the allergen source that dissolves rapidly on contact with the mucous membranes of the body's respiratory tract and penetrates the epithelial lining. The allergen is taken up and presented by an antigen-presenting white blood cell to other white blood cells called plasma cells, which

are capable of making IgE. The plasma cells produce IgE antibodies locally in the mucous membranes and sensitize nearby mast cells, which are found in large quantities in the respiratory tract.

The IgE antibody is a member of a group of proteins called immunoglobulins that all contribute to the functioning of the immune system. IgE has the capacity to bind avidly to particular molecular receptors on mast cells and related white blood cells called basophils. Once bound to a mast cell or basophil, IgE remains stable for an extended time, possibly for years. After the mast cell has become sensitized with about 100 or more IgE molecules capable of recognizing the specific allergen that stimulated their production, subsequent exposure to the same allergen causes the mast cell to become activated. Activation entails a sequence of biochemical reactions culminating in the release of a host of chemicals from storage granules in the cell, a process called degranulation. The granular contents include a large number of chemical mediators that trigger the allergic response.

Depending on the tissue in which mast cell degranulation occurs, the allergic response differs. If the allergen enters the nose, the nasal mucous membrane becomes pruritic (itchy), swells, and discharges glandular proteins, while the local blood vessels dilate and become more permeable (leaky) to fluid. These responses cause the sneezing, itchiness, runny nose, and nasal congestion of allergic rhinitis. If the allergen penetrates the lungs, the responses include vascular permeability, glandular secretion, vasodilation, and inflammation due to an influx of white blood cells, resulting in asthma. If the allergen penetrates the skin (*e.g.,* contact with poison ivy), another place where mast cell population is high, the same vascular permeability and vasodilation may take place, resulting in local swelling or more extensive hives or eczema. Recently several major advances have increased medical understanding and control of allergic diseases.

Stopping allergy at the IgE receptor

The fundamental difference between IgE and other immunoglobulins is the capacity of IgE to sensitize mast cells and basophils. Such sensitization not only allows these cells to respond to subsequent allergen exposure but also protects IgE from breakdown, extending its life from days to months or years. The IgE receptor, itself a protein, consists of three different types of amino acid chains—one alpha chain, one beta chain, and two gamma chains. The genes encoding each of the subunits recently have been isolated, and a model for the structure of the IgE receptor has been suggested. Furthermore, insertion of these genes into cultured cells lacking IgE receptors has endowed the cells with the ability to express IgE receptor in quantity. Thus, medical researchers now have knowledge of the precise sequence of amino acids that constitute the IgE receptor as well as the means for making large amounts of the receptor for study.

Current work is aimed at producing peptides (short amino acid chains) resembling fragments of IgE that can bind to the receptor and so block IgE binding. In this way it may be possible to prevent allergic sensitization at the outset and thereby reduce or prevent allergic diseases.

Recognizing differences in mast cells

Mast cells are found in tissues throughout the human body, primarily in the connective tissues and generally around blood vessels. Some tissues, for example, those exposed to the external world, are richer in mast cells than other tissues. The highest numbers of mast cells are in the skin; in the mucous membranes of the respiratory, gastrointestinal, and reproductive tracts; and around the blood vessels that provide nutrition to larger blood vessels. Mast cells possess a single nucleus, have abundant secretory granules, and carry on their surface the high-affinity receptor for IgE.

From earlier experiments with laboratory animals, it became clear that mast cells in the skin are different from those in the mucous membranes. This difference, or heterogeneity, has been convincingly demonstrated in humans by means of two approaches. The first involves the use of antibodies that bind specifically to one or the other of two enzymes found within mast cell granules: tryptase and a chymotryptic proteinase. Employing these antibodies has revealed that skin mast cells contain both tryptic and chymotryptic proteinase enzymes (and so are designated CT mast cells), whereas mucosal mast cells contain only the tryptic enzyme (and so are designated T mast cells). Thus, one can distinguish by immunohistochemical techniques the presence of two mast cell populations in the body.

This work has been extended by electron microscopy to reveal distinct differences in the morphological features of the granules in CT and T mast cells. Granules of the CT mast cell in skin show a distinct lamellar (thin-layered) internal pattern, and they remain intact upon release from the mast cell. The T mast cell granules show a peculiar spiral pattern, and they dissolve within the cell prior to discharge. The CT mast cell is known to degranulate upon exposure to a number of substances, such as neuropeptides, that do not affect the T mast cell. Current research suggests that the T mast cell can proliferate in response to regulatory substances, called cytokines, that are released by lymphocytes when an allergen challenges the immune system. Moreover, it appears that T mast cells in the respiratory mucous membranes of asthmatics and rhinitis sufferers are increased in number as a consequence of their disease. Current work also suggests that the recently introduced corticosteroid sprays and inhalants (e.g., beclomethasone [Beclovent, Vancenase]), which work topically on the mucous membranes, act in part by reducing the number of mast cells, thereby counteracting the proliferative response and explaining a part of the mechanism by which corticosteroids act in the treatment of allergic diseases.

Improved antihistamines

While a large number of chemical mediators are released from or generated by mast cells during allergic responses, histamine, one of the most potent and prevalent of them, has been recognized for nearly a century. Histamine stimulates a number of actions in the body that may be classified by the cellular receptor to which histamine binds to elicit the reaction. When histamine interacts with an H1 receptor, it stimulates a variety of responses associated with classical allergic diseases. In contrast, interaction with the H2 receptor stimulates gastric acid secretion among other actions. As it turns out, prevention of histamine's interaction

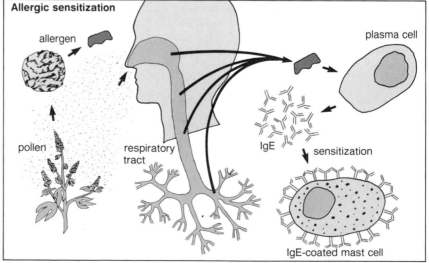

A person may become sensitized to an allergenic airborne substance— in this case, plant pollen—after exposure to it over an extended time. The allergen, a protein on the surface of the allergen source, enters the respiratory tract, where it is presented to plasma cells. The plasma cells make IgE antibodies capable of recognizing the specific allergen that stimulated their production. The IgE goes on to sensitize nearby mast cells by binding avidly to receptors on the mast cell surface. From about 100 to as many as 300,000 IgE molecules may participate in sensitizing a single mast cell.

Allergic sensitization

allergen

plasma cell

pollen

respiratory tract

IgE

sensitization

IgE-coated mast cell

Source: Michael A. Kaliner, National Institutes of Health

Photographs, Marc Friedman, Georgetown University Medical School

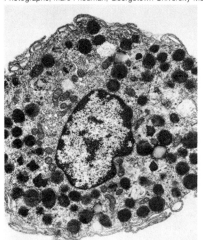
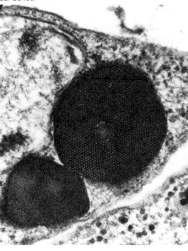
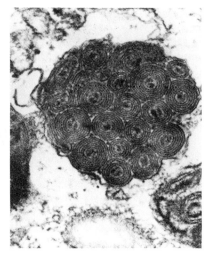

Micrograph of a mast cell from the nasal mucous membranes (left) reveals numerous dark granules, which carry mediators of the allergic reaction. Other micrographs point up differences in visible features between a granule of a skin mast cell (center) and one of a lung mast cell (right). Recognition that skin and mucosal mast cell granules differ structurally and in other ways has shed light on the mechanism of allergies and their response to treatment.

with both the H1 and H2 receptors is required for avoiding the profound blood pressure drop (hypotension) that occurs during anaphylactic shock.

Antihistamines that prevent histamine's interaction with the H1 receptor have been commercially available for 40 years. They have proved remarkably safe and effective and are among the most common drugs sold. Until recently antihistamines had one major restrictive side effect—they caused sleepiness. Within the past few years a new generation of H1-receptor antihistamines, which avoids this drawback, has become available. The mechanism for antihistamine-induced sleepiness has been shown to be the ability of the traditional antihistamines (*e.g.,* diphenhydramine [Benadryl]) to cross the blood-brain barrier—a protective mechanism that prevents most substances dissolved in the blood from entering the brain—and inhibit histamine-mediated alertness. The nonsedating antihistamines do not cross the blood-brain barrier. These agents (*e.g.,* terfenadine [Seldane]), available by prescription, have proved effective against allergic rhinitis and may prove to have a role in treating urticaria, eczema, and asthma as well. Owing to their effectiveness and lack of side effects, they have become the largest class of antihistamines prescribed. In 1989 astemizole (Hismanal), a nonsedating antihistamine taken only once a day, was approved for use in the U.S.

Late-phase allergic reactions

Until recently, allergic processes had been thought to be short-lived responses. Thus, immunologists traditionally classified the sudden-onset, IgE-mediated aller-

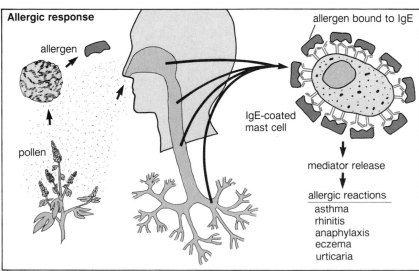

Once a person is sensitized to an allergen, reexposure to the same substance can set off an allergic reaction. On entering the respiratory tract, the allergen binds to IgE-coated mast cells and activates them, causing their release of the chemical mediators of the allergic reaction. The mediators then interact with surrounding tissues to produce the symptoms of asthma, rhinitis, anaphylaxis, eczema, or urticaria.

Source: Michael A. Kaliner, National Institutes of Health

gic processes as immediate hypersensitivity in contrast to the slowly evolving inflammatory reactions (due primarily to the interaction of allergen with lymphocytes rather than with antibodies), which were classified as delayed hypersensitivity. This simplistic concept has been redefined by recent appreciation of the late-phase allergic reaction. It is now known that when a mast cell degranulates, the immediate allergic response that it provokes is only the first stage of a multisequenced reaction. The late-phase reaction consists of infiltration by eosinophils and neutrophils (types of white blood cells) at the site of mast cell degranulation beginning several hours after the immediate allergic reaction and persisting 6–24 hours or more. These cells are attracted to the site by mast-cell-derived mediators including inflammatory factors and other mediators having cell-attracting ability. It is likely that basophils, which are the circulating counterpart to mast cells, also infiltrate, thereby providing additional histamine-containing cells at the site of the allergic response. Late-phase reactions produce swelling, which appears 4–12 hours after the initial allergic event. They occur in asthma and allergic rhinitis, causing persistent airflow obstruction in asthma and further increasing the sensitivity of the airway to asthma-provoking stimuli. This latter effect, called airway hyperreactivity, is thought to play a major role in asthma and has become an important target for therapy, since bronchodilators are effective in treating only the early-phase reaction. Topically applied corticosteroids prevent or reverse the late-phase allergic response and thereby reduce or prevent an increase in airway hyperreactivity.

Effectiveness of allergy immunotherapy

Immunotherapy, also called desensitization or hyposensitization therapy, is one of the oldest treatments for allergic diseases. It involves the progressive administration of extracts containing the allergens to which allergic individuals are sensitive. Thus, by injection of progressively larger quantities of the inciting allergen, the immune response to the allergic substance is changed. Ordinarily, allergic individuals exclusively produce allergen-specific IgE antibodies, which bind to mast cells and thus sensitize the individual toward that antigen. Subjects undergoing allergy immunotherapy, however, produce progressively less IgE antibody and instead make more of another class of antibody, immunoglobulin G (IgG). Whereas reduction in the production of IgE and the increased production of IgG antibodies appear to confer protection to individuals undergoing immunotherapy, the mechanism has yet to be understood.

The most careful studies of the effectiveness of immunotherapy have involved treatment of patients having allergic rhinitis due to such airborne allergens as ragweed, grass, and tree pollen and dust. A second major source of information about immunotherapy has been studies of the treatment of patients subject to a systemic allergic reaction when stung by bees, hornets, and related insects. In both instances at least 85% of patients receiving proper immunotherapy have experienced improvement. Allergic rhinitis patients have had milder symptoms and have required less medication for relief. For patients sensitive to insect stings, stings following treatment have not caused systemic reactions; thus, immunotherapy has been lifesaving. With respect to asthma, there have been few careful trials of immunotherapy, with the exception of desensitization to cat allergen. The identity of cat allergen has proved to be salivary proteins, which have been isolated and are available for immunotherapy. Of cat-allergic patients treated with high-dose immunotherapy, 85–90% have shown a reduction in asthmatic symptoms and in underlying airway hyperreactivity. It should be noted that immunotherapy for diseases other than those mentioned either has not been evaluated or has not been proved safe or effective.

Current treatment of allergies

Medical science is experiencing a wave of enthusiasm both for new studies of the underlying causes of allergic diseases and for their application to improving therapy. Thus far the results have contributed significantly to an understanding and to treatment of all the allergic diseases, especially allergic rhinitis and asthma. The major beneficiary of this research has been the allergy victim; the afflictions of more than 95% of allergic rhinitis sufferers can be adequately and quickly controlled, while those of nearly all asthmatics can be managed by combinations of therapy.

In the treatment of either allergic rhinitis or asthma, the same principles apply; the patient deals with the disease specifically by avoiding the allergen source, by receiving allergy immunotherapy, and by taking medication that interferes with basic processes of the disease. Drugs include cromoglycate (cromolyn sodium), which inhibits mast cell degranulation, and corticosteroids, which reverse many of the processes initiated by mast cells and also reduce mast cell numbers. One major new insight in therapy has been the appreciation that topical corticosteroids act, in part, by dramatically reducing mast cell population in the mucous membranes. Symptomatic approaches to the treatment of allergic disease are also employed. For allergic rhinitis symptomatic therapy generally consists of nonsedating antihistamines and possibly decongestants. For asthma there are bronchodilators, which relax smooth muscle, reduce airway swelling, and reduce secretion of mucus. The combination of symptomatic therapy and specific treatment approaches available today represents a dramatic improvement in the ability of medicine to help people with allergies to remain functioning and comfortable.

—*Michael Aron Kaliner, M.D.*

Not Guilty by Reason of Insanity

by Linda E. Weinberger, Ph.D., and H. Richard Lamb, M.D.

The insanity defense represents one of the most controversial areas within the criminal justice system. It arouses a great deal of criticism from the general public as well as the legal and medical communities, particularly when the media report cases of people who committed heinous crimes but were not held criminally responsible. This not only may infuriate the general public but may also confuse its perception of the criminal justice system. People may believe that the insanity defense is a widely used ploy to get "guilty people off." In actuality, the insanity defense is infrequently used by defendants, and it is perceived by many defense attorneys as the "defense of last resort." For one thing, it is difficult to establish; moreover, some attorneys believe the defendant will undergo more restrictions and negative consequences if found insane than if found guilty and sentenced.

The insanity defense is based on the fundamental assumption in Anglo-American law that humans possess both a rational mind and free will. It is assumed that an individual is the "average reasonable" person and, thus, that if an individual commits an illegal act, he or she did so knowingly and voluntarily. Therefore, the individual should be held criminally responsible and punished. This satisfies the moral sense of the community and serves the objectives of criminal sanctions; *i.e.,* rehabilitation, deterrence, and retribution.

A civilized society also recognizes that there are certain people for whom blame and punishment would be unconscionable. Such individuals would include children and persons who were functioning under a kind and degree of mental disorder that rendered them incapable of criminal intent, or mens rea (Latin: "guilty mind"). Mens rea is a necessary element for criminal liability; as such, the defendant's state of mind at the time of the offense must be considered to determine if it is one for which culpability or exculpation is just.

Insanity defense: historical perspective

The concept that certain mental conditions should relieve an insane person from criminal responsibility has ancient origins; however, a specific legal standard or rule for insanity did not exist until the mid-19th century.

By the time of Henry III of England (1207–72), defendants who committed a crime while "mad" were frequently granted a pardon by the king. Henry de Bracton, a medieval jurist, defined a madman as one who "does not know what he is doing, who lacks in mind and reason and is not far removed from the brutes." Juries would consider this description when deciding whether to acquit defendants as insane. By the 16th century the concepts of "good" and "evil" had been introduced into the law; people who could not distinguish between the two were found insane. In 1724 Judge Robert Tracy elaborated on Bracton's definition and pointed out that not all madmen should be considered insane—only those who are "totally deprived of understanding and memory, and doth not know what he is doing, no more than an infant, than a brute, or a wild beast." In 1800 the case of Hadfield accepted delusions as the basis for an insanity acquittal. James Hadfield, an old soldier, attempted to assassinate King George III because of a delusion that his destiny was to attain a martyr's death.

It was not until the case of Daniel M'Naghten in 1843 that a standard test for insanity was accepted and applied. M'Naghten was a Scottish woodturner who suffered from persecutory delusions. He intended to assassinate the prime minister of England, Sir Robert Peel, because he believed Peel was his major persecutor. Instead, M'Naghten killed Edward Drummond, the prime minister's secretary, whom he mistook for Peel. Medical testimony was introduced at the trial that determined M'Naghten was not of a sensible mind at the time of the act. The jury acquitted him by reason of insanity; however, Queen Victoria and the public at large expressed outrage because it appeared to them that M'Naghten had been conscious and aware of what he did. Fifteen common-law judges then were asked to address the matter, specifying under what circumstances an insanity defense should apply. What emerged from this assembly was a test for insanity that was to be known as the M'Naghten rule; the rule holds that for a person to be not guilty by reason of insanity, it must be proved that the defendant was "labouring under such a defect of reason, from disease of mind, as not to know the nature and quality of the act he was doing; or if he did know it, that he did not know he was doing what was wrong."

The M'Naghten formula was adopted in both Great Britain and the U.S. Some legal theorists and judges, however, were reluctant to restrict a defense of insanity to cognitive disabilities only, thereby ignoring deficiencies in self-control. Consequently, some courts in Britain as well as state and federal courts in the U.S. found people insane if they met either the M'Naghten rule or a standard known as "irresistible impulse." There were various interpretations of what constituted the irresistible-impulse test across jurisdictions, but generally defendants were acquitted as insane if they committed the offense because they could not control their conduct as a result of a mental disease.

Until 1954 the M'Naghten rule, used alone or in conjunction with a form of the irresistible-impulse test, was the insanity standard for every jurisdiction in the U.S. except New Hampshire. New Hampshire adopted a different rule in 1870, in which the question of insanity was addressed according to "whether the accused was suffering from a mental disease or defect and whether the criminal act was the result of the disease or defect."

Recent developments

During the almost 100 years since the M'Naghten formulation, the specialty of psychiatry has expanded and has had a significant impact both on the way society views mental disease and on how mental illness affects a person's thinking and behavior. An outgrowth of this development was the Durham rule, or "product test," which was a reformulation of the New Hampshire rule and was introduced by Judge David L. Bazelon in the case of *Durham* v. *United States* (1954): "simply that an accused is not criminally responsible if his unlawful act was the product of mental disease or mental defect." The Durham rule was intentionally designed as a broad standard that would encourage the admission of psychiatric evidence to explain how the defendant's mental disease or defect caused this person to commit the criminal act. The Durham rule, which was used as the standard for insanity in only a handful of jurisdictions, was greatly criticized for its vagueness as well as the latitude and dominance given to psychiatrists interpreting the rule. It was eventually rejected by Judge Bazelon in 1972.

As the Durham rule was undergoing mounting criticism, the American Law Institute (ALI) drafted an insanity defense in its Model Penal Code of 1962. This stated that an individual would be acquitted by reason of insanity if "as a result of mental disease or defect he lacks substantial capacity either to appreciate the criminality [wrongfulness] of his conduct or to conform his conduct to the requirements of the law." This new standard, known as the ALI rule, was a more liberal combination of the previously established M'Naghten and irresistible-impulse tests. The ALI rule requires only substantial, instead of total, incapacity for a finding of insanity. In addition, ALI uses the term appreciate, which requires more complex mental functioning than "knowing" or "understanding," which were sufficient for a judgment of sanity under M'Naghten. Also, the ALI rule specifically excluded individuals known as psychopaths, stating: "The terms 'mental disease or defect' do not include an abnormality manifested only by repeated criminal or otherwise anti-social conduct." The ALI rule gained considerable support and

In 1843 Daniel M'Naghten attempted to kill the prime minister of England but killed his secretary instead. The public was outraged when M'Naghten was acquitted as insane, as it appeared that he had been aware of his act.

was eventually adopted verbatim or in a modified form in about half the U.S. states and in all federal jurisdictions. In focusing on the volitional as well as the cognitive aspects of incapacity, this test has much in common with the European codes. The Italian penal code, for example, relieves a person of responsibility when he or she "is deprived of the capacity of understanding or volition."

It should be noted that in some states there are defenses in addition to insanity that are available to mentally disordered defendants, but these are not "complete" defenses; i.e., total exoneration from criminal responsibility. These defenses are usually considered when the defendant's mental condition at the time of the offense was not severe enough to meet the standard for insanity. Some defenses may provide for mitigation of penalty ("diminished responsibility"), or they may provide for treatment, if necessary, *after* sentencing ("guilty but mentally ill").

The role of the expert witness

In the U.S., state and federal jurisdictions are free to choose their standard for insanity. Generally, a defendant is presumed sane unless he or she admits having committed the offense and presents evidence that he or she was insane at the time. The defendant must undergo an evaluation by a psychiatrist or psychologist (some states also allow physicians who are not psychiatrists), who then offers an expert opinion about the defendant's mental condition and its relation to legal insanity.

The term legal insanity is not specifically defined, nor does it appear in the American Psychiatric Association's official publication, the *Diagnostic and Statistical Manual of Mental Disorders*. "Legal insanity" merely refers to a mental disease or defect resulting in incapacities such that the accused is relieved from criminal responsibility. The law is intentionally nonspecific so that those who are most knowledgeable and experienced about psychiatric matters may have the freedom to present relevant information to the judge or jury. Unfortunately, what often occurs is that an expert applies his or her own meaning to the terms without accompanying explanations. This creates disagreement among the experts and confusion for the judge or jury. For example, some experts believe that if a defendant was mentally ill during the offense—particularly if the illness was severe, such as a psychosis—that alone is sufficient for offering an opinion that the defendant was legally insane. Such an expert may fail to explain how the mental illness produced impairments in the mental and emotional processes or behavioral functions mentioned in the relevant insanity standard (*e.g.*, the person knows the nature and quality of the act, appreciates its criminality, and can conform his or her conduct to the requirements of the law).

The expert's chief contribution is in describing the defendant's mental disease or defect and how it related to the accused's criminal behavior. Although a retrospective analysis has many drawbacks, these may be lessened if the expert relies not only on the defendant's self-reports but also on the reports of others and if the defendant's past history as well as current test findings are considered. The expert should explain in jargon-free language the defendant's mental condition; that is, how it originated, developed, and influenced the defendant's mental, emotional, and behavioral functioning such that the defendant committed the offense. The following is a hypothetical case of what an expert might consider and present to a judge or jury for a defendant pleading insanity.

The expert explains that the defendant has a long-standing documented history of mental illness, which has been getting progressively worse, and he has been psychiatrically hospitalized on numerous occasions. His illness includes hearing voices of people who are not actually present, including God, which often command him to perform certain acts. When he speaks, he usually rambles, shifts quickly from one topic to another, and is typically vague and concrete in his speech so that little meaningful information is conveyed. One form of treatment he receives when hospitalized is antipsychotic medication that controls his hallucinations and assists him in communicating more effectively.

When he robbed the bank, the defendant was living in a low-rent hotel and not taking his medications. Witnesses in the bank stated the defendant was talking to himself, would frequently look upward, and was dressed in a disheveled manner. They said he did not seem nervous but did appear bizarre. The defendant presented a note to the teller requesting that she give him $268.73, which was written on the back of an envelope addressed to him. The defendant told the expert during the clinical interview that God had deposited this amount of money in the bank in an account to help the poor and that God told him to retrieve it and wait for further instructions. After the teller gave him the money, he sat down on the floor and waited to hear from God but did not receive any instructions because the devil's agents (security guard and police) intervened and removed him from the bank. He explained that these were agents from the devil because they were dressed in dark clothes and wore shiny symbols (badges) that could hypnotize people.

The expert explains to the judge or jury that the defendant was suffering from a serious mental disorder (schizophrenia), which rendered him so impaired that he could not distinguish right from wrong at the time of the offense. The voices he heard and his false beliefs, based on his mental illness, led him to commit the criminal offense and think that he was not doing anything illegal. He was unable to recognize that he was mentally ill and experiencing psychotic symptoms. He believed the money he requested was God's and that God commanded him to act on His behalf. The defendant said that he had no intention of keeping the money for himself but would use it as God instructed to perform a good deed by helping the poor.

Further material the expert offers in support of the defendant's psychotic condition rendering him insane is that the defendant was not afraid and made no effort to escape, conceal his identity, or act in any way that would connote he knew he was committing a wrongful act. His misperception that his good deed was thwarted because of the "devil's agents" further highlights his disturbed thinking.

Many medical and psychological experts are reluctant to offer conclusions regarding the defendant's sanity because they view this as a moral question and not a medical one. These experts, however, are not the ones who decide if the defendant was insane. Their function is to assist those who do make the decision (the judge or jury) to better understand the defendant and his or her criminal conduct. Studies have found that when an expert critically examines a defendant's sanity and offers well-reasoned opinions, the courts tend to agree with the expert.

Some realities of the insanity defense

No extensive nationwide studies on the insanity defense have been conducted in the U.S.; however, the limited research carried out by individual states has produced similar findings. Generally, it has been found that the insanity defense is raised in fewer than 1% of all felony cases. For those defendants who enter an insanity plea, the success rate has ranged from 25 to less than 1%. In recent years the number of defendants raising insanity defenses and being found insane has increased, but it still remains exceptionally small.

Many people believe that the insanity defense is pleaded almost exclusively in murder cases in an attempt by the defendant to avoid capital punishment. While most studies have found that the largest percentage of those found insane were charged with murder or attempted murder (20 to 50%), defendants plead insanity to a wide variety of other crimes as well. Usually there are more felony cases than misdemeanors in which defendants are found insane, and crimes against persons are more prevalent in judgments of insanity than crimes against property. Recently, however, the seriousness of crimes for which defendants have been acquitted by reason of insanity has decreased; there is a lower percentage of homicides, and the percentage of nonviolent crimes has increased.

With respect to the characteristics of insanity acquittees, the majority of them are diagnosed as psychotic and have had a history of previous psychiatric hospitalizations. Prior arrests are also frequently found. The acquittees are usually in their late twenties to late thirties and thus older than the average criminal defendant. Most of them have less than 12 years of formal education and are generally unskilled or semiskilled. There are more men than women who are found insane, but of those, the proportion of women charged with murder is higher than that for men.

The insanity defense is not viewed as favorably by defendants and their attorneys as the public might believe. When an insanity plea is entered, the defendant acknowledges that he or she committed the offense because of an impairing mental disease. Many people, including those who are mentally ill, are reluctant to accept mental illness because they do not understand it or they fear the social, economic, or legal consequences of the label. In addition, the mentally ill defendant is often reluctant to have his or her illegal conduct viewed as causally related to mental impairments; they may perceive the conduct as rational or as an expression of religious or sociopolitical beliefs. Finally, an individual who is found insane may be committed to a mental hospital for treatment for a period that exceeds the length of time he or she would have served in a jail or prison if found guilty and sentenced.

Commitment and discharge of insanity acquittees

For most of U.S. history, insanity acquittees were automatically institutionalized for indeterminate periods and given few due-process considerations. It was not uncommon for insanity acquittees to spend the rest of their lives hospitalized or remain in hospitals for a period exceeding the criminal sentence that would have been imposed had they been found guilty. This was particularly true for less serious offenses, which may account for the high proportion of serious crimes among insanity acquittees; persons who had committed less serious crimes (or their defense attorneys) may have been less inclined to use the insanity defense.

During the 1960s and '70s, this lack of attention to due process changed after a number of legal challenges for the rights of mental patients were mounted. Treatment interventions were then substantially improved, and standards of mental illness and dangerousness were formulated to determine when an acquittee should be committed and when discharged. Some states set maximum terms, based on the crime, for which insanity acquittees could be committed and implemented conditions for outpatient treatment.

Currently only a few states have mandatory commitment laws that require all insanity acquittees to be committed to a hospital. The majority of states provide for a hearing shortly after the individual is found not guilty by reason of insanity to determine if the individual should be committed to a mental hospital or released. In these commitment hearings, almost every state and all federal jurisdictions consider the acquittee's dangerousness (*e.g.,* to self, to others, and to property). If the acquittee is committed, various designated people may initiate the acquittee's discharge hearing, including the acquittee. All federal jurisdictions and most states require a court hearing to determine if the acquittee should be discharged when he or she has been "restored to sanity" (*i.e.,* no longer deemed in need of treatment and no longer dangerous).

Committed acquittees commonly are treated with psychiatric medications, participate in group and individual treatment, and receive vocational counseling and rehabilitation and various kinds of education. A few states provide for a maximum term of commitment that is equal to the maximum sentence the individual would have served in a jail or a prison for the crime. Some states have maximum terms but also use extensions that are usually based on civil (as opposed to criminal) commitment criteria. During the extended period, the acquittee may be granted more rights and privileges as well as more frequent evaluations and reviews than previously given.

Some states commit insanity acquittees for indeterminate periods. This practice was upheld by the U.S. Supreme Court in *Jones* v. *U.S.* (1983). Michael Jones was arrested in Washington, D.C., in 1975 on a misdemeanor charge for attempting to steal a jacket from a department store. He was committed to Washington's public mental hospital, St. Elizabeth's, for an evaluation of his competency to stand trial (*i.e.,* to determine his understanding of the nature and purpose of the criminal proceedings taken against him as well as his ability to cooperate rationally with his counsel in presenting a defense). About six months later, a hospital psychologist reported that Jones was competent to stand trial as described above. The psychologist also reported that he suffered from a major mental illness, paranoid schizophrenia, and that his alleged offense was "the product of his mental disease."

The court declared him competent to stand trial, and the criminal proceedings resumed. He pleaded not guilty by reason of insanity. The court then found him not guilty by reason of insanity and again committed him to St. Elizabeth's Hospital. Fifty days later a release hearing required by statute was held. On behalf of the prosecution, evidence was presented by a hospital psychologist that Jones was still suffering from paranoid schizophrenia and that "because his illness is still quite active, he is still a danger to himself and to others." Jones's attorney conducted a brief cross-examination and presented no evidence on Jones's behalf. The court accepted the testimony and returned Jones to the hospital. He was hospitalized for more than a year before a second release hearing was conducted. Jones asserted that he had been hospitalized beyond the maximum period he would have been detained had he been found guilty (one year) and therefore demanded to be released unconditionally or recommitted under civil commitment standards. He was denied these requests and appealed his case first to the District of Columbia Court of Appeals and then to the U.S. Supreme Court.

In upholding his indefinite commitment, the U.S. Supreme Court explained that the insanity acquittee is detained not for purposes of punishment as warranted for the criminally responsible person but for treatment considerations. Imposing detention and treatment on insanity acquittees is based on treating their mental illness in addition to protecting them and society from future dangerous behavior. The court saw "no necessary correlation between the length of the acquittee's hypothetical criminal sentence and the length of time necessary for his recovery."

Studies have found fairly consistently that the acquittee's period of hospitalization is usually related to the seriousness of the crime. It is unclear if this is at least in part a function of the severity of the ac-

The insanity defense has long been the subject of controversy. The widely held belief that in actuality it is a cunning ploy used to get "guilty people off" is the subject of a cartoon from the 19th century.

The Bettmann Archive

quittee's mental illness or is primarily the hesitancy to discharge serious offenders.

In the majority of states and in all federal jurisdictions, an acquittee may be treated in both inpatient and outpatient settings. Typically, an acquittee is "conditionally discharged" by the court to an outpatient program after a period of hospitalization if the acquittee's mental condition is such that under prescribed care he or she would not be a danger to the community or self. If acquittees do not continue to meet and adhere to the outlined conditions, their outpatient status is revoked and they are returned to the hospital. Rearrest usually leads to revocation. Studies have found rearrest rates ranging from 13 to 31%, with a wide variety of offenses. The following is an example of the successful outpatient treatment of an acquittee who was conditionally discharged.

A 29-year-old single woman was found not guilty by reason of insanity of a charge of assault with a deadly weapon. The patient, who had been living on the streets, had knocked an elderly woman to the ground and attempted to take her purse. At the time of the offense, she was delusional and hallucinating and exhibited a marked thought disorder. She had experienced at least seven state hospitalizations since she was 20 years old and had been consistently noncompliant with medications and with any other kind of outpatient treatment. She had one prior arrest and conviction for grand theft of an automobile. After 20 months of forensic hospitalization for her criminal acts, the patient began court-mandated outpatient treatment. The emphasis was on monitoring her medications, having her live in a supervised setting (a board-and-care home), and having her keep appointments and work in a sheltered workshop. Her sister was named as payee and money manager for her Supplemental Security Income checks, which was extremely helpful in dealing with the patient's problems of many years' standing in managing money. The patient's medication was dispensed to her at the board-and-care home. The outpatient treatment staff viewed their major role as adding structure to the patient's life. She continued to exhibit signs of thought disorder, confusion, and lack of spontaneity and responsiveness, but after receiving four and a half years of mandatory outpatient treatment, she was still stabilized and able to live in the community.

Despite the various hospital and outpatient treatment programs developed for insanity acquittees, follow-up studies have found that up to 41% will require subsequent hospitalizations under civil commitment statutes. In addition, most studies report that the recidivism rates of insanity acquittees, generally ranging from 15 to 37%, are similar to matched convicted groups. Frequently, the acquittee's subsequent arrests are for less serious offenses, but many include assault, burglary, larceny, and robbery.

Controversy resurfaces

In recent years the insanity defense has again been the subject of much controversy. Rearrests of insanity acquittees and such highly publicized cases as John Hinckley's insanity acquittal for the attempted assassination of U.S. Pres. Ronald Reagan in 1981 have encouraged both lay and professional people to call for the abolition or revision of the insanity defense. New laws were enacted in which the tests for insanity returned to more narrow standards, such as those of M'Naghten or its variations. Presently, all U.S. federal jurisdictions use a modified M'Naghten standard, while the states are almost evenly divided between forms of M'Naghten and the ALI rule. Several states use the irresistible-impulse test in conjunction with forms of M'Naghten. In addition, 14 states have adopted "guilty but mentally ill" statutes (making treatment available *after* sentencing) in an attempt to decrease insanity acquittals. However, research in Michigan, which had a guilty-but-mentally-ill statute even before the Hinckley acquittal, has found that the number of defendants acquitted by reason of insanity did not change after the guilty-but-mentally-ill verdict became available.

Despite the considerable criticism that the insanity defense has recently experienced, all states have recognized the importance of psychiatric evidence in criminal proceedings. The landmark case *Ake* v. *Oklahoma* (1985) illustrates this. In 1979 Glen Ake, an indigent, was charged with murdering a couple and wounding their two children. On arraignment his behavior was so bizarre that the court ordered him to be examined by a psychiatrist. The psychiatrist diagnosed Ake as a probable paranoid schizophrenic, and upon the psychiatrist's recommendation, the court committed Ake to the state mental hospital to evaluate his competency to stand trial. Less than six months after his indictment, the hospital's chief forensic psychiatrist informed the court that Ake was not competent to stand trial. At a hearing the court ruled that Ake was a "mentally ill person in need of care and treatment" and declared him incompetent to stand trial.

Ake's treatment at the hospital included antipsychotic medication, which stabilized his condition. Approximately six weeks later, he was returned to the court as competent, and the criminal proceedings resumed. While Ake was hospitalized, no inquiry had been made about his mental condition at the time of the offense. Ake's attorney entered a plea of not guilty by reason of insanity, and because Ake was indigent, his counsel requested that the court appoint a psychiatrist to conduct such an inquiry or provide funds for the defense to arrange for one. The court rejected the request.

Ake's sole defense was insanity, and although experts who had seen him at the hospital testified, none had examined him for sanity with regard to the alleged offense. Therefore, no expert testimony was offered by either the defense or the prosecution about whether Ake was insane. The jury returned a guilty verdict on all counts. At the sentencing phase, the prosecution relied on the previously presented testimony of the state hospital psychiatrists that Ake was dangerous. The

jury sentenced him to death for each of the murders and to 1,000 years in prison for shooting with intent to kill. Ake appealed the sentence on the grounds that as an indigent he should have been given the services of a court-appointed psychiatrist. The Oklahoma Court of Criminal Appeals rejected his argument.

He further appealed his case to the U.S. Supreme Court, which reversed the conviction and sent the case back for a new trial. In its highly important decision, the Supreme Court held that "when a defendant has made a preliminary showing that his sanity at the time of the offense is likely to be a significant factor at trial, the Constitution requires that a State provide access to a psychiatrist's assistance on this issue, if the defendant cannot otherwise afford one." Further, the court stated that through their "process of investigation, interpretation and testimony, psychiatrists ideally assist lay jurors, who generally have no training in psychiatric matters, to make a sensible and educated determination about the mental condition of the defendant at the time of the offense."

Addressing the public's concerns

The public's concern about insanity acquittees' risk for future dangerousness can best be addressed if better supervision and treatment interventions are provided. It is essential, therefore, that treatment staff be experienced and vigilant in working with mentally disordered offenders. In addition, the transition of an insanity acquittee from hospital to community is always better achieved if outpatient care and monitoring are available and if staff are not reluctant to report a patient's noncompliance with treatment. At present there are a few model programs (in Oregon and Maryland) that other states may consider adopting.

The Oregon program has been described as preserving "the medical, moral, and legal values of the insanity defense, while simultaneously honoring the growing contemporary consensus that security measures should be substantially improved for insanity acquittees." Oregon has established a Psychiatric Security Review Board whose primary goal, as directed by statute, is the protection of society. Thus, prompt revocation of a patient's release into the community when indicated is emphasized. Moreover, the review board has jurisdiction over the patient for a period as long as the term of the maximum sentence he or she would have served if found guilty. The Oregon system also stresses continuing treatment of released patients as well as the use of supportive services.

Sensationalizing successful acquittals only contributes to misconceptions and lack of confidence in the criminal justice system. The media have been notably "guilty" of such treatment. The defense of insanity was founded on humanitarian principles. These principles should not be abandoned.

Awards and Prizes

Hundreds of honors and prizes are bestowed each year by organizations and private individuals for high achievement in medicine. Some acknowledge fundamental discoveries that have added to an understanding of the human body and disease processes, while others recognize clinical advances, new technologies, improved drugs and vaccines, and other accomplishments of more immediate benefit to health. The sampling below of major awards given in 1988 highlights but a few of the successes in both basic and applied medical science.

Nobel Prize

The 1988 Nobel Prize for Physiology or Medicine recognized three researchers in the commercial pharmaceutical industry who pioneered rational approaches to drug design. Two of the winners, Gertrude Elion and George Hitchings, worked together for more than 40 years at the Burroughs Wellcome Research Laboratories in New York and North Carolina to develop custom-designed pharmaceuticals that preferentially attack abnormal cells and disease-causing microorganisms in the body. Their approach, which exploited differences in the biochemistry of normal human cells and that of cancer cells, viruses, bacteria, and parasites, gave modern medicine an arsenal of agents against some of humankind's most common afflictions, including leukemia, gout, malaria, and immune disorders. The third winner, Sir James Black, based much of his work on the mechanisms by which natural substances circulating in the bloodstream trigger particular physiological responses in the heart, stomach, and other body tissues. His prizewinning research, be-

ginning in the 1950s at the British firm Imperial Chemical Industries and continuing at a British laboratory of SmithKline Beckman, resulted in the drugs propranolol, used to combat angina pectoris, high blood pressure, and migraine and to aid heart attack recovery, and cimetidine, the first nonsurgical alternative for treating stomach ulcers.

Albert Lasker Awards

Two molecular biologists shared the 1988 Albert Lasker Basic Medical Research Award: Phillip A. Sharp of the Massachusetts Institute of Technology and Thomas R. Cech of the University of Colorado. Sharp discovered that the genetic messages carried in strands of the cell's DNA are interrupted by apparently meaningless stretches called introns, which are spliced out once the genes have been copied into RNA and before they are translated into protein molecules. His work is crucial to understanding gene regulation, a fundamental process in embryonic development, growth, healing, aging, cancer causation, and such viral diseases as AIDS. Cech showed that RNA can act as an enzyme, or natural catalyst, a discovery that may reveal how certain disease-causing agents upset normal cellular processes.

Vincent P. Dole of Rockefeller University, New York City, received the Albert Lasker Clinical Medical Research Award for demonstrating that narcotic addiction is a medically treatable physiological problem and that the withdrawal symptoms of heroin addiction can be controlled with regular doses of methadone. The Albert Lasker Public Service Award went to U.S. Sen. Lowell Weicker, Jr. (Rep., Conn.), for his longtime advocacy of increases in federal funding for biomedical research and public health programs.

Three academic researchers and a U.S. legislator received Albert Lasker medical awards in 1988: Vincent P. Dole (left) for clinical research, Thomas R. Cech (second from right) and Phillip A. Sharp (right) for basic research, and Sen. Lowell Weicker, Jr. (second from left), for public service.

Albert and Mary Lasker Foundation

General Motors cancer research prizes

Four investigators who contributed significantly to the understanding, diagnosis, and prevention of cancer received General Motors Cancer Research Foundation prizes. Sam Shapiro of the Johns Hopkins University, Baltimore, Md., and Philip Strax of the University of Miami, Fla., split the Charles F. Kettering Prize for work that established the importance of mammography in the early detection of breast cancer. Alfred G. Knudson, Jr., of the Fox Chase Cancer Center, Philadelphia, took the Charles S. Mott Prize for his theory of the way gene damage can lead to both rare hereditary childhood tumors and more common adult forms of cancer. Yasutomi Nishizuka of Kobe (Japan) University was given the Alfred P. Sloan, Jr., Prize for his discovery of a cellular protein, protein kinase C, that exerts a powerful effect on cell behavior and, in turn, is sensitive to environmental substances known to promote cancer.

—*Charles M. Cegielski*

Birth Control

In recent years a number of contraceptive-related developments have occurred that are likely to have bearing on the birth-control practices of women and men for many years to come. Older contraceptive methods have undergone considerable change and, in certain instances, new concerns have been raised regarding their safety. Additional techniques have become available, and others are still undergoing evaluation.

Update on oral and other hormonal contraceptives

More than 63 million women around the world and at least 13 million women in the United States alone rely on oral contraceptives (OCs) for prevention of pregnancy. As more and more laboratory and clinical data have been gathered and analyzed on the low-dose combination and multiphasic oral contraceptives, it is becoming increasingly clear that they are very safe for the vast majority of women.

Taking the Pill until menopause. It is now being recommended that women who have reached what has been considered the cut-off age for taking the Pill—40—who do not smoke, and who have no risk factors for cardiovascular disease be allowed to continue to take OCs for five or possibly ten more years. In fact, there is growing speculation that since the newer low-dose products have few to no adverse metabolic effects, their use could be continued until menopause—usually occurring around age 50. Women could then begin hormone replacement therapy (HRT). (For the majority of postmenopausal women, HRT's benefits far exceed any potential dangers.) Moreover, given the proven health benefits of OC use, particularly the reduction in the risk of ovarian and endometrial cancers, benign breast disease, ectopic pregnancy, and even

osteoporosis, the typical lapse of up to ten or more years between taking oral contraceptives for birth control and HRT to offset the side effects of menopause—as well as to prevent bone thinning and reduce the risk of heart disease—may well be counterproductive.

Breast cancer risk? During the past two years an old concern was again raised of a possible connection between the use of oral contraceptives and the development of breast cancer. Three new studies published in 1988 and several more in 1989 suggest such a relationship. However, many older, larger, and more comprehensive studies—including ones conducted by the World Health Organization, the National Institute of Child Health and Human Development, and the U.S. Centers for Disease Control (CDC)—have failed to demonstrate this risk, even in women considered to be at high risk.

In January 1989 the U.S. Food and Drug Administration (FDA) convened its expert advisory committee to evaluate the potential implications of the newer studies. The committee did not find them of sufficient statistical validity to recommend any changes in the prescribing or labeling of OCs, although additional research in this area was encouraged and will soon be under way. Unfortunately, inflammatory media cover-

Before having her prescription for oral contraceptives filled, a young woman compares Ortho-Novum $^1/_{50}$, costing about $15, with a generic equivalent, Genora $^1/_{50}$, at $9. Both contain one milligram of norethindrone and 0.05 milligram of mestranol.

Courtesy, Cos-Medic Discount Drugs; photograph, Cathy Melloan

age of the alleged breast cancer risk caused considerable alarm for women and their health care providers.

In May 1989 a study conducted in England suggested a link between OC use in women under age 36 and breast cancer. Again, these results were not considered conclusive by either the British Family Planning Association or the National Association of Family Planning Doctors in England. The authors of the study also said the findings needed to be kept in perspective, pointing out that women under 36 are not a high-risk group for developing breast cancer, so even if risk for the disease were increased by OC use, the incidence of actual breast cancers would still be low. In addition, the suggested increased risk was not reflected in epidemiological surveys carried out in England. A further study of women 36 to 45 is being conducted by the same British group to help resolve the vital issue of whether there is in fact an OC-breast cancer link in the higher-risk group.

Generic OCs. Another new development is that a number of companies have been looking at the feasibility of manufacturing and selling generic OCs. The stated objective in this instance has been to lower the price of these agents, the costs of which have risen dramatically in recent years. In September 1988 the first such product, N.E.E. $\frac{1}{35}$, a generic version of Ortho Pharmaceutical Corp.'s Ortho-Novum $\frac{1}{35}$, was marketed in the U.S. by Lexis Pharmaceuticals, Inc. The cost of the generic OC is approximately one-third less than that of the brand name product. Like the brand name products, generic OCs still require a physician's prescription.

Advertisements for N.E.E. $\frac{1}{35}$ have appeared in popular magazines, such as *Glamour,* directed at women readers. Such direct-to-consumer advertising of prescription drugs has both supporters and critics in the medical community. Critics argue that advertising prescription medications to patients emphasizes economic considerations in a sphere where they are not appropriate. The American College of Obstetricians and Gynecologists, however, believes such ads can provide sound information about OCs that many consumers otherwise lack.

The FDA has established minimum standards for all generic drugs, and the generic OCs that have been evaluated to date have been found to be within the accepted ranges of deviation. Nonetheless, it is still too early to be able to assess accurately the ultimate impact of the various generic OCs that have become available on the overall marketing and use of oral contraceptives.

Agents being tested. Several potentially very valuable hormonal contraceptive agents have still not received FDA approval, despite many years of evaluation. Most of these are delivered by non-oral routes of administration—including Depo-Provera, a contraceptive given by injection once every three months (which is already

widely used in more than 80 countries), subdermal implants, and vaginal rings, although one subdermal implant (Norplant) is probably close to being approved. In addition, research continues on variants of these methods, on male contraceptives, and on contraceptive vaccinations, but considerably more time will be required before they become generally available.

Intrauterine devices update

After a lapse of more than two years, copper intrauterine devices (IUDs) are now available once again in the United States. All but one of the earlier IUDs (the Progestasert) had been removed from the marketplace between 1984 and 1986 by their manufacturers. One of the major reasons for their removal was the rapidly escalating costs of litigation involving IUDs. One type of IUD (the Dalkon Shield), a plastic device with a multifilamented tail that allowed wicking of bacteria into the uterine cavity, had been associated with a high incidence of infection. Lawsuits stimulated by the adverse publicity regarding the Dalkon Shield caused product liability insurance for all IUDs that were judged both safe and effective by the FDA to become either entirely unobtainable or prohibitively expensive.

The device that is generally considered the best of the copper IUDs, the Copper T 380A, developed by the Population Council, was not marketed in the U.S. following its approval by the FDA in 1984. In October 1987, however, the council issued a license to GynoPharma Inc. to manufacture and sell the device. This device, known as the ParaGard, is now widely available to American women, many of whom had been going to Canada and Europe in the interim to obtain copper IUDs.

The availability of two types of IUDs has been welcomed by both consumers and health care providers because for certain individuals they represent the contraceptive of choice. The prime candidates are women who have had at least one child, are of middle to older reproductive age, are living in a stable monogamous relationship with an uninfected partner, and are at low risk for sexually transmitted diseases (STD). IUDs are particularly valuable for those who are unwilling or unable to use other forms of birth control but who meet the criteria for IUD insertion. Those who are *not* candidates for IUD use are women with multiple sexual partners or a history of pelvic infections, bleeding disorders, or previous ectopic pregnancies.

Three particular factors have fostered wide use of the ParaGard. First, it has been demonstrated to have a failure rate of less than 1%, similar to that of OCs. Second, it is considered safe, no increased risk of either pelvic inflammatory disease or secondary infertility being found in one study when patients met the proper selection criteria. Finally, several recent studies have shown that in almost all instances, IUDs have their actions in the reproductive processes prior to fertilization, effectively removing the widespread allegations of their being abortifacients (inducing abortion).

The other available IUD—the progesterone-releasing Progestasert—alters the uterine environment, causing a loss of normal cyclical activity of the endometrium, which inhibits sperm survival and implantation. The device, which must be replaced once a year, is rated as being 94% safe as well as 94% effective. With proper patient selection, side effects and complications of both types of available IUDs are rare.

New barrier contraceptives for women and men

Barrier methods of contraception, which became less favored by women and their partners when the non-coitally related oral contraceptives and intrauterine devices became available, are now increasing in popularity again. One old technique has been revived, and new ones are now being studied. There are two major reasons for these changes in attitudes and behavior. First, there are numerous fears, some of which are often greatly exaggerated, about the actual and potential side effects of oral contraceptives and intrauterine devices. Second, there are very real concerns about the rapid spread of a number of serious and even fatal sexually transmitted diseases, which barrier methods can help prevent.

Cervical cap. Cervical caps and diaphragms were the major forms of birth control used by women prior to the development of the Pill and IUDs. However, their use declined rapidly and, in fact, for many years caps were no longer made in the U.S. In February 1988 data on the Prentif Cavity-Rim Cervical Cap were presented to the FDA's expert device panel. The panel recommended its approval. This cap was originally made by the British manufacturer Lamberts (Dalston) Ltd. and is now being marketed in the United States and Canada by Cervical Cap (CxC), Ltd., of California.

The Prentif cap is made of natural rubber and fits over the cervix like a thimble. With the addition of a spermicide, the cap provides a chemical as well as a physical barrier. The cap must be inserted before intercourse and remain in place for eight hours afterward; it is reportedly easier as well as less cumbersome to use than a diaphragm. Overall effectiveness is about equal to that of a diaphragm—82–84%.

At the time of the manufacturer's presentation to the FDA, it was noted that a certain number of women had developed abnormal Papanicolaou (Pap) smears early in the use of the cap. For this reason the FDA required additional data on Pap smears after three months of use. It is still unclear at the present time whether there is any clinical significance to this particular observation.

Variations on condoms. One of the barrier methods of contraception currently being evaluated is the "female condom," a 15-cm (6-in) tubular plastic device with a rim at the closed end that fits into the upper vagina and with one at the outer open end that partially covers the perineum, the area below the vagina and above the anus. The device was originally developed in Europe; in 1989 it was marketed in Great Britain, where it is called the Femshield and is sold in individual prelubricated packages, similar to male condoms.

The major advantage of this product is that it gives maximum protection to both the male and the female by interposing a large surface area between the ejaculate and the vaginal secretions as well as any infections on the genitals of either partner. Acceptability studies have shown that men like this device since they do not need to have an erection prior to using it, as with the traditional male-employed condom. Studies are now being carried out in order to establish the female condom's rates of protection against pregnancy and sexually transmitted diseases.

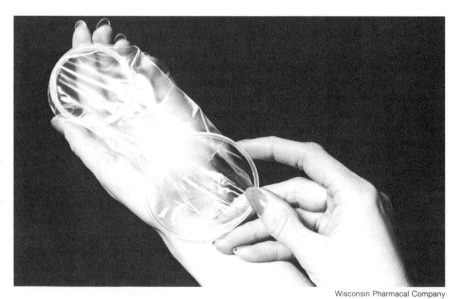

A revival of interest in barrier contraceptives has led to the development of several new products. The "female condom" consists of a polyurethane sheath that has a plastic ring at the closed end, which fits into the woman's upper vagina and holds the device in place, and a thinner ring at the outer, open end, which rests just outside the vaginal opening. Of 28 volunteers in London who used the female condom in a premarketing trial, six out of ten men and eight out of ten women said they preferred it to the male variety.

Several not-yet-available adaptations of the traditional condom are currently receiving considerable media attention, including devices called the "minicondom," or "microcondom," and the "bikini condom." The FDA's definition of a condom has two parts. One, it is a sheath that covers the entire shaft of the penis and, two, it protects against both pregnancy and STD. The minicondom, used by the male partner, covers only the glans of the penis; the "bikini condom" has a rim that is placed in the upper vagina and is attached to a pouch of plastic that is inserted up into the vagina, covering the vaginal walls.

When reviewing these products in March 1989, the FDA's expert device panel recommended that they not be called condoms because neither of them meets the definition and use of this term would be confusing to consumers. The terms glans cap and female vaginal pouch were suggested as possible alternatives. The panel also stated that the data presented to it on these devices regarding the prevention of pregnancy and STD were inadequate. It recommended that additional studies be undertaken before the devices are reevaluated for FDA approval.

Spermicides and STD. In laboratories in the past few years, it has been shown repeatedly that the most commonly used spermicide—nonoxynol-9—will destroy almost all of the major STD organisms. Studies currently under way are attempting to see if the same effect of this barrier method of contraception can be demonstrated in humans. To date, one article has been published documenting that the spermicide-containing contraceptive vaginal sponge reduces the risk of acquiring gonorrheal and chlamydial infections, although there appears to be a concomitant increase in susceptibility to candidiasis infections. Additional data will be forthcoming over the next few years as other studies are concluded and their data analyzed.

—*Elizabeth B. Connell, M.D.*

Cancer

Americans would die from cancer at a rate of almost one a minute in 1989, according to statistics compiled by the American Cancer Society (ACS). Deaths for the year, the ACS estimated, would total 502,000, up from 494,000 in 1988 and 483,000 in 1987. Cancer was expected to account for one of every five deaths from all causes in the United States in 1989.

Comparisons with death rates in the rest of the world are difficult to obtain. The 1988 *World Health Statistics Annual* published age-adjusted death rates for the latest years available. In 1986 the U.S. had 163 deaths per 100,000 males and 109 per 100,000 females. The highest death rates for females occurred in Denmark (138 per 100,000), Scotland (135), and Hungary (130). For males the highest rates occurred in Luxembourg (228), Hungary (235), and Belgium (205).

According to the ACS, about 1,010,000 new cases of cancer would be diagnosed in the U.S. in 1989. An estimated 405,000 of these people will still be alive in 1994 owing to advances in treatment methods and knowledge about the underlying causes of the diseases.

Radiation treatments

Radiation, surgery, and drugs serve as the army, navy, and marines in the war against cancer. Beams of radiation smash the genetic machinery of malignant cells, stopping or slowing uncontrolled growth. X-rays and the more energetic gamma rays burn out tumors as well as relieve pain and stop bleeding. However, such irradiation destroys healthy tissue on its route to the tumor. To limit destruction, physicians often reduce the radiation dose, but this tactic sometimes fails to kill all the diseased cells.

To solve the problem, physicians have been experimenting for about 15 years with beams of protons, which can deliver a higher dose of radiation to tumors than to surrounding healthy tissue. Protons and neutrons are invisibly small particles that make up the nuclei of atoms. Neutrons are used to disrupt cancer cells, but not all physicians agree that these expensive subatomic bullets offer better treatment than do the less costly X-rays. Protons, however, can be focused sharply enough to destroy a tumor with minimal damage to surrounding healthy tissue.

Physicians now use imaging devices that allow them to locate a tumor precisely in three dimensions. Proton beams then can be aimed like an automatic rifle at a bull's-eye on a target. The beam speeds to the tumor with an energy low enough not to damage noncancerous tissue. When the protons hit the target, they slow down and release more energy, eradicating the tumor.

Protons cannot be generated as easily as X-rays. Complex, high-energy machines are required for smashing atoms and releasing these particles. Patients with deep tumors of the type best attacked by this treatment must travel to research centers where atom smashers are located. For many of the 6,000 patients who have done this, the trip was worthwhile. At a Harvard University facility, for example, physicians have been successful in treating tumors that grow inside the eye—a type of cancer known as ocular melanoma. The standard treatment for this malignancy involves removing the eye (enucleation), but even after this drastic measure, cancer reappears in 65% of patients. In contrast, physicians at Harvard have treated 96% of their ocular melanoma cases without removing the affected eye, and 75% of those treated experienced no loss of vision.

Sixty-eight patients with chordoma, cancer of the brain stem, also have made the trip to the Harvard Cyclotron Laboratory's cancer treatment facility, and more than 50 of them were alive five years after proton

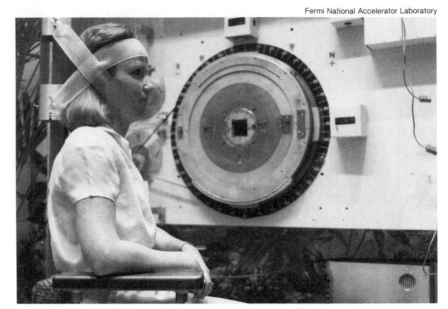

A cancer patient sits positioned for neutron-beam irradiation treatment of the head and neck area at Fermi National Accelerator Laboratory, Batavia, Illinois. Recently the laboratory completed construction of a 6-meter (20-foot)-diameter proton accelerator—the first of its kind in the United States to be designed exclusively for medical purposes—for installation at the Loma Linda (California) University Medical Center.

Fermi National Accelerator Laboratory

therapy. The survival rate of chordoma victims treated with X-rays is roughly half that number.

Such results motivated the Loma Linda (Calif.) University Medical Center to commit $40 million for construction of the first proton-beam facility in the U.S. designed exclusively for medical purposes. (In England a new proton-beam facility at Clatterbridge Hospital, near Liverpool, was scheduled to begin treating patients in 1989.) The Loma Linda atom smasher, or accelerator, was built at Fermi National Accelerator Laboratory, Batavia, Ill. The circular, 6-m (20-ft)-diameter machine will accelerate protons to the necessary energy, after which they will be beamed into four treatment rooms. By varying the energy of the beams, radiologists precisely control the depth to which protons penetrate the body. James M. Slater, head radiologist at Loma Linda, believes that proton therapy will substantially reduce the 100,000 deaths a year in the U.S. caused by inoperable deep tumors that do not respond to conventional radiation treatment.

Mammography benefits

Much lower levels of X-rays are employed to detect rather than destroy tumors. One detection technique—mammography—can be a lifesaver for women 50 years of age and older. Studies by the National Cancer Institute (NCI) conclude that among women in this age group, annual mammograms reduce deaths from breast cancer by 30%. For women aged 40–49, the guidelines agreed upon by the NCI, the ACS, and several other groups call for mammography at one- to two-year intervals.

Mammography provides greater benefits today than in the past because of the availability of increasingly sensitive imaging techniques. Also, less radiation is used in these newer methods, making them safer. The

NCI maintains that the screening methods available today can detect 90% of cancers in women aged 40 to 49 years, compared with 39% in the late 1960s.

Despite the various guidelines and recommendations, a 1987 survey conducted by the Centers for Disease Control (CDC), Atlanta, Ga., found that only 29% of women older than 49 had had a mammogram within the previous year. These results agreed with those of a Gallup poll conducted in December 1987, which revealed that 60% of women aged 40 and older had not had a mammogram during the previous one to three years. Data from a National Health Interview Study, collected in 1987, also showed that only 31% of women older than 39 had been screened within the previous year. This was good news in that it represented an increase from 1983, when only 22% of older women underwent screening. All surveys indicated that black women were less likely than white women to have a mammogram.

Another benefit of mammograms was revealed in April 1989 when the ACS announced that women with a high percentage of dense breast tissue are more likely to develop breast cancer than women with primarily fatty breasts. The amount of dense tissue can be determined by mammograms, thereby identifying women who may be at higher risk.

Aggressive treatment of breast cancer

The earlier breast tumors are detected and the smaller their size, the better chance a woman has of long-term survival after surgery. Treatment varies from removing the breast (mastectomy) to local excision of the tumor (lumpectomy) followed by radiation. The ACS predicted that one of every ten U.S. women would develop breast cancer and that the disease would kill about 43,000 females (and 300 males) in 1989.

An estimated 142,900 new cases were expected to be diagnosed during the year. If the cancer remains localized, survival rates approach 100%; if it spreads, survival plunges to 60%.

Physicians once believed that tumors successfully removed by surgery would not recur if the cancer showed no evidence of having spread to the underarm lymph nodes. Such cancers are referred to as lymph-node negative. It is now known, however, that about one in every four women diagnosed as lymph-node negative dies when the cancer later spreads—about 19,000 deaths annually.

Four new studies indicate that 5,000 of these patients could be saved each year with additional drugs or synthetic hormones. Two of the studies, done by the National Surgical Adjuvant Breast and Bowel Project, examined the medical records of 3,323 women with lymph-node-negative cancer. In the first study, of those who received chemotherapy (the drugs methotrexate and fluorouracil) after surgery, 80% remained disease-free after four years, compared with 71% of those who got no additional treatment. The second study concluded that 83% of those who took the antiestrogenic hormone tamoxifen were symptom-free, compared with 77% of those who were not so treated. In a third study 84% of the patients who received chemotherapy and 69% of those who did not remained free of the disease after three years.

If you haven't had a mammogram, you need more than your breasts examined.

A mammogram is a safe, low-dose X-ray that can detect breast cancer before there's a lump. In other words, it could save your life and your breast. If you're a woman over 35, be sure to schedule a mammogram. Unless you're still not convinced of its importance. In which case, you may need more than just your breasts examined.

Find the time. Have a mammogram.

AMERICAN CANCER SOCIETY

Give yourself the chance of a lifetime.

American Cancer Society

Finally, an international team of researchers in Switzerland published a study of 1,275 women in which the disease-free numbers were 77% with chemotherapy versus 73% without it.

Because of these and other similar findings, the NCI in May 1988 issued an alert advising physicians to offer adjuvant therapy (treatment given in addition to the primary therapy) to women following surgery for lymph-node-negative breast cancer. The alert spawned controversy. One group of physicians protested that treatment of the 70,000 women diagnosed each year with lymph-node-negative breast cancer would mean that 50,000 of them would be taking powerful drugs or hormones unnecessarily. The group claimed that as many as 100 women would die from side effects of the medication and that the treatment would cost an estimated $338 million. Other physicians insisted that the benefits of adjuvant therapy would extend beyond the four years covered by the studies and that these benefits exceeded the risk. Speaking for the latter group, Vincent T. DeVita, former director of the NCI and now head of the Memorial Sloan-Kettering Cancer Center, New York City, said that "the 30% chance of recurrence, with the inevitability of death, . . . is terrifying to most women who have cancer in the prime of their lives, and the risk of death from the toxic effects of these . . . treatment programs is minuscule by comparison."

The best care: available to all?

The U.S. General Accounting Office (GAO) looked at aggressive cancer treatments in another light. This congressional agency questioned whether the advances in chemotherapy made at universities and major cancer research centers actually reach patients treated by ordinary physicians.

The GAO looked at data on women younger than 51 whose breast cancer already had spread and who thus were most likely to die if not treated. The agency concluded that although the use of chemotherapy had tripled since 1975, 37% of young breast cancer patients were not getting the best of care. There were three possible reasons: first, their physicians did not order chemotherapy; second, the women did not receive the most effective combination or doses of drugs; third, the benefit from the advanced treatments is too small to be detected statistically.

Bruce A. Chabner, director of the NCI's division of cancer treatment, found fault with the GAO study on the basis of the third possibility. He said that the expected improvement in survival, calculated from a number of scientific studies, should be about 10%. However, there were too few patients in the GAO study for this improvement to be detected.

The GAO study was not limited to those with breast cancer. Advanced multidrug therapy, experts believe, can extend the lives of those suffering from small-cell lung cancer. Yet 25% of patients go without it, the study stated, probably because physicians do not know about this therapy, or they give the wrong drugs or combination of drugs.

Fifty percent of men afflicted with one type of testicular cancer (nonseminoma) did not receive the most effective known chemotherapy in 1985. The GAO said that this might be because these patients elected surgery and monitoring rather than risk the side effects of powerful drugs. Twenty percent of those with Hodgkin's disease and non-Hodgkin's lymphoma—cancers involving the lymph nodes—also missed getting the best care. The GAO could not explain why.

Silicone implants

Women who lose a breast to cancer may choose to restore their appearance with an implant of silicone gel placed under the remaining tissue. Others choose such implants to enlarge their breasts. The latter account for the vast majority of the estimated two million women who have submitted to the procedure in the past 25 years. All these women became considerably alarmed in November 1988 when Dow Corning Corp., a major manufacturer of silicone gel, announced that implants of the kind used in humans had caused cancer in 23% of rats tested in a study.

The American Society of Plastic and Reconstructive Surgeons quickly issued a statement noting that women with breast implants have undergone follow-up examinations for 25 years, and the type of cancer found in the rats has never been reported in these women. The Mayo Clinic Health Letter agreed and pointed out that when any foreign substance is injected into rats, cancer frequently develops in some of the animals. However, the Public Citizen Health Research Group, a consumer advocate organization in Washington, D.C., demanded that the Food and Drug Administration (FDA) ban silicone gel implants. The FDA refused to do so, saying that a panel of scientists had concluded that the results of the Dow rat study were not relevant to humans and failed to prove that the implants posed any risk of cancer for women.

Researching cancer's causes

Researchers continue to find evidence that a virus may be the cause of childhood leukemia. This evidence is consistent with findings that implicate viruses in the development of certain types of adult leukemia. Viruses also are linked with cancers of the liver, lymph nodes, nose, pharynx, and cervix and other genital areas. Cancer specialists note that only ten years ago, it could not have been said that viruses cause cancer. Now, however, it is known that 20% of world cancers are virus-induced.

That observation indicates both progress and frustration in solving the riddle of these diseases. Though viruses appear to be involved in many cancers, no one understands the details of how they might cause

malignancies. Do they disrupt the genetic machinery of cells? Other cancers—those of the breast, colon, lung, and bone—have been tied to the presence or absence of certain genes. During the past ten years, researchers have linked the development of tumors to activation of so-called oncogenes. More recently researchers discovered a class of antioncogenes that seem to suppress cancer. In the latest studies breast cancer has been linked to the absence of an antioncogene. This gene appears to be on the same chromosome as genes associated with some forms of colon, lung, and bone cancer. Nonetheless, the activation of oncogenes and inactivation of antioncogenes must be only part of the story. Rates of breast and colon cancer vary dramatically from country to country.

Cancer risk also appears to have a geographic component. As noted, women in Denmark and men in Luxembourg have the highest rates of cancer incidence. People from high-risk nations decrease their chances of getting certain cancers by moving to low-risk nations, and vice versa. Some cancer specialists are now saying that without the necessary environment, few people will develop these kinds of tumors, but in suitable surroundings, those with a genetic predisposition will be at high risk.

A young cancer fighter

Untangling the various contributing causes of cancer—heredity, viruses, and cancer-causing radiation and chemicals in the environment—will require the work of many talented and dedicated researchers. The public thinks of such people as highly educated Ph.D.'s and M.D.'s who study and do research for many years before they make a contribution to knowledge about cancer. This is not necessarily so. Roy Bateman, Jr., did it at the age of 14.

The ninth grader had earned a reputation as a computer whiz in his Huntington Beach, Calif., neighborhood. His next-door neighbor, cancer researcher Glenn Tisman, thought that Bateman might help him with a computer analysis of blood samples from patients receiving chemotherapy for colon cancer. The two worked to follow the progress of nine people who received the experimental treatment.

Bateman provided so much help that Tisman included him as a coauthor of the paper that the scientist wrote to describe the work. Bateman then read the report at a meeting of the American Federation for Clinical Research in 1988. His presentation included X-rays of a patient whose tumors apparently had been significantly reduced by the treatment. Tisman concluded that the drug combination he used has potential for fighting colon cancer. Bateman concluded that he wants to pursue a career in medicine. The audience concluded that cancer research needs more people like Bateman.

—William J. Cromie

Cancer Chemotherapy: Chance and Design

by Robert Chilcote, M.D.

Cancer is a word of considerable emotive force. It conjures up images of an alien growth, ungovernable by one's will or body defenses. A major advance in cancer biology has been to find that cancer is "foreign." When cancer starts, the very genetic structure of a single cell, its DNA, is transformed to produce a cell that differs from any other in the patient's body—different, indeed, from any other normal human cell. This single transformed cell divides to create daughter cells; these cells in turn divide, forming a clone. As descendants of the original cell, all cells within the clone carry the cancer-causing mutations. The diagnosis of cancer becomes evident when the rapidly growing cells become a palpable mass or their presence interferes with the function of important body organs.

With chemotherapy many cancers can now be cured, particularly lymphoid leukemias and lymphomas of children and adults. Why, though, is chemotherapy toxic to these cancer cells and not to the patient's normal cells? Why is chemotherapy that is effective for one cancer ineffective for others? Moreover, what causes a cancer in a patient once sensitive to a particular therapy to later develop resistance to that therapy? Cancer genetics—the study of the chromosomal material of cancer cells—is now providing some insights, as the following case illustrates:

Allen, a senior in high school who was active in sports and nearing graduation, developed an irritating cough. He and his family at first thought he had the flu. Eventually he could not get his breath after walking only a short distance. The night before he was prompted to go to the emergency room, he slept upright, propping himself up with several pillows. In the emergency room he responded to the doctor's questions in short phrases rather than sentences, pausing in between to breathe. One could see his nares flare and the skin between his ribs retract as he worked to breathe. The lymph nodes of his neck were also enlarged; his blood counts were low; and examination of a stained film of his blood showed circulating tumor cells.

A chest X-ray showed a huge mass behind his breastbone encasing the heart and compressing the trachea, the tube that allows air to enter the lungs when one breathes. A biopsy of a lymph node in his neck, performed under local anesthesia, confirmed a cancer of lymphocytes termed non-Hodgkin's lymphoma. Additional blood tests and a bone marrow examination showed that the lymphoma, a form of leukemia, had disseminated widely, making chemotherapy—rather than radiotherapy or surgery—the treatment of choice. A chromosomal study of Allen's lymphoma cells—termed a karyotype—showed, among other abnormalities, a subtle deletion of the ninth chromosome.

Allen received tablets of prednisone and intravenous injections of vincristine, cyclophosphamide, and methotrexate through a catheter implanted under his skin that ran directly into a large vein. The injections were given every week at first and then every few weeks for almost two years. Chest X-rays showed that the mass shrank dramatically over the first few weeks of chemotherapy—obviating the need for radiotherapy—and his swollen lymph nodes and abnormal blood counts returned to normal in a month. Although initially his hair fell out, it eventually grew back. He had such other complications as ulcers in his mouth for several weeks, and on other occasions his blood counts were low, but these too recovered completely. His chemotherapy did not prevent his attending school, and he graduated on time. Like many others in recent successful efforts against some types of cancer, he was cured.

Not all patients with lymphoma are cured, however. Indeed, when such patients relapse, only a small proportion will respond to therapy with long-term remissions. Thus, the best chance for a cure occurs when the correct therapy is chosen at the time of diagnosis. Why were Allen's lymphoma cells more sensitive to the chemotherapy than his normal cells? And why is therapy that is effective for this lymphoma ineffective for most other cancers?

Chromosomes and sensitivity to chemotherapy

The answers to such questions are far from complete, but researchers have several clues. First, it was learned from successes in the treatment of infectious diseases caused by bacteria that the manner in which the metabolism of these organisms differs from human cells can be exploited, and the bacteria can be attacked with antibiotics. The differences between bacterial metabolism and human cell metabolism are ultimately determined by dramatic differences between the bacteria's DNA and the DNA in human chromosomes. Such differences made the discovery of agents against bacteria relatively easy. For example, penicillin kills all streptococci in the body by depriving this germ of its protective cell wall. Since no human cells have this structure, it does this with no toxicity to the patient. As is true with bacteria, the DNA in chromosomes of cancer cells differs from that of normal human cells; the differences, however, are far more subtle. Although it is virtually certain that major chromosomal changes are present in nearly all cancers, in only a few instances have major metabolic differences between cancerous and normal cells been detected.

Genetic abnormalities in cancer cells can be seen through the microscope by means of special stains that highlight the cells' 23 pairs of chromosomes in a karyotype. Detailed study of karyotypes of lymphomas and leukemias over the past several years has allowed cytogeneticists—scientists who study the relationship between chromosome activities and heredity—to catalog certain recurring abnormalities. In Allen's lymphoma/leukemia, karyotype abnormalities have guided molecular biologists to detect losses of a small portion of the DNA on the short arm of chromosome 9. This loss of DNA reduces the production of an enzyme termed MTAP, which is important—but not absolutely necessary—to synthesis of new DNA for the cell to divide. MTAP reutilizes building blocks of cell chemistry called purines to make the DNA that is necessary for cell division. Loss of this pathway—the salvage pathway—is not crucial to the cancer cells since all cells normally have an alternative path for making purines, called the de novo ("from the new") pathway.

These two pathways are analogous to construction of a new building. Bricks can be reutilized from demolished buildings (salvage), or one can make new bricks for construction (de novo). If one source is blocked, the cell becomes dependent on the other. This vulnerability can be exploited in cancerous lymphoma/leukemia cells by blocking the remaining pathway with inhibitors of the de novo pathway. This mechanism may explain the effectiveness of antimetabolites such as 6-mercaptopurine and methotrexate, compounds known to block de novo synthesis. Work on such compounds resulted in the 1988 Nobel Prize for Physiology or Medicine for George Hitchings and Gertrude Elion.

One can see how chemotherapy with an antimetabolite is specific for cancer cells—in particular, cancer cells with a distinct chromosome abnormality. Since the mutation that caused the loss of the cancer suppressor gene and the salvage enzyme occurred in the original cell that led to the malignancy, all cells in the clone have this occult vulnerability. Methotrexate, by blocking the remaining de novo pathway, kills the cancer cells while sparing the normal cells, which survive by using their salvage pathways. The specificity against lymphoma/leukemia over other types of cancer can be accounted for by variations in chromosome abnormalities; i.e., not all cancers will have a defect in chromosome 9. Experiments to support or disprove this model are under way.

Acquired drug resistance

Just as bacteria can mutate and develop mechanisms for resisting antibiotics, it has now become clear that through mutation, cancer cells can acquire resistance to chemotherapy to which they were once sensitive. One class of mutations increases the function of genes that produce proteins that normally detoxify noxious compounds. These detoxification mechanisms were in all likelihood necessary for life to have evolved in a world whose normal environment contains many compounds innately toxic to cells.

Although these mutations are rare—occurring only once in many millions of cell divisions—such a mutation may occur even before therapy has been administered. Among the important forms of resistance mutations are those that exclude chemotherapy from the cell's interior. One such mutation produces channels in the cell's membrane that actively pump chemotherapy drugs out of the cell, decreasing the drugs' net concentration within the cell; thus, chemotherapy doses once effective in killing the cancer cell can no longer be obtained. Even though cancer cells lacking this mutation are eradicated, a single drug-resistant cell may persist, eventually to form its own clones with numbers sufficient to make it the predominant cell type in the malignancy. It then becomes impossible to give an effective dose of chemotherapy to eradicate these clones without seriously harming the patient.

Such resistance can even develop simultaneously to multiple drugs that differ in their structure and mode of action. These so-called multidrug-resistance genes, or MDR genes, may militate against the success of current chemotherapy protocols that are otherwise effective against some cancers. The cells in these clones with the MDR mutations—invisible because of their small numbers among the bulk of the entire tumor—resist drugs that kill their progenitors. Using current techniques, one cannot detect these clones until they number in the hundreds of millions—a "relapse" detectable as a palpable mass or abnormal blood element.

The propensity of cancer cells to mutate makes it important to treat cancer quickly and vigorously, eradicating all cells before any can develop resistance. Even a single cell can regrow to form the original bulk of cancer. This phenomenon is well known in cancer treatment clinics, where patients who receive an incorrect treatment protocol for their type of disease and thus relapse are then resistant to therapy.

Chemotherapy in the future

There may be ways to combat drug resistance in the future. In the laboratory, researchers are using agents known to poison the energy pumps of MDR channels, thereby thwarting this avenue of defense and restoring the cell's innate sensitivity to chemotherapy. However, these research trials are just beginning with patients. Researchers are also trying to discover other chromosomal mechanisms by which tumors become sensitive to drugs in the first place. This quest will be aided by the study of cytogenetics and molecular biology of tumors. Application of these findings to discovering new metabolic vulnerabilities of tumors will be aided by progress in mapping the human genome—a major medical undertaking that is now under way.

Dentistry

For more than a century, the science of dentistry has steadily advanced as services, materials, and techniques have improved. During the past decade there has been an explosion of dental research and development. The application of technology and electronics to dentistry has created a revolution that is just beginning to be felt.

These innovations are, to a great extent, the direct result of including computers in the gathering and interpretation of information. The utilization of computers permits vast amounts of data to be rapidly acquired, and as a result the dentist has access to a more thorough analysis of the patient's existing problems. Furthermore, since the programs are visually oriented, patients themselves can become part of the treatment process. This is particularly important when one considers that many of today's dental problems are preventable.

Most importantly, the techniques described below are noninvasive; that is, they do not do any harm to the patient. They are completely painless and can cause no side effects.

Computer-assisted dental imaging

One of the most difficult tasks for a dentist is to provide the patient with a means to visualize the end result of a proposed treatment plan. The dentist uses dental terminology and the knowledge developed through years of experience and study. The patient, lacking this background, is often more confused after the explanation than before it. Drawings, schematics, and models may perplex the patient even more. Before-and-after photographs of similar procedures can be helpful, but they lack the personal touch of informing the patient as to what can be expected in his or her particular case. The computer-assisted dental imaging (CADI) system can solve these problems by projecting the patient's own teeth (or face) onto a screen and thereby demonstrating directly the possible improvements.

CADI is easy to operate but does require artistic skill on the dentist's part. A video camera takes a still picture of the patient, and this information is stored in the computer while the picture is presented on a color screen. The dentist then draws in changes with a special stylus on an imaging board connected to the computer. As they are being made, these changes are seen on the color screen by both the patient and the dentist. Once the desired appearance has been achieved, the dentist can evaluate the treatment necessary for the patient and estimate the cost and the time involved.

CADI allows the patient and the dentist to create and evaluate a treatment plan together. Working as a team, they can make the necessary modifications and reach a consensus on irreversible procedures in advance of treatment. Thus, for the first time the patient is intimately involved in the decisions that will shape his or her smile before the dental work is started. In fact, several different shapes, sizes, or shades of teeth can be examined on the computer screen in order to evaluate which would result in the best appearance. Various types of treatment can be previewed in a presentation format that a person who is not trained in dentistry can readily grasp.

The versatility of this system is such that photographic printouts can be made of the different treatment proposals, and several of them can be viewed at the same time. The patient and dentist can then compare the possibilities, discussing the benefits and drawbacks of each. Once a desired (and feasible) result has been agreed upon, the dentist has a clear and approved objective; the patient, fully understanding the potentials and limitations of treatment, has a means of comparing the proposed and actual results.

CADI systems display the teeth and the surrounding tissues in great detail. Poorly brushed and flossed areas are not particularly pleasant to view. This often has the effect of motivating patients to improve their home oral hygiene procedures. Continued development of CADI systems is leading not only to a better visualization of treatment but also to a consumer-driven demand for more and better dental cosmetic procedures.

Radiovisiography

Over the years it has become accepted procedure that no dentist will begin treatment without first evaluating the patient's problems by means of radiographs, also known as X-rays. Recently, however, radiation of any kind has come to be perceived as a potential health hazard. While it is extremely unlikely that the minuscule amount of dentally administered radiation will cause problems of any sort, the dental profession has looked for ways to reduce patient exposure.

A recently developed technique known as radiovisiography not only reduces the X-ray dosage by approximately 80% but also provides more useful and easily readable information to the dentist. It involves the computer enhancement of X-ray images that can be seen on a monitor or printed onto paper.

Radiovisiography consists of three separate but interconnected components. The "radio" part comprises a conventional X-ray unit and an intraoral electronic X-ray sensor. The "visio" portion consists of an imaging unit that can reproduce the images picked up by the sensor and a video monitor to display them. The "graph" part is a high-resolution thermal printer that enables the dentist to keep a permanent record of the images.

The sensor that is placed inside the patient's mouth is the same size as film for an ordinary dental X-ray, although it is somewhat thicker. Inside the sensor is a screen that absorbs the X-rays and in turn emits light impulses that pass through fiber-optic filaments to a charge-coupled device (CCD). The CCD emits electronic impulses to the imaging unit, which then digitizes the signals and memorizes the whole image.

Once the image information has been stored in digital form, it is a simple matter to change the contrast or brightness to aid in diagnosis. Should the dentist desire a closer look at a particular area, a zoom feature permits enlargements of up to eight times. While the current model presents only black-and-white images (with 256 intermediate shades of gray), future devices will include color images that will provide even more information. The system is instantaneous; there is no need to wait for the development of film. This is important in procedures where an X-ray image is required before the next step is begun.

The large size of the radiovisiographic image on the monitor allows patients to gain a better understanding of their dental problems. For the first time, the X-ray is large enough to be viewed by both the dentist and the patient together. The existing conditions and future care can be discussed. Radiovisiography will expand the horizons of dental diagnostics. Dentists in the future will diagnose problems earlier, more thoroughly, and more confidently.

Computerized occlusal analysis

Occlusion can be defined as the relationship of the upper and lower teeth. While this may seem to be a straightforward concept, there has been much discussion about exactly what happens when the teeth come into contact with one another. It is important that the teeth function harmoniously. If one tooth is bearing too much of the load, it can be weakened and eventually lost. An improper bite can damage not only the teeth but the supporting bone and gums as well.

Initially, it was believed that there were points on the teeth that met during the biting process. However, research has indicated that biting is a complicated procedure, involving not only vertical motions of the jaw but horizontal and diagonal ones as well. Consequently, the relationship between opposing teeth consists of a series of points and slides, all of which are in continuous flux throughout the action of biting.

The amount of information required for treating malocclusion (or improper biting) used to be overwhelming. The only way dentists could determine the areas that were contributing to the problem was to place a colored strip of paper in between the upper and lower teeth while the patient chewed. The resulting smudges of color on the teeth indicated the spots that were in greatest contact. The smudges could not, however, indicate the magnitude of the problem.

The recent introduction of computerized occlusal analysis (COA) has improved the consistency with which dentists can treat problems resulting from malocclusion. COA is achieved by the gathering, analysis, and display of bite information by a specially designed computer. The data are obtained when a patient bites on a thin sensor. The sensor transmits the messages of force and direction to the processing unit. There the information is digitized and displayed on a monitor as a diagram of the teeth with vertical bars, much like the bars on a graph, arising from some of the teeth. The bars represent the areas where there is force during biting; their height is proportional to the amount of the force. Thus, both the location and the magnitude of biting forces are clearly shown.

Using COA the dentist can determine if the patient's teeth are functioning as a group or whether certain teeth are bearing the brunt of the bite. This type of evaluation is particularly important when the dentist is doing extensive reconstruction of the patient's dentition, such as long-span bridges.

TMJ (temporomandibular joint) problems are quite common. Many people suffer from clicking or cracking of the jaws or pain in the jaw muscles. These conditions may be caused by an imbalanced bite. If the origin can be reliably and positively identified, the solution will not be far away.

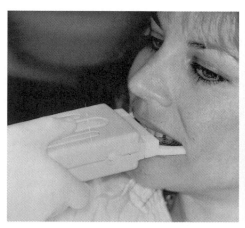

With the aid of a computer, occlusal problems can now be more accurately diagnosed. A sensing device in the patient's mouth transmits information to a computer that analyzes the contacts between teeth and displays the data visually.

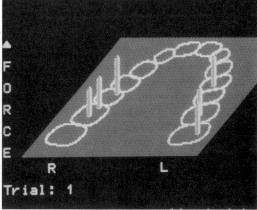

Tekscan, Inc., Boston, Massachusetts

Diane Rekow, University of Minnesota

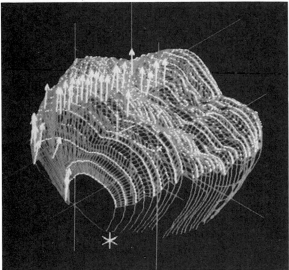

Using a series of photographs of a tooth taken from different angles, a computer builds up a three-dimensional image, which will be used to create a crown that is very much like the natural tooth.

The application of COA is not limited solely to people who still have their natural teeth; at times, wearers of partial or complete dentures also experience difficulties in biting and chewing. In those cases in which the discomfort is caused by an incorrect relationship of upper and lower dentures, COA can assist in determining the exact location of the problem. This allows the dentist to modify only those areas that require change.

As the dentist is in the process of adjusting the bite, sequential images can be displayed on the monitor to evaluate the progress of treatment. A bite history of the patient can be established to determine if any destructive patterns are emerging. Thus, COA is very useful in correcting malocclusions but is even more

important in providing a means to better analyze and understand the function of biting.

CAD/CAM

Computer-aided design and computer-aided manufacturing (CAD/CAM) is another name for advanced robotics. It is one of the most fascinating new dental applications of the decade.

A review of the sequence of events that occurs in the preparation of a crown (also known as "cap") will help explain the role of CAD/CAM in dentistry. The dentist first prepares the tooth. This involves a partial reduction of the outer layers of the tooth. An impression is taken to provide a negative image of the prepared tooth. An impression of the opposing teeth is also taken. These impressions are poured with dental stone to create stone duplicates of the patient's teeth. A wax or plastic bite wafer is made in the patient's mouth to relate the upper and lower teeth during the biting process. The models and the wafer are sent to a dental laboratory, along with a coloring guide that will assist a technician in the fabrication of a crown. Each of the above steps involves the transfer of information from one material to another, during which precision may be lost or error introduced.

It can take a week or longer for the finished product to return from the laboratory. The dentist must make a temporary crown that covers the prepared tooth during this period. This procedure also is a time-consuming one.

The preparation of the tooth is accomplished as before, but CAD/CAM eliminates all the steps afterward. The apparatus consists of a specially designed camera, an image-processing computer, and a milling machine. The camera has a wandlike extension that easily fits inside the mouth. It includes a laser source that projects light on the desired subject and a fiber-optic tube that passes the images back to a camera.

The traditional technique for making a crown requires the dentist to use a puttylike material to take an impression of the prepared tooth base (left) on which the crown will rest. A computer-aided technique (right) eliminates the need for an impression; the dentist "maps" the tooth base with an optical probe in the patient's mouth.

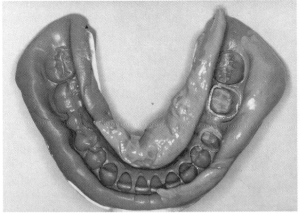
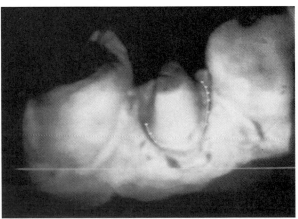

(Left) Kerr Manufacturing Company; (right) Francois Duret, Hennson Technologies, Inc.

"It's your dentist, Charlie. He says it's been five years!"

At least three different images are recorded (from various angles), and they are transmitted to the image-processing computer. From these images the computer creates a three-dimensional electronic diagram and presents it to the operator for verification. The dentist can view the tooth from any direction by visually rotating the diagram on the monitor.

When the dentist is satisfied that the image is correct, the information is sent to the automated milling machine. It contains all the tools that are required for grinding, shaping, and polishing a finished crown for the prepared tooth. The milling begins with a block of acrylic, metal, or porcelain. The computer's impulses indicate to the milling machine where and exactly how much to grind the block. The accuracy of the milling is within 30 microns ($30/10,000$ of a centimeter). Within approximately 45 minutes the crown is ready for testing on the patient's tooth. Then, after being colored to match the existing teeth, the completed crown is bonded to the patient's tooth.

The impressions and all their potential for inaccuracy have been eliminated. The working time has been reduced from a week or longer to an hour or two. The temporary restoration is no longer necessary. And the finished crown is as accurate as the best that human technicians can achieve. This type of technology is as expensive as it is innovative, but with time and continued refinement the costs should be reduced to a level where most dentists will be able to afford it.

Dental caries: a disease in transition

The high-tech revolution in dentistry is helping to eradicate many forms of disease and discomfort, but dentists' old nemesis, dental caries (cavities), continues to develop in the general population. It is interesting to note the evolution of the distribution of this problem.

Dental caries was long considered to be an essentially inevitable disease. However, recent surveys indicate that children—in North America at least—are enjoying a remarkable decline in their numbers of cavities. The progress has been steady during the last 50 years, and recent data indicate that the incidence of caries has been reduced as much as 70%.

Dental comparisons are based on the DMFS index. This is the sum of the decayed, missing, or filled permanent tooth surfaces found in each mouth. This index provides a cumulative record of the lifetime caries experience of an individual. The 1940s DMFS was approximately 10.5 in a study of seven selected cities. By 1980 a similar examination revealed a DMFS of 3.1. These dramatic improvements are the direct result of a number of events over the intervening years.

The addition of minute amounts of fluoride (one part per million) to the drinking water was possibly the most significant step in decreasing tooth decay. This method for improving the strength of the tooth's structure is suitable while the teeth are developing—*in utero* and during the first years of life. Water fluoridation was first attempted in the 1940s; it was more widely established in the 1950s and 1960s.

In the 1950s fluorides were introduced into mouthwashes or gels that are used to harden the surfaces of teeth that have already erupted into the mouth. In the 1960s similar fluorides were incorporated into toothpaste formulations.

At the same time, dentists and manufacturers of dental care products were jointly promoting, and heavily advertising, effective preventive care. This created a general awareness of the importance of dental health and demonstrated the means to achieve it.

In the 1970s school fluoride programs were started. Under their teachers' supervision, children used fluoride mouthwashes. The weekly program was easy to install, was inexpensive, and provided a better means of reaching more children and adolescents.

Fissure sealants were introduced in the 1980s. These are fillinglike materials that are bonded into the crevices and grooves of teeth to prevent food and caries-causing bacteria from being lodged in these difficult-to-clean locations. Sealants are not recommended for teeth that already have fillings but can be used on teeth with early signs of decay.

All of the above measures have resulted in a welcome reduction of decay among children and adolescents. It seems, however, that adults are taking over where children have left off in regard to the frequency of caries.

The interpretation of statistics on tooth decay in adults is complicated by several factors. Adults are living longer, and they are permitting fewer teeth to be removed. Perhaps because today's adults were not brought up in the same high-fluoride environment as their children, they tend to be prone to recurrent caries throughout life. Also, as people age, they are more likely to have medical problems. Both the conditions and the medications used to treat them may reduce the body's ability to fight dental decay. In addition, with advancing years the coordination and concentration required for toothbrushing and flossing may be reduced.

Still another factor is that as people age, their gums recede. This exposes the soft root surfaces to the foods and bacteria in the mouth. Less calcified than enamel, these areas are more prone to decay; hence the term root caries. The increased incidence of root caries in the aging population will probably be the greatest challenge preventive dentistry will face in the 1990s. Fortunately, various fluoride applications are showing early promise in the prevention and treatment of this condition.

—George A. Freedman, D.D.S.

Diabetes

Diabetes is beginning to receive the attention it deserves as a common, serious disease that can be managed successfully—or be devastating. The results of this higher profile are evident everywhere: more diabetes research, more willingness of people with diabetes to address their problem and deal with it successfully, and more understanding on the part of both professionals and people with diabetes as to just what constitutes good care.

More than 12 million people in the United States have diabetes, and almost half do not even know it. All told, it costs the U.S. economy more than $20 billion per year, much of it in avoidable medical and disability costs. There is reason, furthermore, to suspect that diabetes is underreported as a cause of mortality. The

human suffering and financial burden caused by diabetes will, ultimately, be eliminated when the disease can be prevented and cured. Such scientific accomplishments do not just happen, though; they evolve over time from a broad-based biomedical research effort, which can lead to a basic understanding of the disease and the piecemeal development of new treatment approaches.

There is a great deal farther to go on the road toward discovering a cure; just waiting for this cure is futile. With proper education and involvement, people can live healthy lives today by taking advantage of the best care possible while supporting the scientific effort to improve current state-of-the-art therapy. The past decade or so has seen remarkable progress.

Diagnosis and screening

Diabetes mellitus has been known since antiquity, the name drawn from the Greek (diabainein, "to pass through") and the Latin (mellitus, "sweetened with honey"). The name refers to the excessive thirst and urination and the presence of sugar in the urine that are characteristic of the disease. There are fixed criteria for the diagnosis of diabetes. Usually diabetes is discovered when there are typical symptoms (frequent urination, thirst, weight loss) and a clearly high blood sugar level (a daytime level greater than 200 milligrams per deciliter or a fasting level greater than 140 mg/dl). On occasion, doctors have to resort to a more detailed oral glucose tolerance test to diagnose diabetes. There may be borderline test results, but there is no such thing as "a touch of diabetes"; an internist or endocrinologist can determine definitely whether a person has it. The estimated five million people with undiagnosed diabetes should be found.

When should there be screening for diabetes? There is little reason to screen normal populations of people, since both the yield of new diagnoses and the benefits will be small, but high-risk people should be screened. A questionnaire has been developed by the American Diabetes Association to determine who is at high risk. Essentially, people should be screened who are obese, have diabetes in a first-degree relative, have had diabetes in pregnancy, are in a high-risk minority (black, Hispanic, native American), have a history of unsuccessful pregnancies, or have had suggestive symptoms (frequent urination, thirst, weight loss). All pregnant women should be screened for diabetes between the 24th and 28th week of pregnancy.

Advances in understanding diabetes's many causes

All types of diabetes involve high blood sugar concentrations (hyperglycemia), which cause the classic symptoms, and all types are characterized by inadequate action of the polypeptide hormone insulin. Nevertheless, the different types of diabetes have very different causes and clinical features.

Diabetes

Insulin is synthesized in the beta cells of the islets of Langerhans of the pancreas and is necessary for normal utilization of glucose (a sugar) by most cells in the body. Diabetes in all cases is characterized by insufficient insulin action. This insufficient action may be due to complete absence of insulin or resistance by the body's cells to insulin's action, with inadequate pancreatic secretion for overcoming this resistance. In unusual circumstances, then, diabetes may be caused by surgical removal of the pancreas or by diseases such as iron-overload (hemochromatosis), in which iron deposits replace normal pancreatic tissue. Most often, though, the underlying cause of diabetes is more obscure.

Type I, insulin-dependent diabetes mellitus (IDDM), which used to be called juvenile onset diabetes, is characterized by specific obliteration of the pancreatic beta cells. Without the ability to secrete insulin from the pancreas, the person must take it by injection.

The most common form of diabetes, now referred to as type II, non-insulin-dependent diabetes mellitus (NIDDM), formerly called adult onset diabetes, accounts for about 90% of all diabetes. Its cause is entirely different from that of IDDM. Insulin is secreted by the pancreas—but not quite normally—and, most important, there is resistance of the body's cells to insulin's effect, coupled with subtle changes in the secretion of insulin by the beta cells.

There have been dramatic advances recently in the understanding of both IDDM and NIDDM. Much of this research has been stimulated by simple, basic questions.

Heredity in diabetes

Is diabetes hereditary? Does it run in families? Is a parent responsible for a child's diabetes? Will a sibling get it if one child in a family has it? These questions are understandably raised by anyone faced with diabetes in the family, and they probe medical scientists' basic understanding of the disease. Some answers are starting to emerge.

Most diabetes is to some extent hereditary, but heredity is more important in causing NIDDM than IDDM. If a child has IDDM, there is only a 5–10% chance that a sibling will get it; if a parent has IDDM, there is only a 1–2% chance that the child will develop it. (This risk, incidentally, is independent of whether the mother had diabetes during pregnancy. Diabetes in pregnancy does not cause diabetes in the child; the risk that the child will develop IDDM is in fact slightly more if the father has it than if the mother does.)

With NIDDM there is about a 10–15% chance that an offspring will develop the disease (usually as an adult, and highly dependent on whether the person becomes obese). If one of a pair of identical twins has NIDDM, there is more than a 90% chance the other will develop it, whereas the risk of IDDM in both

identical twins is about 50%. IDDM and NIDDM are very different diseases not only in their inheritance but in their causes as well as treatment options.

Diabetes in pregnancy

When the diagnosis of diabetes is made first in pregnancy, it is called gestational diabetes. Whether it was known before or is first discovered during pregnancy, there is very good reason to control the blood sugar closely throughout the pregnancy—keeping it as close to normal as possible (less than 140 mg/dl) at all times. Such control reduces the chance of miscarriage and perinatal complications. The baby of a mother with poorly controlled diabetes is characteristically large (over 4½ kg [10 lb]) yet suffers many of the complications of prematurity.

About 75% of the time, gestational diabetes resolves after delivery; thus, the woman no longer has diabetes. Since a history of diabetes during pregnancy does indicate borderline pancreatic function, however, there is a significant chance that the woman will relapse and develop diabetes over the next decade or so. The best way for the woman to avoid this is to maintain normal body weight. Diabetes is uncovered so often during pregnancy because the placenta produces hormones that counteract the action of insulin.

Autoimmunity in IDDM

The causes of insulin-dependent diabetes are less well understood, although progress is being made. In 1901 Eugene Opie, a medical student in the first graduating class of the Johns Hopkins University School of Medicine, Baltimore, Md., first noted the destruction of beta cells in the islets of Langerhans as a cause of diabetes. Until recently, it was thought that this beta cell damage in IDDM came on suddenly (as the symptoms do), simply from a viral infection of the pancreas.

New research suggests that beta cells are destroyed by a process called autoimmunity. For complex and poorly understood reasons, the person's immune system turns on its own tissues, considering the beta cells "foreign," and destroys them. The evidence for this theory is strong. For example, people with IDDM are more likely to have other autoimmune diseases, such as thyroid disease or a patchy loss of skin pigmentation called vitiligo. Furthermore, about 80% of people with IDDM have antibodies against their own beta cells, whereas very few nondiabetic people do. Normal children with these antibodies are about 150 times more likely to develop diabetes than are other children.

Why do some people have this autoimmune self-destruction of their own beta cells? The answer is not clear, but there are clues suggesting a combination of hereditary and environmental factors. The genetic evidence includes inheritance of certain HLA genes known to be involved in immune processes. Over 90%

of Caucasians with IDDM have either HLA-DR3 or HLA-DR4 or both. Characterization of these genes, located on the short arm of chromosome 6, is not a routine clinical test, and their presence by no means assures that a person will develop IDDM. In the susceptible individual, there is still a major environmental influence necessary to trigger diabetes. This factor is poorly understood but may be a virus. It is clearly *not* a matter of eating too much sugar as a child.

The ability to use anti-islet cell antibodies and HLA typing to predict IDDM has therapeutic implications. Medical scientists have been led to ask if diabetes can be headed off if it is known who is likely to develop it. Since the drug cyclosporine A is known to be remarkably effective in suppressing the immune system and, assuming the theory that the problem in IDDM is immune attack of the beta cells is correct, can cyclosporine be used to abort that attack? Several research trials have tested this hypothesis by taking advantage of a "honeymoon period" in which, after the first symptoms of IDDM, the person's own beta cells temporarily recover. Giving cyclosporine very early after the initial diagnosis of IDDM, during this honeymoon period, appears to prolong the temporary beta cell recovery. Diabetes does recur, however, at least when the drug is stopped. Furthermore, cyclosporine is a highly toxic drug, with major side effects including kidney damage. Given this toxicity, cyclosporine's risks appear to outweigh its potential benefits unless it is given as part of a carefully supervised research study.

Many questions remain to be answered about immunosuppression as an approach to preventing IDDM. What if immunosuppression were accomplished before any significant destruction of the beta cells rather than after the first episode of frank diabetes? What if there were a drug that could suppress only those specific antibodies that attack the beta cells rather than suppressing the entire immune process? What if immunosuppressive drugs were free of serious toxicity or side effects? The limitations of cyclosporine A, just one of the immunosuppressive drugs available today, should not dampen enthusiasm for the future. The study of autoimmunity and immunotherapy in IDDM is a fertile area, and it is very likely that one day the disease will be sufficiently well understood that it will be possible to intervene early and successfully.

NIDDM: a persistent enigma

While the causes of NIDDM remain obscure, certain facts are evident. It is clear, for example, that NIDDM is closely tied to obesity. The higher an individual's body weight, the greater the chance of developing NIDDM. And the more obesity in a nation, the higher the prevalence of NIDDM. Sudden economic development (with sudden dietary excess) in a nation causes the sudden emergence of NIDDM as a major health problem; this has been seen, for example, in Saudi Arabia. Impover-

ished nations with high rates of undernutrition, on the other hand, tend to have low rates of NIDDM.

It is also understood now that there are different kinds of obesity, roughly categorized as upper- and lower-body obesity. Upper-body obesity, usually acquired later in life and consisting of abdominal fat, is defined by a waist-to-hip circumference ratio of greater than 85:100. Recent research suggests that upper-body obesity is a more important cause of insulin resistance and diabetes than is lower-body obesity.

The basic cause (pathogenesis) of insulin resistance in NIDDM remains ill-defined. The insulin produced is almost always chemically normal, but the cells simply do not respond normally to it. Laboratory research has looked intensively at the interaction of insulin with its receptors on the cell surface and at intracellular events, including the "recruitment" of proteins that transport sugar (glucose) across the cell membrane in response to insulin. No single answer has emerged to explain insulin resistance in NIDDM.

There is also evidence suggesting that while the pancreas does secrete insulin in NIDDM, this secretion is slow and inadequately sensitive to small changes in blood glucose. A normal pancreas senses even tiny changes in blood glucose and secretes a burst of prepackaged insulin within seconds. The pancreases of people with NIDDM, however, often fail to provide the normal early response of insulin secretion.

Two defects, therefore, are known to occur in NIDDM: sluggish pancreatic insulin secretion and tissue resistance to secreted insulin. It is unclear which of these problems comes first, but the therapeutic implications of what is known are clear; since obesity itself causes insulin resistance, NIDDM is best treated with a good diet and establishment of normal body weight. If diet has been tried extensively without success, a second line of therapy—that of helping to push the pancreas along with an oral hypoglycemic agent (pills)—may be tried. Only if both diet and pills are not sufficient—*i.e.,* if the person's pancreas still cannot do the job—might the pills have to be replaced by insulin injections. In all cases of diabetes, diet is the first treatment.

Today's diabetic diet

The diabetic diet is a good diet for almost anyone. By sticking with foods prescribed as part of a diabetic diet, the whole family does itself a favor by eating more healthy foods, as well as showing support for the person who has diabetes. Furthermore, there are some new trends in diabetic diets that can make sticking to this prudent diet no sacrifice at all. The diet should be individually tailored to include the foods that each family customarily prefers; usually this is done in consultation with a professional dietician.

Complex carbohydrates—starches, as distinguished from simple table sugar or other concentrated sweets—are no longer considered taboo. Absorbed slowly, they cause a gentle, predictable rise in blood sugar level. In IDDM this rise can be successfully "covered" by a form of short-acting insulin (either regular or semilente). In NIDDM blood sugar control is actually improved when complex carbohydrates are included in the diet, rather than severely restricted as they once were. The accepted recommendation for most people with diabetes is to have 50–60% of all calories as complex carbohydrates. "Sweets" (*e.g.,* candy, cake, cookies) should be minimized (protecting the teeth and waistline as well as the blood sugar level), but they may be consumed on occasion if the individual carefully self-monitors his or her blood sugar level.

Nutrition research has discovered that all carbohydrates do not raise blood glucose equally. The "glycemic index" of a food describes how much a given quantity of it will raise blood glucose compared with the rise caused by the same amount of white bread. In real life, though, many factors come into play, particularly how much of the food is eaten, what other foods are part of the meal, how much insulin is given, and so forth. Therefore, most complex carbohydrates are safe to substitute, one for the other, according to standard exchange lists.

Dietary protein is relatively fixed in the usual American diet, constituting between 12 and 25% of total calories. This may have to be modified when kidney disease is present, but there is insufficient evidence for recommending across-the-board changes in nor-

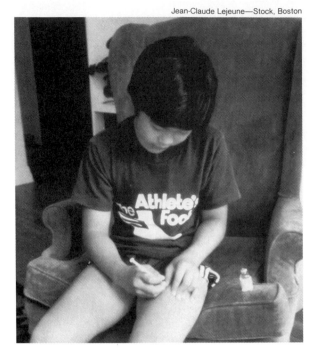

For a young person with insulin-dependent diabetes, starting insulin treatment is always a difficult hurdle. But children soon discover that daily self-injections are painless, and with the therapy they feel much better.

The diabetic "exchange lists" divide foods into starch, meat, vegetable, fruit, milk, and fat. Each group includes foods that have similar amounts of carbohydrates, protein, fat, and calories; foods within a group may be used as "trade-offs," or "exchanges," in daily meal planning. Most people with diabetes can enjoy in moderation a number of formerly taboo foods, which are now included as exchanges.

Sweets—no longer forbidden		
food	amount	exchanges
angel food cake	1 average-size piece	2 starch
cake, no icing	1 average-size piece	2 starch, 2 fat
cookies	2 small	1 starch, 1 fat
frozen fruit yogurt	1/3 cup	1 starch
gingersnaps	3	1 starch
granola	1/4 cup	1 starch, 1 fat
granola bars	1 small	1 starch, 1 fat
ice cream, any flavor	1/2 cup	1 starch, 2 fat
ice milk, any flavor	1/2 cup	1 starch, 1 fat
sherbet, any flavor	1/4 cup	1 starch
snack chips, all varieties*	1 oz	1 starch, 2 fat
vanilla wafers	6 small	1 starch

*400 mg or more of sodium if two or more exchanges are eaten
Source: *Exchange Lists for Weight Management* © 1989 by the American Dietetic Association and the American Diabetes Association, Inc.

mal protein intake. Dietary fat appears to have more consequences for health.

It is clear that most Americans eat too much saturated fat, mainly in the form of fatty red meats, high-fat dairy products, and fried foods. A gram of fat has more than twice the calories of a gram of carbohydrate or protein. And saturated fats increase the total cholesterol level in the blood, contributing to a high incidence of heart attacks and stroke.

Food surveys find that most Americans are reducing their saturated fat intake, and the rate of heart attacks is decreasing. Since the person with diabetes is already at increased risk for vascular complications, however, he or she should make a special effort to avoid saturated fat. With a total fat intake of about 30% of total calories, no more than half should be saturated. Blood cholesterol levels should be checked to determine whether total cholesterol and LDL-cholesterol ("bad cholesterol") are high or HDL-cholesterol ("good cholesterol") is low. This simple blood test will provide guidance on how rigorous a low-saturated-fat diet should be and whether medications may perhaps be necessary for lowering blood cholesterol. Most people, however—even those with a normal blood cholesterol—would be wise to lower their saturated fat intake.

As with most areas of medical research, there is controversy surrounding dietary recommendations. Some experts feel that diets higher in unsaturated fats

Novo-Nordisk A/S

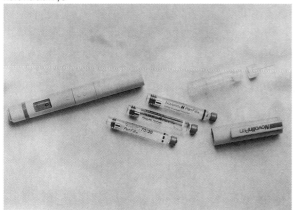

Designed like a fountain pen, the NovolinPen uses cartridges containing insulin—available in three preparations—and single-use disposable needles. A dial enables selection of the appropriate individual dose.

and lower in carbohydrates are at least as healthy for the person with diabetes. There is general agreement, though, on the need to avoid large amounts of concentrated sweets, to avoid saturated fats, and to have blood fats (lipids) checked periodically.

Insulin treatment: many improvements

All people with IDDM, and as many as one-third of people with diagnosed NIDDM, require insulin treatment in order to control their blood glucose. The decision to start insulin therapy is a difficult one for any person to accept, largely because it involves frequent injections. Almost all people, however, quickly learn that with modern syringes these injections are very tolerable and that the treatment, when necessary, makes one feel remarkably better. Moreover, insulin therapy continues to improve year by year.

Human insulin is now generally available, the first commercial product to come from recombinant DNA technology. It is somewhat more expensive than conventional beef-pork insulin, and if a person's disease has been well managed with standard beef-pork product, there is no need to change. For people beginning treatment with insulin and for those who have become allergic or highly resistant to beef-pork insulin, however, human insulin has advantages.

An important advance in insulin therapy is the ability to customize doses to each person's needs. This can be done by mixing short-acting (*e.g.,* regular or semilente) with longer-acting (isophane [NPH] or lente) preparations. If the person learns his or her requirements well, self-adjusting the dose according to current need may be recommended. If unusual exercise is anticipated, somewhat less insulin may be required; if a larger-than-usual meal is to be ingested, more insulin may be necessary. Such adjustments, however, are safe only when the person has learned the basics

of self-adjustment from a qualified health professional, and only with close following of blood glucose concentration by self-monitoring.

Newer developments in insulin delivery include the use of a device about the size of a fountain pen and the use of an external insulin infusion pump. The pen device (*e.g.,* NovolinPen) may be carried in a pocket; the insulin is delivered from a cartridge in amounts determined by turning a dial. A person may take one fixed type of insulin such as regular or a fixed ratio of NPH and regular (70:30) in multiple daily doses.

The external insulin pump is available for those who want to achieve tight control by careful adjustment of insulin flow rates. About the size of a beeper, these pumps are worn on the belt and have a catheter attached to a needle in the abdomen. They have the advantage of delivering a steady basal flow of insulin, which is supplemented at each meal by the patient's programming how much insulin is needed on a small keyboard. It is absolutely essential, however, that the patient perform self-monitored blood glucose several times daily to be sure the pump is delivering.

A new direction in insulin research is the development of insulins with more predictable durations of action. "Designer insulins" have been made through substitution of individual amino acids for usual human insulin. Whether they will prove to have practical utility remains to be seen.

Since insulin's discovery, people with diabetes have yearned for an way to take it without injections. Normal stomach acids degrade insulin when it is given by mouth, so there has never been a useful oral preparation. Recent experiments have found that insulin mixed with a detergent can be absorbed when it is sprayed into the nose. However, this route of administration may run into difficulties when used repeatedly, and its overall efficacy remains to be established. Three major areas of research that could lead to practical insulin delivery without daily injections include pancreas transplantation, implantable mechanical insulin infusion systems, and other implantable systems.

Pancreas transplantation

Theoretically it is possible to transplant the intact pancreas (with all its islet cells and large mass of tissue devoted to making digestive enzymes) or to separate out and transplant the beta cells of the islets of Langerhans alone (since only the beta cells produce insulin). Virtually all experience in human pancreas transplantation has used the intact pancreas. While research on islet cell transplantation continues actively, there are such technical problems as how to harvest enough viable beta cells to produce enough insulin and how to keep them from being destroyed by the host immune system.

Clinically, pancreas transplantation has now been successfully accomplished many times. A major drawback, however, is that strong doses of immuno-suppressive medications (such as cyclosporine A and prednisone) are necessary to keep the recipient from rejecting the "foreign" pancreas, and the complications of this immunosuppression are not insignificant. Therefore, most transplant centers will consider pancreas transplantation only if the person also needs a kidney transplant, since kidney transplantation requires immunosuppression. Pancreas transplantation is not, then, a reasonable way to treat early diabetes; the seriousness of the surgical procedure and the requirement for immunosuppression far outweigh the benefit of not having to take insulin.

Future insulin-delivery systems

Several pumps have been developed that can be implanted under the skin and controlled from the outside, delivering insulin in carefully regulated patterns according to the person's estimate of need. By means of aerospace technology, with support from the National Aeronautics and Space Administration (NASA), one such pump was developed at the Johns Hopkins University Applied Physics Laboratory and tested in animals and humans at the Johns Hopkins Diabetes Center. It is roughly the size of a hockey puck and is surgically placed under the skin in the abdomen.

As of mid-1989 this pump had been used experimentally in 18 people with IDDM, the longest experience being over two and one-half years. It is important to note that no mechanical insulin infusion pumps measure blood glucose automatically; the person with diabetes still has to do that by the usual methods and then decide for the pump how much insulin is necessary. With the implanted pump, however, refilling the reservoir requires just one essentially painless needle prick every two months (done without anesthesia). Although the approach has been used in only a few people, results thus far have been encouraging.

Other implantable systems under development include pellets and islet cells grown in semipermeable membranes. Pellets can be made of various polymers that will bind insulin and release it slowly. The pellets could be placed under the skin with a minor surgical procedure. The challenge in this line of research is to find a way to release the insulin in varying rates, rather than just as a constant flow. People with IDDM, especially, require highly variable flow rates—increasing after each meal, decreasing between meals.

The semipermeable membrane approach would put live, transplanted beta cells in a membrane, which could allow them exposure to the blood glucose concentration but protection from the host's immune system. In this way, the islets would secrete insulin according to need but avoid being rejected. As with all research, the idea is simpler than the execution, and this approach is one of many whose ultimate success is yet to be determined.

Social, financial, and legal concerns

As public understanding of diabetes has increased in recent years, people with diabetes have become far more open about what they need and deserve in order to cope with their illness. In its most successful form, this openness begins with the individual's acceptance of diabetes as part of his or her physical makeup— something that, like unusual height or other physical attributes, is just a fact of life, not a reflection of self-worth. It is most important for friends, family, and co-workers to provide support, helping the person with diabetes live in a normal social environment.

While the financial costs of having diabetes may be considerable, reimbursement for these costs has improved. To take advantage of financial reimbursement, it is important, first, to have adequate health insurance coverage. Most often, such coverage is obtained through group policies or "entitlement" programs. Group policies are usually offered in larger employment settings, and people with diabetes should carefully consider the health care benefit options when choosing a job. Entitlement programs are government sponsored, such as Medicare for the elderly, Medicaid for the poor, Veterans Administration benefits, or Indian Health Service benefits. Given adequate health insurance, the person with diabetes should be in a position to have most expenses covered. In the case of expensive equipment items (pumps or glucose meters, for instance), it may be necessary to have a letter from a physician specifying the medical necessity of such equipment.

It is also important for people with diabetes to avoid discrimination in employment or licensing. Federal and state laws now protect against unfair discrimination; in general, this means that the person with diabetes should be considered eligible for any employment and any license for which he or she is individually qualified. There are still exceptions; diabetes will keep a person from being accepted into active military service, for instance, and a history of serious insulin reactions could make a person ineligible for employment in which confusion would be catastrophic. Nevertheless, diabetes as such should not be the determining factor. The American Diabetes Association has experience in dealing with these issues and can be helpful to people who are concerned about discrimination.

—*Christopher D. Saudek, M.D.*

Disasters

It is rare that many months pass without the news of a major disaster occurring in some part of the world. The year 1988 proved to be no exception. During the year, the Office of U.S. Foreign Disaster Assistance (OFDA) responded to 78 independently declared disasters worldwide. This agency provides assistance only in those situations that surpass the capability of

Morocco was one of the countries hardest hit in the spring of 1988 when regions of northern and western Africa faced one of the worst locust plagues the world had seen in three decades. Swarms of destructive desert locusts multiplied as heavy rains facilitated their breeding. The effort to control the ravenous pests was led by an international team of experts and field staff, and countries around the world donated millions of dollars' worth of insecticides.

the local government to provide adequate relief, as assessed by U.S. Foreign Service personnel stationed in that country. For this reason, neither disasters occurring in the U.S. nor those of lesser impact occurring overseas are included in this figure. Among those serious enough to warrant U.S. assistance were locust infestations in Africa (12 countries); floods in Africa, Latin America, and Asia (14); civil unrest (8); earthquakes in the Soviet Union, India, Nepal, and China; war and displacement in southern Sudan and Mozambique; refugees in Ethiopia, Rwanda, and Malawi; and assorted hurricanes, cyclones, volcanic eruptions, droughts, wars, and epidemics.

Although the publicity that follows a disaster is short-lived, the impact—direct and indirect—of a catastrophe on the lives of the affected population is often long-term. Extensive experience with the human and environmental consequences of disasters has been gained in recent years by various agencies and individuals. Systematic studies and increased documentation of these events has led to improved understanding and accelerated efforts to improve both the preparedness for and response to disasters of all kinds. Nevertheless, the lessons learned from the past are not always put into practice during the excitement and chaos that characterize the aftermath of an acute emergency.

It is important to emphasize that both prevention of disasters and mitigation of their impact on the population are possible if resources are allocated to emergency preparedness. Accordingly, many governments have recently developed preparedness plans that will enable them to prevent the worst effects of disasters and to respond efficiently to disasters once they occur. These governments have been helped in this task by the UN Disaster Relief Organization (UNDRO), the

World Health Organization (WHO), the Office of the UN High Commissioner for Refugees (UNHCR), the League of Red Cross and Red Crescent Societies, UNICEF, and other international agencies.

Disasters may be categorized according to their mode of onset as "sudden-impact" or "gradual-onset" and further by their etiology as "natural" or "man-made." In many instances, disasters that are combinations of these categories occur at the same time, as will be apparent from the discussion of disasters in 1988.

Armenian earthquake

At 11:41 AM (Moscow time) on Dec. 7, 1988, an earthquake registering 6.9 on the Richter scale struck the northern part of the Armenian Soviet Socialist Republic. Occurring in a known earthquake zone, this was the strongest quake in the region in over 80 years. The town of Spitak (population estimates vary from 15,000 to 40,000) was completely leveled, and half the buildings in Kirovakan (population 165,000) were demolished. In all, 56 villages were totally destroyed, and an additional 100 sustained serious damage. Over 21,000 residential buildings, 83 schools, 84 hospitals, and hundreds of stores and public buildings were totally or partially destroyed. In addition to the loss of cattle and other livestock, damage to the agricultural sector was estimated at more than $3 billion, while physical damage to the area was valued at more than $13 billion. As of December 1988 the death toll was estimated at nearly 25,000, and more than 150,000 were injured. At least 510,000 people were rendered homeless, and in the first few weeks more than 100,-000 people were evacuated from the area.

Medical services in the affected area were disrupted because of the death or injury of medical personnel

289

A young girl was rescued some three days after an earthquake struck the Armenian Soviet Socialist Republic in December 1988. The quake destroyed most of the region's health facilities, and many local medical personnel were killed or injured. Although help came from all corners of the world, most of the foreign rescue teams arrived on the scene too late to have an impact. Additionally, the millions of dollars' worth of donated medical and surgical supplies could not be put to immediate use; medications, for example, arrived in small packages with instructions in unfamiliar languages, and thousands of hours were needed just to sort them.

and the destruction of most health facilities. All relief resources had to be brought in from outside the affected area. The world's response was immediate and dramatic; search dogs, medical workers, medicines, surgical supplies, food, clothes, and blankets were donated by governments, international agencies, and voluntary organizations from at least 53 countries. More than $100 million worth of material assistance was provided during the three weeks following the earthquake.

Lessons from Armenia. Earthquakes are characterized by their poor predictability, high lethality, narrow geographic focus, and rapidity of onset. Of all the common natural disasters, earthquakes present the highest risk of death to those affected. Data compiled by the OFDA show that the numbers of people affected by and deaths due to earthquakes have been increasing since 1960. This may be due to rapid urbanization in certain high-risk zones (such as Mexico) and the unregulated housing construction in some of these cities. Unreinforced masonry (including adobe) is the most hazardous building material and can be expected to collapse during an earthquake. Poor building design has contributed to high mortality in urban earthquakes. Japan is one of the few high-risk countries to have an effective warning and evacuation system, as well as excellent community education programs.

Most deaths and serious injuries occur during or soon after the earthquake, and the overwhelming cause is trauma due to partial or complete collapse of man-made structures. Studies have revealed that young children and the elderly are most at risk of death or serious injury. The disruption to health services caused by the Armenian quake was typical of this kind of disaster. The same problem occurred after

the Mexico City quake of 1985 and, thus, the major long-term threat to the health of the population may be the result of the lack of functioning health services. In addition, major damage to the water supply, markets and food storage facilities, and communications systems usually occurs. Epidemics of acute, infectious diseases are the exception rather than the rule, and the threat to public health posed by the many corpses in the area is usually exaggerated.

The priorities of earthquake relief are the following: (1) rapid assessment of the extent of damage and injuries; (2) establishment of medical triage centers; (3) search-and-rescue operations for trapped victims; (4) appropriate surgical treatment of injured survivors; (5) reestablishment of communications; (6) evacuation of survivors to safe areas and provision of shelter for the homeless; (7) establishment of clean water supply and adequate food supply channels; (8) disease surveillance; (9) reestablishment of primary health care services; and (10) reconstruction and rehabilitation.

The flood of foreign medical personnel unfamiliar with local conditions and of supplies and equipment that are often inappropriate may hinder local relief efforts. For example, 450 people (more than 90% of survivors trapped in destroyed buildings) in Armenia were extricated within the first two days by 1,000 Soviet rescue workers who had been mobilized immediately. Only two persons were extricated by U.S. relief workers, although their dogs aided in the detection of several others. Most foreign medical teams arrived on the scene after the period when they might have been of greatest benefit. Many donations were inappropriate to the needs of the situation; for example, large numbers of medications in small packets, with brand names and instructions for use in unfamiliar languages. The sorting and distribution of such medicines can consume thousands of man-hours and clog vital supply lines.

Treating the injured required appropriate surgical skills, supplies, and facilities. Although there is often considerable pressure to vaccinate the entire population against certain diseases (such as typhoid fever), this is not usually a priority; establishment of a clean water supply is a more effective public health measure. Sheltering and feeding survivors requires culturally and technically appropriate supplies. The rebuilding of shattered communities is largely an architectural, engineering, and sociological task and requires little medical input, except in planning the reestablishment of health services. Seismic and geologic experts are often needed to provide both short- and long-term assistance during the recovery period. In Armenia these specialists were among the first requested by the Soviet government.

Thus, the health consequences of an acute natural disaster such as an earthquake may be lessened by careful assessment of the initial impact and provision of relief based on that assessment. Donations not only should be based on good intentions but should reflect the real needs of disaster victims. Many lives could undoubtedly be saved by thorough preparedness; most earthquake zones are known, and all construction in these areas should comply with safety guidelines. Community education and contingency plans based on the known risks of earthquakes would also contribute to effective disaster mitigation.

Floods in Bangladesh

In August 1988 heavy rains in the state of Assam in India, in Bhutan, and in other areas of the Himalayas caused flooding of the Brahmaputra-Jamuna, Meghna, and Ganges rivers in Bangladesh, displacing more than 25 million people from their homes. Flooding is a recurrent problem in Bangladesh, the most serious in recent history having occurred in 1974. The floods affected both urban and rural areas and covered approximately one-third of the total land mass. The poor were generally the most severely affected since they lived on marginal, low-lying lands and 50% of the population depended on daily-paid agricultural labor for their livelihood. While several hundred people were drowned in the acute flooding, the major immediate health risks derived from the lack of clean drinking water in urban areas and the lack of food supplies in rural areas. Long-term health effects were likely to stem from crop damage and a resulting deficit in food production.

Lessons from Bangladesh. Floods are moderate on the scales of predictability, lethality, scope, and rapidity of onset. The number of people killed in relation to the population affected is fewer than is the case for earthquakes and hurricanes. Their scope of damage, however, is generally wider and more pervasive. The relief program in Bangladesh quite correctly focused on reestablishment of a clean water supply, disease surveillance, monitoring of the nutritional status of the affected population, and provision of food aid to those in need. It is believed that detrimental health effects, due to malnutrition, might occur in this population for up to nine months following the floods. Initially, there was considerable pressure to perform mass vaccination of the population; however, epidemics are not common after floods, and the relief priority sensibly remained the provision of clean water, a more effective measure for preventing such diseases as cholera

Jacques Langevin—Sygma

In 1988, 14 floods in Africa, Latin America, and Asia were serious enough to warrant aid from the U.S. Office of Foreign Disaster Assistance. In August torrential rains hit Khartoum, the capital of The Sudan, and the swollen waters of the White and Blue Nile rivers were unleashed on the area. The capital was already overwhelmed by vast numbers of people living in squatter settlements—refugees of civil war and those seeking relief from starvation in the southern part of the country. Typically, this natural disaster took its greatest toll on these poorest and most vulnerable inhabitants.

and typhoid fever. Long-term prevention of flooding in Bangladesh is a formidable, but not impossible, challenge involving not only protection of low-lying delta land but also reversal of the deforestation and soil erosion afflicting the upland rain catchment areas of Bhutan and India.

Floods in Khartoum

In August 1988 severe flooding occurred in Khartoum, the capital of The Sudan, which is situated at the confluence of the White Nile and the Blue Nile rivers. Over 200 mm (8 in) of rain fell in 24 hours—more than twice the average annual rainfall—causing severe ground flooding and disrupting communications, food and water supplies, sanitation, transport, and health services. Approximately 127,000 dwellings were destroyed, leaving some 750,000 people homeless. Most of the worst-affected areas of the capital were squatter settlements where more than a million people had sought refuge from the civil war and mass starvation in the southern part of the country. The squatter settlements were a disaster waiting to happen; the influx of displaced southerners into the capital had been resisted by government authorities, and virtually no services (water, sanitation, communications, health, or education) had been provided to these people prior to the flooding.

The relief program was a mixed success. Many useful donations, such as shelter materials, food, and certain medicines, were flown into Khartoum immediately following the crisis. Unfortunately, many of these items—particularly food—failed to reach the people most in need—those in the squatter settlements. The Sudanese Ministry of Health set up a disease surveillance system, which demonstrated an increase in the incidence of both diarrheal diseases

and malaria. Health authorities concentrated on treating diarrhea with oral rehydration solution, vaccinating young children against measles, and treating malaria. The surveillance system revealed a high rate of malnutrition among children in the squatter settlements, a situation that probably existed before the flooding but that might have deteriorated owing to the disruption of food supplies.

Lessons from Khartoum. Natural disasters often have the greatest impact on poor segments of society. Not only does their poverty give them little physical protection from sudden events such as earthquakes, hurricanes, and floods but their meager resources also make them completely dependent on external assistance. The Sudanese government had not provided adequate support using its own resources to the displaced persons in Khartoum prior to the floods. Thus, a gradual-onset disaster was compounded by the terrible destruction wreaked by the heavy rains on the poorly built, flimsy houses of the displaced persons. Relief efforts quite rightly focused on this high-risk population, although certain local political factions attempted to obstruct the channeling of food aid to these people.

Hurricanes Gilbert and Joan

Hurricane Gilbert swept across the Caribbean on Sept. 11–19, 1988, and caused severe structural damage in Jamaica, Haiti, and the Yucatán Peninsula of Mexico. Before the storm hit the Yucatán Peninsula, the U.S. National Hurricane Center estimated wind gusts up to 320 km/h (200 mph). Measured surface winds in Cozumel were reported at 240–260 km/h (150–160 mph). In Jamaica approximately 810,000 people were affected by the hurricane, their houses either destroyed or heavily damaged. A total of 500,000

An airplane at Jamaica's Kingston airport ended up wedged between trees after being tossed and downed by Hurricane Gilbert, which hit the island on Sept. 12, 1988; heavy rains and winds up to 320 kilometers (200 miles) per hour caused massive destruction and affected an estimated 810,000 inhabitants. Gilbert also caused major damage and hundreds of deaths in Haiti and on Mexico's Yucatán Peninsula.

(Left) After a bomb exploded on Pan Am Flight 103 on Dec. 21, 1988, the plane crashed into a residential area of Lockerbie, Scotland; the "sudden-impact, man-made disaster" killed all 259 persons aboard. By contrast, there were 184 survivors among the 296 persons aboard a DC-10 that crash-landed in Sioux City, Iowa, on July 19, 1989 (right); even before the pilot made his final approach, an emergency rescue team was in place.

were made homeless, and 45 deaths were reported. In Haiti 50 deaths and 300 injuries were reported, and in Mexico there were 200 deaths and 530 injuries. Evacuation of certain areas of Mexico, especially in the Yucatán Peninsula, was quite successful in preventing further casualties, although structural damage was heavy. Scarcely two months later, Hurricane Joan left a trail of destruction from coast to coast in Nicaragua, affecting 185,000 people and causing 116 deaths.

Lessons of Gilbert and Joan. Hurricanes, or cyclones, are sudden in onset but are usually more predictable and affect a wider area than earthquakes. Of all acute disasters, hurricanes have a ratio of deaths to affected population second only to earthquakes. Deaths and serious injuries may be due to trauma inflicted by flying debris or collapsed man-made structures; however, most hurricane deaths are due to drowning in the floods that often result from severe storm surges. Major preventive measures consist of early detection, careful tracking, the issuing of timely warnings, and the evacuation of those in the path of the hurricane. In agricultural countries like Jamaica, the damage to crops may lead to long-term food deficits, malnutrition, and the other health consequences of flooding, as discussed above.

Sudden-impact, man-made disasters

This category includes sudden chemical or nuclear disasters (such as the accidents at Bhopal, India, and the Chernobyl nuclear power plant in the U.S.S.R.); rail, boat, and airplane accidents; terrorist attacks; outbreaks of civil strife; major fires; and industrial accidents. The most dramatic examples of this category during 1988 occurred when civil disturbances took place in the African countries of Somalia and Burundi.

During May and June, fighting broke out between Somali government forces and the rebel Somali National Movement in the northwestern part of the country. In the aftermath, which included extensive bombing of three towns—Hargeysa, Burao, and Berbera—an estimated 20,000 people died and approximately 800,000 people were displaced, 300,000 of whom fled into neighboring Ethiopia. Little is known of relief efforts inside Somalia, as access was barred to almost all foreigners. As is often the case, the exodus of refugees into camps in the adjacent country led to an emergency relief program there. (Refugee relief is discussed below.) In Burundi serious intertribal violence occurred in mid-August, leading to massacres of the civilian population. The final death toll is unknown but is thought to be at least 5,000. This violence, in turn, led 55,000 ethnic Hutu to flee to nearby Rwanda, where international relief aid was provided.

No major chemical or industrial accidents occurred during 1988; however, several incidents involving airplanes occurred, including the much-publicized bombing of a Pan Am Boeing 747 jet over Lockerbie, Scotland, which killed 259 passengers and crew and 11 people on the ground. Although such incidents usually leave few or no survivors, many countries have developed preparedness plans that involve the evacuation, triage, and treatment of mass casualties. The major long-term health effects of these acute disasters relate to the displacement that follows war and civil strife.

Sudden epidemics

Acute outbreaks of infectious diseases often overwhelm the public health response capacity of the affected countries, particularly less developed ones. The most common of such epidemics, frequently requiring

293

external assistance, are cholera, meningitis, certain hemorrhagic fevers, and yellow fever. During 1988 the worst epidemic reported was that of bacterial meningitis, with approximately 18,000 cases reported in The Sudan, 7,500 cases in Chad, and 7,000 cases in Ethiopia. An estimated 2,000 deaths resulted. The response to this epidemic, which affected three countries in what is called the "meningitis belt" of sub-Saharan Africa, comprised intensive surveillance, vaccination of the population in areas of risk, case-finding, and treatment of cases with appropriate antibiotics. Epidemics of this disease tend to occur every ten years in each of the 15 or so countries situated in the "belt." Careful surveillance and early detection of the outbreak require international cooperation and a willingness by Western donor governments to respond promptly and generously with sufficient vaccines and drugs.

Gradual-onset disasters

Drought, war, locust plagues, and ecological changes (desertification, deforestation, soil erosion) tend to have two outcomes in common: loss of access to food and mass migration by the affected populations. This migration may take two forms—flight into neighboring countries, where the people are often given refugee status, or internal displacement within the affected community's own country. The UNHCR estimates that 14 million refugees are receiving assistance today, mostly in Africa, Asia, and Latin America. In addition, an estimated five million people are displaced within their own countries.

During 1988 alone 708,000 new refugees sought asylum in four countries (Ethiopia, Malawi, Rwanda, and Turkey). These refugees fled war or civil strife in Somalia, Mozambique, Burundi, and Iraq, respectively. Assistance continued to be given to refugees who had arrived in The Sudan, Pakistan, Iran, Somalia, Thailand, Honduras, and many other countries prior to 1988. With the exception of Turkey and Iran, all these countries with large refugee populations are poor (with per capita gross national products of less than $400); thus, the quality of care provided to refugee populations depends largely on the relief assistance that is provided by the international community. The influx of refugees from Burundi into Rwanda took place with relatively few deaths; by December 1988 all had been successfully and voluntarily repatriated to their former homes. In Malawi, Mozambican refugees also experienced very low mortality rates and minimal malnutrition, as did ethnic Kurds who fled from Iraq to Turkey. In Ethiopia more than 300,000 Somali refugees were living in remote and poorly serviced camps, dependent on both water and food being transported long distances over poor roads. Malnutrition prevalence rates in this population deteriorated following their initial influx in July, and by the end of the year, 25% of children under the age of five years were identified as malnourished. Death rates in these camps have not been documented.

Assessment of care for refugees and displaced persons. The quality of care provided to new refugees in 1988 varied, depending to some degree on the extent to which lessons learned from past experience were put into practice. In several situations during the past ten years, refugees have experienced unusually high malnutrition prevalence and high death rates. Many young children have died of malnutrition, measles, diarrhea, malaria, and pneumonia—all either preventable or easily treated with low-cost medicines. The most important relief needs of these populations are adequate food supplies, clean water and sanitation, measles vaccination, oral rehydration therapy for diarrhea, and a basic primary care system with good coverage, standard treatment schedules and drugs, and training of community health workers.

The fate of internally displaced populations (who are usually fleeing war) may be even worse than that of refugees. Since these populations are not protected by international conventions, relief workers are often refused access to them by hostile governments or rebel forces. The worst example of this scenario occurred in southern Sudan, where an estimated 250,000 civilians displaced by a civil war died during 1988. In one displaced persons camp, El Meiram, the death rate reached a staggering 2% in the last week of August 1988, the highest ever recorded in a civilian relief camp setting. Other long-term internally displaced populations in Mozambique, Sri Lanka, and El Salvador require appropriate assistance; however, the long-term solution to this problem is not medical. It requires international protocols that guarantee these people protection from unfriendly armed forces and access to international assistance, free from political constraints and conditions.

1988 in focus

The vast majority of the communities affected by disasters in 1988 were in the third world. With the exception of Armenia, less developed countries bore the brunt of the year's natural and man-made disasters (hurricanes, floods, locust plagues, drought, war, and civil strife). Among the poor of these countries, displaced populations perhaps suffered the greatest. Deprived of their livelihood, they were totally dependent on the generosity of outsiders. These disasters will continue to occur and contribute to the already major obstacles to economic development in the third world. Development planners need to take account of this reality and to incorporate disaster preparedness into national development plans; otherwise, unnecessary setbacks will recur when either Nature or Man goes on the rampage.

—Michael J. Toole, M.D.,
and Ronald Waldman, M.D.

Earthquake Preparedness: California Faces Its Faults

by Sandra Blakeslee

On Sept. 19, 1985, a devastating earthquake struck Mexico City; 250 buildings collapsed, 10,000 people died, and 30,000 were injured. Three years later, on Dec. 7, 1988, a far more lethal earthquake hit the Soviet republic of Armenia. Six cities and towns collapsed, killing more than 25,000 people. Another 13,000 people were injured and 510,000 were left homeless.

In both instances, television cameras captured dramatic images of rescue workers pulling dazed and bleeding men, women, and children from the rubble. More than a dozen nations dispatched emergency assistance and medical supplies. As the days passed and moans beneath the rubble faded, the world looked on, stunned by the pictures of human suffering, structural ruin, and lost hope.

For the 20 million Californians living on or near the infamous San Andreas Fault, however, the images were especially vivid and frightening; as every resident knows, California is "earthquake country." A cataclysmic temblor, colloquially referred to as "the big one," is inevitable. With Mexico City and Armenia as shocking reminders, Californians wonder aloud: Are we ready? How bad will it be? When and where will it happen?

How earthquakes are measured

There are at least 20 different scales for measuring earthquakes. The best known Richter scale has recently fallen out of favor among seismologists owing to several shortcomings. First, the scale is designed to give the size of an earthquake only at its epicenter. It measures local waves detected at short distances. Second, the scale is logarithmic. For every increase of one number, an earthquake is ten times larger in amplitude. Thus, a 5 is ten times larger than a 4 and 100 times larger than a 3. Because the Richter scale measures only local waves, it cannot, as designed, measure the power of earthquakes above a magnitude 6. This is because the actual shaking, in terms of amplitude and ground motion, does not increase very much in earthquakes above magnitude 6. What does increase is the time that the shaking lasts, the area affected, and the amount of ground rupture—aspects more accurately measured by surface waves or combinations of various wave types. Thus, the shaking one feels in a magnitude 8 earthquake is about three times stronger than what is felt in a 6 and not 100 times stronger, as the Richter scale would suggest.

When seismologists report earthquake magnitudes above 6 on the Richter scale, they are using extrapolations from other scales to arrive at the higher number. One such measure, the Kanamori scale, is a more precise indicator of energy released in an earthquake.

"The big one"—how soon and how big?

Latest predictions from the U.S. Geological Survey are not reassuring. There is now a 60% chance of a magnitude 7.5 or larger earthquake—"the big one"—on the San Andreas Fault near southern California in the next 30 years. There is a 50% probability of an earthquake with a magnitude larger than 7 (serious, but less destructive than "the big one") occurring on portions of the San Andreas near the San Francisco Bay area within that same time period.

Moreover, there is a 20% chance that a magnitude 7 earthquake will take place on other faults—some identified and others still hidden—near San Francisco or in downtown Los Angeles within the next ten years.

Geologists agree that earthquakes tend to occur in patterns that can be gleaned from the geologic record. Advances in radiocarbon and tree-ring data have enabled researchers to date the past ten large earthquakes on the San Andreas Fault near Los Angeles to the years 677, 737, 797, 997, 1048, 1100, 1346, 1480, 1812, and 1857. When these dates are averaged, it appears that large earthquakes occur on the San Andreas near Los Angeles about every 131 years. That being so, the region is due for a major earthquake now.

On closer examination, however, scientists find considerable variability between earthquakes. Five of the nine intervals are less than 100 years long. Three of the remaining four intervals are two to three centuries long. Thus, it seems that earthquakes occur in groups of two or three events over a short period of time followed by longer periods of quiescence. It is not yet known, however, if southern California is in the middle of a long quiescent period or nearing another peak in an active period. It is a game of wait and see.

Indeed, the idea has been gradually dawning on seismologists that the most destructive earthquake, in terms of lives lost and property damaged, might not be "the big one" on the San Andreas Fault—which lies mostly outside of California's major metropolitan areas. Rather, the deadliest earthquakes—"the worst ones"—could occur on smaller faults, capable of magnitude 7 events, that run smack under city streets, oil refineries, dams, high-rise buildings, and other urban structures.

The notorious San Andreas

This does not mean the San Andreas Fault is not frightening. Like all large faults, it is capable of generating truly great earthquakes that wreak havoc over hundreds of square kilometers. Moreover, some segments of the San Andreas are considered more dangerous than others. The most worrisome is a 100-km (62-mi)-long segment that runs through the Coachella Valley near the southern end of the fault. A major earthquake has not occurred there in more than 300 years. The least dangerous is a 300-km (186-mi) segment on the

northern reaches of the fault. It last broke in 1906.

The San Andreas Fault is a 965-km (599-mi) fracture zone between two gigantic plates—massive blocks of the Earth's crust riding atop a hot, sticky underlayer called the mantle. One plate comprises the North American continent and adjacent parts of the Atlantic Ocean floor. The other plate consists of a major portion of the Pacific Ocean floor and a strip of the California coastline attached to it. These so-called North American and Pacific plates are grinding past one another, with the Pacific plate headed in a northwesterly direction, at a rate of 56–60 mm (2.2–2.4 in) per year. Both plates are driven by forces stemming from the creation of new crust billowing out from deep within the Earth at mid-ocean ridges.

Because the plates are scraping past one another, the San Andreas Fault generates what are called

location	date	magnitude	deaths	injuries	property damage
Costa Mesa	April 7, 1989	5.0	0	0	minor
Santa Monica area	Jan. 19, 1989	5.2	0	several	minor
Pasadena	Dec. 3, 1988	5.0	0	23	minor
Imperial County	Nov. 24, 1987	6.6	0	94	$2.7 million
Whittier	Oct. 1, 1987	5.9	8*	200+	$358 million
Chalfant Valley	July 21, 1986	6.4	0	0	$436,500
Oceanside	July 13, 1986	5.4	1	28	$720,000
Palm Springs	July 8, 1986	5.6	0	0	$5.3 million
Morgan Hill	April 24, 1984	6.2	0	27	$10 million
Coalinga	May 2, 1983	6.7	0	47	$31 million
Eureka	Nov. 8, 1980	7.2	0	8	$1,750,000
Owens Valley	May 27, 1980	6.2	0	4	included below
Owens Valley (3 separate earthquakes)	May 25, 1980	6.1 / 6.0 / 6.1	0	9	$2.1 million
Livermore	Jan. 24, 1980	5.5	1	44	$11.5 million
Imperial Valley	Oct. 15, 1979	6.4	0	91	$30 million
Gilroy-Hollister	Aug. 6, 1979	5.9	0	16	$5 million
Santa Barbara	Aug. 13, 1978	5.1	0	65	$7,310,000
Oroville	Aug. 1, 1975	5.7	0	0	minor
Pt. Mugu	Feb. 21, 1973	5.9	0	several	$1 million
San Fernando	Feb. 9, 1971	6.4	58	2,000	$511 million
San Francisco	March 22, 1957	5.3	0	40	$1 million
Eureka	Dec. 21, 1954	6.5	1	unknown	$2 million
Bakersfield	Aug. 22, 1952	5.8	2	35	$10 million
Kern County	July 21, 1952	7.2	12	18	$50 million
Santa Barbara	June 30–July 1, 1941	5.9	0	unknown	$250,000
El Centro	May 18, 1940	7.1	9	unknown	$6 million
Long Beach	March 10, 1933	6.3	115	hundreds	$40 million–$50 million
Santa Barbara	Nov. 4, 1927	7.0	unknown	unknown	unknown
Santa Barbara	June 29, 1925	6.3	12–14	unknown	$6.5 million
San Francisco	April 18, 1906	7.8	700–800	unknown	$400 million
Owens Valley	March 26, 1872	7.7	27	56	$250,000
Hayward	Oct. 21, 1868	6.8	30	unknown	unknown
San Francisco	Oct. 8, 1865	6.3	unknown	unknown	$500,000
Fort Tejon	Jan. 9, 1857	7.6	1	unknown	unknown
San Francisco	June 1838	7.0	0	unknown	unknown
San Francisco	June 10, 1836	6.8	unknown	unknown	unknown
San Juan Capistrano	Dec. 8 and 21, 1812	6.9/7.1	over 50	unknown	unknown
San Diego	Nov. 22, 1800	6.5	unknown	unknown	unknown
Orange County	July 28, 1769	unknown	0	unknown	unknown

*One death from 5.3 aftershock on Oct. 4, 1987

Source: U.S. Geological Survey, National Earthquake Information Center, Denver, Colo.

strike slip earthquakes. The effect can be simulated by holding one's palms together, as if praying, and moving the left palm up in the direction the fingertips are pointing.

Scientists note that if the San Andreas boundary were smooth and even, there would be frequent small earthquakes as the plates slid along their relative paths. But the boundary is not even. From its southern end at Baja California, the San Andreas travels north until it seems to run into an obstacle—the Sierra Nevada mountain range. There the fault bends sharply to the west and follows a route above the Los Angeles Basin until it again turns northward. All along this bend in the San Andreas are numerous fault zones and a series of east-west mountain ranges pushed up by the relative motion of the plates. This "dog leg" portion of the San Andreas is "locked." That is, it tends not to break until it accumulates a great deal of strain—up to 6-m (20-ft) worth. Measurements show that this locked portion of the San Andreas is, on average, moving only 35 mm (1.4 in) a year. The remaining 20 mm (0.8 in) in overall plate motion is taken up by the many other faults in the region.

After turning north again, the San Andreas runs a straight course through central California—giving rise to frequent, small earthquakes as the plates creep past one another—until it takes another westward turn, or dog leg, below the San Francisco peninsula. This northern section of the fault is also locked. Like the southern section of the fault, it is prone to infrequent large-magnitude earthquakes.

These locked portions of the San Andreas Fault lead to further earthquake hazards. For example, it is now generally recognized that the Los Angeles Basin—a flat expanse of land ringed by mountain ranges—is a former bay that has been raised above sea level by a maze of thrust faults underneath the basin. These thrust faults, which can be visualized as deeply buried ramps of rock that grind past one another at steep angles, are powered by the colliding forces of relative plate motion as Baja California (riding on the Pacific plate) crashes into the mountain ranges above the Los Angeles Basin. In other words, the land underneath the Los Angeles Basin is highly compressed and fractured because of the way in which the San Andreas is configured.

Geologists now believe that dozens of such "faults in the basement" exist beneath the Los Angeles metropolitan area and that they generate damaging earthquakes every few decades. Most thrust faults have not been mapped because, unlike strike slip faults, they tend not to leave surface traces when they rupture.

Predicting damage

As the San Andreas and its companion faults have become better known, government officials have tried

Seismologists now believe that the most destructive California earthquake may occur not on the San Andreas Fault (a segment of which is shown above) but on smaller faults directly below major metropolitan areas.

to assess the likely impact of major California earthquakes. According to a 1980 federal report, an earthquake on the San Andreas near Los Angeles, depending on the time of day, would kill 3,000 to 14,000 people, cause 12,000 to 52,000 serious injuries, and result in $17 billion in property damage. A similar event near San Francisco would cause between 3,000 and 11,000 deaths, 12,000 to 44,000 serious injuries, and $38 billion in property damage. Recent reports have increased property damage estimates to above $60 billion in both cities.

A magnitude 7.5 earthquake on the Newport-Inglewood Fault near downtown Los Angeles could kill 4,000 to 21,000 people, injure between 18,000 and 84,000, leave another 192,000 homeless, and cause $62 billion in damage. Such an earthquake would not last as long as one occurring on the more distant San Andreas, but it could do as much or more damage.

Los Angeles quake—a worst-case scenario

What would a major earthquake in Los Angeles be like? Engineers predict that most modern high-rise buildings will ride out the shaking. Buildings will sway dramatically, perhaps putting impossible strain on those designed with open-air ground floors, multiple towers, and split-level configurations that leave weak spots. Flying glass will be everywhere.

Buildings that are 10 to 15 stories high may not do as well as taller structures. Engineers are afraid

At a day-care center in San Francisco, youngsters practice "drop and cover" during an earthquake drill. It has been predicted that if a major earthquake occurs along the San Andreas and its companion faults near San Francisco, there will be 3,000 to 11,000 deaths, 12,000 to 44,000 major injuries, and more than $60 billion in property damage.

In this emergency planning, local officials are sending an urgent message to the public. Individuals will be on their own for the first 24 hours and probably for the first three days after the main shock. Everyone must expect to camp out as aftershocks further weaken structures. Families should have on hand a week's supply of food and 53 liters (14 gal) of drinking water for a family of four. They will need first aid kits, flashlights, candles, blankets, battery-powered radios, and wrenches to turn off gas and water lines. No one knows how many southern California families have undertaken these preparations.

Every large corporation and business in Los Angeles, however, has made preparations for "the big one." Most high-rise buildings and factory complexes have complete emergency plans calling for self-sufficiency in the first 72 hours after the earthquake. In April companies conduct earthquake drills and train employees in first aid and other emergency measures.

The 166 hospitals in Los Angeles County are ready. After reporting via two-way radio to a central office to announce that they are up and running, the hospitals will literally lock their doors. This is to avoid having hundreds of people descend at once on emergency rooms. Instead, the hospitals will set up casualty collection points outside their facilities to treat earthquake victims, using a triage system—the most needy are helped first.

The Red Cross has been assigned the job of providing mass care for victims. After the earthquake, designated schools and public parks will be opened as emergency shelters. The Red Cross is in the process of training more shelter managers at the local level. While most schools have enough food for two to three days, the Red Cross has agreements with fast-food chains to bring in more food to the shelters as needed.

After a large earthquake state officials plan to mobilize their southern California headquarters at Los Alamitos, an army reserve base with an airfield and communications hub. Bulldozers, dogs trained in rescue, and other resources will be made available to communities via local EOCs.

Finally, the federal government will make resources available as needed. This includes help from the public health, transportation, housing, and commerce departments, as well as the military (for search, rescue, reconnaissance, and safety). Eventually, federal authorities will set up a disaster information center where people can apply for federal and state assistance.

Another Armenia unlikely

Most disaster experts do not think that Los Angeles or San Francisco will sustain the kind of structural losses seen in Armenia. In the wake of that recent earthquake, engineers from the Soviet Union and many other nations identified a serious problem with local construction methods; cement was diluted with too much sand; welding was inferior; and some prefabricated structures and building codes did not anticipate seismic activity. Not all prefabricated buildings failed, however. Those with frames survived surprisingly well. Design, rather than workmanship and prefabrication, made all the difference.

Another lesson concerned coordination of international aid. Many relief teams flown into Armenia got there too late, contributed little, and added to the confusion. As the California planners know, it is best for outsiders to wait 48 hours or so until local disaster officials can say precisely what they need and where and when they need it.

In the meantime, at the Universal Studios Theme Park in southern California, a new ride has opened. It features a terrifyingly real 45-second simulated earthquake in a San Francisco subway tunnel. The crowds love it, although some California residents who have taken the ride say they are not amused.

Drug Abuse

As the decade of the 1990s begins, a solution to the plague of drug abuse and addiction that has swept the United States and most European countries is not in sight. Even the U.S.S.R., Switzerland, Spain, and Japan, where previously only alcohol abuse had been of concern, now report significant levels of illicit drug abuse. Crack—the inexpensive, smokable by-product of cocaine—has become the number one drug-abuse problem, and its use is no longer limited to a single geographic area or demographic group. All segments of society are suffering from the direct or indirect effects of crack.

While only a year ago there was still public debate about the seriousness of the drug epidemic in the U.S., the nation now is seemingly united in its concern. In 1988 Congress created an Office of National Drug Control Policy and declared that it would be national policy to achieve a drug-free America by 1995. While there is no unified agreement on the proper solution to the problem of drug abuse, virtually no one feels it will go away by itself. For the first time, many federal law-enforcement and social service agencies have made drug abuse issues a priority. However, as the number of addicts has increased nationally, smaller amounts of federal and state money per user have been allotted for prevention, education, and treatment.

Despite these serious negative trends, however, small victories in the war against drugs have been won. Attitudes about drugs and experimental drug use are shifting, and illicit drug use in adolescents has stopped rising, although it is still at high levels. Many school systems now begin mandatory antidrug education in elementary grades, and many grass-roots organizations have expanded their efforts to bring drug-education programs into disadvantaged areas, where the drug plague is the worst. One effective antidrug campaign has been sponsored by the Partnership for a Drug-Free America, a nonprofit business association, which organized a national effort, supported by $150 million, to use donated television and radio time and print space for powerful public-service ads discouraging drug use.

Drugs in the workplace are a major focus of government activity. Industrial leaders claim that drug and alcohol abuse have led to economic losses totaling over $100 billion a year. Government reports show that employees who use drugs have far higher rates of absenteeism, utilize more health benefits, and are less productive than those who do not. Several major transportation disasters have been caused by employees under the influence of drugs. For example, in an Amtrak accident that resulted in the deaths of 16 people, one engineer tested positive for marijuana use. Even the environment has not been spared. The captain of an oil tanker that ran aground in Alaska, causing the worst oil spill in history (more than 240,-000 bbl), was alleged have been legally intoxicated at the time of the accident.

There have been a few new developments in the treatment of drug addiction. Recent studies have indicated that in some cases outpatient treatment for drug and alcohol abuse is as effective as and is far less costly than inpatient treatment. Studies also indicate that the type of drug problem, the motivation and social support system of the abuser, and other environmental factors play as large a role as the treatment method in determining success. Other studies released in the past year revealed a clear genetic involvement in some cases of alcoholism and other forms of addiction.

Meanwhile, a controversy has developed around the lack of qualified counselors to treat the complicated multiple addictions of many crack, heroin, and alcohol users—even if public funding for such treatment were available. Further, the number of mentally ill persons addicted to drugs and needing specialized care has increased.

A potential research breakthrough is a treatment for cocaine overdose that involves the lowering of the body temperature. If such a treatment becomes available, it might stem the tide of emergency room deaths. Further clinical tests are needed, however, to confirm the applicability to everyday use.

The Partnership for a Drug-Free America runs full-page, hard-hitting newspaper ads that mince no words about the dangers of addiction.

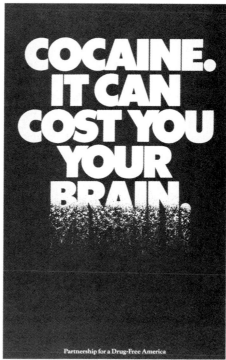

The Media-Advertising Partnership for a Drug-Free America, Inc.

Most of the cocaine that ends up on U.S. streets comes from Colombia, where it is prepared from coca (above left). Despite sophisticated tracking operations, about 90% of the drugs smuggled across U.S. borders are undetected. In 1989 a major bust in New York netted $1 billion worth of Southeast Asian heroin packed in rubber tires.

Cocaine: from bad to worse

In the U.S., public optimism in the battle to reduce cocaine use gave way during the past year to official frustration. One Drug Enforcement Agency (DEA) official summed up the prospects for controlling the cocaine wars of today: "We may look back on this in three years or so and long for the good old days of 1989." The main reasons for this negative attitude are the inability of law-enforcement agencies to reduce the amount of cocaine entering the country and the spread of crack use to almost every region in the country. One indicator of the problem is the increased number of ports of entry. Until recently, most cocaine entered the U.S. through Florida. Now Arizona and California have joined the Southeast as major ports of entry. In 1986, 2,028 kg (4,467 lb) of cocaine were seized at the Arizona-Mexico border. By 1988 seizures had grown to 10,285 kg (22,654 lb), a 407% increase. In California 838 kg (1,845 lb) were seized in 1986. In 1989, 8,989 kg (19,799 lb) were seized, a dramatic 973% jump. Entry into Florida has not ceased, but the rate of increase in cocaine seizures in the past three years was a comparatively low 152%.

Some progress in slowing the rate of drug entry has been made through the use of sophisticated high-tech radar tracking stations. Various U.S. agencies, including the Customs Service, the DEA, and the Coast Guard, reported major seizures totaling over 110,000 kg (250,000 lb) of cocaine in 1988. Nevertheless, the sharp drop in the street price of the drug shows just how little of the cocaine entering the country is intercepted. In 1985 cocaine cost $45,400 per kilogram. Today the cost is less than $9,100.

According to Customs Service reports, because enormous amounts of cargo enter the U.S., only about 10% of the cocaine and other drugs flowing across the borders can be detected. Air and shipping routes are the primary entry methods for most drugs, yet with more than 34 million shipments of merchandise entering the U.S. per year, only a small portion can be inspected closely. Furthermore, because of the number of people entering the U.S. each year (over 310 million people in 1987, for example), it is virtually impossible to check all personal luggage that could contain drugs.

Cocaine enters the U.S. in a highly organized and sophisticated fashion. Powerful drug cartels produce the drug, primarily in Colombia. These organizations smuggle the cocaine into the U.S. by boat through Florida and overland through Mexico. Customs officials have found drugs in the hollows of religious statues, in welded steel beams, in furniture, inside imported cars, and among dozens of products capable of holding a kilo of cocaine or heroin.

The quantity and inexpensiveness of this drug have created a frightening pattern of violence and murder. Virtually no city in the U.S. remains unaffected. From 1987 to 1988 the New York City murder rate rose by 10.4%, while in Washington, D.C., law-enforcement officials could barely keep count of the crime victims. In the early months of 1989, the Washington murder rate soared by 55.1% over the same time period of the previous year. Police estimated that 85% of the cases were directly related to drugs, and they reported that drugs were found on the bodies of half of those murder victims.

New information about the violent effects of crack and other drugs has reinforced the feeling among many public officials that the problems caused by cocaine—and especially crack—use cannot be solved simply through reduction in supply or by legalization. A 1988 study conducted by 1-800-COCAINE, the national cocaine help line, showed that 50% of the crack-using callers acknowledged that they had committed serious crimes ranging from murder and robbery to rape and child abuse. In the past, most criminal activity surrounding drug use had been linked to the need to avoid the pain and suffering of withdrawal, as in the case of heroin users. Almost two-thirds of the crack-using callers who acknowledged criminal behavior, however, committed their crimes while high on the drug, not while in withdrawal. Researchers have also been shocked to discover that there was virtually no difference in the criminal behavior between the 200 female and 450 male callers surveyed.

Another significant trend during the past year was the decline of cocaine use in the middle class. Use has percolated down through all the various strata of society over the past decade and has settled on the urban poor. Data from surveys, including that of the cocaine help line, confirm that the majority of those seeking help for drug problems are unemployed, are uneducated, and smoke cocaine or take it intravenously. A survey sponsored by the Partnership for a Drug-Free America and the National Institute of Drug Abuse (NIDA) found sharp declines in cocaine and other drug use among college students. The NIDA study showed an almost 50% decrease in recreational use, which respondents attributed to fear of the dangers of drugs.

While the urban middle class had reduced its drug use, the market for crack and other drugs seemed to be increasing in rural America. In a survey of 100 southern U.S. sheriffs, 83 said that crack was a significant problem. In eastern Georgia, for example, a town sheriff arrested 100 crack dealers, a ratio of one dealer for every 200 citizens. In addition to crack, a new form of amphetamine—"crank"—was also appearing in the rural U.S. The problems of drug use in rural areas have strained local law-enforcement authorities, who are unequipped to deal with the heavily armed drug dealers. In one Alabama community, 40 drug dealers were on trial in a single week.

Cocaine and AIDS

Injection of drugs, including heroin and other opiates, has been clearly linked to an increased risk of AIDS (acquired immune deficiency syndrome) infection, according to several studies. Reports from several sources, however, including the *Journal of the American Medical Association,* indicate that intravenous use of cocaine also increases the risk of AIDS significantly. Even crack use may increase the risk. One reason is that the practice of exchanging sexual favors for

drugs increases with cocaine use, linking the two main methods of AIDS virus transmission—shared needles and unsafe sexual practices. This trend has increased the incidence of AIDS infection in the heterosexual population and seems to be the main route of infection for many cocaine addicts.

In the U.S. the number of AIDS cases linked to IV drug use is on the rise. Recent studies at the Centers for Disease Control indicate that 27% of all AIDS victims are also intravenous (IV) drug users. In some areas the infection rate linked to both heroin and cocaine use is even higher—40% in New York City and 60% in Newark and Jersey City, New Jersey. According to a study carried out in San Francisco, in areas where AIDS has been linked to homosexual practices, AIDS infection has also increased in the drug-addicted nongay population.

Pregnancy and drug use

Drug-addicted babies are another by-product of the epidemic of addiction. The National Association for Perinatal Addiction Research and Education (NAPARE) in Chicago estimates that as many as 375,000 children will be harmed by their mothers' drug use during pregnancy. The study reports that 11% of all women giving birth use one or more illegal drugs during pregnancy. NIDA estimates that use of both illegal and legal drugs—alcohol and tobacco—is widespread among women of childbearing age in the U.S. Some eight million women between ages 15 and 44 smoke cigarettes or marijuana, drink, or use cocaine, NIDA says. Each of these substances has been directly linked to birth defects. NIDA reports that 15% of these women use these drugs at levels that can alter fetal development during pregnancy.

Cocaine, a toxic drug in adults, is even more dangerous to an unborn child. The drug, which causes increased central nervous system stimulation, quickly crosses into the placenta after injection and is converted into an even more potent form, norcocaine. Because the drug remains in the amniotic fluid, the fetus is exposed to it two to three days longer than is its mother, who clears the drug from her bloodstream in 48 hours.

Infants born to cocaine-using mothers are smaller, weigh less, and are at higher risk for a number of abnormalities, including strokes and genitourinary abnormalities. Cocaine increases the risk of spontaneous abortion and premature and dangerous labor. In addition, infants exposed to cocaine *in utero* run a ten times greater risk of sudden infant death syndrome.

The number of babies addicted to drugs at birth doubled last year in Illinois (about 85% of the cases were in Chicago), tripled in the past two years in Los Angeles, and increased ten times in the same period in Miami. The NAPARE study also cites an increased incidence of drug-impaired infants in rural Oregon, Minnesota, and Illinois. The trend in nonurban areas is so pervasive the study has now been expanded to cover smaller suburban and rural centers that previously had not been testing pregnant women for drug use.

The effects of this trend are both medical and economic. For example, in California one of the state's largest health maintenance organizations (HMOs) pulled out of its San Francisco program because of the cost of the soaring amount of drug use among pregnant women. Costs of caring for a drug-exposed baby are estimated to be 50–100 times higher than the cost of caring for a healthy infant. Drug-exposed newborns stay in the hospital six times longer than healthy babies, often in the neonatal intensive care unit. Social services are strained by the problems of drug addiction in both mothers and infants. Another disturbing trend has been the abandonment of these babies. In 1987–88 there were over 300 abandoned in New York City hospitals.

Teenage drug use: some good news

If a beachhead has been established in any front in the drug war, it is among the young. For the second year in a row, drug use among high school seniors declined in 1988. Drug use by the young still remains an area of major concern, however. The 14-year National High School Senior Survey of 16,000–17,000 seniors in 135 high schools, conducted by the

Many schools now begin antidrug education in elementary grades. In Brooklyn, New York, schoolchildren are shown samples of illicit drugs and drug paraphernalia by police officers who instruct them about the dangers of drug use.

David M. Grossman—Photo Researchers

University of Michigan's Institute for Social Research and sponsored by NIDA, indicates that while seniors have reduced their use of drugs, experimentation with drugs, tobacco, and alcohol among younger adolescents is high. Furthermore, this annual study does not measure drug use among high school dropouts, many of whom live in the inner-city areas most affected by the crack epidemic.

The most significant aspect of the trend toward less drug use is the continued drop in cocaine and crack use among high school students, along with a significant change in attitude toward use of these drugs. The proportion of seniors who said they believed that there was a great risk associated with cocaine experimentation was over 50% for the first time. An even greater proportion, 69%, acknowledged a great risk with even occasional use.

The use of marijuana has declined significantly. In 1978 almost half of all seniors reported some use. That statistic has now fallen to about one-third. Over three-fourths of high school seniors also view marijuana use as very risky. The decline in use of hallucinogens, stimulants, tranquilizers, and opiates (except heroin use, which has remained at 0.5% for years) indicates that the antidrug message is finally affecting students' views of all drugs except alcohol and tobacco.

While there was a statistically significant drop in alcohol use among seniors—from 41 to 35% in the past six years—use still remains high, with over 64% reporting that they had had at least one drink in the month preceding the survey. Tobacco use, however, has been unaffected by the change in illegal-drug-use habits. Today 29% of all high school seniors smoke cigarettes on a daily basis, a rate that has remained unchanged for six years.

A national study conducted by NIDA among eighth and tenth graders in the fall of 1987 is reflective of trends in adolescent drug use:

● 51% of eighth-grade students and 63% of tenth graders have smoked cigarettes

● 77% of eighth graders and 89% of tenth graders have tried alcohol. More than 25% of tenth graders reported having had five or more drinks in the two weeks prior to the survey

● 15% of eighth graders and 35% of tenth graders have tried marijuana

● 5% of eighth graders and 9% of tenth graders have tried cocaine, and approximately one-third have tried crack

Despite these statistics, over 80% perceived either a moderate or serious risk from use of these drugs, and over 70% said their friends would disapprove if they used any of these drugs on a regular basis.

Supply is clearly not a problem for young people. Over 80% said they could get cigarettes and alcohol easily; 57% indicated they could obtain marijuana and 27% could obtain cocaine easily.

"So this is how he knows if we've been bad or good! . . ."

Sponsors of the study point out that the reduction in drug use has occurred despite an increase in the drug supply and easy access to drugs. They conclude that if proper resources are diverted to education, a reduction in demand will lead to achievement of the national goal of a generation of drug-free young people.

Drug testing

Drug-testing policies, especially as a preemployment screening tool, vary among companies. Initial surveys conducted in 1987–88 by the U.S. Department of Labor of 7,502 companies with about 4.5 million employees showed that fewer than 1% faced any sort of drug testing.

On March 21, 1989, the U.S. Supreme Court ruled favorably on two drug-testing cases for the first time. The cases concerned both public safety and the right of the federal government to create a drug-free workplace. Drug-testing programs for railroad workers and for U.S. Customs Service employees were upheld by 7–2 and 5–4 decisions, respectively.

The railroad workers' case came on the heels of several fatal accidents, including one where 16 people were killed in the crash of an Amtrak metroliner and three Conrail freight engines outside Baltimore, Md., in January 1987. The engineer, who ultimately pleaded guilty to manslaughter, tested positive for marijuana and admitted having smoked it prior to the accident. The test case, however, involved regulations passed by the Federal Railroad Administration mandating testing after any major accident. The court ruled that the testing program did not violate the employees' constitutional rights under the Fourth Amendment, which protects citizens from unreasonable search and seizure and guarantees other rights of privacy. The justices balanced the right of the public to protection against injury against the rights of employees in an industry where safety regulations are pervasive and well known to those employees. The justices concluded that "the expectations of privacy of covered employees

are diminished by reason of their participation in an industry that is regulated pervasively to insure safety." The court indicated that a drug-testing program would act as a deterrent to drug use and that testing was needed because employees might become impaired and involved in an accident before a supervisor had an opportunity to observe their behavior.

The U.S. Customs Service case, decided by a one-vote margin, involved the right of the service to test employees seeking transfer or promotion to certain departments, including those who work with classified materials or are involved directly with drug interception. Also, employees who must carry a firearm as part of their job were required to be tested. The justices ruled that public safety and public interest outweighed the rights of the individual. Employees involved in preventing the flow of drugs into the U.S., the court said, "should expect effective inquiry into their fitness and probity." The same standards should be applied to those who carry guns, the court ruled, since the effectiveness of their duty depends primarily on their judgment and coordination. The court did not rule on drug testing for employees who simply handle classified materials, which may include messengers, clerks, or such professionals as accountants or lawyers, and returned this part of the case to a lower court of appeals for further study. The increase in drug testing and the effect of the U.S. Supreme Court cases lend ammunition to the federal government's drive for a drug-free workplace. The Department of Transportation has instituted a random drug-testing program. The Department of Agriculture and the Treasury Department test applicants, and all army and navy personnel are required to undergo random testing.

As both of these cases were narrowly defined, experts in constitutional law hold that the jury is still out on other private and government testing programs. Some 40 additional drug-testing cases are still pending in lower courts.

—*Mark S. Gold, M.D.*

study. The same Swiss study also found a previously unreported excess of testicular cancers among electricians. The numbers in this study were too small to allow any definitive assessment, especially about the possible risks to electricians of leukemia or brain tumors, as have been suggested by similar studies. A report from France reviewing epidemiological studies of the health effects of electricity generation and transmission equipment found an increase in the risk of one form of leukemia among electrical workers, a finding consistent with other studies. The possible link between exposure to electricity and electricity-generating equipment and the development of cancer continues to be a subject of ongoing investigation and concern.

Mental stress—human and financial costs

A 1988 report based on a study by a British agency, the Health and Safety Executive, concluded that mental health stresses cause 30 to 40% of all sick leave from work. Among the findings of this study were that an employee's mental health can be affected by such factors as over- or underpromotion, too much or too little work, relocations, changes in the work environment or among the people one works with, irregular or long hours, lack of autonomy, monotonous work, and the possibility of potential violence at the workplace. A number of warning signs were noted as possible indications that an individual might be suffering from undue job stress—irritability, unsociability, unusual absenteeism, changes in personal appearance or behavior, increasing use of cigarettes, alcohol, or drugs, and other signs of depression.

In the U.S. stress was also becoming recognized as an increasingly important problem in the workplace; in 1988 approximately 14% of occupational disease claims were stress-related, compared with fewer than 5% ten years earlier. The average cost of an insurance claim for mental stress is now approximately $15,000, and about $100 million is paid out in such claims each year. The cost to industry, including absenteeism and losses in production, is estimated at more than $100 billion each year. A study of how stress affects airline pilots indicated that corporate difficulties have a significant effect on the mental well-being of pilots of specific air carriers.

Air pollution: getting worse

Data published by the EPA in April 1989 showed that the air was even dirtier than had been previously believed. It was estimated that more than 1.1 billion kg (one kilogram is about 2.2 lb) of toxic materials were emitted into the air of the U.S. in 1987 and that more than half came from only ten states. Leading the list was Texas, with nearly 105 million kg of toxic pollutants released into the air each year. The biggest single contributor to toxic materials in the air is the chemical industry, which is responsible for close to 410 million

kg per year. Isolated findings of the release of some unusual materials were also noted in the EPA report. In Kansas, for example, almost 32,000 kg of the nerve gas phosgene were released into the air in 1987. In Indiana more than 63,500 kg of methyl isocyanate, the substance that killed thousands in Bhopal, India, were released. Also included on the list of pollutants were 107 million kg of carcinogens, such as benzene and formaldehyde, and 240 million kg of neurotoxins, such as trichlorethylene and toluene. The EPA has estimated that 2,000 new cases of cancer each year can be attributed to airborne toxic substances and that people who live near chemical plants are at higher risk than others of developing cancer.

While clean-air efforts seemed to be stalled nationally, in March 1989 southern California adopted a revolutionary 20-year plan to eliminate air pollution in the Los Angeles area. The "L.A. plan" will ban a variety of products that affect the environment, from aerosol hair sprays to barbecue lighter fluid. The plan calls for the use of cleaner fuels in internal combustion engines, requires employers to promote carpooling by workers, and would eventually require cars and buses to be electrically powered. The most drastic provisions

In January 1989, after officials in Milan, Italy, issued a warning that air pollution had reached alarmingly high levels, some residents (and their pets) donned protective masks before venturing out of doors.

AP/Wide World

In 1989, as the Los Angeles skyline threatened to disappear into the smog, a 20-year plan to eliminate air pollution was unveiled. Under the proposed regulations, motor vehicles with gasoline engines would eventually be banned.

of the L.A. plan, those designed to reduce auto and industrial emissions, are so strict that many observers thought they would prove both impractical and unfeasible. Others characterized the plan as a "blueprint for the future" and predicted that similar programs would be adopted by other local governments.

Getting rid of garbage

In 1988, for the first time, major regulatory action was proposed by the Environmental Protection Agency to control the disposal of municipal garbage. Approximately 78% of solid-waste landfills in the United States are owned by local governments, 17% by private organizations, 4% by the federal government, and 1% by states. Many are small; half are four hectares (ten acres) or less in size. Evidently only 15% of landfills have any type of liner, and only 5% have systems for collecting substances that might leach into the surrounding soil or groundwater. It is thought that at least 25% are currently violating groundwater-protection standards. The EPA proposals include developing inspection programs; strengthening requirements for daily covering of landfills to control rodents, insects, fires, and odors; establishing gas-monitoring stations to detect the presence of methane (which could cause explosions and fires), with concomitant systems for removing the gas; and prohibiting open burning and discharge of harmful wastes into surface waters. Initial estimates of the costs of carrying out these proposals run to about $44,000 per landfill, which corresponds to an average of $11 per household per year—or $880 million for the nation. Some jurisdictions, such as the cities of Minneapolis and St. Paul, Minn., have initiated far-reaching waste-management programs, including ordinances aimed at banning the use of polystyrene drink cups and food packaging, which are not biodegradable and cannot be recycled. Plastic products currently make up about 7% of the garbage in the U.S. and will double in quantity by the next century. The most commonly recycled items at the present time are aluminum and paper.

Also of growing concern during the past year was the disposal of toxic materials. Hundreds of hazardous-waste sites were added to the list of those

eligible for federal funds, bringing to more than 1,000 the number of sites authorized for cleanup under the Superfund program. Numerous episodes of contaminated needles, dressings, and other medical paraphernalia washing up on shorelines and on beaches were reported in the summer of 1988. In New York and New Jersey, some beaches were closed because of the fear that AIDS, hepatitis, or other infectious diseases might be spread by the contaminated materials. These incidents led to the enactment in November 1988 of a law setting up a pilot program under which the EPA will monitor the disposal of infectious wastes in ten states. In other states and many municipalities, stricter laws were instituted for tracking used needles, syringes, and other medical debris from the point of origin to final disposal.

A related issue was the growing practice by companies in developed countries of contracting with poorer nations for unused land in which to bury toxic industrial wastes. Dumping costs at hazardous-waste landfills are high in Europe and the U.S., and some third world countries would like to take advantage of this lucrative market. The governments of these countries are generally opposed, at least officially, to the importation of toxic wastes, even at a handsome profit. In March 1989 leaders from more than 100 nations met in Basel, Switz., and drafted an agreement to limit the shipping of wastes from one country to another. Among its provisions, the accord calls for written permission from the recipient country.

Serving up lead poisoning

In 1988 the U.S. Food and Drug Administration, through its *FDA Drug Bulletin,* told physicians to be on the lookout for possible cases of lead intoxication caused by improperly fired lead-glazed ceramic ware. Although the problem has been recognized for some years, the FDA found in 1988 that almost 5% of all ceramic ware products sold commercially in the United States violated FDA guidelines. All of these violations involved imported products (approximately 60% of dinnerware sold in the U.S. is imported). In FDA tests ceramic ware from Mexico, Italy, Spain, Portugal, and Hong Kong was found to leach excessive levels of lead into food and beverages. The countries accounting for the greatest proportion of the market share of U.S. imported ceramic ware include Japan, China, South Korea, Taiwan, the U.K., West Germany, and Italy. Japan, it was noted, has strict quality-control measures, and Japanese ceramic products are generally safe. An agreement has also been signed with China to ensure that no Chinese-manufactured ceramic ware exported to the U.S. will leach unsafe amounts of lead. FDA investigators noted that although ceramic ware imported through formal channels is monitored and tested, the items that pose the greatest problem are those taken to the U.S. by travelers on business

The Statue of Liberty seems to look down unwelcomingly on this mound of garbage being taken by barge to a Staten Island landfill. Finding places to dump solid wastes is now a major environmental problem in the U.S.

or pleasure trips. In terms of this kind of informal importation, products from Mexico were cited as a special problem. Mexico is unique because its ceramic products are often made in cottage industries rather than in large, centralized facilities and are therefore difficult to regulate or control.

Alar(m) about apples

Clearly, there was much in the news in the past year to provoke consumer anxiety. Without a doubt, however, the subject that captured the most dramatic headlines and roused the most heated controversy was the issue of toxic and potentially cancer-causing pesticide residues on fresh fruits and vegetables. Production of the most widely publicized of these chemicals, daminozide (Alar), was discontinued by the manufacturer as of June 1989; U.S. apple growers had already voluntarily agreed that they would not use it on the fall 1989 crop. Grapefruit growers in Florida announced that they would cease the use of lead arsenate, a chemical used to hasten the ripening of fruit, as of the 1988–89 growing season. (Lead arsenate was not being used in other grapefruit-growing states.) In addition, the EPA barred the use of the fungicide captan on some 40 different fruits and vegetables because residues found on these foods might pose a "significant" risk of cancer, but it continued to allow the chemical to be used on another 20 or so fruits and vegetables (including cherries, tomatoes, and lettuce) because residues in these foods were low enough that the cancer risk was deemed "negligible."

—*Arthur L. Frank, M.D., Ph.D.*

Perils of the Packinghouse: *The Jungle* Revisited

by Christopher Drew

More than eight decades after Upton Sinclair's novel *The Jungle* (1906) exposed the brutal, filthy, and sometimes lethal working conditions in Chicago's slaughterhouses, the health and safety of U.S. meatpacking workers has once again become the focus of a national scandal. Sinclair's tale of death, disease, and gruesome injuries in the largest U.S. meatpacking plants sparked legislative reform and generated real improvements in workplace safety that were effective into the 1970s. In recent years, however, the leading meat companies have revolutionized their production processes, increasing speed and volume of production to levels undreamed of in Sinclair's time—and undoing in only a few short years progress in health and safety that took over half a century to achieve.

Of profits, pain, and progress

Throughout most of the 20th century, it was the job of slaughterhouse workers to split cattle and hog carcasses into halves, quarters, and other large chunks. The meat was then shipped to grocery stores, where skilled butchers sliced it into steaks, chops, roasts, and other cuts, according to customer specifications. During the past 15 to 20 years, however, the meatpacking industry has transformed its operations so that butchered animals are reduced to individual cuts of meat at the plant itself, boxed, and shipped to the supermarket ready for sale. The butchering process is now divided into hundreds of separate jobs that require each worker to perform the same task, or set of tasks, over and over again as quickly as possible.

An average worker may make as many as five knife cuts every 15 seconds—or nearly 10,000 cuts in an eight-hour day. Standing elbow to elbow on either side of a steel conveyor belt, meat cutters reach out, snag a moving slab of beef or pork with a metal hook, lower the meat onto a stationary table, make a specific cut or series of trims, and drop the meat back onto the belt—all with split-second timing. The largest plants process up to 300 cattle or 1,000 hogs an hour; all the while, clanging chains pull the chilled hunks of meat past each carving station on the way from the killing floor to the packaging and shipping departments at the other end of the plant. These fundamental changes in production have enabled the dozen or so largest packing companies, which prepare three-fourths of the meat served on America's tables, to enhance their profits and drive less efficient competitors out of business. At the same time, however, working conditions in the packinghouses have worsened significantly. On-the-job injuries, in particular, have increased dramatically as a direct result of the new production methods. At the core of the problem is a type of injury that results from the physical stress of performing the same action over and over again. These repetitive motion injuries, as they are called (another name is cumulative trauma disorders), are not unique to packing plant workers or even to those who labor on factory assembly lines. They are also common among such diverse groups as musicians, data processors, professional athletes, and supermarket checkout clerks. Their advent in the meatpacking industry is relatively recent, however.

One of the "most hazardous" industries

In all, 52,000, or about 38%, of the nation's nearly 136,000 slaughterhouse workers suffer some type of job-related injury or illness each year, according to U.S. Labor Department statistics. The injury rate—200 people hurt each working day—is more than three times the average for all U.S. factories. Labor Department figures also show that from 1973 through 1987 the number of workdays lost each year to injury or illness at the meat plants rose by nearly 150%, to 339.7 days for each 100 workers. During the same period, the average for all manufacturing plants increased by only 40%, to 95.5 days per 100 employees. Meatpacking thus ranks with construction, mining, and shipbuilding as one of the nation's most hazardous industries. This ominous finding has rekindled public accusations that the meat industry, which boasts annual sales of more than $50 billion, exploits its workers.

Each year as many as 40% of the workers at some packing plants suffer injuries from the constant stress of the machinelike motions they perform. The most common packinghouse injuries range from tendinitis, in which tendons—usually in the arm or shoulder—become inflamed, to carpal tunnel syndrome, in which tendons in the wrist swell and exert pressure on a major nerve that passes from the arm to the hand. Some workers also suffer from "trigger finger," an inflammation of the tendon sheaths, which causes one or more of the fingers to freeze in a curled position as if gripping a pistol trigger. Tendinitis can normally be cured with rest, but a significant number of cases of carpal tunnel syndrome and "trigger finger" require surgery, which in many cases leaves patients with a permanent loss of some percentage of the flexibility or feeling in their hands or wrists. As a result of these injuries, many packinghouse workers quit or are fired when the pain makes it impossible for them to keep up with the pace of production or to handle simple domestic chores. In rural areas where other jobs are scarce, it is not uncommon to find workers who have had several surgeries desperately clinging to their packinghouse jobs in much the same way veteran professional athletes cling to their careers—with the help of braces, splints, and painkilling drugs.

Meatpacking workers face other hazards as well. Each year thousands nick themselves with knives, slip and fall on greasy floors, or wrench their backs lifting heavy baskets of meat. Some develop respiratory problems from exposure to ammonia and other gases used in the refrigeration process. And a few lose limbs—or die—while trying to operate or repair machinery used to chop, grind, or package meat.

New crackdown

Recent exposure of these hazards has prompted the U.S. Occupational Safety and Health Administration (OSHA) to launch a new campaign for improved safety in the meatpacking industry. As a first step, the agency levied some of the largest fines in history against major U.S. meat companies. In October 1988 OSHA announced a $4.3 million fine against John Morrell & Co., alleging that the company had knowingly exposed its meat cutters to injury caused by repetitive job motions. The rate of incidence of cumulative trauma disorders in the Morrell plant at Sioux Falls, S.D., was nine times higher than the industry average, the worst such condition "in any industry to date," in the words of John Pendergrass, then assistant labor secretary in charge of OSHA. The government charged that Morrell not only knew of the serious health hazards and was aware of the tragic toll on its workers but chose to ignore them. A few months earlier OSHA had imposed a slightly smaller fine against another giant meat company, IBP, Inc., for "willfully" exposing workers at its Dakota City, Neb., plant to serious risk of repetitive motion injuries.

Special province of immigrant labor

Several parallels to social and economic conditions around the turn of the century help explain why meat company executives could afford, during much of the 1980s, to be less rigorous about the health and safety of their workers than managers in other industries. One was a surge in immigration—legal and illegal—from Mexico and Southeast Asia. One-quarter to one-half of the workers in some U.S. meat plants today are relatively recent immigrants; they typically speak little English and are reluctant to complain about working conditions for fear of losing their jobs. The recession in the early 1980s and the collapse of the farm and energy sectors of the economy in the middle of the decade also helped to swell the numbers of job seekers in the Midwest, Texas, and Colorado, where most of the packing plants are now located.

Indeed, ever since the 1870s, when the invention of refrigerated rail cars made it possible to ship fresh meat over long distances, packinghouse work—difficult, dirty, and dangerous—had been viewed as the special province of whatever wave of immigrants happened to be the newest and most eager for jobs. The first to arrive were the Germans; then came the Irish. During the time Sinclair spent in Chicago in 1904 researching his book, many of the workers in the largest slaughterhouses were of Eastern European extraction—Bohemians, Poles, Lithuanians, Czechoslovaks. Chicago was at that time the meatpacking industry's hub, a convenient point midway between the farms and ranches to the west of the Mississippi River, where most of the livestock was raised, and the country's major population centers east of the Mississippi. Most of the immigrants had embarked on the arduous voyage across the Atlantic spurred by dreams of the riches described to them by recruiting agents for the "Beef Trust," the five huge companies that dominated the sprawling complex of stockyards, packing plants, and rail-freight stations on Chicago's South Side. Many of the newcomers ended up living in squalid boarding houses "back of the yards."

Work in the meatpacking industry has always been difficult, dirty, and dangerous. A photograph taken in a Chicago plant in the early 1900s shows cleaver-wielding meatcutters wearing not a single item of protective gear.

Leslie F. Orear

Standing shoulder to shoulder at their carving stations along the production line, these workers in a modern meatpacking plant may make as many as five knife cuts every 15 seconds—or nearly 10,000 cuts in an eight-hour day. Repetitive motion injuries— painful ailments caused by trauma to overused joints and muscles—are common in packinghouse workers.

Working at breakneck speed

Sinclair and other critics of the time believed that some of the accidents in the meat plants resulted in part from the relatively crude methods used to increase the pace of production. One common technique, dreaded by most workers, was known as "speeding up." Company foremen would pick out the most adept men and push them to work at breakneck speed for a limited time on the most demanding cutting and trimming jobs; thus, the slower or less able workers were pressured to wield their knives at greater—and riskier— speeds if they wanted to hold onto their jobs. Injuries inevitably resulted from "speeding up."

Other accidents occurred because the packinghouses failed to provide workers with proper safety equipment. Sinclair wrote that the unprotected hands of men who split carcasses and stripped slabs of meat from bones were "crisscrossed" with knife cuts; some had slashed their own thumbs so many times that they were "a mere lump of flesh against which the man pressed the knife to hold it." Men who pulled hides off of animals would scrape their fingers so badly that their fingernails fell off. All of the packinghouse workers had to battle infections caused by germs from the uncooked meat.

Following Sinclair's sensational exposé, government investigators looking into the dangerous working conditions found that "luggers," men who carted about pieces of meat weighing about 90 kg (200 lb) or more, strained their arms and backs; that sausage makers periodically mangled their fingers in the grinding machines; and that the people who operated stamping and labeling machines sometimes lost their hands in the process. Few, if any, of the plants kept doctors or nurses on the premises. Severely injured workers were sent to the nearest hospital emergency room. An unknown number died each year from work-related infections and accidents.

First wave of reform

The Jungle's revelation of unsanitary conditions in the meat plants caused a public sensation and prompted Congress to pass landmark legislation to strengthen the government's food-inspection system. The book also fortified union efforts to gain leverage within the meat companies, and it helped set the climate for passage of reform legislation in most states, creating the worker's compensation system to provide monetary relief for people injured on the job.

The meat companies responded to these developments by introducing new safety equipment and, gradually over the next several decades, improving upon it. The protective steel-mesh gloves and aprons and the high-impact plastic wrist guards worn today by meat cutters are examples of advances born out of this movement for reform. Over the years, however, the meat companies also grew tired of bickering about wages with the main meat cutter's union and of being constantly scrutinized by powerful big-city newspapers. In the 1960s many of the companies began moving their plants from Chicago to small towns in the Midwest and the Southwest, where they could diffuse the union's power and conduct their business under less watchful eyes.

Revolution on the "disassembly" line

In 1966 a relative newcomer to the industry, Iowa Beef Processors, now known as IBP Inc., opened its revo-

313

lutionary plant in Dakota City, centered around a new "disassembly" line designed to ship "boxed beef"—steaks and other cuts—completely trimmed and ready for sale. IBP's innovations sent the industry into a state of turmoil. The old-line companies, which still shipped quarters and sides of beef, realized that these new techniques would reshape the industry; they would have to adopt them or go out of business. The upheaval that followed lasted into the 1980s, and by the time IBP's methods had become the norm, more than 1,000 packing plants had closed and many others had forced steep wage concessions and heavy layoffs on union locals, which feared that their own plants would be closed as well.

Between 1967 and 1987 the number of workers in the U.S. meatpacking industry declined from 187,100 to 135,700. During the same period, however, the new processes enabled the industry to increase the output per worker by roughly 80%. The profits of some of the top meat companies soared. IBP, today the biggest producer in both beef and pork, saw its net profits rise by 67%, to $67.9 million, from 1983 through 1987. The desire for this kind of fiscal gain also brought some of the biggest and best-financed U.S. corporations into the meat business; Occidental

David Kellen, whose job was to rip fat from hog flanks, first developed symptoms of carpal tunnel syndrome in 1978. Even after he had undergone multiple surgeries to correct the problem, some pain and weakness remained.

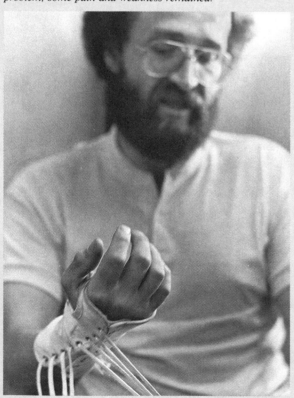

Paul F. Gero; © 1988 Chicago Tribune Company

Petroleum Corp. bought part ownership of IBP, Inc.; United Brands Co., a food and insurance conglomerate, acquired John Morrell & Co.

Toll on two workers: typical

Packinghouse workers and their doctors first noticed serious problems with repetitive motion injuries in the late 1970s. By the mid-1980s these disorders had become fairly common at many plants among workers with knife-wielding and other jobs that required extensive use of the hands.

David Kellen, 41 years old, and Elizabeth Peters, 39, one of a growing number of women working in packinghouses, were among the first employees at their plants to develop such injuries. Kellen, whose job at the Morrell plant in Sioux Falls required him to rip sheets of fat from the flanks of more than 200 hog carcasses an hour, first felt the pain in his hands in 1978. There was a tingling sensation in his fingers and numbness in his wrist. At night the pain made it difficult for him to sleep. Peters, who boned up to 360 hams per hour at a Wilson Foods Corp. plant in Cherokee, Iowa, recalled getting out of bed several times each night to run warm water over her hands to relieve the pressure. During the day she noticed that her hand fell asleep when she held a book, used a knife, or tried to write with a pencil.

Kellen and Peters eventually were diagnosed as suffering from carpal tunnel syndrome in both wrists. Both had multiple operations to correct the problem. Peters also had surgery to repair a "trigger finger" and to relieve a problem in one elbow, again caused by repetitive motions she performed on the job. Both Kellen and Peters returned to the meat plants after their operations because they could not find other employment in their areas that matched the packinghouse wages, which average $9 to $10 an hour, or, with overtime, some $20,000–25,000 a year.

"Railroad-track" scars

Other workers charge that some companies look for excuses to fire them once injuries begin to interfere with their ability to work. Some plants have annual employee turnover rates as high as 80%, and workers who have been let go after having surgery for carpal tunnel syndrome say the "railroad-track" scars on their wrists discourage other industrial companies from hiring them. Some end up in much lower paying jobs; others seek retraining for clerical positions through federal- and state-financed programs.

Injured workers also contend that the meat companies—and the company doctors, usually small-town practitioners who depend on the plant for much of their practice—refuse to give them time off after the surgery or rush them back to work prematurely. OSHA inspectors reported that 880 of Morrell's 2,000 workers in Sioux Falls had developed repetitive motion

Robert Drea

Two Hispanic workers in the only remaining Chicago beef slaughterhouse represent the latest in a long line of immigrant laborers who have earned their livings in the meat industry, doing jobs others shun.

injuries in the one-year period from May 1987 to April 1988. The inspectors found that 817 of these workers had been given no time off for the injuries to heal; 63 others had been returned to work within an average of 1.1 days after surgery. OSHA said its doctors believe workers should be given 30 to 60 days to recover after such surgery.

The companies—negligent or merely "slow"?

In a legal review process that could take a year or more, Morrell has contested the fine levied by the government in 1988. Its company chairman complained that federal regulators had singled Morrell out, imposing "arbitrary" standards for what he termed was clearly a national, multi-industry safety problem. At ConAgra Inc., the second-largest U.S. meatpacking company, the president of the red meats division acknowledged in an interview with the *Chicago Tribune* in October 1988 that the industry had probably been "slow" to recognize that the increase in cumulative trauma disorders was a problem intrinsic to the work itself and not the result of people being hired "off the street" who were not accustomed to such work. He added that company executives may simply have thought that packinghouse work, by its very nature, is "tough and hard and dangerous."

Such acknowledgements are the exception, however. Like Morrell's chairman, executives at several other leading companies strenuously deny that known health and safety risks were disregarded. Nonetheless, by early 1989 Morrell and the other large firms had launched extensive projects to redesign job motions and test new equipment designed to reduce the stress and strain on workers' bodies.

Seeking a solution through ergonomics

Meatpacking, as noted earlier, is not the only industry in which repetitive motion injuries are a problem. In recent years these disorders have become a threat to workers on auto assembly lines, to typists and word processors, even to supermarket checkers, who must flick their wrists repeatedly while passing cans or boxes over price-reading electronic sensors. OSHA officials say, however, that the force necessary to cut through chilled meat and the speed of work on the meat-cutting line combine to make the injury situation in the meatpacking plants at once the "most extensive and intensive" of any industry.

The best hope of eliminating the problem is believed to lie in redesign of tools and reengineering of the work itself along ergonomic lines. (Ergonomics—human factor engineering—is the science that studies the relationship of people to modern technology and to their environments.) IBP, as part of an agreement to reduce the fine imposed by OSHA, has hired an ergonomist to analyze job motions in its plants and advise the company on how to reduce worker injuries. The company estimates that engineering changes at the Dakota City plant alone could cost $1 million to $2 million. Several other companies—including ConAgra, Morrell, and Wilson Foods Corp.—also have hired ergonomists and have established in-plant health centers, staffed by nurses and physical therapists, to teach strengthening exercises and to supervise the use of whirlpools and other therapeutic devices. The American Meat Institute, an industry trade group, has budgeted $500,000 for research into such projects as the redesign of knife handles and ways to vary the heights of work stations.

True reforms yet to be realized

These efforts represent the most extensive research to date into ways to eliminate the risk of repetitive motion injuries. Meat company executives predict that their program could serve as a blueprint for improving worker protection in all industries. Union officials, on the other hand, are doubtful that research will get to the heart of the problem. Deborah Berkowitz, safety director for the meat cutter's union, says she welcomes the companies' "more open attitude" about safety. Given the industry's long history of health and safety problems, however, she and other observers remain skeptical about the commitment of the meat companies to protecting workers. It remains to be seen whether meatpacking will be able to shed its image as one of the nation's most hazardous industries.

Eye Diseases and Visual Disorders

In both developed and less developed societies, eyesight is a very precious sense, and visual disorders are a very common problem. In the United States alone, some 6.4 million new cases of eye disease occur each year. At least 11 million people have impaired vision that cannot be corrected by glasses; 800,000 of them are considered legally blind. Studies of the eye and the disorders that affect it have intensified over the past few years, with new findings occurring at a very rapid rate and offering hope for better understanding, diagnosis, and treatment of many problems.

New ways to measure visual function

The measurement of visual acuity is familiar to all who have visited an eye care practitioner or who have been tested in school or at a motor vehicle bureau. The traditional measurement of visual acuity is based on the eye chart invented in The Netherlands by Hermann Snellen in 1862. The ability to identify letters of

The Pelli-Robson eye chart (below) tests the eye's ability to discern faint images. Unlike conventional eye charts, which measure visual acuity only, this new test was designed to detect early signs of eye disease. An inability to see faint images is indicative of damage to retinal cells, which can figure in such disorders as diabetic retinopathy, optic nerve disease, and glaucoma and can lead to blindness. The new test can be performed in minutes in the clinician's office.

various sizes at a fixed distance is the basis of the test. One problem with the Snellen acuity chart has been that the letters used vary in their difficulty of recognition. The letter *C*, for example, is more difficult to identify than the letter *E*. Recently developed visual acuity charts have solved this problem by using ten uppercase letters that are essentially equal in difficulty of identification. One such system that has gained wide acceptance is the visual acuity chart used in what is known as the Early Treatment Diabetic Retinopathy Study; this test has proved easy to use and yields highly reproducible results.

Most measurements of visual function use a system in which black letters are sharply contrasted against a white background. Such a system may not detect subtle changes in vision that occur in many eye diseases, however. While visual acuity may be close to normal, contrast sensitivity testing reveals abnormalities in many ocular disorders, including diabetic retinopathy (retinal damage that is a symptom of diabetes), optic nerve disease, and glaucoma. The measurement of the contrast sensitivity helps to evaluate more fully the visual function of an individual.

Machines to test contrast sensitivity have been expensive as well as difficult and time consuming to use and therefore not conducive to everyday testing of patients. Recently, however, other methods have been developed for clinical use. One of these is the Pelli-Robson letter chart (named for its developers, Denis Pelli at Syracuse [N.Y.] University and John Robson at the University of Cambridge), which uses "disappearing" letters combined with a traditional eye-chart configuration. The letters become fainter in appearance as one reads down the chart; contrast sensitivity is determined by the faintest letters that can be read. This clinically relevant test can be performed in minutes in the clinician's office.

Studying myopia in chickens

In the United States about 100 million people wear either glasses or contact lenses, and 70 million of these people are nearsighted. In order for an individual to see clearly, the eye's complex optic system must focus a sharp image on the retina, the structure in the back portion of the eye that converts the light image into an electrical impulse that is relayed to the occipital lobe of the brain, thus permitting perception of the image. If the eye has a significant refractive error, then the image on the retina is not well-focused—*i.e.,* one perceives an image that is blurry. If the eyeball itself is too long, the focused image falls in front of the retina; this is termed myopia, or nearsightedness. If the eyeball is too short, the focused image falls behind the retina; this is termed hyperopia, or farsightedness. Ophthalmologists' understanding of the underlying mechanisms leading to myopia and hyperopia or to the development of an emmetropic eye—*i.e.,*

Investigators have shown that the placement of "defocusing lenses" on the eyes of young chickens will affect the growth of the eyes—thereby correcting for the induced nearsightedness or farsightedness. These studies have shown for the first time that the eye may not be genetically preprogrammed to grow to a certain length; rather, formed vision after birth may play a key role in determining the eye's ultimate length. Further research is likely to provide even better understanding of growth factors affecting early eye development.

one with no refractive error—has been limited. Some researchers believe that the end result is genetically determined, while others have suggested that the environment plays the dominant role in determining the eye's shape.

Recent work studying the development of the eyes of young chickens has led to remarkable observations concerning the refractive needs of the eye. This research indicates that eye growth is dependent on the opportunity of the eye to perceive patterns in its field of vision. It has been shown that eyes that are covered during their growing state will become markedly myopic—*i.e.,* the eyes become very long. When these eyes are no longer deprived of the opportunity to see visual patterns, they return to the emmetropic state. When corrective lenses that place an image in front of the retina are worn by a chick, the shape of the eyes will conform to the power of the "wrong prescription" lens and thus will correct fuzzy images. Likewise, if a lens placed in front of the chick's eye causes an image to be focused behind the retina, the eye will then grow to adjust to this new situation. These effects appear to be locally determined, so that if a lens that affects only half of the back of the eye is placed before the chick's eye, then only that part of the eye affected by the lens will enlarge.

These studies have for the first time provided information to suggest that formed vision after birth may play an important role in determining the length of the eye and that the eye may not be genetically preprogrammed to grow to a certain length. If the same mechanism that affects the eye formation of the chicken is at play in humans, according to Howard C. Howland, one of several researchers at Cornell University, Ithaca, N.Y., who have been studying vision in chicks, "it would mean that placement of lenses on the eyes of young children could conceivably affect the

growth of the eyes." The Cornell researchers believe that with further insights into the most common cause of visual disturbance in the U.S., it may be possible to confirm a biochemical basis for regulating vision. This could lead to new drug treatments that would enhance or decrease the growth of eyes so that they could reach an emmetropic state.

Update on contact lenses

Today more than 21 million Americans wear contact lenses, a 50% increase over the 14 million who wore them in 1980. Contact lenses have been available to the public for over half a century, but over the past few years dramatic advances have occurred in the technology related to their manufacture. The popularity of contact lenses reflects their wide applicability. They can be used as a replacement for glasses to correct refractive errors occurring either naturally or after cataract surgery or for such purely cosmetic indications as changing eye color.

The important considerations for any contact lens include comfort, a lack of damaging effects on the cornea, and its permitting a sufficient amount of oxygen to reach the eye. A contact lens capable of correcting the refractive error of the eye first became available to the general public in the 1930s. The first contact lenses used widely were the hard variety, which were originally made of polymethylmethacrylate. This type of lens is still worn by about 1.5 million individuals today. These lenses are difficult to get used to and, because they do not permit sufficient oxygen exchange between the cornea and the environment, cannot be worn for an extended period of time. They can also cause abrasions of the cornea as well as changes in the corneal curvature and in the cells in the deeper layers of the cornea. They do, however, give generally the best visual clarity of all types of lenses, are the easiest to clean, and usually last for years.

While hard lenses sit on the tear surface covering the eye, soft hydrogel lenses, a more recent development, sit directly on the corneal surface itself. Easier to wear, these lenses have the advantage of permitting much better oxygenation of the cornea than do the conventional hard type. Oxygen transmission is essentially dependent on the water content and central thickness of the lenses; thus, the greater the water content and thinner the central portion of the lens, the greater the oxygen permeability. Most soft lenses now on the market have a water content of 55–80%; others compensate for less water content by having very thin central areas (less than 0.04 mm).

Soft lenses have become by far the most popular contacts and are worn by at least 15 million Americans. About 11 million Americans wear the soft lens type that requires daily removal and cleaning.

In the early 1980s the U.S. Food and Drug Administration (FDA) approved soft lenses for extended wear, meaning that the lenses did not need to be removed daily and could be worn up to 30 days before removal for cleaning and disinfecting. Today such extended-wear lenses are available for correction of myopia, hyperopia, and astigmatism; about 3.5 million Americans wear this type of lens.

While soft lenses are comfortable to wear, they have certain disadvantages. The visual correction may not be as sharp as with hard lenses and can change with each blink. Soft lenses also tend not to last as long as hard lenses; e.g., they can rip easily if not handled very carefully. Another problem is that the cornea can be deprived of oxygen, especially during sleep; consequently, the cornea can swell as much as 6 to 12%.

A number of infections are associated with soft lenses. A condition called giant papillary conjunctivitis occurs in 10–15% of patients wearing soft hydrogel lenses, frequently requiring a refitting with a new soft or hard lens. Soft lenses tend to collect deposits of protein, fats, and calcium; thus, they require treatment with enzymatic cleaners every few weeks. Additionally, proper disinfection of these lenses is essential for their safe use. Thermal and chemical disinfection methods are used; the choice of method depends mainly on the water content of the lens.

A very serious complication of all contact lens wear but particularly of soft contact lenses is that of corneal infections caused by bacteria, fungi, or protozoa. A common bacterial pathogen found in corneal infections associated with soft contact wear is *Pseudomonas aeroginosa,* a particularly destructive and often difficult-to-treat organism. This may be related to the selective bacterial adherence of this organism to either the contact lenses themselves or the deposits that collect upon them.

A recent concern has been the finding of acanthamoeba keratitis, mostly in the extended-wear soft contact lens group. This infection characteristically appears as a ring infiltrate in the cornea. It is frequently not amenable to antibiotic therapy, necessitating that a corneal transplant be performed in order to remove the diseased tissue. Sometimes the infection will recur in the transplanted tissue. In many cases those developing this complication do not properly disinfect their lenses, thereby increasing the risk for this very serious but still relatively rare complication. Because of this risk, in June 1989 the FDA issued a formal caution that extended-wear lenses should not be worn for more than a week without being removed and disinfected.

Soft hydrogel lenses have the disadvantage of collecting deposits of protein, fats, and calcium; thus, they require frequent enzymatic cleaning. The photographs below show the extent to which deposits can build up after one month on daily-wear (left) and extended-wear (center) lenses, even if prescribed cleaning practices have been followed. Minimal buildup is seen on a disposable lens (right), which is worn only one week, then replaced.

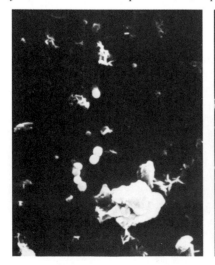 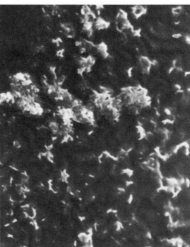 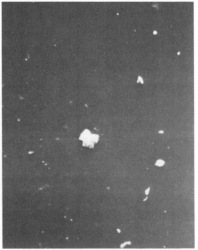

Vistakon, a Johnson & Johnson company

Acuvue® Disposable Contact Lenses are purchased in multipacks; each pair is worn for one week, then thrown away. This new system offers greater convenience than other currently available extended-wear regimens.

New contact lenses are being developed to overcome some of the problems outlined above and to make their use even more convenient. Bifocal lenses have been introduced to help older patients both read and see at distance with the same contact lens. To date, though many variations of bifocal contacts have been attempted, the results still need to be improved. New polymers for soft lenses that will be more durable in spite of a high water content are also being developed. Several new hard gas-permeable lenses have also recently been developed. These include silicone-acrylate copolymers, which are extremely oxygen permeable and are being tested for extended wear. Two other lens developments include silicone resin lenses, which are highly durable as well as gas permeable, and fluoropolymer lenses, which have been shown to cause less overnight corneal swelling than the soft hydrogel lenses that are presently widely used.

Recently a disposable extended-wear contact lens has been placed on the market; these lenses are worn for one week and then thrown away and replaced with new, clean lenses. Though costing somewhat more on a yearly basis than standard extended-wear lenses, this system helps solve the disinfection problem and therefore improves eye care, according to its manufacturer. Many contact lens wearers cannot use this lens, however, because at present it is available only in predetermined sizes.

Although the overall rate of serious complications related to contact lens wear is below 1%, refinements of this important means by which so many people see well are continuing and will likely improve and expand the options available in future years.

New concerns about sun exposure

Cataract formation and changes in the retina with aging (age-related macular degeneration) are two of the major causes of visual handicap in the United States. Both of these disorders have taken on even greater import as the population ages and continues to maintain an active life-style, as more people participate in outdoor recreational activities, and as the protective ozone layer in the atmosphere possibly thins. Accordingly, research has focused on eliciting the factors that may make individuals susceptible to both cataracts and aged-related macular degeneration. One area of major interest has been the role of environmental factors—in particular, ultraviolet (UV) radiation.

Ultraviolet radiation is greatest at high altitudes and low latitudes; environments with highly reflective backgrounds, such as snow, sand, and water, increase the eyes' exposure to UV radiation. The UV spectrum is from 100 to 400 nanometers (a nanometer [nm] equals a billionth of a meter), with visible waves beginning at 400 nm. The cornea—the transparent, front portion of the eye—absorbs UVB radiation below about 300 nm, while the lens will absorb the UVA spectrum from about 300 to 400 nm. The capacity of the lens to absorb UV radiation increases with age as the presence of a yellow pigment in the eye increases.

Cataracts alter the vision of at least 3.5 million Americans. A cataract occurs when the normally transparent lens located inside the eye begins to develop opaque regions. These opacities can form in the front (anterior) portion of the lens, within the body (cortex) of the lens, or along the back portion (posterior subcapsular region) of the lens. Although posterior subcapsular cataracts are the least common of the three types of cataract, they account for an estimated 40% of the cataract surgery cases in the U.S.

In one recent study of watermen working on Maryland's eastern shore, high exposure to UVB radiation was associated with a tripled risk of cataracts. Refined statistical evaluation of the Maryland watermen study, however, indicates that the results could not definitively support this observation, and the increased number of cataracts noted could be due to chance alone. Another study compared individuals with posterior subcapsular cataracts with a similar group of individuals (control group) who did not have cataracts; a high exposure to UV radiation was found to be associated with an increased risk of subcapsular cataracts. There are growing indications that age-related cataract formation is due to multiple factors; the actual role and importance of UV light still need to be determined.

Age-related macular degeneration affects almost 30% of the population between 75 and 85 years of age, with 104,000 people in the U.S. considered legally blind because of the disorder. In the normal eye the retina receives almost no UV light since structures in the front portion of the eye absorb this type of radiation. However, if the eye is aphakic, meaning that the lens has been removed, usually because of cataract formation, the retina may be subjected to ultraviolet radiation. Because of this potential risk in patients who are aphakic, the vast majority of intraocular lenses (implants) placed into eyes during cataract surgery are designed to absorb UV light.

While the role UV radiation plays in the development of age-related macular degeneration still is not clear, work has shown that it has the potential to harm the retina. Recent work in the laboratory suggests that strong light may injure the retina or its supporting structures; one potentially important mechanism for such an effect is thought to involve oxidative chemical reactions that can damage the retinal pigment epithelium, a single layer of cells just under the retina itself. The center of the retina, the macula, is the portion of the back of the eye that enables the best vision. The retinal pigment epithelium is necessary for the normal functioning of the retina, and therefore damage to this layer can lead to macular lesions. Both light and oxygen can trigger these damaging oxidative chemical mechanisms.

Because the body has such naturally occurring antioxidants as vitamins C and E, as well as glutathione, experiments have been undertaken that supplement a medium in which retinal pigment epithelial cells are grown with glutathione; this has been shown to prevent damage due to chemically induced oxidation. A similarly protective response can be seen with vitamin E. Additionally, visible blue light (with a wavelength of 515 nm and below) has been found to cause damage to the backs of monkeys' eyes; placing a filter that blocks the entry of light with a wavelength of 515 nm or below in front of the monkeys' eyes has prevented this damage.

Well-controlled clinical studies have begun, and further studies will be undertaken to determine whether these observations truly reflect a real risk from either ultraviolet or blue light. Most evidence to date suggests that the development of such changes in the retina is multifactorial. Other associations that have been made with retinal damage include eye color, hand grasp strength, smoking, lung infections, exposure to chemicals, and a history of cardiovascular disease. There is not yet a full understanding of the causes of the retinal damage that occurs in age-related macular degeneration; however, a good rule of thumb is that if the sun's rays are strong enough to cause a sunburn, then the eyes should be protected with sunglasses that block a significant amount of UV light.

New therapeutic approaches

New treatments for ocular diseases are being developed at a rapid pace. Two major concepts have regulated the development of new ocular drug therapies. The first involves therapies that are more specific in their effect, so as to avoid side effects; the second, new ways to apply drugs to the eye more efficiently.

Collagen shields. Disorders of the eye surface are very commonly seen by the ophthalmologist. Drops that are applied directly to the surface of the eye (usually onto the cornea) have proved to be an extremely effective way to deliver medication. However, in some cases drops need to be given on a very frequent basis (every one to two hours) to have a significant effect on the disease being treated. One example is keratoconjunctivitis sicca, or so-called dry eye syndrome, a very common disorder that can occur either as an isolated ocular disorder or with diseases affecting other parts of the body. The lack of tears or a change in their quality will lead to a series of problems—from

A recent epidemiological survey conducted by a team of researchers from the Johns Hopkins University, Baltimore, Maryland, found that men who worked on the Chesapeake Bay had a tripled risk of developing cataracts. This and other studies have suggested that cumulative exposure to ultraviolet B radiation may be one key factor that contributes to the formation of certain types of cataracts.

James L. Amos—Photo Researchers

pain, light sensitivity, and redness to increased infections and an ultimate irreversible loss of the clarity of the cornea with a resultant drop in vision. Treatment usually involves applying eye lubricants, with applications sometimes as frequent as every 30 minutes.

The use of corneal shields as one way to overcome the necessity of applying drops on such a frequent basis is currently under investigation. These shields are made from collagen, which in humans is the most widespread natural protein found in the body. Collagen makes up a major portion of the eye as well. A transparent collagen shield can be made to fit the contour of the cornea. An important characteristic of these shields is that their gellike consistency enables them to act as a sponge, absorbing large quantities of a medication, such as a lubricant. When this gellike substance is placed on the eye of a patient with dry eye syndrome, a slow release of the lubricant within the shield will occur. With time (e.g., 24 hours) the gel is completely dissolved, and a new collagen shield can be inserted. This approach could be used for the application of other medications to the eye, such as antibiotics in the treatment of severe corneal infections and ulcers of the eye. Although collagen shields are being evaluated for many different potential treatments of the eye, they have not yet been approved by the FDA for general use.

Glaucoma therapy. The eye's pressure is determined by the production in the eye and subsequent drainage of aqueous humor. A normal pressure is needed for the structures inside the eye to function properly. If the delicate balance of production and drainage is disrupted, then the ocular pressure can go either above or below normal. When the pressure goes up, it is usually due to poor drainage from the eye. This decrease in outflow of aqueous humor can result from damage to the drainage area (trabecular meshwork) either after eye surgery or due to inflammation of the eye; it can also occur spontaneously owing to unknown factors. The result of this increased pressure in many cases is that the nerve fibers that carry the visual message to the brain are destroyed; this is manifested as a change in the field of vision. It is from these changes that glaucoma is diagnosed. If the process continues, the eye's central vision can become involved, resulting in blindness. In the United States 1.6 million individuals are visually impaired by glaucoma, and 62,000 are blind because of it.

Drug therapy generally is the initial glaucoma treatment—first with medications applied locally to the eye and then with oral medications. In cases where the visual field continues to show changes in spite of continued medical therapy, surgery is frequently recommended. For many reasons the initial surgical drainage procedure may not prove successful, and the chance of success of subsequent procedures is markedly lower than the initial surgical intervention.

This is frequently due to excessive scarring over the drainage site. New approaches have therefore been devised to aid in maintaining the increased drainage that is created with surgery.

One such approach involves the application to the eye of 5-fluorouracil, a potent compound that is used in the treatment of certain cancers; 5-fluorouracil helps prevent the development of scarring over the surgically created drainage site. Injections of this agent around the exterior of the eye must be given on a daily basis for several days immediately following surgery. A large multicenter study is currently under way in the United States to test this drug's efficacy as an adjunct to the surgical treatment of glaucoma and also to assess the potential side effects.

Another approach to maintaining a patent drainage site in high-risk glaucoma cases has been to place a "stint" into the wound in order to permit continued drainage. This concept is quite old, and many different types of stints, or drainage tubes, have been used over the years. A new form of stint that has shown particular promise is called the Molteno implant, named after Anthony Molteno, the ophthalmologist who developed it. The implant requires that a small hole be made in the eye into which is placed a tube that leads to a drainage system that is stitched to the outside of the eye itself but is covered by the upper lid. In cases of severe, difficult-to-control glaucoma due to various causes, this drainage system has been reported to keep the intraocular pressures of eyes constant. This approach needs to be studied in well-designed, long-term clinical trials with larger numbers of patients.

Treatment of uveitis. Intraocular inflammatory disease, or uveitis, is the cause of about 10% of visual handicaps in the United States. Inflammation inside the eye can be due to infection or to such internal changes in the body's immune system as autoimmunity (the body attacking itself). Whatever the underlying cause, inflammation inside the eye can be categorized anatomically as involving the anterior, middle (intermediate), or posterior portion of the eye. Anterior uveitis is the most common type of uveitis seen—causing pain, redness, and blurring of vision—and can lead to cataracts, glaucoma, and changes in the cornea. Intermediate and posterior uveitis generally cause no pain but can lead to a marked drop in visual acuity because of opacities in the vitreous. These types of uveitis can also lead to irreversible changes in the vasculature of the retina and the retina itself.

The treatment of infectious disorders involving the eye depends on the type of infectious agent. Of considerable recent concern has been the infection of the retina that is seen in patients with immunodeficiencies, in particular those with AIDS (acquired immune deficiency syndrome). It has been estimated that about one-fifth to one-quarter of adults with AIDS will develop cytomegalovirus retinitis. This virus is present in a very high percentage of healthy adults but is kept in check by an intact immune system. Once the immune system becomes defective—because of AIDS or an underlying cancer or as a result of therapy for transplantation—this opportunistic infection can occur in the eye. Previously no good therapy existed for this infection, which can lead to blindness. Recently the antiviral agent ganciclovir (Cytovene), which interferes with the virus's ability to replicate, has appeared to be effective in most cases and is now approved for widespread use in treating this disorder.

Unlike the types of uveitis for which the causative agent is known, there are other sight-threatening disorders for which no causative agents can be identified. For these endogenous forms of uveitis, therapy has centered around the use of corticosteroids, frequently given by mouth, and, in extreme cases, cytotoxic agents—drugs that were first used in cancer therapy—which have significant side effects. A better understanding of the underlying mechanisms that lead to ocular inflammatory disease has suggested that in some endogenous cases of intermediate and posterior uveitis, one portion of the immune system appears to play a dominant role. These observations have led to the use of cyclosporine (Sandimmune) in the treatment of some of these sight-threatening disorders. Cyclosporine, originally used to prevent the rejection of transplanted organs, affects the T-lymphocyte portion of the immune system, the arm of the immune response that does not involve antibodies in effecting an inflammatory response. When given orally, cyclosporine has proved especially effective in the treatment of Behçet's syndrome, a disorder that affects many parts of the body, including the eye, provoking severe, explosive inflammation. Though relatively uncommon in the United States, it is the most common type of endogenous uveitis in Japan and is very commonly seen in Mediterranean countries. Presently cyclosporine's use as an agent to be applied locally to·the eye for the treatment of various types of uveitis of unknown origin is being evaluated.

—Robert B. Nussenblatt, M.D.

Gastrointestinal Disorders

Numerous insights into gastrointestinal diseases and their treatment have been revealed in recent years. While no startling breakthroughs have appeared, a variety of alternative treatments, some of which are more free of trouble and complications than conventional methods, have been developed.

Evaluating results of clinical trials

Innovative therapy is not always more effective, safer, and less costly than older approaches. In order to evaluate the results of any new treatment, one must have some understanding of the elements of the sci-entific method and of the discipline of statistics. Thus, before the results of a drug trial, for example, can be considered generally valid, it is important to know how patients who participated in the trial were selected, how their disease was diagnosed, and how the effects of treatment were measured. Furthermore, one must be convinced that once patients were selected, they were assigned at random to treatment groups and both they and their physicians were unaware which medication was being administered (thus fulfilling the requirements of the double-blind method). Finally, once the results have been collected and compared for the new and old therapy or for a group receiving a new drug and one receiving no treatment at all, it is essential to know whether any differences recorded are statistically significant—i.e., that they could not have been expected to have occurred by chance alone. Few treatments "cure" everyone with the same disease the way penicillin cures everyone with pneumococcal pneumonia, and it is essential to know whether a new treatment that cures 85% of patients with a given disease is indeed significantly better than the old treatment, which may have cured only 70%. Properly applied statistical formulas can test for the significance of differences, but even so, different results are often reported from studies that were essentially the same but were performed in different localities.

Whatever the reason for these inconsistencies—whether they are due to differences in the populations studied, to variations in the methods by which the results were analyzed, or to some unrecognized phenomenon—it is the recognition that such differences may occur that causes many thoughtful physicians to adopt new treatments slowly, only after they have been widely tested and approved. This reluctance to adopt newer methods applies particularly to the management of many digestive disorders, where older treatments are often quite effective, the disease being treated is not life threatening, costs of new treatment may be very high, and side effects of the "latest" therapy may not have been fully revealed. Thus, while innovations described in the medical literature may sound attractive, it may be some time before they are widely adopted. Some may be found by wider experience to be flawed.

Relief from constipation

Americans continue to be a bowel-conscious population and adhere to the belief that a proper daily bowel movement, or one at least every second day, is essential to well-being. By and large this concept is correct; regular movements without great strain appear to be associated with fewer rectal complications, such as hemorrhoids and anal fissures or tears. It also appears that diverticulosis of the colon (the presence of numerous small pouches in the wall of the colon, particularly the portion just above the rectum) is often preceded by long periods of constipation. Fortunately, strong cathartics are less popular today than in preceding generations; instead, people seeking relief from constipation have turned to the ingestion of increased amounts of vegetable fiber. This constituent of many foods is largely indigestible, retains water, and makes stool soft and bulky and therefore tends to relieve or prevent simple constipation. Its use is harmless, although large amounts may lead to episodes of bloating and discomfort. Psyllium laxatives (Effersyllium, Konsyl, and Metamucil) are also highly effective in producing bulk and are often easier to ingest than some cereal products.

Bowel retraining by means of biofeedback is enjoying some success among patients with constipation that does not respond to fiber and simple laxatives alone. It has been found that some constipated children, and by extrapolation probably adults as well, actually contract instead of relaxing their anal muscles during efforts to defecate. This paradoxical action seems to defeat the secondary effort of voluntary straining that is essential to normal bowel action. Through biofeedback these patients can be taught how to relax their anal sphincters; the technique shows promise in relieving the problem of chronic constipation.

Dissolving gallstones

Stones in the gallbladder are very common. In most patients in the U.S. and in people of the Western world in general, gallstones are composed largely or solely of the fatty substance known as cholesterol. They appear in people who secrete more cholesterol in their liver bile than their bodies are able to solubilize. The excess cholesterol precipitates around a core of mucus or cells cast off from the mucous membrane of the gallbladder or bile ducts, forming flakes and eventually stones. Women who have been pregnant, obese people, diabetics, and people from certain American Indian tribes tend to develop gallstones earlier in life than others do.

Reliable studies have shown that most gallstones cause no symptoms and may be left untreated. They are often discovered inadvertently during ultrasound or computed tomographic (CT) studies of the abdomen or during abdominal surgery for other disorders. Occasionally pain resulting from other diseases, such as peptic ulcer or irritable bowel syndrome, is wrongly attributed to gallstones. It requires considerable clinical discrimination in these cases to determine which disorder is indeed responsible. If gallstones are truly symptomatic, they generally cause pain in the upper right quadrant of the abdomen, often extending into the back or up to the right shoulder. Attacks of pain may last for hours but do not occur often and are not usually associated with chronic constipation or diarrhea. If complications occur, such as fever, chills, or jaundice, one can be more certain of the diagnosis of

symptomatic gallbladder disease since such findings do not appear with the other diseases mentioned. Physicians, however, are understandably reluctant to wait until the patient begins experiencing these complications before administering specific treatment for the gallbladder disorder.

Traditional treatment for stones has been the surgical removal of the gallbladder (cholecystectomy). Removing the stones alone usually does not solve the problem; they will almost certainly recur at a later date if the gallbladder is retained. While this operation is not risky in otherwise healthy patients, it does require hospitalization for up to a week and three to six weeks of convalescence. The risks of surgery increase in elderly patients and when such complications as jaundice or infection are present.

Several alternative methods of treatment for gallstones have been developed recently. Because bile acids (substances derived from the cholesterol produced in the liver) have been shown to be essential for the dissolution of cholesterol in bile, it was hypothesized that feeding bile acids to patients might increase the level of bile acids in bile and provide an environment suitable for dissolving cholesterol gallstones. Administering them by mouth actually reduced the concentration of cholesterol in bile when clinical tests were performed, but the postulated mechanism was found to be in error. Rather than increasing, the total concentration of bile acids did not change, but the profile of bile acids showed increased amounts of the type being administered.

The first bile acid used for cholesterol-gallstone dissolution was chenodeoxycholic, or chenic, acid (Chenix). This is one of two major primary bile acids produced in the liver. It was well tolerated by most patients but produced diarrhea in many, and in a very few patients, slight chemical signs of liver damage were found. Complete solubilization of gallstones was noted after one or two years in only 15–20% of patients. The treatment was most successful in patients whose gallstones were small, were not calcified (hardened by the deposition of calcium), and contained a high percentage of cholesterol. In others the drug was largely ineffective. Furthermore, chronic inflammation of the gallbladder appeared to limit the efficacy of chenic acid, and stones tended to recur shortly after the medication was discontinued.

Recently another bile acid, ursodeoxycholic acid, or ursodiol (Actigall), which appears in very small amounts in humans (but is the major bile acid in bears), was found to be moderately effective in dissolving cholesterol gallstones. Furthermore, its metabolic products are less likely than those of chenic acid to harm the liver, and it also appears to cause less diarrhea. Otherwise, the effects of ursodiol on gallstones are the same as those of chenic acid, although there is some evidence that better gallstone dissolution is attained when the two bile acids are given simultaneously.

Efforts have also been made to dissolve gallstones rapidly by introducing a strong solvent directly into the gallbladder through a small-diameter catheter introduced into that organ through the skin and liver. The solvent, methyl *tert*-butyl ether (MTBE), is washed into and out of the gallbladder on a fixed schedule; treatment periods average just over five hours daily for one to three days (average total length of treatment, 12.5 hours). Stones appear to be capable of dissolution proportional to their content of cholesterol. Recurrences of stones have been noted in a few patients as long as 16 months after treatment, but the toxic effects of MTBE appear to be small. This chemical method of management is an attractive alternative to surgery for patients who have symptomatic gallstones but refuse traditional surgery or cannot be operated upon because of other serious disorders.

Several sessions of ultrasonic (shock-wave) lithotripsy have been found to be successful in pulverizing cholesterol gallstones in perhaps a third of patients, especially those with only a few small stones. After these sessions patients may have a few attacks of pain due to the passage of stone fragments, but these episodes are not usually associated with more severe complications. While giving bile acids along with and after lithotripsy appears to lessen the incidence of pain, the long-term value of ultrasound treatment for gallstones and the frequency of recurrences after successful dissolution by the shock-wave method are still uncertain.

With so many alternative types of treatment now available, how does an otherwise healthy patient with symptomatic gallstones choose the most reliable therapy? To the conservative physician, surgical cholecystectomy by an experienced and competent surgeon working in a respected hospital is clearly the best choice. Any type, size, or number of stones can be treated by surgery; complications are almost negligible; the recurrence rate of stones is tiny; and the requisite period of convalescence is short. For the patient who is physically at great risk for abdominal surgery because of severe disease of the heart, lungs, or liver, some of the other treatment options described above may well be preferable. These recommendations may change if alternative methods become more widely applicable and successful. For now it is reassuring to know that productive research into this problem is continuing.

Treatment of liver disease

Cirrhosis of the liver is a serious condition that may have a variety of causes: prolonged and heavy use of alcohol, exposure to toxic drugs or chemicals, infections with certain viruses, autoimmune processes, or inborn metabolic errors. Cirrhosis is characterized pathologically by progressive fibrous scarring of the liver following the inflammatory destruction of liver cells. There is also a variable amount of irregular regrowth of liver cells in large or small nodules, often producing pressure on blood vessels and leading to poor circulation of blood through the liver. Regenerating nodules often do not function as normal liver tissue, in part because their blood supply is compromised and their normal relationship to bile ducts is disrupted. The death rate from progressive cirrhosis is very high, and specific methods of treatment are not generally available, except for alcoholics in whom prompt and total abstention can often quickly halt the progression of the disease.

Treatment for most cases of cirrhosis today is aimed primarily at the management of complications, such as bleeding from distended veins in the esophagus

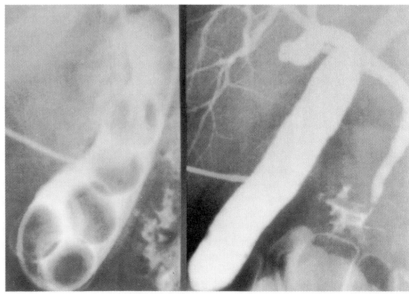

A new procedure that dissolves gallstones offers an alternative for patients who are not candidates for surgical removal of the gallbladder. The new method involves introducing a solvent, methyl tert-butyl *ether (MTBE), directly into the gallbladder. These before-and-after X-rays show a dramatic difference; after two days of MTBE treatment, the patient's previously stone-filled gallbladder appears clear and unobstructed.*

Reprinted from *Mayo Clinic Health Letter* with permission of Mayo Foundation for Medical Education and Research, Rochester, Minnesota

(esophageal varices) or brain damage secondary to dysfunction of the liver. Efforts have been made for years to find drugs that reduce inflammatory changes and the formation of fibrous tissue in the diseased liver. In a 1988 report, a team of doctors in Mexico suggested that cirrhotic patients of all types do better, live longer, and have fewer complications when treated with a common and inexpensive drug called colchicine. In their 14-year clinical trial of colchicine treatment, the Mexican researchers reported that median survival was 11 years in the group treated with the drug, compared with 3.5 years in the placebo group. In some treated patients, biopsies of the liver showed evidence of improvement. Colchicine has long been used in the treatment of acute gout, and it was selected for this study because of its anti-inflammatory effects and its ability to reduce the formation of scar tissue.

While the results of this study appear to be phenomenal, a word of caution was introduced by the authors of an editorial accompanying the report in which they noted a number of factors that may have affected the outcome of the study. For example, although patients were selected at random to receive colchicine or the placebo, those in the control (placebo) group appeared to have more severe liver dysfunction at the start of the trial. Another problem was that 20% of the patients in both groups could not be traced in the follow-up period. These considerations might have skewed the results, making the treatment appear more successful than it actually was—not an uncommon problem, as indicated above in the discussion of statistical and clinical trials. At the very least, however, colchicine deserves further study in the treatment of cirrhosis because of this report and because of other studies indicating that it may benefit patients with a specific kind of cirrhosis—primary biliary cirrhosis (PBC), which is thought to be immunogenic in origin. Heretofore there has been no satisfactory treatment for PBC, and patients faced the slow but inevitable progression of the illness, often with a fatal outcome; transplantation of the liver was their only hope. Now, with the use of colchicine and possibly with methotrexate, an immunosuppressive agent, there is the possibility of slowing or even stopping the progress of the disease.

The bile acid ursodiol is also beginning to find a place in the treatment of PBC and in another immunologically determined liver disorder, primary sclerosing cholangitis (PSC). In fact, its usage for these disorders may be more important than its place in the dissolution of gallstones. Patients with PSC become jaundiced because of inflammatory damage to the bile ducts that lead from the liver to the upper small intestine. These ducts become narrowed by scarring, and bile no longer able to pass readily into the intestine backs up into the liver, from which it regurgitates into the bloodstream. This process also leads to liver damage and ultimately to progressive cirrhosis.

Studies in the U.S. have shown that rats subjected to sudden blockage of the bile ducts are protected from experiencing damage to the liver if they are treated with ursodiol. Recently patients with such chronic biliary obstructive diseases as PBC and PSC have been treated with ursodiol in a number of medical centers and have generally responded well. Jaundice tends to disappear, and blood tests indicative of liver damage improve significantly. Occasional patients do not improve, however, and biopsies of their livers may show little if any change for the better. It is believed that ursodiol reduces the level of toxic bile acids secreted by the obstructed liver, probably without affecting the underlying cause of the obstructive process. Thus, while the use of ursodiol in certain selected patients may be quite beneficial, its final place in the therapy of these chronic disorders of the liver has not yet been established.

Ulcer update

In the past few years considerable research has examined the possible relationship between the bacterium *Campylobacter pylori* and disease of the digestive system. It is now generally agreed that many cases of gastritis (inflammation of the mucous membrane that lines the stomach) are associated with and almost certainly caused by *C. pylori* and that eradicating the bacteria with antibiotic drugs will cure the condition. In one study a medical investigator knowingly swallowed a living culture of *C. pylori,* developed abdominal pain three days later, had biopsy-proven gastritis (*i.e.,* the organism was detected in a gastric tissue sample) shortly afterward, and slowly responded to therapy. The organism can often be found by biopsy, or its presence can be presumed after an enzyme (urease) known to be produced by the bacterium is found in the stomach. A fairly simple breath test involving a radioactive tracer can confirm the presence of urease. Still, despite these many studies, researchers do not believe that *C. pylori* is the cause of *all* cases of chronic gastritis. In different studies the organism has been found in as many as 95% of cases or as few as 62%.

C. pylori has also been associated with gastric and duodenal peptic ulcers in many cases. While it is not yet clear that the bacterial infection causes the ulcer, there is suggestive evidence from at least one study that successful treatment of the infection with antibiotics was associated with healing of the ulcer. This occurred in 92% of the cases. In only 21% of these cases did the ulcer recur in the year after healing. In a control group treated with cimetidine (Tagamet), a histamine-blocking agent widely prescribed for ulcers, 70% of the patients experienced healing of their ulcers; in none of these patients was the *C. pylori* infection eradicated, and more than 90% suffered a relapse within a year. Although these data are im-

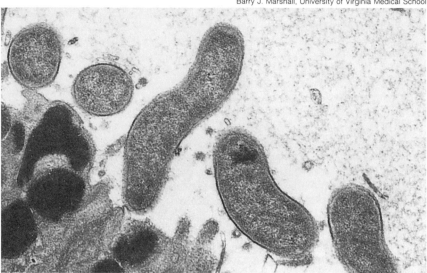

Barry J. Marshall, University of Virginia Medical School

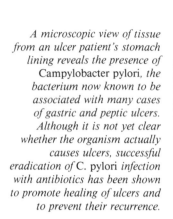

A microscopic view of tissue from an ulcer patient's stomach lining reveals the presence of Campylobacter pylori, *the bacterium now known to be associated with many cases of gastric and peptic ulcers. Although it is not yet clear whether the organism actually causes ulcers, successful eradication of* C. pylori *infection with antibiotics has been shown to promote healing of ulcers and to prevent their recurrence.*

pressive, most conservative physicians would like to see more evidence supporting the proposition that all peptic ulcers should be initially treated with antibacterial agents before they abandon the well-established treatments that rely primarily on reducing the secretion of stomach acid.

There are now four histamine-blocking agents for the treatment of peptic ulcer on the market in the U.S.: cimetidine, ranitidine (Zantac), famotidine (Pepcid), and nizatidine (Axid). These drugs function by blocking the histamine receptors on acid-secreting gastric cells, thus preventing the stimulating action of histamine on the cells. Acid secretion is thereby reduced. All of these drugs are quite effective in ulcer healing; each may be administered successfully in single daily doses; and there is little reason for preferring any one over the others. These drugs are also useful in treating esophagitis (irritation of the esophagus) caused by the regurgitation, or reflux, of stomach acid in patients with weakness of the lower esophageal sphincter ("hiatal hernia"). Further, in patients whose ulcers have healed, there are persuasive data indicating that reduced doses of these drugs can prevent recurrences over a long period of time. It is unfortunate that these useful ulcer medications are often needlessly administered for the treatment of digestive symptoms of uncertain cause. Informed laypersons should not hesitate to question their physicians about such prescriptions.

A new prostaglandin agent, misoprostol (Cytotec), has been found to be extremely effective in preventing the gastric and duodenal damage that often occurs in patients taking nonsteroidal anti-inflammatory drugs (NSAIDs) for arthritis and rheumatic diseases. Prostaglandins are substances naturally produced by the body that have the ability to reduce acid secretion in the stomach and to protect the stomach from ulceration. Because of its apparent ability to increase the resistance of the mucous membrane of the upper gastrointestinal tract to NSAID-caused damage, misoprostol has been called a "cytoprotective" agent; it is indeed much more effective in preventing NSAID-caused damage than are the histamine-blocking agents mentioned above. A few words of caution: misoprostol causes diarrhea in many patients, is expensive, and is not needed by every patient taking NSAIDs. However, for those patients who cannot take antiarthritic drugs because of associated gastrointestinal problems, misoprostol is a great boon. Because of its potential to cause abortion, there was some controversy over the approval of misoprostol in the U.S. The package label carries a warning that the drug is contraindicated for women of childbearing age unless they are at high risk of complications from NSAID therapy.

—*Harvey J. Dworken, M.D.*

Genetics

In June 1989 scientists from around the world met at Yale University for the 10th International Workshop on Human Gene Mapping. At the end of the session, they announced that since their last meeting in 1987, the number of genes located to specific sites on the chromosomes had grown from 1,000 to 1,700. The number of genes discovered in the interval was much larger than expected, and the rapid acceleration in the rate of genetic discoveries in recent years will undoubtedly necessitate more frequent "inventories" of the genetic map. The newly reported data will be added to those already on file at the Yale-Howard Hughes Human Gene Mapping Library, an international repository for information on the human gene map.

Workers in the field of clinical genetics continue to produce satisfying practical applications of the ever expanding knowledge of inherited diseases and of the workings of genetics at the molecular level. This is particularly true in diagnostic medicine: two of the most common genetic conditions—cystic fibrosis and fragile-X syndrome—can now be predicted before birth with a high degree of accuracy. In both cases the diagnostic tests depend heavily on the techniques of molecular genetics. Current genetic research is also helping in the understanding of other major maladies, such as schizophrenia and Alzheimer's disease, which, it is now believed, may exist in either inherited or nongenetic forms.

More fundamentally, the techniques of molecular genetics are now beginning to open new avenues in cancer research and basic biology. The discovery of the first human antioncogene a few years ago spawned a new generation of cancer studies that may bring fresh insights to the understanding of breast cancer. The discovery of a "homeobox" in human genes has provided a new perspective on the study of embryonic development.

Cystic fibrosis gene: search ended

In recent years a number of important hereditary diseases have become diagnosable before birth, and new ones are being added to the list at an unprecedented rate. Cystic fibrosis (CF) is the most common fatal genetic disease of the Caucasian population. In the U.S. alone, about 30,000 children and young adults are affected. Now scientists have identified the CF gene and its defective protein product.

It was established in 1985 that the CF gene is lo-

cated on a particular segment of chromosome 7. In September 1989, after an intensive four-year search, scientists from the University of Michigan and the Hospital for Sick Children, Toronto, announced that they had identified the gene and the mutation responsible for a vast majority of CF cases. Once all the mutations are known, virtually anyone should be able to find out if he or she is a carrier of the CF gene.

Even without this information, geneticists had been able to estimate with 99% accuracy whether a fetus had CF in cases where the family had a living CF child. This was accomplished by comparing DNA from the parents, the fetus, and the affected child. A less direct, and therefore less accurate, kind of analysis was used in cases where a child with the disease had already died and no cell lines had been preserved. The procedure was based on the observation that most CF-affected families share a whole block of genes on chromosome 7. The presence of these in the fetus therefore signals a high probability that the CF gene itself is also present.

The decoding of the gene that causes CF does not necessarily mean that a cure for the disease can be found. Most likely the main benefit in the next few years will take the form of a nationwide voluntary screening program for the detection of carriers. Similar voluntary programs have already reduced the incidence of Tay-Sachs disease and sickle-cell anemia. With the gene for CF isolated and cloned, geneticists will be able to develop an accurate test that will identify carriers of the CF gene and

Using a scanning tunneling microscope, a device capable of tracing the contours of a single atom, researchers have produced the first picture of pure DNA, the fundamental genetic material. It reveals in unprecedented detail the double-stranded helix first described in 1953 by James Watson (pictured with DNA model) and Francis Crick.

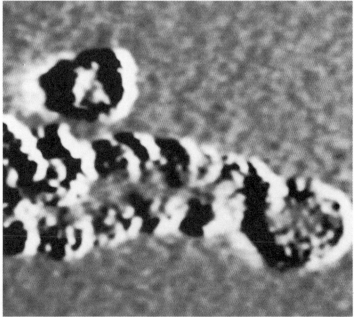

(Left) Don Preisler/The Washington Times; (right) Lawrence Livermore National Laboratory and Lawrence Berkeley Laboratory

Roger H. Kobayashi, UCLA School of Medicine

A youngster with cystic fibrosis (CF) receives inhalation therapy, which helps to break up the thick mucus that interferes with breathing in those who have the disease. The discovery in 1989 of the gene responsible for CF will eventually lead to greatly improved treatment; however, the most immediate application of the new finding will be in the development of accurate methods for detecting carriers. As many as 12 million Americans may carry the CF gene.

be able to predict a couple's risk of having an affected child. This latter capability is important because of the high carrier rate (about one in 25) in the Caucasian population, which accounts for the fact that most CF babies are born into families with no previous history of the disease.

Fragile-X syndrome: a partial success story

Fragile-X syndrome is another extremely important disorder that can now be diagnosed prenatally. It is one of the most common genetic causes of mental retardation, second only to Down syndrome. An effective fragile-X screening program would benefit a large number of families, but such a program is not yet available.

Fragile-X syndrome was first described in 1969 as being associated with a lesion on the X chromosome, which, given certain technical conditions, is visible with an ordinary light microscope. It is precisely these technical conditions—the need to manipulate the culture in which cells from the affected individual must be grown for chromosome analysis—that make the diagnosis difficult. This has inspired a search for molecular probes that would work directly on DNA samples from individuals at risk, including female carriers. A number of medical centers and commercial laboratories now perform prenatal diagnosis and carrier detection of fragile-X syndrome with an accuracy rate of at least 90%. For reasons that remain unexplained, chromosome analysis often fails to detect female carriers; therefore, the probe must be used.

Disorders located on the X chromosome virtually always affect only males—because males have only one X chromosome (plus a Y). Thus, a defective gene

on the X chromosome cannot be compensated for by the presence of a normal counterpart on a second X chromosome, as it can in females (who have two X chromosomes). For this same reason, females are almost never affected by such disorders, but they may have affected sons if they are carriers of the gene. In the case of fragile-X, males with the defective gene may be of normal intelligence, but their daughters may have fragile-X-positive sons. The diagnostic problem is made even more difficult by the fact that a larger-than-expected number of girls with the fragile-X lesion are subnormal in intelligence—a confusing situation that rightfully earns this syndrome its scientific reputation as a "genetic nightmare." A major improvement in the understanding of the entity is expected when investigators locate, isolate, and clone (*i.e.,* produce identical copies of) the fragile-X gene, which may or may not be coincidental with the microscopic lesion.

Neurofibromatosis: success through international efforts

The discovery of the gene for neurofibromatosis—a condition often but incorrectly referred to as elephant man's disease—is one of the most impressive cooperative efforts of the international genetic research community. Less than two years after the British organization LINK (Let's Increase Neurofibromatosis Knowledge) held a seminal meeting in England in 1987, the National Neurofibromatosis Foundation in the United States was able to help launch a prenatal diagnosis program. In that short time span, scientists were able to narrow the location of the neurofibromatosis gene to a minute piece of the long arm of chromosome 17 and to amass molecular probes capable of diagnosing the disease with an accuracy approaching 97–98%. Investigators involved in this collaborative effort credit free exchange of information—data as well as probes—with the remarkable progress.

Neurofibromatosis Type I (NF1 to geneticists) is a relatively common genetic disorder that may be characterized by freckle-like pigmented spots (so-called café-au-lait spots) and tumors of the skin, nerve tumors, and skeletal deformities. It is usually inherited as an autosomal dominant trait. Persons with the disease have a 50–50 chance that their offspring will also be affected. In addition, the disorder often appears spontaneously (de novo) in a child whose parents are themselves both free of the disease and can thenceforth be inherited by the affected child's progeny, with the same 50–50 odds. The new prenatal diagnostic test is for couples with a familial history of the disease only.

Unfortunately, while prenatal diagnosis can confirm the existence of the disease, it cannot predict the severity of the symptoms in a given individual. Many persons have only a few café-au-lait spots or no obvious symptoms at all, whereas their children may be seriously disfigured and disabled, and vice versa. This fact confronts parents and genetic counselors with a considerable dilemma in the event of a positive prenatal diagnosis.

For all the clinical variability, however, evidence so far suggests that all degrees of NF1 are caused by the same gene. The high rate of spontaneous mutation leads to speculations that it is a very large "megagene"; scientists are also entertaining the possibility that the NF1 gene is an antioncogene, which in its normal state acts as a suppressor of the disease.

Blood test to screen for Down syndrome?

Because of the small but real risk of miscarriage (calculated to be about 0.5%) following amniocentesis or chorionic villus sampling, women under 35 are not considered candidates for these procedures unless they have already borne a child affected by Down syndrome and therefore face a risk of recurrence greater than the risk of miscarriage from the test procedure. Overall, however, it is women in their twenties who bear most of the babies with Down syndrome and other chromosomal abnormalities because, in the statistical sense, they are the most fertile group. Investigators continue to seek less invasive ways of predicting the outcome of pregnancies, and the α-fetoprotein (AFP) blood test—already accepted as an effective screen for the group of abnormalities known collectively as neural-tube defects—has aroused considerable interest as a possible method for detecting Down syndrome pregnancies as well.

Introduced in the U.S. in the mid-1980s, the maternal serum α-fetoprotein (MSAFP) screening program has gained wide acceptance as a means of identifying pregnancies in which all is not going well. The test measures the levels of AFP in the prospective mother's blood. Very high levels of AFP may indicate that the fetus has anencephaly, spina bifida, or other neural-tube defects, which can cause varying degrees of permanent paralysis. Low levels of AFP often signal a fetus with Down syndrome. All abnormal levels require a battery of further tests, sometimes including amniocentesis, to diagnose the condition of the fetus as accurately as possible.

On the basis of the finding of an association between Down syndrome and abnormally low AFP levels,

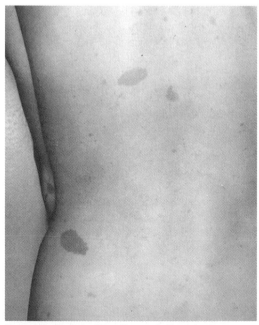

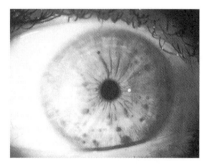

Neurofibromatosis Type 1 (NF1) is a relatively common genetic disorder that can now be diagnosed prenatally with an accuracy of 97–98%. The clinical manifestations of the disorder are highly variable and may include brownish, freckle-like skin spots, known as café-au-lait spots, and iris nevi, unusual clumps of pigment in the iris of the eye; because of this variability, NF1 often eludes diagnosis.

some investigators believe that slightly elevated AFP levels suggest that a fetus *does not* have Down syndrome. How safe is this assumption? Should a woman decline amniocentesis if her AFP level is not abnormal, even if she is over 35 and has a well-documented statistical risk? Ernest B. Hook, a physician and population geneticist at the School of Public Health at the University of California at Berkeley, cautions that experience with MSAFP in the diagnosis of Down syndrome is very limited. He also points out that the U.S. Food and Drug Administration has not approved existing commercial MSAFP kits for use in diagnosing Down syndrome.

Several investigators in England and the United States have proposed developing a combined screening test for all younger women that would detect Down syndrome fetuses with better than 60% accuracy. (The MSAFP test alone would spot only perhaps 25%.) Besides α-fetoprotein, these researchers recommend that the blood levels of two other substances, human chorionic gonadotropin and unconjugated estriol, be measured as well and that all three values be used together to identify more accurately those younger women who should undergo amniocentesis for chromosome analysis. There is little doubt that amniocentesis should continue to be recommended to all pregnant women 35 years of age and older.

Chorionic villus sampling: a vital, newer option

Couples wishing to avail themselves of prenatal diagnosis for any of the ever growing list of diagnosable conditions will soon have a new option in transabdominal chorionic villus sampling (CVS). The transabdominal method is recommended in obstetric situations that do not lend themselves to the more common, vaginal (transcervical) access to the fetal tissues, and it may indeed be the preferred method when the physician is experienced in the procedure.

CVS has been in use for about six years, and it is the procedure of choice for high-risk pregnancies when early, first-trimester results are important. The risk to mother and fetus is about the same as for amniocentesis, the older method of prenatal diagnosis, which is not performed until the second trimester. Some 50,000 CVS procedures have been performed worldwide since the technique first became available, about half of them in the United States, generally at major medical centers. Because the chorionic villi yield cells from a fetal membrane, not from the fetus itself, false normal results may be obtained when a chromosomal abnormality present in the fetus does not involve the membrane. Likewise, a chromosomal anomaly in cells of the chorion need not mean a defect in the fetus. Therefore, in a number of cases, CVS findings must be confirmed later by amniocentesis or fetal-blood sampling, both of which examine fetal cells proper.

Is there a schizophrenia gene?

For many years scientists have been asking if there is a gene for schizophrenia. And if so, is it on chromosome 5, as some suspect, or on one of the sex (X or Y) chromosomes? Late in 1988 Timothy Crow, a psychiatrist in Middlesex, England, speculated that such a gene could be located on either the X or Y chromosome, in the so-called pseudoautosomal regions. Unlike other parts of the sex chromosomes, these regions engage in DNA exchange during the formation of egg and sperm. Crow's theory accounts for several observations that have been made over a period of years: (1) compared with women, men tend to have an earlier onset of schizophrenia; (2) their clinical history is usually more severe than that of women schizophrenics; (3) pairs of schizophrenic siblings are more likely than not to be of the same sex; and (4) extra chromosomes are found relatively often in persons with this disease.

Molecular approaches, more direct than Crow's clinical analysis but still rather roundabout, have concentrated on chromosome 5 ever since researchers made the serendipitous discovery that two related persons with schizophrenia (as well as unusual physical characteristics) had a duplicated segment of chromosome 5. In London, researcher Hugh Gurling and his colleagues studied the chromosomes and medical histories, together with genealogical records, of more than 100 members of seven families with numerous schizophrenic members. They concluded that a single abnormal gene, located on chromosome 5—dominant and incompletely penetrant (sometimes skipping a generation)—could be responsible.

In Scotland still another team of investigators, using a similar but not identical approach in the study of 15 families in Edinburgh, could not confirm close linkage of schizophrenia and chromosome 5. Similarly, Swedish and U.S. researchers, led by Kenneth Kidd and James Kennedy at the Yale University School of Medicine, were unable to confirm a link. Their finding, based on some 30 schizophrenic patients, may simply mean that other chromosomes—and different genes—may be involved in different individuals, making the task of finding the cause of schizophrenia considerably more difficult.

More than one form of Alzheimer's disease?

Molecular genetics has in recent years made significant progress toward elucidating Alzheimer's disease but at the same time discouraged expectations of finding an early cure. The report by a group at Harvard Medical School in 1987 indicating that the gene for one familial form of the disease is located on chromosome 21 was confirmed by researchers in London but was challenged by scientists in Seattle, Wash.

Late in 1988 Gerard Schellenberg and colleagues at the University of Washington School of Medicine reported that they could find no link between early-onset Alzheimer's and the chromosome-21 region identified earlier by the Harvard group. It is possible that, like schizophrenia and many other disorders with genetic components, familial Alzheimer's disease is genetically heterogeneous—that is, different genes, and possibly even different chromosomes, could be responsible in different families. The Seattle study involved 15 families, about half of them belonging to a single extended family. The finding of such a large kindred could very well provide the opportunity to isolate—not just locate—the disease-causing gene and clone it for further investigation. In the meantime, however, another group of investigators, at St. Mary's Hospital Medical School in London, was continuing to study families with a history of Alzheimer's disease. In March 1989 they reported that genetic analysis of six families with a history of the early-onset form of the disease confirmed the presence of a defective gene on chromosome 21.

Approaching the task from a different direction, several scientists have found that chromosome 21 also carries a gene that directs the synthesis of the precursor to amyloid beta protein. This is the substance that makes up the structures known as plaques, which are found in particular in the brains of people with early-onset Alzheimer's disease and are also seen in the brains of healthy, very elderly persons. A gene for another amyloid deposit, the protease inhibitor alpha-one antichymotrypsin, was identified as well. Neurofibrillary tangles, which are also characteristically seen in the brains of people with Alzheimer's disease, were recently shown to contain the *tau* protein, a component of cell microtubules, which are present in practically all forms of life. Further study of these structures may shed some new light on all forms of Alzheimer's disease, whether they have a hereditary component or are due to causes as yet unknown, and on the aging process itself.

Anticancer gene: how general?

Retinoblastoma, a childhood tumor of the eye, is not a common form of cancer, but the gene responsible for the disease is conceptually important because it was the first human antioncogene to be identified. This gene, as the name antioncogene implies, does not cause retinoblastoma; rather, it prevents it. Moreover, its absence or mutation seems to predispose individuals to other primary malignancies—including fibrosarcoma, melanoma, and osteosarcoma. Mothers of children with osteosarcoma are at an increased risk of breast tumors. Many scientists want to know whether the retinoblastoma gene, isolated and cloned in 1987, has general anticancer, tumor-suppressing effects.

Recent work by a group at the University of Southern California School of Medicine led by Yuen-Kai T. Fung indicates that only specific types of cancer in-

In 1989 W. French Anderson, Steven A. Rosenberg, and R. Michael Blaese (left to right) performed the first human experiment in gene transfer. The goal was not to alter genetic makeup but to assess progress of a new cancer therapy.

volve the retinoblastoma gene. In some of the breast tumors they studied, there was an abnormality of the gene, whereas in other types of cancer—cervical carcinoma, hepatoma, Wilms' tumor—there was no obvious change in the gene. Other studies indicate that lung and colon cancer may also belong to the group of malignancies suppressed by the retinoblastoma gene. In recent months a number of experiments have suggested that the protein produced by the gene has a role in regulating the expression of other cellular genes and may also mediate the tumor-forming effects of some viral-transforming proteins.

Gene transfer: finally, a precedent

Gene transfer in humans is a subject that is very much in the news, but as an approved and widely used treatment, it is still very much in the future. The first human experiment in gene transfer took place in May 1989. In this case, however, the introduction of foreign genes into a human body was intended not to remedy a genetic defect but to monitor the progress of cancer immunotherapy. The project, which aroused

This fruit fly developed two sets of wings as a result of a mutation in certain crucial genes, called homeoboxes, which regulate the harmonious development of the insect's body segments. Scientists recently discovered that mammals have homeobox genes nearly identical to those identified in the fruit fly; from that discovery they have concluded that body development—and the differentiation of organs and tissues—is governed by a similar mechanism in all organisms.

considerable controversy, was given the go-ahead by the Recombinant DNA Advisory Committee of the National Institutes of Health (NIH) in 1988 and was finally approved by the NIH itself early in 1989. This precedent is expected to eventually pave the way to actual gene-transfer therapies.

This first experiment, which was offered to ten patient volunteers with terminal cancer, involved adding a bacterial gene to special high-potency immune-system cells used in cancer therapy. The objective is to track the cells after they are administered to the patients and monitor their ability to attack and shrink massive tumors. The cancer therapy itself is still in the experimental stage. It has been administered to 15 patients with advanced melanoma. In eight of these patients the tumors shrank to half their original size. One patient had a complete remission. However, six did not improve at all—possibly because the special anticancer cells never reached their target. With the bacterial gene serving as a marker, investigators hope to learn what happens to the altered immune-system cells after they are introduced into the patient's body and how long they remain effective.

The bacterial gene itself in this instance has no therapeutic value and indeed is not the object of concern to informed critics of the experiment. Rather, it is a virus, used to insert the gene into the immune-system cells, that is the cause of some reservations about the experiment. The virus, as well as the gene, ultimately ends up in the patient's body. The NIH investigators, Steven A. Rosenberg, R. Michael Blaese, and W. French Anderson, tested the virus system in animals and were able to convince the NIH regulatory body that the experiment posed no meaningful risk to the patients or to the medical personnel who treat them. Whether the experiment will succeed remains to be seen.

Homeoboxes: new keys to development

Molecular geneticists have begun to concentrate their attentions on some of the key genes that orchestrate the harmonious development of tissues into organs—and perhaps their discordant development into tumors. Late in 1988 several teams of investigators, separately and simultaneously, identified a new universal sequence through which proteins attach to DNA and direct it either to be expressed or to remain silent. Not surprisingly, the sequence belongs to the category called homeoboxes, which were originally identified in the genes of the fruit fly six years ago. In the fruit fly embryo, it was discovered, there are genes that can be manipulated to make a pair of legs develop on top of the fly's head, where antennae are supposed to be. Homeoboxes got their name from the term homeosis—replacement of one bodily structure by a corresponding structure from another body segment. They are similar in composition, whether they come from insect, sea urchin, frog, or human, and for that reason alone, they were immediately assumed to play a fundamental role in the life process.

The new homeobox was found in mammalian proteins that activate the transcription of a specific gene and in a worm protein that regulates the development of nerve cells. It codes for a protein sequence, called a homeodomain, some 75 amino acids long. All of the proteins that have homeodomains share the property of binding to DNA. This finding confirms the notion that not only the identity of body segments but development from egg to organism comes under the control of homeotic genes. Homeodomains appear to be the very parts of homeotic proteins that physically bind to genes and thereby turn some genes on and turn others off, thus deciding the developmental fate of proliferating cells.

—Alena Leff

332

Great Expectations: New Outlook for Down Syndrome

by Lynn Nadel, Ph.D.

Until fairly recently, children with Down syndrome were routinely institutionalized, usually on the recommendation of physicians or other authorities, who advised parents that such children would never learn to take care of themselves in even the most minimal ways. In the grim atmosphere that prevailed in most custodial institutions, the narrow future forecast for these youngsters became a self-fulfilling prophecy. They learned little, were capable of little, and, because of medical conditions associated with the syndrome, usually died before reaching adulthood.

The outlook for infants born with Down syndrome today is quite different. They will probably be brought up at home, in a typical family atmosphere, go to school with "normal" children, participate in sports, and learn to do some kind of work. Furthermore, many can expect to live to be senior citizens. These gains have been based on a combination of advances in medical treatment, progress in understanding human development, and much dedication on the part of parents, educators, physicians, and others who have contributed toward the enlargement of the horizons of people with Down syndrome.

Surviving to adulthood

Down syndrome (DS) is a genetic disorder that affects both mental and physical development. It was first described in 1866 by a British physician, J. Langdon Down. People with DS have a distinctive physical appearance; they are also mentally retarded. The cause of Down syndrome, most commonly the presence of an extra chromosome 21 (making a total of three instead of the usual pair—hence the alternate name trisomy 21), was discovered in the late 1950s. It has been known for more than 50 years that the chance of having a baby with DS increases with the mother's age, but it is now established that the father's genes also can contribute to the genetic defect that results in DS. Scientists do not yet know exactly what produces the extra chromosome or how it translates into the various features characteristic of the syndrome.

Children with Down syndrome are distinguished by certain distinctive facial features—a flat nose bridge, slanted eyes, and protruding tongue—and soft muscle tone in the rest of the body. Nearly 40% of infants born with DS have a heart defect and a tendency toward an otherwise rare form of childhood leukemia.

Many DS children also have problems with hearing and vision and suffer from speech disorders.

Today the average life expectancy for people with DS is 55 years, a considerable departure from the outlook earlier in the century. Around 1910 children with DS survived only to the age of nine on average, many dying at an early age from the congenital heart defect. The discovery of antibiotics made it possible for physicians to treat the many kinds of infections children with DS often succumbed to, thus increasing the average life-span to about 20 years. Surgical repair of heart defects and successful treatment of other clinical problems, along with a wider integration into society, have in recent years produced a marked improvement in life expectancy for people with DS. Interestingly, with increasing numbers of DS individuals now surviving into their forties and fifties, it has become clear that the incidence of Alzheimer's disease is higher in this group and that its onset is earlier than in the remainder of the population. Though nearly all individuals with DS past the age of 40 have changes in brain tissue resembling those seen in Alzheimer's disease, it is now thought that only 35–40% of these individuals actually suffer the dementia characteristic of this disease. The apparent link between DS and Alzheimer's disease is currently the object of much scientific research and speculation.

Mental retardation: variable in nature and degree

In addition to the typical physical abnormalities, Down syndrome is also characterized by mental retardation. The severity of retardation in DS individuals has, however, been generally overestimated. As noted above, children with DS were once thought to have such limited potential that they were routinely institutionalized. However, recent years have brought new insights into the nature of the mental retardation associated with Down syndrome and its variability from one individual to another. It is now clear that many individuals have significantly greater potential than was previously thought. Basic research into the nature and cause of the retardation, coupled with efforts to stimulate the intellectual and sensory development of DS babies, has created a climate of great hope in the scientific community and among parents of these children.

This is a fortunate development for the more than 250,000 families in the U.S. that are directly affected

After three years of working with computers, six-year-old Matthew Costea (pictured with his sister) showed average reading comprehension for his age. Computers have also been used experimentally to help toddlers with Down syndrome learn to communicate; early results have generated considerable excitement. This kind of success, as well as other new insights, has prompted many educators to revise their thinking about the nature and extent of the mental retardation associated with the syndrome.

by Down syndrome (many more are involved in support, education, and health care). Of all the genetic disorders linked to mental retardation, DS occurs most often—approximately once in every 800 live births. It spares no race, class, or ethnic group. As noted above, it is now known that there is a wide variation in the degree of mental retardation, ranging from minimal to severe. Many of those who have already reached adulthood have not realized their full learning potential because as children they were not considered capable of learning very much.

Innovative programs developed within the past 10–20 years have brought about a change in this situation. The majority of individuals recently born with DS are now considered to be mildly to moderately retarded; this improvement in status is due primarily to the movement away from institutionalization and toward the bringing up of DS children at home. Though they have a slower rate of development than normal children, they can, if given the chance, learn to walk, talk, dress, and bathe themselves and work in a supportive atmosphere. A large percentage are able to function in society with a considerable degree of independence.

Benefits of early stimulation

These advances might appear surprising to some people. In the past it was believed that an individual—whether of average intelligence or greater or less than average—was born with a certain immutable amount of potential. However, considerable basic research on brain and cognitive development in both humans and nonhumans has demonstrated that certain kinds of stimulation can have quite beneficial effects on intellectual functioning. For example, animals reared in stimulating environments that have a variety of objects for them to explore and interact with are found to have more fully developed brains than do those reared in

empty, sterile environments. Compared with animals that are talked to, played with, and handled only rarely, animals that receive extra handling and other forms of attention early in life also have better-developed brains and lower rates of brain-cell death during the aging process. Likewise, human infants who are held and talked to develop differently from infants who have little contact with others.

When these principles have been applied to DS babies, it has been shown that supplementary sensory and motor activity very early in life improves their mental and physical status. Outside of the home, extra stimulation provided by health care professionals and teachers has also been shown to have benefits. Indeed, the kinds of changes now being observed in DS children demonstrate strikingly that the earlier animal research probably has broad applicability for developmentally disabled individuals. Continuing basic research of this kind is likely to yield insights into the actual mechanisms of improvement and, perhaps, some understanding of the nature and most optimal timing of early sensory, motor, and cognitive stimulation. Before specific strategies can be developed to improve the capacities of children with DS, however, there must be some further insight into their specific abilities and disabilities. The average learning capacity of individuals with Down syndrome is something that has not yet been determined; young children currently in early stimulation programs are still making progress, and it is not yet known what their limits will prove to be.

Understanding the world of objects

Initially it was thought that the mental retardation associated with Down syndrome was general in nature, affecting most or all forms of thinking, learning, and remembering, including speech, perception, and motor function, or movement. This presumption of an across-the-board deficit in cognitive abilities contributed to the view that persons with Down syndrome were largely unable to learn. Recent research, however, has made it abundantly clear that DS is selective rather than general, affecting some forms of cognition more than others. One of the aims of basic research is to determine which abilities are impaired and which are largely unaffected.

Many early researchers chose to focus their attention on the problems of language development in Down syndrome. Difficulties in communication place individuals at a considerable disadvantage, whatever their intellectual abilities, and it is essential to define accurately the extent and nature of the disability in communication if progress is to be made in improving the life prospects of individuals with DS. However, recent studies of cognitive development indicate that children with DS suffer from more than just communication difficulties. What is more, it is possible that problems in early, prelinguistic development could set the stage for subsequent language disorders.

One particularly critical area of early cognitive development concerns the acquisition by the infant of an understanding of the nature of physical reality and the laws that govern events in the external world. One may consider, for example, some of the things infants must learn about objects in order to understand the ways in which events unfold in the world. They must learn first of all that objects have their own existence—that is, objects continue to exist even when they are out of sight. Infants must also learn that objects obey fundamental laws of space, time, and causality. Acquisition of this kind of information about objects is critical to the acquisition of many more advanced concepts about the world. Without knowledge of this "object concept," young children would fail to appreciate the basic workings of their world, and it would not be surprising if they subsequently failed to communicate adequately about that world.

The development of knowledge about objects has been carefully studied in both normally developing and developmentally delayed infants. There are several reasons for the interest in this process. First, this aspect of development is often considered to exemplify all forms of cognitive development and, indeed, to predict with some accuracy subsequent intellectual function. Second, the development of an object concept is universal across all cultures, children showing much the same pattern of understandings (e.g., that objects that are dropped fall downward) and misunderstandings (e.g., that something that disappears no longer exists). Finally, variations in rearing conditions are known to have a marked impact on the emergence of understanding about objects; thus, were there to be some difficulty in acquisition of the object concept in children with DS, it might be amenable to improvement by a change in the immediate environment.

Results of a recent study of the acquisition of the object concept in children with Down syndrome, conducted at the University of Edinburgh, provide cause for both optimism and caution. It appears that DS individuals are not as severely impaired in acquiring the object concept as would be predicted on the basis of previous studies of their intellectual development. However, their knowledge about objects is not learned and fixed in memory as firmly as it is in the memories of normally developing infants, and thus it is not as likely to be available for subsequent use in the acquisition of other, more advanced, cognitive skills. This poses a serious problem for those who are creating learning programs for DS youngsters. They will have to develop techniques to help these children to consolidate their learning about objects, thereby providing a foundation for future knowledge.

Understanding numbers

Another area of cognitive development that has been explored recently concerns how children acquire knowledge about numbers. Researchers at the University of Pennsylvania have shown that such development in normal children reflects the presence of certain inborn principles that help to organize otherwise ambiguous information provided by the child's experience; that process leads to the emergence of appropriate knowledge about numbers and how they are used in counting. That is, all normally developing children seem to have, as part of their genetic endowment, a certain kind of abstract knowledge about the properties of numbers, knowledge that enables them to figure out how the number system works when they are subsequently exposed to the typical, yet highly variable, experiences of early life. Children with DS do not seem to benefit from the innate presence of these principles, i.e., simple counting of objects does not come naturally to them, and as a result they react in an entirely different fashion to experiences where numbers are involved. This finding, too, poses problems for those developing strategies for helping DS youngsters. The fact that children with DS react to situations in which enumeration is required in an abnormal fashion means that innovative methods will have to be found to teach them basic principles about numbers and counting. As with the acquisition of the object concept, standard methods of instruction apparently will not work.

Problems of language acquisition

The lessons acquired from the study of nonverbal forms of cognition contribute in an important way to the understanding of what might be going wrong with language development in those with Down syndrome. Research in the past decade has made it clear that not all aspects of language capacity are equally affected in people with DS. Language skills acquisition parallels that of skills concerning numbers; DS individuals suf fer from an apparent lack of certain innate principles needed for acquiring language, principles that guarantee that most children acquire language normally, even when exposed to highly variable learning environments. Further, the things DS children *do* learn about language are not understood by them in the systematic way observed in normally developing children and hence are not as helpful in providing an impetus to further learning.

In most normal children, language development takes a great leap when they are about 20 months of age. It is at this time that children begin to string single words together into small "sentences." Concomitant with this emergence of so-called syntactic skills (those aspects of language having to do with rules of word order and the meaning that attaches to grammatical constructions), there is a virtual explosion in the number of new words being used. Children with Down syndrome seem relatively normal at the earliest stage of language learning, acquiring their first words at about the same time and rate as other children. However, acquisition of syntax and the "word-acquisition explosion" do not occur at a normal rate. In fact, where it might normally take a child a few days or weeks to move from one stage of syntax to another, for a Down syndrome child this simple transition can take months or even years. Thus, the DS youngster reaches various plateaus in the language-learning process, representing long intervals during which very little apparent progress is made.

Recent work suggests, however, that language learning need not follow this course—gains in language capacity have even been demonstrated in DS individuals in late adolescence. Most promising, perhaps, is the possibility of using computers to help in the language-learning process. Though much research remains to be done, early findings indicate that working with computers can have a marked impact on the communications skills of some children with Down syndrome, as will be discussed in more detail below. Computers will not, of course, replace the steady involvement of parents and teaching professionals. Many aspects of the learning process are facilitated by social interaction and the emotional nurturance provided by direct human contact.

The Down syndrome child and the family

A factor that may contribute to the developmental difficulties seen in youngsters with DS is the way in which parents interact with these children. It is an established fact that the nature of interactions between parents and infants plays a critical role in the development of social and cognitive skills; if the parents of children with DS treat them in an atypical way, this could account for some of the abnormalities observed in their development; it could also offer another opportunity for improvement.

Even when parents are carefully prepared to treat DS children in a normal fashion, they do not always do so. Subtle differences emerge, partly reflecting the desire of parents to "make it easier" for the DS child and partly reflecting the inadequate feedback these children provide to their parents. For example, researchers at the University of Oslo showed that, compared with mothers of normally developing children, mothers of infants with Down syndrome engage in more direct, close-up physical stimulation of their babies but less stimulation involving speech that refers to objects and actions on the part of the infants. Such differences presumably reflect the fact that children with Down syndrome react more immediately and obviously to more direct forms of stimulation, such as hugging and holding, than to less direct forms of interaction, such as talking. Unfortunately, such differences can establish patterns of parent-child interaction that might be detrimental to the child's development. Evidence suggests that these abnormal interaction patterns contribute to delayed language development in DS children; establishing a more normal pattern will be a critical part of any successful intervention strategy.

Another issue of concern is the way in which children with DS interact with and affect their normal siblings. In the past, parents were fearful that raising a DS youngster at home would have a negative impact on the other children in the family, a consideration that contributed to the tendency to institutionalize children with DS. These same fears continue to be an issue for families choosing to keep a DS child at home, as most are now doing.

Until recently there was little information about this subject; however, a study recently completed at the University of Toronto indicates that normally developing siblings are often more supportive of a sibling who has DS than they typically would be with a normally developing sibling. The normally developing siblings in the Toronto study were more nurturant of their brothers or sisters with Down syndrome and showed more affection, approval, comfort, and reassurance, as well as sharing behaviors and other forms of help. Researchers were not sure how to account for this finding; possibly, the parents had made extra efforts to promote positive sibling interactions, or perhaps the children with Down syndrome encouraged more nurturing behavior on the part of their normally developing siblings. In any event, the general picture is one of largely normal, or even more positive than normal, relations between normally developing children and their brothers or sisters with Down syndrome.

Using computers to communicate

Given an adequate understanding of the nature and extent of the cognitive deficits associated with Down syndrome, what are the possibilities for real improvements in the capabilities of people with DS? As noted

Mario Ruiz

Seeing 13-year-old Mary Boss on the soccer field with her classmates at the Greenwood Lake (New York) Middle School is testimony to the benefits of mainstreaming. Clearly, both Down syndrome youngsters and their "normal" peers gain from the shared learning experience.

above, a great deal of interest has been generated by the early results of experiments using computers to help DS children overcome some of their difficulties in communication.

Many youngsters with Down syndrome have some degree of hearing loss due to recurrent middle ear infections. Speech comprehension may be further compromised by problems with information processing within the auditory system itself. Computers, however, can produce synthesized speech at a rate children with Down syndrome can handle. Furthermore, synthesized speech is completely consistent in pronunciation and can be repeated over and over, without fatigue to the "speaker," which helps children improve their articulation skills. Studies of DS children suggest that their visual capacity is often less adversely affected than their hearing; computers can provide pictures along with words, thereby increasing the likelihood of comprehension. Motor skills are also compromised in many children with Down syndrome, making writing and articulation more difficult. Computers can be used in such cases to help children communicate more effectively, providing a means of expressing thoughts and ideas they could neither write nor speak with any fluency.

Preliminary results of the use of computers in these and other ways are quite promising, though it is still too early to be sure just what will work best in most cases. Toddlers using computer software capable of generating speech have begun to imitate precise pronunciation; other children have moved from this early stage to the use of word combinations and simple sentences. For these children, working with computers has been quite effective in promoting language understanding and production. Some older children have been taught to use computers as writing tools. In a project at the University of California at Los Angeles, DS children wrote 30-page books with the assistance of computers. They were first shown examples of books other children had written and were helped with the early stages of learning to use the machines, choosing topics to write about, and remembering what these topics were. At first they required a great deal of help in translating their fragmentary thoughts into sentences and typing these sentences on the keyboard. In the best cases, however, real improvements in both writing and speaking skills emerged from this experience, and the children made considerable gains in their ability to go from thought to written expression. Most exciting, perhaps, were the positive changes in feelings and attitudes that accompanied these successes. Finding a way to communicate not only increased interaction among the children but also increased their self-esteem.

Overall outlook: optimistic

There is as yet little evidence that these gains in functioning are long-lasting or can carry over to other cognitive skills; this does not mean that these attempts to help DS children learn are ineffective, only that the methods best suited to a wide range of children have not yet been worked out. In the next few years, there will be a great deal of research in the application of computers to the learning process in children with Down syndrome, focusing not only on the children but also on the involvement of families and professionals. Any effective program is likely to depend upon the continuing efforts of parents, other relatives, and concerned helpers. It will probably be only one part of a larger program that will include special education within regular classroom settings—there are clear indications that mainstreaming children with Down syndrome (*i.e.,* sending them to regular public schools to attend classes with normally developing children) is beneficial both to them and to their classmates.

Certainly, as they demonstrate to themselves—and to others—their ability to cope with and benefit from computers, these youngsters will gain in self-esteem. As their lives improve in many ways, children with Down syndrome will be faced with new possibilities, and with new problems as well. The overall picture, however, shared by most parents and involved professionals at this time, is one of careful optimism for the future.

Heart and Blood Vessels

While cardiovascular disease remains the greatest killer in the industrialized world, increased emphasis on the prevention of atherosclerosis and new therapeutic approaches for victims of heart attacks have been responsible for substantive decreases in the number of deaths from cardiovascular disease during the last several years. Also in the last several years, a new and fertile area of cardiovascular research has focused on understanding the process of blood vessel growth. Researchers are currently seeking ways both to promote and to inhibit blood vessel growth; the former holds the promise of facilitating healing and providing blood flow to tissues deprived of oxygen and nutrients, while the latter could potentially prevent or control certain diseases.

Prevention of heart attacks

Cigarette smoking, high blood pressure, high cholesterol, diabetes, and male sex are associated with an increased risk of coronary heart disease. It has recently been proved that it is possible to lower the risk of coronary heart disease by lowering blood cholesterol. Since the achievement of weight loss in obese individuals and the institution of an exercise program in sedentary men have salutary effects on the cholesterol pattern, it is hoped that either of these methods will lower the risk of coronary heart disease.

Obesity, defined as a weight greater than 20% above "ideal" body weight, unfavorably affects the balance of cholesterol in the blood and, when analyzed independently of its effects on cholesterol, is a relatively weak risk factor. A recent study from Stanford University's Center for Research in Disease Prevention compared two methods of weight loss in overweight men: reduction of energy intake by restricting intake of calories from food versus increase in energy expenditure through the initiation of an exercise program (primarily running, an average of 19 km [11.8 mi] per week). Over the course of a year, both methods were equally effective in reducing weight and lowering blood cholesterol. Thus, either method might thereby reduce the risk of coronary heart disease.

Treatment of heart attacks

The use of drugs to dissolve blood clots in the circulation, thrombolytic therapy, has revolutionized the treatment of myocardial infarction (heart attack). Myocardial infarction generally results from the formation of a blood clot in a narrowed coronary artery. When thrombolytic agents are administered early in the course of a myocardial infarction, restoration of blood flow to the portion of myocardium (heart muscle) that is downstream from the occluded artery has been shown to limit the extent of damage to the heart, decrease the likelihood of death resulting from the heart attack, and

In Seattle, Washington, trials are under way to determine whether it is appropriate for paramedics to deliver thrombolytic therapy on-site to heart attack victims when they are directed through the treatment by emergency room physicians.

improve the overall pumping function of the heart in those who survive. The use of thrombolytic agents has been shown to decrease the mortality associated with a heart attack by 20% and, when used in conjunction with aspirin, by 40%.

When a portion of heart muscle is deprived of its blood supply, the probability that it will recover decreases as the length of time required for reestablishing blood flow increases. There is a several-hour "window of opportunity" for the use of thrombolytic agents beyond which the likelihood of salvaging the injured heart muscle is low and the risks of thrombolytic therapy—such adverse reactions as bleeding, allergic reactions, and fever can occur—are not justified. Moreover, early initiation of thrombolytic therapy (within the first hour of an evolving heart attack) has been demonstrated to produce an even greater (50%) reduction in mortality.

So that this "window" can be taken advantage of, investigations are presently being conducted to determine the feasibility of initiating thrombolytic therapy prior to hospital arrival. Preliminary results of studies in Paris, France, Tel Aviv, Israel, and Seattle,

Wash., indicate that approximately one-third of patients believed to be having a heart attack when first seen by paramedics are, according to current medical guidelines, candidates for thrombolytic therapy. In these cities highly sophisticated emergency medical services systems are in place; electrocardiograms can be recorded and interpreted by mobile-unit personnel or transmitted by cellular telephone to hospital emergency room physicians. When treatment for these patients is initiated in the ambulance, 40 to 70 minutes can usually be saved without a significant increase in the number of complications. Thus, in patients with evolving myocardial infarction, administration of thrombolytic therapy en route to the hospital is feasible under certain circumstances. It is unclear, however, whether these methods could be safely expanded to cities where emergency medical services systems are not available or are not as sophisticated as those in Paris, Tel Aviv, and Seattle. Further studies will be necessary to clarify this issue.

Saving lives—and dollars

After successful thrombolytic therapy, the clot precipitating complete blockage of a coronary artery is dissolved and, if treatment was started early enough, the heart attack is aborted. However, the conditions initially responsible for engendering blood clot formation are not altered by dissolution of the clot. Generally these factors include severe narrowing of an artery by an atherosclerotic deposit, or plaque, with sluggish blood flow or the presence of a plaque that has complex and intricate surface features, predisposing to plaque injury and blood clot formation. Therefore, since the age of thrombolytic therapy dawned in the early 1980s, the conventional wisdom has been that the artery related to the heart attack should be scrutinized and, if need be, mechanically opened or surgically bypassed, after successful treatment with a thrombolytic agent, in order to prevent recurrent heart attack or death.

Accordingly, common practice has been to subject patients to coronary arteriography (cardiac catheterization) within 48 hours after treatment with a thrombolytic agent. In this procedure slender, flexible tubes are inserted into an artery in an arm or leg and passed upstream to the heart. The catheters are inserted into the origins of the individual coronary arteries, and X-ray "movies" are taken (cineangiography) while a solution that is opaque to the X-ray beam (contrast medium) is injected into the artery being studied. Through the use of this technique, much can be learned about the geometry, configuration, and location of blockages in the coronary vessels.

If the artery related to the heart attack is found to be severely narrowed, then balloon angioplasty is generally performed at the same time, if possible. Balloon angioplasty, properly known as percutaneous transluminal coronary angioplasty (PTCA), involves the place-

ment of a small balloon across the partially blocked artery. When inserted, the deflated balloon has a low profile. Upon inflation, the distended balloon fractures and compresses the atherosclerotic plaque, leading to expansion of the internal vessel diameter. Balloon angioplasty is not performed if the critically blocked segment is too long, difficult to reach, or located at a tortuous area or branch point of the artery. Likewise, the PTCA technique is not attempted if abrupt occlusion of the vessel (which occurs as a complication of balloon angioplasty in about 5% of attempts) would be likely to have catastrophic consequences because the vessel in question plays a key role by supplying blood flow to a major portion of the heart muscle. Under these circumstances, the patient is often referred for coronary artery bypass surgery. Coronary artery bypass surgery involves opening the chest, temporarily stopping the heart, and surgically connecting an alternative source of blood to the diseased vessel beyond the point of narrowing.

Thus, treatment of an evolving heart attack with a thrombolytic agent has often committed patients to cardiac catheterization within 48 hours, then frequently to balloon angioplasty or coronary artery bypass surgery or, in some cases, to both. The risks and benefits of this treatment strategy were recently examined in a study involving over 3,200 patients at 50 hospitals in the United States, and to the surprise of many, the conventional wisdom was shattered. Patients with evolving heart attacks of less than four hours' duration were treated with heparin, aspirin, and recombinant tissue plasminogen activator (t-PA), a thrombolytic agent produced through genetic engineering. Heparin, an anticoagulant substance produced naturally by the body, cannot dissolve previously formed blood clots but prevents the formation of new clots. Aspirin, by chemically altering platelets and rendering them less likely to clump together, also prevents new clot formation, as aggregation of these blood elements plays a key role in initiation of the clotting cascade.

In the study, patients were randomly assigned to one of two treatment groups. In the first group coronary arteriography and, if necessary, balloon angioplasty were performed routinely within 48 hours of thrombolytic therapy; this group thus received "invasive" treatment. In the second group these procedures were not carried out unless the patient developed symptoms suggestive of inadequate myocardial blood flow or unless signs of compromised blood flow were detected by an exercise test carried out on a stationary cycle prior to hospital discharge; this group, then, had "conservative" treatment. After six weeks patients who received invasive treatment fared no better than those who received conservative treatment. Approximately 6% of patients in both groups sustained an additional heart attack, and only 5% of patients in each group died. In addition, there was no difference in heart function between the two groups at the end of six weeks. Conservatively treated patients more commonly developed signs of insufficient blood flow, either spontaneously or during the exercise test prior to discharge, in which case coronary arteriography and balloon angioplasty were performed when necessary.

These results indicate that after thrombolytic therapy in patients with an evolving myocardial infarction, it is safe to withhold coronary arteriography and balloon angioplasty—performing them only if and when the need arises. The ramifications of this study, both medical and economic, are enormous. First, the fact that 95% of the patients survived a heart attack is extraordinary and represents an astounding medical achievement. This rate far surpasses the highest rates of survival attained prior to the era of thrombolytic therapy, only a few years ago. Second, this improvement in survival was accomplished without the routine use of costly coronary arteriography and balloon angioplasty.

Many community hospitals are not equipped to perform cardiac catheterization, balloon angioplasty, or bypass surgery. Had the results of the study gone the other way, the cost of implementing the changes necessary for providing optimal care to victims of heart attacks would have increased substantially. These changes would likely have included frequent interhospital transfers of patients, the proliferation of resources needed for performing these specialized procedures, or both. A study from two medical centers involved in the investigation (encompassing about 10% of the total patients) addressed the economic advantages of conservative therapy. Conservative treatment reduced the total hospital charges per patient by approximately $3,000. Extrapolating these savings to the total number of patients who sustain myocardial infarction in the U.S. in a year, they estimated an annual savings of $700 million to $4.2 billion, and this figure does not include the staggering costs that would be incurred in providing added hospitals with facilities for cardiac catheterization and bypass surgery and the trained personnel to use them.

Growing blood vessels: fertile research

The heart and all other living tissues are critically dependent on an uninterrupted supply of blood flow for their existence. As blood flow is essential for life, blood vessels are necessary to transport the blood to and from the tissues. The formation of new blood vessels is termed angiogenesis, and much has been learned about this important process during the last few years. Because angiogenesis may exert either a positive or a negative role in the maintenance of health, it is presently being actively investigated.

The process of angiogenesis. The circulatory system is composed of branching tubes; those that carry blood away from the heart are termed arteries. As the vessels diverge, their diameter decreases progressively until the smallest of arteries, the arterioles, are reached. Further branching results in the formation of capillaries, which are the smallest flow-conducting units of the circulatory system. Capillary diameter is approximately eight micrometers, so small that red blood cells are slightly compressed as they traverse it in single file. At the level of the capillary, oxygen and carbon dioxide are exchanged, and metabolites are exchanged with the tissues. Capillaries coalesce into venules, the smallest of veins, which merge into progressively larger veins on their way back to the heart. The entire circulatory system, including the heart, is lined with the endothelium—a "carpet" of endothelial cells. Immediately beneath the endothelium is the basement membrane, a thin supporting layer.

In the embryo, capillaries begin their development between the sixth and seventh week of gestation. During normal growth and development, proliferation of blood vessels parallels, or occurs at the same time as, tissue growth. In adults there is minimal turnover of blood vessels under normal circumstances, and angiogenesis occurs only rarely. There is, however, one

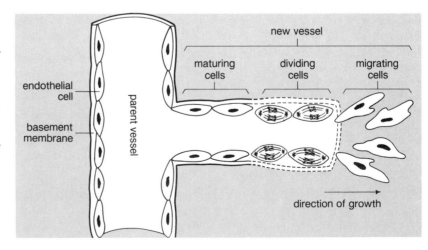

The sprouting of a new capillary from a larger parent vessel, a process called angiogenesis, is depicted schematically. At the first stage of growth, enzymes disrupt a small region of the basement membrane of the parent vessel, and cells of the vessel's endothelial lining migrate out and toward their destination. Cells behind the migrators actively divide to supply large numbers of themselves for new endothelium. At the rear, nearest the parent vessel, are maturing endothelial cells; in this area new basement membrane is synthesized, and supporting cells form.

important exception; angiogenesis occurs in a cyclic fashion in the corpus luteum of the ovary and in the endometrium of the uterus in menstruating women. Otherwise, blood vessel growth occurs only in situations associated with wound repair, in certain disease states, and possibly during the adaptation of the body to exercise or to high altitude.

During the first stage of angiogenesis, the basement membrane is enzymatically disrupted. Interestingly, one of the enzymes involved is t-PA, the same enzyme sometimes used to dissolve blood clots during heart attacks. Endothelial cells migrate from the parent vessel (generally the venule; *i.e.,* the smallest veins) toward the angiogenic stimulus—the area to receive flow from the new blood vessels—during the next stage of development. As sprouts are formed, the cells elongate, loop, and ultimately become encircling as the vascular channel is formed. While this is occurring, endothelial cells succeeding the front of the looping cells actively divide to increase the available number of cells. Finally, a new basement membrane is synthesized, supporting cells form, and the vessel enters a mature, quiescent stage.

Implications for promoting healing and inhibiting disease. The most intriguing unanswered questions about angiogenesis relate to an understanding of what the initiating factors are and, once begun, what causes the process to cease. As indicated above, angiogenesis may exert a positive or a negative role in the maintenance of health. In conditions of ischemia, where the flow of blood is inadequate to meet the metabolic demands of the tissue, the growth or enlargement of blood vessels is advantageous. Such conditions include coronary heart disease, ischemic limbs, persistent wounds, and states in which blood flow to the brain is compromised. It is also reasonable to assume that promotion of blood vessel growth would facilitate the healing process in burns, fractured bones, skin grafts, and the heart *after* myocardial infarction.

Conversely, inhibition of vessel growth has important ramifications in the treatment of disease. Tumors are quite dependent on blood vessel formation and generally will not grow much beyond one millimeter in diameter without concomitant ingrowth of blood vessels. Some forms of blindness occur as a result of the proliferation of blood vessels on the retina, notably diabetic retinopathy and retrolental fibroplasia, caused by oxygen toxicity in premature infants. In some forms of arthritis, psoriasis, and other disease states, continuous inflammation and blood vessel growth may play a primary causal role. Thus, through the suppression of angiogenesis, these diseases have the potential to be controlled or cured.

Discovery of angiogenic factors. Angiogenic factors are substances that facilitate the formation of blood vessels by (1) promoting degradation of the basement membrane, (2) inducing replication (division) of endothelial cells, and (3) causing endothelial cell migration. The first of the factors involved in the angiogenesis process was isolated from tumors in the early 1970s, and subsequently a number of factors with angiogenic potential were isolated from a wide variety of normal tissues. In 1983 it was discovered that some of these factors had a strong affinity for the anticoagulant heparin. This property expedited the purification of the multiple substances with heparin affinity and the characterization of them into classes of structurally related heparin-binding growth factors, the prototypes of which are called acidic and basic fibroblast growth factor (FGF). Both classes are polypeptides, and they induce blood vessel formation *in vitro* (in the laboratory) and *in vivo* (in intact organisms). Angiogenin, a polypeptide unrelated to the heparin-binding growth factors, was isolated from a derivative of human tumor cells in 1985. It too is a potent stimulator of angiogenesis, but its principal effect may be indirect since it does not directly cause endothelial cell division. Transforming growth factor beta (TGF-β) is a two-chained polypeptide that stimulates angiogenesis *in vivo* but inhibits the process *in vitro*. Its actions seem to depend on the recruitment of additional cells, and it may play a regulatory role in angiogenesis.

Heparin and angiogenesis. Heparin and certain fragments of heparin modulate angiogenesis, possibly because they avidly bind to acidic and basic FGF, which protects them from degradation and potentiates their actions. If one of the coronary arteries of an experimental animal is subjected to intermittent, brief occlusions, blood vessels eventually form natural bypass channels, or collaterals, around the obstruction. If heparin is given to the animals, the growth of these collaterals accelerates.

In one investigation patients with coronary heart disease who developed angina (chest pain from heart ischemia) with exertion began a treadmill exercise program. Half of the patients were treated with heparin by vein 10 to 20 minutes prior to exercise, while the other half were not given heparin. After 20 periods of exercise, the patients given heparin were able to exercise longer before developing chest pain than their untreated counterparts. Although this was an extremely small study, it may have practical implications for some patients with coronary heart disease.

Future possibilities. Can angiogenesis factors be used to facilitate the growth of new blood vessels in an ischemic limb or the heart? If so, could it be done without causing blood vessel growth in unwanted places or causing tumors to develop? Could capillary formation be blocked so as to kill tumors, prevent blindness, or mitigate arthritis? Rapid progress is being made in answering these challenging questions, and it is hoped that control of angiogenesis will soon be within grasp.

—Ellis F. Unger, M.D.,
and Stephen E. Epstein, M.D.

Special Report

Life After Heart Transplantation: Adjusting to the Miracle

by Peter A. Shapiro, M.D.

"John, it's the hospital calling. We think we've found a heart for you. We'd like you to come in right away. Can you be here in an hour?"

Across the United States, several hundred people are desperately waiting to hear these words. They are the patients with diseased or failing hearts, already evaluated and approved for transplantation, who now wait only for a suitable donor organ to become available. Not so very long ago, this scenario would have been considered science fiction. In fact, it is only in the past decade that heart transplantation has become a proven, accepted therapy. Yet despite its reality, the procedure has retained the air of a miracle inspiring both awe and fear—the transfer of life itself from one person to another.

Although experimental transplantation of the hearts of animals dates back to the first decade of the 20th century, it was not until the mid-1960s that success in canine heart transplantation was established sufficiently to allow South African surgeon Christiaan N. Barnard to perform the first human heart transplant operation, in Cape Town in December 1967. This operation was a technical success, and the patient lived for two and a half weeks before ultimately succumbing to a lung infection. So intense was public curiosity that reporters, prevented by guards from entering the transplant unit of the hospital, offered hospital staff cash payments for photographs of the patient, and Barnard became an international celebrity. From this beginning there ensued a frantic leap into clinical transplantation at several medical centers in the United States and elsewhere around the world.

In search of a miracle

For those involved in cardiac transplantation in the United States, the years 1968 and 1969 were ones of great enthusiasm followed by a period of disillusionment and exhaustion. Patients dying of heart disease caught wind of a possible miracle cure and sought out the few medical centers offering the procedure. A pioneering spirit was evident in both patients and medical staff. This new treatment, so unproven and so dramatic, was noted to attract two types of patients: first, the desperately ill, grasping at straws, and second, exhibitionistic individuals who wanted to share the publicity and excitement of transplantation.

In order to be ready at a moment's notice, poten-

tial recipients, often accompanied by family members, moved from their homes to accommodations closer to the hospital. Psychiatrists and psychologists studying these early patients observed that small subcultures developed at these medical centers, consisting of patients awaiting donor hearts, recent heart recipients, and their families. These groups had their own informal communications networks, shared preoccupations, and spontaneously created support groups. Patients tended to endow the transplant surgeons, men of forceful and charismatic personality as a rule, with godlike power. While waiting for suitable donor hearts, patients and families wondered who would be next and found themselves listening with a mixture of guilt and hope for ambulance sirens that might portend the availability of a heart.

The dramatic nature of the transplantation process created a sense of crisis and fostered an atmosphere in which patients and families were forced to reexamine their relationships and life course. Some families grew stronger; others came into open conflict. At the same time, while providing each other with moral support, patients and families searched for an edge in the competition for the "next" heart. Hopes were fueled by reports of someone's feeling strong enough to return to work, or to swim or play golf, while news of another's rejection episode or death created waves of depression. Typically patients would react by dissociating themselves from these "failures" with such rationalizations as "He didn't care for himself properly," "He started smoking again," or simply "I'm not as sick as he was." The mass media were a constant, intrusive presence, and television or radio news bulletins might inform a family of a change in their loved one's status before the patient himself or the doctor had had the opportunity to do so. Privacy was hard to come by.

Earliest recipients

Although most of these early patients were described in the immediate postoperative period as mildly euphoric, up to one-third of them experienced psychotic reactions and severe confusion, while others showed more subtle impairment of intellectual function. Recipients commonly had fantasies about the donors of their new hearts. Gender differences between donor and recipient caused anxiety for some (most of these early patients were male), while others wondered about the personal lives, values, and beliefs of the donor. As if to insulate themselves from some of the highly emotional connotations of having another's heart beating within them, patients commonly conceptualized the heart as "nothing but a pump," disassociating it from the feelings commonly associated with that organ. Yet most patients also expressed gratitude, a sense of obligation to the donor's family, and, because they had been given a second chance to live, a need to "give something back" to the world.

Few had the opportunity to do so, however. Innocent optimism gave way within a few months to the dread of rejection of the transplanted organ. Although transplant surgery was technically feasible, the postoperative management of the heart recipient was overwhelmingly difficult. Of the 148 patients receiving transplants through 1969, 20 died within 18 hours; for the remaining 128, average survival was only 69 days. Thirty-eight percent died within a month of surgery, and only 20 patients survived a year or more. By 1971, after developing a cumulative experience of almost 200 patients, heart transplantation programs in the U.S. had largely come to a halt.

Cyclosporine and the "modern era" of transplantation

At Stanford University, under the direction of Norman Shumway, researchers continued over the next decade to make advances in operative technique, in the management of the immune response and the use of antibiotics to fight infection, and in other aspects of postoperative care. Survival rates for transplant recipients gradually improved. In the early 1980s introduction of the immunosuppressant medication cyclosporine, a substance derived from fungi, greatly enhanced control of the process by which the body rejects foreign tissues, and patient survival improved dramatically. This development ushered in what could be called the modern era of heart transplantation—indeed, the modern era of organ and tissue transplants.

In the United States the number of centers performing heart transplantation grew from 37 in 1984 to over 100 in 1988. Seventy-nine centers perform heart transplants in other parts of the world. The number of procedures grew exponentially in the 1980s: 62 cases in 1981, 103 in 1982, with a near doubling of the cumulative total each year since then; approximately 2,200 heart transplantations were performed worldwide in 1987. By mid-1988, the registry of the International Society for Heart Transplantation listed more than 6,800 people who had received heart transplants.

About 90% of patients are male; their average age is 43 years. Cardiomyopathy (disease of the heart muscle) and atherosclerotic coronary artery disease are the most common disorders leading to transplantation. Current statistics indicate that 90% of adult patients survive at least 30 days after surgery, 80% one year, and well over 70% more than five years. For patients on the most intensive medical regimen, five-year survival is as high as 84%. Infection, cardiac failure, and acute and chronic rejection of the transplant remain the leading causes of death. Survival statistics for children are not as favorable; only 60–70% of children undergoing heart transplantation can expect to survive for three months.

Selection process: "on trial" for life

For most patients the first suggestion that heart transplantation might be necessary seems unreal and has a quality of science fiction about it. The fact that a physician would recommend such a drastic procedure underscores in a dramatic and terrifying manner the severity of the condition and its grim prognosis. Some patients respond to the news with denial, others with depression or anger. Commonly, second opinions are sought. Next, patients begin to do research, seeking out transplant patients in their community or contacting a transplant program. Application to a program may take anywhere from weeks to months to complete, during which the medical center requests and reviews personal and medical data. Meanwhile, the patient waits, perhaps suffering progressive symptoms of heart failure requiring emergency hospitalizations or simply living in a state of limited physical activity but without alarming signs of deterioration. Typically, financial and family strains increase as the patient is able to contribute less and less. Anxiety mounts.

By the time of evaluation for acceptance into a transplant program, the patient often has developed a sense of being on trial for his life. By now he has accepted the notion that without a transplant he will likely die sometime in the next year or so. In desperation he wonders, "Will I be rejected? What does it take to be accepted?" He worries about what might be held against him—a history of cigarette smoking or alcohol abuse, for example, or other preexisting medical conditions that might affect his suitability as a candidate for a transplant. Some patients express ignorance or misconceptions about the procedure and are uncertain of their desire to undergo it. For them the evaluation period is an important opportunity to learn more—to see survivors and ask questions. Frequently they express amazement at the vigor of the recent transplant patients they meet. Although efforts are made to explain the risk and uncertainty of outcome, most patients become optimistic that if only given the chance, they will succeed with a transplant.

Potential heart recipients undergo a variety of evaluations—cardiac, neurological, psychiatric, social work, and physical therapy. Tests or trials of medication may be ordered before a final decision is reached. In general, transplantation will not be offered if there are other, less drastic therapies that can be tried first or if the patient suffers from other medical conditions (such as serious circulatory problems, malignancies, or chronic infections) that would vitiate the benefit of transplantation. A patient might also be turned down because the medical team feels that he will be unable to adhere to the rigorous requirements of the postoperative treatment program; for example, by failing to keep scheduled medical appointments, to take necessary medications, or to participate in physical therapy.

The emotional toll of waiting

A period of anxiety and depression follows—waiting. Depending on the patient's weight, blood type, and severity of illness, he may wait from days to months for a suitable donor organ to become available. By conservative estimate there are more than 15,000 people in the United States who could benefit from a heart transplant. Only a small fraction of these ever come to a transplantation program. Still, every year hundreds of patients die while on transplantation waiting lists. In 1987, to ensure fairness, the U.S. Congress empowered a national organ-distribution system, the United Network for Organ Sharing (UNOS), to control and coordinate assignment of suitable organs for transplantation. The problem now is not one of inequitable distribution but rather one of demand exceeding supply.

The strain on family members may be intense during this phase of the process. Their wishes that a heart will become available may lead to guilt at hope for the death of a suitable donor. The waiting period may be punctuated by "false alarms," instances when a patient is summoned to the hospital and prepared for surgery, only to have the operation canceled at the last moment after the proposed donor organ is found unsuitable. The emotional toll of such an event is clear.

The postoperative period: the "honeymoon" and after

At transplantation the patient's chest is opened to allow access to the heart. The heart itself is divided through the right and left atria; the pulmonary artery and aorta are divided; and the new heart is sewn into place. The patient returns to an intensive care unit and is connected to various tubes, monitors, and a mechanical ventilator, or respirator. Frequently the patient awakens from anesthesia while still partially paralyzed by muscle-relaxant medication. As the patient's respiratory system recovers, he can be weaned from the ventilator. In most cases patients are sitting up in bed, eating, and beginning rehabilitation within one to two days after surgery. If all goes well, the patient will be ready for discharge in one to three weeks, depending on the medications he is taking and the difficulties encountered.

Barring complications, this is a time of euphoria for the patient, the "honeymoon" phase, which ends abruptly when the first complication sets in. If significant problems do arise, the emotional state of patient and family rises and falls with the course of the patient's progress. Patients typically experience disappointment, anger at caretakers for failure to live up to their idealizations, and guilt at the strain their illness is imposing on family and friends; often these feelings merge into a general state of depression. However, most patients find that their mood improves as their general sense of well-being grows.

Other psychological problems that may occur in the immediate postoperative period include delirium, anxiety, and medication-related mood disturbances. About 4–18% of patients experience actual delirium. Milder cases of transient confusion or intellectual impairment occur in a much larger number of cases. These disturbances are due to side effects of steroid medication (given to prevent rejection of the transplant) and to abnormal metabolic states that occur occasionally following heart surgery. Severe brain injury, such as stroke, occurs rarely. Occasionally a patient may develop a psychotic illness while in the intensive care unit. One 22-year-old man, doing well seven days after surgery, suddenly developed the belief that closed-circuit television cameras in the room were broadcasting his activities to the White House, where his condition was being monitored by the president. This kind of disturbance can be effectively treated by a combination of drug therapy and moving the patient out of the stressful atmosphere of the intensive care unit.

Postsurgical psychosis is less common today than it was in the early days of human heart transplantation, when it affected up to one-third of patients. Many factors are believed responsible for the decreased incidence of psychosis, including improvements in the surgical process itself, better psychological preparation of patients, and the fact that heart transplantation is now an accepted and proven therapy, the positive results of which are plainly visible in the persons of healthy long-term survivors. There is less sense of leaping into the unknown than there was 20 years ago.

Anxiety during the postoperative period is commonly more evident in the patient's behavior than in self-reported or acknowledged symptoms. A patient will occasionally develop a phobia about the postoperative need for oxygen or become psychologically dependent on the oxygen. Periodic biopsy of the heart tissue, performed by means of a catheter inserted via a neck vein, is one of the primary methods of checking on the status of the new heart. These biopsies are begun in the postoperative period and are occasions of considerable anxiety for a great many patients. The large doses of steroids used immediately after transplantation sometimes cause disturbing changeability of mood. Patients' irritability at this time can be distressing to family members and staff. Finally, discharge from the hospital itself can cause patients to feel extremely anxious.

Will van Overbeek

Fellow heart transplant recipients celebrate Valentine's Day together in 1988. Their confident expressions would seem to testify to the feeling of most heart transplant patients that the considerable risks of the procedure are, after all, well worth taking.

Return to normalcy?

Upon discharge from the hospital, the patient may be asked to follow a fairly rigorous regime, including walking 4.8 km (3 mi) each day, following a low-cholesterol and low-salt diet, taking up to a dozen medications on a complex schedule, and returning to the hospital for evaluation twice a week. Rejection of the new organ may occur without any early symptoms; hence the need for regular, repeated biopsy of heart tissue. The dosage of cyclosporine is adjusted frequently to maintain satisfactory blood levels of the drug.

This is a time of conflicting emotional demands for the patient, who may be impatient for life to return to normal, while others treat him as a fragile curiosity. On the other hand, the patient may be fearful and overanxious about his health while others become impatient with his invalidism. Efforts to return to work, resume family roles, and re-form social connections must be juggled with the tasks of health maintenance and management of medical problems that may arise without warning at any time. Gradually the schedule of medical surveillance and reevaluation eases, and the patient returns, over the space of several months to a year, to a more normal life, in which the care required for maintaining the transplant is just part of the routine.

To the extent that the patient had had previous long-standing personality problems or chronic feelings of depression before transplantation, such problems and feelings are likely to recur in this phase of adaptation. Despite many patients' belief to the contrary, having a heart transplant is not likely to magically solve their problems of living. On the other hand, many patients feel imbued with a greater sense of purposefulness and need to be useful to others as a result of the opportunity afforded them. Although most patients realize that it would not be helpful to them to personally thank the family of their donor, they express their gratitude in volunteer work and support of other cardiac patients, let go of old concerns that no longer seem important, and, in general, try to experience life with more emotional warmth and love.

Health status: key to quality of life

Since the late 1970s, studies from several centers in the U.S., Great Britain, and Australia have reported successful physical rehabilitation of more than 80–90% of one-year heart transplant survivors. Most patients describe themselves as at least moderately satisfied with their physical well-being and quality of life, although personal appearance, sexual function, and finances are commonly noted as problems. Without a doubt, the most important determinant of the quality of life as perceived by the patient after surgery is his or her health status. Quality of life is negatively associated with the number of physical symptoms present—the fewer the physical problems, the greater the patient's satisfaction. Patients surviving heart transplantation face a number of likely medical problems. About 10–20% of transplant recipients experience damaging rejection reactions or fibrous tissue infiltration that damages the heart muscle; as many as 35–50% may develop coronary artery obstruction within three to five years of transplantation. These complications may be disabling to the point of requiring retransplantation. Hypertension (high blood pressure) is common, and treatment carries with it all the side effects associated with antihypertensive therapy, including depression and sexual dysfunction. The continued use of immunosuppressive drugs raises the heart transplant patient's risk of developing infections due to pathogens against which the immune-competent individual can normally mount an effective defense—*Pneumocystis carinii,* cytomegalovirus, *Herpes simplex* virus and other agents—as well as increasing the risk of lymphomas and other malignancies. Other

345

problems may include tremor (a side effect of cyclosporine), excessive hair growth (caused by steroids and cyclosporine), and fractures in bones weakened by prolonged steroid treatment. Chronic pain has been reported to be a problem for some patients.

Body image—fantasy and reality

Up to about half of all heart transplant recipients suffer some distress over body image, arising from two separate sources. The first grows out of fantasies of incorporation of aspects of the donor's person together with the donor heart. For example, a middle-aged male patient may jokingly express the hope that along with the transplanted heart of an 18-year-old man will come the younger man's imagined sexual endurance and prowess. Such fantasies are also frequently reflected in the questions of friends and acquaintances who want to know "if it feels strange to have someone else's heart inside you" or whether some aspect of the recipient's desires, outlook, or ideas have been replaced by those of the donor. Most patients say no to the latter question, just as they ultimately deny the emotional impact of having within themselves a vital organ of another person. A variety of defense mechanisms are utilized, such as depersonalization of the donor heart ("It's only a pump") and repression ("I never think about it"). Patients may, however, notice changes in their behavior that are related to unconscious fantasies about the donor. For example, a patient who developed a fear of driving and another who became scrupulous about seat belt use both believed their donors had been killed in motor vehicle accidents. Remarkably few patients admit to having dreams about their transplants or donors, although in the early days of transplantation, nightmares of the new heart being taken away were occasionally reported. Perhaps such dreams are usually too anxiety-provoking to be recalled after awakening.

The second, and more common, source of distress over bodily appearance focuses more on actual physical changes associated with transplantation. In one generally positive study, in which 89% of patients rated their quality of life favorably, 20% reported tremor, 25% changed bodily appearance, and 30% changed facial appearance, which disturbed them "quite a bit" or "extremely." Overeating and altered metabolism due to steroid drugs lead to pronounced weight gain in many patients. Steroids may also cause a puffy appearance of the face and torso. Cyclosporine, as noted above, causes excessive hair growth on the face and body; it may also produce unsightly overgrowth of gum tissue. Facial acne due to steroids is common. These side effects are especially difficult for schoolchildren and young women, but they bother nearly all patients to some extent. When accompanied by teasing and social rejection, the changes in appearance are all the more difficult to cope with.

Special problems of adjustment

Employment. About 50% of transplant patients are able to return to full-time employment in their previous capacities. Others, while they view themselves as able to work, are not able to get jobs. Most heart transplant recipients face great difficulty and frequently encounter economic disincentives if they attempt to return to work. More than one-third of physically rehabilitated transplant recipients are "insurance disabled"—unable to obtain employer-sponsored health insurance and, therefore, dependent on their disabled status to maintain their government-sponsored health insurance. Some patients work "off the books"—*i.e.,* in unofficial positions that do not entitle them to company benefits. Being unable to return to desired work engenders anger and demoralization.

Family relationships. For the patient's spouse and family, transplantation is usually the answer to a prayer and an occasion for hope that a difficult ordeal is over. Usually a patient's improved health reduces strain and makes family relationships easier. Unusual reactions do occur, however. Recovery may be the occasion for a release of pent-up feelings of anger, and a previously stable-appearing family may fall apart. Spouses who felt obligated not to leave the marriage when their partner was ill may now feel justified in going. Conversely, a patient who was resigned to a bad marriage may feel ready to leave the marriage when his or her health improves. Paradoxical depres-

After receiving a heart transplant in 1985, Mary Peters was able to rejoin her husband in favorite outdoor activities. The necklace she wears bears a cross and a heart, symbolizing her feeling that her new heart is "God's miracle."

Bill Hogan; © 1987 Chicago Tribune Company

sion may develop in family members after the patient's recovery is assured, as "mourning" for the loss of the patient as he was—which may have been deferred in the hope that he would again return to that state—finally occurs. Family conflict may also occur because of the decreased authority of a formerly ill parent, who, following recovery, attempts to regain control over the family.

Psychiatric problems. Many patients experience problems of adjustment after discharge from the hospital. The tasks of resuming social roles, sexual function, work, and leisure activities may all be complicated by feelings of anxiety and fear. Depression affects a substantial proportion of heart transplant recipients in the first year after surgery. Moodiness and irritability are troubling side effects of steroid medication for the first several months until the dosage has been reduced to maintenance levels. Many patients complain of slight impairment in memory or intellectual function, although investigators have not yet documented lasting deleterious effects of transplantation on mental function.

Heart transplantation centers vary in the amount of psychological counseling routinely provided to post-transplant patients. Most centers offer patients educational meetings and opportunities to express personal concerns. Support groups, some of them professionally led, are widely used. Nurses and social workers do most of the screening and counseling. Postoperative psychiatric screening—and intervention, when found necessary—is routine in some programs, while others provide psychiatric care only when an overt psychological problem develops.

Sexual function. Up to half of all male heart transplant recipients have some problem with sexual function. Causes of sexual dysfunction include fear, psychological problems, marital conflict, medication side effects, and persistent physical disorders. Couples vary in the degree of importance they attach to resuming sexual relations, but for most this is a desirable goal of transplantation, and difficulties in attaining it are frustrating. Interestingly, the responses of patients surveyed by questionnaire in Great Britain and Australia suggest that this problem is less common outside of the United States. It is unclear if this is due to cultural differences regarding expectations for sexual function or reticence in expressing dissatisfaction—or whether there is an actual difference in sexual function of heart transplant patients in these countries.

Problems of children. Children undergoing heart transplantation face its associated problems with a special vulnerability. Unlike adults, children may not have developed the capacity to intellectually master the trauma being experienced and to achieve a kind of distance through intellectualization, sublimation, and deferring gratification. It may be especially difficult for children to incorporate the donor heart into their concept of themselves. For example, while adult patients may have fantasies about how the donor's personality might exert an influence over them, they commonly deny that they worry about the personal qualities of the donor; when asked about this concern, adult patients usually say something like, "As long as the heart works, I don't care who it's from." Children, on the other hand, may object to a prospective donor heart if the personal characteristics of the donor seem too hard to assimilate. One preadolescent girl inquired whether, were she to receive the heart of an Asian donor, she would awaken speaking Chinese. Teenage boys, in particular, seem concerned that they receive a male heart. Most teenage boys have concerns about their masculinity, and the idea of placing something "female" inside them provokes great anxiety.

Children who survive heart transplantation tend to be able to function at an appropriate level for their age, including returning to school and normal physical activity. Children with heart transplants have won academic honors, participated in high school sports (even heavyweight wrestling), and gone to overnight camp. However, they have also suffered depression at being rejected because of their changed physical appearance or being held back in school, thus losing touch with peers.

Some youngsters experience neuropsychological deficits from medication-induced seizures and postoperative brain damage. As noted above, adults have social problems associated with the excessive hair growth and swelling of the face and torso that are side effects of their medications; children suffer these effects, too. Adult patients, however, are much better able to buffer the effect of others' reactions and to intellectualize about them. Children, lacking these defenses, may avoid others or develop "school phobia," which may retard their social and intellectual development. Physical growth may be delayed or reduced in some cases.

A risk worth taking

Heart transplantation may be a miracle come true, but it is hardly a panacea. Its reality—like that of many other successful medical therapies—is one of putting up with unpleasant side effects in return for a substantial benefit obtained at considerable risk. Heart transplantation means trading in one set of problems, those associated with terminal heart failure, for another, those of the heart transplant recipient. For most patients this appears to be a worthwhile trade-off. Getting a new heart does not seem to produce any drastic, permanent changes in an individual's emotions, personality, or outlook on life, despite the alternating periods of depression and euphoria the patient may experience along the way. Still, most heart transplant recipients, imbued with a new sense of purpose, seem determined to make the most of their hard-won second chance at life.

Home Health Care

At one time physicians routinely made house calls. As the technological sophistication of medicine grew, however, its practice shifted to hospitals and doctors' offices. Now continued developments in the rapidly evolving health care field have made the home setting once again acceptable—even preferable—for the delivery of some medical care. Home care then is a new name for an old idea.

Patients today are receiving services at home that range from physical therapy for an elderly person recovering from a stroke to ventilator assistance for a young victim of amyotrophic lateral sclerosis (Lou Gehrig's disease). For some chronically ill or disabled patients, home care services are as basic as assistance with bathing, dressing, eating, shopping, and other so-called activities of daily living, or ADLs. The ADLs, taken together, determine a person's ability to live at home independently with safety and security.

Impetus for care at home

The resurgence of home care is a response to social and economic changes that have enhanced the availability and desirability of home treatment and to

Soaring hospital costs mean that patients are being discharged "quicker and sicker"; home health care can provide the extended medical services they may need.

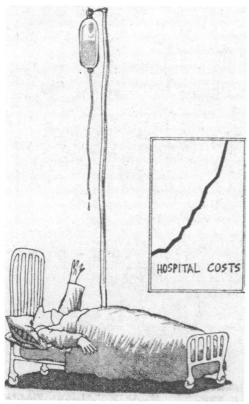

HOSPITAL COSTS

technological developments that have made possible the home delivery of increasingly sophisticated forms of medical care. Scientific advances in medicine have extended the average life-span. In the U.S. the over-65 population is now almost 30 million and is growing twice as fast as the population as a whole, with the over-85 age group growing the fastest. In their later years many people suffer chronic and debilitating illnesses (*e.g.,* diabetes, hypertension, heart disease, arthritis, Alzheimer's disease) that require ongoing treatment and impede independent functioning.

Meanwhile, the cost of medical care has soared. Americans spent $425 billion on health care in 1985, compared with $132.7 billion a decade earlier. The most expensive treatment is, by far, in hospitals and nursing homes. Consequently, the primary payers for this increasingly costly medical care—private insurance companies and government insurers, such as Medicare and Medicaid—are encouraging earlier discharge from hospitals and avoidance of nursing home placement. Financial constraints have shortened the average length of hospital stays for older persons from 14 days in 1968 to 8 days in 1985. Patients are thus being discharged "quicker and sicker."

As a result of these discharges, many patients still have unmet medical and psychological needs when they go home. These discharges are anxiety provoking for patients' families, who must attempt to locate appropriate extended-care services. On the other hand, many patients view with favor the opportunity to recuperate in familiar, noninstitutional surroundings. In some instances care at home can actually expedite recovery. As patients and their families have become more comfortable with home care, physicians, too, have become more experienced and not only accept but encourage care at home as an appropriate and therapeutic alternative for their patients.

Besides the skyrocketing costs of institutional care and physicians' growing acceptance of the home care concept, today's technology greatly facilitates the transition from hospital to home for patients whose conditions have been stabilized. For example, patients can continue intravenous (IV) therapy at home, receiving medications, nutritional support, or blood products that must be delivered directly into a vein.

What is home care?

Home care encompasses a wide range of services that function to promote health and preserve quality of life for patients. In almost all surveys in which patients are given a choice, they prefer being treated at home. A child with a bone infection and an elderly person with terminal cancer share the same goals; they want to be with family, in familiar surroundings, with greater control over their situation than is possible as a hospitalized patient. Home care provides this safety and comfort.

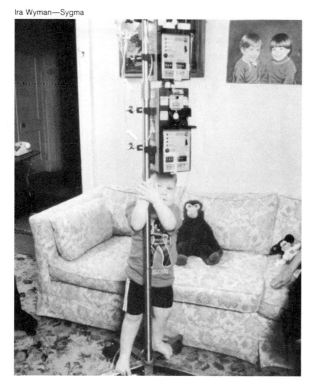

High-tech equipment enables a child with chronic, life-threatening diarrhea to grow up at home instead of spending years in the hospital. He is fed through a tube inserted in his chest; his mother keeps track of his fluid intake and output. "As soon as he came home, he was a happier baby," his mother reported.

Home care agencies offer a broad array of medical and rehabilitation services as well as nonmedical support services. For example, stroke patients, after initial hospital recovery, can receive rehabilitation therapy at home (*e.g.,* to regain the use of limbs or speech) for

weeks or months as necessary. Similarly, a surgical patient may complete recovery at home with visiting nurses changing dressings as needed. Professionals providing home care include physicians, registered nurses, nurses' aides, physical and occupational therapists, speech and hearing pathologists, nutritionists, social workers, and homemakers to aid with ADLs. The equipment used ranges from walkers, electrically operated beds, commodes, and adult diapers to ventilators, home dialyzers for patients with renal failure, and home intravenous devices.

Home care is appropriate not only for the severely disabled, such as victims of stroke and patients with Alzheimer's disease, lung disease, cancer, and multiple sclerosis (MS), but also for patients with milder conditions whose symptoms interfere with ADLs. For example, mild osteoarthritis can cause a faltering or unsteady gait. People with this condition may be able to drive an automobile and otherwise live quite independently, but they may be fearful of bathing because they are at risk of falling. Such a fear can lead to poor personal hygiene, which then lowers self-esteem, and in the absence of intervention, overall health may deteriorate. Home health professionals can provide simple, inexpensive equipment assists—such as a shower transfer bench or a bathtub grab bar—which restore safety and comfort during bathing and thus preserve the patient's independence.

Similarly, the embarrassment and inconvenience caused by the problems of incontinence (leaking urine or stool) can reduce mobility and decrease social interactions of otherwise well-functioning elderly persons. Sometimes there is a specific medical cure for this problem; other times there is not. Regardless, home health professionals can make available an array of devices, including bedside commodes, urinals, and adult diapers, to minimize disruption from incontinence. Re-

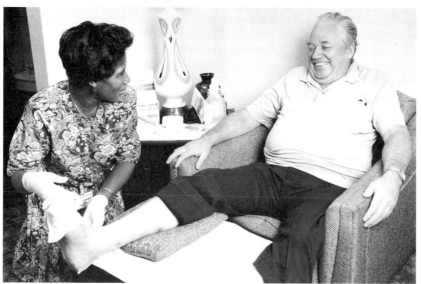

A Chicago man accidentally scalded his right foot when he put it in water that was too hot; because he has poor circulation in his feet due to diabetes, he was unable to judge the water temperature. His burn caused a serious infection (gangrene) that required regular tending and dressing changes for many weeks. Attended at home by a registered nurse and a nurse's aide from Illinois Masonic Medical Center's home care program, he received both the kind of scrupulous care that was required for his infection to heal and monitoring of his diabetes. Once a week he visited the medical center to have his foot checked by his physician.

sponding to the problems of urinary incontinence not only improves the quality of the person's daily living but also can prevent the development of pressure sores—a common problem in those who are confined to a bed or wheelchair—which can create enormous financial and social burdens on the patient and family.

The home care needs of mildly impaired persons are often overlooked because these people have fewer contacts with medical personnel. Regardless of the overall level of functioning, a patient who is experiencing difficulty with any of the routine ADLs or who feels insecure or unsafe at home may be a candidate for home health services. A person should not be denied access to these services because he or she is ambulatory and functional. Unfortunately, physicians and insurers rarely acknowledge the needs of this group of patients.

Seeking and evaluating services

Home care is provided by both for-profit and not-for-profit agencies and companies in most communities. Some are associated with local hospitals; others are parts of large national chains; and still others are free-standing, independent local organizations. The best sources of information about home care agencies are hospital discharge planners, family physicians, case managers, and community social service directors.

Word-of-mouth recommendations are a good way to determine quality when evaluating home care agencies. There are also accreditation processes for home care. Home care agencies can be voluntarily inspected and evaluated by the Joint Commission on Accreditation of Healthcare Organizations, based in Chicago, or the New York City-based National League for Nursing. In addition, many states have their own set of regulations with which home care agencies must comply; Medicare also certifies agencies that accept its patients.

Because home care is different from care in the hospital, these accreditation inspections and licensing procedures can assure only a certain degree of compliance with ethical and medical standards of high-quality care. In the hospital there is round-the-clock patient care, with numerous professionals having contact with patients, providing at least the opportunity for ensuring that patients receive appropriate and high-quality care. In contrast, most home care workers are providing services alone, without close supervision. In the hospital the doctor sees the patient daily and has direct contact with the nurses, whereas in the home the doctor may see the patient at only infrequent intervals and have only minimal contact, by telephone, with the nurses.

Despite these potential problems, home care has been relatively free of the abuses and scandals that characterized the nursing home industry in its early years. Likewise, in an era of a medical malpractice

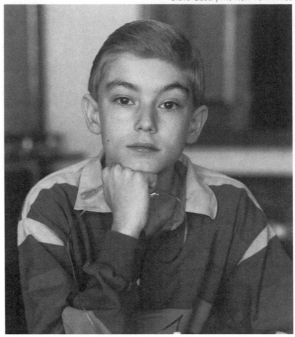

Thanks to a microprocessor-controlled pocket-size pump that continuously administers antibiotics to fight potentially fatal lung infections, this 13-year-old cystic fibrosis patient is able to lead an active life and avoid costly hospital treatments.

crisis, there have been few claims against doctors or agencies involved in home care. This speaks to the quality of the service provided, the human element embodied in home care, and the degree of patient satisfaction.

Benefiting from technology

In the past five to ten years, much of the technology that is associated with the hospital has become commonly available in the home. For example, a person who is totally dependent on a respirator can be safely managed at home by the family and nurses. Owing to advances in technology, once family members have been adequately trained, they can often provide almost all the care the patient needs.

Intravenous antibiotics. Intravenous treatments at home are now common. Virtually any infection that responds to IV antibiotic therapy can potentially be treated at home. For example, children with osteomyelitis (an infection of the bone) can be hospitalized for a few days and then medicated intravenously at home for an additional two to four weeks. Likewise, many skin, respiratory and urinary tract, and wound infections can be treated at home with intravenous antibiotics. Patients treated at home recover as completely and as rapidly as those who receive hospital treatment. Moreover, home care reduces the possibility of certain complications, particularly hospital-acquired infections.

Infusion pumps and new antibiotics have vastly facilitated complex care at home. Infusion pumps are computerized mechanical devices with battery backup that are attached to IV systems that at specified intervals deliver a certain amount of medication into the patient's veins. These pumps are compact, highly reliable, and fairly easy to operate. The patient or family manages most of the process with training and assistance as necessary from nurses and regular follow-up by the patient's physician.

Until a few years ago, most antibiotics had to be administered every four, six, or eight hours. However, new drugs—ceftriaxone (Rochephin) is one—can be given once a day and frequently can be injected intramuscularly, avoiding altogether the need for intravenous equipment. As an example, five years ago a child with cystic fibrosis received a 10–14-day course of antibiotics in the hospital; today the same child can potentially be treated at home with a daily injection in the buttocks given by a visiting nurse or by a parent who has had proper instruction.

It is important to point out, though, that not all patients are suitable candidates for home intravenous or intramuscular antibiotics. Their condition must be stable; they must have access to adequate help at home; and they must be free of other medical problems requiring special monitoring or treatments that would be difficult to manage at home. The inherent severity of their disease and anticipated complications also affect eligibility. Because home intravenous antibiotic treatment can save about 50% of what comparable treatment would cost in the hospital, these economies have been a major impetus to the growth of this form of medical therapy.

Pain management. A great many patients with terminal cancer experience pain as part of their disease. Often pain relief is all that medicine has to offer. In the past when these patients spent their final days in the hospital, it was frequently primarily for relief of pain. However, new techniques of managing pain—many of which are more effective than older methods and have fewer side effects—can be used in the home setting.

There are several ways of giving morphine, the mainstay of managing severe pain. It can be administered either at specified time intervals or continuously. In addition, it can be given by intramuscular, intravenous, or subcutaneous (just beneath the skin surface) routes. When the drug is given at intervals, patients often report that just after receiving the injection, they have pain relief but feel sleepy. Later on as the medicine wears off, they are no longer groggy but begin to feel pain again.

Continuous subcutaneous morphine injections provide an alternative way of relieving severe pain. A slow continuous infusion means that the blood level of the drug never goes too high or drops too low. Patients actually receive less medicine this way than by other routes; they have better pain relief; and they feel less sleepy. The method is quite simple. A very small, almost painless needle is inserted just beneath the skin surface, usually on the front of the chest. This is attached to a battery-operated pump about the size of two decks of cards, which continuously infuses a small dose of morphine. The needle is changed once a week, and the entire process can be managed by the patient or a family member.

Nutritional support. Patients who are not able to eat or absorb nutrients through their intestine can receive total parenteral nutrition at home. All of the necessary calories and other nutrients can be given by vein. The infusions can be given during sleeping hours, allowing patients who are completely functional to work during the day.

IV fluid and blood therapies. Patients requiring intravenous fluids or electrolytes (electrically charged salts and acids that regulate the body's water volume and level of acidity) to correct imbalances can also benefit from IV therapy at home. In addition, those requiring whole blood or blood components (*e.g.,* packed red blood cells, white blood cells, platelets, plasma, or albumin) can be managed at home in a similar fashion.

Preventive care

Preventive care is an integral part of the office practices of family physicians and internists, but this care is often inaccessible to less ambulatory or homebound patients. Nevertheless, these patients are subject to the same largely preventable diseases as other, more functional patients, and they also need the same routine physical examinations, tests, and screenings as other patients.

For example, a 45-year-old woman disabled by MS has the same requirements as other middle-aged women for routine breast and gynecologic examinations, mammograms, and Pap smears. Being homebound—with MS or any other disease—confers no protection against breast or cervical cancer. With thought and some planning by family members and health professionals, such routine care can be provided. A Pap smear, for example, can be taken in the home by a nurse equipped with a flashlight and a disposable plastic speculum. In addition to cancer screenings, patients can arrange to have dental care as well as appropriate immunizations (*e.g.,* flu and pneumococcal vaccines) at home.

Patients with AIDS

AIDS (acquired immune deficiency syndrome) is a disease deserving special mention. Many large city hospitals are being flooded with AIDS patients of all ages. There are two reasons this overcrowding is going to worsen. First, it is predicted that the number of AIDS patients will increase substantially. Second, with research progress and the development of new and better drugs that prolong life for these patients, more people with AIDS will live longer. The reimbursement situation for AIDS patients remains in flux, with federal legislation changing and each state dealing with the cost-of-care issues differently.

Home care for this growing group of patients could be particularly advantageous. The opportunistic infections to which AIDS patients are susceptible—such as *Pneumocystis carinii* pneumonia—can require long courses of therapy. The same is true of drugs used to suppress the virus that causes AIDS. Often these patients are medically stable and remain hospitalized only to receive intravenous medicines. In the terminal stages of the disease, all that can be offered is supportive care, and the hospital environment can be a sterile, uncaring setting. By contrast, being at home could be comforting and emotionally salubrious.

Care partners

Family members usually assume the largest burden of caring for a chronically or severely ill relative at home. The term care partner rather than caretaker or care giver recognizes that these people are in a form of partnership together. Providing additional home care personnel enhances the health and quality of life for the patient while alleviating the burden on the care partner.

In the case of an older patient, the care partner may be an aged spouse or a middle-aged child. One of the greatest burdens on middle-aged persons today is assuming responsibility for an elderly parent while still caring for their own family. This dilemma is often called the "sandwich phenomenon."

The stresses on care partners can lead to depression, irritability, ambivalence, and fatigue, as well as exacerbating the care partner's own medical problems. To prevent burnout and to relieve the burden on the care partner, nurses, aides, homemakers, and others can and should be enlisted to assume some of the chores either regularly or occasionally. Home care staff can also meet the needs of the patient that the care partner may not be able to handle properly.

This kind of respite care—an important way to give care partners a break—is available from home care agencies and hospice programs. Although hospice programs are geared toward terminal illnesses, the concept of respite care is applicable to any home care patient and family. Hospice volunteers visit patients at home, and in some communities hospice inpatient units admit patients for short stays while family members vacation, meet business responsibilities, or simply rest.

Both home care agencies and hospice programs encourage care partners to seek support and relief. Doing so not only refreshes the family members, making it easier for them to continue, but also helps alleviate the guilt that patients almost invariably feel over becoming emotional and physical burdens to their loved ones.

Not for everyone

Home care, it should be pointed out, is not for everyone. An important relationship exists between the patient, family, physician, and home care personnel. In some communities adequate home care resources may not be available; in others, physicians may not yet have accepted the concept and thus may not consider home care part of their responsibilities.

Even if all the players are in place and a well-thought-out care plan has been drawn up, home care still may not work. In some families the interpersonal dynamics make it difficult to sustain a caring relationship during illness. When somebody gets sick, particularly a spouse, it is easy to forget that there are perhaps 30,

Helen Coppola (center) stays at the Northfield Manor nursing home in West Orange, New Jersey, while her daughter and son-in-law, with whom she lives, take a three-week vacation in Europe. This kind of respite care gives those who care for an elderly person at home a needed break; it also ensures that people like Helen who need help with some of the activities of daily living are well cared for and do not feel they are a burden.

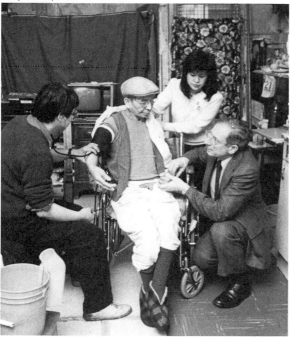

Ka-Lam Pang, a 68-year-old Chinese stroke victim who lives in a small apartment in New York City and speaks little English, is visited by a health care team—a physician, a nurse, and a translator—from St. Vincent's Hospital, who make sure his medical and personal needs are being met.

40, or even 50 years of living together that preceeded the acute event. If the sick person had previously been the one who managed all or most of the household necessities, the well spouse may simply be unable to take over the care of the partner and the home as well. Also, chronic illness can generate intense feelings of ambivalence, anger, and depression in spouses or other family members. These issues should be explored when home care has been recommended or is being considered.

Another problem is created when the patient feels extremely guilty about being a burden and insists on being placed in an institution. It is a difficult decision: honor the patient's request or the family's wishes?

Additional reasons home care may not work include poor compliance on the part of the patient or the care partner with taking prescribed medications or following prescribed therapies. Such noncompliance creates a dangerous situation for the patient and a liability for the professionals. Finally, despite today's sophisticated technology, there are some medical problems that simply cannot be adequately treated in the home.

Reimbursement

Reimbursement for home care services is in a state of flux, with both expansion and curtailment of different services. Currently most insurance coverage for either public or private home care is limited—usually to ser-

vices for short-term, acute situations—and is not for long-term continuous care. An example of expanded coverage is that payment by Medicare for home intravenous antibiotics was approved, effective in 1990. Although home care agencies are usually eager to explore payment options for services the patient requires, there are often a great many restrictions that may be a stumbling block for those seeking services. Even if home care would be less costly and even if it seems eminently reasonable for the services to be covered, unfortunately they may not be.

No place like home

Demographic shifts are creating a large adult population with modest and major disabilities that are amenable to home care. A 1984 survey found that one-fourth of people over age 65 had some difficulty cooking, cleaning, shopping, bathing, or performing other daily living activities. The proportion rose to one-half among people over age 85.

Assisted by technological advances and patient and physician acceptance of the concept, the home care industry is flourishing, and its range of services is expanding as new needs are recognized. The lower cost of medical care in the home setting, in comparison with care in hospitals and nursing homes, will, it is hoped, ensure continued support for the home care option by consumers and others who finance medical treatment. Home care does more than just save money; there is an enhancement of the quality of life patients experience if they are able to remain in their own homes instead of living in institutions.

In the U.S. home care is a growing movement that is fast becoming an integral part of the health care system. It responds to medical needs, is consistent with current economic realities, and is usually the emotional choice of patients and their families.

FOR FURTHER INFORMATION:
American Academy of Home Care Physicians
4600 West 77th Street, Suite 200
Minneapolis, MN 55435

National Association for Home Care
519 C Street NE
Washington, DC 20002
(202) 547-7424

National Hospice Organization
1901 North Fort Myer Drive
Arlington, VA 22209
(703) 243-5900   (home and respite care)

American Association of Homes for the Aging
1129 20th Street NW
Washington, DC 20036   (respite care)
—*Lawrence H. Bernstein, M.D.*

Infectious Diseases

The worldwide epidemiological patterns of infectious disease continue to evolve and change. In the U.S. there has been a recrudescence of some long-known diseases, among them tuberculosis and syphilis, and a growing recognition of relatively new infectious agents, such as human T-cell lymphotropic virus, type 1 (HTLV-1), and anisakis, a parasite transmitted in raw fish. Advances in technology have brought about new types of infection; infections of artificial joints, for example, are now an increasing problem. Medical science continues to find new ways to treat infections—creating more potent antibiotics and better antiviral agents—but the development of organisms resistant to medication poses a continuing challenge.

TB: old health threat renewed

Despite the advances that have been made in the treatment of tuberculosis (TB), approximately eight million new cases are reported annually around the world, and three million people die of the disease each year. The incidence of TB in the United States is less than in most countries—and until just a few years ago was declining steadily. Recently, however, the incidence of TB has been rising. The 22,768 new cases reported to the U.S. Centers for Disease Control (CDC) in 1986 represented a 2.6% increase over the 1985 number. Slightly fewer cases were reported in 1987 (22,517), but this was hardly indicative of any appreciable decline. Twenty-four percent of the new cases reported in 1987 were in persons born outside the U.S., an especially high prevalence being reported in Asian immigrants. A factor of even more concern to public health officials, however, was the increasing incidence of TB among certain populations of native-born Americans—including prison inmates, homeless people, migrant farm workers, intravenous drug abusers, and minorities. The proportion of TB cases in nonwhites rose from 24% in 1953 to 49% in 1987. The tuberculosis bacillus is particularly suited to transmitting the disease among the poor, especially people living under crowded conditions.

Several reports published in 1988 and 1989 attributed the recent increase in TB to intravenous drug abuse and concomitant infection with HIV (human immunodeficiency virus), the AIDS virus. One such report focused on TB incidence in a population of current and former drug abusers enrolled in a methadone program in the Bronx, N.Y. Of those who were infected with the AIDS virus, 23% also carried tuberculosis bacteria. Another 20%, who tested negative for the AIDS virus, were shown to be TB carriers. Two years later active TB had developed in eight of the HIV-infected people but in none of the others. The authors of the report noted that people whose immune systems are weakened by HIV usually develop TB as a result of

activation of a long-standing infection rather than new exposure to the disease. They recommended that intravenous drug abusers who carry the AIDS virus be treated prophylactically with the antituberculous drug isoniazid.

Minority groups and drug addicts are particularly difficult populations for public health efforts to reach; prevention and even treatment of infections are problematic in these groups. The situation is further complicated by the fact that tuberculosis must be treated for a much longer time than most other infections. In the past, treatment regimens consisted of two antituberculous drugs to be taken for a year. Recent studies of newer medications indicate that a shorter course of therapy may be effective, but a six-month course is the minimum. This is a long time in a transient population such as the homeless or migrant workers or in a population that is known to have difficulties complying with a medical regimen. Because of inadequate or intermittent treatment, it is not unusual for persistent infectious tuberculosis to develop in some people. Drug-resistant organisms also develop. As a result of the increasing number of cases of tuberculosis in U.S. inner-city populations, the disease has spilled over to other urban dwellers; there has been, for example, a clear increase in incidence of TB in children in some major metropolitan areas.

The AIDS virus undermines the body's immune system, thus making the treatment of TB much more diffi-

A tuberculosis patient is examined at Harlem Hospital in New York City. The disease, in decline until a few years ago, is now on the rise; at greatest risk are the homeless, minorities, and persons infected with the AIDS virus.

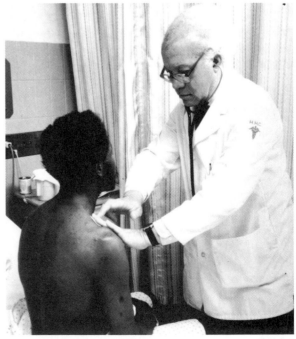

Mario Ruiz

354

Drug abuse—especially the use of crack, which is often the object of sex-for-drugs barter—accounts in large measure for the rising incidence of syphilis in the United States. Public health officials also see evidence of a possible link between syphilis and AIDS; sexually transmitted diseases that cause genital ulcers may facilitate the transmission of the AIDS virus.

cult. Because of the immune defect, the TB organism is seldom eradicated. Treatment may be necessary for life, and the infection is often fatal despite the use of multiple antituberculous drugs.

In addition to *Mycobacterium tuberculosis,* there is another form of tuberculosis—called *Mycobacterium avium intracellulare*—that often infects persons with AIDS. Although it is a common environmental organism, it is found only rarely in people whose immune systems are not compromised. When the organism establishes itself in AIDS patients, it can often be recovered at random from the bloodstream because there is no immune response to counteract it. While *M. avium intracellulare* is not usually fatal in itself and is not communicable, it undoubtedly contributes to the debility of the individual who is infected with it. Unfortunately, the antituberculous medications presently available are not very effective against this organism and are generally not used, as their toxicity outweighs their benefit.

In 1987 the Department of Health and Human Services established an advisory committee for the elim-

ination of tuberculosis in order to develop a strategic plan for the U.S. as a whole. The goal is to reduce the incidence of TB to less than one case per million population by the year 2010, with an interim target of 3.5 cases per 100,000 by the year 2000. It is the hope of the advisory committee that advances in biotechnology will produce better diagnostic and therapeutic measures than those now existing. A second step will be aggressive application of these new methods to clinical practice and public health. If this plan is to succeed, it will require the cooperation of local health departments and practitioners throughout the entire country and improved methods of reaching the more problematic populations, especially the indigent and drug abusers.

Syphilis, drugs, and "unsafe sex"

Syphilis has been recognized since the 16th century. Its spread has been facilitated by military conquest, increasing international travel, and a gradually more sexually permissive society. Penicillin injections, which can cure the disease, have been available since the 1940s. Despite this therapeutic advance, syphilis persists and is now increasing in incidence. In fact, the rate of incidence of syphilis in the U.S. now equals that of 1982—the highest rate since 1950. In 1987 there were 35,241 cases of primary and secondary syphilis reported in the U.S. This represents a 25% increase over the previous year and a rate of 14.6 cases per 100,000 population.

The greatest part of the increase seems to be concentrated in urban areas, with cities in California, Florida, and New York accounting for more than 50% of the total number of cases and about 80% of the increase. Minority groups are disproportionately af-

Incidence of syphilis in California, 1988*		
population group	number of cases	percentage
white males	601	9
white females	289	4
black males	2,002	30
black females	1,658	25
Hispanic males	1,448	22
Hispanic females	432	7
other	191	3
*provisional data		

Source: California Department of Health Services, Sexually Transmitted Disease Section

fected; black males, for example, have an incidence rate of 145 cases per 100,000—ten times the national rate. This recent rise in syphilis is strongly linked to heterosexual transmission. In contrast, there has been a clear decline in the incidence of syphilis (as well as gonorrhea) in the homosexual population, presumably due to the institution of "safe sex" practices because of the threat of AIDS.

According to CDC reports, the increase in heterosexual transmission of syphilis is associated with prostitution and drug abuse, particularly the abuse of crack, which is often the object of sex-for-drugs barter. Prostitutes, drug abusers, and their sexual contacts are now major risk groups. Some of the increase may be attributed to the use of spectinomycin to treat penicillin-resistant gonorrhea. While this drug is effective against gonorrhea, it is not able to kill the syphilis spirochete as penicillin does. Recent recommendations by the CDC have suggested that the antibiotic ceftriaxone be used instead for gonorrhea because it also can kill incubating syphilis. Public health officials are concerned that the increased incidence of syphilis may be due in part to the diverting of health resources from medical treatment of persons with syphilis and tracing of their sexual contacts to the prevention of AIDS. From a public health perspective, however, the two diseases—AIDS and syphilis—are related. Several studies published in 1988 suggested that sexually transmitted diseases that cause genital ulcers (syphilis and herpes simplex, type 2) increase the likelihood of the transmission of AIDS. When syphilis does occur with AIDS, the immune deficit makes it harder to treat. Earlier in the AIDS epidemic, some physicians had speculated that syphilis might be responsible for some of the clinical manifestations of AIDS, but this does not appear to be the case.

There are three reasons why the new outbreak of syphilis is of particular concern. First, because of the prominence of heterosexual transmission, the chances that the disease will spread to the fetus of an infected woman, producing congenital syphilis and its associated deformities, are much greater. In fact, there has already been an increase in the number of cases of congenital syphilis reported in New York City. Second, the increase in syphilis among heterosexuals also suggests an increasing level of unsafe sex practices associated with drug abuse and prostitution in inner-city neighborhoods. This creates an ideal setting for transmission of HIV. Finally, the presence of syphilis in this segment of the urban population may facilitate the transmission of HIV through syphilitic genital ulcers, which are usually painless but, as noted above, are believed to provide a ready path for transmission of the AIDS virus.

It is not clear what exactly is to be done about this recrudescent disease. The Public Health Service had to abandon its goal of reducing the incidence of primary and secondary syphilis to 7 cases per 100,-000 by 1990. It appears that more specific plans to deal with the inner-city and minority populations are needed. It is also apparent that there will be no lessening of syphilis transmission without a reduction in drug abuse and prostitution.

Concerns about the human retrovirus HTLV-I

The first human retrovirus discovered was given the name human T-cell lymphotropic virus, type I (HTLV-I). It was first isolated in 1978 but was not reported until 1980. Since that time HTLV-II and HTLV-III (the latter now called human immunodeficiency virus, type 1, or HIV-1—or simply HIV) have been identified. The discovery that AIDS is caused by HIV launched a massive

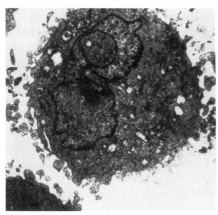

Although the human retrovirus HTLV-I (shown in photomicrograph below) is relatively rare in the U.S., the country's blood banks now screen donated blood for it as well as for the viruses that cause hepatitis-B and AIDS.

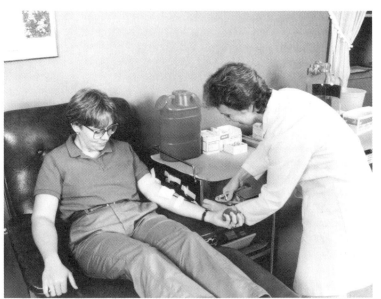

(Left) National Cancer Institute; (right) David York—Medichrome/The Stock Shop

international research effort that has already brought some insight into the workings of retroviruses. Still, much remains to be learned, and new retroviruses continue to be discovered.

HTLV-I, while clearly a human retrovirus, is quite different from HIV in that it does not produce AIDS and does not inevitably result in fatal illness. Instead, it causes an unusual type of blood disease called T-cell leukemia or lymphoma. It has also been associated with a progressive neuromuscular disease, called tropical spastic paraparesis, in which nerve damage usually causes a progressive weakness and spasticity of the leg muscles and often loss of bowel or bladder control. The disorder has also been reported in Japan and the Caribbean. Like HIV, HTLV-I is believed to have originated in Africa, although in a different area. Presumably it then spread to and became endemic in areas in the Caribbean and Japan.

HTLV-I appears to be more easily spread than HIV, at least in southwestern Japan, where in some areas up to 30% of the population have antibodies to the virus; women are infected as frequently as men. Sexual transmission is likely, and there is a clear association of the virus with blood transfusions. Unlike HIV, however, HTLV-I does not appear to be transmitted by infusion of blood plasma or serum factors (the liquid fraction of the blood), probably because it is more closely associated with blood cells.

In the U.S. the incidence of antibodies to HTLV-I is less than one in 1,000 and is often associated with prior residence in the Caribbean or intravenous drug abuse. Despite this low prevalence of HTLV-I antibodies, however, there has been concern about contracting the virus through blood transfusion. Recent studies of more than 20,000 transfusions suggest that the possibility of receiving blood contaminated with HTLV-I (0.024%) may now be higher than the risk of contracting HIV-1 (0.003%), as all donated blood in the U.S. has been tested for HIV-1 since March 1985. To combat the potential for further HTLV-I transmission via transfusions, broad-scale epidemiological studies are being conducted to determine the incidence of the disease in the U.S.; in 1988 the Food and Drug Administration (FDA) licensed tests for the antibody to the virus, which are now being used in most blood banks. The test is similar to the ones used to detect antibodies to HIV and also requires duplication of a positive result (*i.e.*, any blood sample found to contain antibody must be tested a second time and produce the same result) and confirmation with a backup test before a positive result is confirmed. Blood donors who test positive for the virus will be notified of the result, but it is not clear yet what the next step will be.

Parasitic infections from raw fish

Parasitic disease occurs in every form of life. Parasites afflict a large part of the world's human population—particularly in less developed countries, where poor sanitation and primitive methods of sewage disposal are common. Ascariasis, schistosomiasis, hookworm disease, and other intestinal parasitic infections account for much more human disease than cancer, heart disease, and stroke in most countries of Africa and Asia. In North America the spread of these organisms has virtually been eliminated by modern methods of sanitation.

Over the past few years, with increasing consumption of fish in the United States and a growing taste for sushi and other Japanese delicacies has come an increased incidence of parasitic infection. Human infection may occur as the result of eating either raw or insufficiently cooked, smoked, or marinated fish. The fish parasite that most often affects humans is the roundworm called anisakis. Common parasites in marine mammals, the worms live in the bowels of seals and walruses, where they lay their eggs. The eggs pass out into water and are then taken up by fish or squid and become encysted in muscle tissue or body cavities. When the fish is eventually eaten, the larvae migrate out of the cyst and, if ingested by humans, can develop into adult worms in the individual's stomach or become attached to the bowel wall. Symptoms of anisakiasis may include nausea, stomach pain, and indigestion. If the larvae perforate the bowel wall, peritonitis can develop. In some cases the worms migrate up from the stomach to the mouth and are regurgitated or coughed up—often as quite a surprise to the unknowing "host." Anisakis worms in the stomach can be removed by means of an endoscope passed through the mouth.

Another relatively common fish parasite that infects humans is eustrongylides. Like anisakis, it is associated with saltwater fish, but fish-eating birds rather than mammals are its usual host. This parasite has been previously reported in fishermen who inadvertently ate bait fish; there have also been reported cases of bowel perforation after the eustrongylides larva was ingested with sushi.

Fish parasites are so common that there is virtually no way to avoid eating them. The way to prevent human disease is to make certain that the parasite in the fish is not ingested alive. Either cooking a fish for ten minutes at 65° C (149° F) or freezing it at less than −20° C (−4° F) for five days is an effective measure. Supermarket fish have usually been frozen long enough that the parasites are not viable by the time the fish is sold. However, fresh fish are sometimes flown directly from the site of the catch to major distribution points. If the consumer does not plan to cook fish immediately, it should be frozen.

Artificial joints: infection risk

The development of artificial joints represents a dramatic advance for people with severe, crippling arthri-

357

tis. Hips and knee surfaces can now be replaced, allowing a person to walk who might otherwise be confined to a bed or wheelchair. Even the joints of the fingers and toes can be replaced with joints made of metal or other material. While the outcome of joint replacement can be a dramatic improvement when all goes well, the risk of infection is significant. Approximately 1–2% of all artificial joints become infected with bacteria. These infections are particularly difficult to eradicate because of the presence of the implant itself—a "foreign body" within the body's own tissues, which provides an opportunity for bacteria to escape destruction by the body's normal defense mechanisms. Standard antibiotic therapy is not sufficient to reach and destroy bacteria hidden within the complex surface layers of the implanted material. The most frequent bacteria to cause infections in artificial joints are the staphylococci; the more virulent *Staphylococcus aureus* (a common cause of wound infections) and the more common *Staphylococcus epidermis* (a normal inhabitant of the skin that seldom causes infection without a foreign body) play a major role. The infection may be introduced at the time of surgery, when organisms from the skin enter the wound via the initial incision. The prosthetic joint can also be "seeded" by bacteria in the bloodstream that have not yet been filtered out by the liver and spleen. Bacteria may enter the bloodstream from skin sores, or they may be introduced during the course of dental work or diagnostic procedures such as colonoscopy.

Once an infection has become established, there are two treatment options: (1) removal of the infected joint, followed by fusion of the bones on either side, or (2) removal of the joint, aggressive intravenous antibiotic therapy for a period of weeks, and then replacement with a new joint. There is an ongoing debate among physicians about the value of prophylactic antibiotics—for example, the taking of penicillin before and shortly after dental work—for people with artificial joints.

Resistance to antiviral drugs

Developing effective medication for treating viral infections is a difficult task; viruses live within normal human cells, and anything that damages the virus is likely to harm the cell. Nevertheless, great strides have been made in the past decade with the development of acyclovir (Zovirax) to treat herpes simplex infections, zidovudine (also called azidothymidine, or AZT; Retrovir) to treat HIV infection; ribavirin (Virazole) for infection caused by respiratory syncytial virus; and ganciclovir (Cytovene) to treat cytomegalovirus infections. There have been encouraging studies of the use of interferons for a variety of viral illnesses and new antiviral agents foscarnet, dideoxyinosine, and dideoxycytidine for HIV infections. Other antiviral drugs are under active investigation.

With the increased use of antiviral agents, however, the potential exists for viruses to develop resistance mechanisms—just as many bacteria came to be resistant to penicillin. In fact, with viral infections the development of resistant strains is even more likely than it is with bacterial infections because the antiviral agents now available often are not able to eradicate the viruses but simply lessen the severity of the disease or suppress the infection. The herpesviruses, for example, persist within the body's cells despite antiviral therapy and may cause renewed infection at any time. Recurrent or prolonged use of antiviral agents such as acyclovir may contain the spread of disease, but it also applies selective evolutionary pressure in favor of mutant strains that are resistant to acyclovir. The development of drug-resistant viruses is particularly likely to occur in an immunosuppressed patient, such as one with AIDS.

During the past year there have been reports of herpes simplex viruses that are resistant to acyclovir and of cytomegalovirus resistant to ganciclovir. There have been indications that HIV may become resistant or refractory to zidovudine therapy. While many of the resistant mutant viral strains may not be as virulent as the original strains, they can still cause significant disease in an immunosuppressed person.

It is difficult to scientifically test the resistance of a given virus; usually simple clinical indications are all that is possible. At present most available antivirals still appear to be effective and useful. Unfortunately, the future of antiviral drugs is likely to follow a course like that of the antibiotics—a gradually escalating battle between the organisms and the drug developers. In the long term, the best way to deal with infection is to prevent its occurrence rather than to try to treat or manage it once it occurs. The eradication of smallpox through vaccination is perhaps the best example of how successful this approach can be.

—Alan D. Tice, M.D.

Medical Education

Currently in the United States persons 65 years of age and older represent more than 12% of the overall population; this percentage will rise to 20% by the year 2030, amounting to approximately 65 million persons. Until very recently most physicians in the United States were inadequately trained in geriatric medicine. With the current population trends, it has become increasingly essential that geriatrics be incorporated into the education of physicians. In response to these demographic changes, several educational efforts have been initiated to teach physicians how to best care for older persons.

Within the past few years, several notable events have indicated that the discipline of clinical geriatrics is "coming of age." Geriatrics is a relatively new specialty,

Ethan Hoffman

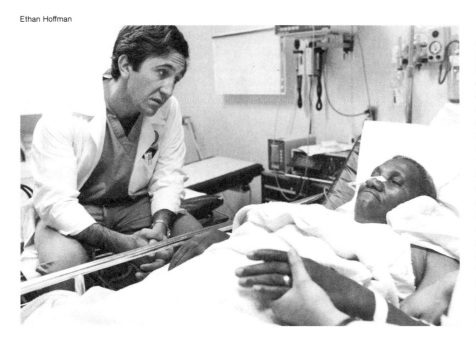

Until recently most physicians in the United States were inadequately trained in the care of elderly people. With the current population trends, however, it has become essential that geriatrics be incorporated into the education of physicians. The specialties of internal medicine and family practice now require as part of their residency training formal teaching and supervised experience in geriatric medicine. This and other efforts that are presently under way are aimed at improving the ability of doctors to deliver high-quality care to the 35 million elderly persons who will enter the 21st century.

and very close attention has been paid to ensuring that its growth is well planned. In the United States the federal government and several professional organizations have recently implemented efforts to assure high standards of education in geriatric medicine. For example, the Accreditation Council for Graduate Medical Education (ACGME), which reviews and accredits residency and fellowship programs, has addressed geriatrics at both the residency and the fellowship training levels.

Geriatrics in internal medicine and family practice

In a document issued in September 1988, the ACGME stated that internal medicine residency training must include formal teaching and regular supervised experience in geriatric medicine. Family practice residency training has had a similar requirement for a number of years. These mandates are believed to be very powerful incentives in the effort to make specific training in geriatrics an integral part of all residency programs. In fact, the family practice mandate has resulted in the implementation of formal curricula in geriatrics in 80% of family practice residency programs, compared with only 36% of internal medicine programs. Training in geriatrics during residency is particularly important in these two specialties because physicians in internal medicine and family practice provide about two-thirds of all hospital care and over 95% of nursing home care for older persons.

A second step that the ACGME has taken is the accreditation of geriatrics fellowship training programs in both internal medicine and family practice. Fellowship training requires at least two years of additional training beyond residency, with specific concentration in geriatrics. Until this accreditation process, any hospital or medical school could establish a geriatrics fellowship program without adhering to any specific standards. The accreditation process, begun in 1988, requires documentation of training, adequate faculty and training sites, and a formal site visit to verify these efforts. Fellowship training programs are particularly important to the discipline because they are the source of future faculty members in geriatrics.

Support for geriatrics training and aging research

The federal government has been increasingly involved in the evaluation of geriatrics education. For the last 15 years, the Veterans Administration has funded Geriatric Research, Education, and Clinical Centers (GRECCs) to attract outstanding professionals to teach and to conduct research on aging in a clinical environment. Currently there are ten GRECCs located nationwide. The federal government recently has begun to reexamine its role in supporting the costs of graduate medical education (residents and fellows). In response to the rising Medicare budget deficit and the proliferation of subspecialists (many of whom do not focus on the care of elderly persons), legislation was enacted to limit the number of years of Medicare-funded postgraduate training. This decision, however, allowed an exemption for the training of geriatricians. Congress has called for a report that would examine the advisability of continuing or possibly expanding that exemption. The adequacy of faculty supply in geriatrics at all levels of medical education will be studied as part of that report. Meanwhile, the government has recently supported a number of geriatrics centers nationwide in order to promote faculty development in geriatric medicine and dentistry through federally funded fellowship programs.

Growing knowledge base on aging

The American Geriatrics Society, the largest professional organization for geriatricians, has just completed its largest educational effort to date—the Geriatrics Review Syllabus. This study guide is aimed at practicing physicians who would like to improve their knowledge of geriatrics. It includes an overview of the most current literature regarding principles of caring for elderly persons; such geriatric syndromes as incontinence, memory loss, and pressure sores; geriatric psychiatry; and diseases of particular importance in the elderly population, such as arthritis, diabetes, and high blood pressure. In addition, the syllabus includes self-assessment questions and annotated critiques for participating physicians.

The knowledge base of geriatrics has also been consolidated through a series of consensus conferences sponsored by the National Institute on Aging, a branch of the National Institutes of Health. These conferences bring together a panel of respected medical scientists with a variety of backgrounds and special skills to hear testimony by experts in one specific subject area. The panel then reviews the testimony and presents a draft of a "consensus statement," which is read to the experts who have testified and those interested physicians and other health professionals who have attended the conference. After listening to questions and suggestions, the panel revises its statement, which is subsequently published by the government and mailed to physicians nationwide. To date, consensus conferences have been conducted to examine several geriatrics topics, including urinary incontinence, diagnostic tests for dementia, and comprehensive geriatric assessment.

Geriatric medicine certification

Perhaps the most important recent development in geriatrics is the new Certificate of Added Qualifications in Geriatric Medicine (CAQGM) that is available to board-certified internists and family practitioners. This certification process was adopted jointly by the American Board of Internal Medicine and the American Board of Family Practice, the first collaboration by these two boards to recognize a discipline by establishing common standards. Similar efforts toward certification of additional qualifications in geriatrics are also under way by the American Board of Psychiatry and Neurology.

Certification recognizes physicians who have additional expertise in geriatric medicine. A doctor becomes certified as a geriatrician by passing a written examination and demonstrating substantial clinical background in the care of elderly persons. The clinical background requirement demands either formal fellowship training or several years of substantial clinical experience in the care of elderly persons. The latter will be a pathway toward certification only until the early or mid-1990s, after which all candidates for the CAQGM will be expected to have completed fellowship training. All candidates for certification, regardless of training or specialty, must complete the same one-day written examination. The first examination was administered in April 1988, and examinations were scheduled to be offered every two years thereafter. The 1988 examination was taken by approximately 4,000 physicians, almost evenly divided between family practitioners and internal medicine specialists. Most of the physicians taking the examination did not have formal training in geriatrics. Slightly more than half of those sitting for the examination passed the test; thus, as of 1989 there were approximately 2,200 certified geriatricians nationwide. The certification is valid for seven years, at which time geriatricians will have to take another examination in order to remain certified.

Shortage of geriatrics faculty

Although the certification process for geriatricians provides a precise number of how many physicians have expertise in geriatrics, it also demonstrates a major problem facing the discipline—a shortage of qualified faculty in geriatrics. Many physicians who are now certified geriatricians have chosen to practice medicine solely rather than teach geriatrics or conduct research in aging. Several studies have suggested that 1,000–2,000 geriatricians are needed for academic geriatrics alone—i.e., to teach geriatrics both to physicians-in-training and to practicing physicians through continuing medical education. Furthermore, a recent survey suggests that in internal medicine training alone an additional 500 geriatrics faculty may be needed now, and another 500 may be needed within five years. Although some success has been noted in the efforts to increase the number of geriatricians through fellowship training, fewer than 100 physicians completed geriatrics fellowships in 1987, compared with more than 1,700 fellows completing cardiology training in that year.

Part of the problem has been a dearth of qualified applicants for geriatrics fellowship program positions. Geriatrics lacks the glamour and generous reimbursement of high-technology specialties. Furthermore, because it is a relatively new field, there are few role models and senior faculty mentors to encourage physicians to enter the discipline. Nevertheless, the efforts described above are being implemented, and there is a strong sense of "gathering steam" within the academic geriatrics community. The federal government, professional organizations, and physicians are responding to the "geriatrics imperative" that has resulted from demographic changes in the population. This response will undoubtedly improve the ability to deliver high-quality health care to the 35 million elderly persons who will enter the 21st century.

—David B. Reuben, M.D.

Exercise Medicine:
How Much Do Doctors Know?

by Jim D. Whitley, Ed.D., and Kenneth L. Nyberg, Ph.D.

A rather dramatic change of emphasis in health care promotion has occurred in the United States during the last decade. Increasingly, members of the medical profession are urging individuals to assume more responsibility for their own health care. They are recommending the practice of what is called preventive medicine. Basically it is a form of holistic, self-help medicine in which the individual voluntarily engages in a sound program of good health practices. For many people this attempt to achieve and maintain good health requires extensive behavior modification leading to significant changes in life-style.

Why preventive medicine?

The major force behind this current nationwide drive to promote preventive medicine is the desire to reduce the incidence of coronary heart disease (CHD), which is the leading cause of death among middle-aged and older men in the U.S. and most developed nations in the Western world. Although females are less likely to suffer from this disease, they are experiencing an increase in incidence.

The primary pathological condition associated with heart attacks is a progressive narrowing of the coronary arteries called atherosclerosis. Atherosclerosis is not a disease restricted to middle-aged and older individuals. Pathological changes that are thought to lead to this condition are commonly found in early childhood. It is estimated that by the age of 20, approximately 75% of males exhibit symptoms to a significant degree. This is supported by the results of autopsies of young Americans (average age in the early twenties) killed in the Korean and Vietnam wars; moderately advanced coronary atherosclerosis was found in over 70% of Korean War victims and in 45% of Vietnam war casualties—5% were in the advanced stages of the disease. If this condition manifests itself in the early twenties (in men) and preventive measures are not taken to retard or stop its progress, the possibility of experiencing CHD in the forties is greatly enhanced. (Women begin experiencing high rates of heart disease after age 50.)

Life-style and CHD

What are the causes of CHD? Several long-term population studies have identified risk factors (primary and secondary) associated with the premature development of heart disease. High blood pressure, high blood fats (low-density lipoprotein cholesterol and triglycerides), and cigarette smoking have strong relationships with heart disease and are considered to be primary risk factors. Those considered as secondary are obesity, diabetes, stress, physical inactivity, age, gender, and heredity (family history of heart disease).

The greater the number of these factors that individuals have, the higher the level of risk they assume. Most of them are interrelated and have interactive effects. For example, obese people who are sedentary tend to have elevated blood fats and suffer from high blood pressure and diabetes. Also, some experts believe that individuals with Type A personalities (time conscious, hard working, aggressive, and competitive) who operate in stress-producing environments are susceptible to hypertension.

One of the most encouraging factors in the fight against CHD is that individuals can exert control over all of the risk factors except gender, age, and family history by practicing good health habits.

The exercise antidote

Emerging from this new approach to health care promotion has been a strong emphasis on the importance of exercise. With the exception of the advice to stop smoking, no other good health practice has received as much popular attention during the last ten years. The positive aspect of this emphasis is an increased public awareness of its potential health-related benefits. The public is informed daily about exercise information from newspapers, television and radio, and health and fitness publications. One result of this media "blitz" is that fitness has become big business. It was estimated that in 1987 Americans spent $30 billion on products, equipment, and services related to exercise and fitness. The money was spent on such items as athletic shoes, exercise clothing, equipment (e.g., bicycles, weights, and rowing machines), memberships in health clubs, corporate fitness centers, diet and exercise books, special diet programs and products, aerobic dance classes, and exercise tapes and videos.

The negative part of the exercise revolution is that much of the information received by the public is not factual; some of it is misleading—even dangerous. It is produced by a growing field of "instant experts" in exercise medicine who have little educational background, training, or experience in exercise physiology and sports medicine and whose interests tend to be commercially motivated. Many of the claims they make for their programs and products are nothing more than quick fixes whose bases are in exercise magic, miracles, and myths. Tragically, in a growing number of cases, the advice concerning exercise given by these self-appointed experts has resulted in serious injury and, in extreme cases, even death. Laws should be passed that would hold unqualified individuals accountable for the malpractice of exercise medicine.

What medical schools are *not* teaching

Where can the average person, the nonathlete who wants to become physically fit, obtain scientifically sound information about exercise? Who is qualified to prescribe a cardiorespiratory fitness program that will result in health-related benefits for the general public? Many would assume that medical doctors, with their knowledge of the basic physiological systems (cardiac, circulatory, respiratory, muscular, and skeletal), would be the leaders in the promotion of cardiorespiratory fitness—one of the most important components of preventive medicine—and in its proper prescription.

Unfortunately, this is not the case. As a result of an extensive review of 92 U.S. medical school bulletins conducted by these authors and published in the October 1988 issue of *The Physician and Sportsmedicine*, the following was reported: only four medical schools (4%) offer exercise medicine as part of required course work (course topics rather than separate courses); in 31 schools (34%) exercise information is offered only on an elective basis; and 57 schools (62%) offer no formal instruction at all. The results of this study closely agree with the findings of a similar investigation completed in 1975 by E. J. Burke and P. B. Hultgren. They reported that only 12 of the 74 U.S. medical schools that responded to their survey offered a course geared to exercise as preventive medicine. They estimated that in most schools an average of only four hours was devoted to the study of exercise. Further, the findings from similar surveys conducted in both Canadian and British medical schools indicate that the lack of attention to exercise medicine is international in scope.

The significance of these findings is that the situation has not improved in U.S. medical education since 1975; doctors are no better trained in exercise medicine or qualified to prescribe it now than they were then. The continued absence of exercise medicine in the medical school curriculum is particularly difficult to understand because of the growing research literature in this area indicating the health-related benefits from cardiorespiratory fitness, the public's increased awareness of these benefits, and its desire for valid exercise information. The increase in scientifically based research, particularly since the early 1970s, has been impressive. Studies conducted by qualified professionals (*e.g.,* researchers in physical education, exercise physiology, and sports medicine) are regularly being published in reputable scientific journals.

Reasons for promoting cardiorespiratory fitness

The long-term adoption and practice of a properly prescribed cardiorespiratory fitness program can result in the reduction of the following major risk factors. High blood pressure has been reduced significantly in hypertensive individuals. High blood lipids (cholesterol and triglycerides) have been reduced. In terms of cholesterol, low-density lipoproteins—the "bad guys" that carry cholesterol to the interior walls of blood vessels—have been found to be reduced, while high-density lipoproteins—the "good guys" that are involved in removing excess cholesterol from the blood and tissues—are increased. Cigarette smoking has either been drastically reduced or completely stopped in people who exercise regularly.

All of the controllable secondary risk factors (obesity, diabetes, and stress) can also be beneficially affected by cardiorespiratory fitness. Obesity, which is known to contribute to the development of certain diseases, can be reduced not only through the reduction of caloric intake from proper dieting but also by increased caloric expenditure from exercise. Persons with diabetes can be helped through exercise, which

Table 1: **Exercise medicine offered in 35 U.S. medical schools***

separate courses	number
exercise physiology	5
sports medicine	3
advanced exercise physiology	1
seminar in exercise physiology	1
sports medicine (skiing)	1
athletic medicine	1
rehabilitation medicine	1
total	13

exercise topics taught in other courses	
exercise response	6
physical fitness	5
physiology of exercise	2
exercise stress test	2
sports medicine	1
exercise and nutrition	1
exercise ECG	1
cardiac rehabilitation	1
rehabilitation exercise	1
total	20

*Of 92 medical schools surveyed, 57 offered no formal instruction.

From Jim D. Whitley and Kenneth L. Nyberg, "Exercise Medicine in Medical Education in the United States," *The Physician and Sportsmedicine*, vol. 16, no. 10 (October 1988), p. 95. Reprinted by permission of *The Physician and Sportsmedicine*; copyright McGraw-Hill, Inc.

reduces their need for insulin. Exercise has been shown to be effective in reducing the side effects of diabetes in individuals who have this disease under effective control. Stress associated with job-related tension and anxiety, particularly in competitive, hard-driving high achlevers (Type A personalities), can also be reduced by exercise.

"Get some exercise"

Unfortunately, because of their lack of knowledge about exercise, it is common for physicians to instruct their patients to "get some exercise." They fail to provide specific prescriptive information concerning the type, frequency, duration, and intensity of that exercise. Fortunately, they do not tell their patients to "take some drugs." When prescribing drugs, they are very careful in specifying the type and dosage to be taken.

On a more positive and encouraging note, there is a small but growing number of physicians who are becoming knowledgeable about fitness and who are qualified to prescribe fitness programs. In fact, a few of these doctors, such as Kenneth H. Cooper, Allan J. Ryan, George Sheehan, and James M. Rippe, have become acknowledged experts and leaders in the field of exercise medicine. These experts did not, however, obtain their knowledge in medical school. In most cases it was gained as a result of their interest, research, and active involvement in a personal exercise program. The latter is important in the promotion of fitness because doctors who engage in exercise are more likely than their more sedentary colleagues to prescribe exercise for their patients.

The development of *The Walking Doctors Directory,* which will be published for the first time in the spring of 1990, is a meaningful step in the promotion of exercise medicine by doctors. It is a statement by doctors that cardiorespiratory fitness is a significant component of preventive, self-help medicine, and it further legitimizes exercise for the general public. The physicians who will be listed in the directory are those who walk themselves and who are likely to educate their patients about the many health-related benefits of cardiorespiratory fitness as well as prescribe walking as a form of either preventive, rehabilitative, or therapeutic exercise.

In addition to the assorted small groups of doctors who are concerned about their patients' exercise needs, the most qualified and knowledgeable professionals in exercise medicine are exercise physiologists and properly trained physical educators. Increasing emphasis in the education and training of current physical education students is being placed on exercise physiology—particularly in the area of cardiorespiratory fitness. Generally, this includes studying the research literature, administering and interpreting the results of various exercise tests (including stress testing), and properly prescribing exercise programs.

Exercise questions of pregnant women

Many women are frustrated when they become pregnant because their obstetricians do not advise them about what the safe limits of exercise are. Yet research indicates that compared with sedentary women, the majority of those who engage in regular, moderately intense exercise during pregnancy tend to (1) experience less fatigue and discomfort during labor, (2) have faster, easier deliveries with fewer complications, and (3) recover faster after childbirth.

Pregnancy does not reduce the body's ability to receive muscular and cardiorespiratory benefits from exercise. For women who were physically active before pregnancy, there is no need to reduce their activity during the first six months of pregnancy (except for reasons of nausea during the first trimester). However, during the last three months, when weight gain makes certain movements difficult (even dangerous), high-impact activities like running and aerobic dancing should be replaced by lower-impact exercises such as swimming.

There is also no reason why previously sedentary women should not start an exercise program during pregnancy, providing they start slowly with a low-intensity program like walking and gradually increase the speed and distance for conditioning.

Proper exercise, when combined with such other positive health habits as good diet and nutrition and refraining from smoking and the use of recreational drugs, should not compromise the birth of a normal, healthy child. Gynecologists should be better prepared to provide this information to their patients. In 1987 the American College of Obstetricians and Gynecologists (ACOG) drew up a set of guidelines in order to help practitioners advise their patients about safe and appropriate levels of physical activity during pregnancy. A subgroup of the ACOG has formed the Sports Gynecology Society, which has approximately 300 members nationwide. These are obstetrician-gynecologists who are especially attuned to the exercise needs of women, particularly during pregnancy.

Exercise physiology versus sports medicine

While there has been increased interest in exercise by the medical profession, that interest is related more to sports medicine for competing athletes than to the promotion of cardiorespiratory fitness (as a form of preventive medicine) for the general public. There is a significant difference between exercise physiology and sports medicine. Exercise physiology deals largely with the effects of work and exercise on human physiological systems and capacities, a major component of which is cardiorespiratory fitness. In contrast, sports medicine deals primarily with conditioning for sports participation—the prevention, treatment, and rehabilitation of athletic injuries and the return of athletes to competition.

Since the early 1970s a growing number of universities in the U.S. have established sports medicine programs for physicians. They provide a variety of experiences and training (rotations, residencies, and fellowships) for doctors who wish to specialize in sport medicine. Because of the continued growth of athletics (for both sexes, all age groups, and all levels of competition), it is important that medical specialists be prepared in this area. Because sports has become big business, particularly at the collegiate and professional levels, there is increasing pressure to return athletes to competition as soon after injury as possible. This requires an adequate number of surgeons trained in the latest surgical techniques and in the use of new instruments created by continued advances in science and technology.

In the field of exercise medicine, the medical profession is moving toward a greater emphasis on sports medicine than on the promotion of general fitness. This is not surprising, considering the importance contemporary society places on competitive athletics. Also, it can be very rewarding financially for team doctors who are successful in corrective and reconstructive surgery and in prescribing effective rehabilitation programs. The fast return of star athletes to competition can mean millions of dollars in revenue for a college or professional team. Although society also has placed great importance on cardiorespiratory fitness, it has received much less attention from the medical profession.

Doctors' attitudes and beliefs about exercise

What are the reasons for the failure of American medical schools to include exercise medicine in their required curricula? Certain beliefs held by leaders in medical education appear to have contributed to this situation: cardiorespiratory fitness does not play a significant role in preventive medicine, *i.e.,* the reduction of CHD risk factors; there is insufficient scientific evidence to support health-benefit claims made for exercise; it is not the responsibility of doctors to prescribe exercise for their patients; information about exercise should be obtained outside of medical school; and the medical school curriculum already is overcrowded—with little room for additional requirements. Perhaps the major reason for this absence of exercise medicine is that medical school education has been primarily concerned with pathology rather than the promotion of wellness through preventive medicine.

Doctors' attitudes and beliefs about health care promotion reflect the fact that they did not learn about exercise in medical school. In surveys designed to determine doctors' preferences concerning health care practices, generally only about 30% consider exercise to be very important. Even more discouraging is the finding that about the same percentage of the respondents feel that it is unimportant. Typically, of those interested in learning more about preventive medicine, only about 20% indicate that they would take a course in an exercise-related topic.

What medical schools should be teaching

Considering the medical profession's growing support for preventive medicine, it is surprising and unfortunate that medical schools have not included formal instruction in exercise medicine in their required curricula. Exercise medicine, like other branches of medicine, is becoming increasingly specialized; general medical training in such areas as cardiology, physiology (circulation), and respiration will not provide doctors with sufficient preparation for prescribing sound exercise programs that promote cardiorespiratory fitness. This will require specific education and training.

The primary reason for the inclusion of exercise medicine is the growing amount of scientific evidence that shows the health-related benefits of exercise and the significant role played by cardiorespiratory fitness

Table 2: **Major health benefits from cardiorespiratory fitness related to the reduction of CHD risk factors**

heart function
- greater contraction strength
- increase in stroke volume
- increase in cardiac output
- increase in coronary blood flow
- lower resting and exercise heart rates
- faster recovery to resting heart rate

blood circulation, composition, and chemistry
- increase in blood volume
- increased blood supply to muscles
- decrease in peripheral resistance
- decrease in systolic and diastolic blood pressure
- decrease in blood lipids (triglycerides and cholesterol)
- more efficient transport of blood gases (oxygen and carbon dioxide)
- more efficient exchange of gases in muscles

lungs and respiration
- stronger and more efficient respiratory muscles
- increase in oxygen consumption (aerobic capacity)
- increase in functional lung volumes and capacities
- increase in diffusion of respiratory gases

muscular system and body composition
- increase in muscular strength and working capacity
- improved limb range of motion and joint flexibility
- decrease in adipose fat tissue
- increase in lean body mass (muscle tissue)
- increase in weight loss and proper weight maintenance

other factors
- improved body image and self-concept
- reduction of stress and tension
- increase in ability to relax
- decrease in depression

(as a part of preventive medicine) in the reduction of CHD risk factors. In terms of the future, other important reasons for adding this subject to medical education will be the continued growth of the fitness movement, the future escalation of health care costs, and the increase in life-span. Caution must be taken with the latter point. While it is clear that exercise can improve a person's health, there is some, but not conclusive, evidence to indicate that it increases the length of life.

It is time now for the medical profession to educate its future practitioners about the beneficial effects of exercise and how it should be prescribed so that they can take the leadership role in its promotion. This would not only help legitimize its acceptance as a major component of health—which would encourage greater adoption by the public—but also counteract the invalid information presently disseminated by unqualified individuals.

Specifically, medical schools should require every student to take a short course in exercise medicine. Minimally, it should be 15 hours in length and cover five major components: a review of the research literature dealing with the health-related aspects of exercise; guidelines for proper prescription of cardiorespiratory fitness programs; stress testing (treadmill or bicycle ergometer) and interpretation of exercise electrocardiograms; analysis of blood fat panels for levels and types of cholesterol and triglycerides; and effective counseling techniques for the promotion of fitness—with emphasis on behavior modification (life-style changes)—combined with sound nutritional practices.

Exercise prescriptions

Properly educated doctors should then be qualified to prescribe appropriate exercise for their patients as follows. Individuals 35 or older who are planning to start a regular cardiorespiratory fitness program or to significantly increase the intensity of their exercise should be advised to have a complete physical examination, including a stress test and a test for blood fats. In fact, this is good advice even for younger people, particularly those who have led a sedentary life and would like to begin a strenuous exercise program.

Individuals should be instructed to start slowly and to gradually increase their level of exercise intensity. For those who are middle-aged and sedentary or who are older, it might take as long as 15 to 20 weeks to achieve a training effect; for more active, younger participants, it might require only 10 to 12 weeks. People should be counseled not to become discouraged if they do not receive immediate benefits from training. They should not expect to become fit after a short training period when they have been physically inactive for most of their lives. They should be made to realize that it will take a major change in life-style (proper exercise and nutrition), practiced over many years, to achieve and maintain the health-related benefits of fitness.

The guidelines that doctors should follow in prescribing cardiorespiratory fitness programs for normal, healthy individuals are based on age and level of fitness. Individualized exercise prescriptions should consist of the following six major components.

• *Warm-up:* a five-minute period that includes slow, static stretching of the major muscles involved in the selected activity and related light exercises (*e.g.,* light calisthenics for jogging).

• *Frequency of training:* three to five days a week—three days as the minimum, five days for additional weight loss or maintenance of desired weight.

• *Duration of training:* 30 minutes of continuous aerobic exercise is generally recommended, but duration depends on the intensity of the activity; caloric expenditure (300 calories per workout) or distance can be used for target values—for example, a distance of 4.8 km (3 mi) would be covered by an individual who jogs 1.6 km (one mile) in ten minutes at a caloric expenditure of ten calories per minute.

• *Intensity of training:* to determine the training target heart rate, one subtracts one's age from 220 and takes 60% of this value for a low fitness level, 70% for a medium level, and 80% for a high level—thus, for a 35-year-old individual, the target heart rate is 111 beats per minute for low fitness level, 130 for medium, and 148 for high; as fitness level improves, individuals should increase training heart rates by moving to the next level. One may measure exercise heart rate—taken at the radial artery (at the wrist) or the carotid artery (on the side of the neck) after five minutes of exercise—by counting the number of heartbeats in ten seconds and multiplying by six to obtain the minute value.

• *Type of training activity:* any activity that uses large muscle groups (preferably total body), is performed continuously, and is rhythmic and aerobic in nature—*e.g.,* brisk walking, jogging, swimming, cycling, cross-country skiing, dancing, and rowing.

• *Cool down:* a five-minute period consisting of activities of reduced intensity (walking after jogging or jogging after running) followed by slow static stretching of the major muscles involved in the activity.

Closing the educational gap

The importance of medical students' being knowledgeable about exercise medicine cannot be questioned. Doctors should know the major research findings concerning the health-related benefits of cardiorespiratory fitness (presented in Table 2). The medical profession should start now to take a greater leadership role in providing the public with valid information about cardiorespiratory fitness. How much longer will it take for medical schools to close this educational gap—to accept this important responsibility?

Medical Ethics

During the past year biomedical ethics saw significant developments in many areas. In particular these concerned the beginning and the end of life. A new controversy—the use of human fetal tissue for transplantation—was the subject of a special report, while an old controversy—abortion—went before the United States Supreme Court once again. At the same time, the movement toward making it easier to discontinue life-prolonging treatment of incompetent patients was slowed by the verdicts in two recent court cases, while a group of physicians asserted that it was morally acceptable to assist patients who wanted to commit suicide. Bioethical issues concerning the time between the beginning and the end of life were also addressed when the state of Oregon looked to citizen groups for guidance on the rationing of health care.

Beginnings of life

Tissue from human fetuses has been used in research for over 50 years. As a source of human cell lines, human fetal tissue has been used notably in vaccine preparation—including the polio vaccine. The current public controversy in the U.S. began when the National Institutes of Health (NIH) asked Robert Windom, assistant secretary for health in the Department of Health and Human Services, to approve a research proposal that would allow tissue from electively aborted fetuses to be transplanted into the brain of a patient suffering from Parkinson's disease, a progressive disease apparently caused by deterioration of tissue in a particular area of the brain, the substantia nigra. Windom's response in March 1988 came in the form of a list of ten questions about the science, ethics, and law of such research. To formulate answers to these questions, the NIH convened a special committee, the Human Fetal Tissue Transplantation Research Panel, composed of physicians, scientists, ethicists, religious leaders, lawyers, and members of the public. The 21-member panel held hearings on Sept. 14–16, 1988, met twice after that, and then submitted its report on Dec. 14, 1988.

A substantial majority of the NIH panel favored approval of continued research on fetal tissue transplantation. They found that research on animal models had proceeded sufficiently to offer hope that transplants of fetal tissue might benefit sufferers from at least two diseases: Parkinson's and insulin-dependent diabetes mellitus. Tissue transplants also held promise for a few other conditions—Alzheimer's and Huntington's diseases, spinal cord injuries, and deficiencies in neuroendocrine glands. Alternatives to fetal tissue, such as fetal cell cultures that could be grown almost at will in the laboratory by means of bioengineering techniques were possibilities but were still a decade or more away.

On questions of law, the panel noted that except for the few states that banned all experimental use of human fetal tissue, research that abided by the safeguards it had urged would not violate any state or federal laws.

The panel's most controversial judgments had to do with the ethical questions. In the view of some panel members, using human fetal tissue in research was not morally problematic; at the opposite end of the spectrum, a handful of panel members believed that any use of human fetal tissue from elective abortions was inextricably tied to abortion itself and, therefore, a great evil. The bulk of the panel seemed to occupy a middle ground, regarding abortion as a difficult issue but judging that with appropriate safeguards the use of tissue collected after elective abortions could be effectively separated from the moral dispute over

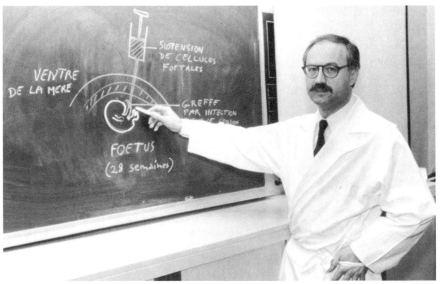

In June 1988 the first in utero transplant of human fetal cells took place in Lyon, France. The recipient was a 28-week-old fetus who had inherited a fatal immunodeficiency disorder; ten months later there were signs that the infant's immune system would become normal. Lyon immunologist Jean-Louis Touraine (right) described the procedure at a meeting in Paris in March 1989. The medical use of aborted fetuses is a promising but highly controversial area. In the U.S. the primary ethical controversy concerns the connection between human fetal tissue transplants and abortion.

In January 1989, when the U.S. Supreme Court announced it would hear Webster v. Reproductive Health Services, *pro-choice demonstrators expressed their fear that the abortion option would be revoked. In a narrow decision on July 3, the court upheld severe state limits on abortion.*

abortion itself. The panel recommended that a decision whether to allow the use of fetal tissue for research be made only after the decision was made to abort. They further recommended that the potential use of the tissue for research not be permitted to affect the timing or manner of the abortion. The panel members also urged that no financial inducements be given either to the woman deciding on an abortion or to the persons or institutions performing the abortions. Fetal tissue was to be treated in the same way as other organ or tissue donations: the donor or donor's family would receive no money; the institution would be allowed to recover only those costs associated with recovering the tissue itself. Finally, the panel recommended that "the pregnant woman should be prohibited from designating the transplant-recipient of the fetal tissue." This would be done to discourage women or their families from having abortions with the intent to provide fetal tissue for a family member or from becoming pregnant with the intent to abort for the same purpose.

In the waning days of the Ronald Reagan administration, even as the NIH panel was deliberating, Gary Bauer, a domestic policy official, urged the president

to proclaim a ban on all fetal tissue research. Bauer's advice, however, was not taken. On Jan. 19, 1989, James Wyngaarden, director of the NIH, transmitted the panel's report to the Department of Health and Human Services with his own recommendations (which have not been made public). By the late summer of 1989, no official decision had yet been made by the assistant secretary's office as to whether the moratorium on such research ought to be lifted.

The primary ethical controversy in human fetal tissue transplantation was whether it was actually tied to the ethics of abortion. The members of the NIH panel who did not accept the majority's conclusions asserted that human life begins at conception, that abortion therefore is murder, and that the use of tissue from aborted fetuses is inextricably tied to that murder.

The legality and ethics of abortion continue to be the subject of great social unrest and heated debate. Once again, that debate entered the august precincts of the Supreme Court. The case was *Webster* v. *Reproductive Health Services.* At issue was a 1986 Missouri law that imposed several restrictions and conditions on abortion. Among other things, the law stated that "the life of each human being begins at conception." It required that all abortions after 16 weeks' gestation be performed in a hospital, that after 20 weeks' gestation the fetus's viability be determined by tests that assess gestational age, weight, and lung maturity, and that there be no use of public funds, employees, or facilities for abortions except those necessary to save the life of the mother. It also banned the use of public funds to counsel women regarding abortion.

Lower courts overturned all provisions of the law except that prohibiting the use of public funds for abortions other than those to save the life of the mother, which was upheld by a federal court of appeals. Missouri did not appeal to the Supreme Court to have the entire law reinstated—only a portion of it; it also asked for a reconsideration of the court's decision on some of the issues in the landmark 1973 case, *Roe* v. *Wade,* which legalized abortion nationwide.

On July 3, 1989, the court announced its decision in the Webster case. By a five-to-four vote, the justices reversed the decision of the Missouri court and reinstated much of the statute. Although the majority's opinion contained language that indicated that at least four justices were opposed to some of the basic tenets of *Roe* v. *Wade,* this decision did not explicitly overturn that landmark case. Justice Sandra Day O'Connor sided with the majority in reinstating the Missouri law but argued that it was not necessary to reconsider *Roe* v. *Wade* in this instance.

The Webster decision is expected to lead state legislatures to greatly increase their activity on abortion. However, the U.S. Supreme Court will have more to say as well; it has accepted three new abortion cases for its next term.

Concern about abortion also figured in another controversy; in September 1988 China and France approved the marketing of a new antiprogesterone "abortion pill" known as RU-486. Produced and distributed in France by the firm Groupe Roussel-Uclaf, RU-486 can be taken in conjunction with another drug, prostaglandin, to prevent implantation of a fertilized egg or cause implanted eggs to be shed, resulting in a very early abortion. Many family-planning groups and physicians consider the drug a safer and less expensive alternative to surgical abortion.

Opposition by antiabortion groups caused the firm to withdraw the drug from the market briefly. The French government, which owns a large share (36.25%) of the company, apparently urged it to reverse its decision, which the firm did two days later. In the U.S. opponents of abortion continue to battle against the drug, referring to it at times as "the death pill" and threatening boycotts against the American subsidiary of Hoechst A.G., the West German firm that owns the majority stake in Roussel-Uclaf. At the present time the drug is sold only in France and China, and no plans to introduce it in the United States have been announced.

The intensity of the battle over RU-486 is probably best understood in light of the general public's ambivalence about abortion. What some people find most objectionable are late abortions and, in certain cases, the reasons why abortions are sought. While RU-486 would not affect the reasons for abortion, it would make it possible to have abortions very early in pregnancy, at a time in embryonic development when many people find abortion much less objectionable. If the great bulk of abortions took place in the first few weeks of pregnancy, public sentiment against abortion might be diminished.

Calling it "the death pill," opponents of abortion have bitterly opposed the drug RU-486, which was first marketed in France and China in September 1988. The pill is taken in conjunction with another drug, prostaglandin, and causes a very early abortion.

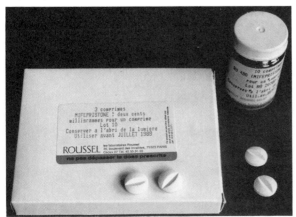

Torregano—SIPA

The end of life

In two important recent decisions, courts slowed what had seemed to be an irreversible movement toward allowing life-prolonging care to be withheld or withdrawn from patients who could no longer speak for themselves. Over the past two decades, the right of conscious and rational adults to refuse medical treatment has become well established. Such "competent" people have gained the legal right to refuse treatment, and health professionals have the responsibility not to impose unwanted treatment. At times, initial treatment refusals are a product of misunderstandings or disguised messages to family or health professionals. However, when the physician is convinced that the refusal is sincere and the patient is competent, then the patient's wishes must be respected. The situation is greatly complicated when patients cannot declare their own desires, as the cases of Nancy Cruzan and Mary O'Connor illustrate.

Cruzan was 25 when she was thrown from her car in January 1983. Although she was not breathing when rescue workers found her, they were able to restore breathing ten minutes later. Since then, she has lain unconscious. Her diagnosis is "persistent vegetative state," characterized by a permanent and irreversible lack of consciousness or responsiveness. So far as can be determined, no one accurately diagnosed as being in a persistent vegetative state has ever regained consciousness. The brain stem, however, can survive the death of the upper brain, or lack of consciousness. Since the brain stem controls breathing and regulates aspects of homeostasis, Cruzan was not legally brain dead. Because she could not take food, a tube had to be inserted surgically into her stomach. In 1987 her parents asked that the feeding tube be removed. A trial court judge agreed that her parents had the right to make such a decision. Before her accident Cruzan had expressed to a friend reservations about living in a state of seriously compromised health; the judge gave this some weight in the decision.

Missouri's Supreme Court disagreed. In a four-to-three ruling, the state's highest court rejected the reasoning employed by courts in other states and asserted that the state's interest in preserving life, in the absence of countervailing considerations such as great pain or other burden on the patient, justified intervening to prevent Cruzan's parents from stopping her artificial nutrition and hydration. The Missouri court did allow that people who provide clear and convincing evidence of their wish to refuse treatment can have that wish respected even after they become incompetent. In the Cruzan case the court apparently felt that the evidence fell short of this fairly demanding standard. In July 1989 the U.S. Supreme Court agreed that in its next term it would hear the appeal of Cruzan's case by her parents.

O'Connor was the victim of multiple strokes, leaving

her in a severely demented and physically incapacitated condition. She had watched her husband and two brothers die of cancer and had expressed to a colleague at work and to her daughters her desires to avoid being maintained by technology and to retain her dignity when death came near. She came to the attention of the New York court system at the age of 77. According to her two daughters—both nurses—O'Connor had ceased to recognize or respond to them during their daily visits. When the hospital requested permission to insert a feeding tube, the daughters refused. The hospital petitioned the court.

The trial court refused the hospital's request, as did the appellate division. New York's highest court, however, the Court of Appeals, reversed the lower courts' rulings and ordered the feeding tube put in place. In so doing, the Court of Appeals took the unusual step of overruling the trial court on an interpretation of fact—whether there was "clear and convincing" evidence about what O'Connor would have wanted. Typically appellate courts limit themselves to interpretations of law and accept the lower courts' decisions on matters of fact. It was true, O'Connor's daughters admitted, that she had never spoken explicitly about refusing nutrition and hydration. As Judge Richard Simons wrote in his dissenting opinion, however, "Mary O'Connor expressed her wishes in the only terms familiar to her, and she expressed them as clearly as a lay person should be asked to express them. To require more is unrealistic, and for all practical purposes, it precludes the right of patients to forgo life sustaining treatment."

By setting such a rigorous and difficult standard of proof for determining a patient's wishes from prior statements, the Court of Appeals may have effectively closed that door in the vast majority of cases. It did endorse another method—the "durable power of attorney"—by which an individual can designate another person to decide on one's behalf. New York allows such statements to be written with "springing power"—that is, they become effective only when the person cannot speak for himself or herself.

It remains to be seen whether the Cruzan and O'Connor rulings signal a reversal in the trend toward easing nontreatment decisions for incompetent patients or are anomalies or perhaps merely indications that state courts are settling into preferred methods for handling decisions about incompetent patients.

At the same time, a group of respected physicians has written favorably about assisting the suicides of some of their patients and discussed sympathetically the practice of active euthanasia in The Netherlands. On March 30, 1989, a dozen physicians published "The Physician's Responsibility Toward Hopelessly Ill Patients" in the *New England Journal of Medicine*. The article came out of a meeting sponsored by the Society for the Right to Die. In that article 10 of the 12 doctors affirmed "that it is not immoral for a physician to assist

in the rational suicide of a terminally ill person." They admit a number of difficulties with their position: that the rationality of people in the late stages of terminal illness may be compromised by the disease or by drugs; that patients may fail to understand what can be done to relieve their anguish; that it may involve secrecy or deceit with family, nurses, and other physicians. Without further argument, however, they offer their conclusion that assisting suicide can be morally acceptable.

The same article points out that active euthanasia by physicians has been practiced openly in The Netherlands since 1984. Many Dutch physicians believe that euthanasia may sometimes be the most reasonable action to limit the suffering of dying patients. According to some sources, in The Netherlands 5,000 to 10,000 acts of euthanasia are performed each year (generally through injection of a barbiturate combined with a curare compound, a paralyzing agent). The authors mention a few of the objections that have been advanced against active euthanasia in the United States, including the reluctance of physicians to perform it, but their primary explanation for the lack of open use of active euthanasia is not moral principle but fear—fear of civil litigation or criminal prosecution. They conclude noncommittally that "the medical profession and the public will continue to debate the role that euthanasia may have in the treatment of the terminally or hopelessly ill patient."

Between life and death: bioethics and public policy

Control over treatment, especially over the circumstances of an individual's dying, has been a concern for many people. Interest in this and other issues helped spawn a series of public-professional dialogues on bioethics, which have recently taken a very interesting turn.

Oregon was the site of the first community bioethics project in 1983. The goal in Oregon and a dozen other states and regions with similar community movements was to engage the public in discussions about bioethical issues of concern to them. In some cases the dialogues led to new legislation. The Vermont Ethics Network, for example, lobbied for a new durable power-of-attorney law that would provide for medical decisions to be made for competent persons who become incompetent (much as the New York Court of Appeals suggested in the O'Connor case).

In Oregon, though, attention turned to allocation of scarce resources, specifically Medicaid dollars. Medicaid is a federal program intended to provide health care to the poor. States have considerable discretion in how they will use Medicaid funds. The current controversy began in 1987 when the choice posed to the Oregon legislature for the coming two-year period was either to fund transplants of bone marrow, hearts, livers, and pancreases for the state's poor or to use that

The Oregonian

Leukemia victim Coby Howard (left) was denied a bone marrow transplant because the Oregon state legislature had decided that Medicaid dollars should be spent on basic care for the needy rather than on costly organ transplants.

same money for basic health care needs of the same population. Some 1,500 women could receive prenatal care for the available money; that same amount would buy 34 transplants. The legislature decided to fund basic care for poor children and pregnant women.

Though two adults were denied transplants, public sentiment was not much aroused until Coby Howard, an attractive seven-year-old boy, was denied Medicaid coverage for a bone marrow transplant—his last hope for treatment for acute lymphocytic leukemia. Although private efforts had raised a reported $70,000 of the $100,000 the procedure would cost, Howard died before it could be done. Among the consequences of his death were lawsuits, an attempt to organize a boycott on organ donation by the state's poor, and considerable national media attention to Oregon's health policy choices.

One of the criticisms of Oregon's actions in this case was that it had inappropriately singled out organ transplantation from all other health interventions, some of which may be as or more expensive and even less likely to be successful. In response, the president of the Oregon state Senate, the state's community bioethics group, and a bioethics consultant held a

series of meetings around the state. They then set up four focus groups—each consisting of a nurse, a social worker, and three physicians. They asked each of the groups to rate health-related interventions on a ten-point scale. Among those things earning the highest rating—a ten—were immunizations for the young and old and prenatal care, not surprisingly. Also rated ten, however, were infant car seats and transportation to health care facilities. Smoking-cessation programs received a six (because there is little evidence confirming their effectiveness), while transplants and infertility treatments were each rated three. Following this, a bill incorporating the rating scheme and requiring that Medicaid funds be spent in order of descending priority was being considered by the Oregon legislature.

Reactions to the events in Oregon are just beginning to form. On the one hand, the Oregon project enhances public awareness that health care is rationed. In the U.S. it is rationed by insurance, wealth, or income, while in Great Britain, Canada, and other countries with national health care, it is rationed by national budgets and regional priorities. (The United States and South Africa are the only two industrialized nations that do not assure that health care is provided for all citizens in need of it.) The priority rankings in Oregon appeared to give attention to such factors as the cost and effectiveness of the intervention, the numbers of people affected, and the centrality of the need, which are all things that most thoughtful analyses of health policy regard as important.

There are disquieting features as well. Oregon's rationing program affects only those who qualify for Medicaid—the poorest of the state's poor. (Only 43% of those below the poverty line in the state receive Medicaid at all.) Those fortunate enough to have private insurance can get any treatment their insurance will cover or that they can pay for themselves. Only the poor are subject to the legislature's rationing. There may also be problems with the process by which priorities were assigned. It is unlikely that the subjects of the rationing—the state's poor—had much of a voice in determining what forms of health care they would or would not receive. At least among the four selected groups, the decisions presumably were made by employed professionals, not those directly affected by the decisions. Finally, although the values that influenced the ratings may have been reasonable ones, precisely which values were chosen and the relative weights assigned to each are absolutely crucial. It is not clear how these were determined or if Medicaid recipients' judgments were given much force.

As it enters the public policy arena, the community bioethics movement will need to give a great deal more attention to its own presuppositions and will need to listen to a wider range of voices. With power comes responsibility.

—*Thomas H. Murray, Ph.D.*

370

Unscrupulous Researchers: Science's Bad Apples

by Drummond Rennie, M.D.

During the first week in May 1989, newspapers reported widely a case of alleged scientific misconduct, known as the "Baltimore case"; a congressional subcommittee held hearings to look into whether a disputed scientific paper—a study of the immunity of genetically altered mice—that was published in the journal *Cell* in April 1986 was fraudulent. The prime target of the allegation was a highly respected immunologist and a Nobel laureate. Those attending the hearings included scientists, administrators, government officials, journalists, and lobbyists. The attention paid to this case and the fact that two other congressional committees held hearings on scientific misconduct in June 1989 make it clear that whether biomedical research workers report their results honestly is very much an issue of concern to the public at large and to the elected representatives of the public. Why?

In general, all scientists are so imbued with the remorseless skepticism of the scientific method and with the code of trust, without which the whole scientific enterprise would founder, that they are incredulous when misconduct by one of their colleagues is alleged. Yet, it seems to be a part of human nature to love a scandal; such scandals are particularly enjoyed when they affect the sort of person who is generally held in high esteem—a scientist or physician, for instance. Moreover, people may secretly relish the contemplation of fraud in fields such as science and medicine because, though they comprehend few of the technical details, everyone understands the temptation to get something for nothing and take a shortcut to fame.

Science has moved from being a small activity supported by private donors to being a large industry, supported primarily by government moneys and carried out in institutions that receive significant federal funding. Congress consists largely of lawyers. They, perhaps more than the rest of the population, tend to be profoundly suspicious of scientists. They rightly see themselves as guardians of the public purse, with every right to investigate how public funds are used. They may, however, fail to understand the essential process of science—let alone the rigors and technicalities of a particular research project.

History

Although there are many examples from earlier times, only three instances of discrete scientific fraud from the past half century are cited here—one from biomedical science, one from psychology, and one from geology.

In 1974, while on his way to see his chief, Robert Good, at Memorial Sloan-Kettering Cancer Center, New York City, William Summerlin opened the modern era of scientific fabrication by improving the results of his experiments in which the skin of black mice was transplanted onto white mice. He touched them up with a black felt-tip pen. The investigation that followed revealed in addition that Summerlin's experiments with rabbits involving the transplantation of corneal tissue (xenografts) were also flawed, not least because he never performed the step in the protocol involving actually doing the transplantation, which accounted for the excellent condition of the rabbits' corneas.

Some of the extraordinary difficulty people have in comprehending that fraud could be taking place was articulated by the distinguished English immunologist Sir Peter Medawar, who served on the investigating board looking into the Summerlin case. He later wrote about Summerlin's rabbits: "Through a perfectly transparent eye this rabbit looked at the board with the candid and unwavering gaze of which a rabbit with a clean conscience is capable. I could not believe that this rabbit had received a graft of any kind, not so much because of the perfect transparency of the cornea as because the pattern of blood vessels in the ring around the cornea was in no way disturbed. Nevertheless I simply lacked the moral courage to say at the time that I thought we were the victims of a hoax or confidence trick."

Such fraudulent activities can have major consequences for patients, science, and society. Sir Cyril Burt died in 1971 at the age of 88; the obituary in *The Times* (London) eulogized him as "the leading figure in Britain in the application of psychology to education and the development of children and the assessment of mental qualities." His research included a comparison of identical twins reared apart and a 40-year study of 40,000 fathers and sons in an unidentified London borough "proving that intelligence invariably followed the father's occupational status." The import of his research was profound. His conclusions were applied to two acts of Parliament, one resulting in sexual segregation of mentally retarded persons and the other in discriminatory practices in education.

It has since been proved that Burt, a strange and

lonely man, simply fabricated his results; he even fabricated his two co-workers as well as his experimental subjects and drew some of his "data" from theoretical normal curves. It is interesting that Burt was the founding editor of the *British Journal of Statistical Psychology*. He abused the editorial privilege egregiously: he published 63 articles under his own name; he often altered other authors' texts to add favorable references to his own work; and he contributed at least 40 reviews, notes, and letters under pseudonyms. Indeed, if an editor of a scientific journal wants to be fraudulent, he can ensure that there are literally no checks on him at all.

In 1987 at a geological congress in Calgary, Alta., a paleontologist, John Talent of Macquarie University, North Ryde, Australia, first alleged that for 20 years Viswa Jit Gupta, a geologist at Panjab University, India, took fossils to trusting experts from all over the world, convincing them that he had found the fossils in a variety of ill-defined sites in the Himalayas and inviting these experts to describe the fossils and to join him in publishing the findings. In this way, Gupta, who is thought to have obtained the fossils from rock shops or museums, is said to have published over 300 papers (an average of more than one a month) and has completely confused the paleontology of the entire region. By mid-1989 the case had gathered considerable steam but had yet to be fully investigated. If fraud is proved, this will be a disaster for Gupta's coauthors, who not only must try to salvage their reputations but must see to the huge task of putting the record straight.

Fraud or error?

For convenience, the words fraud and misconduct are used interchangeably here, even though "fraud" has specific legal requirements, some of which would be very hard to prove in court despite the fact that the norms of scientific behavior have been clearly breached. Most would agree, however, that it is misconduct to fabricate results, to falsify data, and to commit plagiarism.

Plagiarism, at first glance, is the dullest of crimes. A decade ago, however, Elias Alsabti elevated plagiarism to the status of an art form. This Iraqi deceiver would lift papers from Japanese journals and republish them in Europe, pausing only to substitute his own and one or two fictitious names for those of the real authors. He published one person's grant application three times in three different journals simultaneously, adding his own name and a "Ph.D." for decoration. He published at least one article under his own name in Japan before the real author got into print at all. Between 1977 and 1980 alone, he published 60 papers, and with his lengthy list of publications, he conned his way into numerous medical research positions at several U.S. institutions.

This profligate fraud is amusing until one examines the consequences. Plagiarizers steal an author's most precious commodity—his intellectual property—and they do so for personal gain. In one sense, all fabricators have to plagiarize; if they invented everything out of their heads, no one would believe them. The only way they can be convincing is by copying so that their fabricated "results" are similar to the real data of others. In this regard, the reaction to the recent case of Shervert Frazier is particularly interesting. Frazier was general director and psychiatrist in chief of McLean Hospital, a private psychiatric facility associated with Harvard Medical School, and had been director of the National Institute of Mental Health (NIMH) from 1984 to 1986. When it was discovered that large sections of articles and chapters that he had authored in the 1960s and '70s had been plagiarized from other sources, Daniel C. Tosteson, dean of the Harvard Medical School, forced him to resign. Ironically, Tosteson has since been subjected to attack for doing to a distinguished psychiatrist (who, it must be remembered, became distinguished partly by plagiarizing the work of others) what Tosteson would have been criticized for *not* doing to a student. One has to wonder if plagiarism is acceptable if the perpetrator is senior enough and if the articles were, as in this case, review articles (*i.e.*, roundups of research by numerous authors). This sort of double standard makes scientists particularly vulnerable to charges that they do not take the problem of misconduct seriously. Moreover, despite his admission of guilt, less than three months after his resignation Frazier was reappointed as a staff psychiatrist at McLean.

Beyond plagiarism, fabrication, and falsification, there is considerable argument about what constitutes misconduct. Merely to define it as deviation from the norm is dangerous, simply because revolutionary advances are almost bound to deviate from what is accepted. Any definition must allow for honest error; without that allowance, no one would dare to enter research, which, by definition, is an adventure into the unknown.

This is well illustrated by the furor in mid-1989 over the purported discovery of "cold fusion" or "test-tube fusion" by chemists B. Stanley Pons of the University of Utah and Martin Fleischmann of the University of Southampton, England. These scientists said that they had discovered an entirely new way of producing heat by causing deuterium to undergo fusion within palladium electrodes. Scores of other laboratories tried—and with one exception failed—to duplicate these results. Someone must be doing things wrong if the results cannot be repeated, but no one is alleging fraud. The "fusion confusion" was actually normal in the process of science, though in this case it was carried out in the full glare of the press.

Nonscientists often have great difficulty in distin-

A widely publicized case of alleged scientific fraud stemmed from the accusation that a six-author paper published in 1986 contained "serious misstatements." Margot O'Toole (right) made the charge while working in the lab of one of the authors. The prime targets of a protracted and bitter investigation, however, have been Nobel laureate David Baltimore, another of the authors (left), and science itself.

guishing error, without which science cannot proceed, from fraud, which destroys science. This difficulty seems to be at the heart of the "Baltimore case." A paper describing the way that a gene transplanted into a mouse exerted its effect was published in 1986 in the journal *Cell* and had six authors. A postdoctoral fellow, Margot O'Toole, who worked in the research lab of one of the coauthors, Thereza Imanishi-Kari, at the Massachusetts Institute of Technology, alleged that the paper contained results that were not backed up by laboratory data. Her complaints were exhaustively investigated by three different inquiries; none found anything but error. An inquiry by the National Institutes of Health (NIH) in February 1989 concluded that there was no evidence of "fraud, misconduct, manipulation of data, or serious conceptual errors" in the paper. Furthermore, the conclusions of the *Cell* paper have held up in the face of other work; *i.e.,* after other labs have tried to confirm or refute the work.

Alleging fraud: politics and the "Baltimore case"

In May 1989 it was announced that the "final" inquiry would be reopened because of allegations that the Secret Service had found new evidence that laboratory documents were falsified. Why should there have been so much attention paid to this particular paper? Why should this case have been chosen out of the hundreds of other cases that government officials claim to be told about? It was the efforts of overenthusiastic and ambitious congressional aides, abetted in this instance by two self-appointed fraud-busters from the NIH, Walter Stewart and Ned Feder, that caused the case to be so much in the limelight. Many scientists believe that Stewart and Feder listened to O'Toole's complaint, saw one of the coauthors, David Baltimore, as a very "big fish," and set out to get him.

No case alleging scientific misconduct has drawn the lines between scientists and politicians more clearly. Baltimore's research has widely expanded the knowledge of diseases of the human immune system. In 1975 he shared the Nobel Prize for Physiology or Medicine for fundamental discoveries about the behavior of normal cells, cancer cells, and enzymes. His discoveries provided the conceptual foundation for examining how viruses cause tumors in humans. Scientists see the charges against this esteemed researcher as an ignorant attack on the very way science is conducted. They bitterly resent the allegation of error and the heavy implication of fraud. They know that a scientist often has to follow hunches in the face of contradictory evidence, and that it is often the intuition of the scientist that decides which data are to be used. They are angered by the highly publicized attacks on their fellow scientists, who are given no opportunity to defend themselves or, if hauled up to give evidence, are assumed to be guilty and bullied unmercifully. They are appalled that the politicians are so plainly out for "blood." Many scientists also resent Stewart and Feder, whom they regard as misguided and who, having been given the protection of powerful members of Congress, have no option but to harass the biggest targets they can find in their crusade to purify science.

Politicians, on the other hand, see either error or fraud as a waste of public moneys. They believe that by parading and then berating scientists they see as delinquent in public forums, and in some cases in front of television cameras, they are doing their elected job of serving the public at large. They assert that fraud is common, which they may well believe, and as no one has ever done an audit to assess the real prevalence of fraud in the sciences, their unbacked assertions cannot be rebutted convincingly. They point out that no matter how objectionable scientists may find the activities of whistle-blowers like Stewart and Feder, the two have done science a very great service in drawing everyone's attention to serious deficiencies in the way scientific research is conducted and papers are written and published.

The role and the fate of whistle-blowers

It would seem that people on the whole strongly approve of whistle-blowers in *other* occupations but turn on them automatically, savagely, and without regard to the facts when they threaten one in their own line of work. The consequences of fraud may be terrible. So, too, the mere leveling of an allegation of fraud may end a career—and possibly many careers. In February 1987 Howard Eisen, a prominent scientist at the NIH, drew attention to the fact that data in a manuscript being prepared for publication had been faked by a junior (who promptly fled). Eisen did experiments that confirmed the fakery, reported the misconduct, and then, in the middle of the investigation that he had instigated, and apparently overwrought that it should have happened in his laboratory, committed suicide.

In medical research the chief concern is whether patients are harmed. The recent case of Stephen Breuning is curiously reminiscent of that of Burt. Breuning's papers constituted a very large proportion (one-third) of the medical literature on the drug treatment of children with severe mental retardation and greatly affected treatment policies. Breuning had worked in the lab of Robert Sprague, a psychopharmacologist at the University of Illinois. In December 1983 Sprague realized that Breuning could not have done all the patient interviews he said he had done. Sprague investigated and found irrefutable evidence that Breuning was fabricating results, and he reported this to the NIMH. Sprague was rebuffed but persisted, and Breuning's parent institution, the University of Pittsburgh, Pa., was forced to hold an inquiry. Numerous discrepancies and improper research practices (no protocol, "lost" data, "lost" patients, and so forth) were uncovered. Breuning was unable to produce any data at all for the three years' work that had made him the world leader in the field, nor could he remember the names of any of his patients. He actually confessed to submitting false abstracts and grant proposals. The investigating committee wrote to the dean at Pittsburgh that on the basis of "the irregularities noted above we feel that it is essential for you to formally investigate Dr. Breuning's research practices." The dean, however, in defense of Breuning, wrote to the NIMH, which had given Breuning grant money, that the committee could find "no serious fault" and ended: "I have no grounds to take action against him relative to his activities while a member of our faculty."

As seems to be the melancholy tradition, Sprague himself was then put through a two-week on-the-spot investigation of his laboratory but, showing tremendous courage, he persisted in his allegations. The final NIMH investigation of Breuning was completed three and a half years after the complaint, and it showed a pattern of repeated and egregious fraud. The judge who sentenced Breuning five years after Sprague's first allegations said he had never seen a more clear-cut case of fraud. Sprague, a man of integrity and tenacity, whose career Breuning had almost wrecked, up to then had been fully funded. After his whistle-blowing actions his funds were cut off.

Reasons for scientific subterfuge

Why some scientists are frauds is no more easily explained than what makes criminals. The excuse invariably used by those who are caught is that there is a pervasive "publish or perish" attitude in the ranks of academia and that they are driven into cheating by the unbearable pressures of competition. If this were a reasonable excuse, however, society would as readily condone stealing by needy bank tellers. It is true that papers are the measurable product of scientists, but the number of published papers required for promotion has been shown to be small, and the number of papers published by many who are guilty of fraud vastly exceeds this. For example, John Darsee at Harvard Medical School published over 100 papers in just three years, and Robert Slutsky at the University of California at San Diego in a year's time published an average of one paper every ten days. Universities are now altering their policies so that very few papers are actually considered at the time of promotion.

It is distressing that a high proportion of those convicted of fraud have been physician researchers. Of 26 reported cases of scientific misconduct between 1980 and 1987, 17 had M.D. degrees, compared with 6 Ph.D.'s, 1 M.D./Ph.D., 1 M.S. degree, and 1 with no degree. Perhaps this reflects the fact that basic scientists get better formal training in the methods and mores of science. Physician researchers are generally selected from among the best medical students and residents. They are frequently much older than their counterparts in other sciences when they enter research and are often assumed to know how to do it all already and, therefore, often receive (and feel they need) little supervision. Moreover, after their long training, they may be in a rush to get on in their careers.

The discovery of misconduct

Most instances of scientific misconduct are detected in the laboratory. It is widely and mistakenly imagined that peer review of papers submitted to journals

When the Secret Service examined the laboratory notebooks of Thereza Imanishi-Kari, whose data and credibility have been attacked in the "Baltimore case," it found that dates on some pages had been altered by overwriting in different inks.

From Eliot Marshall, "Secret Service Probes Notebooks," *Science*, vol. 244 (May 12, 1989), p. 644; © 1989 by the AAAS

for publication will sniff out any misconduct. Of 26 cases of misconduct between 1980 and 1987, by far the largest number (13) were detected because a coworker reported suspicious or irregular practices in the laboratory; only 3 of these 26 were detected by editorial peer review. Peer review is an excellent system for adjudicating questions of science, but any author can easily invent suitably believable data. Thus, for example, when the question has to do with whether the patients from whom the data are supposedly drawn existed in the first place, only tracking down and interviewing the actual patients will settle the matter.

The fraud perpetrated by Darsee at Harvard is a case in point. The Jan. 15, 1981, issue of the *New England Journal of Medicine* published an article by him—the leading paper in the issue—reporting on a large kindred (group of related individuals) having cardiomyopathy—a disease of heart muscle. Darsee and his coauthor, S. B. Heymsfield, described decreased myocardial levels of taurine, an amino acid, evidenced by a high output of taurine in the urine. On the surface it would seem impossible that this paper was fraudulent—first, because Darsee had a coauthor and, second, because it would not be possible simply to invent every one of the 46-member kindred, as well as all the data on each of the related individuals. Further, the paper ended with an acknowledgement thanking by name three individuals for referring the patients, doing the amino acid analyses, and performing the cardiac biopsies. Presumably these doctors could vouch for Darsee's work. Shocking as it may seem, however, every one of Darsee's alleged patients—the entire kindred—was invented, and the doctors whose help was so gratefully acknowledged were all fictitious characters, too.

In many ways it is remarkable that the Darsee fraud was discovered. As a rule, editors do not have the mandate, the training, or the inclination to undertake the kind of investigation that is necessary for detecting fraudulent research. Nor do they have the staff or the money. What editors can do is insist that all the authors of papers submitted for publication attest to the fact that they did indeed contribute to, and can take responsibility for, the whole paper and that they are able to produce the primary data if asked. While this will not prevent fraud, it will remind scientists of their responsibilities and prevent coauthors from melting away like scowling Cheshire cats should questions or problems arise.

Another reason it is not a simple matter to discover fraud is that unlike most "bench" experiments— *e.g.,* "test-tube fusion"—which should be possible to replicate in the laboratory, for most clinical as well as psychosocial research it is not possible to replicate findings in order to certify their validity. Discrepant data, sometimes in successive studies by the same researcher, are regarded as not unusual. They are often explained as being due to biological variability. Further, no one perpetrating fraud in clinical-medical or psychosocial research would try to present revolutionary findings; that would guarantee discovery. A canny cheat would simply invent a slightly shaggy version of someone else's paper—the fake results being good but not too perfect.

Audits: a way of policing science?

How prevalent is the problem of scientific misconduct? It is not clear whether it is increasing, although certainly the greatly increasing numbers of scientists and the interest of the media together make it seem that there is an epidemic of fraud. As Patricia K. Woolf, a sociologist at Princeton University, has said, critics of science focus on the numerator; they say the number of cases of egregious fraud and the complaints of whistle-blowers are but the tip of the iceberg. Scientists, by contrast, focus on the denominator—*i.e.,* the vast numbers of scientists, of grants awarded, and of papers published. They maintain that fraud is due to the activities of a few bad apples.

One way to find out how prevalent the problem is would be to do an experimental audit—on-the-spot examinations of research laboratories to find out whether published results are backed up by data. There are good precedents for such a course of action; the U.S. Food and Drug Administration (FDA) requires audits of research bearing on the approval of drugs. Such audits show a rate of serious violations of proper research procedures in around 10% of studies examined. A similar figure is found by the audits that the National Cancer Institute does of the trials it sponsors. This does not mean that there is necessarily intentional fraud in all cases—merely that in these studies the procedures were such as to vitiate the results.

Certainly audits have their place. The fact is, however, that auditing is an intrusive, expensive, and— above all—inefficient way of revealing what is usually found to have been suspected already. Though it seems to be a reasonable way of policing the system and of establishing the prevalence of scientific fraud, it is not probable that it will become general policy.

Responding to misconduct

The response of institutions to allegations of fraud and misconduct over the last 15 years has varied considerably. In many cases universities have been caught completely off guard. Allegations were met by disbelief and followed by strenuous efforts to avoid any serious inquiry, to protect the accused regardless of possible guilt, and to punish the whistle-blower. So spectacular and pervasive have been such cases as those of Darsee and Breuning, for example, and so impressed have people been by the extent of their crimes despite the prestige of their institutions that senior scientists have at last acknowledged that scientific misconduct is a real, as opposed to merely a political, problem. Following the lead of such institutions as Harvard and the University of California at San Diego, which had been forced to set up their own procedures to deal with cases of fraud on their premises, most institutions have devised some sort of process that emulates the following ideal.

First, the institution must fully understand that the long-term health and reputation of the institution and of science as a whole are inseparable and that any allegation must be treated with respect and dispatch. The inquiry must be pursued, no matter where it might lead, to a resolution of all the issues surrounding the allegation. Institutional "circling of the wagons" is a disastrous strategy, especially at a time when Congress is alleging widespread fraud, cover-up, dissembling, stonewalling, and persecution of the accuser. The institution must have a published set of procedures to be followed, speed being emphasized. There must be a clearly identified, sympathetic, knowledgeable, discrete, and senior faculty "point man" (or woman) to whom any person can go with a complaint. This person should decide whether there is a real possibility of misconduct.

If there is any merit in the allegation, or if the accuser is still unsatisfied, the matter must be moved up rapidly to a committee to which various experts can be added; this committee will be empowered to investigate and report to the chancellor or president of the university or the head of a research institute, and it will be given legal protection. At this stage the granting agency of the accused must be informed that an allegation of misconduct has been leveled.

To protect the reputations of everyone, the inquiry must be kept confidential. Throughout, the accused and accuser must be kept fully informed, and when a conclusion has been reached, there must be proper and public disclosure. If there has truly been misconduct, the guilty scientist must not be allowed to resign quietly in exchange for a dropped investigation or institutional silence lest, as has often happened, these criminal activities be repeated at another institution that will have hired the scientist in ignorance.

If fraudulent work has been published, the literature must be corrected. The guilty scientist must be instructed to inform the journals that published his or her work and request them to publish a retraction notice in a form that will be indexed. If the author of a fraudulent paper refuses to do this, the institution must take on the task, and the institution must be responsible for vouching for the integrity of every paper previously published by that scientist.

Punishing the guilty

Finally, once fraud has been determined, the granting agency must be informed of this outcome and a suitable punishment exacted. In the past it had usually been considered that since a scientist's reputation was all he or she had, the loss of credibility would end his or her scientific career. Other penalties are now being devised; for example, loss of federal funding and dismissal. In addition, since it is a crime to tell lies to the government, scientists who use fraudulent results in grant requests, for example, are now going to prison.

Also in the past, physician researchers who have been found guilty of scientific misconduct in carrying out clinical research have been allowed to leave the medical schools where they cheated and then have gone into full-time private medical practice. This is, of course, bizarre; most patients would consider that nothing could be more important than the ethical attributes of their physician. There are already moves under way to prevent this, which will depend on the sharing of information between institutions and state boards of registration.

A final word

The recent burst of publicity has had the good effect of making the scientific community come up with ways to prevent fraud. There has to be a strong emphasis on the teaching of good research practices, accompanied by close and graduated supervision of junior research workers. Lax rules have been tied to the prevalence of foul play in medical research. All scientific researchers are being given notice of the sort of practices that are unacceptable and of what the consequences will be if they are discovered. A new law, signed by Pres. George Bush in April 1989, guarantees the rights of federal whistle-blowers. Institutions are beginning to realize that secret bargaining for resignation in exchange for silence on the part of the institution will not be allowed.

It is not surprising to find that scientists are human and that some will cheat. As in all fields, there are those who will cut corners or fabricate data in the hope that such steps will lead to self-advancement. Whatever the frequency of such cheating, the public must be aware that it can happen. The scientific community must be quicker and more open in its response to allegations of fraud and must try to overcome a natural tendency to blame the messenger. After all, the one who alleges fraud is bringing to light a problem with the quality of science that could seriously undermine the public support of an absolutely vital activity. It is a problem, therefore, that must be taken very seriously.

Neurology

The treatment of cerebrovascular disease has long been regarded as an essentially futile pursuit. Preventive measures, particularly control of high blood pressure, unquestionably can reduce the incidence of stroke, but once a stroke occurs, little can be done for the patient beyond immediate supportive measures and sensible rehabilitative techniques. Recently, however, animal and human studies have raised the hope that specific therapies, if applied soon after a stroke, may improve the eventual neurological outcome.

Minimizing stroke damage

A stroke, or cerebrovascular accident, is usually the result of blood clots forming within the arteries of the brain or traveling there from other sources, such as the heart or the large arteries in the neck. The result is ischemia, or lack of blood flow to areas "downstream" from the arterial obstruction. Unless blood flow is restored within minutes, either by dissolution of the clot or an increase in blood flow from nearby arteries or collateral vessels, brain tissue dies, and the victim may experience sudden paralysis, speechlessness, numbness, loss of consciousness, or other symptoms. Some brain cells at the edge of the "dead" area may be injured but may ultimately recover. Stroke therapy is aimed at reopening blocked arteries and increasing the survival of cells that are injured but not immediately killed by the stroke.

Besides tactics for minimizing the destructive consequences of ischemia, other therapeutic approaches are being developed for the immediate treatment of stroke. Since ischemia appears to be a direct result of sudden occlusion of an artery, some researchers have been developing strategies for quickly "unplugging" such occlusions. When large blood vessels are involved, surgical removal of blood clots has been tried; at best, the results have been mixed. The fact that many occlusions are in small but vital arteries in inaccessible places, as well as the need for therapeutic action within minutes of diagnosis, has stimulated the search for drug treatments for removal of clots.

Clotting of blood is a normal phenomenon; without it even a minor injury would cause death by hemorrhage. Like many normal physiological systems, blood clotting is under the control of two balanced processes working in opposite directions, one causing the blood elements to form clots and the other helping to dissolve them. Diseases affecting this normal equilibrium may cause inadequate clotting (e.g., hemophilia) or excessive clot formation.

Tissue plasminogen activator (t-PA), a naturally occurring protein found in blood, helps produce plasmin, a clot-destroying substance that normally acts to keep the healthy balance between clot formation and clot dissolution, or thrombolysis. Thrombolytic (clot-dissolv-

ing) therapy with t-PA has been shown to improve outcome in patients who have had an acute myocardial infarction, or heart attack, caused by occlusion of arteries that supply blood to the heart muscle. Its successful use in myocardial infarction has prompted trials of t-PA in acute stroke with the hope that prompt dissolution of an arterial clot might lead to restoration of blood flow and subsequent return of function in brain areas wounded but not killed by the temporary reduction in blood supply.

In the 1960s attempts at reducing clots in stroke victims by using other thrombolytic agents (streptokinase, urokinase) had mixed results. A few patients improved, but brain hemorrhage was a frequent complication, and enthusiasm for such therapy withered. More recently, however, the availability of t-PA produced in the laboratory via cloning (currently marketed under the trade name Activase), along with the development of new techniques for delivering treatment to the exact site of a clot via small tubes, or catheters, has rekindled interest in clot-dissolving therapy. So far, only a small number of patients have been treated, but results are encouraging. X-rays confirm that the occluded artery was reopened in 90% of these stroke victims, and clinical improvement was seen in about 60%. The effects of some mild strokes subside naturally, however, so studies of large numbers of similar patients who, for the sake of comparison, receive different treatment or none at all will be needed to prove or disprove the usefulness and safety of t-PA in stroke.

The cell death that occurs in ischemia is thought to be due to the toxic effects of calcium leaking through injured cell walls into the cell. Drugs called calcium channel blockers, originally developed to relieve chest pain from ischemic heart disease, may reduce calcium influx into brain cells during a stroke and thus interfere with one of the basic mechanisms of cell injury and death. One such drug, nifedipine (Adalat, Procardia), is now used in the early treatment of heart attack and shows some promise in reducing the extent (and therefore the effect) of strokes when given shortly after the onset of symptoms. Clinical studies of stroke treatment with nimodipine (Nimotop), another calcium channel blocker, are under way.

Changing patterns of stroke incidence

Epidemiology is a science whose subject is the frequency of a given disorder and its distribution in the population by age, race, or other group characteristics. Studying the incidence (the number of new cases per given unit of time) and prevalence (the number of existing cases at a specific time) of diseases has provided important clues to the causes of many disorders, including such diverse maladies as multiple sclerosis, coronary artery disease, and AIDS (acquired immune deficiency syndrome).

Stroke is the third leading cause of death in the

Photographs, Richard Coppola, National Institute of Mental Health, Neuroscience Center

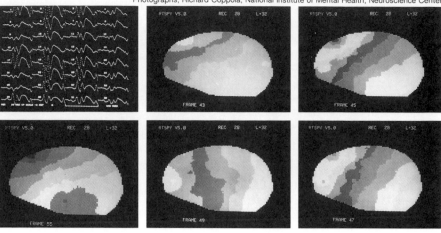

Through the use of computers, an electroencephalogram (top left), the traditional means of displaying brain activity, can be translated into color-coded maps that display changes in brain activity over time. This series (clockwise from top center), reproduced in black and white, shows changes taking place during an epileptic seizure.

United States. Since at least the 1940s, epidemiologists have been reporting a declining incidence of stroke. The risk of stroke increases, however, as people get older, and as medical treatment increasingly prevents early death, especially from infectious diseases and cancer, a larger proportion of the U.S. population is living to older ages. Incidence rates for age-related diseases such as stroke are therefore adjusted for the age of the population; figures are usually given as numbers of strokes per year per specific age group.

The shrinking incidence of stroke appears to be a worldwide phenomenon. Surveys in England, the United States, Australia, Israel, Japan, and Norway have found that both major types of stroke, hemorrhagic (caused by rupture of blood vessels) and ischemic (caused by obstruction of vessels), declined from the 1950s at least until 1980. After that date some surveys show a leveling off of the decline (*e.g.,* Denmark), and others actually demonstrate an increase. For example, in Sweden strokes in women increased from the years 1975–78 through 1983–86. So far, the age-adjusted decline in death rate from stroke in the United States appears to be continuing.

Although the worldwide lowering of stroke incidence over the past 40 years is indisputable, no one knows exactly when the decline began. Diagnostic criteria change over time, and some diagnoses even come into and go out of fashion. "Apoplexy," for example, is not a current diagnostic term but at one time would have been used to identify sudden death from stroke, heart attack, or even cardiac arrhythmia.

The timing of the decline in stroke is an important consideration in attempts to postulate a reasonable cause for it. Most often cited, for example, is the recent improvement in the control of hypertension (high blood pressure). Aside from age, high blood pressure is the most significant risk factor for stroke, and it would be reassuring to think that a relatively simple measure, such as helping people to control their blood pressure, would reduce stroke risk. It is possible, how-

ever, that other factors—such as reduction of smoking and changes in dietary and drinking habits—also play a role. Continuing epidemiological investigation may provide an explanation of how these factors, or others still unknown, work together to affect stroke incidence.

Brain mapping: useful diagnostic tool?

Computers, which seem to have left no area of medicine untouched, have recently been applied to extend the use of an old neurological tool, the electroencephalograph (EEG). The EEG, unlike a scan or X-ray, is not an anatomic imager but rather displays brain function by recording tiny electric potentials caused by neuronal (nerve cell) activity, transmitted by means of electrodes attached to the patient's scalp. This information has traditionally been displayed as an array of wavy lines similar to a cardiogram, which must be interpreted by a highly trained "reader."

Modern microprocessing has now made it possible to transform these tracings into color-coded "maps" of brain activity that can present visually compelling pictures of brain function. So-called brain activity mapping, or brain mapping, holds great promise as a tool for quantifying brain function, for measuring the responsiveness of various brain areas to sensory stimulation, and for applying complex statistical comparisons between areas within a single brain or between the brains of diseased and healthy individuals. Some electroencephalographers hope that brain mapping will eventually enable them to detect abnormalities in function not easily seen on a traditional EEG tracing and perhaps to find new diagnostic applications for EEG. Others caution that the diagnostic claims for brain mapping have not yet been fully substantiated. While statistically detectable differences have been found between the brain maps of a healthy population and some study groups, including those with dyslexia, schizophrenia, depression, and dementia, the applicability of such findings to the diagnosis of an individual patient is much less clear. In fact, the clinical use of brain mapping is proliferating despite the questions that remain about the appropriate diagnostic use of the technology. Exactly how useful brain mapping will ultimately prove remains to be seen.

AIDS and the nervous system

While surveys of large numbers of adults with AIDS find neurological disorders in about 40%, careful postmortem pathological studies reveal signs of nervous system involvement in 70 to 80% of adults who die of the disease.

One of the hallmarks of infection with the human immunodeficiency virus (HIV), which causes AIDS, is susceptibility to other infections, and the central nervous system is often a target. For example, toxoplasmosis, a parasitic infection, is the most common cause of an abnormal mass within the brain in people with AIDS, although it is a rare infection in other contexts. Toxoplasmosis can sometimes be treated successfully with sulfa drugs and corticosteroids but requires lifelong therapy to prevent recurrences. Cytomegalovirus (CMV) infection is also rare in people with normal immune function but is relatively common in people with AIDS. CMV can cause an encephalitis-like illness, spinal cord dysfunction, or eye infection leading to blindness. Cryptococcosis, a fungal infection, can cause chronic meningitis and has been known to be the first symptom in many patients who develop AIDS. An inexorably fatal type of encephalitis called progressive multifocal leukoencephalopathy results from infection by the JC virus, a common human papovavirus that rarely causes disease in other than immunocompromised individuals.

About one out of every 50 AIDS patients develops an otherwise rare brain tumor called lymphoma. In almost half of these cases, there are multiple lymphomas. A brain biopsy is necessary for diagnosis, and this invasive procedure is often readily undertaken because once diagnosed, these tumors usually respond well to radiation therapy.

The HIV organism itself often invades the central nervous system, causing clinical symptoms in up to 75% of those with AIDS. HIV encephalopathy is best described as a chronic encephalitis that slowly causes progressive mental symptoms such as memory difficulties, confusion, and loss of cognitive abilities. The disorder can sometimes be so severe as to incapacitate the patient. In other cases the HIV organisms appear to attach to the spinal cord, causing paralysis and sensory loss in the legs and sometimes loss of bladder control.

Nerves and muscles may be affected in several ways at any stage in an HIV infection, sometimes with grave consequences. Peripheral nerves (i.e., those outside the central nervous system) may become acutely or chronically dysfunctional in either a widespread or a localized pattern. Most common is a slowly progressive, diffuse peripheral neuropathy causing weakness and numbness of the feet or hands. In other cases one or several individual nerves are affected. Still other patients have weakness that appears to be due to the involvement of muscles, which can be easily seen upon muscle biopsy. The causes of these various neuromuscular syndromes are obscure and possibly highly varied. Toxic, nutritional, immunologic, and infectious factors have been invoked as explanations, but little has been proved. Treatment of these conditions depends on the specific syndrome and varies from drug therapy with steroids and zidovudine (also called AZT; Retrovir) to plasma exchange.

Brain tissue transplants: still experimental

The term brain transplant has recently been applied in a literal but slightly misleading fashion to some simple yet imaginative surgical procedures designed to correct localized deficiencies in brain function. In the early 1970s, as basic scientists began to provide more detailed information about natural mechanisms of brain repair after injury, experiments were initiated that entailed the insertion of small pieces of normal brain tissue from one animal into damaged brain areas of another animal of the same species. Rejection of the foreign tissue is not a major problem in such procedures because the brain is relatively isolated from normal immunologic surveillance mechanisms and is said to be an immunologically "privileged" area.

Much of the brain's normal activity is the result of direct cell-to-cell connections by means of chemical "signals" (neurotransmitters) elaborated by one cell onto the surface of another. Most of these connections are fully developed early in life, and the adult human brain has little natural capacity to form new connections. Fetal brain tissue, which still has the ability to grow and make such contacts, appears to be particularly suitable for transplantation as long as cells in the transplanted fragment are capable of making the specific chemical needed by the deficient "host" area. Such transplants can by no means duplicate the complex cellular connection matrix of normal brain tissue, but the elaboration of a deficient chemical and its diffusion through a localized area in which it is needed appear to improve or restore function in some cases.

More than 20 years ago the brains of patients with Parkinson's disease, a movement disorder, were found to have a deficiency of an amino acid called dopamine due to degeneration of the nerve cells that normally produce it. Oral administration of a dopamine precursor called L-dopa was found to improve parkinsonism by raising the level of dopamine in both the blood and the brain, including the deficient brain areas. The success of L-dopa treatment is often dramatic but frequently partial, short-lived, or uneven, probably because of the oral route of delivery and the unwanted effects of dopamine on other, normal brain regions.

K. S. Bankiewicz,
Surgical Neurology Branch, NINCDS, National Institutes of Health

Parkinsonism affecting the left side of the body has been experimentally induced in this monkey. By implanting dopamine-producing tissue from the brains of monkey fetuses into the brains of similar experimental animals, researchers have been able to produce improvements in function.

Reasoning that the replenishment of dopamine activity in the deficient area of the brain might be accomplished with the use of transplanted tissue, a Mexican surgeon took dopamine-producing tissue from the adrenal glands of a small group of patients with Parkinson's disease and inserted it near the appropriate areas in their brains. Since the adrenal glands are located in the abdominal cavity near the kidneys, transplanting the glandular tissue into a patient's brain requires two major operations done simultaneously. (Every person has two adrenal glands and can lose one gland without permanent side effects.) In 1987, in widely publicized announcements, the surgeon reported dramatic success with this procedure.

A consortium of other surgeons immediately set out to duplicate this work. Unfortunately, the results of this much larger group of transplants were not very encouraging. Postoperative courses were sometimes stormy, and after months of careful follow-up only a small number of patients appeared to be better, usually with only modest gains in their functional abilities.

Most specialists in this area now agree that more laboratory work is needed before further human brain implants are done. The same scientists agree, however, that similar procedures have great promise for the future and may someday be used to treat spinal cord injuries, epilepsy, and other neurological disorders.

—*Donna Bergen, M.D.*

380

Nursing

Over the past 40 years rapidly increasing knowledge and new technologies have reshaped the role of nurses. In Florence Nightingale's time nurses' main assessment tools were visual observation, touch, sound, and smell. Today nurses monitor the electrical impulses of the heart, measure blood pressure through special lines placed in arteries and veins, administer powerful intravenous drugs, manage a complex array of life-sustaining equipment to keep people alive whose bodily functions have temporarily failed, and routinely initiate emergency treatment and resuscitation. Specially trained nurses deliver babies and provide comprehensive general medical care to ambulatory patients, including the prescribing of certain drugs.

The changing face of nursing

The institutions where most nurses practice have also been transformed over the past four decades, and nurses' roles and responsibilities have changed accordingly. Hospitals, the major employers of nurses, have evolved from modestly sized community institutions managed by nurses or voluntary groups to multimillion-dollar enterprises employing a broad array of personnel and providing a wide range of medical and social services. Nursing homes, which began as custodial residences for the frail elderly, have become medical institutions where nurses are the primary professionals responsible for the care of people with complex chronic health problems and significant functional impairment. Even nursing care delivered to people at home has increasingly shifted from assisting new mothers and providing instruction in well-child care to treating seriously ill people who in another era would have been hospitalized. Now homebound patients requiring complex health services include those receiving intravenous drugs and tube feedings, respirator-dependent children and adults, and an increasing number of people with serious chronic and debilitating diseases, such as cancer and AIDS (acquired immune deficiency syndrome).

Nursing education has also been substantially reshaped during this period of rapid change in health care, partially because of the explosion of knowledge and medical advances but also in response to nurses' changing career aspirations. In just three decades nursing education has moved from being predominantly apprentice training in hospital schools into mainstream institutions of higher education—community colleges and four-year colleges and universities. Like other women, nurses view their employment as a lifelong career commitment rather than as temporary work to generate a second income. Consequently, the majority are seeking identification as professionals with career advancement opportunities and advanced educational credentials.

Cause for ferment

New responsibilities, the changing needs of sick people, and changing career aspirations of nurses all require modifications in the traditional relationships between nurses and physicians and in the institutions where nurses work. However, relationships between health professionals and organizational arrangements for the provision of health care are deeply embedded in traditions that are not easily modified. Change has not come easily, and considerable ferment has resulted.

Nurses make up the largest single group of health professionals; in the United States they number over two million. Nurses are the most versatile health care providers in terms of the scope of their expertise and the range of roles they perform well. They provide comfort to the child in pain as well as making lifesaving decisions on behalf of the critically ill. When necessary, they substitute for physicians and, at the other extreme, provide housekeeping and clerical services. Nurses have been described as the "glue" that holds all the disparate parts of a fragmented health care system together. Nurses provide the only around-the-clock professional presence in health care institutions; all other providers come and go. As institutions have grown in size and complexity, nurses have become the frontline managers as well as the care givers. In many ways the very successes of nurses in such a wide variety of roles, along with their altruistic values, have contributed to many of the problems that the profession of nursing currently is facing.

Nursing shortages—an intractable problem

For years one of the most intractable problems plaguing nursing has been recurrent nursing shortages. The intuitive solution—increasing the supply of nurses—has not been effective in solving the problem despite very large increases in enrollments in nursing schools over the past three decades. In the past decade alone, the number of employed nurses in the United States has increased by 50%, far outstripping the growth of the population, which has increased less than 10%. Since 1984 nursing school enrollments have been declining. Nevertheless, the number of new graduates each year still exceeds the number of retirees, and the number of practicing nurses is continuing to increase despite the decline in enrollment.

A contentious debate has emerged about the causes of and solutions to the shortage. Federal government estimates—based upon objective criteria, such as the size and age structure of the population, disease patterns, and health services utilization trends—suggest that the country has a sufficient number of nurses in the aggregate to meet national needs not only now but also throughout the rest of this century. This projection is seriously at odds with reports from hospitals and nursing homes of a widespread nursing shortage. In 1988 over three-quarters of all hospitals reported a shortage of nurses; almost one in five described the shortage as being severe. In urban areas 30% of hospitals reported being forced to leave hospital beds vacant in 1987 as a result of the nursing shortage; 15% of rural hospitals reported this problem. A majority of nursing homes also reported difficulty in recruiting nurses.

In order to reconcile the differences between federal estimates of an adequate supply of nurses and employers' reports of recruitment difficulties, the U.S. secretary of health and human services commissioned a group of experts in 1988 to study the problem and to make recommendations for its solution. The secretary's commission concluded that the shortage of nurses was real and widespread and estimated that some 137,000 registered nurse positions were unfilled in hospitals and nursing homes.

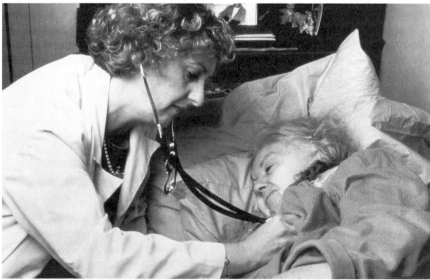

Doug Menuez

Nursing is an occupation in transition. Many nurses are trying to sustain their traditional contributions while at the same time achieving more autonomous roles in health care. With the burgeoning of home care, due in large part to soaring hospital and nursing home costs, many nurses are delivering their expert services to patients in their homes. Nurse practitioner Mary Baker, who heads an enterprise called Chicken Soup Plus in Sacramento, California, makes a house call to a 91-year-old patient.

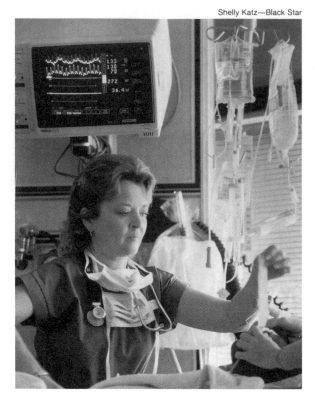

Intensive care nursing, which includes managing a complex array of life-sustaining equipment, is one of the specialty roles that have grown out of the vast changes in medical technologies in hospitals.

Misconceptions abound

There are several misconceptions about the causes of the present national nurse shortage. One is that nurses are dissatisfied and have left nursing in large numbers. In reality, nurses have a high employment rate—over 80% of registered nurses work, which is substantially higher than the 54% rate for all American women. Also contrary to popular belief, fewer than 5% of nurses work outside the health profession.

Another misconception is that so many new jobs for nurses have been created outside the hospitals that fewer nurses are left to work in hospitals. Hospitals, however, continue to employ two-thirds of a growing pool of nurses. In fact, hospitals have dramatically increased the number of nurses employed and the ratio of nurses to patients. Hospitals now have more nurses per patient than ever before. The answer to the often-asked question of where all the nurses have gone is that they are working in hospitals.

The rationale provided by hospitals for the employment of so many additional nurses is that the average patient in a hospital today is much sicker than in years past and therefore requires more intensive nursing care. To an extent this is correct. For example, almost 40,000 new intensive care unit beds were added in hospitals throughout the nation over the last decade.

However, as a result of changing hospital reimbursement policies that encourage shorter patient stays and new technologies, particularly in surgery and noninvasive diagnostic procedures, that enable a much larger share of patients to be treated on an outpatient basis, in 1988 hospitals provided 51 million fewer inpatient days of care than they did in 1982. The average American hospital has only two-thirds of its beds filled, and many are operating at only half capacity because there are no longer enough patients to fill all of the nation's hospital beds. Thus, even if the patients on average are sicker, the reduced volume of care would be expected to offset this in terms of the number of nurses required.

Nurses—a "good buy"

A kind of paradox seems to be at the heart of the nursing shortage—the more nurses that are available for employment, the more nurses employers want. The secretary's commission concluded that the national shortage of nurses has been caused by rapidly growing employer demand for nurses, not by a decline in the number of nurses willing to work. The commission concluded that much of the increased employment of nurses had resulted from a strong employer preference for registered nurses over other kinds of workers, which had resulted in a large-scale substitution of registered nurses for ancillary personnel, particularly in hospitals. Registered nurses were substituted for less educated and skilled licensed practical nurses and nurses' aides in patient care positions. At the same time, reductions in ancillary hospital support personnel of all kinds—including clerical, secretarial, and management staff; various technicians; and patient transport services, housekeeping, dietary, pharmacy, and central supply personnel—increased the nonclinical responsibilities of nurses. So-called time-and-motion studies confirm that nurses are spending, on average, only about one-third of their time in direct patient care, with much of the remainder spent coordinating inefficient or understaffed ancillary services and completing paperwork that could be more efficiently handled by computer systems.

In essence, then, there is a growing consensus that the current nursing shortage is the result of the widespread use of nurses for many functions that do not require their unique expertise. The problem is not that nurses have new job descriptions; rather nurses are faced with increasing responsibilities that are not formally nursing but are essential to assuring patient care of acceptable quality.

Many observers outside the health care field are perplexed by this explanation of the shortage. Noting that the U.S. is a free-market economy, they ask why the laws of supply and demand do not operate to correct the nursing shortage over time. In theory, when the demand for a given category of worker exceeds the supply, wages rise and additional recruits are attracted into the field to bring supply and demand into balance. Nurses, however, are in a captured labor market in the sense that the hospital industry is their major employer. Employers providing nursing jobs in ambulatory settings or businesses have no trouble recruiting nurses because of the regular work hours they offer. Nursing homes are not able to compete with hospitals for nursing staff on the basis of wages because of their weaker overall financial position. Since there is not a large demand for nurses outside the health care system—as there is for secretaries or computer programmers—if nurses want to work, most have to accept the conditions offered by hospitals.

Most communities have a limited number of hospitals. There has been a long-standing belief among hospital administrators that wage competition does not attract additional nurses to a local labor market but simply increases hospitals' operating costs over time. In recent years hospitals have been pressed by government and private insurers to contain costs, and nurses' wages appear to be more vulnerable than the wages of other health care workers to cost-containment initiatives. A major reason why hospitals have been able to substitute so many nurses for other personnel is that nurses' wages have not kept pace with wages in the rest of the economy. Thus, over time

A crucial factor in the present nursing shortage affecting U.S. hospitals is that nurses are forced to function in areas—e.g., handling endless paperwork and coordinating inefficient ancillary services—that do not require their expertise.

Jack Manning/The New York Times

nurses have become a more and more economical source of labor relative to alternative personnel. Since nurses are so versatile in a hospital context, require little supervision, and have a strong professional work ethic, from a strictly economic point of view it makes good management sense for hospitals to hire as many as possible, which is exactly what has happened.

Undesirable working conditions

Not all hospitals are equally attractive places to work. Some are located far from where nurses may live, often in high-crime inner-city areas. Public hospitals, in particular, are facing the numerous problems of crowding, inadequate supplies and equipment, aging physical plants, lack of amenities, and sometimes noncompetitive wages. When suburban hospitals with more attractive working conditions "stockpile" nurses because nurses are such a good buy at present wage rates, the less attractive hospitals and nursing homes are left with an insufficient supply and acute shortages.

One of the most unattractive aspects of nursing is the requirement of shift rotation. When hospital staff vacancy rates are examined, it is clear that most of the vacant positions that make up the current shortage are in inner-city hospitals and on night and weekend hours. One consequence of reducing ancillary support staff throughout the hospital and leaving nurses to fill in is that the number of nurses required for staffing the hospital on unpopular night and weekend shifts increases. It is a common practice for many departments—such as pharmacy, central supply, medical records, patient transport, and housekeeping—to maintain less than 24-hour staff coverage even though patient care is provided around the clock. Placing more responsibility on nurses to provide ancillary services during unpopular hours increases the number of nurses required and leads to considerable discontent and high nurse turnover.

Seeking solutions

Many solutions to the nursing shortage have been proposed. The secretary's commission, having concluded that the underlying cause of the shortage was excess demand for nurses, advanced recommendations designed to moderate demand.

Raise wages? The commission recommended that nurses' wages be increased on the assumption that employers would reduce inappropriate use of nurses at higher wage rates and that recent lagging nursing school enrollments would increase when news of higher wages reached the potential applicant pool. On the two coasts, where there is currently strong competition among hospitals for patients to fill empty beds, hospitals have also been bidding up nurses' wages. In those markets where wages have increased substantially, employer demand seems to be moderating, as was anticipated by the commission. Whatever the trends in market wage rates, the commission urged hospitals to restructure staffing patterns by increasing ancillary personnel in nonclinical support service roles and to consider more creative use of assistants to nurses as a strategy to enable nurses to spend more time in direct care of the sickest patients.

Registered care technologists—a new breed of bedside care provider? The American Medical Association (AMA) has proposed, as a solution to the nursing shortage, to train a new category of bedside care givers, called registered care technologists (RCTs), to substitute for nurses. Nurses and many physicians have opposed the AMA plan on the premise that care givers with more limited training than nurses would compromise the quality of care in today's fast-paced hospitals and contribute to further fragmentation of care. The commission also rejected the AMA proposal on the basis that the shortage has been caused by excess demand and preference for nurses, not by a shortage of bedside care givers. Employers have shown a preference for registered nurses over some 900,000 licensed practical nurses who are already trained and have experience in hospital and nursing home care. The commission concluded that the RCT proposal did not address the root causes of the nursing shortage and thus was not likely to be a solution.

Hiring foreign nurses to solve the U.S. nursing shortage is fraught with problems. It depletes health care resources in countries where there is a greater need of nurses. Moreover, foreign nurses may work for lower wages, thus diminishing U.S. nurses' wages and worsening the shortage.

Jim Cruz/The New York Times

The unilateral nature of the AMA proposal and the pursuit of it in spite of vigorous opposition from nurses have increased tensions between nurses and physicians. Nurses perceive physicians' motivations on this issue to be based on their desire to control both the training and the practice of nursing personnel. In addition, many nurses have suggested that the AMA proposal is another example of the unwillingness of some physicians to accept the more influential and autonomous roles nurses have forged in U.S. health care in recent years. As of the summer of 1989, it appeared that nursing had effectively derailed the RCT proposal. Even though the AMA continued to pursue the idea, no mainstream hospital had volunteered to serve as a pilot training site for the proposed new care givers.

Import foreign nurses? Many institutions facing severe nursing shortages, particularly inner-city and public hospitals, have resorted to recruiting nurses from abroad. This strategy is fraught with problems, however. The nursing shortage is a worldwide phenomenon. The U.S. already has a far greater supply of nurses than other countries do, and recruitment of foreign nurses further depletes health care resources where there is a greater need of nurses than that in the U.S. Moreover, foreign nurses are willing to work for lower wages than U.S. nurses. This has a dampening effect on American nurses' wages, which, as was discussed above, is a major factor underlying the current shortage. Also, the countries that export the most nurses tend to be less developed countries, where there are very different standards of medical care, technology availability, and educational programs than in the U.S. and where English is not the dominant language. Thus, there are serious concerns about the quality of care provided by a substantial share of foreign-trained nurses. Moreover, immigration laws restrict the period that foreign nurses are permitted to stay in the U.S., which limits their utility.

Importing foreign nurses can be seen as only a short-term emergency measure to alleviate the worst problems in a limited number of institutions and will never be anything but a marginal solution to the U.S. shortage. Hospitals in the U.S. employed over 760,-000 full-time-equivalent nurses in 1987. One hundred thousand or more nurses would have to be imported to make a substantial difference in the U.S. shortage on a national basis. Israel, one popular target for U.S. nurse recruiters, for example, has only about 20,000 registered nurses in the entire country.

The success of nursing

The nursing shortage in the U.S. is in a very real sense the product of nursing's success. Nursing has evolved into an all-purpose occupation with almost limitless opportunities in the broader health arena. Technological advances in medicine have enabled nurses to

The nursing shortage has spawned a growing number of nurses who work in temporary positions in short-staffed hospitals. This "traveling nurse" practices her special skills in the neonatal unit of a Long Island, New York, hospital.

creasing status of nursing in the medical hierarchy.

Another career-advancement track for nurses that is beginning to flourish is management and administration of large health care institutions and enterprises of all kinds. More nurses are seeking dual graduate education in both nursing and business to cope with the realities of administering million-dollar businesses. Nurses are also assuming major roles in government regulatory programs, insurance claims review, preadmission hospital and nursing home screening programs, and other positions where professional judgment is required regarding the appropriateness of medical care.

Nursing is an occupation in transition. It is attempting to emerge from a tradition-laden past that seems no longer functional in a world of high technology and changing social attitudes. Nurses are trying to sustain their traditional nursing contributions while at the same time achieving more autonomous roles in health care. With changing disease patterns—including the AIDS epidemic and an aging population with long-term chronic illnesses—and continued technological advancements in medicine, there is little doubt that nurses and nursing will be of even greater importance in the future.

—*Linda H. Aiken, R.N., Ph.D.*

Pathology and Laboratory Medicine

As the last decade of the 20th century begins, the medical specialty of pathology is undergoing profound changes that, in terms of the way the discipline is practiced, may prove to be the most dramatic since the late 18th century, when the anatomic bases for disease were established, and the late 19th century, when the microscope began to be used for medical diagnostic, rather than biological research, purposes. The specialty of pathology evolved directly from the desire of practicing physicians to learn more about the mechanisms of disease. Pathology grew along with the development of the autopsy, beginning with the work of Giovanni Battista Morgagni (1682–1771); Morgagni dissected the bodies of his patients who had died, and he attempted to make correlations between his postmortem anatomic observations and the signs and symptoms he had documented while they were alive and under his expert care.

Now, two centuries after Morgagni, pathology is taking another enormous step that could well be as revolutionary for the practice of medicine as his contributions were. Pathologists are peering deeper into the cell—beyond the level of resolution of the light and electron microscopes—in order to utilize the structural alterations of deoxyribonucleic acid (DNA) and ribonucleic acid (RNA) as a means of establishing specific clinical diagnoses.

develop specialized expertise that carries greater status in society than nursing's more traditional roles of caring, comfort, and empathy. Technology in health care, for the most part, has been labor intensive and nurse intensive in particular. Technological advances have expanded nurses' roles and responsibilities and increased physicians' reliance on them. Physicians in the U.S. have developed practice styles combining hospital- and office-based practice. Unlike many other countries, the U.S. does not have large numbers of institutionally based, full-time salaried physicians. The expanding roles of nurses in the management of complex medical technology and in the care of critically ill patients have enabled U.S. physicians to combine office practice with subspecialty, high-technology hospital care. The increasingly complex medical technologies associated with new surgical procedures—including organ transplants—and technological advances that have forged such new fields as neonatology (the care of premature infants) would not have been possible if nurses had not assumed central clinical decision-making roles in the absence of physicians at the bedside. Specialization is key to differentiation and status in an occupation as large as nursing. Thus, technology has been an important force in the development of the various speciality roles for nurses and in the in-

Pathology's diverse subspecialties

Pathology is both a clinical and a laboratory-based discipline. The autopsy, of course, is the study of organs and tissues of an individual after death. Among the subspecialties of pathology that derived from autopsy pathology are forensic pathology, which deals with murders, accidents, large-scale catastrophes, and other medical problems that affect society as well as the individual; neuropathology, which is concerned with those conditions that affect the brain and nervous system; and pediatric pathology, which concentrates on diseases of children.

Concomitant with improvements in surgical technique and entirely on the basis of the firm foundation of the clinical-pathological correlations established in the autopsy room, the specialty of surgical pathology developed. All tissues removed at surgery are examined by the pathologist to determine the nature of the disease process. The surgical pathologist must then answer certain questions; for example: Is the diseased tissue an inflammation, such as appendicitis, or is it a tumor? If a tumor, is it benign or malignant? Has it been completely removed? Has it spread to lymph nodes? The pathologist must further classify the tumor since therapy must be tailored to its specific nature.

Giovanni Battista Morgagni demonstrated that pathological changes in the internal organs are responsible for symptoms of disease. This plate is from one of his treatises that established pathological anatomy as an exact science.

New York Academy of Medicine

In the 1930s George Papanicolaou was studying the female hormonal cycle in laboratory animals by evaluating the changes of individual cells obtained from the vagina during the menstrual cycle. When this technique was applied to humans, it became apparent that abnormal, as well as normal, processes could be effectively evaluated without the necessity of a biopsy or other surgical procedure. This was the beginning of the subspecialty of cytopathology. At that time carcinoma of the cervix was one of the leading causes of death in women. With the widespread use of the Pap smear technique for early detection and treatment, this dread disease has become a relatively uncommon cause of death. In the last decade cytopathology has greatly enlarged its scope by utilizing extremely thin needles to obtain minute samples of cells from the deep organs, such as the pancreas or the lungs. This technique of "fine needle aspiration" yields material from which the cytopathologist can effectively evaluate conditions that previously could be evaluated only after a surgical operation.

These three closely related fields—autopsy pathology, surgical pathology, and cytopathology—are all based on the evaluation of material with the light microscope and, in a few cases, the electron microscope. They also use even more sophisticated equipment and techniques in order to evaluate diseases. For example, it is now possible to identify specific proteins within cells with the aid of monoclonal antibodies that are developed specifically to react with those proteins. These antibodies are marked with a color indicator in order to make them visible with a microscope. In this way a variety of specific cell components—some of them diagnostic of a given disorder—can be identified even when the identity of the cell itself is not easily established.

Molecular pathology: exciting new possibilities

In the last few years, with the use of tools from molecular biology and the application of them to the study of human afflictions, even more exciting methodologies with seemingly endless potential have been developed. For some years it has been possible to measure the total amount of DNA and RNA within the cells. Now specific characteristics of DNA, RNA, and intracellular proteins can be determined through the artificial disruption of the helical structure and the annealing of complementary nucleoprotein—to which a colored indicator has been applied—either to a single chain or to part of a chain. In this way viruses that are infecting cells can be recognized by a match of their specific DNA or RNA structure—even when they are present in only minute concentrations.

Specific gene or protein segments responsible for the development of a specific disease process can be isolated, allowing physicians to come closer to the specific molecular basis of human disorders. One ex-

Photographs, Lynn McLaren

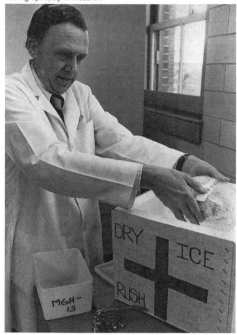
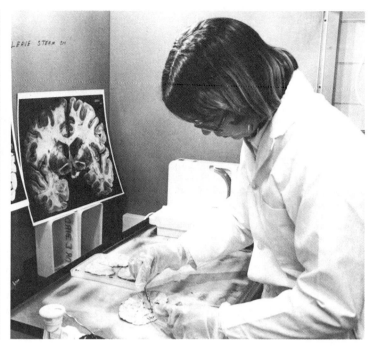

*A neuropathologist from Harvard Medical School unpacks a frozen brain at the Brain Tissue Resource
Center; a research assistant dissects the brain tissue into specimens that will be distributed to investigators for
neuropsychiatric research. The center, established in 1978, receives about 200 donated brains a year.*

ample of this is in the study of oncogenes, segments of the genome thought to be responsible for the transformation of normal cells into tumor cells. Each tumor could very well have a distinct oncogene that is responsible for its development and that may also be a reliable indicator of its clinical behavior. Therapy in future years will be designed to correspond to specific behavioral characteristics of tumors as evidenced by their molecular identity. These same techniques are also used to study and evaluate the full range of inherited disorders.

One of the recently developed methods applied to the study of human disease is the polymerase chain reaction. When there is an insufficient amount of nucleoprotein material to be measured, it is possible to increase the material in a test tube by adding appropriately matched oligonucleotide segments, which, under controlled conditions, replicate and produce sufficient copies of the original material to enable it to be identified and quantified. In this way, for example, a cell could theoretically be infected with a single virus, or it could contain only a part of a single virus, and yet iden-

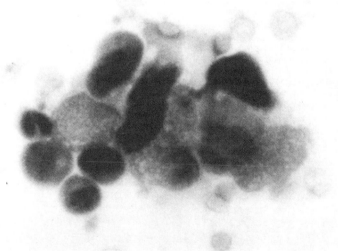

*An experimental technique
that relies on immunologic
and chemical reactions enables
early detection of breast cancer
metastases. Cells from the bone
marrow, a likely site for the spread
of breast cancer cells, are prepared
with a fluorescent stain that has
an affinity for breast tissue cells.
A pathologist uses a microscope to
look for cells that give off a glow—
a sign that breast cancer cells have
invaded the marrow. The test can
detect one breast tissue cell in
100,000 bone marrow cells. The
photomicrograph shows a cluster
of cancer-related cells in the bone
marrow of a patient whose breast
cancer has spread.*

Michael P. Osborne and Richard J. Cote, Memorial Sloan Kettering Cancer Center

tification of the viral material would still be possible.

The applications of molecular pathology to the study of human disease are only beginning to be explored and, at the present time, are available only in large medical centers and research institutes. However, these methods and their improvements will become commercially widely available and a part of the armamentarium of every pathologist within the next decade, enabling specific and completely accurate diagnoses in every community.

Will the methods now used in autopsy pathology, surgical pathology, and cytopathology become obsolete? Clearly, the answer is no because the overwhelming majority of human afflictions are exceedingly well evaluated by these reliable approaches. Instead, many of the patient problems that are now relatively difficult, or even impossible, to understand will be resolved. Further, the new methods of molecular pathology will complement, rather than replace, the pathologist's present abilities. The diagnosis of breast cancer will still be established through examination of the tissues or cells, but in the near future it will be possible by the usual microscopic methods to classify tumors that are seemingly identical into better defined subgroups; such specific tumor identity will enable better prognoses to be established and greater precision to be employed in the design of therapeutic approaches. Greatly improved quality of care will be the result of these advances.

The once distinct disciplines that make up pathology are becoming more similar as they all embrace the new molecular pathology. The same techniques that help to identify the oncogene in the DNA of a resected carcinoma have been used to recognize the virus causing a pneumonia or to construct the abnormality responsible for a hereditary disorder.

Advances in laboratory medicine

The pathologist also carries the responsibility for other laboratories in the modern hospital, all of which are developing improved means of caring for patients. As pathology evolved into a distinct specialty of medical practice and concentrated on the evaluation and care of hospitalized patients, other laboratory disciplines were also being recognized. The utilization of the full range of laboratory techniques was a natural outgrowth of pathologists' desire to learn as much as possible about a disease process. Clinical chemistry, microbiology, hematology, immunology, and immunohematology (blood banking) fell under the umbrella of the pathologist.

Clinical chemistry: new speed and precision. In the early part of the 20th century, only a few blood components were analyzed in the laboratory. This was both because the technology was limited and, more importantly, because the significance of most of the materials that can now be identified was unknown. Just

as Morgagni correlated anatomic derangements with specific signs and symptoms, hundreds of physicians and other scientists have made associations between specific chemical components, immune responses, or microorganisms and a disease. Analyses often took hours to days and required the most precise technique and concentrated attention of the pathologist and technologist. In the 1950s methods of chemical analysis became automated, and there was concomitant improvement in reliability and reproducibility of results. The field of clinical chemistry has developed enormously. Now literally hundreds of substances can be identified with relative ease in a matter of minutes by means of sophisticated computerized instruments. This has made it possible for pathologists to obtain information about a great many substances that can be important in evaluating an individual's health and progress. For example, chemistry laboratories identify and measure certain enzymes that are crucial in establishing the diagnosis of myocardial infarction (heart attack). Pathologists also engage in research designed to identify new, diagnostically important blood components. Among the subdisciplines of clinical chemistry are toxicology, enzymology, and radioimmunoassay; the latter was developed especially for the evaluation of hormone activity.

Microbiology: identifying new infectious agents. The creation of microbiology as a medical discipline followed the work of Louis Pasteur (1822–95). The modern microbiology laboratory is concerned with the identification of bacteria, viruses, parasites, and fungi. It was only after microbiology laboratories were established that effective development and utilization of antibiotics could take place. Specific treatment of an infectious disorder first requires exact identification of its pathogenesis as well as evaluation of the response of the causative microorganism to antimicrobials.

The techniques used by Pasteur are still in use but have been greatly improved. In recent years these approaches have been successfully automated. Greater understanding of microorganism structure and physiology has allowed for the synthesis of highly specific growth media, improving and speeding isolation and maintenance of laboratory cultures. Molecular microbiology is becoming an integral part of the approach to identifying infectious agents, complementing and augmenting existing techniques.

With the advent of antibiotic therapy, it was mistakenly thought that advances in microbiology would slow. Instead, laboratory improvements have helped in the evaluation of newer and better therapies. In addition, new infectious conditions have been recognized—*e.g.,* so-called opportunistic infections, which result from infectious agents that do not affect healthy individuals but cause disease in persons whose immunity is already impaired. Many of the infectious agents that are found in patients with AIDS (acquired immune deficiency syndrome) were unknown or only rarely recognized 20 or more years ago.

Hematology: distinguishing previously unrecognized blood disorders. Hematology is the pathology subspecialty devoted to the study of circulating cells in the blood and in the bone marrow (where blood cells are produced), the many disorders that can affect these elements, and the coagulation of blood. Anemias—reductions in the number of circulating red blood cells—can be due to such nutritional deficiencies as reduced amounts of iron, such inherited disorders as sickle-cell anemia (in which the red blood cell is structurally defective), or even therapies given for another condition (*e.g.,* in cancer patients who receive potent chemotherapeutic agents whose side effects may include bone marrow depression). Leukemias are malignant proliferations of the white blood cells; they are diagnosed through a count of the white cells in the blood—by means of sophisticated computerized devices—and also through study of the blood and the bone marrow under a microscope. The changes in hematology laboratories have paralleled those already described: increasing automation and computerization, greater utilization of molecular technology, and recognition of new diseases and of specific variants of disorders already understood.

Blood banking: the impact of AIDS. The principal change in blood banking in recent years has been in the greater recognition of the potential risks of transfusing blood and blood products, such as red blood cells, plasma, and blood platelets. Blood is a biologically active substance with the potential for carrying antigenically deleterious substances—just as any other transplantable tissue. Certain risks—*e.g.,* that of transmitting hepatitis—have been known for many decades. The AIDS epidemic in this decade has stimulated increasing awareness of the risks of transfusion, and newer tests for detecting blood units at risk have been developed.

In addition to being tested for hepatitis B, all blood donors are now screened for the presence of antibodies to the human immunodeficiency virus (HIV), thought to be the cause of AIDS. A new assay for the human T-cell lymphotrophic virus, type I (HTLV-I), thought to be the cause of a rare form of malignant lymphoma, is also available now and being widely applied. Most recently, investigators have announced the identification of a virus potentially carried in blood products and thought to be responsible for another form of hepatitis known as hepatitis non-A, non-B (NANB) or as hepatitis C. They have also announced that a specific test for this agent may soon be available.

It is clear, unfortunately, that other, as yet unrecognized conditions may be transmitted in this way and, further, that these tests are not perfect since they rely on the presence of an antibody response on the part of the donors. In some instances the infectious agent may be present without an identifiable antibody response either because the individual has not yet developed the antibody or because of a defect in antibody production. Pathologists specializing in transfusion medicine have, in addition to developing better means of testing blood and its products, promoted autologous transfusion, in which a patient stores his or her own blood in preparation for an elective procedure. Clearly, this could not happen if the patient were severely anemic or if there were any emergency need for blood. A few blood banks have offered to freeze blood units, which would allow storage for many years before a specific need arose. Although the advantages of this are obvious, problems in implementing it as a national policy include the fact that most blood centers are not prepared for blood freezing and, even when the technology is available, it is a relatively expensive procedure, requiring considerable personnel time and special storage capabilities.

Immunopathology: explosion of knowledge. Recently, along with the many technological advances in the study of both antibody- and cell-mediated immune reactions, there has been a trend toward combining the testing methods into a single laboratory setting, and thus the specialty of immunopathology has become established. Many new disorders have been shown to be completely or partially based on immune mechanisms. The delineation of the disease systemic lupus erythematosus by Paul Klemperer (1887–1964) was the condition principally responsible for the first explosion in knowledge of immune mechanisms. AIDS serves that role today.

Autopsies: the alarming decline

At one time, in the 1940s and '50s, more than 50% of patients who died in hospitals in the United States were studied after death. This practice contributed to the extraordinary improvements in medical practice that have occurred in the past half century. The autopsy has helped to uncover new diseases, such as Legionnaire's disease and toxic shock syndrome, and has greatly expanded the understanding of previously recognized disorders, such as viral hepatitis and pneumoconioses (diseases resulting from inhalation of industrial dusts). In addition, the widespread utilization of the autopsy, by confirming diagnoses when they were accurate and by identifying misinterpretations when they occurred, allowed for the establishment of many new diagnostic technologies, such as sophisticated imaging techniques. Autopsy utilization allowed for the development of new surgical methods, including modern heart surgery and various organ transplants, by documenting their successful application and recognizing the structural bases for their failures. Also, by confirming efficacy and recognizing deleterious side effects, autopsies enabled new therapies to be evaluated—and their potential hazards to be recognized.

389

Pathology and laboratory medicine

An example of this latter phenomenon was the discovery that the drug methotrexate, used for the treatment of certain cancers and also in patients with severe psoriasis, may be hepatotoxic (causing liver disease), especially at high dosages or with prolonged use.

Inaccurate death certificates. The autopsy rate in hospitals in the United States is now approximately 10%; nine of every ten people who die are *not* studied to determine either the accuracy of the clinical diagnosis, the appropriateness of often-expensive diagnostic methodologies, the effectiveness or side effects of therapies, or the cause of death. It has been repeatedly documented that diagnostic errors occur in at least 15% of cases even in the best of medical centers. This is true even in those hospitals where there is a high autopsy rate—as is the situation in many European centers—and is clearly not because only difficult cases are selected for autopsy.

One of the results of the decline in the performance of autopsies has been that national statistics about death and fatal diseases have become inaccurate. Death certificates are incorrect in at least 50% of cases, even when an autopsy has been performed, since the information obtained at autopsy is often not included in the death certificate. Since so few autopsies are performed, it is reasonable to conclude that national health policy based on death statistics may be inappropriate.

Are autopsies still needed? As the number of "new" diseases discovered at the time of autopsy has diminished, the importance of the autopsy has become better recognized. Because the principal purpose of the autopsy—to provide more knowledge in order to better care for living patients—has not changed, autopsies should be done routinely. In addition to its role in monitoring the quality of medical care, the autopsy can provide an enormous amount of information about the early stages of diseases. Present understanding of coronary artery disease, for example, came largely from the study of these blood vessels in patients who died of noncoronary, as well as coronary, disease. In this way the full range of pathological alterations became recognized, even before they were clinically significant. Further, the ability to recognize the lesions of coronary atherosclerosis radiologically by injection of dyes came only after these techniques were applied during hundreds of autopsies.

The autopsy is very useful for the family of a patient who has died. Obviously, vital information about hereditary disorders can be obtained. In addition, such communicable diseases as tuberculosis may be discovered at autopsy. The autopsy may also help family members immeasurably by relieving them of feelings of guilt that often follow the death of a loved one, and it may even help to reduce the length and severity of the grieving period by assuring them about the reasons for the death and the appropriateness of the medical care given.

Invaluable role in the education of physicians. The autopsy is an integral part of medical education, providing valuable information for medical students, physicians-in-training, physicians-in-practice, and other health care professionals. Unfortunately, the relatively small number of autopsies performed considerably limits this application.

In addition to providing medical students with first-hand exposure to a variety of disorders that they may not have had contact with or may have only limited information about, the autopsy establishes the relevance of studies in anatomy, physiology, biochemistry, and microbiology. It also allows students to copy Morgagni's experience of correlating clinical observations with morphological findings and thus firmly establishing the basis for the patient's physical signs and symptoms. Less well-recognized purposes for the autopsy in the education of the physician-to-be include the opportunity to confront and contemplate death and the opportunity to learn about the potential fallibility of modern medical science (including the limitations of both medical practice in general and distinguished physicians in particular).

This 15th-century woodcut depicts a "Lesson in Dissection." The autopsy remains a vital, indispensable component of medical care. Without it there can be no certain diagnosis or effective evaluation of therapy.

From Carl Zigrosser, *Medicine and the Artist (Ars Medica)*, Dover Publications, 1971; reproduced by permission of the Philadelphia Museum of Art

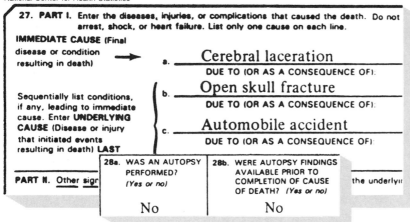

27. PART I. Enter the diseases, injuries, or complications that caused the death. Do not arrest, shock, or heart failure. List only one cause on each line.

IMMEDIATE CAUSE (Final disease or condition resulting in death) →

a. **Cerebral laceration**
DUE TO (OR AS A CONSEQUENCE OF):

Sequentially list conditions, if any, leading to immediate cause. Enter UNDERLYING CAUSE (Disease or injury that initiated events resulting in death) LAST

b. **Open skull fracture**
DUE TO (OR AS A CONSEQUENCE OF):

c. **Automobile accident**
DUE TO (OR AS A CONSEQUENCE OF):

PART II. Other sign...

28a. WAS AN AUTOPSY PERFORMED? (Yes or no)	28b. WERE AUTOPSY FINDINGS AVAILABLE PRIOR TO COMPLETION OF CAUSE OF DEATH? (Yes or no)
No	No

A result of the declining autopsy rate in the U.S. is the inaccuracy of death statistics. In at least 50% of cases, death certificates are incorrect; even when an autopsy has been performed, information obtained during the postmortem examination often is not included on the certificate. Consequently, a new model form has recently been created. The proposed certificate adds instructions and examples to help clarify the cause of death and a place to account for the vital information derived from an autopsy.

The autopsy can also serve these functions for graduate physicians-in-residency and physicians-in-practice. Although there is no scientific proof that the autopsy improves the quality of practice of individual physicians, since an appropriate and reproducible way of testing this has not yet been developed, there is indirect evidence in support of this hypothesis. It has been documented that the diagnostic error rate is lowest in those hospitals where there is a high rate of autopsies. The error rate may be as high as 40% in hospitals with low autopsy rates and as low as 15% in hospitals with high autopsy rates.

Not 100% accurate. Why do hospitals with high autopsy rates not have an even lower rate of diagnostic errors? It appears that 15% is the lowest rate obtainable at the present time. The reasons for this are that diagnoses are often based on noninvasive interpretive techniques and that the types of conditions encountered tend to change owing to such factors as new environmental influences and the increasing age of the population, as well as modern therapies that allow patients to survive previously fatal conditions and thus be afflicted with multiple disorders at the time of death. New therapies themselves can cause abnormalities that might be recognized only at an autopsy. In addition, as discussed above, new conditions, such as AIDS and its many modes of expression, are always being recognized.

Explanations for decline. If these reasons for the autopsy are valid, why has the utilization of the autopsy diminished? There are many explanations. There are those who suggest that diagnoses are usually established before death. This, however, is clearly not true. Even if the principal diagnosis is known in most patients, there may be a second condition that affects the clinical course—which is unknown in approximately 50% of cases—and, of course, the cause of death is often misunderstood.

Many suggest that families will not give permission. In reality, the public is better informed about medical matters than ever before in history, and if an interested physician takes the time to explain the many advantages of the autopsy, permission is likely to be given. In almost all instances religious preferences will not preclude the performance of an autopsy.

Many physicians are reluctant to obtain autopsy permission because they fear that disclosure of some information could be used in a malpractice suit. Despite the increasing litigiousness of contemporary society, there is no evidence to support this fear. Instead, it may be that the lack of an autopsy contributes to a judgment against a physician if a conclusion is reached that the doctor "buried his mistake."

What then are the reasons for the decline in utilization of the autopsy? A number of contributory factors may be relevant: de-emphasis of pathology in general and autopsy in particular in medical schools; de-emphasis of the custom of establishing clinical-pathological correlations in clinical practice; inability of physicians to confront death—perhaps augmented by the lack of exposure to autopsy in medical school; and reluctance to recognize error. The changes in the way hospital medical care is delivered, including the development of multidoctor care, have reduced the level of rapport a patient establishes with any single physician, making it more difficult for both the doctor and family members to discuss autopsy at the time of death. Even if the fear of litigation is not valid, it is often present and may contribute to the failure to seek permission for autopsy.

The pathologist must also be held at least partially culpable. The autopsy is time-consuming, physically demanding, and neither academically nor financially rewarding. The other demands on the pathologist and the support staff, including but not limited to surgical pathology, often take precedence. Even when an autopsy is performed, the completion of study and the preparation of the final report may take so long that the findings are no longer clinically useful for the physician.

Reversing the trend. What is being done to increase the autopsy rate? Organizations, including the College of American Pathologists and the Association of Pathology Chairmen, have been working for the last decade to inform physicians, other health care organizations, health insurers, and government agencies about the problem. There have been successes. For example, policy changes have been effected by the Joint Commission on Accreditation of Healthcare Organizations, which has revised its hospital review criteria, effective Jan. 1, 1989, to include increased emphasis on the autopsy as part of a hospital's ongoing quality-assurance activities. Also, a thoughtful and comprehensive review of the status of the autopsy was published in the Dec. 16, 1988, issue of the *Journal of the American Medical Association.* Further, various clinical specialty-certifying organizations are now requiring minimal levels of autopsy performance before a candidate is accepted for specialist status.

Pathology's paradox. Many of the leaders of American pathology recognize the paradoxical position in which the specialty is now placed. On the one hand, the demands of progress will require the implementation of the most sophisticated techniques of molecular pathology in the evaluation of patients throughout the health care system. On the other hand, the light ignited by Morgagni and fueled by countless others is still holding away the shadows of ignorance and inertia, and a major effort is being applied to enlarge that flickering flame.

Medicine cannot succeed in the 21st century without developing and employing the newest approaches for evaluation of patients. If the information obtained at autopsy in the thousands of hospitals throughout the country is collected, stored, and evaluated in a centralized research facility, the benefits of the autopsy could be greater than they have been at any other time. This will require both enlightenment and financial support.

The autopsy is a vital, indispensable component of medical practice. Without the autopsy, there can be no certainty about diagnoses, no effective evaluation of therapy, and no guarantee of the quality of care a patient has received.

—Stephen A. Geller, M.D.

Pediatrics

U.S. youngsters between the ages of 12 and 17 spend an estimated 21 hours a week in front of the TV set. By the time today's teenagers reach age 70, they will have spent seven years of their lives watching TV. A report on the impact of television on children, issued in 1988 by the U.S. Department of Education, concluded that television viewing had displaced many other activities, among them participating in organized sports, reading comic books, listening to the radio,

and going to the movies. Students often do homework while "watching" TV. There is some evidence that television adversely affects reading achievement, especially during the early elementary school years, and may negatively affect the ability to verbalize certain kinds of ideas; for example, to name alternative uses for an object. According to William H. Dietz of Tufts University Medical School, Boston, a pediatrician who has been following the studies of television's impact on children, the Department of Education's report affirms that youngsters can learn from TV, but it leaves open the question of whether TV displaces other activities or patterns of learning. Dietz and other experts in the field recommend that children be restricted to no more than 14–15 hours of television per week and that parents watch TV with their children as often as possible—or at the very least that they be aware of what their children are watching.

Studies disagree on whether television portrayals of aggressive behavior induce similar behavior in children. In one small Canadian community, where television was introduced in 1973, there was a documented increase in verbal and physical aggression among primary school children. In a more recent U.S. report, published in the journal *Pediatrics* in March 1989, behavioral scientists reviewed 20 field experiments involving a diverse group of more than 2,000 preschool-age, school-age, and adolescent children. The children's aggression levels were assessed before and after the viewing of either aggressive or nonaggressive TV shows. Observation of social interactions among the youngsters revealed no short-term changes in their behavior following the aggressive shows. There is good evidence, however, that exposure to violence on television may increase an individual's acceptance of aggressive behavior in others and blunt his or her sensitivity to violence.

Hyperactivity: ongoing controversies

Hyperactivity is a difficult condition to define and is also one that eludes treatment. The dividing lines between normal behavior, misbehavior, and hyperactivity become blurred in different settings. Even the official name of the condition has been changed twice in recent years—from hyperactivity to attention deficit disorder (ADD) to attention deficit hyperactivity (ADH). In fact, almost the only agreement about this condition is that children who have it are difficult to manage.

Some children seem to be hyperactive almost from birth (or even before birth, mothers may say); in others the behavior manifests itself first in a school setting—or perhaps that is where it is first seen as disruptive. For some unknown reason, hyperactivity is reported more often in adopted children than in biological children.

When hyperactivity cannot be attributed to familial crises (*e.g.,* divorce, separation, abuse) or develop-

The dividing line between normal behavior and hyperactivity can become blurred in different settings. Running nonstop during recess may seem a normal-enough way of letting off steam, but when a child is disruptive in class, overly aggressive toward others, and generally unable to settle down to a task, a diagnosis of hyperactivity may be appropriate. Multimodal therapy—which combines drug treatment with some form of counseling—may be more effective than treatment with drugs alone.

mental retardation, other factors are examined as potential causes or contributing factors. In the past two decades, dietary factors have been prime suspects, especially sugar, food additives and preservatives, caffeine, chocolate, and the like. Designing a controlled study to pinpoint dietary factors presents certain difficulties, among them the problem of providing diets with and without specific ingredients and maintaining the conditions of the so-called double-blind study (in which neither the children nor the researchers know which groups are receiving which diet). Such studies have, nevertheless, been carried out. Unfortunately, the results are contradictory. A report by a Seattle, Wash., group, published in December 1988, found that a high intake of sugar is not related to abnormal behavior; on the other hand, in January 1989 scientists at the University of Calgary, Alta., published a study showing that more than half of a group of hyperactive children improved in behavior on a four-week experimental diet that omitted artificial colors and flavors, chocolate, monosodium glutamate, caffeine, and similar substances.

For many years the drug methylphenidate (Ritalin) has been used to treat hyperactivity. The drug, which is a stimulant when taken by adults, has the reverse effect—calming—on hyperactive children. In hundreds of studies it has been shown to produce short-term beneficial effects, including increased attention span and decreased impulsivity in 70–80% of children with ADH. Cognitive function may or may not improve. The use of Ritalin in the management of ADH, however, has become increasingly controversial, if only because of the rapid increase in the number of prescriptions being written. In Baltimore County, Md., for example, the rate of medication treatment for hyperactive inattentive students has consistently doubled every

five to seven years, so that in 1987 nearly 6% of all public elementary-school students were receiving such treatment. It is not known whether this increase represents overdiagnosis or a real rise in the numbers of hyperactive children or whether physicians are prolonging the treatment, continuing to prescribe the drug as the children grow older. It used to be thought that hyperactivity was a condition that children outgrew; now some authorities believe that youngsters may continue to be hyperactive through adolescence. A certain amount of disruptive behavior and minor crimes committed by teens have been attributed by some to untreated hyperactivity.

In the treatment of ADH, a two- to three-week trial of methylphenidate, given at varied dosages, is usually sufficient for determining whether the drug is beneficial. The medication is commonly stopped during summer, to allow for reevaluation of its effectiveness and to decide if it should be continued. There is no withdrawal effect on discontinuation. In children who have taken the drug for many years, however, there may be a reduction in expected height and weight.

The U.S. Drug Enforcement Administration thinks it possible that methylphenidate, which, as noted above, has amphetamine-like effects, is being diverted to the black market for drug abuse. It is also possible that the medical establishment finds it easier to prescribe a drug than to explore behavioral and other causes of hyperactivity and to try other therapeutic approaches, such as individual, group, or family psychotherapy and remedial tutoring for learning disabilities. Perhaps the best solution will turn out to be a multimodal therapy, which includes a stimulant medication such as methylphenidate for a short period of time as well as help with school performance and some kind of therapy. In 1988 James Satterfield and colleagues of the National Center for Hyperactive Children, Encino, Calif., reported the results of a study of 131 hyperactive boys, half of whom had been treated with stimulants alone and the rest with multimodal therapy for two to three years. Significantly fewer offenses were committed by those in the multimodal group, and institutionalization rates in this group were lower.

Advances in neonatal screening

All newborns in the U.S. are routinely tested for phenylketonuria (PKU), a congenital enzyme deficiency that, if untreated, causes mental retardation, and for congenital hypothyroidism, a thyroid hormone deficiency. In addition, many states screen for other inborn errors of metabolism (such as galactosemia) and for hemoglobin disorders, including sickle-cell disease. Early diagnosis of these conditions enables infants to receive therapy that may be lifesaving or, in the case of disorders involving mental retardation, intelligence-saving. Newborn screening represents a remarkable evolution in the ability to detect and prevent or treat disorders that, although rare, are devastatingly serious if not diagnosed promptly. In recent years advances in newborn screening have also provided valuable information about genetic disorders, helping young couples make informed decisions about family planning.

It is likely that in the coming years additional tests will become routine for newborns, among them tests for congenital adrenal hyperplasia, cystic fibrosis, and biotinidase deficiency, all diseases in which early detection enables optimum treatment. Biotinidase deficiency, a genetic defect in which a missing enzyme results in deficiency of a B vitamin, is manifested by convulsions, ataxia (incoordination), poor muscle tone, developmental delay, deafness, and atrophy of the optic nerve. Daily supplements of biotin, taken by mouth, reverse some of these manifestations. The earlier the diagnosis, the more successful the treatment. The diagnosis of cystic fibrosis not only enables optimum treatment of the affected child from birth onward but may also have an important impact on family planning. Congenital adrenal hyperplasia is a genetic disorder that causes abnormalities of the sex organs and, sometimes, excessive salt loss. Early diagnosis leads to tests to determine the sex of the infant and prevents problems of precocious puberty (early sexual maturation), accelerated growth, and the development of testicular tumors in males in adulthood.

Lungs at risk in preterm infants

Many prematurely born infants who might have died one or two decades ago now survive as a result of advances in neonatal medicine. A number of them, because of the incomplete development of their lungs, require intensive respiratory support in the hospital nursery and even after they are discharged to go home. Now doctors are finding that as a consequence of mechanical ventilation, these infants develop a chronic lung condition called bronchopulmonary dysplasia, or BPD. This new disorder is a direct result of the lifesaving technology that allows small infants to breathe even though their lungs are immature. With the continued use of the ventilator, the baby's lungs become overdistended; the lung tissue may then become fibrous or the lungs may become partially collapsed. When the lungs are so severely damaged, the infant must exert tremendous effort simply in order to breathe. Sometimes, to assist themselves, babies with BPD breathe more rapidly; this, too, expends precious energy. The lungs then produce increased mucus, which makes them susceptible to infection. The pulmonary blood vessels constrict; pulmonary blood

Mechanical ventilation is lifesaving for a premature baby whose lungs are not yet fully developed. As a direct result of this technology, however, the infant can develop bronchopulmonary dysplasia, a chronic lung disorder that requires months of intensive treatment— first in the hospital and then at home. Little is known about the long-term outcome of these infants; studies to evaluate their subsequent growth and development are now under way.

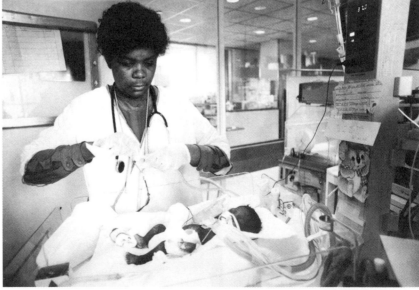

pressure rises; and this in turn physically stresses the heart. BPD affects 13% of infants whose birth weight is low (1,251–1,500 g [3–3.75 lb]) and more than 76% who are under 800 g (1.75 lb) at birth.

The average hospital cost for care of a BPD infant is $142,000. The hospital stay may range from 15 to 65 days and include intensive care, oxygen, a variety of drugs, and respiratory therapy. Because of the huge costs involved, there is great interest in keeping the period of hospitalization of BPD infants to a minimum. Early discharge has other advantages as well: reduced chances of hospital-acquired infections and promotion of close bonding with the family. However, for home care to be successful, parents must have training and backup support from the medical center. The equipment involved is complex. Among the devices parents must learn to use are cardiorespiratory monitors, oxygen tanks and flow meters, nasal tubes, a nebulizer/compressor (to administer inhaled medications), and suction machines. Parents of an infant with BPD also need to understand the various medications (bronchodilators, diuretics) and their purposes. They must know how to administer cardiopulmonary resuscitation and how to feed an infant who has difficulty breathing. In some neonatal centers a nurse coordinator functions as the key person in a team that assists the family in the complex care of the BPD infant.

It may be necessary for the infant to be on oxygen at home for six months or more, and during this time there will be frequent checkups to evaluate the baby's medical progress. As the infant's pulmonary function improves, "catch-up" growth can be expected. Respiratory infections are a frequent concern, however, and may interrupt the child's steady growth. The long-term outcome of BPD children is of special interest because the survival of very small infants with lung disease is a relatively recent development, and only now are data being gathered. A 1982 report of a Providence, R.I., study showed that 52% of infants with BPD showed neurodevelopmental delays at 12 months, and problems were suspected in an additional 24%. However, more recent studies indicate that the developmental delays seen in BPD infants are associated with the low birth weight rather than the pulmonary disease. In a British study (published in 1988) of the intellectual outcome of low-birth-weight babies born in the late 1970s, these infants had lower IQs than normal-weight infants and subsequently were more likely to be performing below average at school. This finding would seem to corroborate the conclusion that birth weight rather than lung disease is the more important variable.

Lyme disease in children

Lyme disease was once regarded as a parochial infection, believed to be confined to the area around Lyme, Conn., where it was first reported in 1975. It was soon

Pfizer Central Research

The tick that carries Lyme disease may be found in heavily wooded areas or in the more tame setting of the suburban backyard. Checking the family pet for ticks is a safeguard not only for the animal but also for its human playmates.

identified in the Northeast, the Midwest, and the West and now has been seen in at least 43 states in the U.S. Cases have also been reported in Europe and Australia. The infection is caused by a bacterium that is spread by ticks. The ticks may be found in suburban backyards as well as in the wooded areas typically associated with the disease and, of course, on dogs.

Lyme disease also used to be regarded as a disease of the joints but now is recognized to involve many anatomic systems. It usually begins (3 to 32 days after the tick bite) with a distinctive localized skin rash called erythema chronicum migrans—sometimes described as a "bull's-eye rash"—followed by other rashes, conjunctivitis (inflammation of the mucous membranes of the eyelids), and sometimes chills, fever, aches, signs of brain and spinal cord involvement (e.g., stiff neck, confusion, hallucinations), or liver, spleen, or other systemic manifestations. These symptoms may continue for several weeks or months, after which there may be late and severe signs of infection, involving the central nervous system, the heart, and any or all joints. Lyme disease is particularly dangerous for pregnant women since the bacteria may cross the placenta and cause fetal or newborn death or congenital malformations.

Children, of course, are especially likely to be ex-

Sam C. Pierson, Jr./The New York Times

A two-year-old Houston, Texas, girl registers dismay as she receives a measles vaccine injection. More than 1,000 confirmed cases of measles were reported in Houston between December 1988 and February 1989. In response to this and numerous other measles outbreaks among preschoolers in inner-city neighborhoods, the U.S. Centers for Disease Control concluded that youngsters in "high-risk" areas should receive not one but two doses of the vaccine. The American Academy of Pediatrics went even further, recommending that all children be immunized twice.

posed to ticks and therefore to Lyme disease. The best treatment is prevention—one expert suggests that children be checked for ticks regularly when playing outdoors in tick-infested areas. Attached ticks should be removed promptly. Protective clothing—high socks, long pants—may help prevent bites; wearing light colors helps make ticks easier to spot. An aerosol spray containing permethrin is available in many lawn and garden stores and may repel ticks. Another repellent believed to be effective is DEET (diethyltoluamide); it is available in lotions, sprays, and other forms. Because DEET is absorbed through the skin and can be toxic, products that contain it should not be used on infants or applied to irritated skin.

If a youngster develops symptoms of Lyme disease or if blood tests indicate that infection has occurred, antibiotics such as tetracycline (or penicillin for children under nine years) are recommended for 10 to 20 days to prevent late complications.

Measles upsurge

After the licensing of the measles vaccine in 1963, there was hope that measles could be eliminated in the U.S., except for cases introduced from outside. In fact, a single dose of vaccine given to most infants over the age of 12 months did reduce the reported incidence of measles to 5% of prevaccine levels in the five years after 1963. However, the number of cases reported to the Centers for Disease Control (CDC) has risen, from a low of 1,497 in 1983 to a high of 6,282 in 1986. Judging by reports to date, the numbers for 1989 will far surpass those of '86; as of July 1989 more than 8,000 cases had already been reported. A significant proportion of these were in individuals over ten years of age and college students, many of whom had previously been vaccinated against the disease.

Measles outbreaks are also occurring among preschoolers and in inner-city neighborhoods. In 1988 a little over 17% of the total number of cases of measles in the U.S. were reported in Los Angeles County, and 64% of the Los Angeles County cases occurring between May and December were in children under five years of age. Many preschool youngsters in the inner-city Hispanic population had not been vaccinated.

The CDC has concluded that additional strategies are needed for reaching inner-city populations, that larger numbers of children must be vaccinated to prevent outbreaks in schools, and that children who live in "high-risk" areas should receive not one but two doses of measles vaccine. The American Academy of Pediatrics (AAP) has gone further. In July 1989 they issued new recommendations calling for two doses of measles vaccine to be given to *all* children after the first birthday. These doses, which are given in combination with mumps and rubella vaccine, should be given at age 15 months and again at entrance to middle school or junior high school.

The outlook for eliminating rubella (German measles) is more encouraging. Between 1970 and 1979 an average of 27 cases of congenital rubella syndrome (a group of birth defects caused by maternal infection during pregnancy) occurred annually in the U.S. By between 1980 and 1985 the average had fallen to seven cases per year. German measles is usually a mild illness in young children, but it is highly infectious. Susceptible women who are exposed in early pregnancy may transmit the infection to the fetus, resulting in anomalies of the eyes, heart, nervous system, and ears and various other defects. In the U.S. the rubella vaccine is commonly given to all children at 15 months of age, in combination with measles and mumps vaccine, and now, in accordance with the new AAP recommendations, will be given again at entrance to middle school or junior high school. The vaccine poses a theoretical risk to the fetus if a woman is pregnant or becomes pregnant within three months after vaccination.

Children after cancer: what the future holds

In the U.S. one child in 600 will develop cancer sometime during childhood. Currently, cancer is the second leading cause of death, after accidents, in children less than 15 years old. The death rate from childhood cancers is declining, however. In the period between 1960 and 1963, the five-year survival rate for all childhood cancers was 28%. In the period 1977–83 it was 62%.

In view of the significant improvements being made in treatment, it has been estimated that by 1990 one in every 1,000 adults reaching the age of 20 will be a long-term survivor of childhood cancer. With more and more young patients surviving, physicians are now becoming increasingly concerned about the aftereffects of the disease itself and of the various treatments. Both the physical and emotional effects of recovery from cancer have been the subjects of recent stud-

Like Ted Kennedy, Jr., now 26, and his fellow basketball player, many survivors of childhood cancer are living to young adulthood. Studies are focusing on how the disease affects their physical and psychological development.

Ken Regan—Camera 5

ies. It is now known, for example, that treatment of brain tumors by means of irradiation adversely affects intellectual development. Moreover, despite efforts to keep the radiation dosage to an irreducible minimum, treatment may cause permanent and irreversible brain damage.

At St. Jude Children's Research Hospital in Memphis, Tenn., 269 adolescents and young adults whose cancer had been diagnosed ten or more years previously were recently evaluated as to their overall sense of well-being; the physicians found it reassuring that in this respect, at least, 90% were rated equivalent to their peers. Follow-up studies then looked at several more specific psychological aftereffects of cancer and its treatment, such as severe behavioral problems or deficient social skills. When the results of the study were analyzed, it was evident that compared with the general population, children who survive cancer have three to four times the deficits in "social competence" (*e.g.,* difficulty getting along with other youngsters in school) and behavioral abnormalities. Interestingly, the study found that impairments in physical appearance as a result of the disease did not increase a youngster's risk of psychological disturbance. The researchers concluded that cancer centers should assess youthful survivors annually and work closely with the children's private physicians when adjustment or other problems are found.

In a similar study, conducted at the Children's Hospital of Philadelphia, extensive analyses of 200 young cancer survivors also found a large percentage (40%) with severe disabilities, including cosmetic problems, growth retardation, and the need for special education. At the August 1988 meeting of the American Psychological Association, psychologists presented data showing that children who survived cancer were more socially isolated and withdrawn than their peers who had never been seriously ill. Most developmental problems were attributed to radiation therapy, but some were associated with chemotherapy and disfiguring surgery. In addition to facing some psychological and social problems as a result of their disease, young cancer survivors are believed to be at higher risk than the general population for developing other cancers later in life.

The concern aroused by these findings is likely to lead to the development of programs in which the long-term outcome for the patient is considered during the initial therapy. Such plans might include not only special techniques to contain radiation within the malignant tissue but also measures such as replacement of amputated limbs with prostheses made from allografts (grafts made of human tissue) rather than from metal or plastic. Supplemental schooling and, where necessary, counseling to assist with adjustment after treatment would be integral parts of such a program.

—*Jean D. Lockhart, M.D.*

Special Report

Compensation for Medical Mishaps: Systems That Work in Sweden and Finland

by Diana Brahams, Barrister-at-Law

In Great Britain and the United States, medical malpractice suits are the only avenue for claiming compensation for injuries arising from medical mishaps. The last decade has seen the situation reach crisis levels. Physicians are increasingly having to practice defensive medicine—sharply limiting their practices to avoid high-risk patients who pose an increased threat of lawsuits. Not only are costs of medical care increasing but access to quality care in a widening variety of clinical situations is becoming blocked; pharmaceutical companies have also been forced to limit their areas of activity to reduce their risk of being sued.

In Sweden and Finland alternatives to negligence litigation for injurious medical and drug treatments have been developed and appear to be working successfully. Although both countries have relatively small populations and strong welfare structures, there are many reasons to believe that their alternative solutions could provide a model for the rest of the world to adopt and follow.

Innovative solutions in Sweden and Finland

In Sweden a patient treatment injury insurance scheme was introduced in 1975 and a drug insurance scheme in 1978. Both schemes are "voluntary" (i.e., not creatures of legislation). However, the pharmaceutical industry set up a scheme only after the government threatened positive intervention if it did not do so. The schemes offer an alternative to adversarial litigation through the courts, via insurance, as a means for patients to obtain compensation for personal injury.

Neighboring Finland watched with interest (and then with envy) to see how the Swedish schemes would work in practice. It was soon clear that they were a success and a vast improvement on litigation, which divided patients from doctors, was slow and costly, and offered patients little expectation of success. In 1978 the Finnish Medical Association petitioned the government for changes that would be along Swedish lines. A committee of inquiry was then set up to look at the alternatives, with a view to amending the existing tort system (in which a civil action is brought for an alleged wrongful act). In practice, however, reform of Finland's patient injury compensation system began in the small private health care sector, and in 1983 a voluntary insurance plan was successfully introduced. In 1984 a voluntary drug injury insurance program modeled very closely on that already operating in Sweden was set up.

Following an unsuccessful attempt to improve the workings of the tort system by the creation of an expert panel that could investigate and quantify medical negligence claims, the Finnish government decided to legislate; in May 1987 a statutory personal injury insurance system that covered all medical treatment failures went into effect. The enabling Patient Injury Act also took the radical step of removing the need for proof of negligence for medical injuries from the substantive law as a whole.

In Sweden, by contrast, the original law requiring proof of negligence remains intact, with the insurance schemes that eliminate the need for proof of negligence operating alongside. Thus, any claimant suing through the courts in Sweden must, if liability is not admitted by the defendant, first prove that the treatment was negligent and then prove that that negligence caused him or her (the claimant) injury. In Finland, however, the plaintiff would not have to prove negligence either in the courts or under the insurance scheme; as of early 1989 had there been no court cases brought in Finland since the scheme was introduced and the law changed in May 1987. This is hardly surprising since the damages payable under the Patient Injury Act would be the same; further, the courts' process would be comparatively slow and costly, whereas a claim made under the act would be promptly dealt with and cost no more than a token fee.

Limit on claims

Both the Swedish and Finnish drug injury compensation plans are subject to caps on claims for any individual in one year and have a total maximum amount that can be paid out overall. Further, in Sweden there are also caps imposed on awards that may be paid under the patient injury insurance and an overall limit for the year. In practice, claimants have been awarded the full rate of damages that would have been payable under a court award. In over 13 years some five cases in Sweden have been fought in court, but only one, in 1987—*Mpanda* v. *Uppsala County Council*—succeeded. This case was brought by foreigners whose son had been injured in a skiing accident. Liability was admitted for a cerebral hemorrhage suffered by the patient, but the plaintiff's parents chose not to accept compensation

398

under the insurance scheme and brought an action through the courts against the county council, seeking higher damages for private nursing care. An award to cover annual costs of nursing care was granted by the court because it appeared to offer the patient a better way of life. Capitalized, the sum ultimately payable could have amounted to as much as $6,840,000. However, the patient died after only one year, so only one annual payment was made. In this particular case, if a lump-sum award had been the rule, as it is in Britain and the U.S., the defendants would have had to provide a massive capital payment that would have given the patient's family an enormous windfall. In the U.S. in 1987, 62 medical malpractice suits reaped awards over $1 million. Such windfalls are considered unreasonable and unjustified.

In Finland and Sweden the treatment injury and drug insurance schemes operate against the background of a welfare state with good, but not total, social provisions that are, in turn, funded by high taxation. Most medical care is provided by the state, although more than half of both nations' dentists are private. In both countries the medical insurance schemes were introduced after national no-fault traffic and work accident insurance schemes had been established. Traffic, work, and medical treatment are all regarded as "endangering activities" that can and should be insured against rather than litigated through the courts.

Increase in claimants

Although the Finnish insurance schemes for medical treatment and drug-caused injuries have been operating for only a relatively short time, it is already clear that the number of patients claiming and receiving compensation each year has greatly increased. Before 1987 only a handful of people made claims and were compensated, but now in Finland (which has a population of 4.9 million), the rate of claims is about 40 per 1,000.

In Sweden (with a population of about 8.4 million), the patient injury insurance claims rates are about 60 per 1,000. In 1974, the last year before the scheme was started, only ten people in Sweden received compensation through litigation. Since then (as of January 1989), the insurance schemes had jointly handled some 60,000 claims. In 1987 Carl Oldertz, vice-president of Skandia Insurance, reported to the VII World Congress on Medicine and the Law in Ghent, Belgium, that as of 1986, under the Swedish patient insurance scheme, 48,167 injuries had been reported (since 1975). Of those, 19,959 were rejected. Among those compensated, 20,066 concerned health care provided by county councils; 7,792 concerned care rendered by private dentists; 129 concerned private doctors' care; 64 concerned care given under company health schemes; and 31 concerned care in private hospitals or nursing homes. Under the pharmaceutical insurance

scheme (from July 1975 to December 1986), 1,900 cases were reported; 1,050 (55%) were rejected. Of those cases, 190 were judged "too minor"; in 320 cases the patient's condition was judged "too serious"; and 17 cases were referred to the patient insurance scheme. The average amount paid in drug-related cases was $8,550.

In the U.K. (population 57 million), the claim rate is about 10 per 1,000, even after allowing for a tenfold increase in medical negligence claims during the last ten years. The Finnish and Swedish experiences thus suggest that there is a large as yet unsatisfied group of patients in any litigation-based system who would claim and be eligible for compensation if a no-fault scheme were introduced.

Funding the schemes

In Sweden and Finland the systems for compensation for medical and drug-related injuries are largely funded by contributions worked out on a per capita basis and paid for by the local medical councils that provide state health care. The professionals and hospitals working in the private sector belong to the same scheme but pay individual premiums that are calculated annually.

The drug industry funds the pharmaceutical insurance programs with payments based on a tiny percentage (0.37%) of the individual manufacturer or importer's gross turnover. Patients injured by contaminated blood products—namely, those who have contracted hepatitis B or AIDS or have become HIV positive—have been compensated by the drug insurance provision. Further, there is no "state of the art" defense in operation; that is, if an adverse result was unforeseeable because of limitations of medical and scientific knowledge at the time, compensation may still be paid. Unexpected and unknown side effects that occur from taking either new or well-established drugs thus will be compensated if an adverse reaction is "unreasonably" severe in relation to the underlying condition being treated. In Great Britain, by contrast, a "state of the art" defense remains an integral part of negligence claims. Thus, competence can be judged only against knowledge available at the time.

Eligibility for compensation

In Sweden to qualify for compensation under the patient injury insurance, the claimant would have to be rendered unfit for work for at least 30 days (in Finland 15 days). Both countries require 15 days off work for eligibility under the drug schemes. Lasting or irreversible impairment; scarring; or disability, death, or loss of earnings over a certain monetary amount will also qualify for compensation. Payments are made for loss of amenities, pain and suffering, and necessary equipment or special housing requirements (e.g., wheelchairs, hoists, or adaptations fitted to a patient's car or premises). Payments for private nursing care are not accepted except in cases where suitable nursing care is not provided by the state sector. Any payment for loss of earnings must take into account other sources of a claimant's income and benefits. Furthermore, no lump sums are payable for loss of earnings; income supplements would be payable monthly or weekly, calculated on an annual basis according to changing requirements. This obviates the possibility of windfalls and shortfalls, which are the norm with lump-sum awards.

What injuries are compensated?

Compensation for injuries arising from medical failure are not paid in cases where the patient's disability was caused by the inevitable deterioration or natural progression of an underlying disease or condition or if a patient's physical condition was a cause of the problem. Nor will compensation be paid if a medically indicated treatment was correctly given, even though an alternative method (e.g., cesarean section instead of a vaginal delivery) might have avoided the injury. However, where the patient's anatomy was unusual (e.g., he had a displaced nerve) and, with the benefit of hindsight, the injury could have been avoided, compensation will be paid. Prescription of an inappropriate drug or quantity of drug that causes injury will be compensated. However, if the drug was correctly prescribed and given, and injury occurs, any claim would have to be made through the drug insurance scheme.

Other exclusions are for injuries that follow inherently hazardous but essential life-saving treatments. A failure to diagnose or to treat a condition appropriately, however, is compensable, as is an injury caused by a diagnostic procedure that later was proved to be inappropriate and unnecessary. For example, this might occur where a patient underwent a mediastinoscopy (i.e., a surgical incision into the mediastinum—the space in the chest between the pleural sacs of the lungs) with the faint possibility of discovering Hodgkin's disease, but later it was found that the patient had tuberculosis, which had been strongly indicated from her symptoms and history. A negligence case based on this particular set of circumstances, in fact, failed in an English court because the doctor's conduct was considered proper by a responsible body of medical opinion.

Infection injuries that arise in a "clean" part of the body may be compensated in certain circumstances but never when they emanate from, say, an infected wound (sepsis) or an inherently unclean area such as the bowel.

As of early 1989 in Sweden, there had been 26 payments made in respect of brain-damaged babies following the birth process—about two per year. Finland had not yet paid out on this basis and was apparently reluctant to do so.

Swedish law does not recognize payment for psychological injury unconnected with physical injury, but Finland is prepared to compensate in serious cases. Thus, in Sweden patients who remained "awake and aware" during anesthesia would not be compensated. (Cases have been reported in which patients have been conscious enough to hear conversations during operations; this might occur with light anesthesia. They may hear things said by the surgical team that are upsetting to them and that may even influence their postsurgical outlook and recovery.) Awards are not granted—first because the initial "hurt" is considered fleeting and second because the ensuing injury complained of is psychological and not physically enduring.

By the end of April 1988, Finland had amassed the details of 852 rejected cases under the Patient Injury Act and 66 rejected cases under the pharmaceutical injury scheme (see Tables, below).

Levels of compensation

In Finland there are no caps imposed on the patient injury insurance; however, in practice, levels of payments made for loss of amenities and for pain and suffering are lower than in Sweden. Payments in both countries are considerably lower than in Britain. For example, the maximum damages payable in 1988 in Britain for pain and suffering and for loss of amenities and so forth was $136,800; in Sweden a maximum equivalent of $68,400; and in Finland $51,300. Social benefits through the welfare system in Sweden ensure that 90% of lost earnings are refunded up to a maximum of $29,070 per annum. In Britain social security benefits are very much lower, so that if a patient injury scheme were enacted, unless the claimant had made private arrangements, the gap that would have to be

Claims rejected under Finland's Patient Injury Act*	
reason	number (%)
injury not associated with treatment and not an infection or accidental injury	178 (21)
injury too minor (as defined)	146 (17)
accident, but not connected with treatment or examination	144 (17)
consequence of necessary risk-taking	124 (14)
unavoidable complication of justifiable treatment	82 (10)
injury happened before act came into force	70 (8)
other	108 (13)

*May 1, 1987–April 30, 1988

Claims rejected under Finnish drugs scheme (of a total 119 claims in 1987)	
reason	number (%)
not a drug injury	29 (44)
injury a reasonably acceptable one	17 (26)
minor injury	7 (11)
other	13 (20)

*From Diana Brahams, "No Fault Compensation Finnish Style," The Lancet, vol. II, no. 8613 (Sept. 24, 1988), pp. 733–736

filled by lost earnings would be much greater and would add greatly to the cost of running a compensation scheme.

No-fault: a misnomer

In the Swedish and Finnish patient treatment injury insurance schemes, while proof of negligence is not required, the term no-fault insurance is something of a misnomer. It is the establishment of an objective fault or error in the patient's treatment (perhaps because the outcome is unexpectedly poor) that is likely to provide the key to compensation for most claimants. However, many clinical errors may and do occur without negligence on the part of the doctor, and in Sweden and Finland injuries caused as a consequence will be compensated (hence the term no-fault), whereas in the U.K. and the U.S. they will not be. (No-fault compensation is also awarded under New Zealand's system—if the patient's injury can be defined as an "accident.")

Advantages of insurance over litigation

Even the fear that a negligence claim may be in the offing is likely to polarize doctor-patient relations and may cause doctors to become evasive and defensive at a time when frankness and sympathy are most important to patients. A failure to provide a detailed explanation or apology can motivate patients into taking legal proceedings when often what they most want initially is an acknowledgement that something has gone wrong and a full inquiry or explanation (although few would refuse compensation if offered it as well).

In Sweden and Finland, as a part of the process of dealing with claims that qualify for consideration, whether or not compensation is awarded, patients are given copies of their doctors' notes with an explanation of what occurred. If it is hospital treatment that the patient is complaining of, the head of the department in question must add his or her comments as well. Serious unexpected medical mishaps are automatically referred to the chief physician of the health district for consideration and possible investigation.

The whole investigative and compensation process is conducted by a team of assessors, who also deal with traffic and employment injury claims. A panel of highly qualified and respected doctors is available for consultation, and a claimant's papers will be sent to an appropriate specialist for assessment concerning both liability and prognosis.

In both Sweden and Finland, the systems work efficiently and cost the patient no more than a very small token fee. Most patients will be given a decision within six months; if the decision favors the patient, he or she will have received the first payment in that same time frame. In Finland the patient can opt for a single check from the insurers, who then will be left to recoup any payments due from state and other benefit sources.

If the patient is dissatisfied with the outcome, either regarding liability or amount of compensation, he or she can appeal and ultimately go to arbitration. At this stage in Sweden some 25% of claimants choose to consult a lawyer for help in presenting their case.

In Sweden, which has had its patient insurance scheme for over 13 years and drug injury insurance for over 10, relationships between doctors and patients have allegedly improved. Swedish law requires a high degree of disclosure of records and notes kept by doctors and hospitals regarding the patient's condition and care. Many doctors believe that a patient who is better informed beforehand will have a more realistic expectation of outcome and be less embittered if the outcome of the treatment is disappointing.

Advocates of the advantages of the tort system argue that fear of negligence suits helps to maintain and improve practice standards. In fact, however, there is strong evidence to suggest that the tort system encourages defensive medical practices. The evidence is strong that no-fault insurance or compensation schemes are much more cost-effective, cutting out the expensive legal process and ensuring that a far higher percentage of premiums are paid to the patients and not diverted into lawyers' pockets.

Drawbacks of the no-fault approach

Although no-fault compensation insurance greatly increases the number of people who can file claims for injuries sustained and is far cheaper to operate than adversarial litigation, it retains some of the social injustices inherent in the negligence system. People who suffer from congenital disabilities or whose injuries are not compensable under the schemes, for example, still have equal needs that are not attended to. Obviously, where social welfare provision is good, the differential will be less than where social welfare is limited or nonexistent and a claim for damages is the only hope of support and provision of medical care and housing.

Further, compensation alone is not enough. It must be accompanied by good peer-monitoring procedures and an independent and readily accessible complaints and disciplinary procedure. (These are not necessarily guaranteed under insurance schemes.)

Whether or not a no-fault compensation system is adopted by those countries that are currently persevering with malpractice suits for medical injuries, the crisis in claim levels means that some kind of reform is needed. Obviously, litigation should be streamlined to reduce costs and delays and bogus claims, but action will have to be taken on the levels of damages payable. If an alternative system such as those in Sweden and Finland were introduced, the damages payable would have to be comparable to existing compensation awards, or the system would founder, with massive claims then appealed through the courts.

Skin Disorders

Dermatology, the medical specialty dealing with disorders of the skin, has been making rapid strides in the control of serious and significant skin diseases. Progressing from an armamentarium largely of creams and ointments, dermatologists have benefited from some of the same breakthroughs in pharmacology, molecular biology, and immunology that other medical specialties have. This progress is well illustrated in the management of psoriasis, a common skin condition affecting about 2.5 million people in the United States, and in the rapidly improving survival rates for patients with cutaneous melanoma.

Psoriasis

Psoriasis is one of the most common skin disorders to afflict the human race. In most populations the frequency is somewhere between 1 and 3%. Fortunately, most individuals are not severely affected. Psoriasis is characterized by raised, scaly patches of skin, commonly located on the elbows, knees, scalp, lower back, and buttocks. Sometimes the nails thicken, become pitted, and separate from the underlying skin. Many patients are socially embarrassed when the condition develops on visible areas. Psoriasis increases in some individuals at times of stress. In some people excessive alcohol intake can worsen the disorder. There are also certain medications that adversely affect the condition. These include drugs to treat malaria (chloroquine); lithium, used in the treatment of psychiatric conditions; and beta-adrenergic blocking drugs, used for high blood pressure, coronary artery disease, and migraine headaches.

Psoriasis appears to result from ill-defined genetic factors, and although a family history of psoriasis is common, the exact inheritance pattern is unknown. While the basic defect in psoriasis is also unknown, it appears that too many keratinocytes (epidermal cells from the outer layer of the skin) are being produced and that these cells do not mature and shed in a normal fashion.

For most individuals the presence of psoriasis is merely a nuisance; a minority complain of itch. However, for rare individuals the disorder may involve the entire skin surface, with the development of total body redness and scaling. When this occurs, problems with temperature regulation often result. These patients may require hospitalization in specialized skin units.

Psoriasis may completely disappear spontaneously. At other times it may worsen for no apparent reason. While there is no cure for psoriasis, there are many treatment options available. The simplest treatments involve the application of moisturizers to the areas of involvement and exposure of the skin to natural sunlight. Moisturizers plaster down the scales, make the thickened skin more flexible, may decrease the production of new skin cells, and help to make the skin more penetrable to the rays of natural sunlight or artificial ultraviolet light sources. Most patients with psoriasis improve during the summer. A small percentage, however—perhaps 10–15% of patients—find that the sun worsens their skin. The treatment of this group of patients may be especially challenging.

Topical treatments. The most common treatment employed for psoriasis is probably the application of topical cortisone (steroid) preparations of varying types and strengths. These are available in cream, ointment, and lotion form. Selection of a form depends on the area in which use is planned. Steroid products are rapidly effective in decreasing the thickness of the scales and the redness of affected areas. Use of topical steroids, while easy and well accepted by the majority of patients, is not without problems. Psoriasis often becomes resistant to topical steroids so that after several weeks of therapy they are no longer effective. In addition, response is rarely complete. Side effects from prolonged use are also a problem. These include thinning of the skin (where the medication has been applied), fixed and dilated blood vessels, stretch marks, and acne. Glaucoma has been reported from prolonged use of potent topical steroid preparations around the eye. Therefore, weak cortisone preparations are recommended for facial skin, and contact with the eyes should always be avoided. Topical steroids tend to be expensive and when applied to large surface areas, if they are of the potent variety, may cause reduction of the normal adrenal gland activity within the body. Steroid medications can be made much more effective by the placement of household plastic wrap for a few hours each day over the areas to which the topical medication has been applied. However, the use of the plastic wrap can lead to the development of a bacterial infection of skin (folliculitis). Plastic wrap also increases the rapidity with which the chronic side effects noted above may appear.

Topical tar products have been used for years and may be useful in individuals with relatively small numbers of involved patches. Response to these medications is usually relatively slow and is often associated with a temporary staining of the skin. The patient's clothing, too, may be stained by the tar treatment; thus, the willingness of patients to use tar-based preparations outside a hospital setting may consequently be reduced. The skin will return to its normal color after the tar treatment has been discontinued for several days. In Europe a non-staining, apparently effective tar preparation is being studied experimentally. If this compound proves safe and effective, it will likely be available in the U.S. within a few years.

Other topical measures may be of help. Sometimes ointments containing such mildly irritating chemicals as salicylic acid are used to help thin down the scales. New agents to reduce the thickness of the skin include ointments containing various acids, such as lactic acid, pyruvic acid, glycolic acid, and tartaric acid. Application of a cream form of urea, a chemical that appears in normal urine as a breakdown product of protein, to the skin surface also can reduce the thickness of the skin. In addition, ammonium lactate (Lac-Hydrin) has been shown to help reverse the abnormalities that occur in the outer layer of the epidermis.

Treatment with light. In patients who respond to the summer sun, sunlamp treatments with ultraviolet B (UVB) light—with a wavelength of 290–320 nanometers (a nanometer [nm] equals a billionth of a meter)—can be used under controlled situations. This indoor therapy is especially useful in the northern parts of the U.S., where only small amounts of natural sunlight are available in the winter. Care should be taken to protect the eyes and to increase the amount of exposure gradually to avoid burns on the skin. Both the duration of exposure and the distance of the body from the light bulbs must be carefully regulated. Artificial ultraviolet light therapy is best administered in a dermatologist's office or a hospital outpatient department, but home units are available and can be safely and successfully used by the patient once the principles of therapy have been learned.

For those patients who fail to respond adequately to regular sunlamp treatments, special treatments using longer wave ultraviolet A light (UVA)—having a wavelength of 320–400 nm—in combination with a photosensitizing drug may be successful. Patients are carefully exposed to the special ultraviolet lamps after ingesting psoralen (8-methoxypsoralen; Oxsoralen). This compound was originally discovered in plants growing along the Nile River. A similar chemical is found in the skin of some fruits, such as the lime. Psoralen must be taken under a physician's supervision, and special UVA-blocking sunglasses must be used during and after treatment to prevent cataracts. Short-term side effects include nausea and easy sunburn development. Experiments are ongoing in the U.S. with another form of psoralen, 5-methoxypsoralen (currently available in Europe), which may have fewer side effects. Chronic psoralen use increases the frequency of skin cancers and produces freckles in unusual locations (*e.g.,* buttocks).

Internal therapies. For patients with extensive psoriasis that has failed to respond adequately to the previously mentioned therapies, a variety of internal medications are available. Among these are drugs originally employed in cancer treatment that reduce the rate of production of cells in the epidermis (outer layer of skin). The most common of these is methotrexate (MTX), which can be taken weekly either in pill form or by injection. MTX must be used under a doctor's close supervision, and regular laboratory tests to monitor the status of the blood and the liver are needed. Some patients with psoriasis also have a disabling form of arthritis that is specific to psoriasis. MTX is also helpful in reducing these arthritic complaints. Patients who receive MTX require liver biopsy at regular intervals because of the potential for some of these patients to develop cirrhosis. Cirrhosis is much more common in individuals who continue to drink alcohol (which is toxic to the liver) while on MTX. This drug should not be used in patients unwilling to abstain from alcohol.

For patients with very severe psoriasis that has failed to respond to other treatments, chemically altered forms of vitamin A—retinoids—have been used. Two of these products, isotretinoin (Accutane) and etretinate (Tegison), have been beneficial in psoriasis. Both of these products seem to produce improvement by thinning the outer layer of the epidermis (stratum corneum) and by promoting improved maturation of the epidermal keratinocytes as they grow out toward the surface of the skin. Both products have major short- and long-term side effects. Etretinate lasts in the body for more than a year and can produce birth defects. Consequently, it cannot be used in women of childbearing potential who are unwilling to maintain contraception for an indefinite period after etretinate use. Accutane, which lasts in the body for about one month, also produces birth defects and is considerably less effective than etretinate. Accutane can be used in women of childbearing potential if an effective form of

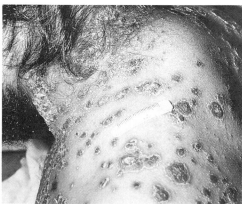
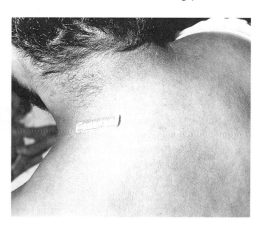

A patient's skin is shown before and after treatment with the drug etretinate, a vitamin A derivative that is often effective in cases of severe psoriasis that have been unresponsive to standard treatments.

Hoffmann-La Roche, Inc.

contraception is used before, during, and after treatment and if a negative pregnancy test is obtained prior to starting the drug. Other short-term side effects are dry skin, dryness and chapping of the lips, conjunctivitis, and hair loss.

Other retinoid side effects—elevation of blood fats (triglycerides primarily) and persistent diminished night vision—have occasionally occurred. The retinoids can be used in combination with the psoralen-ultraviolet light therapy and appear to enhance the rapidity of improvement. The retinoids should be prescribed only by physicians who have special knowledge in their use.

Another unique approach to treatment of severe, unresponsive psoriasis under present experimental evaluation involves the use of cyclosporine, a drug of fungal origin. Cyclosporine is a strong suppressant of the body's immune system and is used in patients with organ transplants to prevent rejection reactions. Fortuitously, it has been shown to improve psoriasis. Since cyclosporine has serious side effects (increased hair growth, high blood pressure, kidney toxicity), its usage is limited to those individuals for whom other forms of therapy have failed. (The most exciting aspect of the apparent beneficial effect of cyclosporine is the possibility that the immune system may be involved in psoriasis and that other, less toxic manipulations may be discovered in the future.)

Present and future prospects. Several new treatments are under investigation for patients with psoriasis. In the U.S. and Japan, creams containing vitamin D have been reported to be beneficial in experimental trials in patients with the mild patch form of psoriasis.

As factors that regulate epidermal growth are identified and their roles understood, more specific approaches will be developed. The ideal drug has not yet been discovered, and no form of therapy is, at present, curative. Treatment of psoriasis, therefore, will remain an individualized effort between doctor and patient, and at times both may be frustrated by slowness of progress or by relapses.

Support groups, such as the National Psoriasis Foundation, can be extremely helpful in providing reliable information on the disease and its treatment. Sharing of information and the support gained through the understanding that others with psoriasis are managing can be as beneficial as some of the therapeutic approaches described above.

Melanoma

Melanoma, the cancer that originates from the melanocytes (the cells in the epidermis responsible for pigmentation), has a bad reputation as the "black cancer." In Aleksandr Solzhenitsyn's *Cancer Ward,* one of the protagonists describes his melanoma as a "merciless bastard." Years ago these tumors were quite uncommon and nearly universally fatal. Over the past 40 years, there has been such a dramatic increase in

Anti-Cancer Council of Victoria, Australia

A poster speaks to sun-soaked Australians, two-thirds of whom are likely to develop some form of skin cancer from ultraviolet exposure. In Victoria the incidence of malignant melanoma has increased nearly 40% since 1982.

their number that melanoma is now one of the more common tumors to occur in the United States, with approximately 27,000 people developing it and 6,000 deaths resulting from it each year. In New Zealand melanoma is the most common cancer affecting the 20–39 age group. If melanoma rates continue to rise at the same rate as in the past, within a decade approximately one in every 100 Caucasians will develop melanoma at some time during his or her lifetime.

The good news is that there has been tremendous progress in the early detection of melanoma, resulting in greatly enhanced cure rates. In 1940 only 40% of patients diagnosed with melanoma were still alive five years later. The five-year survival rate for melanoma patients today is about 80%, and the majority of these patients can be considered cured of their disease. This makes melanoma one of the most curable of the serious cancers. Melanomas should be distinguished from the nonpigmented, rarely fatal common forms of skin cancer, namely, basal cell carcinoma and squamous cell carcinoma. These two types of cancer are responsible for about 500,000 new cases each year in the United States.

Dramatic increase. What is responsible for the startling rise in incidence of melanoma (over 700% increase) over the last 40 years? The major factor has been overexposure to the sun, particularly during sunbathing. Exposures early in life may be important in the later production of melanoma. Very interesting studies in which the melanoma rates have been compared in immigrants to such sunny countries as Australia, New Zealand, and Israel have shown that persons who are born in these countries or who migrate there before the age of ten have much higher melanoma rates than ethnically similar individuals who migrate there later in life. This observation suggests that individuals are more vulnerable to the effects of the sun early in life, or it may reflect the fact that youngsters have greater opportunity for sun exposure (particularly during long summer vacations).

Areas that are covered by clothing during sunbathing—e.g., the breast in women and the genital areas in men and women—are relatively infrequent sites for melanoma. The most frequent body sites for melanoma differ in men and women and relate to areas most often exposed to ultraviolet radiation during sunbathing. In men the most common area of occurrence is the back, followed by the chest and abdomen. In women the most common area is the lower leg from the knee to the ankle, followed by the back.

Who is affected? Melanoma is mainly a problem for Caucasians of light complexion. People with blue or grey eyes, blond or red hair, an inability to tan, and a tendency to sunburn or freckle are those most likely to develop melanoma. Conversely, Asians and American blacks develop the disease only about one-tenth as often as Caucasians. When melanoma does occur in dark-skinned people, it occurs on the lighter areas, such as palms, soles, and nail beds.

Melanoma appears to run in families. Some families seem to have a dominant gene for melanoma, with direct parent-to-child inheritance of the tendency to develop the cancer. In some of these families, a distinctive type of pigmented mole called an atypical mole, or dysplastic nevus, is present, which also appears to be inherited directly from parent to child. People with dysplastic nevi plus a family history of dysplastic nevi and melanoma (in two or more close blood relatives) run a 50% risk of developing melanoma by age 60. Those who have dysplastic nevi but little or no family history of the disease have only a 6% risk. Having 50 or more normal (typical) moles that are two millimeters in diameter or greater is also thought to be an important risk factor. Other factors that may be associated with increased risk of melanoma development are having a raised, pigmented mole (congenital nevus) at birth or taking certain drugs that suppress the body's immunity. A normally functioning immune system is thought to be necessary for the destruction of newly forming cancer cells.

Recognizing melanoma. The importance of early recognition of melanoma is severalfold. First, the tumor has distinct characteristics, which in most individuals allow for recognition at a time when surgical excision is curative. Second, since the tumor appears on the surface of the skin, any individual who is aware of the telltale features has the opportunity to suspect the disease or to make the preliminary diagnosis (any mole that changes in size, shape, or color or that

If melanoma is detected and treated in time, it can almost always be cured. Individuals should check themselves regularly and be alert to signs on the skin such as new moles or moles that change in size, shape, or color.

causes itching or burning should be suspected). Third, unlike many of the other forms of cancer, which disproportionately affect older individuals, melanomas are relatively common in young individuals—occurring in those as young as age 15. (The average age of patients developing melanoma is about 40.)

How are melanomas recognized? Most are larger than the size of the fingernail of the fifth finger, have irregular borders, vary in color, and vary in the distribution of the pigmented speckles. Melanomas are usually not just brown or tan but have other color hues as well. The irregular borders and variation in color and pigment pattern are produced in part by disordered growth of the tumor cells interacting with the patient's immune system, which acts to partially retard tumor growth and to cause regression of the tumor. Most melanomas can grow superficially on the surface of the skin for a number of months or years before penetrating deeply into the skin. It is during this period of superficial growth that melanoma can be recognized and cured surgically.

The recognition of dysplastic nevi is an important skill for all health care workers to develop. It has been estimated that perhaps 7% of the Caucasians in the

United States have these moles. This translates into at least ten million people in the U.S. alone. Atypical moles are often seen when patients have large numbers of moles. Individuals with dysplastic moles may have only a few or as many as 200 of them. These moles tend to occur on the trunk (as do normal moles), or large numbers may occur on just the legs. Sometimes dysplastic nevi occur in both locations. Less frequently they occur on such areas as the scalp, buttocks, and female breasts, where ordinary nevi (moles) are relatively uncommon. Dysplastic nevi are distinguishable from ordinary nevi in that they are frequently larger than the head of a pencil eraser, while most ordinary nevi are smaller. Dysplastic nevi have fuzzy, less distinct borders than normal moles, and their patterns of pigmentation are more irregular and their coloration more varied. Although an individual may be able to detect the presence of a suspicious pigmented spot, because of potential confusion with normal pigmented spots due to other causes, the final evaluation should be made by a physician.

Surgical treatment. In recent years removal of early melanomas has been done in the physician's office or in outpatient operating rooms under local anesthesia, obviating the need for hospitalization. The pigmented area is removed along with at least one centimeter (four-tenths of an inch) of normal-appearing skin surrounding the lesion. More advanced melanomas are removed with somewhat wider margins of normal skin.

The treatment for recurrent (metastatic) melanoma depends on the location of recurrence. If the recurrence is in the area near the initial surgical site, additional local surgery to remove this area is possible. If it is determined that the cancer has spread through the lymph channels to the local lymph glands, surgery can still be performed with a high degree of success. However, when melanoma has spread via the bloodstream to internal organs, the treatment is much more problematic. Various strategies have been developed to treat this situation. Surgical removal may be possible if a single tumor is found in one internal organ. More commonly, however, several tumor deposits are found, in which case the most common form of treatment involves the use of one or several drugs (chemotherapy) that kill cancer cells. Unfortunately, only about one patient in five responds to this treatment, and most of these relapse after a short time.

Immunotherapies for metastatic melanoma. Because melanoma occasionally disappears on its own, attempts have been made to help the patient's immune system fight the metastatic tumor. Various natural body products called biological response modifiers have been used for this purpose. Among these are the interferons and the interleukins. Both substances occur naturally within the body in response to inflammation and appear to help the body fight infection and tumors. The best results from interferon therapy have been comparable to chemotherapy. The interleukins, which showed more promising results when first introduced in an experimental trial at the U.S. National Cancer Institute a few years ago (one of the first patients in the study had complete disappearance of metastatic melanoma), have been disappointing when larger numbers of patients have been treated. Complete responses have been few. In addition, interleukin treatment is not without hazard; many patients experience weight gain and difficulty with fluid regulation.

A newer form of immunotherapy is tumor-infiltrating lymphocyte (TIL) therapy. In this approach the lymphocytes (one of the types of white blood cells) that are found within the tumor are grown in the laboratory following surgical removal of the tumor. Large numbers of these special lymphocytes are then returned to the patient with additional immunologic stimulation from interleukin-2. In several patients also treated at the National Cancer Institute, significant tumor response has been seen. The proportion of patients who responded was higher with this treatment than with other immunotherapies. At present, this approach is highly experimental and available only at a few centers around the United States.

Treatments utilizing pigment cells. Other potential treatments exploit the unique features of pigment cells. One such feature is the existence of a chemical system in the pigment cell for the manufacture of the dark brown pigment, melanin. This melanin-production pathway employs enzymes that do not occur in other cells of the body. When drugs are given that are selectively taken into the pigment cell and, when altered by the melanin-producing enzymes, become selectively toxic to the cell, tumor cells can be destroyed. The drug levodopa, used to treat the neurological condition Parkinson's disease, is one such agent; it becomes toxic to the pigment cells when in high concentration but is relatively nontoxic to other types of cells. Another approach involves attacking the outer cell membrane of the pigment cells, which has unique antigenic sites. It is possible by biotechnological methods to develop specific antibodies that attach to the surface of the cancer cell and carry with them a toxin or a radioactive compound. Such systems appear to work in experiments with cultured tumor cells but to date have not been very effective in people.

Present and future prospects. While it is hoped that new, rational, and more effective modes of therapy will be developed, emphasis should be placed on the prevention and early detection of melanoma by decreasing sun exposure and by screening of individuals at increased risk. Melanoma is a disease in which there is great promise for good outcome if it is caught early. There is also optimism that the future will bring new treatments for the decreasing fraction of patients with advanced disease—perhaps in five to ten years' time.

—*Arthur J. Sober, M.D.*

Sports Medicine

On Sept. 24, 1988, a warm, sunny Saturday in Seoul, South Korea, Ben Johnson accelerated out of the blocks in the Olympic 100-m track event and ran into history 9.79 seconds later. Unfortunately for Johnson, his historic mark was not what he intended. Instead of being remembered as the fastest man alive—winner of a 1988 Olympic gold medal and victor over Carl Lewis and a host of the finest sprinters in the world—he will always be known as the athlete whose downfall exposed the public to the widespread use of anabolic steroids by athletes. Indeed, the crisis of steroid abuse—not only by Olympic athletes but by all ranks of athletes—is the subject that has dominated sports medicine since the events in Seoul.

Scandal at Seoul and the aftermath

Johnson was still savoring his victory, as well as looking forward to cashing in on some $15 million in product-advertising endorsements waiting for him at home in Canada, while his fate was being sealed by a gas chromatograph and mass spectrometer in the International Olympic Committee (IOC)-approved laboratory in Seoul. After the first positive result on a specimen of Johnson's urine, drug testers at the laboratory opened the backup urine sample and again found stanozolol, a water-based oral anabolic steroid sold under the trade name of Winstrol.

It was the second embarrassment of the Olympic season for Canada, which, ironically, had been in the forefront of the movement to get international agreement on drug testing and sanctions. Three Canadian weight lifters also tested positive for steroids and were taken off the team the day they were scheduled to fly to Seoul. After Johnson left Seoul in disgrace, Canada announced it would convene a judicial inquiry to examine the problem of drug use in sports.

The United States, too, had its own problems in the most recent Olympic season. Swimmer Angel Myers was removed from the U.S. Olympic team before it left for Seoul after a positive drug test for nandrolone, another anabolic steroid. Like Johnson, Myers denied drug use, which, according to directors of several of the major IOC-approved laboratories, is a common reaction to a positive finding. Even after the Olympics ended, rumors about the alleged drug use of other U.S. athletes persisted and marred their accomplishments. Unlike Canada, the United States does not subsidize its national athletes and, therefore, has less control. Control of U.S. athletes rests with the individual national sports governing bodies.

The Canadian inquiry began in November 1988. What the long-term impact of the drug scandal will be is not yet clear. If it marks the beginning of realism about the use of performance-enhancing chemicals by athletes, the outcome could be positive. Ontario Associate Chief Justice Charles Dubin, who presided at the hearing, said, "I think it is important to consider whether there are pressures being placed on our young men and women athletes to tempt them to cheat. Have we lost track of what athletic competition is all about?"

Although a Canadian-style judicial inquiry would not be possible in the United States, there is so much evidence that anabolic steroids are being widely used—even by some youngsters—that the National Institute on Drug Abuse (NIDA) held a technical review meeting on steroids in Rockville, Md., in March 1989. This marked the first time the government agency had examined drugs that enhance athletic performance. "The use of anabolic steroids is too consistent with societal values—bigger, stronger, taller, faster—to be eradicated," said James E. Wright in his summation remarks at the NIDA meeting. Wright, an expert on anabolic steroids, is the author of two books on the

Ben Johnson's glory in Seoul, South Korea, was short-lived. In June 1989 he testified before a Canadian commission that since 1981 he had knowingly used banned anabolic steroids in competition.

(Left) Duomo; (right) Canapress Photo

Swimmer Angel Myers was removed from the U.S. Olympic team before it left for the 1988 Summer Games in Seoul because she tested positive for the anabolic steroid nandrolone. Myers denied using the drug and claimed that it was her birth control pills that had been mistaken for the illegal substance.

subject and is the research director of the Adirondack Mountain Foundation, Jay, N.Y. He noted that there is evidence that some of the derangements of body chemistry that occur with steroids are reversible but warned, "These drugs are too powerful not to have some damaging effects associated with long-term use, and it is imprudent to assume that athletes are immune to the deleterious effects that are seen with animals."

Drugs of champions: discovery and evolution

Anabolic steroids are powerful. Although athletes may think of them as wonder drugs, they are male sex hormones—androgens. Man has always longed for something magical and wonderful that would make him another Atlas, Hercules, or Superman. Over the years, many observers suspected that the development of male characteristics—including strength and power—was somehow regulated by the testes. Some tried to prove it. In 1771 John Hunter, from Scotland, transplanted testes from a cock to a hen and confirmed his theory that the hen would become more like a cock. It was not until the 1930s that researchers were finally able to demonstrate that testosterone is the masculinizing hormone that occurs naturally in the body.

Anabolic steroids are not simply artificial testosterone. The term anabolic means "tissue building," and "steroid" is the chemical term for a complex molecule that has a specific pattern of carbon atoms. Each of the different formulations of anabolic steroids has its own chemical pattern. Because plain testosterone would be broken down and inactivated by the liver, chemical modifications had to be made to allow the hormones to remain biologically active. However, all anabolic steroids are derivatives of male sex hormones, and their virilizing effects cannot be entirely separated from the tissue-building effects.

After the steroids were synthesized, the European researcher Ove Boje speculated in 1939 that testosterone might enhance sports performance. Less than a decade later, the Soviets were reportedly using them for that purpose. Shortly thereafter, U.S. weight lifters were given the drugs as part of a study to test their effects. Many weight lifters, however, were so impressed with anabolic steroids that they ignored recommended doses and took them in large quantities.

Anabolic steroid use spread rapidly as athletes who were not using them saw the impressive gains in strength and power made by athletes who were. As early as 1956, Czechoslovak Olympic discus gold medalist Olga Fikotova said, "There is no way in the world a woman nowadays, in the throwing events—at least the shot put and the discus—I'm not sure about the javelin—can break the record unless she is on steroids. These awful drugs have changed the complexion of track and field."

Steroids and the competitive edge

Although the publicity since the Olympics in Seoul has made the public more aware of steroids, there are many widely held misconceptions about the effects of the drugs, which is not surprising, given the fact that some doctors still disagree about whether steroids work at all to enhance athletic performance.

Steroids can be taken by injection or orally, but once inside the body, they mimic testosterone. The body has specific receptors for testosterone that allow the drug to exert its effect. If the receptors are already saturated with testosterone, no further effect will occur until more receptors become available. Under normal conditions the steroid receptors in a man's muscle tissue are saturated by his own testosterone production. In order to get increased bulk or strength, he must develop additional receptors, and he does this by weight training. Weight training forces the muscle tissue to become larger, and thus more receptors are available. Because no muscle building will occur unless more receptors are available, anabolic steroids can be effective in increasing bulk and strength only when athletes have an adequate diet and are exercising. At the Canadian hearings Ben Johnson was described as an almost scrawny lad when he began training at age 15. Anyone who saw pictures of Johnson's heavily developed and bulging muscles at Seoul could see that in a few years his physical development had advanced remarkably.

Women and young boys normally have only low concentrations of testosterone in their bodies—mainly produced by the adrenal glands. When boys reach puberty, their testes begin producing testosterone and masculine characteristics emerge—a deeper voice, facial and body hair, enlargement of the genitals, sexual maturation, and the development of a stronger, more adult physique. When people refer to the "raging hormones" of male adolescents, testosterone is the main hormone they mean.

Women and prepubertal boys do not have saturated testosterone receptors, so they get more immediate—and often very striking—changes in muscles by taking anabolic steroids. In female users other striking changes are caused by the virilizing properties of male sex hormones—for example, facial hair develops, their voices deepen, and their genitals become enlarged. Prepubertal boys may get bodies that look more like those of adult men. However, there is a danger that the epiphyses—growth plates on the ends of their bones—will close prematurely, causing them to be shorter than they might otherwise have been. There is also a concern that flooding a young adolescent male's body with a sex hormone from the outside may adversely affect the normal progress of adolescence.

Muscles alone do not ensure enhanced performance. The current consensus of sports medicine experts, however, is that because steroid-using athletes appear to have a greater proportion of lean muscle in their bodies even when the actual amount of weight gained is small, most have impressive gains in strength.

Today not only Olympic athletes but younger athletes and nonathletes appear to be using steroids. Charles Yesalis, a professor of epidemiology at Pennsylvania State University, presented data at the NIDA meeting indicating that 7% of the respondents in a survey of male high school seniors had tried anabolic steroids. The startling fact was that almost 40% of the steroid users did not participate in any school-sponsored sports. Although the prevalence of anabolic steroid use is unknown, it is apparent that the non-athlete-user group is increasing and that it includes police officers, fire fighters, and young persons in the armed services. Moreover, many athletes who are steroid users like the drug effects so much that they would not want to stop even if it could be guaranteed that their competitors in sports competitions were not using them.

Assessing the hazards

The adverse health effects of anabolic steroids vary; moreover, it must be said that some men have used them for years with no apparent ill effects. The perceived benefits that steroid users say they gain are enhanced physical appearance and capacity to train at high levels; increased strength; enhanced libido, mood, and self-confidence; and feelings of euphoria and well-being.

One scientist at the NIDA meeting commented that the self-confidence is actually more a lack of restraint.

© 1988 Locher; reprinted by permission of Tribune Media Services

Some scary tales involving lack of restraint by steroid users have surfaced within the past year. A psychiatrist reported the case of a steroid-using motorist who became so incensed when the driver in front of him neglected to stop his flashing turn signal that he forced the vehicle off the road, ripped a road sign from the ground, and smashed the window of the offending driver. Many steroid experts have said that more study needs to be given to the psychiatric effects of steroids and that unrestrained aggression may lead the list of potential harmful effects.

Anabolic steroids may cause acne and baldness, which are among the effects considered mild. More seriously, they can impair glucose tolerance and cause changes in blood fats so that there is a decrease in high-density lipoprotein (HDL) cholesterol—the "good" cholesterol—and an increase in unhealthy low-density lipoprotein (LDL) cholesterol. Sperm production declines and may cease altogether, and testicles may become smaller. Steroids have been linked to liver problems, including tumors; there are three case reports in the medical literature of liver tumors in athletes. There are two known reports of strokes in athletes who were taking steroids (both survived) and one of a heart attack in a young man with no other risk factors. Participants at the NIDA conference noted the need for more case reports and well-designed research studies to replace the anecdotal information about the dangers of steroid use.

Only about half of the early scientific studies looking into whether anabolic steroids actually enhance athletic performance established any performance benefit, leading many doctors to conclude that steroids did not work. It is now known that there were flaws in many of the study designs. When doctors told athletes that steroids did not work, athletes simply stopped listening to them. This led to the current situation in which an unknown number of young men and women are taking powerful drugs that cause significant derangements of body chemistry—which may not be entirely reversible—with no medical monitoring or supervision.

Many of the more extreme effects may never be fully understood because scientific studies cannot be undertaken; doctors cannot ethically justify giving athletes the huge doses of steroids they take on their own. Most experts believe that dosages have increased over the years and that many users take far more than they need to get an effect, thereby increasing their health risk.

Curbing the black market

Steroids are easily obtainable, although in the U.S. there is presently a move to make them a controlled substance, which would give the government more control over manufacturers. It also would make it easier to monitor the prescribing practices of physicians. It is estimated that about 20% of steroids used for athletic-performance enhancement are prescribed by doctors, and the other 80% come from the black market. The black market supply consists of steroids smuggled into the country from Mexico and Europe, drugs that are obtained surreptitiously through U.S. pharmaceutical outlets, and "homemade" drugs—which have no guarantee of purity or standards of quality assurance. There may be as many as 500 black market distributors handling the U.S. traffic in steroids.

The government moved to address the problem of steroid trafficking by creating an interagency task force in May 1986. Since then the Food and Drug Administration, the Justice Department, and the Federal Bureau of Investigation have been cooperating to investigate and prosecute cases of illegal use, possession, sale, or distribution of the drugs. There have been arrests and convictions in several cases. A Florida man who was indicted on 21 felony counts of violating the federal Food, Drug, and Cosmetic Act had a black market mail-order steroid business that netted him about $400,000 in less than two years. Two South Carolina companies and five people were indicted for manufacturing and distributing more than a million dollars' worth of steroids that were labeled and distributed under the names of nonexistent European companies.

The interagency task force also has warned pharmaceutical houses to be cautious in filling orders for steroids and has asked to be notified of large or frequent orders. Some experts believe that the voluntary cooperation of manufacturers has helped reduce the quantity of steroids from U.S. sources on the black market.

Testing athletes for drugs: state of the art

If steroid users cannot be dissuaded, can they be detected? Drug testing has become a fact of life in sports competition, and the IOC hopes to achieve international agreement on the testing of athletes before the 1992 Games in France and Spain. While most experts feel that random, unannounced drug testing is the only way to curb steroid use, many athletes object to urinating in the presence of an observer. Donald H. Catlin, director of the Paul Ziffren Olympic Analytical Laboratory at the University of California at Los Angeles and a member of the IOC Medical Commission, has pointed out that he cannot justify testing samples that might have come "from anywhere." When there is any lapse in vigilance in carrying out tests, it has been common for athletes to supply urine samples that are not their own. Indeed, such substitutions were noted to have reached scandalous proportions when weight lifters testified at the Canadian hearings that they had been caught by an unexpected drug check and that their national trainer had provided four of them with drug-free urine samples, which they injected into their own bladders in an attempt to pass the test. In addition, at a training camp the athletes attended early in the summer of 1988, they received advice on how to use masking agents to avoid detection.

The IOC began drug testing at the 1968 Winter Games in Grenoble, France, but the first testing for anabolic steroids was not until the 1976 Summer Games in Montreal. Even then, the testing technology lacked the sophistication it has today. Athletes began taking drug testing seriously after the 1983 Pan American Games in Caracas, Venezuela. With the gas chromatograph and mass spectrometer available, it quickly became obvious that the laboratories could tell reliably who was using drugs. Nineteen athletes (about 5% of the total, as opposed to 1% at the 1984 Olympic Games) were disqualified for using drugs at that event, and many more athletes withdrew from competition or purposely performed so poorly that they did not qualify for competition and thus were not subjected to testing.

Drug testing is an expensive, time-consuming procedure, but modern equipment is so sensitive it can detect one part per billion of a forbidden substance. Most performance-enhancing drugs are metabolized so extensively that laboratories do not look for the drug itself but for metabolic products, and there may be several metabolites for each drug. Although Angel Myers claimed that the laboratory had mistaken her birth control pills for nandrolone, that is unlikely because the number of specific metabolites that can be identified is now so vast.

Anabolic steroids are not the only drugs abused by athletes. A number of drugs are banned by the IOC because they can affect performance. The substances that are routinely tested for by urinalysis include anabolic steroids; corticosteroids, which can reduce fatigue and pain and increase aggressiveness; diuretics, which can reduce weight quickly and mask other drugs; stimulants, such as amphetamines, that

Banned by the International Olympics Committee						
	anabolic steroids	cortico-steroids*	diuretics	stimulants	narcotic analgesics	beta blockers	blood doping (reinjecting one's own red blood cells)
effects	increase muscle mass and strength	increase aggressiveness; reduce fatigue and pain	reduce weight quickly and mask other drugs†	increase alertness and delay fatigue	kill pain and induce feeling of calm	slow the heartbeat and steady body movements	enhances endurance
common sports	weight lifting, football, field events	most sports	weight lifting, boxing, wrestling	most sports, but counterproductive for shooting	shooting and others	archery and shooting	cross-country skiing, biking, long-distance running
testing method	urinalysis	urinalysis	urinalysis	urinalysis	urinalysis	urinalysis	no test available
minor complications	menstrual irregularity, breast shrinkage in women; testicular atrophy, irritability in men	retard healing or foster infections	dehydration; stomach or leg cramps; loss of sodium and potassium	restlessness and anxiety; accelerated heart rate and breathing	worsening of injury	cause asthma symptoms; decrease mental alertness; can lead to impotence	none documented; allergic reactions reported
severe reactions	heart and liver disease; sterility	pituitary- and adrenal-gland dysfunction, leading to glucose intolerance and kidney problems	irregular heartbeats that can lead to cardiac arrest; kidney damage	erratic heartbeats and severe high temperature; addictive	slowed breathing, stupor, or coma with overdose; addictive	heart rate severely slowed	none documented; infections with unsupervised injections

*use permitted as a local anti-inflammatory agent †other masking agents such as probenecid also banned

From a chart by Joe Lartola, *Time* Magazine, Oct. 10, 1988, p. 76; © 1988 Time Inc.

increase alertness and delay fatigue; narcotic analgesics, which can kill pain and induce a feeling of calm; and beta blockers, which slow the heartbeat and can help steady body movements. Blood doping—*i.e.,* reinjecting one's own red blood cells to enhance endurance—is also banned by the IOC, but there is not yet a test for detecting the practice.

If the equipment used since the early 1980s is so sensitive and Ben Johnson had been using steroids since 1981—passing drug test after drug test—what went wrong? The answer is that although the IOC-approved drug-testing laboratories are without peer, they cannot find what is not there. Anabolic steroids are used primarily as training drugs, whereas most testing is done at the time of competition. Athletes, coaches, and trainers have become very sophisticated about hiding the use of performance-enhancing drugs. They switched from the injected form, which is easier on the liver but is stored in body fat and released over a period of time, to the oral agents, which wash out of the system in three to six weeks. Athletes may have their urine tested at private laboratories in order to "fix" the washout times of various drugs. Professional sports contracts allow drug testing at specified times, usually the beginning of training camp. Almost anyone can pass that type of testing. The fact that 6% of National Football League players tested positive in 1988 for steroids indicates that the true incidence of use is very high. In Ben Johnson's case it may never be known whether there was a simple miscalculation about washout time or whether the drug-testing technology simply proved to be better than his advisers supposed. After Johnson claimed that someone had slipped steroids into his drink, the IOC took the somewhat unusual step of announcing that his steroid profile was *not* consistent with one-time use.

It does seem clear that in an atmosphere that promotes winning as the only thing of importance, athletes will continue to search for chemical performance aids. Whether drug-testing agreements will allow the drug testers to keep pace with the drug takers remains to be seen.

—*Virginia S. Cowart*

Veterinary Medicine

Prevention of disease has been an important focus of veterinary medicine, with much recent attention being given to overweight pets and the consequences of their obesity. In an effort to deal with this problem, nutritionists have developed diets that help fat animals reduce weight. Prevention of stress suffered by laboratory animals is also being studied, and recommendations have been made to improve their cages and reduce the noise of nearby equipment.

Two serious outbreaks of disease took place during the past year. Bovine spongiform encephalopathy affected cattle in Britain, and thousands of North Sea gray seals died after being infected by a virus of the same type that causes distemper in dogs.

Fat cats and droopy dogs
The overweight syndrome that causes such concern to so many people in the Western world is not confined to humans. Fat people tend to have fat pets, and obesity causes health problems in dogs and cats similar to those it encourages in their owners. An overweight pet is more likely to suffer from conditions affecting the joints and locomotion, heart and circulatory difficulties, and impaired reproductive potential and to be more prone to skin diseases and the formation of tumors. Thus, increasing numbers of pet owners are consulting veterinarians about weight-related problems in cats and dogs.

As with so many health problems, prevention is better than cure; preventing obesity by providing a puppy or kitten with a proper diet, in the right quantities, right from the start is a great deal easier than curing it. It is in the nature of things, however, that the veterinarian is usually consulted when excessive weight has already become a problem.

While the basic cause of excessive weight is overeating, other factors can be involved. Neutering is one. A recent study in the United Kingdom showed that approximately one-quarter of all dogs that are neutered, male and female, are overweight. The reason is simply that spaying or castrating a dog or cat reduces its

Garfield by Jim Davis; reprinted by permission of United Feature Syndicate, Inc.

The protests of animal rights activists over alleged abuses of laboratory animals are often widely publicized. In response, scientists and public health officials have recently mounted a campaign of their own, calling attention to the advances in the treatment of disease and the sparing of human suffering made possible by the use of experimental animals. This newspaper ad, created by a New York City advertising agency, emphasizes the contribution of animal research to human life and health.

activity and, therefore, its energy expenditure. Eating the same amount of food as before it was neutered can, therefore, make the animal put on weight.

Cutting food intake by starvation is not an acceptable option, and so a number of manufacturers now market specially formulated diets. These are high-fiber, low-fat feeds that satisfy the animal's hunger but provide up to 45% fewer calories. Fed in prescribed quantities, they help to reduce the weight of the animal while maintaining its health. Adding vitamins and trace elements ensures that overall nutritional requirements are maintained. A typical canine reducing diet will contain 7% fat and 25% fiber and will produce 1,100 kilocalories of metabolizable energy per pound. A normal dog food, by contrast, contains 10–25% fat and about 3% fiber and produces 2,000 kilocalories per pound.

Obesity is not the only condition for which prescription diets are available. In recent years studies have been performed to determine the food requirements of small animals. Veterinary nutritionists such as C. A. Buffington, working at the University of California at Davis, have developed research programs in clinical nutrition. Now a whole range of special dietary prescriptions are available.

Foods low in magnesium in order to combat feline urolithiasis (bladder stones), high in the amino acid taurine to help prevent a heart muscle ailment in cats, and low in carbohydrates to deal with diabetes are available. In addition, there are high-energy diets for very active dogs and diets specifically blended to fulfill the different nutritional requirements of both young and old dogs and cats. Properly used, such foods can maximize the health status of pets and help correct a number of potentially disabling metabolic disorders.

Animal welfare

While a large part of the world still regards dogs as no more than a table delicacy, treats living horsepower far worse than its motorized counterpart, and uses farm animals as economic units rather than as creatures with feelings, animal welfare is a major preoccupation in most of the developed countries. Two types of activity are causing concern among welfare groups. One is the development of transgenic animals—those carrying a "foreign" gene injected into the embryo at a very early stage in order to introduce characteristics that will enhance their usefulness as food producers, as laboratory animals, or for some other purpose. The other activity is the use of growth hormone (somatotropin) in an injectable formulation to produce similar ends.

Opinions are divided over the use of such techniques. Proponents argue that transgenic animals could, for example, be developed to produce more meat for a given amount of feed, to be resistant to certain types of disease, and to be high yielders of milk. Such animals, these people believe, would do no more than bring into the technological age the time-honored principles of breeding to improve the species that have been practiced since the dawn of civilization. Such techniques, their supporters maintain, offer the potential for improving the cattle and sheep stocks of less developed countries, with accompanying benefits for their human populations. The opposing camp, however, regards such efforts as, at best, an unjustifiable interference with nature.

No matter how they are viewed, the techniques have a long way to go before they are predictable in their effects. Other than in laboratory mice, success has been mixed, but once a new strain has been

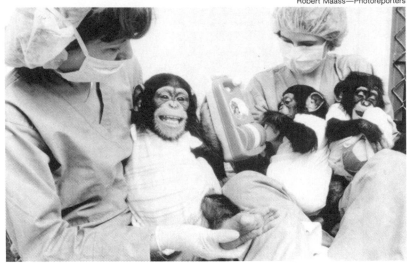

In the U.S., legislation passed in 1985 but not yet in force requires laboratories that use live animals for research to establish animal-care committees, to house the animals decently, and to attend to their psychological well-being. Some research facilities, however, already meet these standards; at a New York University lab where primates are used for medical research, staff members make special efforts to provide for the social needs of experimental chimps.

created, it could be used as a breeding population to produce similar "improved" animals.

Resistance to the use of growth hormones, already commercially available in the U.S., is strong in Europe, where political opposition is likely to cause their use to be banned. The welfare and consumerist lobbies have combined to act against them in spite of the fact that scientific evidence has shown that they do not harm animals when their use is properly controlled.

Laboratory animals have long attracted the activity of animal rights supporters. Concerns center on the type of accommodations provided for the animals and whether their environment is stressful. In particular, it is now believed that noise from nearby laboratory machinery may cause problems. The Universities Federation for Animal Welfare is one of the organizations in Britain investigating the effects of ultrasound created by, for example, oscilloscope equipment. Among a number of groups studying the effects of housing and social environment on laboratory animals, workers at the University of Heidelberg, West Germany, looked at cages in which rats are kept. They found that, given a choice, rats preferred a longer and higher cage than the type most commonly used.

Meanwhile, Donald Broom, holder of the world's first chair of animal welfare, at the University of Cambridge, is seeking to establish a scientific means of measuring animal welfare. Those who regard the approach of many untrained welfarists as overemotional and based on their own feelings rather than those of the animals see this as an essential step to real progress.

Picking a winner

Anyone visiting a bloodstock auction with a view to buying wants to know one thing about any racehorse on offer—if it is a potential winner. Veterinary certification can testify to general health and soundness, but the rest is left to the skilled eye—or to chance.

One of the less easily identifiable of the factors that diminish racing ability is an inherited defect of the larynx (voice box) of foals that interferes with breathing and thus affects performance. Normally the condition, called laryngeal palsy, is detected by means of an endoscopic examination. This involves passing a flexible tube down the esophagus, a procedure not suitable for the auction ring even if the seller would allow it. However, W. Robert Cook of Tufts University School of Veterinary Medicine, Medford, Mass., has devised a simple method for diagnosing this condition. Using his index fingers to palpate the throat over the larynx, Cook claims to be able to assess the degree of muscle wasting present and thus the extent of laryngeal palsy. This is then scored on a scale correlated statistically with racehorse performance.

Other workers in the same field are skeptical, however. They dispute Cook's claim that the condition is inherited, maintaining that it might be due to a virus or to the stress of severe exercise, and argue that it could be corrected surgically. Cook, basing his findings on more than 40 years of extensive research, has remained unmoved.

A related problem in racehorses is that of exercise-induced pulmonary hemorrhage. When a horse is raced, the exertion can be so great that bleeding occurs in the lungs. This sometimes causes blood to flow from the nostrils. Like laryngeal palsy, this affects breathing and, therefore, performance.

Using one of the latest techniques, scintigraphy, workers at Tufts have for the first time been able to study pulmonary hemorrhage in living horses. Scintigraphy involves injecting small amounts of radioisotopes into the bloodstream; this enables sophisticated imaging equipment to produce a computer-enhanced color scan of lung function. The technique allowed the Tufts researchers to compare function before and after exercise and to assess the effect of bronchodilator drugs, which enlarge the airways. It is hoped that effective clinical treatments may be developed from such studies.

Cattle brain disease

A fascinating veterinary problem with international ramifications surfaced in the U.K. in 1987 and was the subject of detailed study. A degenerative brain disease of cattle, small in incidence but invariably fatal, appeared in a number of herds. A link with scrapie, a similar disease in sheep, was suspected. It was deduced that the disease, called bovine spongiform encephalopathy (BSE), was passed to cattle in feed concentrates that incorporated small amounts of processed sheep offal, a source of protein.

A British government committee, chaired by Sir Richard Southwood, a University of Oxford zoologist, was set up to investigate the problem. It confirmed the link with scrapie and reinforced the government ban on the use of offal in cattle feeds. It also concluded that the chances of a human's catching the disease from eating contaminated meat are remote.

BSE also has similarities with chronic wasting disease in mule deer, transmissible mink encephalopathy, and three rare human diseases: kuru, Creutzfeldt-Jakob disease, and Gerstmann-Straussler-Scheinker disease. All take a long time to develop; it is thought that the cattle currently diagnosed with BSE first became infected in about 1981. If the Southwood conclusions prove correct, BSE will be eliminated by about 1996 following the ban on the use of sheep material in cattle feeds. Meanwhile, all affected cattle must be destroyed.

North Sea seals: endangered

A bizarre chain of events has led to the decimation of the North Sea gray seal population. Huskie dogs used for hunting seals in Greenland are believed to have infected seals, which then escaped. The seals developed a disease identical to canine distemper, which they passed on to other seal populations in the course of their natural migration.

The infecting virus, a morbillivirus in the same genus as that which causes distemper in dogs and rinderpest in cattle, was identified by Albert Osterhaus, a veterinary virologist at The Netherlands National Institute of Public Health and Environmental Hygiene. Although suitable vaccines exist and were employed to prove the existence of the virus, they can be used only in seal sanctuaries owing to the difficulty of catching seals in the wild. It is estimated that up to 80% of the seal population in Scandinavia and the U.K. might be lost before the situation stabilizes.

Future prospects

An ambitious program designed to plan the future of veterinary services and veterinary education to meet

A veterinarian at a seal sanctuary in The Netherlands vaccinates an animal against a viral disease related to canine distemper. The seal population in the coastal waters of Western Europe was decimated by the disease during the summer of 1988.

the needs of the 21st century has been set in motion by a U.S. educational charity. The first stage of the operation, a report titled "Future Directions for Veterinary Medicine," has been published by the Pew National Veterinary Education Program of North Carolina and Duke University Press.

Subjected to extensive review by veterinary educational and practitioner groups, the report is the first stage of the four-part program. Stage two is a training scheme to enhance leadership and managerial skills in the 27 U.S. veterinary colleges; stage three will involve the colleges in strategic planning; and the final stage will provide financial support for implementing the plans. The program is part of an initiative designed by the Pew Charitable Trusts of America to reinforce all of the country's health care professions.

The recommendations for veterinary medicine are intended to change the focus from treating animal disease—so-called fire brigade services—to preventing it; to restructure veterinary practice and strengthen veterinary education to better serve the needs of society and the profession itself; and to make research a higher priority. Detailed suggestions as to the way veterinary practice should be organized to make the best use for society of specialized veterinary skills and high-technology equipment have worldwide applications. The Pew exercise is being viewed with great interest in Europe, particularly in the U.K., which is facing a government-inspired review of its veterinary education system.

—Edward Boden

415

HEALTH INFORMATION UPDATE

Instructive and practical
articles about common
health concerns

Wild for Oats

by Diane H. Morris, Ph.D., R.D.,
Ann Ward, Ph.D., and James M.
Rippe, M.D.

An apple a day keeps the doctor away. Almost everyone remembers this adage used mainly by mothers and schoolteachers to encourage obstinate young people to eat right. It reflects a widespread belief that eating a high-fiber food every day promotes regularity and good health. In the late 1980s the maxim to eat an apple a day is still a good one. Regularity is still a concern, and the value of fruits, vegetables, nuts, and wheat and other grains in the diet is well recognized for digestive health. Now, however, there is another, even more urgent, health focus—high blood cholesterol—and today's watchword is oats!

It is hard to say exactly when the oat bran craze began. Certainly oats have been grown for thousands of years, but until the dawn of the 19th century they were used primarily as a pasture crop and as livestock feed. Human consumption of oats, largely in the form of hearty porridges, was widespread only in Scotland and Ireland. Scottish immigrants to the New World took oatmeal with them, but it did not gain widespread acceptance. Samuel Johnson, the English lexicographer, essayist, critic, and poet, is said to have remarked, "Oats—a grain which in England is generally given to horses, but in Scotland supports the people," to which his friend Lord Patrick Murray Elibank is said to have replied, "True, but where will you find such horses, where such men?"

Recognition of oatmeal as a satisfying breakfast food remained unchanged into the 20th century, past the horse-and-buggy era, into the dawn of the computer age. Several popular nutrition books of the 1970s, including those by Adelle Davis, Carlton Fredericks, and Nathan Pritikin, discussed the benefits of a high-fiber diet but placed no special emphasis on oat bran. In the 1980s, however, the results of research studies on oat bran began to appear in major scientific journals. By 1987 the oat bran craze was in full swing. Newspaper articles touted the health benefits of oat fiber, advertisements for oat bran cereals appeared in major magazines and on television, and Robert Kowalski published a best-seller, *The 8-Week Cholesterol Cure,* which featured oat bran muffins as part of a plan to lower blood cholesterol. Before long, cereal manufacturers reported difficulties in meeting the market demand for oat bran, and supermarket managers struggled to keep grocery store shelves stocked with this popular item. Americans were wild about oat bran.

What is oat bran?

Today, oats are in the limelight as a wholesome, nutritious grain, served up as hot and cold breakfast cereals and in a variety of breads, cookies, baby foods, and other products. Perhaps the most popular way to eat oats nowadays is in muffins. Of course, humans do not eat oats the way horses do—as just plain oats. In the grocery store, oats are found primarily as oat bran and oatmeal. What is the difference?

The answer to this question lies in the milling process. "Green oats" delivered to the mill are first cleaned, a process that removes sticks and stems, weed seeds and other grains, stones, dust, and dirt. In the hulling step that follows, oats are sorted by size and dried to loosen and help remove the hard, outer shell called the hull. The hulled oats are then crushed to knock off the hulls, yielding groats. The groats undergo additional refining and finishing to produce a variety of oat products available for commercial use.

Rolled oats, for example, are steamed to be made soft, cut into various thicknesses, and then crushed between rollers to produce flakes. The thickest rolled oats are known to most people as hot, cooked oatmeal. A longer cooking time (more than five minutes) is required for the thick oats. Thinner, smaller flakes result in the rapid-cooking, "instant" varieties of oatmeal and usually require less than two minutes to cook. Rolled oats are not limited to breakfast cereals, however; they are sometimes used as a thickener in soups, sauces, and gravies and as a meat extender in meat loaf and meat patties.

A steaming bowl of hearty oat porridge (or porage, which is the old Scottish name) first became a breakfast staple in the British Isles. It was Scottish immigrants who introduced oatmeal into the New World.

Grinding either groats or flakes produces oat flour; it is frequently added to breads, muffins, cookies, and cereals. Oat bran is the bran-rich fraction produced by sifting coarsely ground oat flour.

Why all the excitement about oat bran?

Oat bran has gained attention as a result of its effects on blood cholesterol levels. In a classic study published in 1963, A. P. De Groot and his colleagues at the Central Institute for Nutrition and Food Research in The Netherlands showed that rats fed a diet containing rolled oats had significant reductions in blood cholesterol. Excitement about this observation prompted the researchers to study the effects of rolled oats on blood cholesterol in human beings. The results were similar; consumption by adult men of 140 g (5 oz) of rolled oats incorporated into bread resulted in a lowering of blood cholesterol over a three-week period. Even so, De Groot's findings did not spark a mad rush to buy oat bran to help lower blood cholesterol because in 1963 physicians and other health professionals were not generally aware of the relationship between high blood cholesterol and heart disease.

Since De Groot's study, though, the beneficial effects of oat bran on blood lipids have been demonstrated by other researchers in a variety of study populations. One study, for example, was undertaken by James W. Anderson and his colleagues at the University of Kentucky; the results of the study were published in 1984. Twenty adult men with hypercholesterolemia, the technical name for high blood cholesterol, were invited to participate in the study that would be conducted on a metabolic ward of a medical center over a three-week period. The metabolic ward setting allowed the researchers to evaluate every aspect of the participants' food intake, activity levels, and fecal (stool) output. In this study, the participants eating 100 g (about 3.5 oz) of oat bran (equivalent to about one bowl of hot cereal and five oat bran muffins) every day showed reductions in blood cholesterol of about 19% over the 21 days.

In another study, conducted in 1988 by researcher Linda Van Horn and her colleagues in the department of community health and preventive medicine at Northwestern University Medical School, Chicago, 236 volunteers were recruited from the Continental Illinois National Bank. These participants, living in their usual home and work environments, included both men and women, aged 30 to 65 years, who were healthy and not overweight. All were asked to follow an American Heart Association (AHA) diet—which is low in total fat, saturated fat, and cholesterol—and received weekly instruction from trained registered dietitians for 12 weeks. After four weeks half of the participants were asked to add to their diet about 60 g (about ⅔ cup, dry) of oatmeal every day in the form of cereal or special oatmeal recipes. The company cafeteria even made oatmeal muffins available for the study participants. The other half followed the AHA diet without added oatmeal. After 12 weeks both groups showed

In the milling process, "green oats" are first cleaned to remove stems, seeds, and debris; then the hard outer shell is removed—yielding groats. Groats undergo further refining to produce the various oat products on the market—e.g., oatmeal and oat bran.

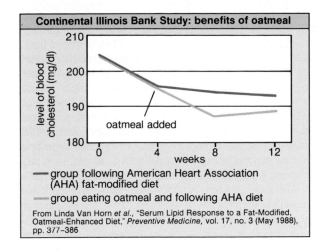

Continental Illinois Bank Study: benefits of oatmeal

— group following American Heart Association (AHA) fat-modified diet
— group eating oatmeal and following AHA diet

From Linda Van Horn et al., "Serum Lipid Response to a Fat-Modified, Oatmeal-Enhanced Diet," *Preventive Medicine,* vol. 17, no. 3 (May 1988), pp. 377–386

substantial reductions in total cholesterol and LDL (low-density lipoprotein)-cholesterol, but the group with added oatmeal had the larger decrease in total blood cholesterol.

These and other studies have demonstrated reductions in total blood cholesterol ranging from 5 to 19% in adult men and women with hypercholesterolemia. In addition, oat bran has been shown to lower blood levels of LDL-cholesterol (the so-called bad cholesterol). The effects of oat bran on HDL (high-density lipoprotein)-cholesterol (the so-called good cholesterol)

and triglycerides have been variable, with some studies reporting a decrease and others an increase or no change in the levels of these blood lipids.

Fad or fact?

Concern about high blood cholesterol levels can quickly be placed in perspective: more than half a million people die annually from coronary heart disease (CHD) in the United States. While such risk factors as having a family history of CHD or being male cannot be controlled, others can be. Three major controllable risk factors for CHD are smoking, high blood pressure, and high blood cholesterol. Other risk factors include being overweight and having a sedentary life-style. In addition, recent studies have established the blood lipid fractions, LDL-cholesterol and HDL-cholesterol, as important predictors of CHD risk. Individuals with elevated levels of LDL-cholesterol and low levels of HDL-cholesterol are at increased risk.

The fact that oat bran has been shown to lower blood cholesterol has important implications for the millions of Americans at risk of heart disease. Why? Because for individuals with elevated blood cholesterol levels, the first line of defense in the fight against CHD is diet.

As part of a nationwide effort to heighten awareness about high blood cholesterol and CHD risk, the National Cholesterol Education Program (NCEP) pub-

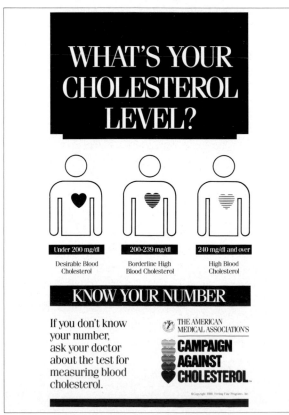

WHAT'S YOUR CHOLESTEROL LEVEL?

| Under 200 mg/dl | 200-239 mg/dl | 240 mg/dl and over |
| Desirable Blood Cholesterol | Borderline High Blood Cholesterol | High Blood Cholesterol |

KNOW YOUR NUMBER

If you don't know your number, ask your doctor about the test for measuring blood cholesterol.

THE AMERICAN MEDICAL ASSOCIATION'S **CAMPAIGN AGAINST CHOLESTEROL**

American Medical Association; © 1988 Feeling Fine Programs, Inc.

Step-one diet for reducing cholesterol by 30 to 40 mg/dl	
nutrient	recommended intake
total fat	less than 30% of total calories
saturated fatty acids	less than 10% of total calories
polyunsaturated fatty acids	up to 10% of total calories
monounsaturated fatty acids	10 to 15% of total calories
carbohydrates	50 to 60% of total calories
protein	10 to 20% of total calories
cholesterol	less than 300 mg/day
total calories = calories needed for achieving or maintaining desirable weight	

lished a set of guidelines designed to help physicians and other health professionals identify and treat at-risk individuals. For individuals with blood cholesterol levels above 200 milligrams per deciliter (mg/dl), the NCEP recommends an initial therapeutic approach involving a low-fat, low-cholesterol diet. This diet plan should be followed earnestly by at-risk individuals for a period of at least six months before drug therapy is considered.

Specifically, the recommended diet plan is a "Step-One" AHA diet. This is a low-fat, low-cholesterol diet plan that emphasizes three dietary changes: (1) reducing the total intake of fat, (2) substituting polyunsaturated and monounsaturated fat for saturated fat, and (3) limiting the intake of dietary cholesterol. It encourages consumption of whole grains and cereals, fruits, vegetables, fish, poultry, lean cuts of beef, and low-fat dairy products as part of a balanced meal plan.

Where does oat bran fit in? Studies have shown that adding oat bran or oatmeal to the AHA diet can result in additional reductions in blood cholesterol over those achieved with the AHA diet alone.

How does oat bran work its "magic"?

The key to oat bran's success is the nature of its fiber. The term fiber refers to materials that make up plant cell walls or that are part of the "cement" within plant cells; these materials resist digestion by enzymes found in the human stomach and intestines. Much of the fiber in oat bran is water-soluble. Water-soluble fibers include pectin found in citrus and other fruits and certain vegetables and gums found in oats, barley, and dried beans. In general, water-soluble fiber lowers blood cholesterol but does not affect stool weight or reduce the amount of time required for materials to move through the gastrointestinal tract (transit time). By comparison, water-insoluble fiber, such as that found in certain vegetables, wheat bran, wheat flour, and cereals, increases stool weight and reduces transit time but does not affect blood cholesterol. Both types of fiber are important in human nutrition. Thus, a consumer concerned about regularity *and* high blood cholesterol levels will want to include both insoluble and soluble fibers in his or her diet. Here is a classic situation where eating a variety of foods—especially fruits, vegetables, and whole-grain cereals—will ensure an adequate intake of both types of dietary fiber.

The exact mechanism by which oat bran helps lower blood cholesterol is not understood. It is possible that soluble fiber, including that found in oat bran, binds cholesterol and bile acids in the small intestine, decreases their absorption, and increases their excretion. The net result is that the liver is forced to make bile acids from stored and circulating cholesterol. Thus, blood levels of cholesterol fall.

An alternative explanation is that soluble fiber is fermented to short-chain fatty acids in the colon. These are then absorbed and serve to inhibit cholesterol synthesis in the liver. The net effect again is a fall in blood cholesterol.

How much oat bran is enough?

Most of the clinical studies done to date have used oat bran at levels ranging from about 35 to 100 g daily. On the low end, two average-size muffins made with oat bran provide about 35 g. To reach an intake of 100 g of oat bran, approximately five oat bran muffins or seven to eight servings of a ready-to-eat oat bran breakfast cereal would need to be consumed daily.

Types and sources of plant fibers		
category	component	major food sources
insoluble	lignin	breakfast cereals, wheat bran, strawberries, eggplant, pears, green beans, radishes
	cellulose	whole-wheat flour, wheat bran, cabbage, young peas, green beans, wax beans, broccoli, peppers, apples
	hemicelluloses	wheat bran, cereals, whole grains, brussels sprouts, mustard greens, beetroot
soluble	gums	oatmeal, oat bran and other rolled-oat products, dried beans
	pectin	squash, apples, citrus fruits, cauliflower, green beans, cabbage, dried peas, carrots, strawberries, potatoes

Adapted from *Fiber for a Healthy Life* (Kellogg Co., 1988)

Dietary fiber content of selected foods (in grams)			
food	total dietary fiber	water-soluble fiber	percentage of soluble fiber
oatmeal, dry, ⅓ cup	2.58	1.33	52
oat bran, dry, ⅓ cup	4.03	2.01	50
All Bran, ⅓ cup	8.61	1.43	17
corn flakes, 1 cup	0.44	0.13	29
whole-wheat bread, 1 slice	1.53	0.34	22
white bread, 1 slice	0.57	0.28	49
carrots, raw, ½ cup	1.76	0.84	48
broccoli, frozen, ½ cup	2.18	0.98	45
kidney beans, canned, ½ cup	5.75	1.45	25
pinto beans, canned, ½ cup	4.34	1.01	23
white beans, canned, ½ cup	4.98	1.50	30
apple, raw, 1 small	2.76	0.97	35
orange, 1 small	1.94	1.13	58
purple plums, canned, ½ cup	2.74	1.19	43

From J. W. Anderson and S. R. Bridges, *American Journal of Clinical Nutrition* 47:440 (1988)

"Wellness Update: Thirty-year-old man starting on the twenty-five-thousand-pound oat-bran muffin he must consume over forty years in order to reduce significantly his risk of death from high cholesterol"

Most experts agree that two-thirds of a cup of cooked oat bran a day is sufficient to reduce blood cholesterol levels. Because oatmeal has less water-soluble fiber than oat bran, more is needed to achieve the same effect—about one cup daily.

Regardless of the form eaten—oat bran or oatmeal—it is not enough to have a serving every day. Other important dietary changes must also be made. This point deserves emphasis because an individual with elevated blood cholesterol levels will probably not see an improvement in blood lipids unless an effort is made simultaneously to reduce the intake of total fat, saturated fat, and dietary cholesterol.

One final note: not all foods made with oats are created equal; some are high in fat and cholesterol. One should always check the recipe. Many muffin recipes, for example, call for whole eggs—a major source of dietary cholesterol. When possible, one should use egg whites or egg substitutes (available in grocery store frozen foods departments) in place of whole eggs in oat bran muffin recipes. Most muffin recipes call for butter, margarine, or vegetable oil. To help control the type of fat, one should choose margarine or vegetable oil over butter; this will reduce the saturated fat content of the muffin. Better yet, one can substitute nonfat yogurt in place of margarine or vegetable oil to reduce both the muffin's fat and caloric value.

Can oat bran save money?

In April 1988 a study was published in the *Journal of the American Medical Association* of the cost-effectiveness of treating individuals with high blood cholesterol levels, defined as greater than 265 mg/dl, with three different agents: cholestyramine, colestipol, and oat bran. Cholestyramine (Questran) and colestipol (Colestid) are prescribed drugs used widely in the management of patients with hypercholesterolemia. The authors estimated the costs, both direct and indirect, of using these three intervention programs over a period of seven years. The estimated per capita cost of therapy on a yearly basis was $1,442 for cholestyramine, $879 for colestipol, and $248 for oat bran. The authors indicated that the major expense related to the use of oat bran was for the cost of medical supervision and not for the product itself. Thus, there appear to be genuine savings to utilizing oat bran as part of a standard therapy to help patients lower blood cholesterol. A decision to replace traditional drug therapy with oat bran, however, should be made only in consultation with a physician.

Oat bran muffins

ingredients:

1 cup whole-wheat flour
1½ cups oat bran
2½ tsp baking powder
1 tsp salt
¼ tsp baking soda
⅓ cup brown sugar, packed
½ cup nonfat dry milk
1 tsp ground cinnamon
½ tsp ground nutmeg
3 tbs olive oil
1 cup plain nonfat yogurt
2 egg whites
1 cup unsweetened applesauce

method:

1. preheat oven to 400° F
2. grease bottom of muffin pan
3. in a large bowl, mix dry ingredients together thoroughly
4. in a separate bowl, beat oil, yogurt, and egg whites together
5. blend in applesauce
6. add wet ingredients to dry and blend just until moistened; do not overmix
7. pour batter into pan
8. bake at 400° for 20 minutes

yield: 12 muffins

nutrition information (per serving [1 muffin])

calories: 170
protein: 6 g
fat: 4 g
carbohydrate: 26 g
cholesterol: less than 1 mg
saturated fat: less than 1 g
sodium: 50 mg

From J. M. Rippe and A. Ward, with K. Dougherty, *The Rockport Walking Program* (New York: Prentice Hall, 1989)

between the mother and the older child diminishes. Schedules change. A stranger or unfamiliar relative may come to stay during the mother's absence. Particularly upsetting to many children is the mother's sudden disappearance to the hospital, provoking worries about her being sick or never returning. All of these factors produce anxiety and confusion.

When the mother comes home with the new baby, her availability to the older child is decreased and she may find the stress of caring for the newborn overwhelming. Frequently she finds herself feeling critical of the firstborn child for not demonstrating greater self-sufficiency. This can strain the relationship and cause the mother to feel guilty for not having enough time and patience to devote to the older child. Some mothers try to compensate by becoming irrationally indulgent toward the firstborn.

The situation is further complicated when the child begins to act out the stress he or she is feeling. Nearly 90% of all young children show signs of stress after a sibling's birth; these include hyperactivity, sleep problems, fussiness at meals, a tendency to cry easily, and regression in toilet training. Interestingly, aggression is rarely directed at the newborn but rather is directed at the mother herself, suggesting that the upset is more about losing contact with mother than about acquiring a sibling. Older children resort to a variety of "naughty" behaviors, such as spilling food or messing up the house, to attract attention. They accuse the mother of not loving them, demand endless bedtime stories, or repeatedly recall their exhausted parents to their bedsides for yet another drink of water. These regressive behaviors are usually transient and disappear within several months. On the positive side, parents frequently observe developmental leaps forward following the appearance of stress; the child may show new forms of independence, surging ahead in toilet training, getting dressed, and being helpful around the house.

Conflict between the children rises sharply after the baby's first birthday. No longer an infant lying helpless in a crib, the baby becomes a walking, biting, pushing, demanding person who can wreak havoc on the belongings and the body of the older child, straining his or her understanding and self-restraint. Conflicts between children who are close in age are extremely frequent. At first, not yet having mastered language, they hit, scream, and snatch toys from one another. Older children use brute force and bullying, while younger ones often instigate in subtle ways and then appeal helplessly to the parents. Parents should not feel guilty when such routine fighting occurs; this stage in children's lives is part of the vital process of learning to win and lose, to give and take, to compromise and realize the limits of one's power. Despite the annoyance and anxiety such fighting triggers in parents, children's conflicts can be a source of social

learning and maturation. Bickering and fighting are not necessarily a sign of a poor sibling relationship.

Getting off to a good start

Research suggests that relationships that begin on a positive note in the children's earliest years have a better chance of being harmonious later in life than those where antagonism and rejection were the rule. When no warmly shared childhood experiences can be remembered, the chances of a warm adult relationship diminish.

The following are some guidelines parents can follow to help ease the transition period.

● Allow the older child to visit the mother and baby in the hospital. This calms fears, allays confusion, and gives the youngster a chance to feel like a participant. Some hospitals have launched "prepared sibling" classes, in which children have a chance to see the delivery room, play with dolls that anatomically demonstrate the childbirth process, and have lessons about feeding, diapering, and being helpful in caring for the baby. They can also talk with other children who are "expecting."

● Make as few changes as possible in the older child's routine. If a babysitter comes to stay while the mother is in the hospital, the older child should have time to become well acquainted with the new caretaker. Changes in eating, play, and bedtime routines should be minimized. There is no evidence that breastfeeding the new baby in front of the older child produces rivalry, but jealousy over "sharing" the mother can be eased by providing an enjoyable activity for the older child while the mother nurses.

● The father's help can be crucial in establishing a positive sibling bond. Studies indicate that when the father spends time with the older child in this early period, siblings get off to a better start, and the older child has fewer adjustment problems.

● Speak to the older child about the baby as a human being, a person with feelings, rather than as a stranger or an "it." Studies have found that when the mother speaks to the child about the baby's needs ("Is he hungry?" "Do you think he is sleepy?" "I think she wants to play with you—see! She's smiling at you!"), empathy develops, and the children are less prone to rivalry in later years.

● Allow the older child to vent his or her feelings. Parents who act as a sounding board for their older child's frustration can reduce the child's anger simply by acknowledging they understand the jealous and angry feelings rather than insisting that these feelings must not exist. ("Of course you were angry! The baby needed all of my time because he wasn't feeling well this morning. Let's make a special time for you and me when I'm finished cleaning up.") When a parent validates the child's right to have a feeling, the need to act out that feeling can be reduced.

Lester Sloan—Woodfin Camp & Associates

Youngsters preparing for the arrival of a new sibling get a lesson in baby care at a California hospital. Experiences like this one can be reassuring to children who are "expecting."

Problems in later childhood and adolescence

Although siblings share an average of 50% of their genes, often they resemble one another only slightly in physical appearance, intelligence, and personality. These differences may seem remarkable to parents, who tend to describe their children as "as different as day and night." Differences observed early in life become sharper in the parents' eyes as the youngsters grow.

While most of these differences are undoubtedly the result of different genetic endowments, they are amplified by the children themselves in the process called "deidentification," in which each child uses the sibling as a point of reference for his own view of himself and thereby becomes a distinct and different person. Two sisters—one bright but not beautiful, the other beautiful but not bright—develop their social identities by "bouncing" their different images off of one another. Each gets to know who she is—and is not—by comparison with the sibling. The comparison can be especially painful when the siblings are close in age. Identification, on the other hand, occurs when one sibling uses valued aspects of a brother or sister's personality as a yardstick or mirror of his or her own image. By trying to be like a sibling, the child can experiment with a variety of roles and images. Rivalry and identification appear most sharply when two siblings are very close in age and are less pronounced when the children are separated by a number of years.

Favoritism

As differences between siblings become more evident, they can produce feelings of inferiority, envy, and doubt, or they can, in a supportive family environment, become something to enjoy rather than to disparage. Children compare themselves—and are compared by family members and friends—in three basic areas: physical-athletic-sexual attractiveness; intellect; and social skill. When one child outshines another in all three areas for many years, the less well-endowed child can develop serious problems of self-confidence. Although few parents admit to having a favorite child, they may find that the talents or personality traits of one of their children make them feel more loved or accepted by that child. Another child's temperament can be difficult, or the child may in some way disappoint the parent. This process, often not consciously recognized, can ferment into the acceptance of one child and rejection of another.

Frequently some physical characteristic of a child may delight or upset a parent; the shape of a nose, the color of the hair, a body build, a way of looking at people, or a tone of voice—all can remind the parents of things they have hated or loved in themselves or in others. Sometimes a child will remind a parent of a relative who was adored or despised. If unchecked, the feelings produced by these kinds of comparisons can lead to serious emotional complications for the less favored child. Favoritism and sibling resentment appear particularly to flourish when the husband-wife relationship is a hostile one.

Coping with antagonism in the later years

Parental influence declines as children get older. However, it is still possible for the parents to limit the extent and pain of sibling conflict. The following are some rules of thumb for parents of older children and adolescents.

● Do not settle the children's battles for them. Parents should instead teach each child how to negotiate, empathize, compromise, and defend his or her territory. Parents should be consultants rather than combatants.

● Set a few basic rules for strictly prohibited behavior. Parents should intervene if there is humiliation, belittlement, or physical violence that could result in injury, inappropriate sexual contact, or abuse.

● Avoid displaying uncontrolled anger when enforcing rules. Parents' behavior should demonstrate that respect for all family members is expected.

● Minimize good-versus-bad distinctions between children. Instead, the differences between them should be celebrated.

● Resist being manipulated into equalizing children's privileges. Parents need to understand that completely even-handed treatment is impossible—different children have different needs and different competencies. A spirit of equal consideration, rather than one of mathematical equality, should prevail.

● Recognize that too much contact between siblings

can produce tension. Help children to enjoy some separate experiences, away from one another.

Special stresses on the family

In the U.S. a divorce rate that had been rising precipitously appears to have peaked around 1980; it is estimated that 40–50% of the children born between the late 1970s and early 1980s will spend an average of five years in a single-parent home. Children face many changes when their custodial parent remarries, often involving new homes, new schools, and sometimes stepbrothers and stepsisters. These stresses force siblings simultaneously toward greater closeness and toward greater possibilities for mistreatment and misunderstanding.

When parents are absorbed in dealing with their own life stresses or when the mother is employed full-time, the children often must look out for one another. An older child may be given considerable responsibility for a younger sibling. Being a caretaker can produce nurturing, parental behavior in an older child, but there is no guarantee that the youngster will not abuse his or her power over the younger child or that the children will not get into trouble together. Caretaker siblings often appear so competent and want so much to help the parent keep the household running smoothly that they do not share their problems with the parents, sensing them to be already overtaxed. Parents can ease this burden in some of the following ways.

- Investing extra time in helping the older child become skillful at managing the younger one and answering all of the older child's questions.
- Making sure that both the younger and the older child have some separate time with a parent.
- Allowing the children an opportunity to get away from one another. Caretaker siblings need time off.
- Working with the children to establish rules and procedures that everyone agrees to live with.
- Showing appreciation and praise for the children's help and cooperation. Children deserve some credit for *not* fighting or *not* messing up the house.
- Making time to call children from work each day after school.

A parent's remarriage (about three-quarters of all divorced parents *do* remarry) inevitably brings losses and changes. Children in newly combined families may still have unresolved anger and sadness as a result of the divorce. Particularly painful to both children and parents are the issues of special favors from the natural parent and perceived maltreatment by the stepparent.

Aggressive, coercive sibling and stepsibling relationships are quite common during marital transitions, particularly among boys living with their mothers. Children express anger toward one another as a way of coping with their own sense of disappointment that the family has split up. For some children, however, acquiring a stepbrother or stepsister can actually serve as a buffer against the stress of divorce or can be the answer to a long-held wish to have a sibling. The introduction of a stepsibling can also create tensions between biological siblings who formerly enjoyed a harmonious relationship. If, for example, a new stepsibling forms a friendship with one sister but not with the other, painful, jealous feelings can develop.

The divorce rate in second marriages is substantially higher than in first marriages, and tension among the children and disagreements between stepparents regarding the children are a major factor in the breakup of these marriages. Parents who deal effectively with stepsibling conflict are able to communicate flexibly and frequently with each other and with their children about issues of fair play. They also recognize that the remarried family can neither replace nor resemble the original nuclear family. Remarried couples who allow the children to express their underlying sense of loss and sadness and who realize that the new life is far more complex than life in the original family may be better able to cope with conflicts that arise between the children. Effective stepparents respect the children's basic attachments to the biological parents and siblings.

Another special stress is the presence in the household of a child who is seriously ill, physically handicapped, emotionally disturbed, or mentally retarded. The "normal" child may be confused about exactly what caused the sibling's problem, and he or she needs clear, early explanations about what the problem is, what can and cannot be done about it, and what the future may hold. It is also helpful for parents to share a limited amount of responsibility for the care of the ill or handicapped child with the normal brother or sister, allowing the "well" child to take some of the credit for the progress and gains of the other. The "normal" child may experience feelings of jealous rage over the amount of time parents spend with the impaired youngster; normal siblings may also feel enormous guilt over their very normality and the many opportunities open to them that the impaired sibling is denied. All of these feelings can be made easier to cope with if parents encourage open discussion and are supportive and accepting.

Help for siblings in conflict

When the tension between siblings appears uncontrollable despite the family's best attempts to resolve conflict, professional help can provide new ways of coping with the problems. Family therapy is particularly useful in helping family members to listen and to try different ways of solving disagreements. Individual therapy can help those who need to better understand an unhappy sibling relationship or whose rivalry reflects deeper problems to be resolved.

Slipped Disk
by Stanley J. Bigos, M.D.

"Slipped disk" is a term that has generated much confusion for both sufferers of back pain and physicians who treat them. Back pain is a very common condition. Approximately 80% of all people will remember at least one episode of back pain by 50 years of age. Often people will attribute their back or leg discomfort to a "slipped," or herniated, disk. However, disk problems can be pinpointed as the cause of leg symptoms in only 1–2% of cases. In fact, for the vast majority of patients with back symptoms, no physical or anatomic cause can be detected.

Spinal disks: structure equals function

The disk is a key component of the normal structure of the spine, which is composed of 24 vertebrae—7 cervical vertebrae in the neck, 12 thoracic vertebrae in the chest and upper back region, and 5 lumbar vertebrae in the lower back. The disks are actually the large joints between the bony vertebral bodies. A disk resembles a jelly doughnut; the outer part, called the annulus fibrosis, is composed of gristlelike material. The inner part, called the nucleus pulposus, is jellylike in composition. This alternating structure of vertebrae and disks encloses and protects the spinal canal, where nervous tissue connects the brain to all parts of the body.

Structure is an expression of function. The functions of the disk are (1) to provide stability to the spine, (2) to act as shock absorber by allowing flexibility when the spine is under stress, and (3) to protect the spinal canal from injury. Actually, very few people have serious problems with their spine, which is evidence that the vertebrae and disks do a very good job of carrying out their duties.

Aging of the spine

The disks tend to age much more rapidly than do other parts of the body, primarily because they lack a blood supply to nourish and regenerate the tissue. While they are less visible than wrinkles, gray hair, and balding, significant aging changes in the disk area occur in most people by the late twenties and in everyone by the early forties.

The first aging changes to occur are cracks in the outer gristle of the disk, the annulus fibrosis. Then the jellylike material of the inner nucleus pulposus becomes similar to crabmeat in consistency. The cracks allow some of this "crabmeat-like" jelly to escape, sometimes pressing against a nerve. Terms often used

for this condition include slipped disk, herniated disk, or herniated nucleus pulposus. Unfortunately, the disk material does not tend to slip back and forth; once out in the spinal canal, it stays there. But, being softer than nerve tissue, the disk material usually accommodates to the shape of the nerve, allowing symptoms to abate.

Disk problems: the symptoms

Are so-called slipped disks the primary cause of back pain? Medical science has not found this to be the case. Studies do show that 35–40% of people in their mid-forties have this herniation of disk material even if they have never had any back or leg pain. However, a herniated disk pressing on a nerve may cause leg pain.

Disk herniation seems to cause a problem only when the inner part of the disk squirts out and traps nerve tissue. This condition most commonly occurs in the disks in the lower part of the back, causing leg symptoms such as aching, numbness, and sometimes lancinating pain, which is characterized by piercing or stabbing sensations and is accompanied by an aching back. "Sciatica" is the term frequently used to describe this set of symptoms because the main sciatic nerve of the leg is involved. Disks also can herniate in the neck region, causing arm pain, and in some rare cases can irritate the spinal cord. Shooting shocks down the spine and legs that occur with neck movement or difficulty controlling urination, bowel, or leg function are important danger signals for anyone with neck pain, as they may indicate pressure on the spinal cord. Disk herniation in the lower back does not present as much danger because the spinal cord does not extend into this region.

Virtually everyone with a true herniated disk who is experiencing leg symptoms will have had previous episodes of back pain. The nature of the pain can vary from a mild ache to excruciating, pulsating pain that can even feel like electrical shocks. The severest symptoms generally last for only a short time, perhaps three to ten days. Pain seems to be produced when the soft disk material decreases the space around the nerve, giving it less room to move and thus causing the nerve to become inflamed. This irritation decreases the nerve's ability to function normally, sometimes causing periods of weakness or numbness that usually abate spontaneously without long-term problems. In rare cases, nerve damage becomes extensive enough to result in permanent or severe loss of nerve function.

What causes herniated disks?

Some medical researchers believe that herniated disks are caused by wear and tear. Unfortunately, almost all people eventually wear out their disks; as previously indicated, this problem is related to the normal aging process regardless of back pain. The catch is that disk aging begins when people are in their twenties and thirties, which is *before* most people have any discomfort. Several factors can speed this aging process. Poor nutrition is one; smoking, which decreases the oxygen supply to all tissues, is another.

Some studies indicate that herniated disk is more common in people who are tall or overweight. Lifting heavy objects often has been blamed as a cause, but studies evaluating workers in various types of jobs show very little association between heavy lifting and problems with herniated disk. In fact, some studies indicate that sedentary workers are at greater risk for herniated disks than are people who perform more

strenuous jobs. This information adds support to the growing recognition that improved muscular stamina may be the real key to protecting people from severe back problems of all types. More importantly, endurance may determine how long a person's activities may be restricted by the common sort of back problems that almost everyone can expect to experience at some time in life.

Who gets herniated disks?

Disk hernias seem to occur when the more fluidlike jelly in the inner portion of the disk is able to squirt out like toothpaste through the cracks in the outer gristle. Herniations do not happen if there are no cracks in the disk and thus are uncommon in very young people. As people age, the inner part of the disk loses much of its water content, thus decreasing the amount of jellylike material available to be squeezed out. For this reason, herniation is less common in the elderly. Herniated disks seem to occur most commonly in the 30–50 age group, affecting men and women about equally.

How long do symptoms last?

Approximately 50% of people recover from common back pain within one week, and 90% recover by six weeks. Most people also recover rapidly from symptoms caused by herniated disks; 50% are over their symptoms within one month, and 90% by three months. Unfortunately, more than half of those who have a first episode of back pain will experience multiple episodes over the next two–three-year period.

Diagnosing disk problems

How is a herniated disk diagnosed? First, a physician takes a thorough history of the problem and performs a physical examination that focuses on how the nerves are working.

Since the majority of working-age people are well on their way to recovery within 30 days, there is little reason to do special diagnostic tests during the first month except in the rare patient with bowel or bladder function impairment or severe and worsening leg function. Such cases will require early evaluation. Narcotic and hypnotic medications also can affect bowel and bladder function, sometimes prompting special tests that are not needed. Patients should ask about potential side effects of drugs they are taking for any medical problem, as physicians who treat back problems must keep potential drug reactions in mind.

If severe pain or other symptoms persist beyond 30 days, special diagnostic tests are warranted and may be very helpful in detecting an anatomic cause. In cases of herniated disk, tests can determine the location and severity of nerve dysfunction. The most commonly used test is electromyography (EMG), which employs electrodes to record the electrical activity in the muscles innervated from different levels of the spine. This

Spinal anatomy

cervical vertebrae

thoracic vertebrae

lumbar vertebrae

sciatic nerve

cross section through disk

spinal cord

nerve root

lamina

disk

annulus fibrosis

nucleus pulposus

disk

vertebra

spinal cord

herniated disk

irritated nerve

test helps to localize the level of the problem and evaluate the severity. Results are most dependable after three to four weeks of leg symptoms. An EMG test may be followed by anatomic studies such as myelogram and computed tomography (CT) scans or magnetic resonance imaging (MRI), a newer sophisticated diagnostic technique. These special studies evaluate the contents of the spinal canal. This information is then correlated with the patient's symptoms and the findings from the physical examination.

An anatomic or physical cause for common back pain is found in a small percentage of cases, while nerve root dysfunction caused by herniated disk can be documented in only 1–2% of patients who have a combination of back and leg symptoms. It is this latter and very small group of patients who may possibly benefit from surgery if they have strong test findings and are slow to recover.

Given these statistics and the likelihood that "I don't know the cause" will be the most frequent result of special tests, neither patient nor physician should apply such terms as sprain, strain, arthritis, myofaciitis (inflammation of the muscle and its fascia), disk syndrome, facet syndrome, or others that are commonly but inappropriately used.

Initial treatment: the importance of exercise

In the early stages of symptoms, treatment of herniated disk is similar to that recommended for most other musculoskeletal problems. The first goal is to gain control of symptoms without the debilitation that results from too much rest. A second goal is to restore function by improving the ability of the back muscles to compensate for any physical abnormality in the spine. Most physicians experienced in the treatment of back pain recognize that the mainstay of early symptom control is reducing the mechanical stress on the back without further debilitating the patient. Too much bedrest and inactivity can severely debilitate the muscles and even the bone. Avoiding sitting can be helpful in controlling symptoms because sitting is mechanically more stressful for the back than standing or walking.

When a patient is experiencing severe symptoms during the initial acute phase of herniated disk, standing or walking for short periods of time (20 minutes for every three hours of lying down) can slow the debilitating effects of rest without risking further damage. It may seem surprising, but standing and walking stress the back only slightly more than lying on one's side. After a few days, even if some symptoms remain, most patients can increase their walking pace to a level that can begin to restore good muscle function. Proper aerobic training over a period of time can increase the endurance of the muscles of the body and back so that they tire less quickly and thus can better protect the back against future episodes of back pain.

Restoring a good level of fitness to the back is similar to the recovery process of an athlete following a knee injury that requires surgical attention. A knee surgeon rarely is able to restore the injured athlete's knee to its original condition. The leg may be useless until the muscles are retrained and conditioned to compensate for knee deficits. Through proper muscular compensation, however, athletes often can return to high levels of function in college or professional sports.

The principles of conditioning are similar for the back. Activities such as speed walking, cycling, swimming, or even jogging—which are all less stressful to the back than sitting—can build endurance in patients with back pain. If pursued with the proper frequency, intensity, and duration (at least four to six weeks of conditioning), these activities are good tools for building sufficient stamina so the muscles can better protect the back and for increasing tolerance for daily activities. Unfortunately, among practitioners there are some who are still caught up in the archaic bias of medical inactivation to treat back problems.

Pain-relieving medications are only an adjunct to conditioning therapy to take the edge off the pain; they do not seem to relieve pain in the spine as effectively as they do pain from other joint problems or, for example, from dental procedures. Most physicians prefer to prescribe combinations of anti-inflammatory agents (*e.g.*, aspirin, nonsteroidal anti-inflammatory drugs) and mild analgesics such as acetaminophen to decrease the likelihood of slowing recovery. Stronger analgesics should be used only for a short period of time when symptoms are most severe. Most symptom-control methods—including thermal modalities, manipulation, and traction techniques—have what are sometimes termed the "hot-tub effect." That is, most of them feel good whether a person has back pain or not, but scientific studies have not verified that they significantly speed recovery or that they will protect the back in the future.

Surgery: rarely recommended

Special diagnostic studies and evaluation for surgery are recommended only for those individuals who are not able to make the transition from symptom control to restorative exercise. A very important point is that surgery is for the most part a luxury to help speed recovery in patients with very strong findings on physical examination and diagnostic tests and who are slow to recover. In fact, surgery for herniated disks was not even recommended prior to 1934. The medical literature before that date does not indicate that patients commonly suffered from severe, long-term problems without disk surgery.

This luxury of surgery should be considered only if careful evaluation of special diagnostic studies strongly indicates that a herniated disk is putting pressure on a nerve root at the level of symptoms and dysfunction.

Furthermore, a misdiagnosis and subsequent surgery on the disk when the nerve root is not under pressure actually has been found to *reduce* the individual's chances of recovery to as little as half that of someone given no treatment at all.

For a patient with strong test findings, surgery can take the pressure off nerve tissue and alleviate the severe leg symptoms, providing the patient with relief. Surgery cannot make the back feel as it did at 18 years of age, however. Some individuals, perhaps expecting too much from surgery, never regain sufficient confidence in their back function that they feel they have been helped by surgery. For this reason, some physicians may ask the patient to complete a personality inventory test that can help identify if the patient will later not consider the surgery as satisfactory as he or she had hoped or expected.

Surgical procedures

For cases in which surgery is considered a potential source of relief for a herniated disk, a preferred surgical procedure is direct nerve root decompression, often termed a laminotomy, subtotal diskectomy, diskectomy, or laminectomy—terms that are explained below. The goal is to reduce the pressure on the tissue by restoring the normal space for the nerve. In recent years some surgeons have used microscopes to aid visualization during the surgical procedure, but the advantage of this technique over the use of less magnification has not been determined.

In all the above-mentioned procedures, the orthopedic surgeon exposes the nerve to determine the cause of pressure. The normally occurring "window," or space, between each vertebral lamina is expanded so the nerve canal can be seen, and the pressure is then surgically relieved. The term lamina refers to the section of the vertebra that covers the posterior portion of the spinal canal. In a laminotomy the surgeon enlarges the window between the lamina of the adjacent vertebrae above and below the herniated disk. A laminectomy is a procedure to remove the entire lamina and the palpable spinous process itself. Diskectomy refers to removal of the disk material that is pressing on the nerve root, which is not necessarily total removal of the disk between the vertebrae.

Over the years, attempts also have been made to decompress the nerve canal indirectly through a variety of other techniques. One that gained considerable publicity is injection of chymopapain, an enzyme from the latex of the papaya tree that may break down disk material and theoretically decrease the amount of material in the disk that is pressing on the nerve. A newer technique, percutaneous diskectomy, uses a large needle to suck out some of the disk material in the hope of taking some of the pressure off the nerve in the spinal canal. These techniques have not achieved universal acceptance and presently are rec-

ommended only when there is a contraindication to direct nerve root decompression.

Chronic back problems

For physicians, employers, insurance agencies, and patients alike, the greatest concern about back pain is the potential for a chronic problem. Fortunately, only about 10% of patients with back pain develop chronic problems. Some blame the recurring pain on unsuccessful surgery; others seem unable to tolerate the fact that the back will never again be "as good as new." In some people back pain may be worsened by stress from other problems, but the pain itself becomes "the straw that breaks the camel's back." Some studies seem to indicate that individuals with chronic back problems who are unable to return to their former occupations are left with few career options. For these people the continuing pain may be worsened by their emotionally frustrating and stressful situation. Psychologist Wilbert Fordyce, a pioneer in the behavioral treatment of pain at the Multidisciplinary Pain Center at the University of Washington, has theorized, "People don't hurt as much if they have something better to do."

Chronic back discomfort also may worsen other life stresses, but the greatest contributor to a chronic problem is the tendency to significantly decrease activity. When symptoms linger, the patient should be urged to take up activities that are mechanically safe and that promote recovery. The best approach is frequent repetitions of low-stress activities to establish and maintain the highest possible level of stamina. While such activity may not completely eliminate pain, it will increase the tolerance for essential daily activities as well as pleasurable ones that can restore some sense of fulfillment to life.

The most important advice for a person with any type of back problem is to avoid debilitation through overresting and to avoid overtreatment with strong medications or unnecessary surgery. Any person with back pain should ask his or her physician these questions: (1) Why and for how long should I limit activities such as working, lifting, and so forth? (2) What activities can I participate in to keep from becoming debilitated while trying to control symptoms? (3) How long should I take any medication that is stronger than a combination of anti-inflammatory agents and acetaminophen?

If a physician recommends surgery, the patient should request specific information about the type of surgery and the findings of special diagnostic tests that seem to indicate the need for surgery. Most importantly, the patient should obtain a second opinion. The most fortunate person restores back function through stamina training and recovers more quickly without facing the risks of surgery.

Are You Abusing (Over-the-Counter) Drugs?

by Robert M. Julien, M.D., Ph.D.

There are two classes of drugs legitimately available for sale in most Western countries: prescription drugs, those obtainable only upon the order of a physician, and nonprescription drugs, commonly referred to as over-the-counter, or OTC, drugs. The fact that a drug is available only upon prescription implies both that its use is reserved for more serious illness and that it has the potential for causing harm if misused or abused. There is, correspondingly, a widespread belief that OTC drugs have little potential to cause complications and are not likely to be misused. This is not necessarily the case, however. In the discussion that follows, these popular misapprehensions will be examined in detail, and some guidelines will be given for the safe use of OTC medications.

Extent of OTC drug use

In 1987 in the U.S. alone, expenditures for OTC drugs totaled $10.5 billion. The average per capita expenditure was $40 per year, or $160 for a family of four. Certainly some individuals ingest proportionately larger quantities than others, and many people routinely take five, ten, or more of these drugs with relative frequency. The categories of OTC drugs used most commonly are analgesics, laxatives, antacids, skin preparations, cough and cold medicines, and vitamins.

Approximately 4% of hospital admissions in the U.S. are the result of adverse reactions to drugs and interactions of both OTC and prescription medications. The exact contribution of OTC drugs to this number is unknown, although an estimate of 25–40% (or 1.5% of hospital admissions) seems probable. As most drug reactions and interactions do not result in admission to a hospital, the total number of adverse reactions is quite a bit larger than the statistics would suggest. Indeed, as many as one-fourth of all patients taking prescription or OTC drugs experience some type of drug reaction or interaction. Fortunately, most are relatively minor and do not result in fatalities; however, they can produce serious crises.

Hazards of self-diagnosis and self-treatment

An old adage says that the physician who treats himself has a fool for a patient. Very early in their training, medical students are cautioned not to diagnose either their own illnesses or those of members of their immediate families. This same advice holds true for lay persons yet, like physicians, many individuals are in the habit of diagnosing their own ailments. This is not to say that a person should not diagnose a headache as a headache and take one or two aspirin tablets for relief. However, taking aspirin in an attempt to relieve a serious headache that, unlike previous headaches, is associated with an episode of blurred vision may mask a possible diagnosis of meningitis or prevent recognition of the transient symptoms that sometimes precede a stroke. While both of these more serious events are relatively rare, they do occur, and any delay in treatment might be life threatening. Self-diagnosis of common maladies is certainly not to be wholly condemned, but when a symptom does not respond rapidly or as expected to the OTC remedy, when symptoms intensify despite treatment, or when the need for the drug is unusually prolonged, then professional help should be sought immediately.

Just as physicians are advised not to diagnose their own illnesses, they are similarly advised not to prescribe treatment for their own ailments. This warning against self-medication also applies to the nonprofessional. Most OTC drugs carry some potential for harm, especially in the case of patients who regularly take one or more prescription drugs for the treatment of chronic illness (e.g., heart disease, hypertension, diabetes, epilepsy, and certain psychiatric disorders). Such people are much more likely than those taking no prescription drugs to suffer adverse effects from self-prescribed OTC medications.

Masking of serious illness

While an OTC drug can alleviate the symptoms of disease, thus making the person feel better, the underlying disease process may not be affected. In fact, it may be progressing all the while, unbeknownst to the individual. For example, aspirin—a priceless and virtually irreplaceable drug for treating a variety of minor maladies—is so effective in relieving the pain and reducing inflammation caused by certain infections that it can mask important warning signs and allow the infection to become worse. A number of similar examples can be cited. Prolonged self-medication of stomach pain with antacid preparations can mask the presence of an ulcer until it grows so large that medical treatment may be much more difficult than if it had been initiated early on. Similarly, the repeated use of OTC gynecological preparations for genital itching or irritation may cover up early signs of serious infection, thus unnecessarily delaying effective treatment. The same is true of prolonged self-medication for "chest tightness" with inhalers or nose sprays, measures that may delay the diagnosis of bronchial asthma until the situation becomes so severe that a respiratory crisis develops. As a rule, symptoms that do not disappear within a few days should be considered a warning of a more serious illness and an indication to seek professional assistance.

Dangers of delaying treatment

Self-diagnosis, self-medication, and the process of waiting for some significant relief to occur involve considerable amounts of time. If the underlying cause of the symptoms is something more serious than the person imagined, the disease process will continue unabated—even though the symptoms may be minimized. There is, for example, the case of a teenage boy who consulted a physician because he had been experiencing headaches that had become worse and worse over time. Upon close questioning, the physician ascertained that these headaches had been quite different in nature from the common tension headaches a teenager might experience. Despite this, the boy had continued to take aspirin in ever increasing quantities; still the headache persisted and intensified. It was clear to the doctor that this was no ordinary headache and that it might even be an indication of a steadily enlarging aneurysm ("ballooning-out") of an artery within the brain, which could rupture, causing a stroke or even death. Furthermore, the aspirin the boy had been taking had exerted an anticoagulant effect, inhibiting the blood's ability to clot and thus potentially exacerbating bleeding into the brain. By not seeking professional help earlier, the teenager had taken what could have been a fatal risk.

Drug action and interaction

The action of a drug ultimately occurs as a result of drug molecules attaching to specialized areas, called receptors, located on the surface of the cells that are responsible for the drug's clinical effects. The intensity of drug action depends on the amount of drug attached to these receptors. Drug interactions can occur whenever two drugs compete for the same receptors. Such interactions usually result in potentiation, or intensification of a drug effect. Many OTC cough and cold preparations and sleep-inducing preparations contain potent antihistamines that potentiate other actions of many prescription medications, including other antihistamines, antipsychotic agents, antidepressant drugs, and antiparkinsonian drugs. Symptoms of potentiation include excessive sedation, blurred vision, dry mouth, rapid heartbeat, cardiac arrhythmias, urinary retention, mental confusion, and even hallucinations.

Whenever two drugs are taken concurrently, there is always the potential for one drug to interfere with the action of the other. As the number of drugs a person takes increases, the potential for drug interactions increases exponentially. As a general rule, drug interactions produce either an increase in the toxicity of one of the drugs or a decrease in the therapeutic effect of one or both of the drugs. More simply, a drug interaction occurs whenever one drug alters the effect of another.

How drugs interact

It might seem surprising that a drug taken to relieve stomach acidity or alleviate a headache could alter the effectiveness of another drug taken to treat high blood pressure. To begin to understand such interactions, it is necessary to recognize that all drugs are handled similarly by the body. All drugs taken by mouth pass into the stomach and eventually into the intestines. From there they are absorbed into the blood and, once in the blood, they are distributed throughout the body until they are present in near-equal concentrations in all body tissues. Thus, even though a drug might act to relieve pain in the head or reduce acidity that is causing stomach upset, it will be found in equal concentrations in brain, muscle, fat, and other tissues throughout the body.

Eventually, as drugs pass through the liver (again, via the blood circulation), they are metabolized, or broken down, by specific proteins, called enzymes, located inside the cells of the liver. In general, most drugs lose their therapeutic and toxic properties when they are metabolized. Finally the by-products of metabolism pass through the kidneys and are excreted in the urine. Most drug interactions, then, occur as a result of the action of one drug to alter the absorption, distribution, metabolism, or excretion of a second drug—as described in the above processes.

Absorption. Antacids are among the most widely used OTC medications. They reduce stomach acidity by neutralizing the acid secreted by the stomach. Antacids that contain calcium, magnesium, or aluminum (that is, almost all antacids commercially available) also have the effect of slowing the absorption of many drugs. In some instances (as with the tetracycline antibiotics) antacids inactivate drugs by physically binding with them to form a nonabsorbable compound. Laxatives that contain magnesium, such as milk of magnesia or citrate of magnesia, similarly bind the tetracyclines and prevent their absorption.

Distribution. As drugs circulate through the body in the blood, large quantities of a drug may be temporarily inactive because they may be tightly bound to albumin, a protein in the plasma, or noncellular portion of the blood. Indeed, between 85 and 99% of some drugs within the bloodstream may be bound to albumin. In such cases only 1 to 15% of the available, circulating drug may be unbound and active. When a second protein-bound drug is taken, it may displace a significant fraction of the original drug already bound to albumin, thereby increasing the active amount of the first drug. Such increases, in turn, can raise the level of pharmacologically active drug in the blood so high as to markedly increase its toxicity. Anticoagulant drugs (the coumarin group is the most widely used) are frequently prescribed as blood "thinners" to prevent the formation of blood clots. Because anticoagulants are approximately 99% bound to plasma proteins, they can easily be displaced by many medications, the most prominent of which include aspirin, the nonaspirin analgesic–anti-inflammatory agents such as acetaminophen, and oral drugs for diabetes. Anticonvulsant drugs prescribed for epilepsy also fall into this category. Any patient taking prescribed medication for treatment of diabetes, blood clotting, chronic inflammation (such as gout or arthritis), or epilepsy should be aware that many OTC drugs can increase the levels of their prescribed medication to a dangerously high amount, which can produce serious toxicity.

Metabolism. The liver's response to the presence of a drug is to manufacture the enzymes needed to break down the chemical structure of the drug into a variety of less active substances. As more of a drug is taken, increased quantities of drug-metabolizing enzymes are produced. Eventually drug tolerance (the need for larger doses to produce the same effect) may develop as the drug is metabolized ever more rapidly. For example, prolonged administration of a barbiturate (such as the sedative phenobarbital) results in increased availability of enzymes to metabolize the drug. As a result, however, tolerance develops both to the phenobarbital and to most other drugs that might be present, because they are metabolized more rapidly.

Excretion. The products of metabolic breakdown are normally excreted from the body in the urine. If a person is taking a drug that affects kidney function, the removal of drugs from the body is altered. Salicylates (such as aspirin) and antacids (such as ammonium chloride and sodium bicarbonate) can affect the actions of prescription medications such as diuretics, antibiotics, and drugs for treatment of diabetes.

Effects of alcohol

Alcoholic drinks contain ethyl alcohol (or ethanol)—a potent drug available without prescription. Ethyl alcohol is a direct depressant of the central nervous system (CNS); it impairs coordination, alertness, and judgment. Excessive impairment of both mental and physical abilities occurs when alcohol is taken with any other CNS depressants. Agents that potentiate the effects of alcohol include tranquilizers, antiepileptics, antipsychotics, antihistamines, blood-pressure-lowering medicines, muscle relaxants, narcotics, and sleeping pills. The result of potentiated central nervous system depression is drowsiness, dizziness, loss of muscle coordination, and reduced mental alertness, all of which may lead to fatal automobile and other accidents and to death from respiratory failure. Drugs that interact with alcohol usually carry a warning on the label: "Do not drink alcoholic beverages while taking this product." It is important that this advice be heeded.

Potential for addiction

Just because a drug can be obtained without a prescription does not mean that it is totally safe or nonaddicting. While development of true narcotic-like addiction is extremely rare with OTC products, both psychological and physical dependency can develop insidiously. What this means is that withdrawal symptoms appear upon discontinuation of the drug, and the person inevitably uses the drug again to treat these symptoms.

Sometimes addiction to an OTC drug is the result of a phenomenon known as rebound effect. Some products, when used for prolonged periods of time, actually interfere with the normal function of the tissues they act upon. When this happens a vicious cycle begins. Larger quantities of the drug, or more frequent dosages, are needed to produce the desired effect. For example, certain potent nasal sprays (used to treat nasal congestion)—in particular those containing oxymetazoline hydrochloride—are extremely effective in constricting swollen nasal blood vessels and shrinking swollen tissues, thus resulting in improved nasal airflow; when a person stops using the spray, the blood vessels again dilate, the surrounding tissues swell, and there is a return of stuffiness, which is most effectively treated by repeated administration of the nose spray. Eventually, with prolonged use of the spray, the blood vessels become fatigued and do not constrict and dilate as quickly and completely. Larger and more frequent doses of spray are then required. In order to break this cycle, the person must stop using the spray and suffer through a rather prolonged rebound period until the drug-induced dependence is finally resolved.

Another example is that of laxative abuse. The body has a remarkable ability to regulate intestinal motility, maintaining a pace that is slow enough to allow absorption of needed food and vitamins but rapid enough to eliminate waste products. Interference with this cycle, through the repeated use of laxatives or enemas, interferes with normal function to the point where cessation of laxative or enema use is followed by a flaccid bowel (*i.e.,* poor intestinal muscle tone) with reduced propulsion. The result is constipation, which is most often treated by reinstitution of laxative or enema treatment. Again, a cycle of dependence—medication use to treat medication withdrawal—has been instituted.

In recent years many potent drugs formerly available in the U.S. only upon prescription have been approved for sale OTC, albeit in lower concentrations. Examples of such medications are:

● the antidiarrheal medicine loperamide hydrochloride (sold OTC as Imodium A-D; available by prescription as Imodium)

● the analgesic ibuprofen (sold OTC as Advil, Nuprin, and Medipren; available by prescription as Motrin)

● the anti-inflammatory drug hydrocortisone (sold OTC as a cream, ointment, or lotion in a 0.5% concentration; available by prescription in many other, more concentrated forms)

● numerous antihistamines, such as oxymetazoline hydrochloride (Afrin), diphenhydramine hydrochloride (Benadryl), chlorpheniramine maleate (Chlor-Trimeton), and brompheniramine maleate (Dimetane)

A number of other drugs are scheduled to become available as OTC products, which creates the potential for their unsupervised use and possible misuse. Little information currently exists for assessing the implications of release from prescription control. Some states, however, have chosen to maintain prescription status for some of these agents, especially those drugs that, taken in high dosages, are subject to abuse.

Points for the consumer to remember

Self-diagnosis and self-treatment may be appropriate for many minor disorders, but professional care is needed whenever symptoms intensify despite the use of an OTC remedy or whenever the effect of the OTC product is less than expected. Careful judgment must be exercised about the effects of OTC drugs; the lack of an expected response to the drug may indicate that the problem is really more serious than was originally believed.

All OTC medications are intended only for brief and intermittent periods of use. Printed directions on the bottle or package always give guidelines for the appropriate and reasonable use of the product. These directions should be read carefully and followed strictly; the product should not be taken more often or for a longer time than specified. This is not new or startling advice—everyone has probably heard it before. Several years ago a study by the New York Pharmaceutical Society found that of 10,000 people surveyed, 85%

either had not followed instructions on drug labels or had not completely understood the significance of the package directions. Whenever the dosage recommendations for OTC medications are exceeded in either size of dosage, frequency, or duration of use, the potential exists for the development of a drug habit or dependency.

OTC preparations can interfere with the action of some prescription drugs, either increasing or decreasing their effectiveness. The physician should always be told about any nonprescription medications the patient is taking so that he or she can decide beforehand if these might interact with drugs being prescribed.

The physician and the pharmacist are important resources for health information. They should be consulted whenever there are any questions about the possible dangers of different kinds of OTC drugs, their side effects, the consequences of their prolonged use, and interactions that might occur when they are taken together with prescription medications.

Only a few drug interactions involving OTC drugs are life threatening. Most produce only disturbing symptoms that can be corrected by a simple adjustment in dosage, which is best done by a physician. Predicting the seriousness of a drug interaction involves consideration of the margin of error associated with the drugs involved. With anticoagulants, diabetes drugs, digitalis, antiarrhythmic drugs, and anticonvulsant drugs, the margin of safety is not great, and drug interactions can have catastrophic effects. Patients being treated for bleeding disorders, diabetes, heart disorders, and even high blood pressure should be cognizant of the fact that even apparently benign OTC drugs (such as mild aspirin-containing pain-relievers and cough and cold preparations) can cause problems, and these individuals should consult a physician prior to even occasional use of such medication.

FOR FURTHER INFORMATION:
Clayman, Charles, ed. *The American Medical Association Guide to Prescription and Over-the-Counter Drugs.* New York: Random House, 1988.
Consumers Union (the Editors of *Consumer Reports*). *The Medicine Show: Consumers Union's Practical Guide to Some Everyday Health Problems and Health Products,* 6th Edition. Mount Vernon, N.Y.: Consumers Union, 1988.
Graedon, Joe, and Graedon, Teresa. *The People's Pharmacy.* New York: St. Martin's Press, 1988.
Julien, Robert M. *A Primer of Drug Action,* 5th Edition. New York: W. H. Freeman and Co., 1988.
Julien, Robert M. *Drugs and the Body.* New York: W. H. Freeman and Co., 1988.
Huff, Barbara B., ed. *Physicians' Desk Reference for Nonprescription Drugs,* 10th Edition. Oradell, N.J.: Medical Economics Co., 1989.

Cardiac Rehabilitation: Exercise for the Heart's Content

by Marc K. Effron, M.D.

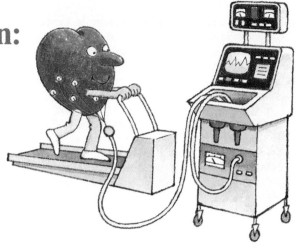

Cardiac rehabilitation is a program of exercise and education designed to help cardiac patients achieve their optimal level of function. Coronary heart disease continues to be the leading cause of death and the major cause of nonfatal serious illness in developed countries. Each year, thousands of Americans suffer a myocardial infarction (heart attack) and must readapt to the requirements of home life and the workplace. Other patients undergo coronary artery surgery, are disabled by angina pectoris, or undergo coronary angioplasty (balloon dilatation of a coronary artery). All these individuals are candidates for a rehabilitative program that assists them in achieving their maximal physical level of function and psychosocial adaptation to their medical condition.

For the first half of this century, treatment of the heart attack patient was characterized by extended periods of bed rest in the hospital and subsequently at home. The medical profession's reassessment of cardiac function and infarct healing (*i.e.,* healing of the area of the heart muscle that is damaged as the result of a heart attack, when one or more of the coronary arteries supplying blood to the heart is blocked) led to earlier mobilization of the cardiac patient and development of postinfarction exercise programs. In the U.S. about one-sixth of survivors of heart attacks—an estimated 100,000 patients per year—participate in cardiac rehabilitation.

Physiology of exercise

The physiological effects of exercise are multiple. Regular exercise leads to a conditioning effect with progressively greater exercise capacity. Functional capacity is often described in terms of metabolic equivalents (METS), a work-load unit; 1 MET represents the metabolic expenditure at rest. Very light work, such as a slow walk, amounts to 2 METS; a brisk walk is approximately 6 METS; jogging may be 7 to 9 METS; and fast running or heavy labor is 10 METS or more. Peak exercise capacity soon after a myocardial infarction may be as low as 5 METS. Exercise training can improve the aerobic capacity of heart patients. The training sessions usually are performed at 60 to 85% of the maximum work-load capacity of the patient.

As an individual exercises and becomes more physically conditioned, oxygen uptake at a given work load decreases, heart rate does not increase as abruptly, and the amount of blood the heart pumps increases. The heart thus performs more efficiently. Pulmonary ventilation also increases with exercise training. Blood lactate shows a slower increase, indicating less of an oxygen debt. Blood volume and hemoglobin concentration increase. Such augmented function of the heart and of the peripheral circulation enables the patient to do more with less energy expenditure. In the angina patient, this may permit resumption of work activities without provoking cardiac symptoms.

Physical training can modify the risk factors regarded as causes of coronary disease. Systolic blood pressure decreases with training. This is, in part, due to a reduction of sympathetic nervous system tone, both during exercise and at rest. Exercise training enhances the serum level of high-density lipoprotein cholesterol (HDL-cholesterol), the component of serum lipids that appears to exert a protective effect on the coronary arteries. Although exercise (without dietary changes) has minimal effect on total cholesterol, the improvement in HDL-cholesterol may prevent or minimize progression of coronary atherosclerosis. Regular exercise may lower glucose levels in persons with diabetes. Exercise may help to attenuate stress, normalize sleep, and reduce psychological depression.

Goals of cardiac rehabilitation

A comprehensive cardiac rehabilitation program facilitates the patient's transition from hospital care to home recovery and finally to the maximum achievable level of function at home or work. The program aids recovery and aims to prevent or minimize recurrence of cardiovascular disease symptoms.

Improvement of functional capacity of myocardial infarction patients enrolled in formal rehabilitation programs is easily demonstrable. Maximum functional capacity is usually achieved after 8 to 12 weeks of participation. Improvement in functional capacity occurs spontaneously after myocardial infarction in most patients, but a supervised program may increase the exercise performance by an additional 15 to 25%. A

435

meaningful increase in work capacity is expected in those individuals with a capacity of less than 7 METS at the time of entry into a program. Even patients with congestive heart failure, who have sustained a large amount of myocardial damage, can show a beneficial training effect.

The majority of patients can achieve the physical capability of returning to work or to their preinfarction activity level. Many will actually pursue a higher level of exercise than before their heart attack, attempting to revise their prior sedentary habits.

Psychosocial benefits of cardiac rehabilitation seem obvious for many patients but are difficult to measure. Fear of recurrent heart problems may virtually incapacitate some myocardial infarction or coronary surgery patients. The classic "cardiac neurosis" patient limits physical activity, does not return to work, and misconstrues any minor musculoskeletal chest discomfort as a warning sign of another heart attack. Cardiac rehabilitation programs provide a structured and supportive environment for the coronary patient. Exercise can be performed in the reassuring pres-

ence of trained specialists, and in most cases regular electrocardiographic monitoring ensures that exercise regimens are not causing harm but rather are fostering improvement. Questions can be answered, and the patient can interact with others who have had similar illnesses and face similar challenges. The program can provide a psychological stepping-stone into a home exercise program or into the workplace.

Cardiac rehabilitation is a setting in which any risk factors for coronary artery disease may be reviewed. Blood pressure, blood sugar and lipid levels, and cigarette habits all are scrutinized. Before or after exercise sessions, participants have available to them educational literature, video instruction, and discussion of goals and concerns with cardiac rehabilitation specialists and other participants. Dietary methods of modifying the risk factors are emphasized most strongly. Weight loss can lower the blood pressure, triglycerides, and blood sugar. Serum cholesterol can be lowered by reduction of dietary fat, particularly the saturated fat found in meat and dairy products. A high level of dietary fiber is emphasized. Oat, rice, and corn

Approximate energy requirements of selected activities				
category	home	occupational	recreational	physical conditioning
very light <3 METS*	washing, shaving, dressing desk work, writing washing dishes driving auto	sitting (e.g., clerical, assembly) standing (e.g., store clerk, bartender) driving truck operating crane	shuffleboard horseshoes bait casting billiards archery golf (cart)	walking (3.2 km/h) stationary bicycling (very low resistance) very light calisthenics
light 3–5 METS	cleaning windows raking leaves weeding power lawn mowing waxing floors (slowly) painting carrying objects (7–14 kg)	stocking shelves (light objects) light welding light carpentry machine assembly auto repair paper hanging	dancing (social and square) golf (walking) sailing horseback riding volleyball (6-person) tennis (doubles)	walking (4.2–6.4 km/h) level bicycling (9.7–12.9 km/h) light calisthenics
moderate 5–7 METS	easy digging in garden level hand lawn mowing climbing stairs (slowly) carrying objects (14–27 kg)	carpentry (exterior home building) shoveling dirt using pneumatic tools	badminton (competitive) tennis (singles) snow skiing (downhill) light backpacking basketball football skating (ice and roller) horseback riding (gallop)	walking (7.2–8 km/h) bicycling (14.5–16 km/h) swimming (breast stroke)
heavy 7–9 METS	sawing wood heavy shoveling climbing stairs (moderate speed) carrying objects (27–40 kg)	tending furnace digging ditches pick and shovel	canoeing mountain climbing fencing paddleball touch football	jogging (8 km/h) swimming (crawl stroke) rowing machine heavy calisthenics bicycling (19.3 km/h)
very heavy 9 METS	carrying loads upstairs carrying objects (> 40 kg) climbing stairs (quickly) shoveling heavy snow shoveling ten minutes (7 kg)	logging heavy laboring	handball squash ski touring over hills vigorous basketball	running (≥ 9.7 km/h) bicycling (≥ 21 km/h or up steep hill) rope jumping

*1 MET = metabolic expenditure at rest   1 kg = 2.2 lb; 1 km = 0.62 mi

Adapted from P. Greenland and J. S. Chu, "Efficacy of Cardiac Rehabilitation Services with Emphasis on Patients After Myocardial Infarction," *Annals of Internal Medicine*, vol. 109, no. 8 (Oct. 15, 1988), p. 652

bran can have a favorable effect on serum cholesterol. As total cholesterol is brought down, the ratio of HDL-to LDL-cholesterol is increased; this ratio is a separate predictor of coronary risk.

While reduction of cardiovascular mortality is a purported goal of cardiac rehabilitation, a significant decrease in mortality has been difficult to prove. Only one of several major, randomized research trials has shown a statistically significant reduction of cardiac mortality attributable to exercise training after infarction. The preponderance of the medical literature on cardiac rehabilitation since 1976, with over 14 randomized trials, indicates no reduction in nonfatal myocardial infarction rate. Although advocates of cardiac rehabilitation may optimistically attribute a mortality reduction to these programs, a survival advantage has not been definitively proved. Moreover, because of differences in programs and other factors, it is difficult to compare studies. Indeed, rigorous proof may be difficult to achieve, considering the marked expense, large patient numbers, and long duration required for performing an interventional study. Even if the ideal research study could be carried out, an important survival difference would not be expected.

Program features

A comprehensive program of cardiac rehabilitation begins during the hospitalization for myocardial infarction or coronary surgery. Education is provided early in the hospital stay. The patients learn about cardiac anatomy, the nature of their illness, the prognosis, and treatment. Physical activity progresses gradually during the hospitalization. A transition is made from bed rest to sitting in a chair and then to ambulation on the hospital ward. After seven to ten days in the hospital, the patient continues progressive ambulatory activity at home. Entry into a formal rehabilitation program may occur as early as one to two months after myocardial infarction or coronary operation.

Exercise training is often accomplished on a treadmill device, although distance walking and stationary bicycle exercise are also used. These forms of exercise emphasize large muscle groups and aerobic conditioning—progressive, sustained activity that improves the ability of the heart and lungs to keep pace with the increased need for oxygen during exercise—and may be supplemented with arm work or isotonic exercise emphasizing muscular contraction. The patient's functional capacity is assessed at the onset of the training program. A graded program of exercise is then designed and implemented. Exercise sessions are usually held three to five days each week for 30 to 60 minutes each. Aerobic exercise is monitored for achievement of up to 85% of the symptom-limited work load or the age-adjusted heart rate (figured by subtracting age in years from 220). As the patients become better conditioned and the aerobic capacity

Although formal cardiac rehabilitation programs help many heart patients achieve their optimal level of function, home exercise programs of walking, jogging, or cycling are often recommended by physicians and can be just as beneficial for motivated patients.

increases, the work load is increased. An exercise session usually includes a warm-up period, an endurance phase, and a cool-down period. The program is continued for 8 to 12 weeks. Most participants reach a plateau effect of maximum benefit by this time.

Most programs affiliated with clinics or hospitals utilize telemetry electrocardiographic monitoring at least during the initial stages of the exercise training. The electrocardiogram (EKG) is monitored for signs of ischemia (poor blood flow to the heart) or arrhythmias. Continuous EKG monitoring during a complete course is advised only for high-risk patients. Blood pressure is measured before, during, and following exercise.

Once a favorable level of functional capacity has been reached, participants are encouraged to develop an individual exercise plan that can be performed at home or as part of a community-based exercise program. Patients are instructed to monitor their pulse during walking sessions and to avoid surpassing 85% of their maximum predicted heart rate.

Program staff members may include specially trained nurses or exercise specialists. They provide regular progress reports to the patient's physician. The exercise capacity achieved by the end of the training program is assessed, and an "exercise prescription" is provided for continued physical training after completion of the supervised program. Generally some sort of follow-up contact is made with patients intermittently during the subsequent months and years. The staff's communication to the physician may bring to light special problems regarding the patient's compliance with exercise orders, new symptoms, uncontrolled risk factors, or psychological problems.

Safety of exercise

Death, nonfatal myocardial infarction, and serious arrhythmias have been described in association with physical exercise. In a study of persons without a history of heart disease, exercise training was associated with a lower overall incidence of sudden death. However, despite this lower risk of sudden death in the exercising group, the deaths that did occur in that group were more likely to take place during exercise than during sedentary activities.

The safety of postinfarction rehabilitation programs has been carefully evaluated. The morbidity or mortality is no greater than that expected for postinfarction patients not involved in a formal program. In cases where ventricular fibrillation (a form of cardiac arrest characterized by ineffective quivering of the heart muscle) has occurred during supervised exercise, there has been a high success rate of resuscitative efforts. When such resuscitated patients subsequently have undergone cardiac catheterization, severe multiple-vessel coronary disease frequently has been found. Appropriate patient selection, early monitoring for signs of ischemia, and adherence to target heart rates are, therefore, important ways to enhance the safety of exercise training in post-heart-attack patients.

Failure to respond well to exercise

Despite encouragement to participate, some patients fail to respond favorably to the rehabilitative efforts. Attitude is the basis for some of these failures, as some patients have not regularly exercised and have no intention of changing their life-style. Others fear that exercise might provoke further cardiac problems. For some patients such fears are difficult to allay despite efforts at education.

Some patients are unsuccessful because of cardiac limitations. Severe coronary disease may cause early fatigue or anginal chest pain early in the exercise protocol. A training effect cannot be achieved without sustained exercise above 50% of the predicted maximum. Although heart muscle dysfunction from extensive infarction may limit physical conditioning, many patients with more moderate heart failure can still show some training effect.

Conditions other than cardiac disease also may limit a patient's participation. Cigarette-induced lung disease, peripheral vascular disease with leg claudication (temporary lameness), uncontrolled hypertension, and degenerative arthritis are common examples.

Selective use of cardiac rehabilitation

Initially developed for postinfarction patients, cardiac rehabilitation has been logically extended to coronary surgery patients. There is also some role for enrollment of selected patients with angina pectoris. Physical training may substantially benefit patients with symptoms of lower extremity arterial disease as well.

In recent years there has been an increase in the number of older patients enrolled in cardiac rehabilitation programs. Previously, patients over the age of 65 were often excluded from exercise rehabilitation. Now many in their eighties are participating and may stand to gain from even small increments in their functional capacity.

Not all myocardial infarction and coronary surgery patients, however, are appropriate for referral to a rehabilitative program. Some individuals will readily progress to a good level of functional capacity without formal supervision. If the patient can already perform at 9 METS after the acute recovery phase of myocardial infarction, little benefit is expected from supervised training.

Close communication between patient and physician may suffice to monitor the patient's activity level in home exercise. A treadmill test in a physician's office can provide further objective information. The physician can provide appropriate literature to educate the patient and can directly monitor blood pressure, lipids, and other risk factors. Some patients are appropriately referred to formal cardiac rehabilitation when they have failed a one- or two-month trial of graduated home exercise.

Unfortunately, the rehabilitation enrollment is sometimes motivated by monetary gain (or recovery of start-up cost) to health professionals and the sponsoring institutions rather than by individual patient need. Hospitals and clinics frequently make expensive outlays for EKG-monitoring equipment even though such equipment has been shown to provide minimal additional safety for the average patient. Over $100 million is spent in the U.S. each year on medically supervised exercise programs. Nevertheless, most coronary patients can regain their functional capacity without any organized participation.

Some patients with an excellent functional capacity have been inappropriately sent to rehabilitation. Others who have met their exercise goals by the 12th week have been kept unnecessarily in programs for several months.

Formal cardiac rehabilitation can be very helpful to selected heart patients. Program participation has been a major factor for some in their physical and psychological recovery from myocardial infarction. Cardiac rehabilitation underscores an evolution in the medical profession's attitude toward exercise for the injured heart. It is not a necessary therapy for all postinfarction patients but should be used by those who their physicians judge will derive the greatest benefit. Successful rehabilitation is determined by this patient selection as well as by the motivation of program instructors. The best programs are able to individualize the physical training for each patient and can adapt the educational material to serve the individual's health care and occupational needs.

Sunbathing: A Dying Ritual

by Joan Lippert

The Incas did it. The Egyptians did it. The builders of Stonehenge did it, too—they worshiped that mysterious celestial source of light and life, the sun. Civilizations *still* worship the sun. The rites of devotees can be witnessed the world over in virtually any location where the sun shines. People wearing scanty clothing that leaves most of their skin exposed gather near a body of water, anoint themselves with oil, and sprawl out on rectangular pieces of cloth. Many of these people emerge from their sunbath with a deeper skin color, ranging from a light tan to a very dark brown or black, depending on the coloring they began with and the length of time they stayed in the sunlight. Fair-skinned individuals who perform the ritual for too long often come away lobsterlike—their red skin is hot and painful, and they suffer dearly. (They are, however, quite likely to repeat the ritual many times in the future.)

There have been periods in history when the ritual has lost its lure. In the late 1800s and the first half of this century, suntanned skin was viewed as unfashionable; parasols, porch swings, and paleness were intimations of leisure and luxury, and only outdoor laborers had tans. Moreover, most people worked indoors six days a week and had no time for tanning.

A change began to take hold after World War II. Among Caucasians in the Western world, a tan became a symbol of prosperity. Air travel made sunny vacation spots accessible to those who could afford the plane ticket, and among the souvenirs these travelers brought home was a tan—a picture that spoke a thousand words. The tan even carried mistaken notions of health. In the 1955 movie *Doctor at Sea*, Miss Colbert (Brigitte Bardot) flirts with a ship's captain, inquiring whether he sunbathes. "I do not," says he (James Robertson Justice), to which Miss Colbert exclaims that he *should* because it is "so good for you." Throughout the 1960s and much of the '70s, the tanned look was in. Women used cosmetics (*e.g.,* pale frosted lipsticks) to heighten their tans. The impression that a tan was synonymous with health had implanted itself in the public mind, and there it largely stayed until the late 1970s and early '80s, when dermatologists joined forces to dislodge it.

A time bomb recognized

Fortunately, sun worship today is again experiencing at least something of a decline. Why? Because it has become apparent that a tan is a time bomb that can go off—in the form of skin cancer—decades after indulgence in sunbathing; there is a 20-year time lag between exposure to ultraviolet rays and the development of skin cancer.

Some half a million Americans, most of them Caucasian, will develop skin cancer this year. The sun will be the cause of almost all the cases. About 5% of these cancers will be malignant melanomas, a type of cancer that is treatable if caught early but deadly if not. Experts offer the ABCDs of melanoma: asymmetry, border, color, and diameter. These skin cancers tend

439

to be asymmetrical; their border is irregular, ragged, notched, or blurred; the color is not uniform and is made up of tan, brown, and black, sometimes with added hues of red, white, and blue; and the diameter is usually larger than that of a pencil eraser. Many malignant melanomas arise from preexisting moles.

Some 80% of skin cancers that Americans will develop in the next year will be basal cell carcinomas, which can appear as an open sore, a reddish patch, a smooth growth, a shiny bump, or a scarlike area. Basal cell carcinomas appear most often on the face and other exposed areas of the body but may show up anywhere. These cancers rarely metastasize, but they can cause trouble by impinging on underlying structures or orifices (*e.g.*, eyes, ears, mouth, or bone). Fortunately, the cure rate for these cancers is high.

The remaining 15% of skin cancers will be squamous cell carcinomas—usually raised pink opaque nodules or patches that may open in the center. These cancers also tend to show up on areas of the skin that have been exposed to sunlight, but they can grow anywhere on the body. About one-third of the squamous cell carcinomas found on the tongue and inside of the mouth have metastasized by the time they are diagnosed. Like malignant melanomas and basal cell carcinomas, squamous cell carcinomas are treatable if caught early.

For decades most dermatologists have issued warnings about the sun and skin cancer, but it was in the past several years that statistics added their loud voices—the consequence of the excessive sunning of the two or three previous decades were beginning to show up as a skin-cancer epidemic. The incidence of malignant melanoma has risen 93% in the last ten years and is increasing at a rate greater than that of any other cancer except lung cancer in women. One in 135 whites can now expect to develop melanoma. This has made headlines in newspapers and filled pages and pages of popular magazines. In fact, most people say they learned about the link between the sun and skin cancer through the media.

Skin cancer warning signs*

- a skin growth that changes in size and appears pearly, translucent, tan, brown, black, or multicolored
- a mole or birthmark that changes color, size, or texture and is irregular in outline
- a spot or growth that continues to itch, hurt, crust, scab, erode, or bleed
- an open sore or wound that persists for more than four weeks or heals and then reopens

*If one notices any of these signs or symptoms, one should see a physician immediately.

Source: The Skin Cancer Foundation

On three occasions during Ronald Reagan's presidency, his nasal skin cancers made the news. His down-home quotes caught the attention of the public in 1985: "I had—well, I guess for want of a better word—a pimple on my nose . . . and it was snipped off. . . . It was indeed a basal cell carcinoma, which is the most common and least dangerous kind. . . . I don't mind telling you all this because I know that medicine has been waging a great campaign to try and convince people to stop broiling themselves in the sun." He admitted, however, that having to avoid the sun was "a little heartbreaking . . . because all my life I've lived with a coat of tan, dating back to my lifeguard days." His wife, Nancy, had had the same kind of cancer removed from her lip in 1982.

Skin cancer consciousness

Studies done in the last few years have placed the cancer consciousness of the public at a very high level; some 87% of the general population, according to a survey by Westwood Pharmaceuticals, and 95% of the respondents to a survey conducted by *Health* magazine in conjunction with the Skin Cancer Foundation knew of the sun's link with skin cancer. Nearly as many also knew that exposure to the sun leads to premature aging of the skin.

Many of these same people, however, did not immediately break off their love affair with the sun. Although a larger number altered their behavior so that they devoted less time to actual sunbathing and were more likely to use sunscreen, these surveys found that about one-third of the respondents still sunbathed with the intent of getting a tan. Eighty-four percent of the *Health* readers used a sunscreen; only half of the Westwood study subjects did. A study by the American Academy of Dermatology (AAD) arrived at strikingly similar conclusions about what people know versus what they do. One need only visit a beach or pool when the sun is shining for confirmation that whether or not people are knowledgeable, sun worship is still a living religion.

A limestone relief, c. 1360 BC, shows the Egyptian King Akhenaton under the rays of the sun god Aton, who "distinguished the races, their natures, tongues, and skins, and fulfills the needs of all." Modern humans also bask in the sun, but they are likely to pay dearly for their devotion.

The Granger Collection

From *The Sun and Skin News*, vol. 5, no. 2 (1988), and *Health* Magazine, May 1988; © 1988 The Skin Cancer Foundation, New York, and Family Media, Inc. Reprinted by permission; all rights reserved

Denying the evidence

Sun damage begins with the breakdown of the collagen and elastin that support the skin, and the results, years later, are premature wrinkling and sagging. These consequences, however—and the surgical procedures for removing skin cancers and the resulting scars—seem far off to tanners. Tanning's adherents are people, say physicians, who believe that skin cancer will never happen to them. Not everybody who smokes two packs of cigarettes a day gets lung cancer, people rationalize. They apply the same exception to the sun, convincing themselves that skin cancer happens to *others.*

Tanners also think a tan looks healthy. This is why tanning salons, some of which claim to confer a "safe" tan, are a special problem. Their safety information is outdated. The sun emits both ultraviolet A (UVA) and ultraviolet B (UVB) rays. UVB rays are the ones that burn the skin; public concern about the risk of burns led manufacturers to shift from machines that used UVB to devices that emit only UVA radiation. It is now recognized, however, that UVA is dangerous, too; experts believe that in the long term UVA causes cancer, and it definitely leads to premature aging of skin. Although a relatively small fraction of people patronize tanning salons, from 1978 to 1987 there was more than a 55% increase in the number

Sun habits		
attitude/perception	% of those who had skin cancer	% of those who did not have skin cancer
perceive a tan as healthy	28	48
perceive someone with a tan more attractive than someone without	56	67
almost always avoid exposure between 9 AM and 3 PM	47	31
reduced sun exposure because of		
● the sun and skin cancer link	75	44
● premature aging	19	29
use sunscreen to		
● prevent skin cancer	68	26
● prevent sunburn	29	54
have annual total body exam	33	11
always protect children from sun	56	38

of such enterprises, with over 18,000 salons now in operation in the U.S.

Because tanners believe a tan looks attractive, they are apparently willing to trade beauty today for whatever may happen tomorrow. They enjoy lying in the sun too much to give it up. Unfortunately, lying in the sun *is* pleasurable: it is warming and relaxing;

"Cathy" by Cathy Guisewite; © 1987 Universal Press Syndicate. Reprinted with permission; all rights reserved

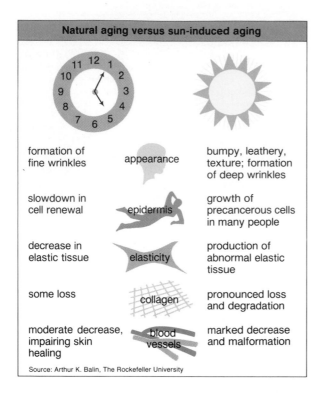

Natural aging versus sun-induced aging

	appearance	
formation of fine wrinkles		bumpy, leathery, texture; formation of deep wrinkles
slowdown in cell renewal	epidermis	growth of precancerous cells in many people
decrease in elastic tissue	elasticity	production of abnormal elastic tissue
some loss	collagen	pronounced loss and degradation
moderate decrease, impairing skin healing	blood vessels	marked decrease and malformation

Source: Arthur K. Balin, The Rockefeller University

one can read, meditate, and imagine oneself on the Côte d'Azur.

Paling popularity

On the bright side, as already indicated, intentionally tanned skin may again be losing its allure. Evidence of this new trend is beginning to be apparent even in the fashion industry. Browsing through the pages of *Vogue, Elle, Seventeen,* and other popular women's fashion magazines, one is unlikely to see any bare skin that is not close to its natural color. In fact, in 1988 two top fashion designers, Donna Karan and Adrienne Vittadini, vowed *not* to use models with suntans. Just as the healthy, amply curvy Christie Brinkley-type body is the mode now—rather than the wispy (*i.e.,* emaciated) Twiggy look—so is truly healthy (*i.e.,* natural) skin.

Today's tanners—those who still deny the evidence—are less likely to have had relatives with skin cancer or to have had it themselves. In the *Health/*Skin Cancer Foundation study, about 10% of respondents had developed some kind of skin cancer. The experience was apparently a sobering one; only 10% of skin cancer patients reported having had a tan in the last year. People with a family member who had developed skin cancer were a bit less cautious; 23% of them had sunbathed. Of people who had not had skin cancer and did not have a relative who had had it, 35% took a chance and toasted themselves in the sunshine. It appears, then, that some people are beginning to get the message and are learning from experience.

Of course, one must question whether the apparent

fashion change will be only a passing trend or will be truly enduring. It is heartening that in the recent past, fashion has in many instances followed public enlightenment about matters of health; to wit, smoking is out, and heart-healthy food and fit bodies are in. If skin au naturel becomes fashionable, this will be a lucky break for today's teenagers, who, more than any other age group, are influenced by styles more than by medical concerns. A recent national opinion survey by the AAD found that a quarter of teenage respondents cited sunning as a cause of skin cancer. In a similar survey two years earlier, only 4% of teens viewed tanning as harmful.

Sun sense

It is absolutely essential for parents, older people, and others to set a good example for these younger members of society. Does this mean people must huddle indoors from now until they die (of something other than skin cancer)? That, fortunately, is further than any one need reasonably go. No dermatologist expects people to stay out of the sunlight entirely. Dermatologists do not even expect their skin cancer patients to live a life of hermitage. They know that would be impractical. Moreover, the sun is *not* a villain through and through. Everyone needs a few minutes of sun-

Selected drugs that can cause photosensitivity reaction	
acetohexamide	lincomycin
amitriptyline	maprotiline
amoxapine	mesoridazine
barbiturates	methacycline
bendroflumethiazide	methotrexate
carbamazepine	nalidixic acid
chlordiazepoxide	nortriptyline
chloroquine	oral contraceptives
chlorothiazide	oxyphenbutazone
chlorpromazine	oxytetracycline
chlorpropamide	perphenazine
chlortetracycline	phenobarbital
chlorthalidone	phenylbutazone
clindamycin	phenytoin
cyproheptadine	prochlorperazine
demeclocycline	promazine
desipramine	promethazine
diethylstilbestrol	protriptyline
diltiazem	pyrazinamide
diphenhydramine	sulfonamides
doxepin	tetracycline
doxycycline	thioridazine
estrogen	tolazamide
fluphenazine	tolbutamide
gold preparations	tranylcypromine
glyburide	triamterene
griseofulvin	trifluoperazine
hydrochlorothiazide	trimeprazine
hydroflumethiazide	trimipramine
imipramine	triprolidine
isotretinoin	

From *The Essential Guide to Prescription Drugs* by James W. Long; © 1989 by Harper & Row, Publishers, Inc. Reprinted by permission of the publisher

light a day to help make vitamin D in the skin. The sun's warmth also promotes wound healing, and ultraviolet radiation has antimicrobial properties that can prevent skin infections. In recent years psychiatrists have demonstrated that sunlight also has profound effects on emotional well-being. The light and warmth of the sun elevate the mood, while sunlight deprivation can cause depression in some people.

Dermatologists encourage people to take the middle road—one that leads to a sensible attitude that most people can live with. The following is their advice on ways to be "sun smart."

● *Stay out of the sun during the peak hours.* Peak hours are between 10 AM and 2 PM (11 AM and 3 PM daylight saving time). While one can tan and burn any time the sun is out, it is safest to schedule a tennis match in the late afternoon or a bike hike in the early morning.

● *Use a sunscreen.* A sunscreen is a lotion or cream that is applied to the skin to protect it chemically. It does this by absorbing the sun's harmful ultraviolet rays. Active absorbing agents used in sunscreens are PABA (para-aminobenzoic acid), PABA esters, cinnamates, benzophenones, salicylates, and anthranilates. A good sunscreen protects against both UVB rays, which are the burning rays, and UVA rays, once thought to be the safer tanning rays but now known to produce long-term skin damage.

Sunscreens come with varying sun protection factors, or SPFs. The SPF is the ratio of the amount of exposure to ultraviolet rays required for causing the skin to redden *with* and *without* a sunscreen. If applied properly, a sunscreen with an SPF of 15 should enable a person to stay in the sunshine without burning 15 times longer than without protection. Although SPF numbers now reach as high as 50, most people are safely protected if they use a sunscreen with an SPF of 15 and reapply it every two to three hours. Moreover, dermatologists warn that a very high SPF, such as 50, may give the user a false sense of security. The U.S. Food and Drug Administration designates five degrees of protection in sunscreen products: an SPF of 2 to 4 offers "minimal" protection; 4 to 6 "moderate" protection; 6 to 8 "extra" protection; 8 to 15 "maximal" protection; and 15 or greater "ultra" protection. One should base the choice of sunscreen on skin type, length of time to be spent in the sunshine, and intensity of the sun's rays according to the time of day and geographic area.

Even on cloudy or hazy days, skin needs the protection of a sunscreen; as much as 80% of burning rays can penetrate clouds. People also need to use sunscreens in winter; snow and ice can reflect as much as 85% of the sun's rays. Skiers in particular should protect themselves. At high altitudes the thinner atmosphere is less absorbent, thus increasing the risk of burning. Each 305-m (1,000-ft) increase in altitude adds 4% to the intensity of ultraviolet light. Further, because the winter air is brisk and cold, skiers and others who recreate outdoors may not feel when they are getting too much sun exposure.

Lips need the protection of sunscreen, too. Skin cancers that develop on lips are common, and they have a greater tendency to metastasize. Many lip balms that protect against chapping also contain sunscreen.

Children especially need protection, but studies have found that they are infrequently made to use sunscreens. In one survey only half of the mothers interviewed applied protection regularly to their children.

Sunscreen should be put on 15 to 30 minutes before going out in the sunshine. This gives the agent time to interact with the skin and set up a shield against ultraviolet rays. It should be applied generously; otherwise, one will get less protection than the bottle indicates. If the same bottle of sunscreen has been traveling around in the bottom of a beach bag for five years, it probably will not offer the full protection it once did. One year is a good limit for keeping a bottle. If one buys a sunscreen that does not carry an expiration date, it is wise to mark the container with the purchase date oneself.

One good way to keep sunscreen protection current is to use the buddy system. If one has perspired

Children are especially vulnerable in the sun. Damage leading to skin cancer can begin with the very first summer sunburn. This ad for one of many sun blocks on the market stresses that parents need to protect their youngsters.

© Eclipse Laboratories, Inc.

or been swimming, one should ask a friend to help refresh sunscreen. The buddy should be reminded to do the same. If alone, one should be brave and ask someone who looks approachable to help reapply sunscreen to one's back.

Currently researchers are using genetic engineering techniques to develop new and better sunscreens, such as a melanin-based agent that may prove to be ten times more effective at preventing sunlight-induced skin cancers than any currently available sun-protection product. Other new products on the horizon are a tanning gauge, which measures the sun's intensity and correlates the intensity with the degree of protection needed by people with different complexions, and an adhesive patch that is worn on the skin and changes color when the sunscreen has washed off or worn down.

● *Use a sun block.* Sun blocks physically stop the sun's rays by reflecting them. These are opaque formulations containing talc, titanium dioxide, or zinc oxide, the traditional white sun block typically seen on the noses, lips, and ears of lifeguards. Sun blocks now come in many hues, such as pink, purple, and other wild colors, and young people especially enjoy playing with this beach "war paint."

Hats, long sleeves, and long pants are sun blocks, too. For clothing to function as protection, the material must be tightly woven and kept dry. A dry T-shirt is a good sun block, but a wet one is not.

● *Wear sunglasses that absorb UV radiation.* Sunglasses, in addition to lowering the chance of getting cataracts, will protect the highly sensitive skin around the eyes. A nonprescription lens that efficiently shields almost 100% of UVB radiation will be labeled "general purpose" or "special purpose," rather than "cosmetic." Skiers should be sure to wear "special purpose" goggles.

● *Do not patronize tanning parlors.* No tan is a safe tan, despite what advertisements claim. Tanning indoors can be deceptive. When using tanning machines, many people expose areas of their bodies that are normally protected. Also, both sides of the body are exposed to rays at once, which intensifies the effect. Even though the glare may not seem harsh, exposure to the UV light emitted by tanning machines can be harmful to eyes, causing retinal damage.

● *Be alert to a potential photosensitivity reaction.* Photosensitivity is an abnormally increased sensitivity of the skin to the harmful rays of the sun. A variety of drugs are capable of causing exaggerated burns or rashes after exposure to ultraviolet light. These include thiazide diuretics, phenothiazine antipsychotics, sulfonamide antibacterials, tetracycline antibiotics, psoralens, and nalidixic acid. Persons taking a prescription medication should be aware of its potential to cause a reaction in the sunlight and should protect themselves properly.

● *Consider alternatives to activities in the sunshine.* This is what the experts call a life-style change. Instead of sunning, one should find other relaxing activities— *e.g.,* taking a bath, meditating, practicing yoga exercises, or listening to music.

● *Think of all the things one can get done instead of wasting time lying around sunbathing.*

● *Fake a tan.* If one "cannot live" without a tanned look, there are safe options, such as bronzing powders or lotions and self-tanning creams like QT and Man Tan. These products use the chemical dihydroxyacetone, which acts by producing a color change when it reacts with proteins on the top layer of skin. The manufacturers have improved their formulas, so one is less likely to get streaks and blotches. The color achieved depends on one's skin color to begin with; people with olive or ruddy skin will get a more realistic (that is, less orange) effect.

Tanning accelerators are lotions that promise to give the user more color from less exposure to sunlight. They contain amino acids used by skin to make pigment. Manufacturers say that using them a few days prior to sunbathing causes cells to do their job of acquiring a darker color more quickly. Dermatologists question their effectiveness, however, and many such enhancers are reputed not to work and may contain potent chemicals that are harmful to the skin.

Tanning pills, claimed by their makers to be a safe substitute for sunlight, contain beta carotene, the pigment in carrots, or canthaxanthin, a food coloring. The pills work by depositing pigments under the skin, but the results are often an unattractive yellow or orange, and color may be very uneven.

● *Check skin for melanomas and other cancers once a month.* People who spend time in the sunshine should examine themselves regularly. This includes inspecting frequently exposed areas, such as the face and hands, as well as less obvious areas on the body, such as the scalp and the spaces between toes. For the former a hair blower can help separate the hair as one checks in a mirror for suspicious lesions. If one notices any unusual spots or growths, one should see a physician without delay.

● *Change one's standard.* Why should people want to alter their skin color anyway? Once upon a time, a tan was a symbol of leisure, and it connoted health. Today the evidence is irrefutable that tans are *unhealthy.* The time has come for all people to be sun smart. To strengthen his patients' resolve, one dermatologist shows them photographs of sun damage and scarring, and he reminds them that operations can be both expensive and disfiguring. He suggests finding a picture of a deeply tanned, deeply lined face and taping it to one's mirror as a reminder. One's own natural skin color, whatever it is, will be very beautiful once one decides to see it that way.

Gum Disease
by L. Anne Hirschel, D.D.S.

Gum, or periodontal, disease, is a stealthy and usually progressive disorder that destroys the tissues that anchor the teeth. Gum disease will afflict 90% of the people in the U.S. at some time in their lives. It is responsible for most tooth loss in adults. Yet in spite of its prevalence—approximately 75% of U.S. adults currently have some periodontal (Greek for "around the tooth") problems, 10% of which are serious—fewer than one-third of those who need periodontal treatment actually seek it. Because it often progresses silently for several years, gum disease is less dramatic than tooth decay, the other most common cause of tooth loss. Whereas cavities are often painful and unsightly, the beginnings of periodontal disease may escape detection unless patients are alerted to early warning signs or the disease is discovered by the dentist or hygienist while still in its incipient stage.

Nature and incidence of gum disease
In a healthy mouth teeth are securely held in place by the gums, or gingiva; the roots of the teeth are firmly embedded in the jawbone. Surrounding each tooth root is a fibrous ligament, the periodontal ligament, which is attached to both the tooth root and the jawbone. These supporting structures—gums, ligaments, and bone—withstand the enormous forces generated each time the teeth bite together, and if properly cared for, they will function for a lifetime. The once-prevalent belief that gums must deteriorate with age and that gum disease and tooth loss are inevitable accompaniments of aging is a myth. In fact, about 30 years ago scientists confirmed that periodontal disease is infectious in nature. They concluded that in most cases of gum disease, plaque—the sticky bacterial film that forms on the teeth continuously—is the primary culprit. If plaque is not removed adequately by tooth brushing and flossing, it hardens to form calculus (tartar). Barnacle-like, calculus clings firmly to the teeth. It can be removed from the teeth only in the course of professional cleaning by a dentist or dental hygienist.

The incidence and severity of periodontal disease increase with age, yet it is seen in all age groups, even in young children. A recent U.S. survey indicated that 92% of the country's schoolchildren have some gum inflammation; 3%, or 1.4 million, of them have periodontal problems severe enough to warrant treatment. The condition is not confined to any particular part of the world, nor is it considered a malady of "modern" times. Neanderthal skulls show signs of loss of supporting jawbone (an indication of advanced gum disease), and it is known that the ancient Egyptians, Greeks, and Phoenicians attempted to wire together teeth loosened by gum disease in order to stabilize them and prevent them from falling out. Current studies show that gum disease is prevalent around the globe, although comparisons of different populations are complicated by the varying methods of collecting and interpreting data. Further, the degree of toothlessness in older people in various parts of the world may be influenced by cultural, social, and religious differences and is not necessarily related only to the incidence of gum disease.

Kinds and stages of disease
The term periodontal disease is actually a catchall name for a variety of gum diseases and stages of disease. In gingivitis, the milder stage of periodontal disease, gums irritated by bacterial by-products found in plaque become inflamed, red, and swollen. They may be tender and bleed when brushed, leaving a telltale clue on the toothbrush—hence the term pink toothbrush. (While gum disease may be present even without noticeable bleeding, bleeding gums are never normal and always signify a problem.) At this stage of periodontal disease, the inflammation is confined to the superficial soft tissues, and if they are properly cared for, the damage is reversible.

Although gingivitis is not invariably followed by the more severe condition called periodontitis (formerly called pyorrhea, Greek for "flow of pus"), gum disease tends to be progressive, and periodontitis frequently develops. The gum tissue pulls away from the teeth, and spaces, or pockets, form between teeth and gums. A vicious cycle develops—continued accumulation of plaque causes a deepening of the pockets, and deeper pockets trap ever more plaque. Within the pockets infection develops. As the body's immune

445

mechanism attempts unsuccessfully to overcome the infection, the connective tissue fibers surrounding the tooth are progressively destroyed. The infection moves into deeper tissues under the gum line, and pockets deepen even further. The gum gradually recedes, and the attachment of tooth and gum weakens. Eventually the supporting bone is resorbed (dissolved), and the tooth, robbed of its support, loosens and finally may fall out or need to be removed.

Unlike gingivitis, which generally precedes it, periodontitis usually does not remain unnoticed, although it may be present for a considerable time before the patient becomes aware that something is amiss. As the tissues are destroyed, abscesses may form, and a milky fluid, pus, may ooze out when the gums are pressed. Pain develops when pus collects in the pockets between the gums and teeth and is unable to drain. The patient may notice an unpleasant taste in the mouth. This, along with persistent bad breath—often more apparent to others than to the patient—can be a tip-off to the presence of gum disease. As the gums recede further and more of the roots become exposed, teeth may actually appear longer. Exposed roots may be sensitive and become susceptible to cavities (root caries). Patients who have not had a cavity for years may therefore be startled to suddenly find they need new fillings. With their mechanical support failing, teeth may begin to protrude, spread out, or change in the way they bite together. Eventually teeth may be lost. Most investigators now believe that periodontitis progresses in bursts of activity followed by dormant periods. There may be active disease in one part of the mouth and a quiescent condition in another. Nevertheless, although the disease may be temporarily dormant, in susceptible individuals it tends to worsen if left untreated.

An estimated 0.1 to 15% of healthy adolescents suffer from a form of periodontitis called localized juvenile periodontitis (LJP), which rapidly destroys supporting bone usually around the first molars (first large back teeth) and incisors (front teeth). LJP is not generally accompanied by notable plaque accumulation or gum inflammation. Scientists now believe that LJP, which afflicts females three times more often than males, has a familial basis. If caught early, it responds well to local treatment and to antibiotics.

During World War I a virulent form of gingivitis, acute necrotizing ulcerative gingivitis (ANUG), or Vincent's infection, was prevalent among soldiers in the trenches and was popularly called trench mouth. The condition is characterized by ulceration, pain, and rapid destruction of tissues between the teeth; there may also be an unpleasant odor. ANUG is seen with some frequency in children in less developed areas of Africa, Asia, and South America but is less prevalent among North American and European children. Predisposing factors include systemic illnesses, viral infections, malnutrition, stress, and lack of sleep.

How general health can affect oral health

Although almost everyone may succumb to periodontal disease at some time, certain systemic conditions—among them diabetes, scurvy, certain blood disorders, and various immunodeficiency diseases (including AIDS)—tend to lower people's resistance to infections and increase the severity of gum disease. In those who have diabetes, the interplay between oral and general health is profound. Uncontrolled diabetes aggravates periodontal disease, and the presence of periodontal infection in turn complicates the effective control of diabetes. Although adults whose diabetes is under good control generally do not suffer undue periodontal disease, the picture is dramatically different for those whose diabetes is not well controlled. Also, because infections, including gum infections, tend to cause hyperglycemia (increased sugar in the blood), any exacerbation of periodontal infection may interfere with maintenance of good diabetes control. For persons with newly diagnosed diabetes, the presence of preexisting severe periodontal disease may complicate

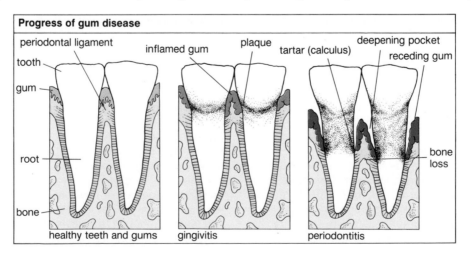

Progress of gum disease

periodontal ligament — inflamed gum — plaque — tartar (calculus) — deepening pocket — receding gum

tooth — gum — root — bone — bone loss

healthy teeth and gums — gingivitis — periodontitis

their initial diabetes control. Diabetes control is further hampered when, because of painful gums, patients select foods that are easy to chew but inappropriate for a diabetic diet.

Hormonal changes that occur during puberty (in both boys and girls) and pregnancy tend to increase susceptibility to gingivitis. About half of all pregnant women experience some gum disease. The condition tends to regress after childbirth but may recur during subsequent pregnancies.

Taking certain medications, including steroids, oral contraceptives, and some anticancer drugs, may affect the gums adversely. In cancer patients a relatively innocuous preexisting periodontitis may flare out of control and even become life-threatening after the initiation of cancer chemotherapy. Fortunately, these acute episodes can generally be prevented with adequate dental care before, during, and after cancer therapy. Patients taking the antiepilepsy drug phenytoin (Dilantin) often have swollen, inflamed gums, although careful oral hygiene can keep the enlargement of the gum tissue to a minimum. Occasionally periodontal surgery may be indicated. Even after successful surgical treatment, recurrence is common if the patient's oral hygiene habits are not scrupulous.

Smokers have been found to have more plaque and calculus accumulation than nonsmokers, and when they get gum disease, it appears to be more severe. Traditionally the explanation offered for this difference was that smokers were less meticulous in their tooth brushing and flossing. Recent studies have shed some new light on the issue. They indicate that the nicotine in cigarettes and smokeless tobacco results in the abnormal growth of gum cells, which may be the reason the gums of smokers fail to attach satisfactorily to the tooth roots after periodontal surgery.

Mechanical irritants—including broken fillings and poorly fitting partial dentures; habits such as tooth grinding (bruxism), which place stress on the tissues; and the stress caused by a faulty bite or misaligned teeth—tend to have a deleterious effect on the health of the gum tissues. They do not, however, appear to be primary causes of periodontal disease.

One focus of current research is the role heredity plays in the development of periodontal disease. It is known, for example, that LJP tends to follow familial patterns, although the exact mechanism is not yet understood. The preliminary results of a recent study based on the examination of 30 pairs of twins indicated that about 50 to 75% of chronic adult gum disease may also be the result of genetic influences. Investigators are also examining the possibility that the causative organisms may be transmitted between household members, although the exact route of spread is unknown; even bacteria in the mouths of pets have been implicated as a source of infection in humans. The extent to which diet and nutritional deficiencies affect periodontal disease is controversial, but it is generally agreed that they are not a primary cause of the condition.

The importance of prevention

Prevention, accomplished by meticulous daily brushing and flossing as well as regular professional cleaning, is the ideal approach to gum disease. In addition to routine brushing and flossing, dentists may recommend the use of certain adjuncts—*e.g.,* employing an interdental brush (a small rounded brush that fits into the spaces between teeth); massaging the gums with a rubber tip, such as those on the nonbrush end of some toothbrushes; flossing with the aid of a special floss holder; and periodic testing with so-called disclosing agents, tablets or solutions containing a harmless dye that colors the plaque clinging to the surface of teeth. These latter products help to detect plaque that the toothbrush may have missed.

Mechanical plaque removal by brushing and flossing is still considered basic to good oral hygiene, but various methods of chemical plaque control—mouthwashes, irrigating devices, and toothpastes that deliver plaque-fighting drugs locally—are being widely promoted. Only a few such products have been sufficiently tested, however, and many have drawbacks. Unless used with an irrigation device, mouth rinses fail to reach plaque clinging in the recesses of deep pockets, and irrigation devices are not an answer in and of themselves, as even the most efficacious irrigators may be difficult to aim accurately. Chemical plaque control is suitable for short-term use or for disabled patients who find brushing difficult, but it is not a substitute for routine brushing and flossing. The tartar-control toothpastes currently on the market control tartar build-up only on the exposed surfaces of teeth up to the gum line (but not under the gums). Many ideas about gum disease have changed in recent years, but plaque removal remains the cornerstone of prevention and of successful therapy.

Diagnosing periodontal problems

Ideally, treatment is keyed to an accurate diagnosis. The diagnosis is based on examination of the gums and teeth, with notation of evidence of inflamed or bleeding gums and tooth mobility; the use of probes for measuring the depth of the pockets of inflammation; and observation of bone changes as revealed by X-rays. Improved diagnostic tools are continually being developed. One recent innovation is a computerized probe that electronically measures the depths of pockets in the gums more gently and quickly than a traditional probe. Measurements taken over a period of time can be compared more accurately than was possible in the past. This information supplies important clues about whether the pockets are deepening, remaining unchanged, or becoming shallower as gum tissue reattaches to the teeth. Computers are also now used in an X-ray technique, digital subtraction radiography, that measures bone changes. The method is up to 30 times more sensitive than visual inspection of traditional X-rays. In the future, laboratory tests for identifying specific causative organisms will probably become increasingly important in treatment planning.

Professional treatment

Periodontal diseases are often treated by general dentists; in more advanced cases the patient may be referred to a periodontist—a dentist who specializes in periodontal disease or who has taken additional courses in the field and may be board certified. Therapy is often a team effort involving several health professionals in addition to the periodontist—the general dentist to correct faulty fillings, crowns, and other restorations; the orthodontist to correct misaligned teeth; the endodontist to treat a diseased tooth pulp; the prosthodontist to replace missing teeth; and in some cases the physician who may be treating the patient for a significant systemic disorder. Regardless of how many health professionals are involved, the patient plays an essential role in controlling the disease. Although with therapy the outlook is generally good, treatment is likely to fail unless the patient practices meticulous oral hygiene not just during the active stages of the disease but for the rest of his or her life. Because gum disease tends to recur, its long-term control involves a lifetime commitment.

Nonsurgical and surgical therapies

In the early stages of periodontal disease, professional cleaning may be all the treatment that is necessary. The teeth are scaled (scraped free of plaque and calculus). If inflamed tissue is present in pockets, it is also scraped away (curettage). Finally, the root surfaces are planed to make them completely smooth. Not all cases can be controlled by scaling and curettage alone, however. Some patients need systemic or topical (locally applied) antibiotics to bring the infection under control. In recent years dentists have been experimenting with placing tiny dosages of antibiotics directly into the gum pockets. In one such technique, antibiotic-soaked fibers are inserted into the pockets for a limited time and then removed. In another relatively new therapy, a tiny biodegradable bead is used; it contains a time-release antibiotic. Nonsurgical treatment may also include splinting loose teeth together to provide more stability.

Nonsurgical therapy is always tried first, but when pocket depths exceed about five millimeters, it often becomes impossible to keep the pockets plaque free or to remove deeply situated deposits of calculus and plaque. Surgery may then be necessary. The objective is to gain access to the inflamed tissues, remove deposits and diseased tissue, and possibly reshape the

tissues and reduce pocket depths. Upon completion of the surgery, the teeth should be as smooth and clean as possible so as to minimize the number of places where plaque can become trapped and to enable the patient to keep these surfaces plaque free. Periodontal surgery is generally an office procedure.

If the disease has not reached the bone, deep pockets in the gums may be corrected by cutting away the outer wall of the pocket or removing it with electrosurgery. This procedure is called a gingivectomy, and it is generally performed on no more than one quadrant or half of the mouth at a time. Dressings placed over the operated area after surgery help to reduce discomfort. They are usually removed after three to five days, at which time the patient can generally resume practicing normal oral hygiene.

When the disease has progressed to the bone, so-called flap surgery may be indicated. A flap of gum tissue is laid back to allow access, and calculus, plaque, and diseased tissue are removed. The bone may then be reshaped, and the gum is sutured (sewn) back in place. The sutures are usually removed 5 to 14 days after surgery. Anywhere from one to four follow-up visits are then generally scheduled at one- or two-week intervals. Other periodontal surgical procedures include the replacement of destroyed bone with transplanted natural bone and synthetic bone substitutes and gum tissue grafting to correct defects or improve appearance. Recent clinical tests of innovative techniques for promoting regeneration of soft and hard tissues destroyed by periodontal disease have shown a great deal of promise. Researchers were excited to see that such regeneration is indeed possible.

Directions for future research

In the hope that gum disease, like tooth decay, will begin to decline dramatically in incidence, dental investigators continue searching for answers to underlying questions: Are some people more susceptible to gum disease than others because their body's immune mechanisms do not respond appropriately to periodontal infections? If so, what is responsible for the defect in immunity? How can persons at high risk be identified before they develop gum disease? What role does heredity play? How can areas of tissue that are in the process of healing be distinguished from areas of active disease? If, as many researchers believe, specific organisms cause specific periodontal diseases—and many of these organisms have not yet been identified—which bacteria are responsible for which disease? Which drugs combat these bacteria most efficiently, and how can these drugs best be delivered? Can researchers develop a vaccine for protection against periodontal disease? Dental scientists are continuing to work toward finding answers to these questions.

Calorie Counting— the Scientific Way

by J. Anderson Williams

You've probably been wondering how they figure out just how many calories there are in, say, a four-ounce Italian sausage. I've been wondering the same thing. You may have been wondering about it for the same reason that I've been wondering about it: maybe they're wrong. Maybe calculating calories is a science about as exact as handicapping horses.
—Copyright © 1986 by Calvin Trillin

Many people are better acquainted than they would like to be with calorie counting for the purpose of weight control. However, as consumers acquire information on the caloric content of the foods they eat from all the various sources of information available to them—books, magazines, food package labels—they may wonder just how reliable all those calorie values are. Actually, accurate information on the caloric content of food is indispensable not only for dealing with obesity but also for dealing with undernutrition and establishing normal nutrition.

What is a calorie?

A calorie is a unit of measure used to describe energy content. Energy can exist in any number of forms; for convenience most energy units are expressed in terms of heat or work equivalents. A calorie, then, is defined as the quantity of heat necessary to change the temperature of one gram of water (about one-fifth of a teaspoon) 1° C (1.8° F). A calorie defined this way is referred to as a "small calorie" and, as its name might imply, indicates an amount of energy too small to readily lend itself to a discussion of the energy value of foods. For this reason, most people, when discussing diet and referring to "calories," are actually referring to "large calories," or kilocalories. A large calorie is equal to 1,000 small calories and is distinguished in scientific notations of caloric content by the use of a capital C. In other words, if a peach is listed as having 40 Calories, this indicates that the peach has 40,000 calories.

Such units as British thermal units (BTUs) and joules are also used to describe energy values but are infrequently used in a nutritional context. It has been proposed that the kilojoule replace the kilocalorie as the unit of choice for discussing the energy value of foods. Such a change would bring the nomenclature used by food scientists into closer agreement with that used by other scientists. The conversion factor for expressing kilocalories as kilojoules, as recommended by the Committee on Nomenclature of the International

Union of Nutritional Sciences, is one kilocalorie equals 4.184 kilojoules, based on the kilocalorie determined at 14.5° to 15.5° C. U.S. government publications now provide energy counts in kilojoules and kilocalories, but Calorie is still the most commonly used food energy unit in the U.S. and abroad.

Calorie chemistry

Calories are stored in chemical bonds and released when these bonds are broken. No matter how a given type of chemical bond is broken, it will always release the same amount of energy. Human bodies biochemically break down chemical bonds in food to release energy. These physiological reactions produce effects similar but not identical to the reactions that occur when something burns. Food contains a variety of bonds, ranging from easy-to-break (high-energy) bonds to bonds that are not broken down in human bodies (and have no utilizable energy).

During the 1800s scientists first began to suspect that each chemical bond had a characteristic energy value. Around the turn of the century, Wilbur O. Atwater, professor of chemistry at Wesleyan University, Middletown, Conn., and chemist for the United States Department of Agriculture (USDA), along with his associates conducted studies that laid the foundation for calorie counting as it is known today. Atwater realized that there are differences in the total energy content of a food and its usable energy. The total energy content of a substance is easily determined but, unfortunately, it is of limited use to nutritionists;

449

meanwhile, the usable energy of a substance is difficult to determine but of great value to nutritionists. Atwater's work was directed toward developing a method of calorie counting that would provide the relative ease of direct laboratory analysis while producing physiologically meaningful energy values. There are a number of ways to actually count calories: bonds can be physically broken by combustion and then the total heat or work obtained is measured; bonds can be biochemically broken and the heat or work available to a living organism measured; or after determination of the number and type of chemical bonds present, the caloric content can be mathematically determined by means of predetermined energy equivalents for each type of bond. Current methods of calorie counting for human nutrition applications have evolved to include elements of all three of these methods.

Determining total calories. The bomb calorimeter is a device that has been in use since before Atwater's time to determine the total energy content of a substance. It consists of a bomb—a small pressure-resistant container—and a calorimeter—a highly sensitive temperature-measuring device. When a calorie determination is to be made, an accurately weighed sample of a given foodstuff is placed inside the bomb. The bomb is then sealed, pressurized with oxygen, and lowered into a bucket of water located inside the calorimeter. An electrical charge initiates combustion of the sample, releasing energy, which, in turn, warms the bomb and the water in the bucket. The calorimeter measures the resulting temperature change, allowing calculation of the total caloric content of the sample.

Determining usable calories. Atwater developed and used "human calorimeters" to gauge the usable energy, or physiologically available energy, of foods. His hu-

man calorimeters were somewhat like bomb calorimeters in that food was "burned" in one unit—a human volunteer—and the resulting change in temperature of the containing unit—a specially designed test room—was measured. However, determining physiologically available energy is much more complicated than determining total energy. Human bodies do not completely utilize the total energy available, and the energy obtained is used in a variety of bodily processes in addition to heat generation. All products of metabolism must be taken into account in physiological tests to determine the amount of energy actually consumed. Because of this, Atwater not only had to determine the apparent caloric content of the food from the temperature change and work done in the test chamber but also had to characterize the caloric content of the food before and after digestion. Later studies included measurement of respiratory by-products.

Determining calories by calculation. Atwater was able to categorize foods according to their usable energy content. He subsequently determined the energy-bearing components of a variety of foods. Through the work of Atwater and others, it has become widely accepted that fats, carbohydrates, and proteins are the predominate sources of available energy in foods (and therefore are the chief nutritional sources of calories) and that even though fats, carbohydrates, and proteins constitute rather broad categories, each individual member of a given category has roughly the same caloric content. Atwater proved that one can make accurate physiological energy-value estimations on food by applying appropriate multiplication factors to the protein, fat, and carbohydrate concentrations of the food in question and then adding up the values obtained. Because the calorie values obtained this way are in such close agreement with physical and physiological values, the Atwater system of calorie calculation has become the method of choice for calorie counting in the United States. The USDA's Agriculture Handbook No. 74 (*Energy Value of Foods: Basis and Derivation*) provides detailed summaries of studies supporting the Atwater system.

The Atwater system of calorie counting

A general formula for the Atwater method of calorie calculation is: caloric content = (4 × protein content) + (9 × fat content) + (4 × carbohydrate content). Properly applied, this formula provides a fairly good rule of thumb for calorie counting. The versions used by food scientists differ in that more exact multipliers than four, nine, and four, respectively, are used, and fat, protein, and carbohydrate definitions may vary with the type of food being considered.

The Atwater system further simplifies nutritional information acquisition by using proximate data to calculate calorie values. A "proximate" analytical method provides an estimate of the concentration of a given

Calculating calories: two methods		
food	calories in 100 g	
	method a*	method b†
beef	273	268
salmon, canned	143	138
eggs	162	158
milk	68	69
butter	716	733
vegetable fats and oils	884	900
oatmeal	390	396
rice, brown	360	356
rice, white or milled	362	351
beans, snap	35	42
cabbage	24	29
carrots	42	45
potatoes	83	85
apples, raw	58	64
lemons, raw	32	44
peaches, canned	68	75
sugar, cane or beet	385	398

*method a: highly specific "ultimate" analyses
†method b: simplified analyses using "proximate" data

Source: USDA *Agriculture Handbook* No. 74

category of compounds by targeting some common characteristic of each compound in the category. Food scientists make extensive use of proximate data because these data provide information of equal or greater value to highly specific "ultimate" analyses (see Table); moreover, they are more easily acquired. Analyses of caloric concern conventionally determined by proximate methods include determinations of fat, protein, carbohydrates, moisture, ash, and some types of fiber. The term crude is used to indicate a proximate analysis.

Routine food analyses in the U.S. are all generally performed in the same manner, whether run by private, public, or independent laboratories. The USDA and the Food and Drug Administration (FDA) rely heavily upon the official methods of analysis of the U.S. Association of Official Analytical Chemists (AOAC). These methods have been validated through collaborative studies and provide accurate and reproducible results for the stated component and sample type, when performed by competent scientists. Use of AOAC methods is required by federal law when laboratory results are to be used in support of nutritional labeling claims.

Sampling. Regardless of the methodology used, the result of an analysis of caloric content is only as reliable as the sample analyzed. The objective of all food sampling is to obtain a representative portion of the total supply of a foodstuff. The techniques for obtaining such a representative sample vary widely with the targeted foodstuff but should account for such variables as seasonal and regional differences in food supplies. The choice of sampling technique is sometimes prescribed by federal law. For nutritional labeling claims—e.g., for a Lean Cuisine Chicken à l'Orange frozen dinner or a can of Campbell's Chunky Chicken soup—a sample must be a composite of 12 consumer units of a product taken from 12 different randomly selected shipping cases. Once the sample has been selected, it must be processed in such a way that representative subsamples for laboratory analysis may be taken without compromising the original chemical composition. This is usually accomplished by the use of commercial blenders or food processors capable of turning foods into a homogeneous paste or fine powder.

Fat. Dietary fat—or, more accurately, crude fat—has come to indicate any material that can be extracted by means of an organic solvent (usually ether). In a simple ether extraction, a prepared sample is thoroughly mixed with ether. Anything that is soluble (i.e., dissolves) in ether is extracted from the food when the food and ether are physically separated by filtration or other means. This mixing and separating is repeated with fresh ether until all ether-soluble material has been removed from the food. When the extraction is complete, all ether that has come in contact with the sample is combined and evaporated under controlled conditions. The residue after evaporation is

crude fat. This residue is weighed for determination of fat content. The calorie factor for fat takes into account the fact that crude fat also contains ether-soluble nonfat components, such as cholesterol and pigments (e.g., chlorophyll); the calorie factor is based on the metabolizable energy of crude fat, not the total energy content of pure fat.

The type and amount of materials extracted are dependent on the pretreatment of a sample and on the type of solvent used. Two different extraction methods applied to the same sample can yield results that differ significantly but that are reproducible within the method itself. This occurs because the fat in food can be chemically bound in ways that make it incompletely soluble in ether (or other solvents) but still available for physiological reactions. Pretreatment of samples frees fats from these combinations and thus facilitates reproducible extractions. AOAC methods for crude-fat determinations generally use one of the following three basic techniques: (1) acid pretreatment followed by ether extraction; (2) alkali pretreatment followed by ether extraction; or (3) direct solvent extraction. The technique used is dependent on the sample type and is usually specified by the AOAC method.

Protein. What is known as the Kjeldahl method of protein determination was developed in 1883 by the Danish chemist Johan G. C. T. Kjeldahl. This method involves converting all the nitrogen in the sample into ammonia—a simple nitrogen-containing compound—by heating the sample with sulfuric acid in the presence of a catalyst. To separate the ammonia from the original sample, this solution is rendered alkaline, and the ammonia is distilled into a trapping solution. The amount of ammonia in the trapping solution is measured, and the nitrogen content is calculated. The protein content is estimated from the nitrogen content by means of an appropriate multiplication factor. Protein determined this way is more accurately referred to as crude protein because nonprotein nitrogen-containing compounds, such as nitrates, nitrites, and free amino acids (the building blocks of protein), are found in measurable quantities in some foods. The presence of nonprotein nitrogen-containing compounds partially negates the underlying assumption of the multiplication factor that all nitrogen present is bound as protein.

The multiplier is the most controversial part of the protein determination. In reality, the relationship between the protein and the nitrogen contents varies with sample type and the growth stage of the sample. AOAC methods generalize by using the factor 5.7 for products in which a major part of the protein is contributed by wheat, 6.38 for products in which a major part of the protein is contributed by milk, and 6.25 for everything else ranging from meat to barley. This can give anomalous results for samples such as pork rinds, in which the measurement of protein content can exceed 100%. Another method involves calculating the protein content from the sum of the individual amino acids in the sample, but this method is laborious, expensive, and not very precise.

Carbohydrates. Carbohydrates are most often determined by taking the sum of the percentages of fat, protein, moisture, and ash and subtracting from 100%. This proximate value is sometimes referred to as "total carbohydrate" or "carbohydrate by difference." Ash and moisture determinations are made by heating a food under controlled conditions. Moisture is the loss in weight observed after a sample is heated near the boiling point of water. Ash is the weight of residue left after a sample is heated at temperatures that burn all the burnable material. A drawback is that carbohydrates determined this way also include other calorie-containing compounds, such as the organic acids found in citrus fruits, and non-calorie-containing components, such as fiber. The fiber contribution to the total carbohydrate value is a subject of dispute among food scientists.

Fiber may be defined as a substance found in plants that is resistant to digestion by human beings. Various types of fiber are recognized. Unfortunately, there is not a single proximate fiber determination that is as well suited to nutritional applications as the proximate methods discussed above. The extent to which fiber inflates the calculated calorie value is a function of the type and amount of plant material in a food. Generally, edible leaves and stems are high in fiber, fruits and vegetables contain moderate amounts of fiber, and animal tissues contain no fiber. For some foods, subtracting fiber from the total carbohydrate count lowers the calculated calorie count; for others there is little change. No single convention has been established for including or excluding fiber from the Atwater calculation method. Therefore, if it is not known whether fiber was accounted for in a calorie calculation, it is safe for consumers to assume that the calorie value given in calorie charts or on a food label represents a maximum; the actual caloric content may be, for example, ten Calories less.

Sources of calorie counts

Two reliable sources of calorie counts in the U.S. are nutritional labels on food packages and the USDA's Agriculture Handbook No. 8 (*Composition of Foods: Raw, Processed, Prepared*). Food manufacturers provide the information on food labels and can use data from their own laboratories or from any of about 25 independent labs to support their claims. However, if the manufacturer's claim differs by more than 20% from the findings of the responsible governmental agency, the manufacturer is required by law to make any necessary corrections. Thus, allowing for differences in samples and various manufacturing uncertainties, a frozen dinner that claims to be "under 300 Calories"

could actually have as many as 360 Calories or as few as 240 Calories. The USDA is responsible for regulating the nutritional labeling of meat, poultry, and egg products, while the FDA has jurisdiction over the labeling of all other foods.

The Agriculture Handbook No. 8 is an extensive set of tables of nutritional information and is widely regarded in the U.S. and other countries as the premier document of its kind. The handbook has evolved to include nearly 100 years' worth of accumulated nutritional data and is constantly being updated by means of the USDA's computerized Nutrient Data Bank. Most of the published calorie values that are found in books, magazines, and newspapers can be traced to the Agriculture Handbook No. 8.

Interpreting calorie values

For the consumer who is concerned about getting adequate nourishment or who is interested in losing or gaining weight, making informed decisions by using available calorie values requires an understanding of the relative accuracy of the values in question and knowing how they were derived. While the best way for the individual to get this information ultimately would be to perform his or her own laboratory analyses, rarely is this a practical suggestion. Therefore, most often the interpretation of calories from available sources involves having a little technical knowledge and doing a lot of situational analysis.

How accurate do calorie values really need to be? Most people are surprised to learn that the method of choice for calorie counting is an approximation based upon approximations; it is likely that the actual calorie value of a given food will differ from the predetermined value. However, provided the predetermined value was obtained responsibly, the average of several "actual values" usually comes close to the predetermined value. The variability in food supplies and the fact that people metabolize food differently preclude a single calorie value appropriate for every circumstance. Luckily, variances between actual and predetermined calorie values are usually slight and rarely a matter of life and death. Therefore, the consumer can rest assured that calorie values determined by the Atwater system are sufficiently accurate to be used as guidelines for most nutrition decisions.

In answer to Calvin Trillin—the writer who has made a career of eating and writing about food and wonders about the calories in an Italian sausage—handicapping and calorie calculating are alike in that one's chances of getting the right result increase dramatically with an intimate understanding of the subject, be it a horse or a food product. However, the energy values of chemical bonds have proved time and time again to be much more consistent than racehorses!

Pressure Sores
by David B. Reuben, M.D.

Along with Alzheimer's disease and incontinence, bedsores rate as one of the greatest medical problems associated with aging. Many names have been applied to this condition, including bedsores and decubitus ulcers (decubitus from the Latin *decumbere,* "to lie down"), but the preferred term is pressure sores because the main cause of the problem is pressure. Pressure sores are classified into four grades; the most superficial of these, grade one, may be simply an ill-defined area of redness or what appears to be a minor scrape. At the other end of the spectrum, a grade four pressure sore may extend into the deep tissue, bone, or muscle.

A common and costly problem

Although pressure sores may occur in bed-bound persons of any age, approximately 50% occur in persons 70 years of age or older. In the healthy elderly population, pressure sores are virtually nonexistent, but with acute or chronic illness the likelihood of developing them increases. An estimated 10–25% of elderly hospitalized patients will develop a pressure sore, usually within the first two weeks of hospitalization. The problem also commonly occurs in 20–30% of nursing home patients, especially in homes that have poor staff-to-patient ratios. People of any age who are immobilized or confined to wheelchairs are also at risk.

Pressure sores are costly, both in terms of medical expenses associated with treating patients with the problem (average $15,000 per pressure sore treated) and in terms of increased mortality. It is estimated that up to 60,000 persons die as a result of these sores each year, and the risk of death increases fourfold in nursing home patients who develop them.

Most often, pressure sores in hospitalized patients are discovered by nurses in the process of bathing and repositioning patients in attempts to prevent the problem, and it is the nursing staff that generally attend to the sores once they develop. Physicians, in general, have been inattentive to the prevention, detection, and management of pressure sores. The topic receives little attention during medical school or residency training, and physicians rarely inspect their bedridden patients carefully at pressure points.

Causes and complications

The primary cause of pressure sores is sustained pressure over a bony prominence, such as the hip or the heel. In usual activities of daily living, very high pressures are generated over bony prominences; *e.g.,* the buttocks, when a person is sitting. After a few moments, this pressure is sensed, often subconsciously, and the person repositions himself or herself to relieve the pressure. This continual repositioning generally prevents the development of pressure sores in healthy persons whose work requires sitting for prolonged time periods and in young adults or children who suffer through an acute illness such as a bout of the flu. Although the skin and the underlying tissue can withstand very high pressure over these areas for short periods of time, irreversible tissue damage begins if this pressure is not relieved within two hours. In fact, quite low pressures, if unrelieved, may cause tissue breakdown. Prolonged pressure stretches and compresses blood and lymphatic vessels, preventing tissue from receiving oxygen and nutrients and impairing removal of waste products. Although the skin is the most commonly noticed breakdown site, damage occurs earlier and to a greater extent in underlying

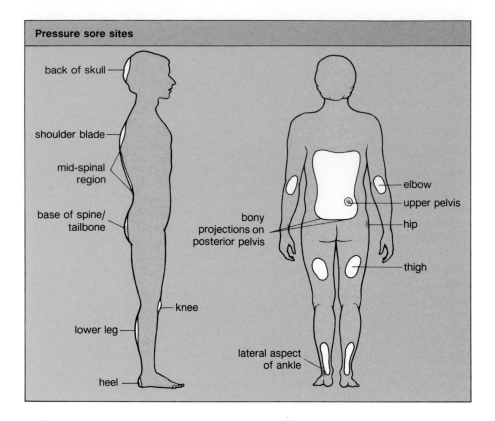

Pressure sore sites

back of skull

shoulder blade

mid-spinal region

base of spine/tailbone

knee

lower leg

heel

elbow

upper pelvis

hip

thigh

lateral aspect of ankle

bony projections on posterior pelvis

muscle and fat. As previously mentioned, grade one pressure sores appear as ill-defined areas of redness or resemble minor scrapes. Grade two sores extend through skin to fat; grade three sores extend through fat layers; and, as indicated above, grade four sores can extend into deep tissue, muscle, and bone. Almost all pressure sites occur below the waist, especially over the sacrum (base of spine/tailbone), pelvis,

trochanter (hip), heel, and lateral aspect of the ankle (*see* figure above).

Some pain may be associated with early stages of pressure sores, and the patient may be upset by these unsightly skin lesions. However, at later stages, pain—both physical and emotional—is generally overshadowed by the debilitating conditions that are responsible for the development of pressure sores.

Positions for preventing pressure sores: (1) supine position—localized pressure chiefly on heels and base of spine; (2) 30° oblique position—optimal: none of the five main ulcer sites in contact with bed surface; (3) 90° lateral position—body weight chiefly on hip; (4) 135° oblique prone position—body weight chiefly on pelvis; and (5) prone position—efficient for younger but not for elderly patients.

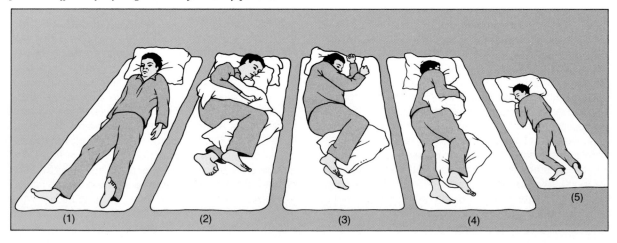

(1)   (2)   (3)   (4)   (5)

Norton pressure sore risk-assessment scoring system*									
physical condition	score	mental state	score	activity	score	mobility	score	incontinence	score
good	4	alert	4	ambulant	4	full	4	none	4
fair	3	apathetic	3	walks with help	3	slightly limited	3	occasional	3
poor	2	confused	2	wheelchairbound	2	very limited	2	usually urinary	2
very bad	1	stuporous	1	bedfast	1	immobile	1	urinary and fecal	1

*Total score is determined by adding the individual scores for the five components.

Adapted from D. Norton, R. McLaren, and A. N. Smith, *An Investigation of Geriatric Nursing Problems in Hospital* (Edinburgh: Churchill Livingstone, 1975; originally published London: National Corporation for the Care of Old People, 1962)

Although pressure is the most important factor in the development of pressure sores, other factors may also contribute to the problem. Shearing forces are caused by the sliding of one layer of tissue upon another. These forces commonly occur in bed-bound patients when the head of the bed is raised, causing the torso of the bedridden patient to slide down while the skin is fixed to the bed by friction. Another contributor is friction, the rubbing of two surfaces against each other, which removes the skin's outer protective layer. For example, friction is created between the patient's skin and the bedsheet when a patient is dragged across a bed. Finally, moisture, whether the result of spilling liquid in the bed or incontinence, promotes the development of pressure sores.

In addition to a person's overall state of health, certain specific conditions increase the risk of developing pressure sores. These risk factors include not only incontinence but also malnutrition, bone fractures (*e.g.,* of the hip), and immobility. Several scales have been developed that incorporate these risk factors to assess an individual person's risk of developing a pressure sore. One such scale, the Norton Score (*see* above), suggests that a patient who scores 14 or less out of a possible 20 is at high risk. Although the accuracy of these scales in predicting pressure sores is far from perfect, they serve to remind the physician and nursing staff of important risk factors to be considered.

Preventing the problem

Given that many of the factors that cause pressure sores can be eliminated, it follows that virtually all pressure sores can be prevented. For patients who are able to walk, frequent ambulation is recommended. Persons who cannot walk should be encouraged to shift their body weight every two hours. For many chronically ill persons, this repositioning must be assisted by family members or other care givers or nursing staff. The optimal position is roughly a 30° angle rather than being turned entirely on one's side (*see* figure on previous page).

Good skin care is also helpful in preventing pressure sores. After bathing, skin should be patted dry—not rubbed—to minimize friction. The skin should be left not too dry or too moist. Excessive use of lotions or creams may actually increase the likelihood of skin breakdown. For the bedridden patient, bathing about every other day is usually sufficient; daily bathing is probably not necessary unless the person at risk is incontinent and needs to be cleaned quite regularly. Although massages are frequently administered by nurses or other care givers, the value of this therapy in actually preventing pressure sores is unclear.

Wheelchair-bound persons, such as paraplegics, are especially prone to developing pressure sores over the ischial tuberosities (bony swellings on the posterior part of the pelvis that are attached to various muscles and bear the weight of the body in sitting). The average user spends over 36 hours a week in a wheelchair.

An open cell polymeric foam material, originally developed for aircraft-seat padding, has been adapted for wheelchairs. A liquid form of the foam is contour-molded to the individual's body; the seat distributes body weight and pressure evenly over the entire contact area, thereby helping to prevent the development of pressure sores.

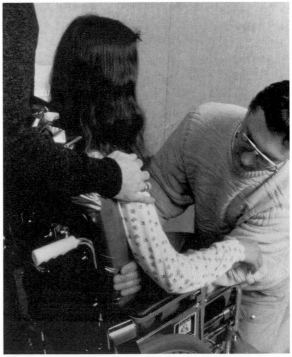

NASA

Of persons with spinal cord injuries, an estimated 25–85% will develop pressure sores at some time; those with spinal injuries are less likely to shift positions regularly because they do not get the messages from the brain that tell them when they have been sitting in one position too long. Wrinkled or coarse clothing (such as tight denim jeans) may aggravate the problem for persons who are wheelchair bound.

Preventive measures include maintaining an upright position in the wheelchair to minimize shearing forces and, to help distribute weight, using special wheelchair cushions, which may need to be custom fit. Many varieties of cushions are available; the most commonly used are air-filled and gel-filled. Some persons also use sheepskin to protect their skin. These cushions, however, are not as effective in the prevention of pressure sores as intermittent complete unweighting—*i.e.,* being out of the wheelchair itself and out of the seated posture. There are many benefits for the wheelchair-bound person in axial loading—or what is known as passive standing. Many paraplegics with strong upper bodies are able to put weight on their legs and support themselves with parallel bars; others use braces or a standing frame device.

Treating pressure sores: from simple to serious

If a pressure sore develops, the first step is to assess the seriousness of the sore. Generally the earlier stages (grades 1 and 2) can be managed with relief of pressure and simple wound care. The use of antiseptic solutions such as iodine and hexachlorophene does not help and may actually impair the healing process. Usually, gauze dressings soaked with saline (a salt-water solution) are applied, allowed to dry, and removed every three to four hours (wet-to-dry dressings). In this process, old damaged tissue is removed, allowing new healthy tissue to begin the healing process. Wet-to-dry dressings are administered by the nursing staff in hospitals and nursing homes. With proper instruction, a person who is caring for a patient at home can also learn to apply such dressings. A variety of biochemical preparations and skin substitutes have been developed for removing tissue and promoting healing, but none of these has been demonstrated to be superior to saline wet-to-dry dressings.

More severe pressure sores (grades 3 and 4) usually demand surgical cleaning of the wound. Because they are open wounds, the most serious pressure sores usually become colonized with bacteria. Aggressive attempts to eliminate these bacteria by using topical antibiotics (creams and ointments) or oral antibiotics are generally unsuccessful and may, in fact, allow more dangerous bacteria to predominate. Thus, antibiotic treatment is generally withheld until there is evidence of infection of the skin, bone, or blood. Treatment of these serious infections usually requires hospitalization and intravenous antibiotics.

Regardless of the grade of the pressure sore, healing is promoted not only by direct care of the wound itself but by the elimination of other risk factors, such as pressure, malnutrition, and moisture. Recent studies have suggested that the use of air-fluidized beds, which simulate a "floating surface of beads" on which the patient lies, may be more effective in healing pressure sores than other kinds of soft, supporting surfaces, such as "eggcrate" foam mattresses, air mattresses, sheepskins, or water beds. Even so, in one study in which air-fluidized beds were used, fewer than one-third of deep pressure sores healed completely when treated for an average of 100 days. Furthermore, air-fluidized beds are expensive and are not widely available. Other devices and mattresses, such as foam and water beds or water mattresses, may be less effective at reducing pressure but are also less expensive and, therefore, may be reasonable alternatives for home use.

Some hospitals also employ heat or cold therapy, ultraviolet treatments, whirlpools, or ultrasound, which may help relieve some patients' sores; however, none of these methods is a proven therapy. A treatment that utilizes electrical stimulation of the skin to dilate blood vessels, thus increasing circulation to the ulcerated area, is another experimental approach that has helped in some cases but must be further tested. Also, some research has suggested that oral zinc and vitamin C may accelerate the healing process, but further studies are needed to confirm these findings.

Seeking new and better treatments

The treatment of pressure sores continues to be an active area of medical research. For example, Italian investigators are studying the effectiveness of laser treatment of pressure sores. Devices such as the air-fluidized bed and such newer methods of supplementing nutrition as intravenous hyperalimentation are encouraging prospects for more effective therapy. Despite these advances, the therapy of established pressure sores is unlikely to ever be fully satisfactory. Thus, the emphasis must continue to be placed on prevention. The mainstays of preventing and treating pressure sores have not changed for decades and include relieving pressure, eliminating shearing forces and friction, and keeping bed surfaces dry.

Hot Flashes: Not for Women Only

by Bruce D. Shephard, M.D.

The hot flashes started when I began skipping periods. It's a feeling of heat that races through my chest, neck, and face. My skin looks flushed, and my hair gets wet with sweat, even if it's cold out.

Flushes—popularly known as hot flashes—are most frequently thought of as a symptom of menopause. Contrary to popular belief, however, they may be experienced by both men and women. They are felt as intense heat and produce a transient, flushed appearance, usually in the upper half of the body. Flushing comes about as a result of something that causes blood vessels in the skin to suddenly dilate (widen). This increases blood flow to the area and causes a sensation of warmth and a red, blotchy appearance in the skin of the affected area. While flushing has various causes and triggering mechanisms, the end result is similar to what happens when the body is overheated and heat-loss mechanisms are activated; blood vessels in the skin dilate, making the skin warm to allow rapid heat loss.

Of the causes of flushing (unrelated to fever), many are associated with alcohol, physical stimulants, certain tumors, various chemicals and drugs, and hormonal changes that are part of menopause.

Alcohol-related flushes

Some people may experience flushing several minutes after consuming an alcoholic beverage. The alcohol-induced flush is apparently more common among certain ethnic groups, especially Orientals, and probably is caused by an aberrant enzymatic pathway in the metabolism of alcohol. Additional symptoms may include rapid heart rate, increased depth of respiration, and decreased blood pressure. Ethnic background is not a factor in this type of flush.

Flushing along with dizziness may occur when alcohol is consumed in the presence of certain chemicals, such as carbon disulfide, trichloroethylene, and dimethylformamide, which are commonly used in industry. Chronic exposure to these organic solvents alone has also been reported to cause flushing.

A number of medications produce flushing as a side effect if alcohol is consumed. In gynecology this occurs most often with the antibiotic metronidazole (Flagyl), which is used to treat certain forms of vaginitis, including trichomoniasis. During the approximately one-week course of therapy, a patient who does not avoid alcohol is likely to experience flushing, vomiting, palpitations, and shortness of breath. Similar reactions

may occur with the antidiabetic drug chlorpropamide (Diabinese) and with certain antibiotics. A severe flushing reaction occurs when alcohol is consumed after a person has taken the drug disulfiram (Antabuse), used in the treatment of alcoholism.

Alcohol may also trigger a flushing reaction when a person has certain tumors. The most common of these is carcinoid, a sometimes malignant tumor that usually affects some part of the digestive tract, especially the appendix. Carcinoids release various chemical substances—e.g., serotonin, bradykinin, histamine, and prostaglandin—that cause the blood vessels in the skin to dilate. Tumors of the thyroid and lymph glands have also been associated with alcohol-induced flushing.

Physical causes of flushing

Certain physical factors cause flushing. Many people experience a mild flushing sensation in response to heat, such as hot liquids or steam baths. This is a normal physiological response; blood vessels near the skin's surface dilate to lose heat. Cold may induce flushing associated with hives (urticaria) in susceptible individuals. Individuals with "cold urticaria" may develop flushing and such symptoms as nausea and fainting in response to prolonged exposure to cold.

Tumors as a cause of flushing

A number of tumors, both benign and malignant, have been found to cause flushing. In addition to carcinoid, tumors in the pancreas, lung, thyroid gland, adrenal gland, central nervous system, blood, and kidney all have been known to produce flushing by releasing various substances that cause blood vessels in the skin to dilate. These tumors often produce other symptoms—such as diarrhea, palpitations, and fainting—thus making the diagnosis a challenging one.

Chemical- and drug-induced flushes

A number of chemicals and drugs may cause flushing. Nicotinic acid, one of the B vitamins and the active ingredient in various cholesterol-lowering drugs—e.g., Lipo-Nicin, Nicobid, and Nicolar—may cause flushing; the effect is dose-related. The flushing is usually temporary and is sometimes associated with headache, sweating, or an upset stomach. Flushing is also a potential side effect of prostaglandins, drugs used both to induce abortion and to "ripen" the cervix before labor is induced in a term pregnancy. Flushing occurs in up to 5% of individuals taking calcitonin-containing products such as Calcimar, used to treat such bone conditions as Paget's disease and osteoporosis. Such pain-relief drugs as the narcotic analgesics morphine and meperidine (Demerol) may produce a variety of cardiovascular side effects, including flushing, rapid heartbeat, palpitations, and faintness. Leuprolide (Lupron), used in chemotherapy for prostate cancer, has been reported to cause flushing in over 50% of patients. In women this drug inhibits the release of luteinizing hormone by the pituitary and thereby reduces estrogen secretion by the ovary. Lupron presently is being used in clinical trials in the treatment of two common gynecologic conditions—fibroids (leiomyomas) and endometriosis—and is likely to become more widely used. Certain chemotherapy drugs, such as tamoxifen (Nolvadex), widely used in the treatment of breast cancer, cause hot flashes in about 25% of patients. Tamoxifen produces these side effects by acting as an antiestrogen; i.e., it competes with a woman's own estrogen for binding sites (where the estrogen molecule attaches and produces its hormonal effects) in such target tissues as the breast. Another antiestrogen drug causing hot flashes, danazol (Danocrine), is used in the treatment of endometriosis, a rather common gynecologic condition causing painful periods and, in some patients, infertility.

Flushing during menopause

Hot flashes are considered the hallmark symptom of menopause, which is reached when a woman has ceased having menstrual periods for one year. Flushes may precede menopause by months or even years; they often develop imperceptibly at first but gradually increase in intensity and frequency as menstrual periods come less and less often. The flush lasts from a few seconds to a few minutes and is usually followed by sweating. It may be associated with insomnia and nervousness. Palpitations may precede the flush, and other symptoms, such as faintness, dizziness, or weakness, may accompany it. Hot flushes occur more often at night but may be triggered during the day by such factors as warm weather or a sudden noise. The symptom occurs in up to 75–85% of all women after natural or surgical menopause (in which the ovaries are removed). The symptom persists for at least one year in 85% of women, and 35–50% of women will experience flushes for more than five years. Flushes tend to become less severe with time.

The general cause of menopausal flushing is a lowered level of estrogen in the blood. Apparently the flush is initiated by a sudden downward setting of the temperature-regulating area within the brain stem. To adjust the body's core temperature to the new, lower set point, heat-loss mechanisms are activated, and sudden sweating and dilation of skin blood vessels result. During a hot flush there is also an increase in oxygen consumption and cheek temperature, as well as about a 15% increase in heart rate. No change in blood pressure has been noted. Aside from menopause, most gynecologic conditions involving hormone changes are unassociated with hot flashes. For example, hot flashes generally do not occur if menses temporarily stop for a few months (a condition called secondary amenorrhea) owing to various stresses, such as illness, a change in job, divorce, or strenuous physical exercise. During such times estrogen levels are basically maintained, preventing flushing.

Prevention, treatment, and relief

While the causes of flushing are complex and varied, the treatment is relatively simple. Drinking ice-cold liquids and maintaining a cool room temperature will help, as will wearing layered clothing in which the outer layer can be peeled off on a moment's notice. Individuals susceptible to drug, alcohol, or chemically mediated flushing must avoid these triggering factors unless the medical benefits outweigh the side effects produced. If the cause of flushing cannot be identified, consultation with a physician is advisable; this symptom can, in rare instances, be the first sign of a (usually benign) hormone-producing tumor.

Menopausal flushes are most commonly and effectively treated by the hormone estrogen—either the oral form (e.g., Premarin) or the estrogen patch (Estraderm). (Today many postmenopausal women also take estrogen for prevention of osteoporosis and of heart disease.) Long-term estrogen use has been associated with uterine (endometrial) cancer, but patients may prevent that by cycling the estrogen with a second hormone, progesterone. The progesterone protects the uterus and perhaps the breast from excessive estrogen stimulation and may itself reduce hot flushes, although not as effectively as estrogen.

In addition to reducing hot flushes, current hormone replacement therapy (combining both estrogen and progesterone) usually has secondary benefits, including decreased insomnia and irritability. Other medications used to reduce hot flushes—including clonidine (Catapres), to lower blood pressure, the antispasmodic Bellergal-S, and male sex hormones—have been less effective and also have unpleasant side effects.

A Matter of Taste

by Richard L. Doty, Ph.D.

Tell me what you eat, and I shall tell you what you are.
—Jean-Anthelme Brillat-Savarin, 1825

The ability to taste is critical for the survival of most vertebrates and plays a key role in their nutrition and social behavior. The widespread human predilection for sweet- and salty-tasting substances and the equally widespread dislike for things that taste bitter or sour reflect inborn mechanisms of ancient phylogenetic origin. It is generally assumed that these sensibilities developed as protective mechanisms. Thus, many naturally occurring poisons are bitter tasting, while foods that are rich sources of calories are often sweet tasting, and salt is needed to maintain the balance of electrolytes vital to body functions. Inborn preferences and aversions can, however, be markedly altered in omnivorous animals (those that eat both plant and animal foods); the capacity to change these basic preferences is an adaptive advantage that allows for the exploitation of novel foods and diverse habitats, as is sometimes required when seasonal shortages occur in specific food sources. Interestingly, data from animal studies suggest that some taste preferences may be learned *in utero* or during suckling and can reflect components of the mother's diet.

Flavor—taste and smell working together

Flavor is by far the single most important factor in determining human food choices. For this reason, dysfunction of the gustatory (taste) system can be very debilitating. Indeed, in extreme cases disturbances in taste function can lead to malnutrition and even starvation and death.

Although the senses of taste and smell work together in contributing to flavor sensations, the two sensory systems are anatomically and functionally distinct. In the case of taste, specific chemicals are detected by the taste buds, which are located within the oral cavity; the derived sensations are largely limited to those of sweet, sour, bitter, salty, and perhaps metallic. In the case of olfaction (smell), a much broader range of chemicals can be detected. The olfactory receptors are located within an area of specialized tissue high in the nose; sensations derived through the sense of smell can number in the thousands.

Most flavor sensations commonly referred to as taste actually result from the stimulation of the olfactory receptors by odor-laden air forced during chewing and swallowing from the rear of the oral cavity into the higher recesses of the nose. The list of foods and beverages whose "taste" is olfactory in origin is extensive and includes such flavors as chocolate, vanilla, grape, lemon, coffee, pizza, chicken, peanut butter, onion, cheese, and pineapple. One can make a simple demonstration of the dependence of such sensations on olfaction by holding the nose while eating or drinking a food or beverage containing one of the above flavors; the "taste" readily disappears (because active movement of air from the oral cavity to the rear of the nasal cavity is prevented), even though the characteristic texture, temperature, sweetness, saltiness, sourness, or bitterness remains.

The taste bud

The human taste bud consists of specialized cells that form a budlike structure with a small opening—the taste pore—through which a taste stimulus, or tastant, can enter. Tastants interact with portions of the membrane covering tiny fingerlike extensions (microvilli) of cells located within the taste bud. This physical interaction, in turn, induces biochemical events that ultimately send impulses to the brain via nerve fibers, signaling the taste sensations. Taste buds are dynamic in that their cells undergo birth, maturation, development of sensory responsiveness, old age, and death all within the time span of a week or two. Connections between the sensory elements of the bud and the nervous system are also dynamic; nerve branches are continuously sprouting new processes, or extensions, to connect to young taste cells and withdrawing such connections from old taste cells. Taste buds are found

459

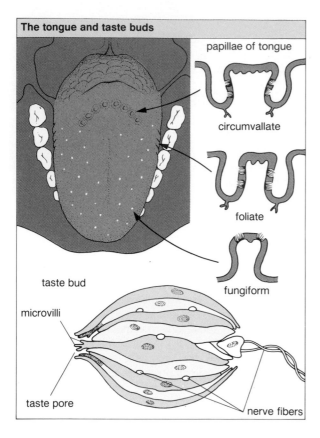

The tongue and taste buds

papillae of tongue

circumvallate

foliate

fungiform

taste bud

microvilli

taste pore

nerve fibers

in all vertebrates and in some, for example, the catfish, are located over the entire surface of the body. In human newborns taste buds are found in large numbers on the inside of the lips and cheeks, as well as on the tongue, palate, and oropharynx (area between the mouth and the esophagus). This distribution changes during development so that by adulthood few taste buds are present on the lips or cheeks.

The majority of human taste buds are located on or around papillae—peglike protuberances distributed across the surface of the tongue. There are different kinds of papillae on different parts of the tongue. Several thousand taste buds are often found distributed among the 200–500 fungiform papillae on the anterior, or forwardmost, part of the tongue. The 8 to 12 circumvallate papillae, located along a chevron-shaped border between the anterior two-thirds of the tongue and the posterior one-third, contain about 250 taste buds apiece. Additional taste buds are located on the soft palate, pharynx, epiglottis (structure that covers the tracheal opening), and upper third of the esophagus. In some humans the foliate papillae, located along the posterior lateral (side) surfaces of the tongue also contain taste buds. Both behavioral and electrophysiological data suggest that the front of the tongue is more sensitive to sweet and salty stimuli, whereas the back of the tongue is more sensitive to sour and bitter stimuli.

Dysfunctions of taste

A number of diseases and medications are associated with dysfunctions of taste; however, total loss of the ability to detect sweet, sour, bitter, and salty sensations is relatively rare. Unlike the olfactory receptors, which are innervated by the olfactory nerves, the taste buds are innervated on each side of the oral cavity by several cranial nerves, which are much less likely than the olfactory nerves to be damaged by trauma. In a recent study of 750 patients evaluated for smell or taste dysfunction at the Smell and Taste Center of the Hospital of the University of Pennsylvania, fewer than 4% had evidence of even partial loss of taste function, despite the fact that 67% complained of loss of taste and smell and 10% reported loss of taste unaccompanied by loss of smell. Typically, such reports of loss of taste reflect loss of flavor sensations resulting from decreased olfactory function.

Despite the rarity of true taste loss, about one-third of the patients in the study complained of strange taste sensations (known as dysgeusias), a condition second in frequency only to pain as a sensory symptom in patients seen by dentists and other oral health specialists. Of these individuals, 40% reported that chemosensory stimulation (*e.g.*, that induced by food during eating) was not required for the elicitation of the strange taste. An upper respiratory infection or cold was associated with 23% of these cases, head trauma with 18%, and nasal sinus disease with 8%. Dental procedures (*e.g.*, tooth extraction), medications, and oral exposure to toxic chemicals (usually the result of an occupational accident or the accidental swallowing of acids, cleaning products, and so forth) accounted for about 8% of the cases. The probable causes of the remaining cases were unknown. Although most dysgeusias were reported as producing sour, bitter, salty, or metallic taste sensations, a number of people complaining about a taste problem did not experience any true taste sensations, suggesting that some kinds of dysgeusia may actually reflect distortions in smell function misperceived as distortions in taste.

The physiological bases for most cases of dysgeusia and hypogeusia (lessened taste sensitivity) are poorly understood; however, there are straightforward remedies for certain taste problems.

● Vitamin and mineral (*e.g.*, iron) deficiencies, as well as certain medications (*e.g.*, antibiotics, cancer chemotherapy agents, and anticholinergic medications), can result in depapillation of the tongue and can be reversed by the taking of the appropriate vitamin or discontinuation of the medication.

● When an individual has fillings and dental prostheses made of different types of metals, electric currents, perceived as metallic tastes, can be set up in the mouth; this problem can be corrected by replacing the fillings or prostheses with ones composed of only a single type of metal or with nonmetallic substances.

● A taste loss is sometimes reported by patients undergoing radiation treatment for head and neck cancer. This is believed to be due to radiation-induced damage to the taste-receptor cells. Usually patients recover their sense of taste within two to four months after the last radiation treatment.

● The lessened taste function associated with cigarette smoking or poor oral hygiene can be reversed, to some degree, by cessation of smoking and improved hygienic measures.

● Taste alterations are sometimes associated with acute liver disease but usually disappear following recovery from illness.

● Fungal infections in the mouth and other oral infections may cause symptoms of lessened or altered taste perception; treatment of the disorder usually restores normal taste function.

Inherited taste deficits

Genetically determined deficits in the ability to detect specific types of tastants have been reported, although such insensitivities are rarely recognized as such by individuals experiencing them. The best example of a deficit of this type is the inability to taste a class of bitter-tasting compounds commonly found in edible plants of the *Brassica* genus, including kale, turnips, cabbage, and brussels sprouts. The prototype taste stimulus of this class is the chemical compound phenylthiocarbamide (PTC; also termed phenylthiourea), which may be either bitter or tasteless depending on the genetic makeup of the individual who ingests it. Among Caucasians in Western Europe and North America, about 30% of the population are nontasters. The percentage of nontasters is much lower in other populations that have been tested. Since such bitter-tasting compounds inhibit the synthesis of thyroid hormone and, as a result, permit the pituitary gland to secrete large amounts of thyroid-stimulating hormone, their ingestion can lead to the development of a goiter (enlargement of the thyroid gland). In a study of people in highland Peru, "tasters"—those who experienced the bitter taste—avoided foodstuffs containing these compounds (for example, bread made from a local grain) and therefore did not have goiters; their nontasting counterparts did. The nontasting gene, however, is associated with protection against malaria, a possible reason why it continues to exist in the gene pool. Some data suggest that PTC taster status is associated with the type of thyroid disorder that persons develop.

Another example of a specific taste deficit that has some medical significance is observed in people with diabetes and some of their close relatives. Patients with late-onset diabetes (type II, non-insulin-dependent diabetes mellitus) not only have an abnormality in insulin release in response to the sugar glucose but are also less sensitive than normal to the taste of this sugar. Some first-degree relatives of these individuals with diabetes, none of whom have diabetes themselves, also have decreased taste sensitivity to glucose but not to the closely related sugar fructose. This observation suggests that late-onset diabetes may be caused by a biochemical abnormality that influences both the endocrine and taste systems. Further support for this hypothesis comes from the finding that one form of glucose (alpha-D-glucose), which is known to be more potent in releasing insulin than another form (beta-D-glucose), elicits stronger sweet taste sensations. More research is needed to test the intriguing hypothesis that the nondiabetic relatives who have decreased glucose taste sensitivity will themselves eventually develop late-onset diabetes.

Taste perception and obesity

Obese individuals have great difficulty inhibiting their consumption of calorically dense sweet-tasting foods. The role played by taste in the development of obesity is, at present, poorly understood. Recent data suggest that markedly obese persons show a greater liking than nonobese persons for complex carbohydrate-fat mixtures (milk shakes, for example) and that their taste sensitivity, per se, is not different from that of their nonobese counterparts. However, in studies using simpler, sweeter test substances (*e.g.*, sweetened water), obese patients reported less of a preference for solutions with higher sugar-concentration levels than with lower levels; furthermore, the rated disliking of such solutions correlated directly with the subject's percentage of body fat. Since sugary-sweet test solutions are generally less palatable than milk shakes and other typical high-calorie food items, it is conceivable that, compared with normal-weight people, obese people are more particular about taste and thereby find these simple sweet-tasting solutions to be relatively less pleasant. Another possible interpretation may be that obese individuals are reluctant to rate sweet-tasting liquids as pleasant in experimental settings where the goal is to achieve weight loss.

Salt taste and health

Salt (sodium chloride), the substance that is widely used as a preservative and seasoning agent, provides the sodium essential for basic bodily functions, including nerve conduction, acid-base balance, cardiovascular tone, and muscle contraction. Not surprisingly, there are both behavioral and physiological mechanisms that maintain an appropriate level of sodium in the body. If too much salt is ingested, the kidney compensates by excreting sodium in the urine. If too little sodium is present in bodily fluids, conservation mechanisms come into play to inhibit sodium excretion.

Salt-deficient animals (including those whose requirement for salt is produced by failure or removal of the adrenal glands) search out sources of salt and show a strong preference for salty-tasting foods or liquids. This is commonly observed in such herbivores as cattle and deer, whose plant diets usually do not contain adequate levels of salt. Similar cravings for salt are observed in human patients whose adrenal glands fail to produce necessary hormones.

Numerous studies link excesses in sodium consumption to essential hypertension (high blood pressure of unknown cause), a condition associated with coronary heart disease, stroke, and congestive heart failure. One widely cited estimate of the sodium requirement of humans is 0.25 g per day; however, the average consumption of salt in the United States is from 6 to 18 g per day. Presumably, this high salt intake is a result of the large amounts of salt that are put into processed foods and the widespread popularity of salty "junk" foods.

Recent data suggest that salt preferences, but not sensitivity to salt, are acquired and thus can be altered by dietary factors. Persons placed on a low-sodium diet (which is, nonetheless, above the minimum level required for good health) exhibit, within a time span of two to four months, a preference for lower levels of salt, whereas people whose dietary sodium is increased actually come to prefer higher levels of salt. However, the preference for increased amounts of salt develops only when salt is added directly to the subjects' food. If the intake of salt is increased by administration of a salt tablet, which is swallowed but not tasted, no corresponding preference for saltier-tasting food is observed. This finding suggests that sensory experience is somehow involved in altering the preference for salt.

Scientists speculate that there may be an association between kidney function and salt-taste sensitivity, possibly analogous to the association between diabetes and glucose-taste sensitivity. Thus, when drops of amiloride (a drug that blocks sodium uptake by the kidney) are applied to an individual's tongue, he or she experiences a decrease or block in salt-taste perception, suggesting that blockage of the sodium channels associated with salt-taste function may be involved in altering salt-taste perception. Whether adding or subtracting salt to foods directly influences either the number or responsiveness of these sodium channels is unknown.

Learned taste aversions

As was demonstrated by the Russian physiologist Ivan Pavlov at the turn of the 19th century in his classic experiments with dogs, salivary and gastric secretions are produced as reflexes in the presence of various sensory stimuli. Possibly because of the unconditional nature of the relationship between oral sensory stimulation and oral and gastric secretory activity, tastes are very potent inducers of alterations within the digestive system; indeed, such reflex action may possibly trigger the preingestive (cephalic) period of insulin secretion, which occurs before food has had time to be digested in the stomach or intestines. Clinically, it has long been known that lemon juice is useful for testing salivary reflexes, for increasing the secretion of saliva, and for aiding in the diagnosis of such conditions as xerostomia (dry mouth).

There are important clinical applications for the finding that aversions to specific food items can be conditioned by the pairing of certain tastes and flavors with unpleasant gastric events, such as nausea and vomiting, even though these events may occur long after the ingestion of the food. Studies show that people develop profound distastes for foods coincidentally associated with gastrointestinal illness (especially protein-rich foods such as eggs, fish, and meat). In addition, strong food aversions readily develop in children and adults undergoing radiotherapy or chemotherapy for cancer, both of which produce nausea as a common side effect. Research performed at the University of Washington has shown that such conditioning is particularly potent for novel food items and can occur even when (1) the new food is presented only once, (2) a number of chemotherapy treatments have been previously administered, (3) an interval of many hours occurs between the eating of the food and the onset of the gastrointestinal distress, and (4) the patient is aware that the nausea and vomiting are a result of the therapy and not of the ingestion of the newly introduced food. Interestingly, the development of an aversion to a new food can block the development of an aversion to more familiar foods eaten at the same time. This finding has an important clinical application: patients about to undergo chemotherapy can be purposely exposed to new foods, which then serve as "scapegoats," protecting familiar foods from becoming targets of learned taste aversions.

The future of taste research

The diverse phenomena described above illustrate the fact that taste disorders are of clinical significance and suggest that quantitative taste testing may prove to be of use in the early diagnosis of diabetes and other diseases. Formal chemosensory testing will undoubtedly become commonplace in major medical centers in the near future, coincident with the growing realization that taste and smell disorders, like disorders of vision, hearing, and movement, have a significant impact on the well-being of the individual. Future research is likely to focus on factors that (1) influence the development of flavor preference, (2) cause age-related changes in taste and smell perception, and (3) enhance the palatability of beverages and foodstuffs. There will also be significant advances in the understanding of the complex workings of the sensory systems of taste and smell.

Taking Drugs Wisely—Concerns for Seniors

by David B. Reuben, M.D.

Although medications provide benefits to the vast majority of elderly persons, the use of prescription and nonprescription, or over-the-counter, drugs by the elderly is not without drawbacks. As people age they tend to be afflicted by an increasing number of diseases and medical conditions. Consequently, treatment regimens, including medications, become more complex. In one U.S. study, the average number of prescription drugs taken by residents in an urban dwelling for senior citizens was 4.5 per person. In addition, the average number of nonprescription drugs was 3.4 per person. Thus, the average total number of drugs per person was 7.9! A similar British study, based on a representative sample of elderly people in the U.K., found that 60% of those surveyed were taking some kind of medication and 20% took three or more prescription drugs. In the U.S. people 65 and over (representing some 12% of the population) consume nearly 25% of all the drugs prescribed, and this percentage is rising. The bill for medications purchased by elderly people in the U.S. is approximately $10 billion per year.

A U.S. government report released in February 1989 went so far as to call "mismedication of the elderly" one of the country's most pressing health concerns. The report cited a number of problems, among them inadequate training of physicians in geriatric medicine, prescription of the wrong drug or wrong dosage, lack of adequate information on medicine labels, and adverse reactions to combinations of drugs prescribed by several different physicians. One of the most arresting statistics in the report was that 51% of the deaths from drug reactions in the U.S. involve people 60 and older.

The use of medications by the elderly is complicated by several factors. First, as mentioned above, older people tend to have more medical problems than younger people do, and they take more medications. These drugs may interact with each other in such a way as to reduce the effectiveness or increase the side effects of other medications being taken concurrently. Furthermore, the likelihood of an interaction between drugs increases with the number of drugs being taken. According to one estimate, in people taking more than five drugs, there is a 7% chance that a significant interaction will occur; for those taking more than ten medicines, the probability rises to 24%.

Drugs may also affect diseases or conditions other than the ones for which they were prescribed. For example, eye drops prescribed for glaucoma may adversely affect heart function in patients who have heart disease with congestive heart failure. This complication is especially common when the patient with several ailments is being treated by a number of different specialists. Each doctor may order a different medication, not knowing what—or how many—drugs the person is already taking.

Drugs and the aging body

A major consideration in the use of medications by elderly persons is the effect of aging on the body's abilities to handle and to respond to drugs; these abilities are termed pharmacokinetics and pharmacodynamics, respectively. Pharmacokinetics includes absorption, distribution, metabolism, and elimination of drugs. Although absorption of medications in elderly persons and younger adults is relatively the same, the distribution of drugs within the body changes consid-

With aging, drug effects change
how the body handles drugs (pharmacokinetics)
fat-soluble drugs may accumulate, effects may be prolonged water-soluble drugs may reach higher blood levels, may be more toxic drugs are metabolized more slowly as liver function declines, effects may be prolonged drugs are excreted more slowly as kidney function declines, effects may be prolonged
effects of drugs on the body (pharmacodynamics)
the brain is more sensitive to sedative effects of drugs blood pressure is more sensitive to medications morphine and other narcotics tend to be more potent

erably, largely owing to increases in the percentage of body fat that occur with aging. As an individual gets older, lean body mass, especially muscle, diminishes and is replaced by fat. On average, between ages 20 and 65, body fat increases from approximately 18 to 36% of total body weight in men and from 33 to 48% in women. Thus, medications that are stored in fat cells will accumulate in increased amounts and will last longer in the body of the elderly person. In contrast, medications that are not fat soluble will tend to concentrate in increased levels in the blood.

The two principal organs that are responsible for metabolism and elimination of drugs, the liver and kidney, both change with aging. Blood flow to the liver decreases, which may delay the elimination of some drugs. In addition, some liver enzymes decrease in activity with aging. Thus, drugs that are metabolized by these enzymes must be reduced in dosage. The kidney experiences a similar decrease in blood flow,

roughly 1–2% per year, and renal function deteriorates with aging in most persons. Unfortunately, routine blood and urine tests may not accurately reflect this decline, and special formulas must be used to adjust drug dosage for age-related kidney-function decline. The overall effect of these changes in liver and kidney function is usually a prolongation of a drug's effect. Accordingly, the dosages of some medications need to be reduced in amount or frequency of administration in all elderly persons. Other medications, such as long-acting tranquilizers, should be avoided entirely in older persons.

Proper prescribing: physicians' problems

Before prescribing medication for the elderly person, the physician must decide whether the disease, condition, or symptom is serious enough to warrant treatment. Frequently the patient's opinion has an important bearing on this decision. For example, an occasional backache may not be bothersome to the point that a person is willing to accept the inconvenience and risk of taking an anti-inflammatory drug, which may offer some relief but may also cause indigestion, bleeding from the gastrointestinal tract, or impairment of kidney or mental function. The effectiveness of the medication for the specific condition also must be considered, and its potential benefit must be weighed against possible side effects and interactions with other drugs. For example, while Alzheimer's disease is serious, effective therapy is not yet available. Thus, medication has little likelihood of producing improvement and usually should not be prescribed.

The costs and convenience of various different medicines within a category of medications also are factors that the physician must take into account. The doctor should consider prescribing generic medications whenever possible, which can result in considerable

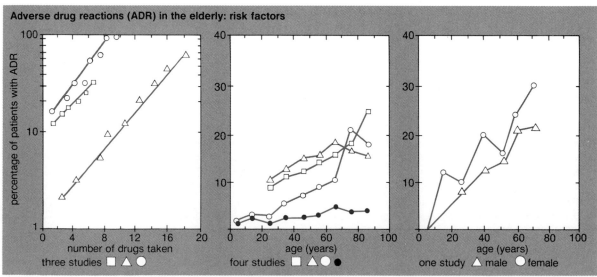

Adapted from Lisa Nolan and Kevin O'Malley, "Prescribing for the Elderly," *Journal of the American Geriatrics Society,* vol. 36, no. 2 (February 1988), p. 145

Cathy Melloan

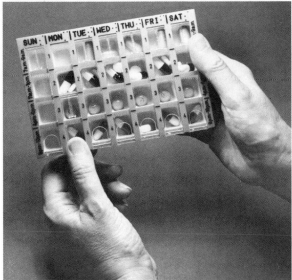

A medication organizer—a seven-day pill box with individual compartments for each day's pills—can help a person who is on a complicated drug regimen to take the right medication at the right time.

cost savings to the patient, who is likely to have limited resources. Medications that can be given once or twice a day are preferable to those that require multiple dosages. For the elderly patient, who may have memory problems or be confused or disoriented, frequent dosage regimens are difficult to maintain; this difficulty is compounded when the person is taking a number of different medications. For example, an individual taking one medication every six hours and another every eight hours must take some medicine at least seven times a day. People of all ages are likely to have difficulty adhering to such a rigorous medication schedule. It is important that the physician keep in mind the patient's physical, mental, and social circumstances when deciding what drugs, and how many, to prescribe.

Comprehension, compliance: patients' problems

Problems with medications for the elderly are not confined solely to the physician's difficulties in choosing appropriate drugs. Patients must understand why each medication has been prescribed; they also must know how to use the medication correctly and be aware of and able to recognize side effects. Noncompliance—failure to take medications properly—is a serious problem, one that has many causes. Some research suggests that up to 21% of all prescriptions are never filled, either because the patient may not believe that the medicine will be of benefit or because the drug costs too much.

In the U.S., until the recent passage of the Medicare catastrophic health coverage, the cost of prescription medications was not covered. Even under the new law the coverage remains limited; Medicare beneficiaries must pay the first $600 per year out-of-pocket (slated to increase to about $700 by 1993) and are reimbursed for only 50% of additional costs (to increase to 80% by 1993).

Other problems have to do with the patient's physical ability to take medicines, including the reading of prescription labels (often difficult for older people with failing eyesight or visual disturbances) and the opening of containers. Child-resistant medication containers unfortunately are also commonly senior-resistant as well. In one study of more than 100 elderly noninstitutionalized men and women, all of the participants were able to open a selection of child-resistant containers; however, none of the child-resistant containers could be opened by *all* of the people. In addition, older people may have difficulty swallowing medications. One study of asymptomatic persons demonstrated that 22% had abnormal swallowing. Causes included neurological disorders (such as stroke and Parkinson's disease), muscle disorders, and anatomic abnormalities.

Finally, if they are unaware of a drug's potential side effects, elderly patients may mistakenly attribute drug-related symptoms to other diseases, for which they then take additional medications. Or they may assume that the unpleasant effect—blurred vision, dizziness, fatigue, confusion—is simply an inevitable part of the aging process and therefore not report it to the physician. Adverse side effects also contribute to noncompliance. Thus, in order to stop what he or she perceives as the untoward effects of a drug, the patient may simply cease to take it.

A quick check of computer data on potentially dangerous drug interactions enables the pharmacist to make sure that the medication being ordered will not conflict with other drugs the patient is taking.

Walgreen Company

Some solutions

The problem of appropriate drug treatment for elderly persons is being addressed at several levels. Pharmacists are playing a more active role in hospitals, nursing homes, and other institutions, as well as in the drugstore setting. The addition of a single pharmacist to the staff of a 100-bed nursing home could save an estimated $70,000 per year and improve the effective use of medications. In the community pharmacists are also taking steps to prevent drug interactions, frequently with the help of computerized systems that scan the medical literature regarding each medication that the patient is taking, warning of possible adverse effects or interactions with other classes of drugs. In the U.S. the prescription records of all Medicare beneficiaries will eventually be entered into a nationwide computer network; having this information on file will aid pharmacists in spotting potential problems of drug interaction.

Patients too are taking a more active role in learning about medications and their side effects. The American Association of Retired Persons, in conjunction with the U.S. Food and Drug Administration, has published a series of free leaflets providing details about more than 350 prescription drugs—explaining how the drugs work and what kinds of precautions should be taken. Increased patient understanding of some general principles regarding the use of prescription drugs will undoubtedly help prevent medication problems.

The goal of drug treatment for elderly patients is safe, effective, convenient, and inexpensive therapy with minimal adverse effects. Reaching this goal will require the cooperation of the pharmaceutical industry, physicians and pharmacists, and patients. Drug manufacturers can contribute by developing safer and more effective medications that can be administered in a convenient manner. Physicians and pharmacists can help by improving the prescribing process to ensure that interactions between two or more drugs are avoided and that appropriate medications are chosen for each specific patient, taking into consideration other diseases, potential for benefit, and associated risks. Patients must take an active role by expressing their wishes when the use of medication is optional, taking their medicines correctly, and watching for and reporting side effects. Like so many other issues in the care of elderly patients, optimizing the use of medications is a team effort, enlisting the skills of various professionals along with the active cooperation of the patient.

Tips for preventing medication problems

1. When going to the doctor's office (or hospital, clinic, or emergency room), the elderly person should take all current medications (including nonprescription drugs) in their original bottles or containers.

2. Nonprescription drugs may have side effects and may interact with prescription drugs. The pharmacist or doctor should be consulted if there are any doubts about the safety of a nonprescription medication.

3. The person taking the medication should understand what each medicine is for and how it should be taken. If the patient is an elderly person who is confused, disoriented, or otherwise mentally impaired, the care giver should be fully informed about the purpose of each drug and the dosage schedule.

4. When the doctor prescribes a new medicine, it is appropriate for the patient to ask whether the new drug may possibly interfere with any of the medicines he or she is already taking.

5. When the doctor prescribes a new medication, the patient should ask for samples or request a prescription for only a small supply of the drug, enough for the first week or two. Then if the drug causes unpleasant side effects or does not work, the patient has not invested a great deal of money in a medication he or she cannot take.

6. Generic drugs are usually less expensive and may be just as effective as brand name drugs. The patient should ask the doctor about the possibility of prescribing a generic drug.

7. If the patient thinks that a specific medication is causing an unpleasant side effect, he or she should report it to the doctor immediately rather than waiting until the next visit or simply ceasing to take the medicine in question.

8. No one should take another person's prescription medications or give other people his or her medicines. Many drugs look alike but have different effects.

Cardiac Catheterization
by Marc K. Effron, M.D.

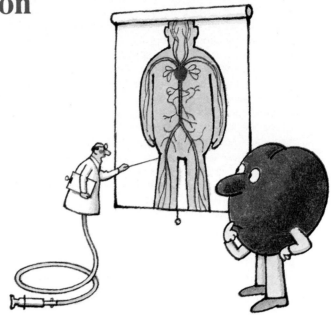

Cardiac catheterization is a diagnostic procedure for evaluation of heart anatomy and function. It is often performed in conjunction with a coronary arteriogram (coronary angiogram) for study of the coronary arteries. Cardiac catheterization has become increasingly common in the United States as an aging population develops coronary artery disease and as new treatment methods warrant the invasive testing.

Once told of the need for cardiac catheterization, a patient may respond with anxiety and trepidation. Yet the procedure can be performed with very little discomfort, usually takes less than 45 minutes, and has a low risk of complications.

Candidates for catheterization

Cardiac catheterization and coronary arteriography are the "gold standard" tests by which the cardiac patient is evaluated and therapeutic decisions are made. Patients in need of cardiac catheterization include those with severe valvular heart disease, certain types of heart muscle dysfunction (cardiomyopathy), or congenital heart conditions (holes between heart chambers or other defects). Coronary arteriography assesses the location and extent of atheromatous obstruction of the coronary arteries (clogging by cholesterol and proliferating cells) in patients with angina pectoris or in those who have had noninvasive test results that suggest the presence of coronary artery disease.

Symptoms of heart disease may be subtle or severe. Shortness of breath or blackout spells may indicate the presence of congenital or valvular heart disease. Pain or a pressure sensation in the chest, throat, or arm may suggest coronary disease. Some patients with no symptoms at all may have a serious heart murmur detected on physical examination. The cardiologist can often make basic diagnoses by the medical history, physical exam, and such noninvasive tests as electrocardiograms (EKGs), echocardiography (ultrasound imaging of the heart), and stress tests—electrocardiographic testing of heart function before, during, and after a controlled period of increasingly strenuous exercise (as on a treadmill). However, if surgical intervention is to be considered, an invasive study by cardiac catheterization will be required in most cases.

Undergoing the procedure

The test is performed by a cardiologist in a hospital cardiac catheterization laboratory ("cath lab"). Hospitals may have from one to six cardiac catheterization laboratories, depending on the case load and scheduling pattern. The cardiac catheterization laboratory is a room dedicated to this type of study and is distinct from the regular radiology suite or operating room. Radiographic imaging equipment is present for fluoroscopy (a method of examining deep structures by X-rays that are projected through the body, casting shadows on a fluorescent screen) and cineangiography (X-ray motion pictures). Hemodynamic monitoring equipment records the pressures in various heart chambers. Technicians are specifically trained in the functions of the laboratory and assist the cardiologist in a "hands-on" manner for manipulation of catheters and injection of contrast medium (dye).

Many elective catheterization studies are now accomplished on an outpatient basis, and the patients leave the hospital usually about seven hours after the procedure. Emergency or medically unstable cases undergo invasive study during an inpatient stay for treatment of the heart condition.

Preparation. The patient is informed of the nature and goals of the diagnostic procedure. Alternatives and risks of invasive testing are discussed. Written consent is usually obtained. Solid food should not be consumed on the day of the procedure, but consumption of fluids and medications may be advised. The patient is further prepared with a mild oral sedative and possibly with an antihistamine to minimize reactions to the radiographic contrast. Once the patient is on the procedure table, the vessel entry site is prepared by shaving and scrubbing with antiseptic soap.

Catheter insertion. Most cardiac catheterizations are

467

Cardiac catheterization

now performed from the right groin area, where the large femoral vessels are easily accessible. With the percutaneous femoral approach, first a local lidocaine anesthetic injection is given, and then a scalpel is used to make a small nick in the skin overlying the artery or vein. The lumen (cavity) of the vessel is located with a needle, and a flexible wire is passed through the needle into the vessel. The needle is then removed and a flexible diagnostic catheter is passed over the wire and up the vessel toward the heart. The patient feels the initial local anesthetic injection, but after introduction of the catheters, there is no discomfort or sensation, since neither the inner lining of the great vessels nor the heart has sensory innervation. The patient remains conscious during the procedure and may watch the progress on television monitors.

An alternative approach via the brachial artery of the upper arm is now used infrequently. The brachial artery is smaller, thinner walled, and technically more difficult to access than the femoral artery. Additionally, complications are more common when this artery is used. The approach requires an actual surgical incision at the front of the elbow as well as dissection to expose the brachial vessels. The vessels are then directly incised to permit introduction of the catheters.

The plastic catheters that are used in both approaches have surface properties that minimize formation of blood clots. An anticoagulant (the drug heparin) is usually given intravenously at the start of the arterial studies. The anticoagulation is reversed at the conclusion of the procedure with an antagonist agent called protamine. While inside the body, the catheters are repeatedly flushed with heparinized saline solution to further prevent blood clot formation.

The actual cardiac catheterization is accomplished by advancing the catheter under fluoroscopic guidance into the heart chambers. A venous entry site leads to the right side of the heart. The right heart catheter passes sequentially through the right atrium and the right ventricle into the pulmonary artery. An arterial entry site leads to the left side of the heart, with the catheter passing retrograde along the aorta into the left ventricle. Heart chambers may be entered in a different sequence if there is a congenital defect or hole in the septum between the atria or ventricles. The exact anatomic location of the catheters is known to the operator by its appearance under fluoroscopy, by the pressure waves that are recorded through the catheter lumen, or by the oxygen content of blood samples drawn through the catheter.

Measuring the heart's performance. The pressures in each heart chamber are transmitted via the catheter to a transducer outside the patient and are recorded on graph paper for later review. These data may also be directly entered into a computer for storage and analysis. The cardiac output, or volume per minute output of the heart, is usually measured by one of two

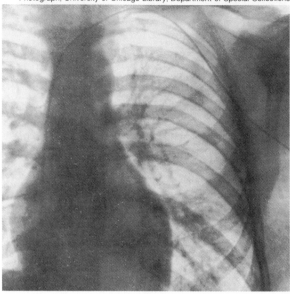

In 1929 Werner Forssmann, a surgical resident in Berlin, boldly performed the first cardiac catheterization on himself. This X-ray shows a long rubber tube inserted into a vein in his arm looping its way to his heart.

methods. The Fick technique requires measurement of the patient's oxygen consumption via collection of expired air with a mouthpiece. This measurement and the difference between arterial and venous oxygen contents permit estimation of the cardiac output. Another method, the thermodilution technique, utilizes a special catheter with a thermistor near its tip. The thermistor is an electrical resistor whose resistance increases as temperature decreases. With this technique, the cardiac output is reflected by the time required for the downstream passage of a certain amount of cool saline.

Pressure recordings, oxygen readings, and the cardiac output permit an evaluation of the heart chamber function, valvular leaks or narrowings, and abnormal communications between chambers. These features of the catheter study are known as hemodynamic measurements.

Angiography. Angiography describes the picture-taking portion of the catheterization study. The radiographic contrast substance is an iodinated compound that is opaque to X-irradiation. The contrast is injected forcefully by a mechanical injector to fill the left ventricle, which is the main pumping chamber of the heart. The patient may briefly experience a warm flush when the dye is injected, but this sensation vanishes shortly. The left ventricular angiogram displays the size and contraction pattern of the ventricle and the degree of regurgitation (leak) at the mitral valve. Other chambers may also be studied by angiography in special instances. Angiographic injection of the proximal aorta, just outside the heart, depicts any regurgitation of the

468

aortic valve. Motion-picture images are recorded on videotape for quick replay and also on conventional film for a high-quality permanent record.

Coronary arteriography. For patients with angina pectoris or related coronary problems, this is the most essential part of the catheterization study. Preshaped catheters are designed to enter the right and left coronary arteries easily when appropriately positioned in the proximal aorta. Contrast medium is injected with a hand-held syringe in order to maintain close control of injection pressure and volume. Arterial injections are recorded from several angles to assure a clear picture of each coronary artery branch and show the degree of vessel narrowing if obstructive disease is present.

Completion of the procedure. After the completion of all hemodynamic and angiographic studies, anticoagulation is reversed and the femoral catheters are removed. Strong pressure is applied to the groin site for about 15 minutes or until there is no sign of bleeding. The patient stays flat in bed for at least six hours and does not flex the leg. The nurse checks vital signs, the entry site, and lower extremity pulses during the six-hour observation period. The patient then may get out of bed and walk about the ward before going home as early as seven to eight hours after the procedure. If the study was performed by the brachial approach, the exposed vessels and incision are sutured closed. Blood flow to the forearm and hand is checked afterward.

Limited activity is usually advised for a day or two after leaving the hospital. Usually the doctor will reexamine the groin or brachial operative sites within the week following the study.

Extensions of the diagnostic study

There are special extensions or modifications of the cardiac catheterization procedure, which add useful diagnostic information for some patients. These include the following:

● Anginal chest pains may result from dynamic spasm of the coronary artery with or without fixed atherosclerotic coronary disease. Coronary spasm can be assessed by what is known as an ergonovine maleate challenge test. Ergonovine maleate is a drug that can provoke coronary spasm in patients with the condition. After baseline coronary arteriograms are done, incremental doses of ergonovine maleate are given intravenously. Symptoms that arise during the test, EKG recordings, and repeat coronary injections are used to detect inducible spasm.

● Percutaneous cardiac biopsy aids in diagnosis of heart muscle disorders and is used to monitor tissue rejection in patients with cardiac transplants. The entry site for percutaneous cardiac biopsy is the internal jugular vein of the neck. A long narrow-gauge bioptome (tissue-sampling device) is positioned in the right ventricle along the dividing wall between the two ventricular chambers. Small one- to three-millimeter snips of heart muscle are removed for examination under the microscope. Patients either feel nothing during the actual biopsy or describe a slight tugging sensation.

● A balloon flotation catheter is used for continuous hemodynamic monitoring in patients undergoing major surgical procedures or in the critical care setting. This type of right heart catheter can be inserted in the operating room or in the intensive care unit. It supplies useful information on heart function and blood volume, thereby guiding the therapy of critically ill patients.

● Electrophysiological studies are performed with electrode catheters in order to evaluate conduction system disease and tachyarrhythmias (rapid heart rhythms). This is accomplished by electrical measurements of conduction times and by tachycardia induction. The need for the implantation of a pacemaker or

Insertion of catheters

aorta
pulmonary artery
left atrium
left ventricle
right atrium
right ventricle
brachial artery insertion
right groin insertion
femoral artery
femoral vein

Most commonly, cardiac catheterizations are performed by insertion of the thin flexible plastic tube into the right groin area, where large femoral vessels are easily accessed. An alternative approach is to insert the catheter into the brachial artery of the upper arm via a surgical incision of approximately 2.5 centimeters (one inch). The patient is mildly sedated but remains awake throughout the procedure.

a defibrillator, as well as a patient's response to drug therapy, can be determined by these studies.

Therapeutic catheterization

Therapeutic interventions as well as diagnostic ones are now performed in the catheterization laboratory. Patients who arrive at the hospital early in the course of an acute myocardial infarction may receive thrombolytic (clot-dissolving) medications, such as streptokinase or tissue plasminogen activator (t-PA), which are delivered intravenously. If the occlusive clot dissolves, myocardial damage is interrupted. Coronary arteriography may be performed electively if the patient remains clinically stable or in emergency situations if coronary reocclusion is impending.

Percutaneous transluminal coronary angioplasty is a procedure that may be used soon after thrombolytic therapy. It entails threading a narrow balloon-tipped catheter down the affected coronary artery and across the narrowed arterial segment. The atherosclerotic narrowing is then dilated open by high-pressure inflation of the balloon.

Percutaneous transluminal coronary angioplasty is also a common treatment for cases of angina pectoris that are resistant to drug therapy. Balloon dilatation is usually followed by two days of in-hospital observation. The patient's experience during coronary angioplasty is similar to that during diagnostic catheterization, although brief chest discomfort may be experienced during balloon inflation. Antithrombotic medication and coronary vasodilators are administered afterward to help maintain the patency of the treated vessel.

Balloon-tipped catheters are also used to treat congenital heart disease (balloon atrial septostomy) and narrowed heart valves (balloon valvuloplasty). Some infants with severely malformed hearts are too small to safely undergo surgical repair of their abnormality. The balloon atrial septostomy procedure creates a hole between the right and left atrial chambers, permitting mixing of oxygenated with nonoxygenated blood and thus sustaining life. Definitive surgical repair can then be delayed until the infant is older and stronger. Balloon valvuloplasty has been applied in children with congenitally narrowed valves as well as in adults with acquired valvular stenosis (narrowing due to fibrotic or calcific obstruction). A balloon catheter essentially tears open the narrowed valve and may obviate the need for open-heart surgery in some patients.

Risks of catheterization

The risk of diagnostic cardiac catheterization studies is relatively low. Minor complications can include an allergic reaction to medicines delivered during the test, allergy-like reactions to the iodinated contrast medium, and bleeding or hematoma formation at the vessel entry site. Iodinated contrast can cause kidney dysfunction, particularly in patients with diabetes or dehydration. Major complications occur only once in every several hundred cases. Stroke, life-threatening arrhythmias, extremity arterial occlusion, myocardial infarction, and death have all been recorded as a consequence of the diagnostic procedure. Risks are higher in the emergency setting and in patients with severely impaired cardiac function. Risks may be minimized by appropriate patient selection and preparation and by proper training and experience of technicians who assist in the cath lab. Studies have shown that risks are lower in medical centers that perform a high volume of catheterizations—i.e., in hospitals having an active laboratory case load. For this reason, cardiac catheterization laboratories should be centralized to permit high levels of activity and to allow catheterization specialists to maintain a high level of skills.

Transcatheter cardiovascular therapeutics—in particular, percutaneous coronary angioplasty—expose the patient to a greater risk than does a diagnostic study. One of 20 coronary angioplasty cases is complicated by coronary artery occlusion. In such cases where a cardiac emergency ensues, the patient is taken promptly to the operating room for coronary artery bypass surgery. The outcome of this emergency "back-up" surgery is usually good, although a small amount of cardiac muscle damage may occur during the time that elapses.

Recognition of these risks is an important part of cardiology practice. The inherent risk of the invasive study must always be weighed against the projected benefits of obtaining the information. Cardiologists must first screen patients, using bedside skills and noninvasive tests to assess cardiac symptoms. If the patient is not a candidate for surgical or angioplasty intervention, then medication can often be tried and adjusted without a catheterization study.

The future: burgeoning applications

The frequency of cardiac catheterization in hospitals today has grown with the burgeoning armamentarium of surgical techniques for treating heart disease. Cardiopulmonary bypass (heart-lung machine) technology in the late 1950s greatly opened the field of cardiac surgery for valvular and congenital heart disease. The cardiac catheterization procedure then became a necessary preoperative test. Coronary arteriography was rarely needed until coronary artery bypass surgery became widely accepted in the early 1970s. Less than a decade ago percutaneous transluminal coronary angioplasty was experimental; it is now a procedure of major import. Thrombolytic therapy of acute myocardial infarction has brought a new and increasing clinical set of coronary patients to the catheterization laboratory. It follows that the future is likely to see many new uses as diagnostic goals and therapeutic capabilities of the cardiac catheter continue to grow.

Food Allergy—Fact or Fancy?

by S. Allan Bock, M.D.

Any discussion of food allergy should begin with a definition of terms. In this area of medicine, the terminology has become so muddled by misuse that it has lost much of its precision and meaning. Because the term allergy has been so misused with respect to adverse reactions to foods, "food hypersensitivity" is currently the best term for documented adverse reactions to food for which an associated immunologic mechanism has been proved. In this article the term adverse reaction will refer to any symptom that can be reproduced by means of objective tests but for which a mechanism is presently unknown. The term intolerance will be used to indicate an enzyme deficiency (absence of an enzyme in the intestine that is necessary for digestion of certain foods).

If a youngster's history of developing a skin rash after eating egg can be reproduced when that youngster unknowingly eats egg or food containing egg, and if a skin test for hypersensitivity to egg is also positive, the youngster has a food hypersensitivity. If a youngster develops chronic diarrhea in association with eating a certain food but no laboratory test tells how or why this is happening, then it is called an adverse reaction. If an adult drinks milk and develops a sensation of bloating as well as diarrhea and it can be shown that the enzyme lactase is deficient in that individual's system, this is called lactose intolerance.

There are a number of categories of adverse reactions to foods. In North America enzyme deficiency leading to intolerance is probably the most common cause of adverse reactions to food. Occasionally, substances such as pesticides that get into foods (*e.g.,* fruits, vegetables, grains, and legumes) can be responsible for adverse reactions. Certain natural constituents of foods—alkaloids in mushrooms, cyanide in the stones of some fruit, oxalates in rhubarb, and hemagglutinins in beans, for example—may also be noxious. Of course, accidental contamination of food by certain microorganisms (*e.g.,* salmonella contamination of eggs) can cause food poisoning, and this is another type of adverse reaction. Aflatoxins, secreted by molds, can contaminate stored grain and stored peanuts. Also, there are substances added to processed foods during preparation, such as the preservative bisulfite, to which a very small segment of the population may have an adverse reaction. Finally, food hypersensitivity, although it gets a great deal of attention from the media—in which it is usually referred to as food allergy—is actually rather uncommon.

Symptoms without hypersensitivity

Many adverse reactions to foods do not occur when the person does not know the food is being ingested but do occur when the food can be seen. This is particularly true for subjective symptoms, such as abdominal pain, muscle aches and pains, and headaches. It is also true for behavioral reactions that seem to disappear magically when blind food challenges (which are described below) are performed. The placebo effect is a reaction that occurs in response to an inactive substance. In many studies, even of very significant symptoms, such as skin rashes (which are easy to see) or pain (which, although hard to measure, is certainly easy for the subject to perceive), the placebo effect may account for the relief felt by as many as one-third of the people involved. This figure points out the potent nature of strongly held beliefs. Because food plays such an important role in society, a person may be more likely to blame a food for his or her symptoms and to be convinced that avoiding that food will bring relief. The power of the human mind to aggravate or alleviate illness must never be underestimated. However, for scientific understanding to advance, rigorous rules of investigation must apply; *i.e.,* a reaction must have a mechanism of action that is demonstrable. During evaluations of alleged reactions to foods, such scientific scrutiny is essential.

Food allergy—fact or fancy?

How common are food reactions?

Unfortunately, there are no accurate figures indicating the frequency of food hypersensitivity. Although estimates vary from fractions of a percent to well over 20% of the population, many of the studies upon which these figures are based have not been scientifically reliable. One study, performed between 1980 and 1985 at the National Jewish Center for Immunology and Respiratory Medicine, Denver, Colo., enabled researchers to accumulate helpful information concerning children from birth to three years of age.

The Denver study examined the incidence of adverse reactions to foods in young children and then determined their natural history; that is, the long-term outcome of the children who had food reactions. Of the 501 children enrolled in the study, contact was maintained with 480 (96%) from birth to their third birthdays. During the first three years of life, 208 of these 480 children had some complaint that a parent, grandparent, day-care provider, or physician thought was due to a food. The vast majority of these complaints occurred during the first year of life. In tests, symptoms were reproduced in about half of the 208 children thought to have a problem; in the other half, symptoms were not reproduced. Of great interest was that 75 children were reported to react to fruit or fruit juice and that 56 of these children had reproducible symptoms. However, the most important finding in these young children was how fast the problem disappeared. Usually, within several months, the reproducible reaction was no longer observed, and the offending food was replaced in the diet. By the time they reached their third birthdays, only four of this entire group of children were still having a food reaction. Hardly any of the reactions—even those that could be reproduced in tests—could be proved to have an immunologic basis. While this study does provide some valuable information about food hypersensitivity in young children, reliable data revealing the true incidence (rate of occurrence of food hypersensitivity in the study group) or prevalence (percentage of food hypersensitivity in the general population) are simply not available.

Food-induced symptoms

Almost any symptom experienced by humans has at one time or another been blamed on food ingestion. Despite this, the number of symptoms that can be shown by scientifically acceptable studies to be due to food hypersensitivity is actually quite small. Such gastrointestinal symptoms as abdominal pain, nausea, vomiting, and diarrhea are commonly observed. "Colic" in young children (which is characterized by paroxysms of acute abdominal pain) has been a controversial area in pediatrics, partly because it is so hard to define. Some rigorously performed studies strongly support the notion that a small number of infants do have colic

when they eat certain foods or when their mothers have eaten those foods before breast-feeding them. Some breast-fed infants will also develop skin rashes in reaction to foods that their mothers have ingested—most commonly egg, milk, and peanut—but such reactions are uncommon.

The most common skin rashes following food ingestion are atopic dermatitis (eczema) and urticaria (hives). Occasionally more extensive swelling, known as angioedema, occurs after food ingestion. If this happens in the throat or mouth, and if the swelling is severe, the reaction can be life-threatening.

A great deal has been written in the lay literature about the association between food allergy and chronic respiratory symptoms in children. Symptoms that on occasion have been reproduced include coughing, wheezing (asthma), runny rose, sneezing, and itchy eyes. The studies performed in this area have shown, however, that respiratory symptoms due to food hypersensitivity are unusual.

The most important and serious reaction that occurs with food hypersensitivity is known as anaphylaxis, a life-threatening constellation of symptoms that can involve any or all of those mentioned above plus a drop in blood pressure, known as shock. Although it is rare, it is a medical emergency when it occurs. In the U.S. a number of people die of anaphylactic reactions to foods every year. Efforts are being made to determine the frequency of such occurrences and to identify people who have these potentially life-threatening reactions so they can be provided with educational information.

Culprit foods

Almost every food has been incriminated at one time or another as a cause of food hypersensitivity. Despite this, however, of foods reproducibly demonstrated to produce adverse reactions in properly controlled food hypersensitivity studies, egg, peanut, milk, wheat, and soy were responsible for 80% of the reactions. If fish, shellfish, and nonlegume nuts (walnuts, pecans, almonds, Brazil nuts, cashews, pistachios, and so forth) are added to the list, then over 90% of the documented food hypersensitivity reactions have been accounted for. It is notable that chocolate is absent from this list. Chocolate is probably the most commonly implicated "food villain." Even modern, up-to-date textbooks in pediatrics, internal medicine, and allergy continue to incriminate chocolate as a major food allergen. On almost every elimination diet used, chocolate appears as one of the culprits. Despite this reputation, chocolate rarely has been found to cause symptoms during double-blind food challenges, and there are fewer than ten well-documented cases of chocolate "allergy" in all of the medical literature in English.

People who are sensitive to egg also need to avoid foods that contain albumin, ovomucoid, and ovomucin.

Those sensitive to milk must avoid products containing casein, calcium caseinate, and whey. Many people who are sensitive to peanut may tend to avoid all legumes, but this is rarely necessary; rather each food stands alone as a possible culprit until it has been proved otherwise.

Diagnosing adverse reactions to foods

Currently, there is only one "gold standard" test for diagnosing an adverse reaction to a food: a double-blind, placebo-controlled food challenge; the person undergoing a challenge and the person administering the challenge and making the observations are unaware of the contents of the challenge. The challenge procedure consists of giving the suspected food on some occasions—increasing the amount each time—and giving a placebo (an inert substance) on other occasions. Thus, the patient does not know when the food has been given.

Elimination diets—removing a single food at a time—can be extremely helpful for determining whether a suspected food or the diet in general is responsible for some symptom. However, the open reintroduction of foods into the diet will often reproduce subjective symptoms because the patient expects it to, as discussed above.

A great deal of information (and misinformation) about skin tests and laboratory tests for food allergy has made its way into the popular press—with the result that allergy skin testing has long received a "bad rap" from those who do not understand how such tests are properly performed and interpreted. Skin testing for any allergy—whether to food, ragweed pollen, or a pet cat or dog—identifies only the presence of proteins called antibodies and thus identifies only the individual's potential for reaction. Many people whose skin tests have revealed antibodies to things they eat or breathe never react to those substances when exposed in daily life.

In skin tests small amounts of test solutions (extracts of food substances) are applied to the skin on the patient's forearm or back, and then a prick is made through the solution. After about 20 minutes the skin is examined for the presence of a wheal and flare (hive) at the site of each test. A hive indicates that the patient has antibodies to that substance. Intradermal injections, a more sensitive test, may be used to test a suspected inhaled substance when the skin-prick test produces no reaction. However, intradermal skin tests should not be used in testing for food hypersensitivity.

Perhaps more confusion exists surrounding the interpretation of blood tests than the interpretation of skin testing. There are many laboratory tests available that detect the presence of antibody but in no way predict a patient's reactivity upon eating the food or being exposed to a certain substance. Yet there are practitioners, some without medical degrees, who

FDA Consumer, May 1989

The most serious reaction that occurs with food hypersensitivity is life-threatening anaphylaxis. An emergency epinephrine kit provides temporary treatment until a patient can be seen in an emergency room.

claim to be able to diagnose food hypersensitivity by an array of laboratory tests. They then provide diets guaranteed to cure any ailment. A very large and lucrative industry has developed around some of these tests and the dietary treatments associated with them. A person concerned about the presence of a food allergy should forgo the more expensive and widely advertised laboratory tests and seek the counsel of a board-certified allergist capable of doing blind food challenges.

The only blood test that is accurate when properly performed and interpreted is the RAST (radioallergosorbent test), which uses radiation. Unfortunately, this test has not been found to be any more sensitive than a skin test, and it is usually far more expensive. Therefore, the American Academy of Allergy and Immunology currently recommends that this test be used only for special problems and not for routine diagnosis. In fact, many insurance companies will not pay for RAST without prior approval.

Prevention and treatment

At the present time, no medication has been demonstrated to be effective in preventing reactions in people who have true food hypersensitivity. The only treatment currently acceptable is avoidance of the food causing the symptoms. However, if a reaction occurs when a culprit food is eaten, there are medications that can be used to treat the symptoms and decrease their progression. These include epinephrine (adrenaline), antihistamines, and corticosteroids.

Some children are likely to outgrow some of their food hypersensitivity reactions, but there is not much information about this problem in adults. Studies have shown that reactions to egg, milk, wheat, and soy are

473

Food allergy—fact or fancy?

most likely to be outgrown. Certain kinds of chronic diarrhea produced in children by milk and soy seem to uniformly be "outgrown" by the third or fourth birthday, whereas chronic diarrhea produced by wheat, known as gluten-sensitive enteropathy or celiac disease, appears to be a life-long condition; the diagnosis must be properly made by a gastroenterologist. On the other hand, children appear unlikely to outgrow their reactions to peanuts and other kinds of nuts. This also seems to be true for adults who have reactions to peanuts and nuts and certain kinds of seafood. Such allergies are the focus of active research, so it is hoped that in the near future, allergy and immunology specialists will have more precise information about why some foods continue to produce reactions while others do not. Unfortunately, the term outgrow is vague, and it is not known precisely what occurs on a biochemical level when a symptomatic reaction to a food no longer occurs.

The proper way to follow patients with documented adverse reactions to foods, especially food hypersensitivity, is to do blind food challenges at specific intervals. The interval between these challenges depends upon the age of the patient and the food in question. Since it is thought that children rarely outgrow their peanut hypersensitivity, the interval between these challenges may be infrequent. On the other hand, milk hypersensitivity much more commonly disappears; therefore, milk challenges should be done at shorter intervals unless the preceding reaction has been extremely severe. It is particularly gratifying to discover that some young children with even the most severe and life-threatening reactions to milk, egg, and soy do lose these reactions as they get older.

Anaphylaxis from a food ingestion can lead to death within minutes—usually 30 or less—if not promptly and effectively treated. Once the food has been identified, the patient needs to be aware of how many places that food may be found. For example, dairy products may be an ingredient in many prepared foods. Peanuts and other kinds of nuts seem to find their way into increasing numbers of dishes, especially as gourmet cooking has become more and more popular. One recently reported fatality resulted from peanut butter in a chili recipe. Any patient with a history of an anaphylactic reaction to a food should carry an emergency epinephrine (adrenaline) kit (prescribed by a physician), usually containing a preloaded injector with a dose of epinephrine, and should proceed immediately to the nearest emergency room after an initial dose of this drug has been administered; symptoms relieved by the first epinephrine injection may recur within a fairly short period of time. Unfortunately, at present there is no way to decrease a person's hypersensitivity to foods by giving injections the way allergists give injections for especially severe allergies to insect bites causing insect venom anaphylaxis.

Controversial tests and treatments
In addition to questionable laboratory tests, there are a number of other popular procedures that have not been shown to have diagnostic efficacy. These include sublingual food drops, extracts administered in order to cause symptoms; neutralization food skin testing, in which food extracts are injected under the skin in order to provoke a reaction and an additional injection is then given in order to "neutralize" it; the cytotoxic food test, an examination of a sample of the patient's white blood cells to which an extract of a specific food has been added; the food-immune complex test, a blood test for the presence of allergen and antibody combined; and applied kinesiology, which involves the measurement of muscle strength after the suspect food has been eaten or after an extract has been applied sublingually.

There are also controversial treatments. A number of different diets are currently popular and eliminate various foods from the diet. Many testimonials and anecdotes support each of these diets, and many adults do have a good response to them and are well adjusted when using them. However, the application of elimination diets to children for long periods of time is not benign. Often children are subjected to dietary fads, eliminating foods that are a common part of the daily diet. Unfortunately, children are rarely asked how they feel about these diets. Too often parents forget to consider that being on a special diet can make a child feel "different" from peers and can create untold problems for children in social situations. Some of these restrictive fad diets may create new kinds of eating disorders in a society that is seeing increasing numbers of such disorders already.

An unproven treatment that is given in various parts of the U.S. and in some other countries is "immunotherapy"—allergy injections that are purported to desensitize people to culprit foods. Many patients will swear to the efficacy of their "food shots." Unfortunately, this seems to be one additional demonstration of the placebo effect. The proponents of this form of treatment need to subject their procedures to the rigorous examination of the scientific method, which they have not done.

FOR ADDITIONAL READING:
Bock, S. Allan. *Food Allergy: A Primer for People.* New York: Vantage Press, 1988.
U.S. Department of Agriculture, Human Nutrition Information Service. *Cooking for People with Food Allergies.* Home and Garden Bulletin No. 246 (January 1988).
U.S. Department of Health and Human Services, Public Health Service, Food and Drug Administration. "Food Allergies—Separating Fact from 'Hype,' " *FDA Consumer* (June 1986).

Air Pollution Comes Home

by Robert Keene McLellan, M.D., M.P.H.

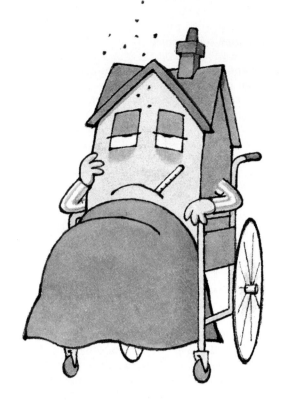

Home, safe home. Ever since humans first spent the night in a makeshift shelter, home has been a safe haven in an unpredictable world and a protection from the weather. Now, however, the security the home once provided is threatened; scientists report that the air people breathe indoors can be more hazardous to their health than the polluted air outside.

There are several reasons why it has become increasingly important to pay close attention to the quality of indoor air at home:

- Citizens of developed countries spend 90% of the day indoors, much of that time at home.
- Those who spend the most time at home are the most vulnerable: babies, pregnant and nursing women, and those who are too young, too sick, or too old to attend school or work.
- Scientific studies show that indoor air contains a range of toxic substances capable of causing cancer, birth defects, asphyxiation (suffocation), brain damage, and chronic respiratory disease. Some of these substances are found in concentrations ten or more times higher than in the most polluted outdoor air.
- It is estimated that every day, the average American inhales approximately 24.5 kg (54 lb) of indoor air. The average American also eats 0.5 kg (one pound) of food and drinks 2.3 kg (5 lb) of water, but unlike food and water, which are closely regulated, indoor air quality is neither regulated nor monitored.

A range of health effects

Because illnesses caused by indoor air pollutants can resemble many common ailments—for example, a cold, the flu, or an upset stomach—environmental causes are frequently overlooked. Environmental illnesses can be broadly divided into two categories: those that occur shortly after exposure and those that become apparent primarily in delayed effects. The most common immediate effect of poor-quality indoor air is irritation of the eyes, nose, throat, and lungs. With sufficient exposure, the skin too may become irritated. Sensitization to allergens in the environment is also common. Typically, a combination of three factors—irritation, recurrent respiratory infection, and allergy—is present, each making the individual more vulnerable to the other. Intoxication (poisoning) may also occur, usually most prominently affecting the nervous system, heart, or lungs. Most of these common acute problems are completely reversible if exposure ceases.

The same agents that in some cases cause these immediate physical reactions may in other cases cause reactions that occur only after a latent—*i.e.,* asymptomatic—period. Substances that produce only latent effects are particularly dangerous for the very reason that no early signs of exposure are present to serve as a warning. Delayed illness can be caused by either brief, high-dose exposures (*e.g.,* to asbestos) or chronic, low-level exposures (*e.g.,* to formaldehyde). The most important diseases in the category of delayed effects of exposure are cancer, fibrosis (scarring) of the lungs, reproductive disorders, and neurological damage.

Perspective on risk

The mere presence of toxins in the home is not sufficient to cause disease. First, a toxin becomes hazardous only when a person is exposed to it; thus, asbestos around pipes may not pose a danger if it is undisturbed. Second, the greater the exposure, the greater the hazard. Finally, whether illness actually occurs depends on the vulnerability of the individual. In general, the very young, the elderly, and those with chronic illnesses are most susceptible. Smoking significantly multiplies the risks associated with exposure to radon and some other toxins.

With rare exceptions (tobacco smoke, for one), most carcinogens found in low levels in the home have not been directly linked to cases of human cancers. Rather, medical scientists calculate estimates of cancer risk by extrapolating from data collected in animal studies or from statistics on human cancers caused by higher, industrial-level exposures. These risk estimates are therefore speculative.

Key indoor air pollutants—a guide

Even the earliest human dwellings posed some hazards to respiratory health; one example is the smoke from an open fire in a cave. Today, however, there are many other factors involved, among them infiltration of outdoor pollutants, emission of toxic substances from construction materials and furnishings, the volume of the living space and system of ventilation, and the habits of the residents. Each of these factors may be altered so as to improve air quality.

Tobacco smoke. Environmental tobacco smoke is one of the best known, most hazardous, and most easily eliminated indoor exposures.

Health effects. Tobacco smoke is known to contain at least a couple of thousand different toxic chemicals, many of which are carcinogenic or highly irritating. Nonsmokers chronically exposed to smoke have an increased risk of lung and cervical cancer; compared with other nonsmokers, they have more respiratory infections and are prone to exacerbation of allergic and other chronic respiratory conditions. Increasing evidence suggests that the lung development of children who live in a household with smokers is stunted.

Controlling exposure. Smoking should be prohibited inside the house or restricted to areas with special exhaust fans. No one should smoke in the same room with a small baby, a pregnant woman, or a person with chronic lung disease.

Asbestos. Asbestos, a natural mineral, has been used in flooring, roofing, and insulation. Although banned from most residential uses in the U.S. since 1978 (and from *all* uses whatsoever in a gradual phaseout begun in 1989), asbestos may be found in some flooring and roofing materials installed in the past decade. Asbestos products are usually classified as either friable (likely to disintegrate with hand pressure) or nonfriable (firmly embedded in a matrix); friable products are the most hazardous because they may readily release asbestos fibers into the air, but nonfriable products may also do this if they are disturbed by scraping, sanding, or chipping.

Health effects. Asbestos is of concern only if it is inhaled. It is known to have caused respiratory and intestinal cancer and severe scarring of the lungs (asbestosis) in asbestos workers as long as 10 to 40 years after exposure. Because asbestos levels at home are at least 1,000 times less than levels in occupational settings, most scientists feel that the chance of an individual's developing an asbestos-related disease as a result of residential exposure would be very, very low (less than one in a million). However, cigarette smoking multiplies a person's lung cancer risk from asbestos exposure by about ten times.

Controlling exposure. Nonfriable asbestos materials are best left undisturbed. There are four alternatives for people who have friable asbestos in their house: (1) do nothing for the moment but continue to monitor the condition of the asbestos-containing material; (2) enclose the area with wallboard; (3) seal it with tape wrap or liquid sealant; (4) remove the asbestos-containing material. Removal should be considered only when remodeling or other considerable activity is planned in the room containing asbestos. Removal of asbestos—or even repair of asbestos-containing materials—carries the risk of creating a significant hazard where one did not previously exist; a professional asbestos contractor should be employed.

Biological contaminants. Living organisms and their toxic products are found in abundance in the air of even the cleanest homes. They include fungi (yeasts, molds, and mildew); dust mites (microscopic animals found in household dust); dander (minute scales from skin, hair, or feathers), urine, and saliva from pet animals; insect parts; pollens; and microorganisms such as bacteria and viruses.

Health effects. Common biological substances found in the air can cause the familiar symptoms of allergic rhinitis—stuffy nose, sneezing, watery eyes—and sometimes asthma. Contact with some agents, such as animal saliva, may cause skin rashes in susceptible persons. Even the home humidifier, usually thought of as contributing to a healthy indoor environment, can actually make people sick. An inadequately cleaned humidifier can aerosolize both antigens, such as mold and mildew, and the toxins produced by the metabolism of these organisms. When high levels of microbial toxins are released into the air, "humidifier fever," a flulike syndrome, may develop within hours. Ultrasonic humidifiers, which many consumers believe to be safer and more efficient than conventional ones, may also pose a hazard if they are not cleaned regularly or if unfiltered tap water is used. As much as 90% of the substances (which may include lead, asbestos, and aluminum) dissolved in tap water is aerosolized by the ultrasonic humidifier into fine respirable particles.

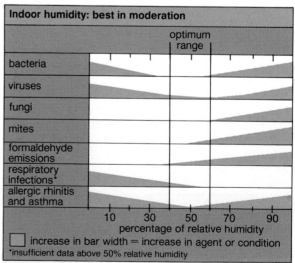

Indoor humidity: best in moderation

percentage of relative humidity

increase in bar width = increase in agent or condition
*insufficient data above 50% relative humidity

Adapted from Sterling *et al.*, "Criteria for Human Exposure to Humidity in Occupied Buildings," *ASHRAE Transactions,* vol. 91, part 1, 1989. Used by permission from the American Society for Heating, Refrigeration, and Air Conditioning

Hypersensitivity pneumonitis (HP) is another condition that may develop; it is similar to, but more severe than, humidifier fever. Symptoms include chest tightness, coughing, wheezing, and shortness of breath. A contaminated ventilation system is a common source of the disease. HP resembles an allergic reaction in that, with continued exposure, less of the antigenic substance is needed for a reaction to be produced. Long-term exposure may lead to permanent, scarring lung disease. People who are not normally allergic may be susceptible to both HP and humidifier fever.

Controlling exposure. The most important step in controlling biological contaminants is controlling moisture. The ideal range for relative humidity in the home is between 30 and 50%. Air conditioners and dehumidifiers are useful for maintaining the ideal range during the summer or in warm climates. Exhaust fans should be used to reduce moisture in bathrooms; clothes dryers should be vented outdoors. Various kinds of sealants and moisture barriers can be used to prevent moisture incursion from outdoors and to keep water vapor from condensing on walls and in attics.

Portable humidifiers should be cleaned carefully each day with a dilute solution of chlorine bleach (one cup bleach per gallon [3.8 liters] of water), undiluted vinegar, or a commercial cleaning product made for this purpose. The water reservoir of a central humidifier should be cleaned weekly. Air conditioners, refrigerator condensation pans, and dehumidifiers should

Ultrasonic humidifiers: what's in the mist?

mineral particles and fragments of microorganisms in ultrasonic mist can cause respiratory infections and allergic reactions

high indoor humidity encourages growth of allergy-producing molds on furnishings

mold and bacteria may accumulate inside water reservoir that is not cleaned regularly

tap water may contain minerals (*e.g.*, lead, asbestos) and dissolved gasses; even distilled water may contain fine particles of hazardous substances

also be cleaned regularly. Steam vaporizers, in which water is boiled before being released into the air, are the healthiest. A central humidifying system is healthier if it is supplied with hot water.

People with allergies may find that installation of central electronic air cleaners, high-efficiency particulate air (HEPA) filters, or electrostatically charged plastic filters is of considerable help in ridding indoor air of allergens. (These methods apply only to forced-air ventilation systems, however.)

Good housekeeping practices can also reduce exposure to biological contaminants. Shower stalls and other damp surfaces should be cleaned regularly with a mild disinfectant (*e.g.*, dilute household bleach). It should be noted that some commercial bathroom cleaning products can be very irritating. Routine dusting and vacuuming may, however, drastically increase exposures for a couple of hours afterward unless special precautions are taken; central vacuums (which exhaust outside), special portable "allergy vacuums," and wet dusting help to minimize the problem.

Combustion gases. No residential combustion appliance—stove, fireplace, furnace, or space heater—provides complete combustion. Incomplete burning of a fuel results in many toxic products, including asphyxiants, irritant gases, particulates (*i.e.*, particles), and carcinogens. The more inefficient the burning is, the more these substances are produced. The type of fuel being used is an important factor, as different fuels are usually associated with different efficiencies. The order of decreasing efficiency is as follows: gas, oil, coal, wood.

Health effects. Because there are so many different types of chemical exposures from combustion gases, adverse health effects are quite varied. In general, the major effects are irritation from nitrogen oxides, sulfur dioxide, particulates, and aldehydes; asphyxiation from carbon monoxide; and the most extreme, development of certain cancers (*e.g.*, from aldehydes and benzo[a]pyrenes).

Irritation usually affects the respiratory tract and eyes. In the most mild case, the symptoms can include burning and stinging of the eyes and nose, nosebleeds, sore throat, and a dry cough. In a more serious case, recurrent respiratory infections, including bronchitis and pneumonia, may occur. Asthmatic attacks may be precipitated in susceptible individuals. Young children are particularly vulnerable and may be at risk for chronic lung disorders. In the extreme case, asphyxiation results in death due to lack of oxygen to the body's tissues. At moderate concentrations of carbon monoxide, even healthy people may have headaches, fatigue, nausea, dizziness, and shortness of breath. All of these symptoms could be attributed to mild illness; unrecognized chronic exposure due to defective combustion appliances is probably widespread. Wood and coal smoke contain several known carcinogens.

Air pollution comes home

Chronic exposure may increase risk of cancer of the respiratory tract (nose, mouth, and lungs).

Controlling exposure. Unvented kerosene and gas space heaters should never be used indoors. Gas pilot lights should be extinguished only by gas company service persons. A gas stove should never be used to heat a house or apartment. Exhaust hoods should be used with gas ranges, and gas clothes dryers should be vented outdoors. Furnaces, chimneys, flues, and filters need to be checked regularly to ensure that they are not blocked. The use of draft assist fans and the provision of outside air by a duct to wood-burning fireplaces can help prevent flue gases from being sucked back indoors.

Formaldehyde. Formaldehyde is a chemical that is used in a great number of construction materials, upholstery and carpeting, glue and sizing, and other products; it is also a by-product of combustion. High temperatures and humidity dramatically increase formaldehyde "off-gassing," or volatilizing of formaldehyde gas from formaldehyde-containing materials. Over time, however, the amount of formaldehyde being emitted declines rapidly. After the first year, emission rates usually decrease by 50%. By two to five years, few formaldehyde-containing products continue to release significant amounts.

Health effects. Formaldehyde is a potent eye, upper respiratory, and skin irritant. It also has the potential for causing or exacerbating asthma and aggravating other types of chronic lung diseases. Other symptoms, including headaches, memory loss, dizziness, fatigue,

chest pain, and rashes, have frequently been reported by individuals living in environments contaminated by significant levels of formaldehyde. The U.S. Environmental Protection Agency (EPA) considers formaldehyde a *probable* human carcinogen (it is known to cause nasal cancer in laboratory rats).

Controlling exposure. There are five effective ways for a homeowner to decrease formaldehyde exposure; they are (1) removing the source of exposure, which is the most effective method but also may be expensive if it involves removing insulation or subflooring; (2) aging the product by placing it in a well-ventilated, heated, nonliving area, such as an attic; (3) treating the source by sealing it with a polyurethane sealant or, in the case of particleboard, enclosing it on all sides with plastic laminate; (4) increasing ventilation by means of an air-to-air heat exchanger (also called a heat-recovery ventilator), a device that draws in outside air but conserves indoor heat; (5) maintaining cool, dry environmental conditions. The latter measure quickly lowers formaldehyde levels, but it also prolongs the time required for "aging" of formaldehyde-containing products.

People who are extremely sensitive to formaldehyde may go to greater lengths to avoid exposure. If possible, in any new construction they should choose building materials, such as exterior-grade plywood, which "off-gas" less formaldehyde than other similar products. In furnishing and decorating they should shop for window coverings, fabrics, rugs, and upholstered pieces made without formaldehyde.

Lead. Sources of lead exposure in a house or apartment include lead-based paint and lead in plumbing pipes and solder. Lead may also be present in the exhaust fumes of motor vehicles using leaded gasoline. Actual contamination of residential air with lead is rare—for the most part it occurs only during remodeling activities that involve the sanding or torching of surfaces painted with lead-based paint. Usually, however, airborne lead settles quickly into house dust, where it can easily be ingested by small children. Lead also enters the home via drinking water, but the amount varies greatly, depending on the local water supply and the age and condition of the plumbing.

Health effects. Lead is a cumulative poison that even at relatively low levels can cause brain, kidney, glandular, reproductive, and nerve damage and even death. At highest risk are young children and, especially, developing fetuses; lead is therefore a hazard to pregnant women and lactating mothers. Lead poisoning is one of the most prevalent—and preventable—childhood health problems.

Controlling exposure. Lead removal can cost thousands of dollars and should be approached with the same caution as asbestos removal. As with asbestos, if lead cannot be removed correctly, it is better not to do it at all. Only trained, qualified professionals should do this work. Local health departments can help homeowners find such persons. An alternative to removal is enclosure of the leaded surfaces behind permanent barriers, such as wallboard or paneling. Painting over lead paint does not provide adequate protection. Some studies have shown that careful biweekly washing of leaded surfaces with a trisodium phosphate (TSP) solution can significantly reduce lead exposure and may therefore be a good interim measure.

Several easy, inexpensive measures can virtually eliminate ingestion of lead-contaminated tap water:

● After water has been sitting in the pipes for several hours (such as in the morning), run the water for a few minutes until it has reached its coldest temperature.

● Never use hot water for food or formula preparation.

● If the water is acidic, neutralize it with an appropriate treatment.

Particulates. Particulates include a wide variety of things—from animal hair to elements of tobacco smoke to soot or mineral particles (produced in prodigious quantities by ultrasonic humidifiers). Aside from the specific toxic effects of certain types of particulates, the total amount of particulate "stuff" that is inhaled also influences respiratory health. Size determines whether and how deeply a particle will penetrate the respiratory tract. Above 15 microns in diameter, particles are generally too large to be inhaled, although they may injure the body's surface by contact. Between 10 and 15 microns, most inhaled particles are deposited in the nose, mouth, and throat, where they may cause irritation. The most important parti-

cles from a toxic perspective are those smaller than ten microns, because they can actually enter into the lungs. The terms used in assessing and quantifying particulate matter are "total suspended particulates" (TSP), which refers to all particles regardless of size, and "respirable suspended particulates" (RSP), those less than 3.5 microns, which reach the deepest, most sensitive parts of the lungs.

Health effects. High-level exposure to RSP can cause a decline in lung function in children. Preexisting respiratory diseases are exacerbated by high levels of RSP, and an increased incidence of respiratory infections can occur. Chronic elevated exposures have been correlated with an increase in respiratory symptoms and chronic respiratory disease in both children and adults. RSP may also increase the toxicity of other pollutants, such as formaldehyde, by carrying them into deeper regions of the lung than they would ordinarily reach.

Controlling exposure. Residential exposure to particulates is especially high in houses and apartment buildings located near busy highways, factories emitting a high level of particulate matter in smoke, and poorly controlled or improperly filtered incinerators. Fences and hedges can be helpful in shielding houses. Devices that keep indoor pollutants from accumulating are helpful—exhaust fans and exhaust vents to the outside for all indoor combustion devices.

Pesticides. Pesticides—chemical compounds used to kill or control animals, insects, and fungi—differ widely in their toxicities, environmental persistence, and tendencies to linger in body tissues. According to the EPA, pesticides are used in as many as nine out of ten U.S. households.

Health effects. The diversity of pesticides is reflected in the multiplicity of their toxic effects, which include irritation of the mucous membranes, acute and chronic neurological damage, cancer, and miscarriage and birth defects. Allergic reactions may be caused by such botanically derived pesticides as pyrethrum, which has similarities to ragweed. The "inert" (*i.e.,* inactive) ingredients of commercial pesticides often include volatile organic chemicals and oils that add their own toxicities. (See *Volatile organic chemicals,* below.) Of particular concern have been the chlorinated hydrocarbons (DDT) and the cyclodienes (chlordane, heptachlor, aldrin, and dieldrin) because of their environmental persistence—it may take decades for them to degrade into harmless substances—and their accumulation in the food chain. Most uses of these products are now banned in the United States. Ironically, the chemicals usually used as replacements are much more acutely toxic to humans.

Controlling exposure. Several measures can reduce or eliminate the risk of pesticides in the home, among them: (1) minimizing the use of pesticides through such alternative measures as insect traps; (2) asking for a list of chemicals to be used by professional exterminators; (3) using pesticides only sparingly and with plenty of ventilation; (4) storing and discarding unused pesticides safely; (5) consulting the local department of environmental protection for advice on safe cleanup in cases of accidental spillage.

Radon. Radon gas is a product of the normal radioactive decay of uranium. As radon gas forms, it seeps upward to the surface of the Earth. Most of it spews directly into the open air and quickly dissipates. Some of it encounters the basements and foundations of houses, entering through cracks, and is then concentrated within the house. Radon also dissolves in groundwater.

Health effects. Radon cannot be seen or smelled. It does not make the eyes burn or cause a headache. In fact, without special monitoring equipment, there is no way to even be aware of its presence. Unfortunately, next to tobacco smoke, radon is the most serious environmental carcinogen known. Not everyone exposed to elevated levels of radon will develop lung cancer, however. Cigarette smoking is one factor that is known to increase susceptibility to the effects of radon. Smokers probably have a ten times greater risk of developing cancer from radon than nonsmokers do. People living with smokers are likely to be at increased risk as well.

Controlling exposure. There are several ways to measure the amount of radon in the air. The simplest come in the form of kits that can be purchased for under $50. Generally, it is not a good idea to take remedial action on the basis of one simple screening test, however. Some follow-up testing should be performed to predict annual levels of exposure. A variety of radon-abatement procedures may be recommended: sealing cracks in basement walls and floors and in foundations, improving the ventilation system, and changing the pressure differential between the house and the surrounding soil. Radon-contaminated water is best treated with aeration devices. Radon abatement can be fairly costly, but most problems can be solved for less than $2,000.

Volatile organic chemicals. Hundreds of volatile organic chemicals (VOCs) pollute the indoor air by volatilizing from building products, home furnishings, and freshly dry-cleaned clothes or through the use of such household products as cleansers and room fresheners. The list of these indoor contaminants includes benzene, styrene, tetrachloroethylene, dichlorobenzene, methylene chloride, and chloroform, as well as the earlier mentioned formaldehyde. Usually any one of these chemicals is present at only very low levels but nonetheless in amounts much higher than in outdoor air. Aerosol products directly introduce large amounts of organic chemicals into the air in a form that causes them to linger for long periods.

Health effects. Any one of these chemicals may have a host of toxic effects, including cancer, repro-

ductive disorders, or intoxication. Very little is known about the interaction of these specific toxins. Several researchers, however, have correlated elevations of the sum total of VOCs with symptoms of "sick building syndrome" (in which several people in a household or office become ill for no ostensible reason), such as irritation of the mucous membranes, fatigue, poor concentration, and dizziness.

Controlling exposure. Some VOC-containing products can be replaced with similar but safer ones. Aerosol products should be avoided. Unused volatile products should be stored as far from living areas as possible.

Is your house contaminated?

The investigation of a house or apartment starts with a good history of the building's construction, remodeling, decoration, and furnishing. The ages and types of products used are clues to the possible presence of hazards. The second step is visual inspection, looking for sources of the toxins listed and described above. Except for radon, laboratory testing is indicated only if a source of a specific toxin is identified and exposure is occurring or has already occurred.

In many cases historical review and visual inspection provide ample evidence of the need for some corrective measures—installing an exhaust fan, for example, or something as simple as disposing of leftover paint. Further steps would depend on characteristics of family members (*e.g.,* their ages, allergies, and chronic diseases) and their hobbies, interests, and other activities that might involve the use of paints, glues, and other sources of pollutants. All in all, improving indoor air quality does not have to be an overwhelming or expensive task.

FOR FURTHER INFORMATION:
Residential health hazards (general)
Bierman-Lytle, Paul, and McLellan, Robert K., with Smith, Ralph Lee. *Home Safe Home: How to Design, Build and Control a Healthy Home.* New York: Nichols Publishing Co., 1989.
Greenfield, Ellen J. *House Dangerous: Indoor Pollution in Your Home and Office—and What You Can Do About It!* New York: Vintage Books, 1987.
U.S. Environmental Protection Agency, Office of Air and Radiation, Consumer Product Safety Commission. *The Inside Story: A Guide to Indoor Air Quality.* Washington, D.C.: U.S. Government Printing Office, 1988.
Nontoxic alternatives
Dadd, Debra Lynn. *Non-Toxic & Natural—How to Avoid Dangerous Everyday Products and Buy or Make Safe Ones.* Los Angeles: Jeremy P. Tarcher, Inc., 1984.
Wallace, Dan, editor. *The Natural Formula Book for Home and Yard.* Emmaus, Pa.: Rodale Press, 1982.

Contributors to the World of Medicine

Linda H. Aiken, R.N., Ph.D.
Nursing
Trustee Professor of Nursing and Sociology and Associate Director for Nursing Affairs, Leonard Davis Institute of Health Economics, University of Pennsylvania, Philadelphia

Donna Bergen, M.D.
Neurology
Associate Professor of Neurological Sciences, Rush Medical College, Chicago

Lawrence H. Bernstein, M.D.
Home Health Care
Physician in private practice, Storrs, Conn.; Assistant Clinical Professor in Medicine, University of Connecticut School of Medicine, Farmington

Sandra Blakeslee
Special Report Earthquake Preparedness: California Faces Its Faults
Free-lance science and medical writer; West Coast Science Correspondent, *New York Times*

Edward Boden
Veterinary Medicine
Editor, *Veterinary Record,* and Executive Editor, *Research in Veterinary Science,* British Veterinary Association, London

Diana Brahams, Barrister-at-Law
Special Report Compensation for Medical Mishaps: Systems That Work in Sweden and Finland
Editor, *Medico-Legal Journal;* Legal Correspondent, *The Lancet,* London

Charles M. Cegielski
Awards and Prizes
Senior Editor, *Yearbook of Science and the Future,* and Contributing Editor, *Medical and Health Annual,* Encyclopædia Britannica, Inc., Chicago

Robert R. Chilcote, M.D.
Special Report Cancer Chemotherapy: Chance and Design
Associate Professor, Department of Pediatrics, University of California Cancer Center and Cancer Research Institutes, University of California at Irvine

Elizabeth B. Connell, M.D.
Birth Control
Professor, Gynecology and Obstetrics, Emory University School of Medicine, Atlanta, Ga.

Virginia S. Cowart
Sports Medicine
Principal, Medical Information Services, LaGrange, Ill.; Contributing Editor, *The Physician and Sportsmedicine*

William J. Cromie
Cancer
Editor, *The MIT Report,* Massachusetts Institute of Technology, Cambridge

Christopher Drew
Special Report Perils of the Packinghouse: The Jungle *Revisited*
National Correspondent, Chicago *Tribune,* Washington, D.C.

Harvey J. Dworken, M.D.
Gastrointestinal Disorders
Professor of Medicine, School of Medicine, Case Western Reserve University; Physician, University Hospitals, Cleveland, Ohio

Stephen E. Epstein, M.D.
Heart and Blood Vessels (coauthor)
Chief, Cardiology Branch, National Heart, Lung, and Blood Institute, National Institutes of Health, Bethesda, Md.

Arthur L. Frank, M.D., Ph.D.
Environmental and Occupational Health
Professor and Chairman, Department of Preventive Medicine and Environmental Health, University of Kentucky College of Medicine, Lexington

George A. Freedman, D.D.S.
Dentistry
Dentist in private practice, Montreal; Vice-President, American Academy of Cosmetic Dentistry

Stephen A. Geller, M.D.
Pathology and Laboratory Medicine
Director, Department of Pathology and Laboratory Medicine, Cedars-Sinai Medical Center; Professor, Department of Pathology, University of California at Los Angeles School of Medicine

Mark S. Gold, M.D.
Drug Abuse
Director of Research, Fair Oaks Hospital, Summit, N.J.,
and Fair Oaks Hospital at Boca/Delray, Delray Beach, Fla.

Michael Aron Kaliner, M.D.
Allergies and Asthma
Head, Allergic Diseases Section, National Institute of
Allergy and Infectious Diseases, National Institutes of
Health, Bethesda, Md.

Sharon Kingman
AIDS
Science Correspondent, *New Scientist* magazine, London;
coauthor of *The Search for the Virus* (Viking Penguin,
1989)

H. Richard Lamb, M.D.
Special Report *Not Guilty by Reason of Insanity* (coauthor)
Professor of Psychiatry, University of Southern California
School of Medicine, Los Angeles

Alena Leff
Genetics
Laboratory Supervisor, Prenatal Diagnosis Laboratory,
New York City

Jean D. Lockhart, M.D.
Pediatrics
Editor in Chief, *Current Problems in Pediatrics;* formerly
Director of Maternal, Child, and Adolescent Health, Amer-
ican Academy of Pediatrics; Belvedere, Calif.

Thomas H. Murray, Ph.D.
Medical Ethics
Professor and Director, Center for Biomedical Ethics,
School of Medicine, Case Western Reserve University,
Cleveland, Ohio; Editor, *Medical Humanities Review*

Lynn Nadel, Ph.D.
Special Report *Great Expectations: New Outlook for
Down Syndrome*
Professor of Psychology and Research Cognitive Sci-
entist, University of Arizona, Tucson; Member, Science
Advisory Board, National Down Syndrome Society

Tom D. Naughton
Accidents and Safety
Free-lance health and science writer, Chicago

Robert B. Nussenblatt, M.D.
Eye Diseases and Visual Disorders
Clinical Director, National Eye Institute, National Institutes
of Health, Bethesda, Md.

Kenneth L. Nyberg, Ph.D.
Special Report *Exercise Medicine: How Much Do Doctors
Know?* (coauthor)
Professor of Sociology and Director and Chief Scien-
tist, Applied Research Center, California State University,
Bakersfield

Drummond Rennie, M.D.
Special Report *Unscrupulous Researchers: Science's Bad
Apples*
Professor of Medicine, Institute for Health Policy Studies,
University of California at San Francisco; Deputy Editor,
The Journal of the American Medical Association (West
Coast)

David B. Reuben, M.D.
Aging; Medical Education
Associate Director, Multicampus Division of Geriatric
Medicine, and Associate Professor of Clinical Medicine,
University of California at Los Angeles School of Medicine

Christopher D. Saudek, M.D.
Diabetes
Associate Professor of Medicine, Johns Hopkins Univer-
sity School of Medicine; Director, Johns Hopkins Diabetes
Center; Director, Johns Hopkins Clinical Research Center,
Baltimore, Md.

Peter A. Shapiro, M.D.
Special Report *Life After Heart Transplantation: Adjusting
to the Miracle*
Assistant Clinical Professor of Psychiatry, College of
Physicians and Surgeons of Columbia University; Assis-
tant Attending Psychiatrist, Presbyterian Hospital, New
York City

Arthur J. Sober, M.D.
Skin Disorders
Associate Professor of Dermatology, Harvard University Medical School; Associate Chief of Dermatology, Massachusetts General Hospital, Boston

Alan D. Tice, M.D.
Infectious Diseases
Private practice in infectious diseases; Clinical Assistant Professor, University of Washington, Tacoma

Michael J. Toole, M.D.
Disasters (coauthor)
Medical Epidemiologist, Centers for Disease Control; Assistant Professor, Master's Degree Program in Public Health, Emory University, Atlanta, Ga.

Ellis F. Unger, M.D.
Heart and Blood Vessels (coauthor)
Senior Investigator, Cardiology Branch, National Heart, Lung, and Blood Institute, National Institutes of Health, Bethesda, Md.

Ronald Waldman, M.D.
Disasters (coauthor)
Director, Technical Support Division, International Health Progress Office, Centers for Disease Control, Atlanta, Ga.

Linda E. Weinberger, Ph.D.
Special Report *Not Guilty by Reason of Insanity* (coauthor)
Chief Psychologist, University of Southern California Institute of Psychiatry and Law; Assistant Professor of Clinical Psychiatry, University of Southern California, Los Angeles

Jim D. Whitley, Ed.D.
Special Report *Exercise Medicine: How Much Do Doctors Know?* (coauthor)
Professor of Physical Education and Member, Center for Physiological Research, California State University, Bakersfield

Contributors to the Health Information Update

Stephen P. Bank, Ph.D.
Sibling Rivalry
Adjunct Associate Professor of Psychology, Wesleyan University; private practice, family and child psychotherapy, Middletown, Conn.

Stanley J. Bigos, M.D.
Slipped Disk
Associate Professor of Orthopedics and Director, Spine Resource Clinic, University of Washington School of Medicine, Seattle

S. Allan Bock, M.D.
Food Allergy—Fact or Fancy?
Staff Physician, National Jewish Center for Immunology and Respiratory Medicine, Denver, Colo.

Richard L. Doty, Ph.D.
A Matter of Taste
Director, Smell and Taste Center, University of Pennsylvania School of Medicine, Philadelphia

Marc K. Effron, M.D.
Cardiac Catheterization; Cardiac Rehabilitation: Exercise for the Heart's Content
Cardiologist, Scripps Memorial Hospital; Clinical Instructor, University of California at San Diego School of Medicine, La Jolla

L. Anne Hirschel, D.D.S.
Gum Disease
Free-lance medical writer, Southfield, Mich.

Robert M. Julien, M.D., Ph.D.
Are You Abusing (Over-the-Counter) Drugs?
Staff Anesthesiologist, St. Vincent Hospital and Medical Center, Portland, Ore.

Joan Lippert
Sunbathing: A Dying Ritual
Contributing Editor, *Health* magazine; free-lance health and fitness writer, Hastings-on-Hudson, N.Y.

Robert Keene McLellan, M.D., M.P.H.
Air Pollution Comes Home
Director, Center for Environmental Medicine, and Vice-President, Ecotek Corp., Hamden, Conn.; Assistant Clinical Professor of Medicine, Yale University Medical School, New Haven, Conn.

Diane H. Morris, Ph.D., R.D.
Wild for Oats (coauthor)
Assistant Professor of Medicine, Division of General Medicine, University of Massachusetts Medical School, Worcester

David B. Reuben, M.D.
Pressure Sores; Taking Drugs Wisely—Concerns for Seniors
Associate Director, Multicampus Division of Geriatric Medicine, and Associate Professor of Clinical Medicine, University of California at Los Angeles School of Medicine

James M. Rippe, M.D.
Wild for Oats (coauthor)
Director, Exercise Physiology Laboratory, and Associate Professor of Medicine (Cardiology), University of Massachusetts Medical School, Worcester

Bruce D. Shephard, M.D.
Hot Flashes: Not for Women Only
Clinical Associate Professor, Department of Obstetrics and Gynecology, University of South Florida College of Medicine, Tampa

Ann Ward, Ph.D.
Wild for Oats (coauthor)
Director of Research in Exercise Physiology and Assistant Professor of Medicine, University of Massachusetts Medical School, Worcester

J. Anderson Williams
Calorie Counting—The Scientific Way
Technical Manager, Woodson-Tenent Laboratories, Inc., Memphis, Tenn.

Title cartoons by John Everds

Index

This is a three-year cumulative index. Index entries to *World of Medicine* articles in this and previous editions of the *Medical and Health Annual* are set in boldface type, *e.g.* **AIDS**. Entries to other subjects are set in lightface type, *e.g.*, astigmatism. Additional information on any of these subjects is identified with a subheading and indented under the entry heading. The numbers following headings and subheadings indicate the year (boldface) of the edition and the page number (lightface) on which the information appears. The abbreviation "*il.*" indicates an illustration.

AIDS, *or* acquired immune deficiency syndrome **90**–253; **89**–461; **88**–254
  Africa **88**–46
  arthritis causation **89**–271
  Bellevue hospital study **88**–43
  blood-bank testing **90**–389
  dementia causation **89**–188
airplane
  accidents and safety **88**–239
  disasters *il.* **90**–293

All entry headings are alphabetized word by word. Hyphenated words and words separated by dashes or slashes are treated as two words. When one word differs from another only by the presence of additional characters at the end, the shorter precedes the longer. In inverted names, the words following the comma are considered only after the preceding part of the name has been alphabetized. Examples:

    Lake
    Lake, Simon
    Lake Charles
    Lakeland

Names beginning with "Mc" and "Mac" are alphabetized as "Mac"; "St." is alphabetized as "Saint."